Marine
Mammals
and
Noise

MARINE MAMMALS AND NOISE

W. John Richardson
LGL Ltd. environmental research associates
King City, Ontario, Canada

Charles R. Greene, Jr.
Greeneridge Sciences, Inc.
Santa Barbara, California

Charles I. Malme
BBN Systems & Technologies Corporation
Cambridge, Massachusetts

Denis H. Thomson
LGL Ltd. environmental research associates
King City, Ontario, Canada

With contributions by
Sue E. Moore and Bernd Würsig

ACADEMIC PRESS

San Diego   New York   Boston   London   Sydney   Tokyo   Toronto

Cover photograph: Dorsal fluke of a sperm whale off the Palos Verdes Peninsula, California. Photo courtesy of Alisa Schulman-Janiger.

This review was funded by

Minerals Management Service
U.S. Department of the Interior
381 Elden Str., Herndon, VA 22070

Office of Naval Research, Code 124
U.S. Navy
800 N. Quincy St., Arlington, VA 22217

and by LGL Ltd., Greeneridge Sciences Inc., and BBN Systems & Technologies

MMS Contract 14-12-0001-30673

This manuscript has been reviewed by the Minerals Management Service and has been approved for publication. Approval does not signify that the contents necessarily reflect the views and policies of the Service, nor does mention of trade names or commercial products constitute endorsement or recommendation for use.

This book is printed on acid-free paper. ∞

Academic Press, Inc.
A Division of Harcourt Brace & Company
525 B Street, Suite 1900, San Diego, California 92101-4495

United Kingdom Edition published by
Academic Press Limited
24-28 Oval Road, London NW1 7DX

Library of Congress Cataloging-in-Publication Data

Marine mammals and noise / by W. John Richardson . . . [et al.].
        p.   cm.
     Includes bibliographical references (p.   ) and index.
     ISBN 0-12-588440-0 (alk. paper)
     1. Marine mammals—Effect of noise on.   2. Marine mammals-
  -Vocalization.   I. Richardson, W. John (William John)
  QL713.2.M27   1995
  599.5'0419143—dc20   95-8190
                                                             CIP

PRINTED IN THE UNITED STATES OF AMERICA
95 96 97 98 99 00 EB 9 8 7 6 5 4 3 2 1

CONTENTS

8 Marine Mammal Hearing   205

9 Documented Disturbance Reactions   241

10 Zones of Noise Influence   325

11 Significance of Responses and Noise Impacts   387

12 Conclusions and Data Needs 425

PREFACE

Concerns about the effects of environmental degradation on marine mammals have increased greatly in recent years. These concerns developed at about the same time as commercial hunting of marine mammals was in rapid decline. At that point, most marine mammals were no longer in danger of extirpation by hunting, but there was increasing awareness that some populations might be susceptible to other human influences. The most obvious problems were incidental take by fishing gear and collisions with ships, and the effects of pollutants: oil spills, heavy metals, pesticides, sewage, etc. However, during the 1970s, concerns about the effects of man-made noise and other forms of human disturbance were mentioned increasingly often.

This increased concern about potential noise effects on marine mammals has manifested itself in several ways. In the United States, government agencies such as the Minerals Management Service and, more recently, the Office of Naval Research have developed substantial programs of research on this issue. These and other agencies have sponsored a number of major field studies. Numerous workshops and meetings have been convened to discuss noise effects on marine mammals. Many Environmental Impact Statements for proposed marine developments have included comments, and in some cases major sections, on potential noise effects on marine mammals. Regulatory agencies have applied restrictions to some marine projects in attempts to protect marine mammals from noise and disturbance.

The question of noise effects on marine mammals has been pursued most vigorously in the United States, but it is an issue in some other countries as well. Agencies in countries such as Australia, Canada, Denmark (on behalf of Greenland), Great Britain, and New Zealand, as well as in the United States, have also sponsored reviews or studies of noise effects on marine mammals, or have established regulations in attempts to reduce disturbance to these mammals.

In 1974, LGL Ltd., environmental research associates, the employer of John Richardson and Denis Thomson, began conducting field studies of marine mammals in relation to proposed oil-and-gas developments. By 1977, LGL had begun more specific studies of the disturbance reactions of arctic marine mammals (Salter 1979), and shortly thereafter LGL began assessing potential noise effects from proposed icebreaking tankers. In 1980, with support from what is now the U.S. Minerals Management Service, LGL began the first of a series of studies of noise effects on bowhead whales. During the 1980 study, biologists at LGL Ltd. began a still-continuing collaboration with physical acoustician Charles Greene, of Polar Research Lab. and later Greeneridge Sciences, Inc. Similarly, in 1981, Chuck Malme and other physical acousticians at Bolt Beranek and Newman, Inc. (BBN), in collaboration with biologists, began a series of systematic studies of the reactions of humpback and later gray whales to underwater noise.

Since the mid-1980s, LGL, Greeneridge, and BBN have worked together in various combinations on many government- and industry-funded studies, impact assessments, and literature reviews concerning noise effects on marine mammals. We have found that comprehensive studies of this type require a joint effort by specialists in underwater acoustics and marine mammals.

The present review has evolved over more than a dozen years. In 1983, Richardson, Greene, and others completed a literature review on the *Effects of Offshore Petroleum Operations on Cold Water Marine Mammals*, including both acoustic and nonacoustic effects, under a contract from the American Petroleum Institute (API) to LGL Ltd. In 1989, Richardson, Greene, Thomson, and others completed an updated second edition, again under API sponsorship. During 1987, the U.S. Minerals Management Service (MMS) awarded a contract to LGL Ltd., assisted by Greeneridge and BBN, to prepare a more comprehensive review of the world literature on *Effects of Noise on Marine Mammals* (Contract 14-12-0001-30362). That review, including literature published up to 1990, emphasized the effects of noise from oil industry activities, but addressed other topics as well. It was released as an MMS contract report in February 1991 (OCS Study MMS 90-0093; NTIS PB91-168914). The authors were the same as those of the present volume.

In 1992, the Office of Naval Research, U.S. Navy, agreed to provide the core funding necessary to convert the 1991 review into a manuscript suitable for commercial publication. The Minerals Management Service agreed to administer the ONR funding, and Academic Press agreed to publish the volume. The scope of the review has been expanded to give additional attention to noise sources other than the oil industry, and the review has been brought up to date through early 1995. LGL Ltd. had general responsibility for the project and specific responsibility for biological chapters, editing, and production of camera-ready copy. Greeneridge Sciences, Inc., and BBN Systems & Technologies, a division of BBN, were responsible for the physical acoustics components.

Sue E. Moore of SAIC Maritime Services Division, San Diego, assisted with Chapter 6, and Bernd Würsig of Texas A&M University, Galveston, assisted with parts of Chapter 11. Both of these contributors reviewed drafts of some other chapters.

This book was planned as an integrated document rather than a series of discrete papers. Chapters 10–12, in particular, depend on material from all preceding chapters. Chapter authors are indicated at the start of each chapter, but all six authors contributed to some or all other chapters. Richardson organized the project, edited the volume, and produced the camera-ready copy.

We thank the many individuals, cited throughout the book, who kindly provided personal communications, preprints of recent work, or copies of difficult-to-locate reports.

We also thank the many people who reviewed drafts of various chapters. Referees for the 1991 version consisted of the late Dr. R. H. Nichols and Drs. W. C. Cummings, A. N. Popper, D. Ross, and R. Schusterman. Dr. F. Awbrey provided constructive comments on the complete draft of this version, and J. T. Clarke reviewed some chapters. Dr. R. A. Davis of LGL reviewed several draft chapters for both versions. Reviewers at the Minerals Management Service included J. Wilson, Dr. R. M. Avent, C. S. Benner, D. P. Moran, and other anonymous MMS staff. We also thank various readers of the 1991 version who provided comments and additional data, or who encouraged formal publication.

Although most comments have been taken into account in some manner, not all suggestions could be accepted verbatim. Any remaining errors and omissions are the responsibility of the authors. We welcome comments and corrections.

Many present or former colleagues had important roles in our studies of noise effects on marine mammals. Among the most frequent participants were Dr. R. A. Davis, C. R. Evans, K. J. Finley, M. A. Fraker, Dr. S. R. Johnson, W. R. Koski, G. W. Miller, and M. A. Smultea of LGL and P. R. Miles of BBN. Drs. C. W. Clark, G. K. Silber, P. Tyack, R. S. Wells, and B. Würsig also participated in a major way in some of our studies. J. P. Hickie contributed extensively to one of our early reviews of this literature.

We thank R. E. Elliott, K. Hester, and B. Griffen at LGL and R. Blaylock at Greeneridge for technical assistance with the diagrams and manuscript. Finally, we are grateful to the U.S. Minerals Management Service and U.S. Office of Naval Research for supporting this review; to LGL, Greeneridge, and BBN for supplementary funding, technical assistance, and time away from our normal duties; to Dr. C. Crumly, M. Larson, and their associates at Academic Press for publishing the volume; and to our families and colleagues for their forbearance.

W. John Richardson, LGL Ltd., environmental research associates
Charles R. Greene, Jr., Greeneridge Sciences, Inc.
Charles I. Malme, BBN Systems & Technologies
Denis H. Thomson, LGL Ltd., environmental research associates

CHAPTER 1

INTRODUCTION[1]

This volume reviews the known and potential effects of man-made noise on marine mammals. Sound, unlike light and other possible stimuli, is transmitted very efficiently through water. Underwater noise created by ships and some other human activities often can be detected many kilometers from the source, far beyond the distances where human activities would be detectable underwater (or even in air) by vision or other senses. The efficiency of underwater sound propagation also allows marine mammals to use underwater sounds as a primary method of communication with one another. Furthermore, toothed whales use echolocation sounds to sense the presence and locations of objects, including prey.

Marine mammals probably obtain much information about their environment by listening to the sounds from other natural sources, aside from members of their own species. Examples may include surf noise (indicating the presence and direction of a shoreline or shoal), ice noise, and sounds from predators such as killer whales.

Concern has arisen that sounds introduced into the sea by humans could have deleterious effects on marine mammals. This could happen through interference with the mammals' ability to detect calls from conspecifics, echolocation pulses, or other important natural sounds. Any sound signal in the water or air is detectable only if the received level of the sound exceeds a certain detection threshold. Within the frequency range of good absolute hearing sensitivity, detection thresholds often are roughly equal to the background noise level at frequencies near those of the sound signal (Chapter 8). If the sound signal reaching an animal is appreciably weaker than the background noise, the signal probably will not be detected. Thus, elevated background noise levels caused by man-made noise may prevent detection of other sounds important to marine mammals.

---

[1] By W. John Richardson, LGL Ltd.

A second potential effect of man-made noise on marine mammals is to disturb their behavior. Reactions can range from brief interruptions of normal activities (e.g., resting, feeding, or social interactions) to short- or long-term displacement from noisy areas.

A third concern is that strong sound might cause temporary or permanent reductions in hearing sensitivity. In humans, exposure to very high sound levels for brief periods or to moderately high levels for prolonged periods (e.g., in the workplace) sometimes causes permanent hearing impairment (Kryter 1985). There has been speculation about the possibility of similar temporary or permanent hearing impairment in marine mammals exposed to high levels of man-made noise (Chappell 1980; Bohne et al. 1985, 1986; ARPA and NMFS 1994).

Most concern about noise effects on marine mammals has involved potential effects of underwater noise. However, airborne sounds are important to marine mammals that emerge from the water into the air, mainly the pinnipeds. Indeed, most data on reactions of pinnipeds to man-made noise deal with their responses to airborne sounds when hauled out on land or ice.

1.1 Types of Marine Mammals

Marine mammals are a diverse group, and the potential effects of man-made sounds depend on the type of animal involved. Marine mammals occur in three orders: Cetacea, Sirenia, and Carnivora. All cetaceans and sirenians are marine mammals. The Carnivora includes some groups that divide their time between the air and the water (the pinnipeds, otters, and polar bear), plus other more strictly terrestrial groups such as the cats, dogs, and other bears.

Appendix 1 lists the common and scientific names of presently-recognized species of living marine mammals, and shows the higher taxonomic groups into which they are classified. Some aspects of the classification, names, and species distinctions are still debatable. However, these details are not very relevant here. We refer to mammals by the common names shown in Appendix 1.

1.1.1 Cetaceans

There are two main groups of living cetaceans: *odontocete* or *toothed whales*, and mysticete or baleen whales. The 68 species (approximately) of living toothed whales are highly diverse, with representatives throughout the world's oceans and in some rivers (Klinow-

ska 1991; Jefferson et al. 1993). Their communication calls are mainly
at moderate to high frequencies (e.g., 1-20 kHz; see Chapter 7). Many
species also have highly developed echolocation systems operating at
high and very high frequencies: 20-150 kHz.

Baleen whales (*mysticetes*) include at least 11 living species, with
representatives throughout the world's oceans (Ridgway and Harrison,
1985). Baleen whales are apparently sensitive mainly to low- and
moderate-frequency sounds (e.g., 12 Hz to 8 kHz), and lack a high-
frequency echolocation system.

Both toothed and baleen whales include some species that prefer
shallow and/or nearshore waters, and other species that prefer deep
and/or offshore waters. Some of the latter species dive to great
depths, where acoustic transmission conditions differ from those in
shallow water or near the surface.

1.1.2 Sirenians

The living sirenians are herbivores that inhabit shallow coastal
waters or rivers of the tropics and subtropics. The three species of
manatees occur in the Atlantic and in New or Old World rivers drain-
ing into the Atlantic (D.K. Caldwell and Caldwell 1985; Reynolds and
Odell 1991; Reeves et al. 1992). The one living species of *dugong*
inhabits the western Pacific and Indian oceans (Nishiwaki and Marsh
1985). The Steller's sea cow, now extinct, was related to the dugong.

1.1.3 Carnivores

The marine Carnivora—pinnipeds, sea otters, and polar bears—
all spend some time on land or sea ice, and some in the water. The
young are born on land or ice, except for some sea otters. Most or all
feeding is at sea.

The *pinnipeds* include three families: 18 living species of Phocidae, which are the "true" or "hair" seals (Ridgway and Harrison,
1981b); 14 species of Otariidae or eared seals, including the fur seals
and sea lions; and the Odobenidae, represented by the walrus (Ridgway and Harrison, 1981a). The pinnipeds call and hear both underwater and in air, and are potentially subject to noise effects in both
media. Pinnipeds are most abundant at temperate and polar latitudes, but a few species occur at low latitudes. Most pinnipeds occur
in salt water, but there are a few freshwater populations. Bonner
(1990), Riedman (1990), Reeves et al. (1992), and Jefferson et al.
(1993) provide up-to-date summaries of data on pinnipeds.

The *otters* include both saltwater and freshwater species. The sea otter lives around the margins of the North Pacific (Kenyon 1981).

The *polar bear* is a circumarctic species found mainly on sea ice or on shore (Stirling 1988a). However, it swims well and is sometimes found in open water far from ice or land. Little information is available about acoustic communication in sea otters and polar bears, and their hearing abilities are unknown.

1.2 Relevant Topics

Many publications dealing with the natural history of marine mammals include comments on observed reactions (or lack of reactions) to boats, aircraft, or other sources of underwater or airborne sound. In most cases it is uncertain whether the animals reacted to noise, visual stimuli, or some other sensory modality. However, these anecdotes give some indications about possible responses (or lack of them) to potentially disturbing human activities.

Behavioral responsiveness of marine mammals to noise has been studied during many research programs, mostly within the past 15 years. A high proportion of this work has been in U.S. waters, largely as a result of the requirements of the U.S. Marine Mammal Protection Act and Endangered Species Act (see Section 1.3). Much of the research was done because of concern that noise from offshore operations of the oil industry and geophysical survey industry might harm marine mammals. Other studies were done because of questions about effects of noise and disturbance from boats, including those involved in oil industry operations, tourism, whalewatching, marine mammal surveys, and (to a lesser degree) general shipping. The limited attention devoted to effects of noise from general shipping is noteworthy, given the numbers, sizes, and high noise levels of many ships (Tyack 1989).

During some recent studies, researchers have documented in a more or less quantitative manner the disturbance reactions of various species of whales and, less often, pinnipeds to several noise sources. These sources have included boats and aircraft, marine seismic exploration and construction, and offshore drilling. Study techniques have included (1) uncontrolled observations of animal reactions to actual noise-producing activities, and (2) controlled experimental tests of reactions to simulated activities. In some studies the levels of noise near the animals were monitored or predicted by acoustic modeling

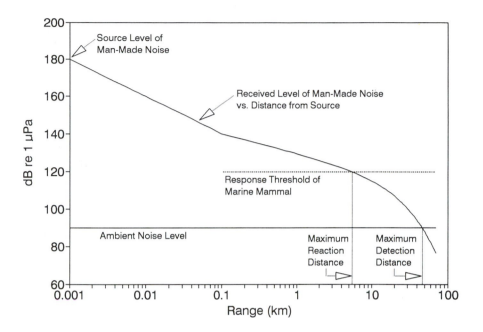

FIGURE 1.1. Theoretical interrelationships of the source level of a man-made noise, distance from the noise source, ambient noise level, and response threshold in determining detection and response distances of a marine mammal. By convention, source level is measured 1 m (0.001 km) from the source. Variations in source level raise or lower the received level versus range curve. Variations in sound propagation conditions change the steepness of this curve. A man-made noise becomes undetectable at about the range where its received level drops below the ambient noise level, which varies greatly with location and time. Overt behavioral reactions often occur only when the received level of man-made noise is well above the ambient noise level. In these cases, the response threshold is well above the ambient noise level, and the maximum response distance is less than the maximum detection distance.

methods, thereby providing information about sound levels and frequencies that do and do not elicit behavioral reactions ("response thresholds"; Fig. 1.1). Chapter 9 reviews these data.

Since about 1990, there has been increased concern about potential effects of underwater noise from military operations and certain scientific activities. Naval operations and research often involve not only ship noise but also high-powered sonars and sometimes explosives. Some underwater acoustics and oceanographic research involves projection of strong, low-frequency sounds into the sea (e.g., Spindel and Worcester 1990; Baggeroer and Munk 1992). Available data are recognized as being inadequate to allow confident predictions about the effects of these types of sounds on marine mammals (NRC/OSB 1994). Various studies of marine mammal reactions to these sounds are under way or planned (e.g., ARPA and NMFS 1994).

Characteristics of man-made sounds have been measured during a few studies of marine mammal disturbance. These data are needed because there is much variation in the levels, frequency compositions, and waveforms of sounds from different human activities. These variations cause differences in the reactions of marine mammals. Many more data on characteristics of man-made noise have come from studies conducted for purposes unrelated to marine mammals: basic acoustical research, studies of ship noise conducted for navy purposes, studies of aircraft noise for noise control purposes, and so on. Chapter 6 summarizes relevant aspects of man-made noise.

Natural background noise (ambient noise) strongly affects the detectability of marine mammal calls and specific man-made sounds. The stronger the background noise, the stronger a sound signal must be in order to be detected (Fig. 1.1). There is a large literature on ambient noise in the sea and air, briefly summarized in Chapter 5.

Attenuation of sound as it propagates through the water or air from its source to a receiver is very important in determining its effects on marine mammals. Sound attenuation rates, exemplified by the slope of the diagonal line in Fig. 1.1, are highly variable and depend on environmental conditions. Where the attenuation rate is large, effects on marine mammals are not expected to extend as far from the noise source as would occur where the attenuation rate is small. Some research on sound propagation has been done during recent studies of the reactions of marine mammals to underwater noise. Far more information on underwater sound propagation has been obtained during basic and military research programs in various countries. Computer models that predict sound attenuation rates under different environmental conditions have been developed, often for naval interests. Chapter 4 summarizes some basic principles of underwater and airborne sound propagation.

Hearing abilities of various marine mammals are another important area of research. Hearing abilities of several species of toothed whales, hair seals, and eared seals have been measured in at least a preliminary way. There are also a few data on hearing by manatees, but no direct data on hearing by baleen whales or sea otters. Such data are important because hearing abilities determine the detectability of natural and man-made noise, and the effects of man-made noise on detectability of natural sounds. Until recently, most studies of the hearing abilities of marine mammals were done for purposes other than evaluating the effects of man-made noise. However, many of the resulting data, reviewed in Chapter 8, are relevant here. Also, some ongoing and planned hearing studies, such as Kastak and Schusterman (1995), were designed specifically to help assess the effects of man-made noise on marine mammals.

Characteristics of calls emitted by many species of marine mammals are known (Chapter 7). The frequencies of these calls identify at least some of the frequencies important to the species. The source levels of the calls are also important; levels and susceptibility to masking by man-made noise are closely related. Unfortunately, specific functions of most marine mammal calls are poorly known. Hence, it is difficult to assess the consequences when man-made noise interferes with reception of these sounds.

Evaluations of the potential effects of underwater noise on marine mammals involve most or all of the foregoing factors. The first publication to attempt such an evaluation was Payne and Webb (1971). On the basis of existing data, they evaluated the detectability of fin whale calls as a function of distance, and discussed the probable effects of increased shipping noise in recent decades. Fletcher and Busnel (1978) edited an important symposium on the effects of noise on wildlife, including a review by Myrberg (1978) on the effects of underwater noise. The Acoustical Society of America (1981) organized, on behalf of the Alaska Eskimo Whaling Commission, a discussion of the need for more specific data of the various types listed here. Several workers used existing data to evaluate the possible effects of noise from proposed liquefied natural gas (LNG) tankers on northern marine mammals (Peterson 1981).

Gales (1982) was one of the first investigators to make specific field measurements to help evaluate noise effects on marine mammals. He measured sounds emitted by drilling and production platforms. He then used existing data on sound attenuation and hearing to estimate the distances within which the oil industry sounds might be audible.

Beginning in the early 1980s, a series of studies was conducted to obtain more specific and coordinated field data on characteristics of man-made noises, sound propagation, and behavioral reactions of marine mammals as functions of distance and received sound level. As more data of these types become available, useful mathematical models of the potential radius of noise influence may become possible. Miles et al. (1987) and Malme et al. (1989) have made the most elaborate attempts to develop "zone of acoustic influence" models for marine mammals. However, as discussed in Chapters 10 and 11, these models have major limitations. Most seriously, present data and models deal primarily with short-term behavioral reactions to noise, on a scale of minutes or hours. Longer-term implications of these short-term effects are generally unknown.

1.3 Regulatory Aspects

1.3.1 The U.S. Regulatory Framework

Much of the concern and research about effects of man-made noise on marine mammals has resulted, directly or indirectly, from the U.S. *Marine Mammal Protection Act (MMPA)* of 1972 and other U.S. laws and regulations. Although these provisions have promoted much research on noise versus marine mammals, research on marine mammals is itself closely regulated in the U.S.A. and some other countries. Some familiarity with the U.S. laws is needed to understand why certain kinds of research have (or have not) been done. We emphasize that the following is a brief and non-technical introduction to a complex topic whose legal dimensions are largely outside our field.

Insofar as we know, no other countries have such extensive regulatory frameworks relating to noise effects on marine mammals. However, the U.S. situation is of interest outside as well as within the U.S.A. The MMPA applies to U.S. citizens in international waters, and thus can affect international projects. Also, some of the U.S. provisions have been emulated in the regulations of other countries.

To promote the conservation of marine mammal populations and their habitats, the MMPA established a moratorium on the "taking" of marine mammals. "Taking" is defined to include harassment as well as hunting, killing, and capturing. However, special exceptions to the moratorium allow "taking" under some conditions. These include "taking" during scientific research on marine mammals (provided a scientific research permit is obtained), and unintentional harassment of small numbers of marine mammals by other human activities (provided an incidental take authorization is obtained).

The U.S. regulatory requirements vary depending on the type of marine mammal. Cetaceans and most pinnipeds are the responsibility of the National Marine Fisheries Service, in the Department of Commerce. Walruses, polar bears, sea otters, and sirenians fall under the Fish & Wildlife Service, in the Department of the Interior.

Species classed as endangered or threatened by the U.S.A. are also protected by the *Endangered Species Act (ESA)* of 1973. It includes some provisions more restrictive than those in the MMPA.

The *National Environmental Policy Act (NEPA)* of 1969 also has major implications with regard to noise effects on marine mammals. NEPA is the U.S. legislation under which Environmental Assessments and Impact Statements are required. Many studies of noise effects on marine mammals have been done to provide data needed for impact statements. Under Executive Order 12114, NEPA applies to many U.S. federal actions outside as well as within the U.S.A.

The MMPA has focused attention on the effects of man-made noise on marine mammals because it defines "taking" to include harassment. Noise-related disturbance is considered to be harassment. Regulations published to implement the MMPA indicate that, for cetaceans and seals, "taking" includes "the negligent or intentional operation of an aircraft or vessel, or the doing of any other negligent or intentional act which results in disturbing or molesting a marine mammal" (50 CFR §216.3). The 1994 amendments to the MMPA define harassment as "any act of pursuit, torment, or annoyance which has the potential" to **(A)** "injure a marine mammal or marine mammal stock in the wild", or **(B)** "disturb a marine mammal or marine mammal stock in the wild by causing disruption of behavioral patterns including, but not limited to, migration, breathing, nursing, breeding, feeding, or sheltering". In practice, U.S. authorities sometimes consider any change in behavior attributable to a human activity to be a "take by harassment" (Swartz and Hofman 1991), and thus subject to prohibition, permitting, or regulation under the MMPA.

1.3.2 Studies Resulting from Regulatory Framework

Some U.S. federal agencies have funded studies to determine whether marine mammals are disturbed (= harassed or "taken") by activities under their jurisdiction. For example, the U.S. Minerals Management Service, which sells and administers leases for offshore oil exploration, has funded many studies to determine the effects of industrial noise and disturbance on various marine mammals. The U.S. National Park Service supported studies of the effects of cruise ships on humpback whales within Glacier Bay National Park (Baker and Herman 1989). The U.S. Air Force funded studies to predict the effects of space launches on pinnipeds concentrating near a launch site (Bowles and Stewart 1980).

Recently, as the scope and requirements of the MMPA have become more widely known and as regulators have expanded their focus, studies of the disturbance effects of U.S. naval activities and of underwater acoustics research have begun. Given the applicability of the MMPA to U.S. citizens in international waters, such studies may be required in any of the world's oceans (e.g., Bowles et al. 1994).

Some U.S. studies have been done to fulfill monitoring requirements associated with incidental take authorizations granted under the MMPA (50 CFR §228). For example, parts of the Alaskan oil industry received authorization to harass small numbers of marine mammals during offshore seismic exploration and drilling programs. Industry must sponsor monitoring studies to assess the "take" during these programs (e.g., Brewer et al. 1993; Hall et al. 1994). An incidental take authorization for rocket launches from Vandenberg Air Force Base, California, requires monitoring of the effects of sonic booms on pinnipeds (Stewart et al. 1993). Potential explosion effects on marine mammals were monitored off southern California during tests to confirm the resistance of a ship to underwater blast (U.S. Navy 1993).

1.3.3 Operational Restrictions

Concerns about noise effects on marine mammals ("take by harassment") have led to operational restrictions on several activities under U.S. jurisdiction. Most of these restrictions have been developed for particular regions and perceived disturbance problems, not for general application in all U.S. waters. For example, many leases for offshore oil exploration near Alaska require support helicopters to fly above an altitude of 1000-1500 feet (~300-450 m), and require seismic exploration vessels to cease operations if bowhead whales are seen within 3 miles (~5 km). In certain areas, seismic and drilling operations have been prohibited at times of year when endangered species such as bowhead or northern right whales were likely to be present.

Whalewatching and some other tourist activities in U.S. waters frequented by whales are coming under increasing scrutiny (Atkins and Swartz 1989). Guidelines for vessel-handling have been developed to reduce disturbance during whalewatching. For Hawaii, the guidelines have been formalized as regulations (NMFS 1987). The number of cruise ships entering Glacier Bay, Alaska, is limited to reduce disturbance to humpback whales. In some Florida waters, motorboat speeds are limited to reduce the risk of collisions with manatees.

Underwater explosions could disturb, injure, or kill marine mammals (Section 9.10). Explosions are sometimes permitted only when a real-time monitoring program—visual, acoustic, or both—has found no evidence that marine mammals are within a specified distance.

In some other countries, similar operational restrictions on certain noisy activities have been imposed. In *Canada*, many marine mammals receive some protection under the Fisheries Act and associated regulations (Waters 1992). Canadian permits for marine seismic surveys prohibit surveys within 500 m of any marine mammal. In recent years, seismic surveys have been discouraged within one of the Canadian summering areas of bowhead whales during the season when whales are present. Seismic surveys are to stop if a bowhead is seen within 4 km.

In *Australia*, all marine mammals receive total or partial protection under various Acts (Tucker and Puddicombe 1988). Some recent Australian permits for seismic exploration within the winter range of southern right whales have included provisions similar to those in U.S. and Canadian permits for seismic work near northern right whales or bowheads. The Australian Whale Watching Regulations of 1990 prohibit aircraft from flying over whales at altitudes <300 m.

In *New Zealand*, the Marine Mammal Protection Regulations of 1990 limit vessel and aircraft operations near whales (Gordon et al. 1992). In *Great Britain*, guidelines are being developed for the use of explosives in areas occupied by dolphins and porpoises (Lockyer 1992).

1.3.4 Regulation of Research

Studies of noise effects on marine mammals are important in defining the types of restrictions that are (and are not) useful in protecting marine mammals from man-made noise. Some of the guidelines and restrictions applied or proposed for application to industrial activities, tourism, aircraft overflights, and acoustical oceanography are based on very meager information (Chapter 9). More research is needed to define which restrictions are necessary and effective in protecting marine mammals (NRC/OSB 1994).

However, the research necessary to accomplish this is itself subject to the regulations designed to protect marine mammals. Many types of research on marine mammals, including studies of noise effects, can only be done if special scientific research permits are obtained from regulatory authorities. These authorities include, in the U.S.A., the National Marine Fisheries Service or Fish & Wildlife Service (depending on the type of animal); in Canada, the Department of Fisheries & Oceans; and in Australia, the National Parks & Wildlife Service. Permits may not be obtainable quickly, and may not be given for some studies that would be permissible if other types of animals were the subjects. For example, few "invasive" physiological studies have been done on marine mammals in the U.S.A. since the MMPA came into effect in 1972.

The U.S. scientific permit system has been the subject of much discussion among scientists and regulators (e.g., NMFS 1993; NRC/OSB 1994). In 1994 it was significantly altered by amendments to the MMPA, which now distinguishes Level A harassment (= injury) from Level B harassment (= behavioral disturbance) (Section 1.3.1). The new provisions considerably simplify the U.S. permit process for scientific research on marine mammals when this would cause no more than Level B harassment to non-endangered species. There is now provision for quick issuance of a research permit if delay could result in loss of a unique research opportunity.

The 1994 amendments also simplify the process under which U.S. citizens can seek incidental take authorizations for activities, aside from research on marine mammals, that might harass small numbers of marine mammals.

1.4 Objectives and Scope of This Book

Our general objectives are to provide the background information on acoustics that is necessary to understand noise effects on marine mammals, to summarize what is now known about these noise effects, and to provide a framework for further studies and analyses. The review is designed to be useful to those assessing noise impacts on marine mammals, and to those planning additional studies of this topic. It should also be useful to nonspecialists attempting to understand and evaluate impact statements and studies for regulatory or other purposes. Emphasis is given to underwater noise, but some attention is given to airborne sounds. The main emphasis is on effects of noise from boats, aircraft, and the offshore oil and gas industry (including seismic exploration), since most of the available data concern those noise sources. However, insofar as the data allow, we also discuss the effects of other noise sources, including icebreaking, sonars, marine construction, and explosions.

The worldwide literature is considered. However, there is an inevitable emphasis on North American work because many of the most relevant studies were done there and because of our greater familiarity with that work. Formally published literature is reviewed in detail. However, we also consider the many relevant technical and contract reports insofar as they are known to us. Unfortunately, much of the relevant information in this field is available only in limited-circulation (and often lengthy) reports. One of our objectives is to provide a guide to and summary of this large body of difficult-to-access information. Many of these reports are available on paper or micro-fiche from the National Technical Information Service (NTIS), Spring-field, Virginia 22161, U.S.A. NTIS catalog numbers known to us are included in the Literature Cited section.

Several types of necessary background information are presented in the early chapters. These are followed by chapters summarizing the available information and hypotheses about specific noise effects on marine mammals. The initial background chapters include the following:

1. Introduction (this chapter)
2. Acoustic Concepts and Terminology
3. Measurement Procedures
4. Sound Propagation
5. Ambient Noise
6. Man-made Noise
7. Marine Mammal Sounds

These background chapters are followed by five chapters that deal more specifically with the effects of noise on marine mammals:

8. Marine Mammal Hearing
9. Documented Disturbance Reactions
10. Zones of Noise Influence
11. Significance of Responses and Noise Impacts
12. Conclusions and Data Needs

The review concludes with an extensive list of Literature Cited, a list of the common and scientific names of all living species of marine mammals (Appendix 1), a Glossary of Acoustical Terms (Appendix 2), and an index.

CHAPTER 2

ACOUSTIC CONCEPTS AND TERMINOLOGY[1]

2.1 Introduction

Sound is what we hear. Waves of sound energy travel through air or water as vibrations of the fluid particles, reaching our ears to exert tiny push-pull pressures on our eardrums. *Frequency* is the rate of oscillation or vibration, measured in cycles per second or *hertz*. The pitch of a sound as perceived by a human is directly related to frequency. Humans are often said to hear sounds ranging from 20 to 20,000 Hz. However, for most individuals the actual range of useful sensitivity is narrower. A *tone*, sometimes called a pure tone, involves a sinusoidal oscillation at a specific frequency. Frequency is the reciprocal of the oscillation *period*, which is the time required for one oscillation. The *wavelength* of a periodic sound is the length of the fundamental oscillation in the propagation medium.

To a physical acoustician,

> Sound is a ... mechanical wave motion propagating in an elastic medium. The waves comprise alternating compressions and rarefactions that propagate at a speed that depends on the relative compressibility of the medium.... . The wavelength of a single tone is related to its frequency by the equation $c = f\lambda$, where c is the speed of sound, f is the frequency, and λ is the wavelength. (D. Ross, personal communication)

Some fluctuations in fluid pressure are commonly called sounds even though they cannot be heard by humans. *Ultrasonic* frequencies are too high to be heard by humans (>20,000 Hz); *infrasonic* sounds are too low to be heard (<20 Hz). Many animals (e.g., dolphins, bats, and dogs) can detect certain ultrasounds. Some animals, including

---

[1] By Charles R. Greene, Jr., Greeneridge Sciences Inc.

elephants, pigeons, and probably some baleen whales, can detect certain infrasounds.

A useful model of the acoustic process is the "*source-path-receiver*" model. This model recognizes that any hearing process involves

- ▸ a source of sound with particular characteristics,
- ▸ changes in sound characteristics as the sound propagates away from the source, and
- ▸ a receiver with specific detection capabilities.

For example, consider a whale swimming near a drillship: the ship is a source of underwater sound, the water (including surface and bottom) is the path from source to whale, and the whale is the receiver.

Source characteristics include variability over time, for example, transient versus continuous; the way in which sound energy is distributed in frequency; and its strength. *Transmission* refers to the propagation of sound through the air, water, or bottom from a source to a receiver. The *transmission path* is the route from source to receiver. The path may include various combinations of air, water, or bottom materials. The path often is not a straight line. Multiple transmission paths (*multipaths*) occur when sound reflects from surfaces along the path, such as the surface and (in underwater sound transmission) the bottom. Rough surface or bottom features cause sound to be scattered, and some underwater sound impacting the bottom is absorbed. *Refraction* (ray bending) can be important in either underwater or airborne sound transmission. In this review the *receivers* of interest are marine mammals. Important receiver characteristics include an animal's hearing sensitivity to sounds at different frequencies and its responsiveness to different types and levels of sounds.

In this chapter we introduce terminology used by acousticians to describe the elements of the source-path-receiver model. Familiarity with these concepts and terms is essential to understand subsequent chapters of the review and to read the technical literature in this field. Three books that provide good discussions of acoustic concepts and terminology are Ross (1976), Kinsler et al. (1982), and Urick (1983).

2.2 *Sound Measurement Units*

2.2.1 *Basic Units*

Most sound receivers are sensitive to *sound pressure*, which is measured in *micropascals (μPa)*. A pascal is a standard unit of pressure in the SI system of units. One pascal is the pressure resulting from a force of one newton exerted over an area of one square meter. Older reports use a different pressure unit, the *dyne/cm²*, also called a *microbar (µbar)*. A bar is the pressure of 0.986923 standard atmospheres. The microbar and micropascal are directly related:

$$1 \text{ micropascal} = 10^{-5} \text{ microbar} \tag{2.1}$$

Acoustic intensity is rarely measured directly but is often discussed. It is important because it is a fundamental measure of propagating sound. It is defined as the *acoustical power* per unit area in the direction of propagation; the units are watts/m². The intensity, power, and energy of an acoustic wave are proportional to the average of the pressure squared (mean square pressure). Acoustics researchers often refer to intensities or powers, but they derive these from pressures squared. Measurement instruments normally sense pressure, not intensity or power. This practice is legitimate for measurements in the same medium (i.e., in water or in air), where constants of proportionality between intensity or power and pressure are the same.

In presenting sound measurements, acousticians use ratios of pressures, or pressures squared, requiring adoption of a standard reference pressure for use in the denominator of the ratio. Early acousticians working on problems in air acoustics adopted a standard pressure of 0.000204 µbar, corresponding to an intensity of 10^{-12} watts/m² or 1 pW/m² in air. This reference was chosen because it is the approximate minimum sound intensity detectable by humans (Table 2.1). Early underwater acousticians used the same reference (rounded to 0.0002 µbar). However, this reference pressure was inappropriate for underwater sound and 1 µbar was adopted. Finally, when the SI system became accepted throughout physics, the underwater sound community adopted 1 µPa as the reference pressure (Table 2.1). For airborne sound it is still conventional to use 20 µPa (0.0002 µbar) as the reference pressure—the approximate threshold of human hearing at 1 kHz (Table 2.1).

For humans, sounds that are faint and barely perceptible have intensities near 1 pW/m², whereas those that are painful are near 10 watts/m². The ear spans this wide range of intensities by means of a complicated nonlinear response (Kinsler et al. 1982). In fact, in judging the relative loudness of two sounds, our ears respond logarithmically. Therefore, acousticians adopted a logarithmic scale for sound intensities and denoted the scale in *decibels*. In decibels, the *intensity level* of a sound of intensity *I* is given by equation (2.2):

TABLE 2.1. Interrelationships of various scales for acoustic measurements; standard reference units are underlined[a]

Pascals	Dynes/cm²	Bars	dB re 1 µPa	dB re 1 µbar	dB re 0.0002 µbar	Typical airborne sounds and human thresholds	Typical underwater sounds and marine mammal thresholds
1,000,000	10^7	10	240	140	214		2 kg high explosive, 100 m
100,000	1,000,000	1	220	120	194		Beluga echolocation call, 1 m
10,000	100,000	.1	200	100	174		Airgun array, 100 m
1,000	10,000	.01	180	80	154	Some military guns	
100	1,000	.001	160	60	134	Sonic booms	Large ship, 100 m
10	100	100 µ	140	40	114	Discomfort threshold, 1 kHz; 500 m from jet airliner	Fin whale call, 100 m
1	10	10 µ	120	20	94		
.1	1	**1 µ**	100	**0**	74	15 m from auto, 55 km/h	Beluga threshold, 1 kHz
.01	.1	.1 µ	80	-20	54	Speech in noise, 1 m	Ambient, SS4, ⅓-OB @ 1 kHz[b]
.001	.01	.01 µ	60	-40	34	Speech in quiet, 1 m	Seal threshold, 1 kHz
.0001	.001	.001 µ	40	-60	14		Ambient, SS0, ⅓-OB @ 1 kHz
20 µ	**200 µ**	**.0002 µ**	26	-74	**0**	Open ear threshold, 1 kHz	Beluga threshold, 30 kHz
10 µ	100 µ	.0001 µ	20	-80	-6	Open ear threshold, 4 kHz	
1 µ	10 µ	.00001 µ	**0**	-100	-26		

[a] Airborne portions adapted from Kryter (1985:8).
[b] Ambient noise in ⅓-octave band centered at 1 kHz under sea state 4 conditions.

$$\text{Intensity Level (dB)} = 10 \log (I/I_0) \qquad (2.2)$$

where I_0 is the reference intensity, for example, 1 pW/m^2. Because intensity is proportional to pressure squared, the *sound pressure level* (SPL) of a sound of pressure P is given by

$$\text{Sound Pressure Level (dB)} = 20 \log (P/P_0) \qquad (2.3)$$

where P_0 is the reference pressure, e.g., 1 µPa. The phrase "sound pressure level" implies a decibel measure and that a reference pressure has been used as the denominator of the ratio.

In summary, when studying underwater sound, we usually measure pressure, not intensity. The reference pressure is now one micropascal (µPa). Earlier publications used one microbar (µbar) or the equivalent unit one dyne/cm^2 or, even earlier, 0.0002 µbar. Sound pressure levels referred to these units are related as follows:

$$\text{SPL (dB re 1 µPa)} = \text{SPL (dB re 1 µbar)} + 100 \qquad (2.4)$$

$$\text{SPL (dB re 1 µPa)} = \text{SPL (dB re 0.0002 µbar)} + 26 \qquad (2.5)$$

For example, an SPL of -40 dB re 1 µbar, or re 1 dyne/cm^2, is 60 dB re 1 µPa (Table 2.1).

Acoustical researchers are not uniformly conscientious about citing their reference units. One finds many graphs with confusing scales simply labeled "dB". Often the caption or text clarifies what is meant. The recommended practice is to cite the reference unit. Some documents use abbreviations such as dB//1µPa instead of dB re 1 µPa.

Pulsed sounds usually should be measured in terms of their energy, not just their pressure or power. Pressure and power measures are often used, but are difficult to interpret because—for a brief pulse—they depend on the averaging time. Energy measures include time as a dimension. Energy is proportional to the time integral of the pressure squared. Thus, sound energy is proportional to and may be described in terms of µPa^2-s. Energy levels are not directly comparable with pressure or power levels. For brief pulses, energy values in dB re 1 µPa^2-s are less than peak pressure levels in dB re 1 µPa. In most cases, energy values are also less than "average pressure squared over the pulse duration", measured in dB re 1 µPa. The difference is variable; energy and pressure units are not directly convertible.

Airborne impulsive sounds are usually measured on an energy basis, integrating the squared instantaneous sound pressure over a stated time interval or event to obtain the *Sound Exposure Level* or

SEL; A-weighting (Section 5.6) is implied unless otherwise stated (ANSI 1994). The energy measurement technique, without A-weights, is sometimes applied in underwater acoustics, but rarely in studies of underwater noise versus marine mammals. Better standardization and reporting of measurement methods for pulsed underwater sounds are urgently needed to permit meaningful comparisons among studies.

Authors discussing effects of explosions on animals often use positive acoustic *impulse* as the acoustic parameter. Positive impulse is the integral of pressure over time, from arrival of the leading edge of the pulse until pressure becomes negative. Impulse is measured in pascal-seconds (Pa·s); as contrasted with pressure, in Pa; or total energy in the pulse, proportional to Pa^2·s.

2.2.2 Sound Spectra

Sound spectra are important because we use them to describe the distribution of sound power as a function of frequency. An animal's sensitivity to sounds varies with frequency, and its response to a sound is expected to depend strongly on the presence and levels of sound in the frequency *band* (range of frequencies) to which it is sensitive.

A sound *waveform* represents the amplitude variations of the sound with time. Sound from some sources has power distributed over a wide range of frequencies. Some sound components may be periodic, consisting of a repeated waveform whose power is concentrated at specific frequencies. The waveform of a *pure tone* is a simple sinusoid. However, other components of sounds from most sources are *continuously distributed* across frequency. Such sound may have a hissing quality at high frequencies or a rumbling quality at low frequencies. The waveforms of these more complex sounds are erratic. If a broadband sound is passed through a *bandpass filter*, which permits only the components between two specific frequencies to pass the filter, the filter output will contain the power, or the mean square pressure, within the filter passband. If the sound is continuously distributed across a frequency range wider than the filter bandwidth, output power decreases as filter bandwidth decreases.

To describe continuously distributed sounds, acousticians use the concept of *power density spectrum*. This is a graph plotting power per unit frequency versus frequency. Because measurements are usually in terms of pressure rather than power, a more common graph is the *sound pressure density spectrum*—the mean square pressure per unit

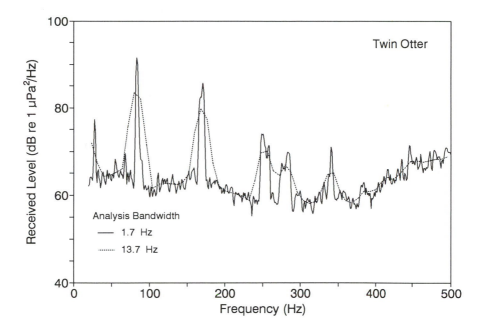

FIGURE 2.1. Effect of analysis bandwidth on sound pressure density spectra. Each line is a computed spectrum for sounds received by a hydrophone at depth 18 m during an overflight by a deHavilland Twin Otter aircraft (altitude 460 m; speed 157 km/h; 9.5 s of recording analyzed). The more variable and smoother lines show, respectively, sound components based on analysis bandwidths of 1.7 and 13.7 Hz. After allowance for analysis bandwidth, calculated levels of the 83 Hz tone were the same (see text).

frequency, in $\mu Pa^2/Hz$ (e.g., Fig. 2.1). To measure sound pressure density spectrum, one could use one narrow filter whose passband is adjustable and whose output is recorded as the passband sweeps across frequency. A better approach is to use a set of contiguously spaced narrow filters spanning frequencies of interest. By using a set of filters, all frequency bands can be analyzed simultaneously.

The mean square pressure density spectrum is obtained by dividing the mean square pressure for each filter band by filter width. The result is sound pressure density versus frequency, in $\mu Pa^2/Hz$. These data become *sound pressure density spectrum levels* when converted to decibels referred to a unit pressure density (e.g., dB re 1 $\mu Pa^2/Hz$). Some authors use a reference unit of 1 $\mu Pa/(Hz)^{1/2}$, which is read as 1 micropascal per $\sqrt{Hz}$. Values referenced either way are numerically the same. Similarly, for pulsed sounds, an overall energy level in dB re 1 $\mu Pa^2 \cdot s$ can be decomposed into an energy density spectrum, with *energy density spectrum levels* at each frequency in dB re 1 $\mu Pa^2 \cdot s/Hz$. For pulsed sounds, these energy values are not directly comparable to sound pressure density spectrum levels.

Nowadays, spectra are usually obtained by computerized analysis techniques rather than analog filters. After digitization, an acoustic waveform may be "filtered" mathematically into its power density spectrum by means of the *discrete Fourier transform*, usually implemented with a *Fast Fourier Transform* (FFT) algorithm.

2.2.3 Levels of Tones

A tone is a sinusoidal waveform for which all power is at a particular frequency. Tones originate from rotating or oscillating objects. For example, something that rotates at 3000 rpm (50 times/s) likely will create a tone at 50 Hz. There may be additional tones (*harmonics*) at integer multiples of this *fundamental* frequency (100, 150 ... Hz). For a multibladed propeller or turbine, the *blade rate* (rotation rate per second times number of blades) is often the fundamental frequency of a harmonic family of tones.

Consider the effect of a constant-amplitude, continuous tone in a sound whose sound pressure density spectrum is determined. The pure tone has all its power at one frequency. As filter bandwidth decreases, the output from the filter containing the tone remains constant. A filter of infinitesimally narrow width, but including the tone, would indicate the power in the tone. Furthermore, the ratio of the finite output power to the infinitesimally narrow filter width would be an infinitely large mean square pressure density. Thus, it is inappropriate to cite a pressure density for a tone, even though it is inevitable that tones will be present in many general sounds.

The effective width of the analysis "filters" is always greater than infinitesimal, and tones appear in the resulting density spectrum graphs as vertical spikes above the background noise continuum (Fig. 2.1). The heights of these spikes depend not only on their strength but also on the characteristics of the analysis—the narrower the filter, the lower the background around the spike (provided the filter is wider than the "tonal" spike). Therefore, researchers reporting a sound pressure density spectrum should also report the width of the analyzing filter. This permits readers to compute the power in the tone for themselves by compensating for the divisor used to compute the density spectrum. For example, if a strong, pure-tone spike shows an apparent amplitude of 110 dB re 1 $\mu Pa^2/Hz$ on a pressure density spectrum graph and the analyzer bandwidth is 4 Hz, the tone level is actually 110 + 10 log (4) = 116 dB re 1 μPa.

The foregoing discussion applies strictly to pure tones or narrow-band sounds with frequency range less than the analyzing filter width. Two common sources of nonzero bandwidth in tones are (1) variations in rotation rate of the source of the tone, and (2) *doppler shift* due to the source's relative velocity with respect to the receiver. For example, the frequencies of tones from an aircraft decrease as it passes over and starts moving away. At any one time, a tone is at a single frequency, but frequency may change within a typical analysis interval of a few seconds.

The effect of analysis bandwidth is shown in Fig. 2.1. When aircraft sound was decomposed into analysis cells 1.7 Hz wide, numerous tones were evident. The strongest was at 83 Hz, with nominal "spectrum level" 92 dB re 1 $\mu Pa^2/Hz$. When corrected by adding 10 log (analysis bandwidth)—10 log (1.7) or 2.3 dB—the result was 94 dB re 1 μPa. When the same sound was decomposed into analysis cells 13.7 Hz wide, the 83 Hz tone was in the filter bin centered at 80 Hz, with nominal "spectrum level" 83 dB re 1 $\mu Pa^2/Hz$. After adding 10 log (13.7) or 11.4 dB, the level was again 94 dB re 1 μPa, as expected.

Some spectrum analyzers in common use are designed to compute the frequency distribution of sound waveforms in which tones are of primary interest. The results, called *power spectra*, do not include a correction for filter bandwidth and the units are dB re 1 μPa. The levels for the tones are correct. They are the sound power levels at tonal frequencies, if the filter bandwidth is wider than the tone and if the tone is strong compared to the continuously distributed background sound power (i.e., >10 dB above it). However, with this type of analysis the continuously distributed sound power is not correctly presented as sound power density spectrum levels (dB re 1 $\mu Pa^2/Hz$), as that requires correcting for the filter bandwidth. This is confusing to acousticians as well as others. Readers of the literature are cautioned to pay close attention to the units of any data describing the distribution of sound with frequency. The values could be either *sound power density spectrum levels*, in dB re 1 $\mu Pa^2/Hz$, correct for continuously distributed sounds but not tones, or *sound power spectrum level*, in dB re 1 μPa, correct for tones.

2.2.4 Octave and ⅓-Octave Levels

Sound pressure density spectrum levels, representing mean square sound pressure per unit of frequency, can be integrated over a range of frequencies (band) to obtain the mean square pressure expected in the band. That is, if we applied a perfect bandpass filter with infinitely sharp lower and upper frequency "cutoffs" to a sound, the filter output would have the same mean square pressure as the integral of the density spectrum over the same frequency range.

Two types of *proportional bandwidth* filters have been adopted as standards: *octave* band and *one-third octave* band filters. In each case, filter bandwidth is proportional to filter center frequency. An octave is a factor of two in frequency. For example, middle C on the music scale is at 262 Hz; the next higher C on the scale, an octave higher, is at 524 Hz. The bandwidth of a 1-octave band is 70.7% of its center frequency. Thus, for center frequency x, a 1-octave band extends from $x(2^{-1/2})$ to $x(2^{1/2})$, or from 0.707x to 1.414x. The bandwidth of a ⅓-octave filter is 23% of its center frequency, that is, from $x(2^{-1/6})$ to $x(2^{1/6})$, or from 0.891x to 1.122x. Standard center frequencies (in Hz) for adjacent ⅓-octave bands include the following:

$$50 \quad 63 \quad 80 \quad 100 \quad 125 \quad 160 \quad 200 \quad 250 \quad 315 \quad 400 \quad 500 \text{ Hz}$$

plus other frequencies lower or higher by factors of 10. Sound levels are often presented for ⅓-octave bands because, in humans and some animals, the effective filter bandwidth of the hearing system is roughly ⅓ octave (Chapter 8).

The sound power in a 1-octave band is at least as high as that within any of the three ⅓-octave bands within that octave. Indeed, it is the sum of the sound powers within the three ⅓-octave bands. Similarly, the sound power in a ⅓-octave band is the sum of that within all 1-Hz bands within the ⅓ octave. (The sum of two sound levels expressed in dB is obtained with equation 2.9—see Section 2.5.) Thus, a ⅓-octave level will equal or exceed the spectrum levels for all frequencies within that ⅓ octave (Fig. 2.2). When interpreting any quoted sound level, it is essential to be aware of the bandwidth over which that level was measured. Unfortunately, this critical information is not given with some published results, making it very difficult to compare them with other studies.

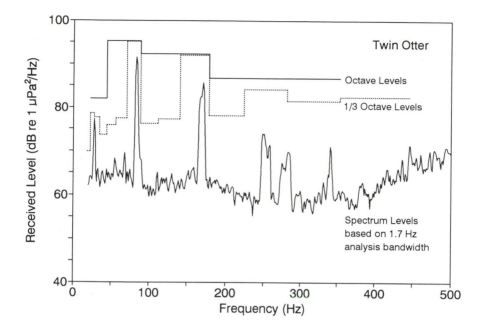

FIGURE 2.2. Comparison of spectral density levels, ⅓-octave band levels, and 1-octave band levels for example of Twin Otter aircraft sound. Spectral density levels represent the sound power in each 1-Hz band, and hence are lower than ⅓-octave levels, which represent sound power in bands whose widths are 23% of the center frequency. Similarly, 1-octave band levels are higher than ⅓-octave levels, because an octave band is three times as wide as a ⅓-octave band at the same center frequency. (Note: ordinate units apply to spectral density levels; for ⅓-octave and 1-octave band levels, correct units are "dB re 1 μPa".)

2.3 *Terms Describing Sound Sources*

2.3.1 *Temporal Properties*

A sound may be *transient*, of relatively short duration having an obvious start and end, or it may be *continuous*, seeming to go on and on. Transient underwater sounds include impulsive transient sounds from explosions, airguns, pile drivers, and sonars. An explosion produces a single transient sound, but airguns, pile drivers, and many sonars produce repeated transients. Sound from a fixed, ongoing source like an operating drillship is continuous. However, the distinction between transient and continuous sounds is not absolute. Sound emitted from an aircraft or a ship underway is continuous, but it is transient insofar as a stationary receiver is concerned. Also, many sounds are not purely transient or purely continuous even at the source. For example, on a drillship, generators and pumps operate essentially continuously, but there are occasional transient bangs and clanks from various impacts during operations.

In describing a transient sound it is useful to present the *peak level* as well as some description of how the sound varies with time— its waveform. The peak level may be described as being a particular pressure, or as a mean square pressure averaged over a relatively short interval. The latter approach allows more reasonable comparisons with mean square pressures of continuous sounds. When transient sounds are so short as to be impulsive, they are best described in terms of their energy levels (Section 2.2.1) and energy density spectra. Some transient sounds, like airgun impulses, occur periodically. For such sources it is also helpful to describe the *duty cycle*, or the fraction of time during which the transients are significant.

A continuous sound or slow transient may be described, for some defined averaging time, by its mean square pressure and its mean square pressure density spectrum. The latter shows the distribution of sound power versus frequency (e.g., Fig. 2.1). It may also be useful to show the corresponding levels in various ⅓-octave and 1-octave bands (e.g., Fig. 2.2).

2.3.2 Amplitude Properties

Source level is defined as the pressure level that would be measured at a standard reference distance (e.g., 1 m) from an ideal point source radiating the same amount of sound as the actual source being measured (Ross 1976). This concept is necessary because sound measurements near large, distributed sources like ships depend strongly on source size and measurement location, and are difficult to relate to levels measured far away. Such *near-field* measurements are generally lower than would be obtained at the same distance from a point source radiating the same amount of energy. The maximum distance of near-field effects can be estimated as

$$d = (f{\cdot}a^2)/c = a^2/\lambda \tag{2.6}$$

Here, f is frequency in Hz; a is the longest active dimension of the source in m; c is sound speed—~1500 m/s in water; and λ is the wavelength in m (Verboom 1992).

The concept of source level introduces the dimension of distance into the description of sound. In general, sound level decreases with increasing distance from the source. To compare different sound sources, it is necessary to adopt a standardized reference distance at which source levels will be determined. Normally, field measurements are made at distances larger than the standard reference distance, beyond the near field. Source level is determined by taking into account the known or expected change in level (propagation loss) between the reference and actual distances. For underwater sounds, a reference distance of 1 m (or 1 yard in older reports) is usually cited. However, in some reports on ship noise the reference distance may be 100 m or 100 yards. In any case, source level is estimated by adjusting the measured level to allow for transmission loss between a standard reference range and the range where the sound was measured. Only in this way can source levels of various sounds be compared.

The present standard units for source levels of underwater sounds are µPa-m for a reference range of 1 m. Many authors state the reference range explicitly, as in "x dB re 1 µPa at 1 m", or abbreviate as "x dB re 1 µPa-m". The units for *source spectrum level* are also µPa-m. The units for *source density spectrum level* are $(µPa\text{-}m)^2/Hz$. Authors sometimes cite a reference unit of "1 µPa at 1 m in a 1 Hz band", which is equivalent to $(µPa\text{-}m)^2/Hz$, or they may even fail to indicate the density spectrum nature of their sound description.

In comparing different source levels, readers must be alert for inconsistencies in reference distances, units, and bandwidths, which are all given in variable ways in the literature. Source levels at reference distance 1 yard can be converted into levels at 1 m by subtracting 0.8 dB. Levels at 100 m or 100 yards cannot always be converted to 1 m using a similar simple "rule of thumb", since propagation losses from 1 m to 100 m or 100 yards vary somewhat. Levels will typically be ~40 dB lower at 100 m than at 1 m, since spherical spreading (Section 2.4) usually applies—to a first approximation—at ranges up to at least 100 m. However, this may not be true in very shallow water or at very low frequencies.

2.4 Terms Describing Sound Propagation

Discussions of sound propagation include two equivalent terms: *transmission loss* (TL) and *propagation loss*. Chapter 4 discusses this topic in greater detail, but some introductory material is necessary to understand parts of that and other chapters. Conceptually, a sound wave traveling from point A to point B diminishes in amplitude, or intensity, as it spreads out in space, is reflected, and is absorbed. If the source level (at 1 m) is 160 dB re 1 µPa-m, the received level at range 1 km may be only 100 dB re 1 µPa; in this case TL is 60 dB. TL is generally expressed in dB, representing a ratio of powers, intensities, or energies of a sound wave at two distances from the source. The distance at which the denominator measurement was taken is the reference distance for TL. Because dB scales are logarithmic, and log (ratio) equals log (numerator) minus log (denominator), TL can be expressed as the difference, in dB, between the levels at the two distances. Strictly speaking, TL is a positive quantity, but it is plotted downward, as in Fig. 2.3. A person viewing a TL graph can visualize the way in which a sound diminishes with increasing distance.

A major component of transmission loss is *spreading loss*. From a point source in a uniform medium (water or air), sound spreads outward as spherical waves. *Spherical spreading* implies that intensity, or the mean square pressure, varies inversely with the square of the distance from the source. Thus, TL due to spherical spreading is given in dB by $20 \log (R/R_0)$, where R_0 is the reference range, normally 1 m. With spherical spreading, sound levels diminish by 6 dB when the distance is doubled, and by 20 dB when distance increases by a factor of 10 (Fig. 2.3).

Cylindrical spreading sometimes occurs when the medium is non-homogeneous. In shallow water, sound reflects from the surface and bottom. At some distance from the source that is long compared to water depth, various reflected waves combine to form a cylindrical wave. Such a wave may be imagined by picturing a short tuna fish can. The top and bottom of the can correspond to the water surface and ocean bottom, and the curved outer surface is the cylindrical wavefront. In some situations (Chapter 4), a near-cylindrical wave can also form as a result of refraction or ray-bending. With cylindrical spreading, the sound intensity varies inversely with distance from the source. A simplified but useful equation for transmission loss with cylindrical spreading is given (in dB) by

$$TL = 20 \log R_1 + 10 \log (R/R_1), \quad R > R_1 \tag{2.7}$$

where R_1 is the range at which spherical spreading stops and cylindrical spreading begins. For ranges $< R_1$, TL is spherical (Fig. 2.3). The preceding equation can be rewritten as

$$TL = 10 \log R_1 + 10 \log R, \quad R > R_1 \tag{2.8}$$

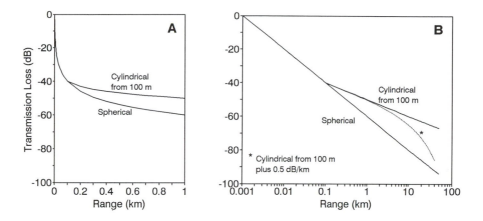

FIGURE 2.3. Sound transmission loss versus distance with pure spherical spreading, combined spherical and cylindrical spreading with transition range 100 m, and (in B only) the latter plus linear absorption and scattering losses of 0.5 dB/km. *(A)* Linear distance scale. *(B)* Logarithmic distance scale.

With cylindrical spreading, sound levels diminish by 3 dB when distance doubles, and by 10 dB when distance increases 10-fold. Thus, levels diminish much more slowly with increasing distance with cylindrical than with spherical spreading (Fig. 2.3).

Sound rays are *refracted* (bent) in accordance with *Snell's Law* when sound speed changes along the ray path (see "Refraction" in Appendix 2—Glossary). Refraction is common in the atmosphere and the ocean when temperature varies with height above ground or depth in the ocean; temperature has a major influence on sound speed. Refraction of sound rays can result in *caustics* or *convergence zones*, which are regions of focused rays and higher sound levels; and *shadow zones*, which are regions of very low sound level (Section 4.3).

As sound travels, some power is absorbed by the medium, giving rise to *absorption losses*. In dB, such losses vary linearly with distance traveled, and absorption loss can be described as x dB/km. Absorption losses depend strongly on frequency, becoming greater with increasing frequencies. *Scattering losses* also vary linearly with distance, but result from different physical mechanisms (Chapter 4). These losses are in addition to the spherical, cylindrical, or other spreading losses previously mentioned (e.g., Fig. 2.3B).

The terms *phase, phase difference, relative phase*, and *phase angle* can be used in comparing two periodic waveforms with the same period. For example, sound components from one source that arrive at a given point via two different propagation paths may differ in phase. Phase refers to the difference in time, or the offset, between two waveforms. If the difference equals the period, or any integer multiple of period, the two waveforms look the same and the phase difference is zero. Thus, it is possible to describe phase as an angle in the range ±180°. For example, if phase difference is ¼ of the period, phase angle is ±90°. The sign depends on whether the waveform of interest is "ahead of" (leads) or "behind" (lags) the reference waveform. For continuous waveforms that are random or nonperiodic, the phase concept generalizes to one of *time delay*, describing the time offset of a waveform and its replica.

2.5 Terms Describing Ambient Noise

Ambient noise is the background noise. There is no single source, point or otherwise. In the ocean, ambient noise arises from wind, waves, surf, ice, organisms, earthquakes, distant shipping, volcanoes, fishing boats, and more (Chapter 5). At any one place and time, several of these sources are likely to contribute significantly to ambient noise. In the source-path-receiver model, ambient noise is present in the medium (water or air) along the path, and it is present at any receiver location.

When the ambient noise level is x dB and there is a sound signal with level y dB, total sound level is

$$L_{x+y} \text{ (in dB)} = 10 \log (10^{x/10} + 10^{y/10}) \tag{2.9}$$

Thus, if signal level and background noise level both equal z dB, total sound level is $(z+3)$ dB. For example, 100 dB + 100 dB = 103 dB. When two levels differ by at least 6 dB, their sum is within 1 dB of the higher of the two component levels, for example, 106 dB + 100 dB = 106.97 dB. These seemingly nonintuitive sums result from the logarithmic nature of decibel scales.

Ambient noise varies with season, location, time of day, and frequency. It has the same attributes as other sounds, including transient and continuous components, tones, hisses, and rumbles. It is measured in the same units as other sounds. However, in measuring ambient noise, it makes no sense to use a reference distance from the "source". There is no one source.

2.6 Terms Describing Sound Reception

Sounds can be received by instruments such as *hydrophones* and *microphones*. They are *transducers* that transform received acoustic pressures into electrical voltages or currents, which may be amplified and conditioned for application to meters, tape recorders, speakers, or earphones. These transducers are characterized by their *sensitivities*, which vary with frequency, by the *electrical noise* they add to received sound, and by their *distortion* properties. Hydrophone sensitivities generally are described in volts per micropascal or in dB re 1 V/μPa.

Animals, including people, have complicated sound reception capabilities. We introduce a few key terms here. More terminology related to hearing is given in Chapter 8. Sonn (1969) compiled a comprehensive lexicon. Other valuable sources include Kryter (1985) and R.R. Fay (1988).

The *absolute auditory threshold* of an animal is the minimum received sound level at which a sound with particular frequency and other properties can be perceived in the absence of significant background noise. The animal can hear a fainter sound if the threshold is low than if it is high. The concepts of auditory threshold and *auditory sensitivity* are inversely related. A low threshold indicates high sensitivity, and vice versa.

Auditory thresholds vary with frequency. A graph of thresholds versus frequency, called an *audiogram*, typically is U-shaped. Thresholds generally are high (poor sensitivity) at low frequencies. From there, thresholds generally diminish (improve) with increasing frequency, up to some frequency range of optimal sensitivity (*best frequency*). Above that range, thresholds increase (deteriorate) with a further increase in frequency. The "best frequency" varies from one species to another. Section 8.2 includes underwater and in-air audiograms of all marine mammal species for which audiograms have been measured; the human in-air audiogram is also shown (Fig. 8.3). R.R. Fay (1988) shows similar data for many other vertebrates.

The terms *critical ratio* and *critical band* deal with the audibility of a pure tone in the presence of background noise. People and animals have varying abilities in this regard. The critical ratio is the ratio of the level of a barely audible tone to the spectrum level of background noise at similar frequencies. Because of the logarithmic nature of dB scales, a critical ratio can be derived by subtracting the spectrum level of the background noise from the tone level. For example, if a tone must be 100 dB re 1 µPa to be detected with background noise of 80 dB re 1 $\mu Pa^2/Hz$ at similar frequencies, the critical ratio is 20 dB (i.e., 100 minus 80). Critical ratios tend to increase with increasing frequency (Section 8.5.1).

Critical bands can be defined in different ways (Section 8.5.2), but in general the critical band around a given frequency is the band within which background noise affects detection of a sound signal at that frequency. Background noise at frequencies outside the critical band has little effect on detection of a sound within that band unless the noise level is very high. Critical bands are often roughly ⅓ octave wide. Hence, it is often useful to summarize man-made noise and ambient noise on a ⅓-octave basis. The process by which background noise may prevent detection of sound signals at nearby frequencies is called *masking*. These topics are discussed in Chapter 8.

CHAPTER 3

MEASUREMENT PROCEDURES[1]

3.1 Introduction

To understand the effects of noise on marine mammals, one must quantify all basic components of the source-path-receiver model as it applies to this problem (Fig. 1.1). This requires data on the noise emitted by a noise source, attenuation rate along the propagation path, and ambient noise near the receiving marine mammal. Information about the receiving marine mammal is also needed: its call characteristics, hearing abilities, and reaction thresholds (Section 1.2). Few components of the source-path-receiver model can be predicted with confidence from theoretical considerations. Empirical measurements are necessary. Even in the case of sound propagation loss, where theoretical or partly theoretical models exist, field measurements are desirable to verify model predictions and to adapt models to local environmental conditions.

The required measurement procedures are diverse and some are difficult. No one researcher will have expertise with all relevant methods. To fully quantify a noise effects model, a collaborative effort by specialists in physical acoustics and marine mammalogy is needed:

- ▸ Standard physical acoustic measurements are needed to determine the characteristics of the emitted sounds, their propagation losses, and the ambient noise. However, in designing the timing, locations, and frequency range of these physical measurements, one needs to take account of the seasonal distribution of the marine mammals of interest, and the frequencies of the sounds that they detect and emit.
- ▸ Measurements of marine mammal calls require familiarity with both the animals and acoustic measurement procedures.

---

[1] By W. John Richardson, LGL Ltd., and Charles R. Greene, Jr., Greeneridge Sciences Inc.

▶ Measurements of the hearing abilities of captive marine mammals are especially complex. They involve acoustical measurement problems, animal care requirements, and either behavioral training (for psychoacoustical testing procedures) or neurophysiology (for evoked potential methods).

▶ Field studies to determine reaction thresholds must obtain coordinated data on marine mammals, human activities, and their sounds—a logistically complex task. One severe complication is the fact that many marine mammals are below the surface and invisible much of the time.

A further complication is that, in many countries, special permits must be obtained in order to conduct studies involving potential disturbance to marine mammals, such as studies of propagation loss and of marine mammal calls, hearing, or reactions (Section 1.3).

Many instruments, procedures, and standards have been developed to measure sounds in air. In contrast, methods for measuring and reporting underwater sounds during studies of marine mammals are highly variable. It may seem that standard in-air procedures and instruments could be used underwater after the microphone is replaced by a hydrophone and suitable waterproofing or cable is added. However, most in-air noise measurements are done to assess noise annoyance to humans, and the instruments apply weightings appropriate to human hearing sensitivity. In contrast, underwater measurements should provide band-level estimates for frequency ranges relevant to the animals under study. Notwithstanding this need to tailor measurement procedures to the species of interest, more consistent measurement methods and more precise reporting of results are possible and urgently needed in studies of marine mammals and noise.

A basic understanding of measurement procedures is helpful in understanding the data concerning noise effects on marine mammals, including the limitations of these data. It is especially important when attempting to design studies to fill some of the many data gaps. Sections 3.2-3.4 describe basic techniques for detecting, recording, and analyzing sounds. Sections 3.5 and 3.6 describe the application of these techniques in making the measurements needed to assess noise effects on marine mammals. Useful general reviews include Kinsler et al. (1982), Urick (1983), and Beranek (1988), plus Burdic (1984) and Nielsen (1991) on signal analysis, and Thomas et al. (1986a) on acoustic recording and/or analysis methods for marine mammal studies.

3.2 Sound Sensors

Sound may be sensed as acoustic pressure or as particle velocity. Most sensors, including our ears, sense acoustic pressure.

3.2.1 Microphones

Microphones are used to detect airborne sounds. Microphones vary greatly in quality, sensitivity, and characteristics. When making quantitative measurements of noise levels and characteristics, it is usually important to use a microphone with high sensitivity, low self-noise, good transient response, low distortion, and wide frequency response. For most purposes, sensitivity should be as uniform as possible across the frequency band of interest. If sounds at very low or very high frequencies (infrasounds or ultrasounds) are of interest, a specialized microphone sensitive to those frequencies is needed. If the microphone is to be used for sound level determinations, its sensitivity must be determined periodically. Ideally, sensitivity should be calibrated versus frequency across the relevant range of frequencies.

An omnidirectional microphone is desirable for routine measurements of ambient noise. It may also be the simplest type of microphone to use when studying the sounds from specific sources. However, for the latter application, a directional microphone can be helpful in isolating the sound of interest from other ambient sounds. If quantitative data are to be obtained via a directional microphone, its directional gain (sensitivity versus angle) at the relevant frequencies must be known and taken into account. Parabolic reflectors are often used in conjunction with omnidirectional microphones to minimize the effect of background noise when recording airborne sounds from distant sources such as animals.

Sound level meters are widely used in airborne acoustics studies. These include a microphone plus electronics to provide a direct read-out and/or stored record of sound level. Many of the overall sound-level data obtained with these meters are A-weighted (Section 5.6) or otherwise adjusted in relation to human hearing processes. These adjustments may be inappropriate for pinnipeds or other animals, whose relative sensitivity to different frequencies is likely to differ from that of humans (Chapter 8). It is generally better to obtain unweighted data for the relevant frequency band, or separate level measurements for a variety of narrower bands such as ⅓ octaves.

One-third octave data can later be combined to obtain an A-weighted or otherwise adjusted overall level if needed.

3.2.2 *Hydrophones*

Hydrophones, the underwater equivalents of microphones, detect underwater sounds. Hydrophones also vary greatly in quality, sensitivity, and characteristics. The desirable attributes for hydrophones generally parallel those of microphones: high sensitivity, low self-noise, low distortion, and uniform sensitivity across the frequency range of interest. If the hydrophone is to be used for sound level determinations, its sensitivity must be determined periodically, preferably as a function of frequency.

Most hydrophones have some directionality. Typically, hydrophones are sensitive to a broad range of frequencies. At frequencies where the hydrophone element is small relative to the wavelength, the element is essentially omnidirectional. Every hydrophone has at least one resonant frequency, and near resonant frequencies some directionality occurs.

Hydrophones are subject to some problems not generally encountered with microphones. Hydrophones must operate underwater, often a considerable distance from the listener or tape recorder at the surface. Just 10 m down the pressure is double the surface (air) pressure. Hydrophones that operate at depths must either be pressure compensated or be "free flooding"—that is, designed so ambient pressure exists all around the element.

Another important feature of hydrophones is their noise performance, which is determined by the hydrophone plus any associated preamplifier. In very quiet environments, it is important to use equipment with low self-noise. Long lengths of cable and high-impedance hydrophones tend to increase the electronic noise level. Sensitive hydrophones often contain preamplifiers near the elements to minimize cable effects. For very long cables, repeaters may be necessary. Typically, preamplifier power is transmitted from the surface via copper wire in the hydrophone cable, sometimes using the same conductors as those that carry the signals (which are at different frequencies). Alternatively, a small battery is built into the hydrophone to power the preamplifier. A sea water return can reduce the required number of conductors, but this may cause interference.

Fiber optics are being used increasingly for long-distance, high-quality, broad-bandwidth transmission of acoustic signals. The signal modulates a laser beam transmitted along a fiber. Usually there is also a single or paired copper conductor to send power to the sensor.

Hydrophone depth should be chosen carefully, taking account of the specific objectives, source location and depth (if there is one specific source), water depth, and frequencies of interest. For underwater sources, received levels of underwater sound tend to be reduced within ~¼ wavelength of the surface (Section 4.5.2)—for example, within ~37.5 m of the surface at 10 Hz or 7.5 m at 50 Hz. Thus, if the sound of interest has low-frequency components, the hydrophone should normally be at least several meters below the surface. However, the bottom can also cause interference, and in shallow water it may be best to suspend the hydrophone near midwater.

Special care is needed to minimize "mechanical self-noise" that occurs when a hydrophone is suspended from a buoy or boat moving up and down on the waves, and "flow noise" that occurs when a current moves past the hydrophone. These problems are most serious when one is recording ambient noise or other relatively weak sounds. Vertical motion can be dampened by suspending the hydrophone beneath a spar buoy drifting near the boat, or by a horizontal plate in an elastic suspension. The tendency of currents to cause cable-strum can be reduced by using a "faired cable" with flagging or other material that breaks up vortices. These self-noise problems are especially difficult to overcome when studying infrasonic (<20 Hz) ambient noise. Bottom-anchored, drifting (D'Spain et al. 1991), or specialized noise-canceling hydrophones may be needed for this application.

Noise interference from nearby equipment or vessels is a common problem. Because of the efficient propagation of sound in the sea, even a distant noise source can interfere with attempts to measure "natural" ambient noise or other weak sources. When the hydrophone is deployed from a boat, it is usually essential to turn off boat motors. Even then, noise from generators or other auxiliary equipment aboard, or wave slap against the side of the boat, may be a problem.

It is usually impractical to use a standard hydrophone from a moving boat because of interference by water flow noise and, in the case of a powerboat, machinery and propeller noise. However, if the sounds of interest have little frequency overlap with those of flow noise or machinery, sounds may be detectable, especially if appropriate bandpass filters are used (Mullins et al. 1988; Sayigh et al. 1993a). Sonobuoys and towed hydrophone arrays also allow acoustic monitoring from moving vessels, as described in the next two sections.

A

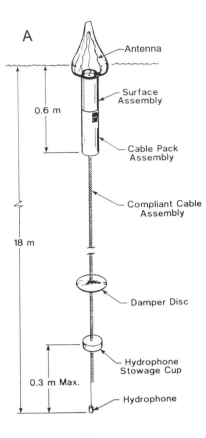

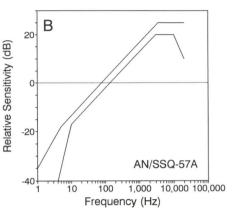

FIGURE 3.1. Naval sonobuoy: *(A)* Appearance of one variety of AN/SSQ-57A sonobuoy after deployment. *(B)* Frequency response envelope for AN/SSQ-57A sonobuoy relative to its sensitivity at 100 Hz. The response of each buoy is required to fall within the range shown here (from U.S. Navy 1985; Horsley 1989). AN/SSQ-41B buoys are similar (U.S. Navy 1979; Greene 1982:269). Spectra of sounds received via these sonobuoys require correction for high-frequency emphasis and low-frequency de-emphasis.

3.2.3 Sonobuoys

Standard naval sonobuoys are designed as expendable devices to be dropped from aircraft in order to monitor underwater sounds (Fig. 3.1A). Most sonobuoys are cylinders 12.4 cm in diameter and 91.4 cm long, and weigh 10-20 kg. In small quantities they cost a few hundred U.S. dollars each, but unit prices diminish for large orders. Their aerial descent is slowed and stabilized by a small parachute or drogue. Upon striking the water, a hydrophone drops to a preset depth. The standard shallow setting is 18 or 27 m, and alternative depths of 120-300 m can be selected. Signals detected by hydrophone are transmitted by VHF radio transmitter to a receiver on the aircraft or elsewhere. The FM transmissions, usually at 136.0-173.5 MHz, are of high quality but low power: often 1-W radio frequency power input to antenna. Depending on antenna heights and surface conditions, telemetry range varies from a few kilometers to a few tens of kilometers. Sonobuoys operate for 1-8 hours, and later sink.

Sonobuoy sensitivity as a function of frequency is designed to fall within a reasonably narrow range, such as ±3 dB across a defined band (Fig. 3.1B). Some types are individually calibrated. Although sonobuoy data are less precise than could be obtained from a high-quality hydrophone, sonobuoys can provide meaningful data on sound level in relation to frequency in situations where hydrophones cannot be used. One important peculiarity is that standard sonobuoys are, by design, much less sensitive to low than to high frequencies (Fig. 3.1B). This counters the usual tendency for underwater noise spectra to contain more power at low frequencies. Thus, raw signals received via sonobuoy have noticeably exaggerated high frequency content, and weak low frequency content. This needs to be taken into account during analysis.

Care must be applied when using sonobuoys to monitor strong sounds. The signals may be distorted and uninterpretable if the received level exceeds a certain frequency-dependent level. The AN/SSQ-57A buoy begins to distort with sound levels >128 dB re 1 µPa at 100 Hz. Special desensitized sonobuoys can be used if high received levels are expected.

Common sonobuoys with omnidirectional hydrophones, such as the AN/SSQ-41B and -57A, are effective from 10 to 20,000 Hz. These buoys, plus suitable radio receivers, are commercially available. They are used extensively in some whale studies, providing data on whale calls, man-made noise received by whales, and ambient noise (e.g., Ljungblad et al. 1982c, 1988; Richardson et al. 1985a-1987b).

Although normally dropped from aircraft, standard sonobuoys can be deployed from ships to monitor ship sounds relative to distance as the ship moves away, or to monitor other sounds after the vessel is far enough away for its noise to be minimal (Bowles et al. 1991). Sonobuoy components can also be used in building special-purpose expendable or retrievable buoys for longer-term monitoring (e.g., Greene 1987a; Horsley 1989; S.E. Moore et al. 1989).

Other specialized types of sonobuoys exist. DIFAR buoys, type AN/SSQ-53B, allow one to determine the directions of arrival of many sounds at the buoy location. However, frequency response is only 10-2400 Hz, and specialized signal-processing equipment is needed to determine directions. In one study, DIFAR buoys were used to determine the directions to distant calling whales, allowing an aircraft-based crew to fly toward and find the whales (Ljungblad 1986). Tests have shown that DIFAR buoys could be useful in noise effects studies (Richardson et al. 1990a). Some other types of sonobuoys, including "active" buoys that emit underwater sounds, are available only for military uses.

3.2.4 Hydrophone Arrays

When several hydrophones are deployed with appropriate spacing, sensitivity may be improved and bearings to sound sources determined. When array dimensions are large enough, differences in time of arrival at various hydrophones may also allow an estimate of the location of the sound source. Localization is valuable in associating received sounds with specific animal or human sources. During marine mammal studies, arrays have been used to study the calling behavior and other activities of several types of marine mammals (e.g., Watkins and Schevill 1974; Clark 1983; Wartzok et al. 1992; Gagnon and Clark 1993), to help census marine mammals (e.g., Thomas et al. 1986b; Clark and Ellison 1988; Sparks et al. 1993), to document the movements of calling animals in relation to noisy human activities (e.g., Clark and Clark 1980; LGL and Greeneridge 1987), and to monitor sounds from human activities (Greene 1987a). It may even be possible to localize silent whales near other calling whales by processing the scattered whale calls received by an array (Makris and Cato 1994).

Fixed hydrophone arrays can be deployed from the bottom, buoys, or ice edges. Floating arrays can be deployed from drifting ships (Watkins and Schevill 1972, 1974). Arrays can also be towed behind moving vessels (Watkins 1981b; Thomas et al. 1986b; Leaper et al. 1992; Sparks et al. 1993). Whatever the method of deployment, it is important to have a mechanism for determining the relative positions of the hydrophones as accurately as possible. For most applications, it is also important to record the signals from all hydrophones simultaneously on different channels of the same recording system. Signals from several hydrophones can be transmitted to a receiving station either by cables (e.g., Tyrrell 1964; Davis et al. 1985) or by radio telemetry (e.g., Greene 1987a; Clark and Ellison 1988).

Sophisticated arrays of hydrophones are widely used by ocean acousticians studying directional and spatial aspects of ambient noise and sound propagation, and there are many operational navy applications. The U.S. Navy's SOund SUrveillance System (SOSUS), based on bottom-mounted hydrophone arrays, provides extensive coverage of the North Atlantic and North Pacific oceans. Additional coverage is provided by SURTASS arrays towed by naval vessels (SURface Towed Array Surveillance System). Together, SOSUS and SURTASS are the basis of the U.S. Navy's Integrated Undersea Surveillance System or IUSS (Gardner 1994). Other countries no doubt operate related systems. Recently, certain IUSS facilities have become accessible to some U.S. marine mammal researchers (Amato 1993; Costa 1993; Clark et al. 1993; see also Section 7.1.6). If this access continues and expands, it could greatly improve our ability to study species whose calls are at low frequencies—primarily baleen whales.

3.3 Sound Recording

Underwater or airborne sounds detected via the sensors discussed previously are normally recorded onto magnetic tape for later analysis. The types of recorders suitable for a given situation depend on the number of sensors, the frequencies of interest, and the types of analysis required.

3.3.1 Standard Analog Tape Recorders

Both open-reel and cassette recorders are widely used. High-quality open-reel recorders provide near-uniform frequency response from ~20 Hz to 20 kHz or more, depending on tape speed. High-quality cassette recorders provide near-uniform response from ~35 Hz to 14 kHz. These recorders can be used to study a somewhat wider frequency range if frequency-specific calibration data are used to compensate for variable sensitivity. However, even within the "near-uniform-response" range, sensitivity may vary across frequency by as much as ±3 dB. Thus, for precise data on sound level versus frequency, raw results for all frequencies should be adjusted using frequency-specific calibration data. With cassette recorders, Dolby or other special noise-suppressing circuitry is needed for good high-frequency (>10 kHz) performance. This circuitry can cause complications when there are strong high-frequency components (Thomas et al. 1986a).

Consistent tape speed is critical for accurate determination of the frequency content of recorded sounds. Electronic speed control is important in assuring reasonably stable tape speed during battery operation in the field.

Several other features are also important. High signal-to-noise ratio and wide dynamic range are critical in recording variable sounds and in determining the levels of weak components accompanying strong components. Even with a high-quality analog recorder, it can be difficult to obtain reliable data for bands containing weak sound components when much stronger components are present in other bands. (Use of a bandpass filter and multiple-channel recording can help.) Additional important features include low distortion, low wow and flutter, and—in multi-channel recordings—good channel separation. Good level meters and a method of setting the recording gain at a consistent level are also important. In general, preparation of analog recordings suitable for quantitative acoustical analysis is a demanding task for a standard analog recorder and its operator.

3.3.2 Specialized Analog Tape Recorders

Most conventional tape recorders are designed to work well in the frequency range of human hearing. However, both infrasonic and ultrasonic frequencies can also be relevant in studies of underwater noise and marine mammals.

Specialized tape recorders must be used if sounds much below 20 Hz or much above 20 kHz are of interest. Battery-operated instrumentation tape recorders are available for field use at frequencies from 0 Hz to 300 kHz, depending on recording method (direct or FM) and tape speed. Infra- and ultrasonic components are not directly audible to the operator. However, they can be monitored indirectly via level meter, oscilloscope, real-time spectrum analyzer, or electronics that translate one frequency range to another (*heterodyning*).

Video cassette recorders (VCRs) can be used as audio recorders. The two standard audio channels of a high-fidelity VCR provide better fidelity in the range 20 Hz to 20 kHz than does a conventional audio recorder. With modifications, the video channel can be used to record acoustic data by either analog or digital techniques.

3.3.3 Digital Recording

Standard Digital Audio Tape (DAT) recorders sample at 44.1 or 48 kHz for frequency response up to 20 kHz on each of two channels. Some instrumentation DAT recorders provide other channel/bandwidth combinations. In comparison with standard analog recorders, DAT units provide more uniform frequency response plus better speed stability, signal-to-noise ratio, and dynamic range (e.g., Stark 1988). They also avoid cross-talk between channels and print-through from one tape layer to the next. DAT recorders designed for scientific use provide flat response down to <1 Hz. Some less expensive battery-operated consumer units also have good response to ≤1 Hz. Given the frequent difficulties in obtaining adequate performance from analog recorders, DAT recorders are recommended for critical recording work at frequencies up to 20 kHz.

A different digital recording technology, Digital Compact Cassettes (DCC), is now being marketed for consumer use. The DCC system is unlikely to be suitable for most scientific purposes. It compresses the digital audio data by discarding some components that are expected to be undetectable to humans.

VCR drive mechanisms have been adapted for high-quality digital audio recording via Pulse Code Modulation (PCM) techniques. Various combinations of bandwidth and number of channels are possible. With a low number of channels, frequency response can extend into the ultrasonic range. Standard DAT recorders can also record a 20-kHz bandwidth of ultrasonic frequencies after special frequency translation. For example, the 20-40 kHz band can be translated to 0-20 kHz and then recorded. Frequency translation can also be used with analog recording, either direct or FM.

Acoustic data can also be digitized and transferred, in real time, into computer memory or onto computer disks. As memory and disk capacities increase, this approach will no doubt become more common.

3.3.4 Amplification

Even with a built-in preamplifier, hydrophone signals usually require more amplification before they can be recorded. Preamplifiers are designed mainly as impedance-transforming devices to better drive the cable and minimize electronic noise. A postamplifier with selectable gain is desirable to maximize the signal match to the tape recorder. At high frequencies, such as those of odontocete calls, high amplification is often required. High-gain amplifiers are prone to oscillation, noise, or both if not carefully designed and built. Thomas et al. (1986a) give further details.

3.4 Sound Analysis

Several standard types of measurements of sounds are commonly needed in studies of either underwater or in-air sounds. The same types of measurements may be needed for ambient, man-made, or marine mammal sounds.

3.4.1 Waveforms

The waveform of a signal or noise is a graph of its strength versus time. The waveform of a continuous pure tone is a sinusoid. Continuous sounds with varying levels and frequency composition have more complex variations. An impulsive waveform typically consists of a brief period of strong oscillation preceded and followed by a relatively steady background signal (Fig. 3.2A). Analyses of waveforms are especially useful in studying noise pulses and other brief transients, including their peak and average levels, shapes, and durations. Waveform shape can also help identify cases when the signals are distorted and unrepresentative.

An oscilloscope can be used to display the waveforms of sound signals from hydrophones, microphones, or tape recorders. Alternatively, the signal coming from a transducer or tape recorder can be digitized with an analog-to-digital converter, and the resulting series of voltage measurements can be plotted against time by computer. In either case, to convert signal voltages into sound levels, one must have calibration data representing the sensitivity of each piece of equipment involved in transducing and manipulating the signal, including hydrophone or microphone, preamplifier and/or amplifier, sonobuoy receiver, tape recorder input and output, and digitizer.

3.4.2 Sound Level

The overall broadband level of a signal coming from a hydrophone, microphone, or tape recorder can be determined in volts by various types of meters. If calibration data are available, this can be converted to an overall sound level. By using an appropriate pair of high- and low-pass filters, the level within a particular frequency band can be determined. However, in modern underwater acoustics and bioacoustics research, data on overall sound level are most often obtained simultaneously with data on level versus frequency through use of spectrum analyzers or their software equivalents (Section 3.4.3).

Sound level often depends on the frequency bandwidth under consideration. The relevant bandwidth will vary with the circumstances, and the bandwidth considered should always be reported. As noted in Section 3.2.1, sound level data from studies of human community noise often are weighted to place most emphasis on frequencies to which humans are most sensitive. A-weighted and other human-related sound level data may be inappropriate for other species.

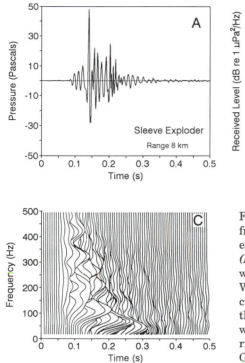
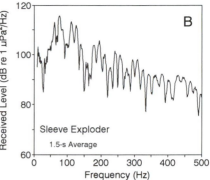

FIGURE 3.2. Underwater sound pulse from seismic survey ship using sleeve exploders 8 km away. *(A)* Waveform. *(B)* Narrowband spectrum (filter bandwidth 1.7 Hz; 1.5-s average). *(C)* Waterfall display. Dominant frequencies diminished over the duration of the pulse, as shown in (C) by a downward shift in peak levels from left to right. Reanalyzed from recordings of Greene and Richardson (1988).

Any sound level measurement is taken over some interval of time. Most level data are actually averages over intervals as short as a fraction of a second or as long as several minutes, hours, or even days. For transient sounds shorter than the measurement interval, the measured value is less than the actual level during the noise event, and the measured value diminishes as measurement interval increases. Thus, for transient sounds, it is important to specify the interval over which a level measurement was taken ("averaging time"). Also, for continuous but variable sounds, it is important to realize that the variability in a series of level measurements will depend greatly on the averaging time for each individual measurement. The longer the averaging time, the less the apparent variability. For example, if ambient noise varies from second to second, but averaging time is several seconds, there will be both quieter and noisier instants than evident from the measurements (e.g., Richardson et al. 1991a:55).

3.4.3 Spectra

Sound spectra depict the distribution of sound power as a function of frequency (Section 2.2.2; Fig. 3.2B). Spectra depict the relative or absolute levels of the sound components at various frequencies. Sound spectra can be either "narrowband spectra", typically showing levels in 1-Hz bands (spectral density levels); or "proportional bandwidth spectra", typically showing levels in bands ⅓ octave or 1 octave wide.

Specialized spectrum analyzers are commercially available. These instruments receive acoustic signals from a tape recorder or other source, digitize them, and compute the spectrum. The frequency range of interest, averaging time, and other parameters are usually selectable. From the narrowband spectrum, ⅓-octave spectra and other derived data can be determined. Results generally can be displayed, plotted, and saved digitally for further processing, such as application of frequency-specific calibration data. Many spectrum analyzers now operate in real time, although there is an upper limit on the frequencies that can be processed in real time.

Spectrum analysis can also be done by general-purpose computers with analog-to-digital (A/D) converters and appropriate signal analysis software. Acoustic signals from a tape recorder or other source are digitized at a rate at least twice the highest frequency of interest. For example, a sampling rate of ≥20,000 times per second would be needed if a spectrum up to 10 kHz is required. These voltage data are then processed with the Fast Fourier Transform algorithm. Frequency-specific calibration data are used to convert the resulting spectra to sound levels on a spectrum level (/Hz), ⅓-octave, and broadband basis, as required. Digitizers and signal analysis software are commercially available for microcomputers and workstations.

When digitizing a waveform, it is essential to sample at a rate at least twice the highest frequency in the waveform. If a higher frequency is present, an artifact appears in the sampled signal spectrum at a frequency given by the sample rate minus the high frequency, a phenomenon called *aliasing*. The sampled spectrum is corrupted by these aliased components. They cannot be distinguished from components truly at frequencies less than half the sample rate. Aliasing is avoided by low-pass filtering the signal at a frequency at or below one-half the sampling rate prior to digitizing.

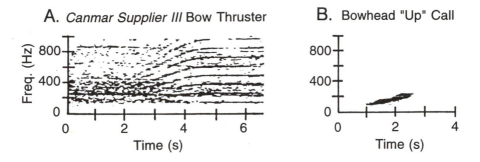

FIGURE 3.3. Examples of sonagrams of underwater sounds. *(A)* Noise from a small ship as its bow thruster began to turn. *(B)* One type of call from a bowhead whale. Sonagrams by C.W. Clark from Richardson et al. (1985c).

3.4.4 Spectrum versus Time

Graphs that show sound level versus frequency and time provide a good way to depict the characteristics of transient or variable sounds, either man-made or from animals (e.g., Fig. 3.3). These graphs, called *sonagrams* or *sonograms*, are widely used to illustrate animal calls and measure their characteristics. Traditionally, they were made using a Kay Sona-Graph, an analog instrument. Nowadays, commercially available digital signal processors can produce similar graphs more quickly and with greater flexibility, often with sound level depicted as a third dimension (e.g., Fig. 3.2C). Sound spectra are computed for successive brief time intervals and are plotted sequentially across or down the display or page. These graphs are often called *waterfall displays*, although that term properly applies only to a particular format of real-time spectrum analysis display. Both analog and digital sonagrams are very valuable tools. However, for quantitative uses, considerable care must be taken to avoid artifacts (Davis 1964; Watkins 1967b; Gaunt 1983; Thomas et al. 1986a; Beecher 1988; E.H. Miller 1992).

3.5 Physical Measurements

All methods described previously are used in studying ambient noise, man-made noise, and sound propagation. This section mentions some approaches and complications that are important in each of these types of studies.

3.5.1 Ambient Noise

Ambient noise is continuous but with much variability on time scales ranging from <1 s to 1 year. To understand the ambient noise of a particular area, one must make many measurements over a wide range of environmental conditions (Chapter 5). Both the average and the variability of these measurements are relevant. Periodic measurements with microphones (in air) or hydrophones or sonobuoys (underwater) provide useful data on ambient noise at particular locations and times. However, it is labor-intensive and costly to obtain long series of measurements with human-tended equipment. Also, the results tend to be biased toward environmental conditions and times of day conducive for fieldwork. Comprehensive ambient noise studies often involve hydrophones or microphones connected to data-logging systems that automatically measure or record sounds at regular intervals over extended periods.

Ambient noise is broadband in character but it can include tones or other narrowband components, often from distant human activities. Thus, both overall broadband measures and power spectra are widely used. Because there is ambient noise at all frequencies from the far infrasonic to the far ultrasonic, the overall ambient level inevitably depends on the bandwidth of the measurement. Thus, it is important to measure ambient noise in the band(s) relevant to the issue at hand. For example, in assessing the maximum radius of audibility of a specific noise source, data on ambient noise at infrasonic frequencies would be relevant if one were dealing with a supertanker radiating infrasounds and with a species able to hear infrasounds. Infrasonic ambient noise would not be relevant in assessing the detection radius around an outboard motorboat radiating noise at higher frequencies. Spectrum levels of ambient noise tend to be high at infrasonic and low frequencies (Section 5.2). Hence, the low-frequency limit chosen for a broadband level measurement can have a strong influence on the result. Ambient noise often tends to decrease with increasing frequency, so the choice of upper-frequency limit may be less critical. One useful way to summarize both the temporal variability and the frequency content of ambient noise is on a percentile basis by frequency (e.g., Fig. 3.4).

Although the ambient noise received at most locations comes from many different sources, more energy may be received from some directions than others (e.g., Wagstaff 1973). The directional properties of ambient noise can influence the detectability of specific sounds of

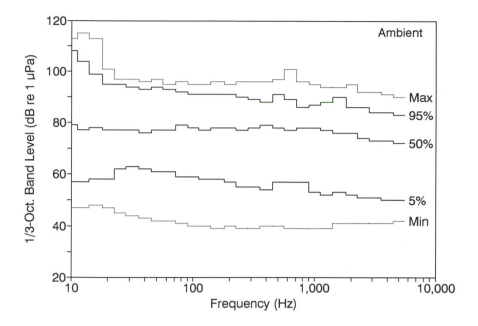

FIGURE 3.4. Variation in underwater ambient noise recorded off Barrow, Alaska, in May 1990. The curves show, for ⅓-octave bands centered at 10 Hz to 5000 Hz, the minimum and maximum ambient noise levels during 61 measurements, and selected percentile levels. From these data, the broadband level for any combination of ⅓-octave bands within the 9- to 5600-Hz range could be derived via equation (2.9). Data of C.R. Greene, Jr., from Richardson et al. (1991a).

interest whose source is in a particular direction. The horizontal and vertical directionality of ambient noise can be studied using arrays of hydrophones or microphones.

3.5.2 Man-Made Noise

Different human activities produce underwater and/or airborne sounds with widely varying level, frequency composition, and temporal pattern (Chapter 6). Hence, many different measurement techniques and schedules can be appropriate in different situations.

To compare the levels of different sources, one needs source level data for a standard distance, normally 1 m. Source level is usually estimated from (1) level measurements taken at longer distances plus (2) estimates of propagation loss between 1 m and the actual measurement distance. This process is necessary to avoid near-field biases, particularly if the source is large (Section 2.3.2). Equation (2.6) can be used to estimate the radius of the near-field zone.

Provided that the measurements are taken outside the near field, it is generally best to collect at least some of the data as close to the noise source as possible. This reduces the size and uncertainty of the adjustment for propagation loss between 1 m and the actual measurement distance. Also, received level is farther above the background noise level at a close-in measurement location. This is important when the natural ambient noise level is high, or other sources of man-made noise are nearby, or the frequencies of interest include those where the source emits rather weak sounds.

In addition to measurements near the source, data from several longer distances can be valuable in understanding the overall noise field near the source. Received sound levels tend to diminish as a roughly logarithmic function of range. Hence, it is often efficient to collect data at ranges increasing by a standard factor such as 2x, for example, 125 m, 250 m, 500 m, 1 km, ..., 8 km, 16 km. Received sound level in one or more frequency bands can then be plotted against range, and the range at which received level drops below the ambient level and becomes undetectable can be determined. It is also useful to plot the narrowband or ⅓-octave spectrum versus distance (Fig. 3.5). This shows frequency-related differences in attenuation rate and in the distances where various components drop below ambient and become undetectable. Such an analysis can also identify any frequency components that do not diminish with distance. These components are usually artifacts from some other source.

When the emitted sound varies over time, a representative series of measurements should be taken just beyond the near-field zone to characterize the variability. The average level over one or more full duty cycles may be a useful measurement. However, it is also important to determine the range of variability, including the peak level and/or the average level during a well-defined short interval around the time of peak level. For low-altitude aircraft overflights, we find that one useful datum is the average level during a 4-s period centered on the time of peak noise. For slowly varying sounds, averaging time is less critical. For noise impulses from sources such as distant explosions or seismic surveys, many measurement procedures have been used, including the peak-to-peak or zero-to-peak level determined from the waveform, average level over the duration of one pulse, average level over a 1-s interval, energy content, and positive impulse.

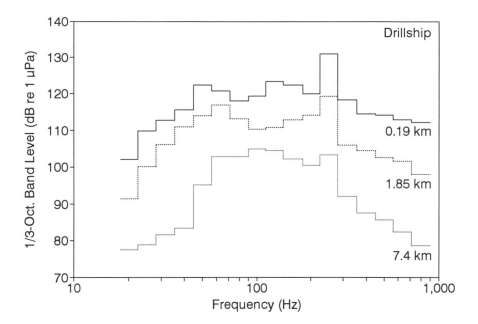

FIGURE 3.5. Received ⅓-octave band levels (dB re 1 µPa) at three distances from the drillship *Canmar Explorer II*. The high level in the band centered at 250 Hz was attributable mainly to strong tones at 277 and 254 Hz. Note the rapid attenuation of low-frequency components with increasing distance; water depth was 27 m and hydrophone depth 9 m. Data of Greene (1987b).

Standard measurement procedures are better defined for airborne sounds relevant to humans than for underwater sounds. This is especially true with transient sounds. It is difficult to compare different studies of marine mammals versus transient underwater sounds, given the inconsistent acoustic data. More attention should be given to this problem, adapting existing standard methods for airborne sound when appropriate. The *Sound Exposure Level (SEL)* concept, an energy measure, may be adaptable to transient underwater sounds. However, for most marine mammals, the A-weighting (Section 5.6) usually applied in measuring SEL will not be appropriate.

It is important to know the operating condition of the source during each measurement. If data are to be obtained at various distances from a source over a period of time, it is desirable to use a sonobuoy or some other method to obtain "control" data at one standard location while measurements are taken at other distances. This allows one to distinguish distance effects from temporal variations in source level. Data concerning the rotation rates of machinery and propellers on the noise source are important in identifying the machinery responsible for tones detectable in the received noise. It can be useful to make in-air noise recordings adjacent to potential noise sources aboard a ship or other noise source. One can then determine whether tones present in the spectra of these sounds are also evident in the overall sound emitted from the source.

Underwater noise received from many sources can depend on direction, source depth, and receiver depth as well as distance (Chapter 6). Many sources, including some ships and drillrigs, emit more noise in certain directions than in others; frequency content may also vary with aspect. Seismic survey gear and most sonars are specifically designed to project as much energy as possible in a narrow range of directions. In these cases, it is desirable to obtain acoustic data at various aspects, and to be aware of aspect angle during each measurement. When source depth is variable, this can also affect the effective source level, especially for low-frequency sources close to the surface. Finally, received level can vary with hydrophone depth; the frequencies of interest and water depth should be considered when selecting measurement depth (Section 3.2.2).

3.5.3 Sound Propagation

Studies of the attenuation of underwater and airborne sound with increasing distance require measurements of received sound levels at various distances from a source of known and standardized sounds (Chapter 4). Measurements should be taken over as wide a range of distances as possible. The optimum distance increments will often form a geometric progression, as noted in Section 3.5.2. Distance from source can be measured with a variety of methods depending on distance and situation. These include direct measurement, surveying, acoustic travel time, radar, LORAN, or GPS.

Measurements taken at several distances from any source of continuous or repeating man-made noise can provide data on propagation loss. However, "sources of opportunity" may emit sounds that vary between the times when measurements can be taken at different distances. Also, the frequency content of their sounds is unlikely to be optimal for measurement purposes. These limitations reduce precision and maximum detection range.

Optimum results are obtained using a standardized source emitting test sounds appropriate to the question of interest. In studies of long-distance underwater propagation, low frequencies are of primary interest, since high frequencies are quickly attenuated by absorption (Section 4.5.1). Small explosive charges produce strong, standardized, low-frequency noise pulses (Section 6.7), and they have been widely used in underwater propagation tests. The receiving equipment can remain at one location while a boat or aircraft is used to drop charges sequentially at various distances. Alternatively, charges can be set off periodically at one location while the receiving equipment moves to a variety of stations. However, even small charges can injure or kill marine animals (Section 9.10.2; O'Keeffe and Young 1984), and indiscriminate use of explosives is not advisable.

Underwater sound projectors are also widely used to broadcast test sounds at selected frequencies. A series of tones at different frequencies can be projected repeatedly, and recorded at a series of distances and (if desired) depths. However, steady tones are especially subject to frequency- and range-specific effects. It is common to use more complex test sounds that are less subject to these effects and that are amenable to special signal processing to improve the ratio of signal to background noise. These test sounds can include frequency-modulated tones or pseudorandom noise containing a set of harmonically related tones, possibly closely spaced, with controlled phase relationships.

Most tests of underwater sound propagation are over distances of tens or hundreds of kilometers. However, propagation tests over thousands of kilometers are possible in some deep-water situations where low-frequency sound is "channeled" and subject to low rates of attenuation (Section 4.3; e.g., Shockley et al. 1982; Baggeroer and Munk 1992). Propagation tests for airborne sound and for high-frequency underwater sound are normally over short distances, given the rapid absorption of these sounds (Sections 4.5.1 and 4.6.1).

Propagation tests are usually done to understand the effects of environmental conditions on sound attenuation. Therefore, environmental factors known to affect propagation should be recorded along the propagation path during the test. For underwater tests, these factors include water depth, vertical profile of sound speed (as determined by temperature and salinity profiles), surface conditions (wave and/or ice characteristics), and bottom conditions (substrate type, depth of any soft layer) (Chapter 4). For airborne propagation tests, relevant variables include the surface material and elevation profile; vegetation; near-surface temperature, humidity, and wind; and the vertical profiles of temperature and wind (Section 4.6). These data are useful in accounting for observed variability in propagation loss, and in fitting semiempirical propagation loss models to observed data.

3.6 Biological Measurements

3.6.1 Marine Mammal Calls

The dominant components of the "communication" calls of most marine mammals are within the 20 Hz to 20 kHz range that can be detected and recorded with widely available recording equipment. However, many sounds produced by blue and fin whales are at or below 20 Hz, and the echolocation calls of toothed whales extend far above 20 kHz (Chapter 7). Specialized recording equipment (Section 3.3) is needed to study these sounds.

When the calls of captive marine mammals are recorded, one can be sure that the sounds are coming from a particular species. When only one animal is present, the age and sex of the calling animal may also be known, along with its distance and orientation relative to the hydrophone. The latter information is important in determining source levels, directionality, and frequency spectrum (Watkins 1980b). However, captive animals may not produce the full repertoire of species-specific calls, and the strongest calls emitted in a small tank may be weaker than some calls by free-ranging individuals.

When calls of free-ranging marine mammals are recorded, a fuller and more representative repertoire may be documented. However, it is often difficult to be certain that a given sound comes from a particular species, let alone from a particular individual of known age, sex, distance, and orientation relative to the hydrophone. Various methods have been used to help determine call source (e.g., Watkins and Schevill 1972; Clark 1980; Tyack 1985). Acoustic localization using arrays of hydrophones and computerized signal processing is useful (e.g., Cummings and Holliday 1987; Freitag and Tyack 1993), especially when combined with simultaneous visual observations (Clark 1983). Even then, it is difficult to obtain reliable estimates of source levels, particularly for directional sounds like the echolocation calls of toothed whales. It is rarely known whether a given call was emitted at the maximum possible source level.

Marine mammal calls are transient sounds whose frequency composition often varies within the duration of the call. Therefore, waterfall or sonagram displays (Figs. 3.2C and 3.3) depicting frequency versus time are the standard method of analysis. However, care must be taken when using sonagrams to study rapidly pulsed calls. Depending on the analysis procedures, pulses at a particular interval can be artifactually displayed as "tones" at frequencies related to that interval (Watkins 1967b). Also, in the absence of appropriate low-pass filtering prior to digital sampling, signal components above the frequency range being analyzed can appear as artifacts within that range (aliasing). Examination of waveforms (level versus time) can assist in studying pulsed sounds.

3.6.2 Marine Mammal Hearing

Auditory thresholds at various frequencies can be determined either by tests with trained captive animals or by electrophysiological tests on captive or beached animals. The former method results in behavioral audiograms showing the estimated absolute auditory threshold versus frequency (Section 8.2). The latter method estimates relative sensitivity to different frequencies.

In the behavioral method, pure tones at various levels and frequencies are presented to a trained animal. If the animal hears a sound stimulus, it usually responds positively; if the tone is not heard or if no sound was presented, as in a control trial, no positive response is expected. An individual animal's audiogram depicts, for various frequencies, the minimum detectable sound level, which is the level to which the animal responds during 50-75% of the trials. (Different researchers have used differing criteria.) Thus, the threshold at a given frequency is a statistical measure, subject to uncertainty. The training and testing processes are time-consuming and are possible only on animals that are amenable to captivity and to operant or classical conditioning (Defran and Pryor 1980; Au 1993:13). Species tested to date have included some of the smaller dolphins and porpoises, hair seals, and eared seals, but no baleen, beaked, or sperm whales (Section 8.2). A study of manatee hearing is underway (Gerstein et al. 1993).

Electrophysiological methods measure the evoked electrical response from the ear or brain upon stimulation with sounds of various frequencies, levels, and durations. A sound that evokes an electrical response may or may not elicit a behavioral response. Evoked potential (EP) methods are valuable in revealing the *relative* sensitivity of some part of the sensory or nervous system to different sounds. However, EP methods may not provide useful data on *absolute* sensitivity or on effectiveness in eliciting behavioral responses. One great advantage is that EP methods rapidly provide many quantitative data from untrained animals. They are potentially applicable to entrapped or beached as well as captive animals (e.g., Carder and Ridgway 1990, 1994). Some early EP studies on marine mammals used deeply implanted electrodes, but recent work has used noninvasive surface electrodes.

Similar behavioral and evoked potential methods can provide data on other capabilities of the auditory system besides its absolute sensitivity. Both approaches have been used to determine the smallest detectable differences in frequency, level, or direction of arrival (Sections 8.3 and 8.4), and in mammal abilities to detect sounds in the presence of background noise (masking studies, Section 8.5).

3.6.3 Marine Mammal Reaction Thresholds

Most existing data on behavioral reactions of marine mammals to human activities have come from uncontrolled field observations of free-ranging animals. Some of the more detailed data have come from a few field studies designed to quantify these reactions under partially controlled conditions. Only a few data on behavioral reaction thresholds have come from captive marine mammals.

Uncontrolled field observations have been reported concerning the reactions of certain marine mammals to aircraft, boats, offshore construction and drilling, marine seismic exploration, explosions, and sonars (Chapter 9). Most of these observations were incidental to studies with other objectives, many were subjective, and received noise levels were rarely measured. Indeed, many of these reactions may have been attributable to vision rather than hearing. Despite these limitations, the results provide the only available evidence about the reactions of certain species of marine mammals to some human activities. Some of the results show reactions of marine mammals to full-scale human activities that cannot easily be simulated in an experiment.

Field experiments can be designed to test the reactions of marine mammals to noise and other stimuli from human activities. Several major studies of this type have been done, mainly on cetaceans (Chapter 9). These tests usually aim to obtain replicated and systematic behavioral observations before, during, and after exposure to man-made noise or some other form of disturbance. The animals may be exposed to the actual human activity and its associated noise, or to a simulated activity. One common simulation method is to use a sound projector to broadcast recorded man-made sounds: a "sound playback experiment". Sounds from the actual or simulated noise source should be recorded near the animals during the experiment, by sonobuoy or hydrophone, to determine received levels. If this is impractical, reliable estimates of received levels should be obtained by site-specific sound propagation models. Ambient noise levels should also be determined just before and after exposure to the man-made noise. It would be ideal if an electronics package attached to test animals could measure the received sound level. There is an ongoing program to develop that capability.

With these types of behavioral and acoustic data, reaction thresholds can—in theory—be determined relative to received sound level and to the signal-to-ambient ratio. However, complications are inevitable: ▶ The logistics of field experiments on marine mammals are usually difficult, and sample sizes are usually small. ▶ Playback and other simulations of full-scale human activity may be imperfect (Ellison and Weixel 1994), leading to questions about the representativeness of the results. ▶ There are often concerns that the animals' behavior was affected by the presence of observers, or their boats or aircraft. ▶ Specialized analysis methods are desirable when the same animals are observed repeatedly over time, since repeated observations on the same animals are not statistically independent. However, if the animals are not individually marked, it is often impossible to determine whether a given observation involves a previously observed or "new" animal. ▶ Improved telemetry tags optimized for these types of studies are needed (NRC/OSB 1994). Various workers are developing improved tags (Costa 1993).

Partially controlled field experiments and uncontrolled field observations both have advantages and limitations. Experimental methods allow controlled comparisons of behavior before, during, and after a simulated disturbance. Observational methods have the disadvantage of no direct control, but the advantage of greater realism when the human activity cannot be fully simulated during experiments. The two approaches are partly complementary, and a few noise-effects studies have incorporated both (e.g., Richardson et al. 1986, 1990b).

Long-term effects of noise on marine mammal behavior are difficult to study. Almost all available data involve observations over intervals of minutes or at most hours. The significance of short-term behavioral responses to the long-term well-being of individuals and populations is rarely known. In a few cases marine mammals have been found to cease using areas heavily disturbed by humans (Section 11.6.3). However, it is difficult to prove that this effect was caused by noise or other aspects of disturbance. We need data on the behavioral and physiological reactions of marine mammals to repeated or ongoing noise exposure. Radiotelemetry may be necessary in many cases.

CHAPTER 4

SOUND PROPAGATION[1]

4.1 Introduction and Relevance

The audibility or apparent loudness of a noise source is determined by the radiated acoustic power (source level), the propagation efficiency, the ambient noise, and the hearing sensitivity of the subject species. This chapter focuses on propagation.

Noise levels produced by human activities in underwater and terrestrial environments are determined not only by their acoustic power output but, equally important, by the local sound transmission conditions. A moderate-level source transmitting over an efficient path may produce the same received level at a given range as a higher-level source transmitting through an area where sound is attenuated rapidly, that is, over a "lossy" path. Likewise, a given noise source operating in different areas, or in the same area at different times, may be detectable for greatly varying distances, depending on regional and temporal changes in sound propagation conditions among other factors. In deep water, depth variations in water properties strongly affect sound propagation. In shallow water, interactions with the surface and bottom have strong effects.

As a result, the zone of acoustic influence for a given source of man-made noise can vary in radius 10-fold or more, depending on operating site and depth, and on seasonal changes in water properties. Hence, sound transmission measurements, analyses, and model predictions are necessary to estimate the potential radius of acoustic influence of noisy human activities.

Site-specific sound propagation data are often lacking when a potentially noisy activity is planned. It is often not feasible to obtain *in situ* sound transmission measurements to estimate how intrusive the new noise will be. However, predictions can often be made even

---

[1] By Charles I. Malme, Bolt Beranek and Newman Inc.

without site-specific propagation data. Predictions are based on prop-agation models developed for both airborne and underwater sound. These models provide procedures for estimating the received noise level as a function of distance, assuming that the source level and characteristics are known (Chapter 6). These propagation models may be purely theoretical, based on physical principles; or semi-empirical, using both physical principles plus field measurements.

Model predictions can be useful for planning and for preparing environmental impact statements, but it is advisable to obtain relev-ant empirical data as well. This is important because of the highly variable and site-specific nature of underwater sound transmission, especially in shallow water, and of airborne sound transmission near the ground.

This chapter describes some sound propagation concepts relevant to noise impact prediction. We discuss theoretical aspects; basic features of deep water, shallow water, and airborne sound transmis-sion; and air-to-water transmission. The summary (Section 4.8) in-cludes some general sound transmission equations. Nonacousticians should read Chapter 2, "Acoustic Concepts and Terminology", before reading this one. The "Glossary" at the back of the book may also be helpful.

4.2 Theoretical Aspects

Efforts to develop theoretical sound transmission models have been under way for several decades. This section mentions some common approaches without attempting to explain equation formula-tions. Later sections include examples of models mentioned here. To apply models to actual situations, large numbers of calculations must often be done. Thus, all but the simplest models must be implemented as computer programs before they can be applied to practical acous-tical problems (Jensen et al. 1994).

The differential equation relating the space and time variables in an acoustic field, the "wave equation", is difficult to solve for real-world situations (Frisk 1993). The method of *normal modes* can be applied in the common case where sound velocity structure in the water column is horizontally stratified (i.e., changes vertically but not horizontally) and where the boundary conditions at the surface and bottom can be specified. The normal-mode method, developed by Pekeris (1948), is useful in calculating the sound field in shallow water where the water column acts as a waveguide for a limited number of propagating modes. The combinations of wavelength and incidence angle that match the boundary conditions determine the most efficient modes of propagation. Normal-mode theory has been expanded to take account of (1) sound speed gradients that vary with depth and (2) bottom layer properties that require both fluid and solid-layer models (Tolstoy 1955, 1960). Alternatively, bottom effects can be included by using experimentally determined plane-wave reflection coefficients, without requiring detailed knowledge of the bottom layer composition (Brekhovskikh 1960).

The problem of solving the wave equation for range-dependent conditions such as sloping or irregular bottoms and range-varying sound speed gradients has been overcome by using an approximation called the *parabolic equation* (Tappert 1977). Computer-implemented solutions to this equation use small incremental steps in range and depth to accommodate changes in propagation parameters without developing large errors. However, in deep water when many modes are propagating, the large number of increments that must be used make this method computationally cumbersome.

In water deep enough for propagation of 10 or more modes, another wave equation approximation called *ray theory* may be used. This requires only that the properties of the medium do not change much over a distance of one acoustic wavelength. The sound field is calculated by tracing paths of rays starting from the source at uniformly spaced angular increments. For each increment in range, each path direction is determined by the ray equations and the local gradient of sound speed vs. depth. Sound intensity is determined by ray density relative to the starting density. Ray calculations of intensity must be modified where they predict infinite intensity, as in focusing regions (*caustics*), or zero intensity, as in *shadow zones* (Section 4.3).

Ray theory is useful in deep water where a small number of rays transmit most of the acoustic energy from a source to a receiver, where there is a direct path from source to receiver, and where only a limited number of surface- and bottom-reflected paths contribute. In water that is shallow but sufficiently deep to permit application of ray theory, the large number of reflected paths involved in most transmission geometries makes it impractical to calculate transmission loss by summation of individual ray contributions. For this application, theoretical and semiempirical transmission models have been developed. These models use principles of ray theory together with measured or theoretical boundary loss parameters. They typically incorporate one or more spreading loss terms, boundary reflection and scattering loss terms, and an absorption term. Specific examples are included in the following discussion of deep and shallow water propagation.

4.3 *Deep Water Propagation*

The theoretical distinction between deep and shallow water concerns primarily the wavelength/water depth ratio rather than depth per se. At frequencies of a few hertz, wavelengths are hundreds of meters and even abyssal depths must be considered shallow water. In contrast, in the kilohertz range where wavelength is <1.5 m, much of the continental shelf as well as abyssal areas may be considered deep. In deep water, water depths are typically >100 times the acoustic wavelengths and sound transmission generally involves few or no bottom reflections. In shallow water, in contrast, bottom and surface reflections are usually dominant components of sound transmission. Despite the wavelength effect, it is common to consider depths <200 m as shallow and depths >2000 m as deep.

In a uniform medium with no nearby boundaries and no absorption loss, sound from an omnidirectional source spreads uniformly outward with a spherical wavefront. Intensity decreases as the area of the wavefront expands. At distances that are large compared with the source dimensions (far field), sound intensity varies inversely as the square of range from the acoustic center of the source. Since sound intensity is proportional to sound pressure squared (Section 2.2.1), sound pressure is inversely proportional to range. In logarithmic terms, this is called a *20 log R spreading loss* or *spherical spreading*:

$$L_r = L_s - 20 \log R \qquad (4.1)$$

where L_r is the received level in dB re 1 µPa (underwater) or dB re 20 µPa (in air),

   L_s is the source level at 1 m in the same units, and

   R is the range in m.

When sound becomes trapped in a sound duct between horizontal refracting or reflecting layers, it is constrained to spread outward cylindrically rather than spherically. *Cylindrical spreading* also occurs when sound is trapped between the surface and bottom in shallow water. In these cases, sound intensity decreases in proportion to the increase in area of the expanding cylindrical wavefront. As a result, sound intensity varies inversely as the range from the source (i.e., as $1/R$), in contrast to the $1/R^2$ that applies with spherical spreading. Sound pressure varies inversely as $\sqrt{\text{range}}$ (i.e., as $1/R^{0.5}$), in contrast to the $1/R$ that applies with spherical spreading. This is the *10 log R spreading loss* of cylindrical sound transmission:

$$L_r = L_s - 10 \log H - 10 \log R \qquad\qquad (4.2)$$

where H is the effective channel depth. The "$- 10 \log H$" term is related to the fact that cylindrical spreading does not begin at the source; spreading is usually more or less spherical from the source out to some distance, and then may transition to cylindrical (Section 2.4).

Sound attenuates much more rapidly with increasing distance with spherical ($20 \log R$) than with cylindrical ($10 \log R$) spreading (Fig. 2.3). A given source can be heard farther away when there is cylindrical spreading along much of the path from source to receiver.

Simple spherical or cylindrical spreading are important theoretical concepts and apply at least approximately to many real-world situations. However, the ocean is not a uniform medium. Variations in temperature and salinity with water depth affect the rate of propagation loss. The speed of sound increases with increasing temperature, salinity, and pressure. This results in distortion of the wavefront as it propagates. This distortion is equivalent to bending (*refraction*) of the sound rays that trace the paths of points on the wavefront. Refraction causes rays to be bent toward the direction of slower sound speed, since the portion of the wavefront traveling in the region of higher sound speed advances faster than the remaining portion. Refraction is a dominant feature of deep water sound transmission. Variation of sound speed with depth controls the ray paths. As a result, the decrease of sound intensity with range is influenced not only by spreading loss but also by concentration or reduction in the ray density due to refraction.

Typically, the sound speed profile can be divided into several horizontal layers (Fig. 4.1A). Characteristics of the surface layer and seasonal thermocline are strongly influenced by solar radiation and by fresh water input from rain, rivers, and ice melt. These factors cause seasonal and geographic changes in sound speed profile (e.g., Fig. 4.1B). In winter, surface cooling forms a thin *surface duct* where sound generated near the surface—for example, from ship traffic—propagates well. Under these conditions, some sound energy from a near-surface source is refracted upward, trapping it within the surface

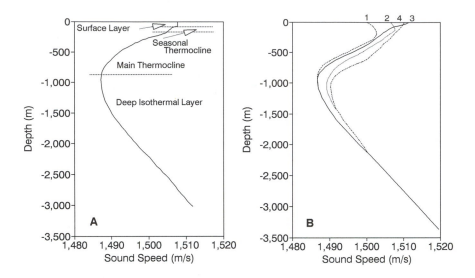

FIGURE 4.1. Typical deep sea sound speed profiles. *(A)* Profile showing layer structure (from Urick 1983). *(B)* Average sound speed profiles in different seasons in an area halfway between Newfoundland and Great Britain: (1) winter, (2) spring, (3) summer, (4) autumn (from Urick 1983, based on U.S. Navy data).

duct. In contrast, during spring and summer the surface warms up, developing a thin upper layer that causes most sound from a surface source to be refracted downward. This results in increased transmission loss for sound propagating near the surface.

Details of surface-layer transmission can be shown in a ray diagram (Fig. 4.2). In this example, turbulence from waves has resulted in a mixed layer of uniform temperature and salinity down to 60 m. The increasing pressure with increasing depth causes sound from a source in the surface layer to be alternately refracted upward and then reflected back downward from the surface. Sound trapped in a surface duct propagates with approximately cylindrical spreading beyond the range where trapping occurs. However, there is some additional loss due to surface scattering and *leakage* of sound energy out of the duct. In the case illustrated, rays propagating at angles steeper than 2.5° below the horizontal are not trapped but are refracted downward. This causes a *shadow zone* below the mixed layer (Fig. 4.2). Received sound levels in this zone are low but not zero. Some sound energy reaches this region by the scattering and leakage processes.

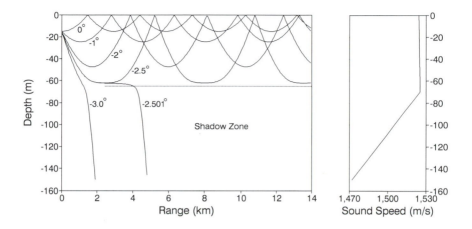

FIGURE 4.2. Ray diagram for sound transmission from a source at a depth of 15 m in a 60-m mixed layer. Sound speed profile at right. Rays are drawn at 1° intervals except as noted.

When the mixed layer near the surface is absent or thin, a negative sound speed gradient may exist at shallow depths. Here a downward-refracted sound field may result in a near-surface shadow zone. This shallow shadow region often has higher attenuation values than found in a deeper shadow zone of the type shown in Fig. 4.2. Sound levels at 24 kHz in the shadow zone may be 40 to 60 dB lower than expected at the same range in the free field (Urick 1983:135).

One of the better known features of deep water propagation is the *deep sound channel*, also known in some older literature as the *SOFAR* channel. The axis of this channel is at the depth of minimum sound speed: typically 600-1200 m at low and middle latitudes (Figs. 4.1A and 4.1B), but approaching the surface in polar regions. The focusing effect of this channel causes near-horizontal sound rays from sources within the channel to be trapped, avoiding the losses that would result from bottom and surface reflections (Fig. 4.3).

The sound transmission efficiency of the deep sound channel is evident from various extremely long-range transmission experiments. For example, noise from 91- and 136-kg high-explosive charges detonated at 732-1800 m depth off Western Australia was clearly detected 19,800 km away near Bermuda, halfway around the earth (Shockley et al. 1982). A recent application involved transmission of low-frequency (~57 Hz) sounds from underwater projectors near Heard Island (southern Indian Ocean) to a set of globally distributed receiving sites

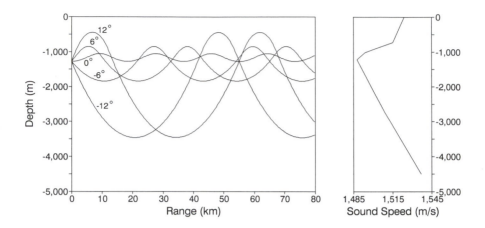

FIGURE 4.3. Ray diagram for the deep ocean sound channel when the source is on the axis. Sound speed profile at right. Rays are drawn at 6° intervals.

up to ~17,500 km away (Section 6.8). The Heard Island experiment tested the feasibility of using sound transmission time to monitor global temperature change (Munk 1990; Baggeroer and Munk 1992; Munk et al. 1994). Heard Island was chosen for two reasons: the relatively shallow channel depth (200 m) at that high-latitude location, and the unobstructed great-circle pathways into many parts of the Atlantic, Pacific, and Indian oceans.

Special cases of the sound-channel effect also occur for near-surface sources in deep water when the surface layer is thin or becomes downward refracting. In this situation, sound from the surface source can be trapped in the sound channel and refracted so that, near the surface, elevated sound levels occur in narrow annuli or *convergence zones*. These zones typically are spaced 56-65 km apart at low and middle latitudes (Fig. 4.4) and closer together at high latitudes, where the depth of the sound channel decreases. Sound levels in convergence zones are typically ~10-15 dB above those expected based on simple spherical spreading and absorption, as illustrated by the mid-Atlantic curve in Fig. 4.6, later.

Another type of sound channeling in deep water occurs in arctic regions, where the cold temperature at the surface causes the minimum sound speed to occur there. All sound rays in the *arctic surface channel* are refracted upward and are then reflected from the under-ice surface (Fig. 4.5). A major source of low-frequency loss in the arctic is conversion of acoustic waves into flexural waves of the ice

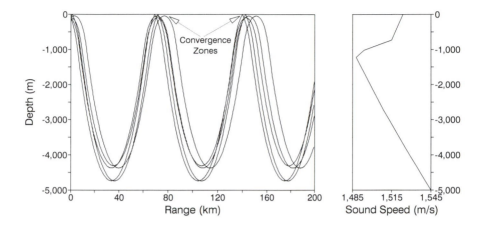

FIGURE 4.4. Ray diagram for convergence zone propagation in deep water; source at depth 90 m. Sound speed profile at right. Rays are drawn at 2-3° intervals from -5° to +5°.

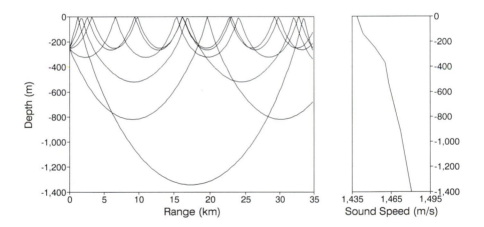

FIGURE 4.5. Ray diagram for deep water sound transmission in the Arctic. Sound speed profile at right. Rays are drawn at 2-4° intervals from -8° to +10°.

sheet. At higher frequencies, under-ice roughness has important effects on sound propagation. Smooth annual ice may enhance propagation as compared with open water conditions. However, with increased cracking, ridging, and other forms of roughness, transmission losses generally become higher than when the water is open. Richardson and Malme (1993) discuss other aspects of arctic sound propagation relevant in predicting effects on marine mammals.

In summary, in deep water with uniform properties, spherical (20 log R) spreading is an important mode of sound transmission. However, water properties are usually horizontally stratified (Fig. 4.1). As a result, for propagation over long distances, sound ducting and sound shadows often occur. In a duct, spreading losses may be as low as 10 log R (cylindrical spreading) when range from the source exceeds a transition range related to duct thickness.

4.4 Shallow Water Propagation

Sound transmission in shallow water is highly variable and site-specific because it is strongly influenced by the acoustic properties of the bottom and surface as well as by variations in sound speed within the water column. As in deep water, variations in temperature and salinity with depth cause sound rays to be refracted downward or upward. However, the shallow depth does not allow most types of sound channeling effects noted earlier for deep water. Refraction of sound in shallow water can result in either reduced or enhanced sound transmission. With upward refraction, bottom reflections and the resulting bottom losses are reduced; with downward refraction the opposite occurs. Thus, sound transmission conditions in continental shelf areas can vary widely, as illustrated by the Scotian Shelf versus Grand Banks data in Fig. 4.6.

The many environmental factors that influence shallow water sound transmission make it difficult to develop adequate theoretical models. One must combine theory with site-specific empirical data to obtain reliable propagation predictions. In recent years, questions about military sonar operation in shallow seas have motivated many field studies. Although many of these data are unavailable, some unclassified results have been published (e.g., Kuperman and Jensen 1980; Akal and Berkson 1986).

When the water is very shallow, with sound wavelengths (λ) comparable to the water depth (H)—that is, where $0.25 < H/\lambda < 2$—sound propagation may be analyzed using *mode theory* or modified mode theory involving solutions of the parabolic wave equation. Mode theory predicts that, if the effective water depth is less than $\lambda/4$, waves are not matched to the duct and very large propagation losses occur. In many cases, however, the bottom consists of water-saturated

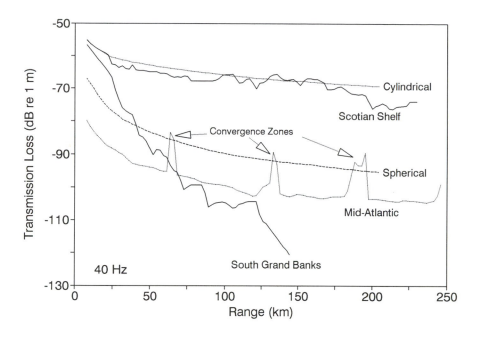

FIGURE 4.6. Propagation loss versus range for 40-Hz sound traveling in deep and shallow waters of the Atlantic Ocean (from Staal 1985). Measurements from two shallow water areas (Scotian Shelf and South Grand Banks) illustrate the large differences that can occur as a result of different environmental conditions. Dotted lines are theoretical predictions for deep water sites.

sediment and is not a discrete reflecting boundary for all the sound energy. In these conditions, propagation of low-frequency energy extends downward into the bottom material. If the composition and layer structure of the bottom are known, or can be estimated, this information, when incorporated into the modal analysis procedure, permits calculation of shallow water sound transmission losses with good accuracy.

The development of efficient computer-implemented solutions of the *parabolic equation* or PE (Lee and Botseas 1982) provides advantages over conventional normal-mode solutions. PE methods can work with range-dependent conditions such as sloping bottoms and spatial variations in sound speed profile. As an example, Fig. 4.7 illustrates sound transmission into a region of decreasing depth, including sound transmission into a penetrable bottom. For accurate solutions, PE methods typically require computation of the acoustic field using incre-

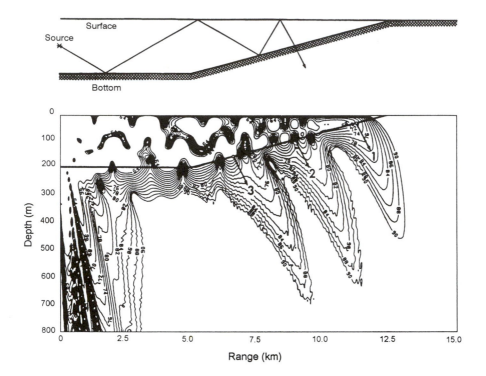

FIGURE 4.7. Output from a Parabolic Equation Model showing sound transmission loss contours for upslope propagation at 25 Hz with three modes excited. Upper profile shows the bottom contour and mode 2 path. Numbered arrows on contour plot indicate three points of maximum mode transmission into bottom material (from Jensen and Kuperman 1980; see Jensen et al. 1994 for color version).

ments of $\lambda/4$ in depth and $\lambda/2$ in range. Solutions involving high frequencies, deep water, or long ranges are computationally intensive and require a fast computer or a patient analyst. PE models are now being used in environmental assessments of some noisy activities (e.g., ARPA and NMFS 1994).

When water depth becomes large compared to the longest wavelength of propagating sound energy ($H/\lambda > 5$), acoustic ray theory may be applied. Ray theory represents the sound field as a sum of ray contributions with each ray following a direct, refracted, or reflected path from the source to a receiving point. In shallow water the reflected paths may be represented as arrivals from a set of *image sources*, which are geometric reflections of the source in the planes of the bottom and surface. The strengths of the image sources are determined by amplitude and phase changes produced by reflection losses. At the receiving point the sound pressure is calculated from the vector sum (accounting for magnitude and phase) of all pressure gradient contributions from the images. When many images are involved and when the bottom reflection losses can be expressed as a function, a closed-form solution for transmission loss can be obtained using an integral to represent the image summation process (Smith 1974). Theoretical models developed in this way provide convenient methods for predicting shallow water transmission loss. Unfortunately, the variability of the water and bottom parameters often restricts the usefulness of these models.

To accommodate the variability of real-world data, semiempirical propagation models have been designed for application to shallow water. One of these, developed by Marsh and Schulkin (1962) and summarized in Urick (1983:178), was based on a large number of shallow water measurements from 100 Hz to 10 kHz. This model includes three basic equations covering different spreading loss conditions. **(1)** Near the source, sound energy spreads spherically outward at the "20 log R" rate—see equation (4.1). **(2)** At intermediate ranges, a "15 log R" loss rate is assumed:

$$L_r = L_s - 20 \log R_1 - 15 \log (R/R_1) \tag{4.3}$$

R_1 is the transition range ($R_1 < R$) where spherical spreading changes to "15 log R" spreading. This equation is a useful approximation when bottom reflection loss is proportional to the grazing angle of the sound ray with the bottom. This has been called *mode stripping* because the higher-order modes with steeper grazing angles are attenuated more quickly than the lower-order modes with shallow grazing angles. **(3)** After this process, only low-order modal energy remains at ranges beyond a second transition range. This propagates as the lowest mode with a cylindrical "10 log R" loss rate. Marsh and Schulkin give criteria based on water depth and mixed layer depth for determining the ranges where each loss rate applies.

It is possible to make reasonable propagation predictions from simple formulas of these types if sound speed is nearly independent of water depth and if the bottom either is flat or slopes uniformly and gradually (Weston 1976). Weston's formulas divide the shallow water transmission path into four regions rather than the three used in the Marsh and Schulkin model. The additional region is located between the spherical-spreading and mode-stripping zones. It is a transitional, cylindrical-spreading region where bottom- and surface-reflected rays contribute more energy than the directly transmitted rays (10 log R). Weston's formulas have been modified by P.W. Smith, Jr. (Malme et al. 1986a), and incorporated into a short computer program that calculates transmission loss when given parameters of frequency, water depth at the source, bottom slope, and two parameters describing the bottom reflection loss. This "Weston/Smith" procedure has been used in predicting reaction distances of some whales (e.g., Section 10.4 and Miles et al. 1987).

4.5 Absorption and Factors Affecting Spreading Loss

Several additional factors can have important influences on sound propagation in both deep and shallow water. These include molecular absorption and interference effects associated with shallow sources or receivers. A sloping bottom or special types of subbottom layers can also affect propagation, especially in shallow water.

4.5.1 Absorption

When sound energy is transmitted through water, a small portion is absorbed by water molecules. Seawater absorbs considerably more sound energy than does distilled water (Liebermann 1949). Viscosity effects are responsible for sound absorption by pure water (Mason 1965). Various chemicals contained in seawater—some in very small amounts—cause the additional absorption. Magnesium sulfate is the main cause of absorption from about 10 to 100 kHz. A second absorption process caused by boric acid ions occurs at frequencies below 5 kHz (Yeager et al. 1973). The latter process is influenced by other chemicals in seawater. As a result, low-frequency attenuation values vary with ocean location and can range from 10^{-2} to 10^{-3} dB/km for frequencies below 100 Hz (Kibblewhite and Hampton 1980). Another low-frequency attenuation process results from scattering of sound by large inhomogeneities in the sound channel. This process results in a nearly constant attenuation of 3.3×10^{-3} dB/km below 100 Hz (Mellen et al. 1976).

Sound energy loss due to absorption is directly proportional to range and is usually given in dB/km or, in earlier literature, dB/kiloyard (1 dB/kyd = 1.09 dB/km). Absorption of sound by seawater increases with increasing frequency; energy loss is approximately pro-

portional to the square of frequency. Absorption is also weakly influenced by water temperature. Furthermore, there is a relatively strong
pressure dependence, with absorption coefficients being reduced with
increasing depth. At frequencies >5 kHz, absorption causes significant
(>2 dB) transmission loss if range is >10 km. At frequencies <1 kHz,
absorption is not significant at ranges <40 km. However, when the
propagation path is thousands of kilometers long, as in some tests
mentioned in Section 4.3, there is significant absorption even at frequencies below 100 Hz. Several empirical formulae have been published to calculate absorption versus frequency (Urick 1983; Browning and
Mellen 1986). One that gives reasonable agreement with data over a
wide range of frequencies (f, in kHz), courtesy of D. Ross (personal
communication), is

$$a = 0.036\, f^{1.5} \quad \text{(dB/km)} \tag{4.4}$$

4.5.2 Shallow Source and Receiver Effects

When the source and/or receiver are very close to the surface, the
surface reflection of the sound interacts strongly with direct sound
radiation. The reflected sound is out of phase with the direct sound.
If the source has strong tonal or narrow-bandwidth components, this
phenomenon produces an interference pattern. It may be observed as
range-dependent fluctuations in sound level at receiving locations
along a horizontal radial line from the source. This phenomenon, the
Lloyd mirror effect, is strongest with low-frequency tones and in calm
sea conditions.

This effect occurs when range from source to receiver is long
enough such that the direct and reflected path lengths are comparable. An interference field develops with alternating maxima and
minima in received level. The boundaries of the interference region
are determined by

$$2(d_1 d_2)^{0.5} < R < 4d_1 d_2/\lambda \tag{4.5}$$

where d_1 and d_2 are source and receiver depths in meters, R is range
from the acoustic center of the source (m), and λ is wavelength of
sound (m) at the frequency of interest (adapted from Urick 1983:132).
Theoretically, with a pure-tone source and a smooth surface, pressure
doubling could occur at the maxima and complete cancellation at the
minima. However, because of wave roughness and finite bandwidth
effects, variations in received level are more commonly <6 dB from
maxima to minima for narrow-band components.

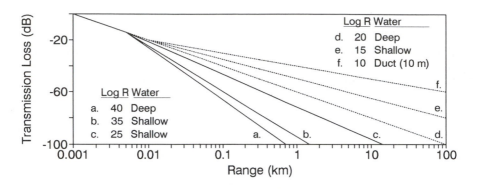

FIGURE 4.8. Theoretical underwater transmission losses when source and/or receiver are within ¼ wavelength of the surface (a, b, c) as compared with loss rates for greater source and receiver depths (d, e, f).

Beyond the interference zone, propagation loss is higher than normal when either the source or the receiver is close to the surface, that is, when their depths are less than ¼ wavelength for the dominant frequencies. With a shallow source, the source and its reflected image become effectively a dipole source with a vertical directionality (Urick 1983:134). In deep water, with both a shallow source and a shallow receiver, spreading loss may be as much as 40 log R, versus the 20 log R expected from spherical spreading (Fig. 4.8a versus 4.8d). In shallow water, the shallow source dipole effect introduces an additional 10 log R spreading loss (Grachev 1983), increasing the loss from ~15 log R to ~25 log R (Fig. 4.8c versus 4.8e). A similar interference effect occurs when the receiving location is within ¼ wavelength of the surface. Thus, propagation from a shallow source to a shallow receiver in shallow water will show ~35 log R spreading loss (Fig. 4.8b).

These types of effects have been reported for several oil industry sounds. Noise pulses from distant seismic exploration are typically several decibels weaker when received at 3 m depth than when received at 9 or 18 m (Greene and Richardson 1988). Similar depth-related differences in received levels were found for low-frequency components of dredge sounds (Greene 1987b).

4.5.3 *Bottom Slope Effects*

The slope of the bottom has a strong influence on sound transmission in shallow water. For transmission from a shallow region into deeper water, the increasing depth permits sound energy to spread out into a larger volume than would have been available if depth had remained constant. This tends to result in a reduced sound level. On the other hand, a downward-sloping bottom causes decreasing angles of incidence of sound rays with the bottom and surface. This results in fewer reflections per kilometer, and thus less energy loss. For most bottom types, the reduction in reflection loss with increasing depth has a stronger influence than the increased water volume.

Hence, the net effect of a downward slope along the propagation path often is lower transmission loss. This effect is most pronounced when neutral or upward-refracting sound speed gradients exist. With these conditions, increasing depth may allow sound transmission to become ducted, in which case it is no longer influenced by the bottom (Section 4.3). Downslope propagation into a duct provides a mechanism for long-range transmission of sound from ships and other near-surface sources over a continental shelf (Ross 1976:283). Thus, spreading loss is initially high in shallow water, but may diminish to ~10 log R when the energy reaches deeper water.

Conversely, for sound transmission upslope into shallower water, the decrease in available volume for the sound energy would theoretically result in higher sound pressure and lower transmission loss. However, an upward slope causes more surface and bottom reflections, and a steeper incidence angle for each reflection. Consequently, there is a net increase in loss rate as sound enters shallower water unless bottom loss is very low. As propagation continues upslope, there is a transition from multimode to single-mode propagation and a shift from 15 log R to 10 log R spreading loss. Although spreading loss is reduced, attenuation from bottom loss may be high because of the many reflections in shallow water. Eventually, depth is reduced to the point where modal transmission is not supported (depth < $\lambda/4$) and the remaining sound energy is attenuated very rapidly.

4.5.4 Transmission over Fast Subbottom Layers

Recent studies of low-frequency sound transmission in the Beaufort Sea have reported very low loss rates in shallow areas where high losses normally would be expected (Greene 1985a, 1987b; Miles et al. 1987). Observed transmission loss typically is near 10 log R plus some additional linear-with-R losses at the longer ranges. There sometimes are intermediate regions where the trend of the data becomes flat or even positive.

These results may be explained by evidence that some bottom materials with high sound speed may permit incident sound to penetrate the bottom and be refracted back out with low loss (Spofford et al. 1983). This process does not depend on a large impedance mismatch such as occurs when sound encounters a rocky bottom. Subsea permafrost or overconsolidated clay layers, which exist below parts of the Beaufort Sea, may have the necessary properties.

4.5.5 *Transmission of Infrasound*

Infrasound (<20 Hz) can be transmitted efficiently in deep water, especially if the source is in the SOFAR channel. There is negligible absorption into seawater (Section 4.5.1). However, because of the long wavelengths, proximity of source and/or receiver to the surface causes more attenuation than for other sounds. Also, infrasound usually attenuates rapidly in shallow water. However, it may be transmitted nearly as well as higher-frequency sound in shallow areas where it can propagate along the bottom and re-enter the water by means of interface motion and scattering from discontinuities (Staal and Chapman 1986). Infrasound at <15 Hz may be transmitted by seismoacoustic interface (Scholte) waves if there is a hard bottom. Thick sediment layers (>50 m) cause high attenuation of these waves, but thin layers (<10 m) cause little attenuation (Rauch 1980).

4.6 *Airborne Sound Transmission*

Airborne sound transmission needs to be considered for two reasons. First, sound from some sources, especially aircraft, travels through air before entering water, and is attenuated along the airborne portion of the propagation path. Second, some marine mammals—pinnipeds and sea otters—commonly occur on land or ice, where they hear airborne sounds and emit aerial calls.

Sound from an omnidirectional source in an unbounded uniform atmosphere is attenuated only by spherical spreading ($20 \log R$) and by absorption of sound energy by air molecules. However, sound from a source near the ground is affected by additional factors. The ground is usually nonrigid and permeable, and propagation near this surface is influenced by reflections and wave transmission along the surface. Interference between the direct, reflected, and ground wave paths causes fluctuations in received level and in frequency composition for near-ground transmission. Also, refraction caused by wind and temperature gradients produces shadow zones with poor sound transmission in the upwind direction, and often produces enhanced transmission downwind.

4.6.1 Atmospheric Absorption

Atmospheric absorption of sound at frequencies below 30 kHz is produced by oxygen and nitrogen molecules. The dominant mechanism is similar to the process acting underwater (Section 4.5.1). The amount of absorption depends on frequency, temperature, relative humidity, and to a small degree atmospheric pressure. The physical relationships between these parameters and absorption are not easily expressed mathematically, but an empirical algorithm has been developed to compute absorption coefficients from these four parameters (ANSI 1978).

At middle frequencies, sound absorption has more influence on sound transmission in the atmosphere than in the ocean. For example, at 1 kHz the underwater sound absorption coefficient is ~0.06 dB/km, whereas a typical value for in-air attenuation is ~4 dB/km. The absorption coefficient increases rapidly with frequency to ~130 dB/km at 10 kHz, depending on temperature and humidity. Hence, only low-frequency sound is transmitted well in air (Fig. 4.9).

4.6.2 Gradient Effects

Near the ground, vertical gradients in wind and temperature cause upward or downward refraction of acoustic wavefronts. Wind speed tends to increase with height because of the diminishing influ-

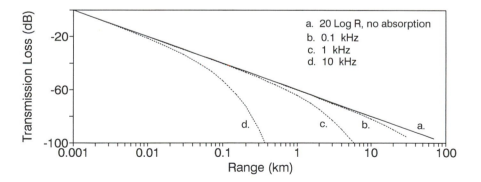

FIGURE 4.9. Atmospheric propagation loss based on spherical spreading plus additional absorption loss at 0.1, 1, and 10 kHz.

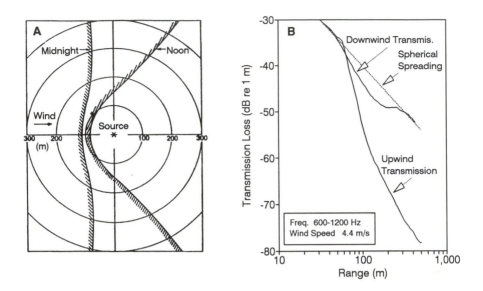

FIGURE 4.10. Effects of temperature and wind on airborne sound propagation
(from Wiener et al. 1954). *(A)* Location of sound shadow near a source during the
day and night. A constant wind is blowing from left to right. The sound shadow
is to the left of the hatched boundary. *(B)* Variations in measured sound pressure
levels in relation to wind speed and direction.

ence of drag by the ground. For downwind transmission, some sound
enhancement occurs because the higher wind speed aloft is added to
the sound speed, bending ray paths downward. For upwind transmission, the higher wind speed aloft acts to reduce sound speed, and
sound rays are bent upward. This usually results in a near-surface
shadow zone some distance upwind from the source. This distance is
determined by the strength of the vertical gradient in wind speed and
by the heights of the source and receiver.

   During a sunny day, air near the ground becomes warmer than
that at high altitudes, resulting in *temperature lapse*. Because sound
speed increases with temperature, sound rays from a source near the
ground are bent upward. If the wind speed gradient is weak, a shadow zone surrounding the source is formed. In contrast, with *temperature inversions*, which often occur at night when the ground cools, air
near the ground is colder than that at altitude and sound rays are
bent downward. This results in enhanced sound transmission along
the ground in all directions.

Under the usual daytime conditions, wind and temperature gradients interact to produce a shadow zone that partially surrounds the source (Fig. 4.10A). The day-night change in the shadow boundary illustrates the effect of a typical day-night change in temperature under a constant wind condition. The location of the shadow zone and the amount of *excess attenuation* within that zone change as the angle between wind direction and sound propagation direction changes (Fig. 4.10B). The amount of excess attenuation (i.e., in excess of spreading loss and absorption) is limited to a maximum of ~28 dB because of sound scattering from turbulence and ground wave transmission.

4.6.3 Ground Effects

Sound propagation near the ground is influenced by the acoustic properties of the surface. Together with the direct and reflected paths, a ground wave path also contributes significant energy at low frequencies. Few studies of ground effects on airborne sound propagation have been reported for habitats likely to be occupied by marine mammals (but see Cummings and Holiday 1983). However, data from near-ground transmission studies in urban areas show that interference between sounds arriving via different paths causes transmission irregularities. For propagation over a hard surface, these irregularities are greater with increasing source or receiver height. Irregularities are minimized if the source or receiver is located near a hard surface where there is pressure doubling (Piercy and Embleton 1974). Measurements over a soft surface such as grass typically show irregular received levels with no pronounced interference pattern. At longer ranges and higher frequencies, transmission is not as good over grass as over asphalt or concrete (Embleton et al. 1976).

Thus, sound transmission in the atmosphere depends on the site and weather. Airborne propagation losses, especially near the ground, cannot be predicted accurately by a general model. Information on path geometry and local conditions is needed in order to use available transmission models successfully. However, to predict the *maximum potential* sound exposure for a given source and range, a simple model including only spherical spreading and atmospheric absorption (Fig. 4.9) is adequate, especially when the source is well above ground level. This model is appropriate for aircraft, which are the sources of airborne man-made noise to which marine mammals are most often exposed.

4.7 Air-to-Water Transmission[2]

Sound traveling from a source in air to a receiver underwater propagates in four ways: (1) via a direct refracted path; (2) via direct refracted paths that are reflected by the bottom; (3) via a "lateral" (surface-traveling) wave; and (4) via scattering from a rough sea surface (Urick 1972; Fig. 4.11). The types of propagation vary in importance depending on local conditions, depth of receiver, and bottom depth. The direct refracted path is important when the receiver is nearly under the aircraft. Snell's law predicts a critical angle of 13° from the vertical for the transmission of sound from air to water. Under calm sea conditions, sound is totally reflected at larger angles and does not enter the water. However, some airborne sound may penetrate water at angles >13° from the vertical when rough seas provide water surfaces at suitable angles (Lubard and Hurdle 1976).

Sound traveling from air to water along the direct refracted path passes through three phases: through air; across the air-water surface; and from the surface to the underwater receiver (Fig. 4.11). To a first approximation, propagation loss in air can be described by simple spherical spreading—a 6 dB decrease per distance doubled (Section 4.6). At the surface, the great difference in acoustic properties of air and water results in most acoustic energy being reflected. However, the sound pressure transmitted to the water is actually enhanced because of a pressure-doubling effect at the interface. Hence, sound pressure at the surface directly beneath the source is twice that expected in air at the same distance if there were no water surface. From the surface to the underwater receiver, sound propagation includes both geometrical spreading and the effects of the divergence of sound energy as it passes through the surface. This results in a complicated distribution of underwater sound pressure that depends on height of source, location of receiver, water depth, and temperature-salinity profile of the water column.

Air-to-water sound propagation has been documented using wave theory (e.g., Weinstein and Henney 1965; Medwin and Hagy 1972) and ray theory (Hudimac 1957; Urick 1972; Waters 1972; Young 1973); see also Chapman and Ward (1990). To estimate underwater sound levels produced by an airborne source over shallow water, an air-to-water

---

[2] This section was prepared by Charles I. Malme, Bolt Beranek and Newman Inc., and Charles R. Greene, Jr., Greeneridge Sciences Inc.

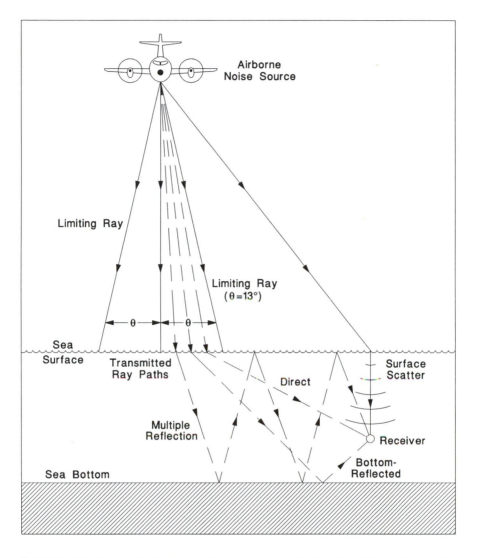

FIGURE 4.11. Ray-path diagram showing various air-to-water propagation paths for aircraft noise (based on Urick 1972).

sound transmission model has been developed using an equation from Young (1973) plus shallow water transmission theory (Malme and Smith 1988). Fig. 4.12, based on this model, shows the difference between the sound level underwater and the "incident" sound. The latter is the level expected at the surface directly under the airborne

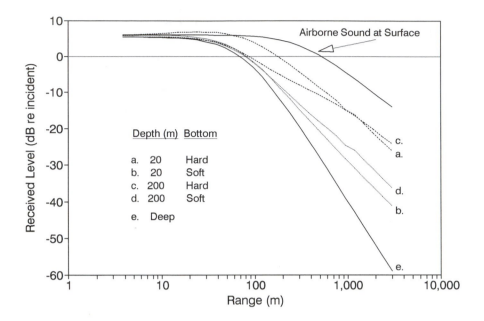

FIGURE 4.12. Theoretical air to shallow-water sound transmission for receiver depth 5 m and source altitude 300 m. Received levels just above the surface (top curve) and received levels underwater are expressed in dB with respect to the incident level expected 300 m directly below the source if the water surface were not there (from Malme and Smith 1988). Assumed bottom loss parameters based on mud (soft) and basalt (hard).

source ("subsource point") if the surface were not there. A source altitude of 300 m and a receiver depth of 5 m have been used for all curves in Fig. 4.12.

Model results are consistent with empirical data (e.g., Urick 1972; Greene 1985a). In deep water, there are high transmission losses between a source in air and an underwater receiver distant from the subsource point. Underwater received levels away from the subsource point are higher in shallow than in deep water. This difference occurs because, in shallow water, sound is transmitted horizontally away from the subsource point by multiple reflections from the bottom and surface. This process is more efficient for hard bottom conditions. Even with a hard bottom, however, underwater noise diminishes more rapidly with increasing horizontal distance than does airborne noise (Fig. 4.12). Consistent with this, under typical ambient noise conditions, an approaching aircraft can be heard in the air well before it is audible underwater (Greene 1985a).

Waves affect air-to-water sound transmission. With sea states of two or higher and frequencies >150 Hz, surface roughness enhances air-to-water transmission at shallow grazing angles (Urick 1972; Barger and Sachs 1975). This results in a 3 to 7 dB increase in underwater sound levels in the direction of wave travel, and a 2-5 dB increase in directions perpendicular to those of wave travel. Near the subsource point, which normally has the highest sound level, wave scattering reduces underwater sound level by 3 to 5 dB.

Transmission of sound energy from air through ice and into water involves generation of several different types of waves in the ice in addition to those transmitted through the ice and into the water. The inhomogeneous nature of saltwater ice makes this process a formidable theoretical modeling problem. At frequencies <500 Hz, where most acoustic energy from aircraft (Section 6.2.1) and surface vehicles is concentrated, the ice layer is acoustically thin and causes little attenuation of sound (H. Kutschale, personal communication). Direct use of the air-to-water transmission model for transmission of low-frequency sound through ice would provide slight overestimates of underwater sound levels from aircraft overflights. Transmission of noise from surface vehicles on ice into the water is a more difficult problem. Sound entering the water through ice is important because numerous species of cetaceans and pinnipeds inhabit regions with some ice.

Air-to-water propagation of sonic booms created by supersonic aircraft was summarized by Cook et al. (1972). Although most energy is reflected upward when it reaches the sea surface, some penetrates into the water and creates considerable acoustic pressure near the surface. The strength of the low-frequency pressure pulse received underwater decreases rapidly with increasing depth. However, even at depths as deep as 100 m, the received level increases significantly with decreasing aircraft altitude or increasing aircraft speed (Sparrow 1995).

4.8 Summary

The potential effects of noise on marine mammals are determined by radiated sound power levels (Chapter 6), sound propagation characteristics, and the auditory and behavioral sensitivity of the mammals (Chapters 8 and 9). The general description of sound propagation in this chapter is intended to assist biologists in evaluating noise effects.

Sound propagation in the sea has been the subject of intensive research. The open literature is voluminous, and there is much additional unpublished and classified information. For specific applications, the information provided in this chapter should be augmented by a detailed review of relevant references.

Sound propagation research has made considerable progress in recent years. Field measurements of sound levels in relation to distance, frequency, and environmental parameters have been obtained in many areas and situations. Based on these data and on theoretical considerations, efficient computer models have been developed. Some models provide sufficient detail to account for many of the propagation processes occurring in the real world. However, most models are designed for specialized applications (often classified) and are not easily generalized for use in predicting potential noise impact ranges for anthropogenic sources. Fortunately, some simple and general relationships can be used to make estimates of transmission loss for many sources and locations, both underwater and in air.

The spherical spreading law with an added absorption loss term can be applied in the cases of (1) air-to-ground transmission from aircraft or other sources at elevation angles greater than 10° and (2) nonducted, direct-path underwater transmission:

$$L_r = L_s - 20 \log R - \alpha R - 60 \tag{4.6}$$

where L_r is received level at range R (km) in dB re 1 µPa (underwater) or dB re 20 µPa (air),

L_s is the source level in the same dB units at range 1 m,

α is the molecular absorption coefficient in dB/km, taken from a table or equation (4.4), and

-60   is a conversion factor related to the change in range units from L_s at 1 m to L_r at R km; it represents spherical spreading (in dB) between 1 m and 1 km.

At frequencies below a few kilohertz, where most industrial noise energy is concentrated, the absorption coefficient is very low in water but higher in air. Thus the absorption term is generally negligible for underwater propagation of industrial noise over the limited ranges where spherical spreading applies. However, absorption can be significant for underwater propagation of high-frequency sounds such as echolocation sounds from toothed whales, or for airborne propagation of industrial or animal sounds. For broadband sources, calculations should be made at several frequencies since the absorption coefficient, and usually also the source level, are frequency dependent. If an over-all broadband received level is required, it can be obtained by summing, via equation (2.9), the results for various narrower bands.

For very shallow water or ducted underwater transmission beginning at a distance R_1 from the source, equation (4.6) is modified to use cylindrical spreading beyond range R_1 plus an additional linear loss factor:

$$L_r = L_s - 20 \log R_1 - 10 \log (R/R_1) - \alpha R - (A)R - 60$$

which is equivalent to

$$L_r = L_s - 10 \log R_1 - 10 \log R - \alpha R - (A)R - 60 \qquad (4.7)$$

where R_1 is the range (in km) where the transition from spherical to cylindrical spreading occurs, and

     (A)   is a loss factor representing duct leakage or modal attenuation in dB/km (Urick 1983:152).

The transition range R_1 depends on the acoustic reflection properties of the bottom or on duct refraction conditions. In the absence of site-specific data, it is often defined as being equal to the water depth or duct width.

For underwater transmission in shallow water where the depth is greater than 5 times the wavelength, $15 \log R$ spreading loss may occur beyond range H:

$$L_r = L_s - 5 \log H - 15 \log R - \alpha R - At[(R/H)-1] + Kl - 60 \qquad (4.8)$$

where *H*   is the water depth in meters,

     At   is an empirically determined factor related to scattering and other losses not accounted for in the mode stripping process, and

     Kl   is an anomaly term related to the reverberant sound field developed near the source by surface- and bottom-reflected energy; involves an apparent increase in source level.

Relationship (4.8) is from the Marsh and Schulkin model (Urick 1983: 178). Values for *At* and *Kl* may be obtained from tables based on their measurements or from empirical data collected at the specific site. With site-specific data, this model can provide good predictions of received levels for that general area. This model will work for sloping bottom conditions if the depths at the source and receiver locations are averaged to determine *H*.

For more accurate transmission loss predictions, various more elaborate models mentioned in this chapter may be appropriate. The reader is referred to the cited sources for detailed descriptions. Acoustical expertise is needed to apply most specialized propagation models. If propagation losses and received levels at long range must be predicted, especially in shallow water, site-specific empirical data on bottom and water properties will be needed. Ideally, direct measurements of propagation loss should be made to validate any propagation model.

CHAPTER 5

AMBIENT NOISE[1]

5.1 Introduction

Ambient noise is environmental background noise. It is generally unwanted sound—sound that clutters and masks other sounds of interest. Ambient noise includes only the sounds that would exist if the sensor were not there. Noise created by the measurement process, including any vessel or vehicle used to deploy the sound sensor, is usually excluded (Ross 1976). Ambient noise may have directional properties. Surf sounds coming from a shore, or distant shipping sounds from a shipping lane, are examples of directional ambient noise. Vertical directionality occurs at deep water sites.

In determining how far away a given sound source can be detected, the level and frequency characteristics of the ambient noise are two primary controlling factors, along with the source level of the sound of interest, its spectral characteristics, and the rate of sound transmission loss between the source and the receiver (Fig. 1.1). As a first approximation, a sound signal is detectable only if it is stronger than the ambient noise at similar frequencies. The lower the background noise, the farther a sound signal will travel before its level diminishes below the background noise level. The potential "zone of acoustic influence" of a man-made sound (Section 10.2.1) is influenced strongly by the levels and types of background noise.

Ambient noise requires the same descriptors as other kinds of sounds. Basic qualities include the following: What is the temporal pattern of the sound—is it continuous or transient? What are its duration and frequency of occurrence? What are its frequency characteristics—is it concentrated at low or high frequencies, and does it contain tones (sinusoidal components)? Or is it relatively broadband, rumbling at low frequencies and hissing at high frequencies? Does it

---

[1] By Charles R. Greene, Jr., Greeneridge Sciences Inc.

contain significant energy at frequencies that human beings cannot hear, either at very low frequencies (infrasonic, <20 Hz) or at very high frequencies (ultrasonic, >15-20 kHz)? What are the directional properties, both horizontally and vertically, of the ambient noise at a specified location? What are its sources?

The published literature on ambient noise is very extensive. Many papers on underwater ambient noise appear in the *Journal of the Acoustical Society of America*. A major review was written by Wenz (1962). An important predecessor paper, still widely cited, is Knudsen et al. (1948). Ross (1976) and Urick (1983) include considerable discussion of ambient noise in the sea, and Urick (1986) is a monograph on this topic. Zakarauskas (1986) reviews literature on ambient noise, especially in shallow water.

We provide a brief introduction to ambient noise in the sea, including its sources, variability, and characteristics in shallow and deep water. Airborne ambient noise is mentioned briefly. The chapter emphasizes topics relevant to later sections concerning noise effects on marine mammals.

5.2 Sources of Ambient Noise in the Sea

5.2.1 Wind and Waves

Wind and waves are common and interrelated sources of ambient noise in all the world's oceans. The spectrum of sound from wind and waves is distributed smoothly with frequency; there are no "spikes" (tones). Ambient noise levels tend to increase with increasing wind speed and wave height, other factors being equal. Ambient noise is often described in relation to sea state (SS). Table 5.1 shows the relationships among SS, wind speed, and the Beaufort Wind Force scale (see also Kennish 1989). The SS and Beaufort scales are not the same, but are often used interchangeably and incorrectly.

Knudsen et al. (1948) summarized typical sound levels versus frequency for sea states 0-6 (Fig. 5.1A). The data were taken at frequencies above 500 Hz from oceanic sites outside harbors, and are probably appropriate for depths on the order of 200 m (Ross 1976). However, the Knudsen curves are widely used to characterize deep water ambient noise.

The Knudsen curves for spectrum level ambient noise have slopes of -5 dB per octave. Thus, for each doubling of frequency above 500 Hz, the ambient noise level in a 1-Hz band typically decreases by 5 dB

TABLE 5.1. Interrelationships of wind speed, Beaufort wind force, sea state, and wave heights on the open sea

Wind speed		Beaufort wind force	World Meteorolog. Organization terms	Sea state (SS)	Wave heights (m)	Description
Knots	m/s					
<1	<0.5	0	Calm	0	0	Glassy
1 - 3	0.5 - 1.5	1	Light air	½	<0.1	Ripples
4 - 6	2.1 - 3.1	2	Light breeze	1	0 - 0.1	Small wavelets
7 - 10	3.6 - 5.1	3	Gentle breeze	2	0.1 - 0.5	Smooth wavelets
11 - 16	5.7 - 8.2	4	Moderate breeze	3	0.5 - 1.2	Slight; small whitecaps
17 - 21	8.7 - 10.8	5	Fresh breeze	4	1.2 - 2.4	Mod. waves, some spray
22 - 27	11.3 - 13.9	6	Strong breeze	5	2.4 - 4	Rough, larger waves
28 - 33	14.4 - 17.0	7	Near gale	6		
34 - 40	17.5 - 20.6	8	Gale	6	4 - 6	Very rough
41 - 47	21.1 - 24.2	9	Strong gale	6		
48 - 55	24.7 - 28.3	10	Storm	7	6 - 9	High
56 - 63	28.8 - 32.4	11	Violent storm	8	9 - 14	Very high
>64	>33	12	Hurricane	9	>14	Phenomenal

(Fig. 5.1A). This is equal to a 0.67 dB decrease in the band level of ambient noise for each successive ⅓-octave band (Fig. 5.1B). The slope is shallower for ⅓-octave bands than for spectrum levels (1-Hz bands) because ⅓-octave bands become wider as frequency increases (width = 23% of center frequency; Section 2.2.4). Because there are three ⅓-octave bands per octave, ⅓-octave levels decrease by ~2 dB/octave.

Wind speed at the sea surface seems to be directly related to noise production (Wille and Geyer 1984). Their data, from water 30 m deep, indicated that wave height is not as directly relevant to noise levels. Use of wave heights to infer noise levels may lead to errors because the sea state is not always fully developed for the existing wind conditions (Section 5.4).

Ross (1976) also developed generalized spectra relating spectrum level ambient noise in deep water to wind force and sea state (Fig. 5.2A). He indicates that, above 500 Hz, the Knudsen models tend to overestimate the ambient levels at each sea state by a few dB. This may be related, at least in part, to the fact that Knudsen's data came from moderately shallow water. More importantly, below 500 Hz the

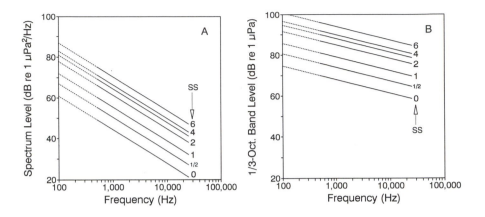

FIGURE 5.1. Ambient noise levels versus frequency and sea state (SS); adapted from Knudsen et al. (1948). Dashed line segments span frequencies for which the curves are extrapolated and may be inaccurate. *(A)* Spectrum levels (i.e., 1 Hz bandwidth). *(B)* Equivalent ⅓-octave band levels.

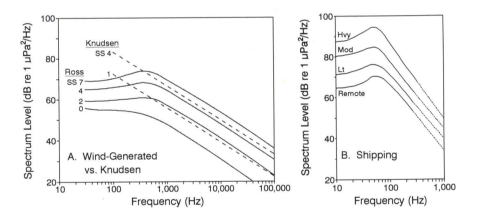

FIGURE 5.2. Spectrum levels of ambient noise in deep water. *(A)* Wind-generated noise as compared with Knudsen levels, for selected sea states (SS). *(B)* Average shipping contribution versus relative amount of shipping in the region (adapted from Ross 1976).

spectra for wind-generated ambient noise in deep water tend to flatten out at values considerably lower than would be predicted by extrapolating the Knudsen curves to frequencies <500 Hz (Fig. 5.2). Note that this considers only wind-generated noise and deep water. When shipping and other sources are considered (Fig. 5.2B and below), typical levels below 500 Hz are higher than those in Fig. 5.2A, and closer to the extrapolated Knudsen curves of Fig. 5.1A.

Wenz (1962) presented a graph of ambient noise spectra attributable to many sources and spanning five decades of frequency from 1 Hz to 100 kHz (Fig. 5.3). This graph shows the wind dependence of ambient sounds plus the typical contributions of many other sources discussed below. The wind contribution often dominates from a few hundred hertz to ~30 kHz (Fig. 5.3). Infrasonic noise at frequencies of 1-20 Hz is caused largely by surface waves (especially in shallow water) and turbulent pressure fluctuations. However, biological sources, distant shipping, earthquakes, and other seismic activities are also major contributors to infrasonic ambient noise.

Wenz (1962:1954) stated an empirical "rule of fives" as an approximation for spectrum levels of wind-dependent ambient noise. Paraphrasing it using units in current use,

Between 500 Hz and 5 kHz, spectrum levels decrease 5 dB per octave with increasing frequency, and increase 5 dB with each doubling of wind speed from 2.5 to 40 knots (5-75 km/h). The spectrum level at 1 kHz in deep water is 51 dB re 1 $\mu Pa^2/Hz$ when the wind speed is 5 knots (9 km/h), and it is 5 dB higher in shallow water.

Wenz stated that this generalization was fairly accurate up to 20 kHz. However, "considerable departure may sometimes be expected, since wind speed is not a precise measure of the actual surface agitation..., nor are estimates of sea state". Varying bottom conditions may also introduce considerable variability from site to site.

Surf noise is a form of wave noise that is localized near the land-sea interface. During heavy surf conditions in Monterey Bay, California, Wilson et al. (1985) made directional measurements at several distances from shore. At a distance of 8.5 km, the received noise level in the 100- to 700-Hz band was about 10 dB higher from directions toward the beach. Surf noise may be prominent near shore even in calm wind conditions.

5.2.2 Other Environmental Sources

Seismic noise from volcanic and tectonic activity can contribute significantly to ambient noise at low frequencies, especially in geologically active areas (Fig. 5.3; Wenz 1962). Such sounds are usually transient. Energy from earthquakes on land or below the sea bottom couples into the water to propagate as low-frequency, locally generated "T phase" waves. Energy from large man-made explosions generates

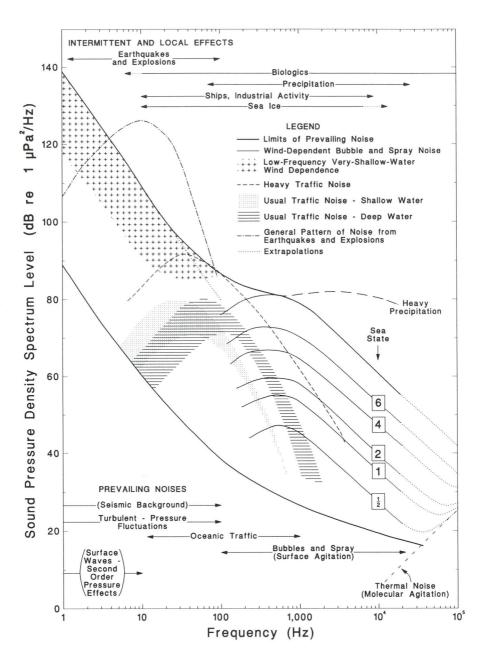

FIGURE 5.3. Generalized ambient noise spectra attributable to various sources, compiled by Wenz (1962) from many references and replotted in presently used units.

the same types of waves. Seismic sources and large explosions emit energy at frequencies up to 500 Hz, although maximum spectrum levels occur between 2 and 20 Hz, with most energy below 100 Hz.

Precipitation noise from rain and hail is another naturally occurring source of ambient noise. Generally such noise is an important component of total noise at frequencies above 500 Hz during periods of precipitation. However, it may be evident at frequencies down to 100 Hz during otherwise quiet times (Fig. 5.3; Wenz 1962).

Biological noise arises in all oceans from a variety of sources. Marine mammals are major contributors (Chapter 7), but certain fish and shrimp can also be significant (Myrberg 1978; Dahlheim 1987; Cato 1992). Frequencies of biological noises extend from ~12 Hz (some blue whale calls) to over 100,000 Hz. Depending on the situation, biological noise can range from nearly absent to dominant over narrow or even broad frequency ranges. When biological noise is dominant in a particular frequency band, it—like any other ambient noise—can interfere with detection of other sounds at those frequencies.

Sea ice noise can be very significant at high latitudes, but its levels are highly variable. There are two important mechanisms: thermal stress, in which temperature changes induce cracking; and mechanical stress, in which ice deformation under pressure from wind and currents causes significant noise at low frequencies. Milne and Ganton (1964) reported significant thermal cracking noise in landfast ice (ice frozen firmly to the shore and sometimes also to the bottom) during winter and spring. The spring noise spectra peaked at ~90 dB re 1 $\mu Pa^2/Hz$ at infrasonic frequencies (0.5-2 Hz). Above 2 Hz, spectrum levels decreased with increasing frequency up to ~20 Hz, above which the levels remained essentially constant up to 8 kHz. In contrast, during quiet times the spectrum levels remained below the Knudsen spectrum for sea state zero. The winter noise spectra included wind-induced noise as well as thermal cracking sounds.

Ice deformation noises were measured by Buck and Greene (1979); see also Greene (1981) and Buck and Wilson (1986). A pressure ridge active over a 3-day period produced tones at frequencies of 4-200 Hz. Source levels for 4- and 8-Hz tones ranged from 124 to 137 dB re 1 μPa-m.

Melting icebergs contribute "seltzer" noise to the background (Urick 1971). Urick estimated that the spectrum level of the iceberg noise was flat at ~62 dB re 1 $\mu Pa^2/Hz$ at a range 180 m from the iceberg, decreasing to about 58 dB at 10 kHz. The noise was attributed to tiny exploding air bubble cavities in the ice or, at deep depths, to imploding cavities.

Although sea ice often creates considerable noise, certain types of stable sea ice can dampen the total ambient noise. With 100% ice cover, noise from waves and surf is absent or dampened. Under these conditions, total ambient noise level can be considerably less than expected under calm open-water conditions (Greene and Buck 1964; Milne and Ganton 1964). Greene, in Richardson et al. (1989), provided a more extensive review of ice effects on ambient noise.

Thermal noise resulting from molecular agitation is important at frequencies above 30 kHz (Mellen 1952). It limits the high-frequency sensitivity of hydrophones. It also limits the effective echolocation range for toothed whales that use very-high-frequency echolocation calls (C.S. Johnson 1979; *cf.* Section 7.2.4). Its spectrum level increases 6 dB per octave with increasing frequency. It is shown as the dashed line in the lower right corner of Fig. 5.3.

5.2.3 *Distant Human Activities*

Many human activities produce noise (Chapter 6). Noise from specific ships and other identifiable human activities is generally not considered part of the background ambient noise. However, the aggregate *traffic noise*, arising from the combined effects of all shipping at long ranges, is included. This traffic noise originates more than 10 km away, and in deep water may include low-frequency components from distances up to 4000 km. Shipping generally dominates ambient noise at frequencies from 20 to 300 Hz. The slope of the spectrum level of distant shipping noise typically diminishes at -9 dB per octave (Figs. 5.2B and 5.3; see Section 5.3).

In coastal regions, the aggregate noise from many distant *fishing boats* may contribute significant sound. Because fishing boats have higher-speed engines and propellers than do ships, noise spectra from fishing boats peak around 300 Hz (Section 6.2.2).

Other sources of man-made sound include industrial plants or construction activities on shore, offshore oil industry activities, naval operations, and various types of marine research involving sound emission (Chapter 6). For example, geophysical surveys employing airgun arrays or other strong transient sources can be very significant contributors to ambient noise, even at very long ranges (Section 6.5). Characteristics of underwater noise from various specific man-made sources are discussed in Chapter 6. The human contribution to ambient noise is primarily at frequencies <1 kHz. Much of the noise emitted by human activities is below 1 kHz, and higher-frequency components attenuate rapidly with distance (Section 4.5.1).

5.3 Deep Water Ambient Noise

Sounds from the foregoing sources combine to produce the overall ambient noise. Urick (1983, 1986) summarized the characteristics of ambient noise in deep water. Fig. 5.4 identifies the spectral slopes expected in five frequency bands.

In deep water, noise from 1 to 20 Hz contains the fundamental frequency components of the propeller blades used on oceangoing ships. At these infrasonic frequencies, noise levels depend only slightly on wind speed. Oceanic turbulence is also an important source of noise in the 1- to 20-Hz band (Wenz 1962; Urick 1983). This turbulence takes the form of "irregular random water currents of large or small scale" (Urick 1983). Below 1 Hz, ambient noise arises from seis-

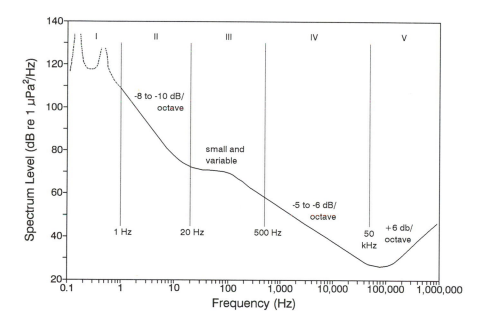

FIGURE 5.4. A sample spectrum of deep-sea noise, showing typical spectral slopes in five frequency ranges (from Urick 1983).

mic sources, turbulence, tides, and waves. In general, ambient noise levels below ~20 Hz are difficult to measure accurately because of cable strum from water currents, bounce motion associated with hydrophone suspension systems and surface waves, and other equipment limitations (Section 3.2.2). Many reports do not include data at frequencies below 10-20 Hz, or include data of dubious accuracy.

From 20 to 300 Hz, noise levels from distant shipping (Figs. 5.2B and 5.3) usually exceed wind-related noise. Above 300 Hz, shipping sounds may or may not be significant depending on the level of wind-dependent ambient noise (Fig. 5.3). From 500 to 50,000 Hz, wind, wave, and (intermittently) precipitation noise dominate. Above 30-50 kHz, thermal agitation may dominate, especially when wind speed is low (Fig. 5.3).

5.4 Shallow Water Ambient Noise

Shallow water is often defined as water <200 m deep, although the definition should depend on frequency (Section 4.3). Zakarauskas (1986) characterized shallow water as an area where acoustic wavelength is of the same order of magnitude as water depth; 200 m is the wavelength at ~7.5 Hz. Ambient noise in shallow water is subject to wide variations in level and frequency distribution, depending on time and location. The three primary sources in most shallow water regions are (1) distant shipping, industrial, or seismic-survey noise; (2) wind and wave noise; and (3) biological noise. In the Arctic, ice noise may dominate at low to moderate frequencies.

A wider range of ambient noise levels occurs in shallow than in deep water under corresponding wind and wave conditions. In shallow water, the highest levels can be higher and the lowest levels lower than those in deep water. Above ~500 Hz, levels are often 5-10 dB higher in coastal than in deep water with corresponding wind speeds (Urick 1983). However, when shipping and biological noise are absent, low-frequency noise levels (<300 Hz) in shallow water can be lower than expected in deep ocean waters (Urick 1983). Differences in sound transmission conditions between shallow and deep regions (Sections 4.3 versus 4.4) are partly responsible for these trends.

Ambient noise levels in shallow waters are related directly to wind speed but only indirectly to sea state (Wille and Geyer 1984). For frequencies of 50-20,000 Hz and wind speeds above ~9 km/h, ambient noise level was better predicted by wind speed than by wave height. Some of the variation in noise level at a given wind speed was attributable to changing wind profiles caused by temperature stratification of the atmosphere. Other references showing the correlation between wind speed and ambient noise level in shallow waters include Worley and Walker (1982) and Zakarauskas et al. (1990).

Bottom conditions have a large influence on shallow water ambient noise (Urick 1983). Bottom conditions have strong and complex effects on sound propagation in shallow water (Sections 4.4 and 4.5). Other factors being equal, ambient noise levels in a particular frequency range tend to be high where the bottom is very reflective and low where it is absorptive.

5.5 *Variability of Ambient Noise in the Sea*

The wide variability in ambient noise levels is shown in the generalized noise spectra of Figs. 5.1-5.3. Ambient noise levels at a given frequency often vary by 10-20 dB from day to day (e.g., Fig. 3.4). In addition, there can be great variability from minute to minute and even second to second (Richardson et al. 1991a:55*ff*). These changes can have dramatic effects on the detectability of other sounds—an important consideration in later chapters.

Variability in ambient noise in the sea is due mostly to variations in the noise sources. Changes in wind speed and wave action have a direct effect on ambient noise, as does variation in the amount of distant human activity and rate of precipitation. There can be strong minute-to-minute, hour-to-hour, or seasonal variability in sounds from some biological sources. For example, in much of the Arctic, calls from bearded seals dominate the ambient noise near 1 kHz during spring, but are rarely heard during other seasons (Section 7.3.1).

Variations in sound transmission conditions also cause variations in ambient noise levels. Ambient noise is expected to be stronger when sound attenuates slowly with increasing distance, and weaker when it attenuates rapidly. For example, the better propagation conditions on the Scotian Shelf than on the Grand Banks (Fig. 4.6; Staal 1985) are probably partly responsible for the higher average ambient noise levels on the Scotian Shelf (Zakarauskas et al. 1990). At a given location, transmission conditions vary when the vertical profiles of temperature and salinity change, and when wave and ice conditions change (Chapter 4). This can contribute to the day-to-day changes in ambient noise level.

In deep water, depth in the water column has little effect on the level of wind and wave noise at low to moderate frequencies (<10 kHz). This is largely attributable to the fact that wind and waves are not point sources of sound. As distance from the surface increases, the surface area from which noise is reaching the receiver increases, countering the effect of transmission loss. However, for higher frequencies (>15 kHz) and surface-originating sounds, absorption losses (Section 4.5) result in diminishing levels with increasing depth.

Anyone planning studies of the reactions of marine mammals to man-made noise at a specific site should consider the likely sources and characteristics of the ambient noise during the study period. For example, noise studies in warm-water areas may encounter the cacophony of snapping shrimp (Everest et al. 1948; Cato 1992) mixed with the sounds of fishing boats. Studies off the Alaskan north coast during May will doubtless encounter choruses of bearded seals, but vessel sounds are unlikely. Continental shelf areas may be subject to geophysical surveys using powerful impulsive signal sources like airgun arrays or, on the Arctic ice, Vibroseis (Section 6.5).

The aggregate ambient noise strongly affects the distance to which mammal calls, specific man-made noises, and other sound signals can be detected. Even within the range of detectability, variation in ambient noise levels greatly affects the prominence (signal-to-noise ratio) of sound signals. Section 8.5 summarizes the available auditory data on masking of sound signals by ambient noise. Section 10.5 discusses the potential effects of nearby sources of man-made noise on detection and reaction distances.

5.6 Airborne Ambient Noise

Readers are familiar with airborne ambient noises through their personal experiences. Wind, thunder, aircraft, road and rail traffic, and biological sources all contribute to the background noise level. Kinsler et al. (1982:279-312) provide a useful overview of environmental acoustics, including its sources and measurements.

Airborne noise measurements are usually expressed relative to a reference pressure of 20 µPa, which is 26 dB above the usual underwater sound reference pressure of 1 µPa (Section 2.2.1). Also, they are often expressed as broadband *A-weighted sound levels* (L_A), expressed in dBA. "A-weighted" refers to frequency-dependent weighting factors applied to the sound in accordance with the sensitivity of the human

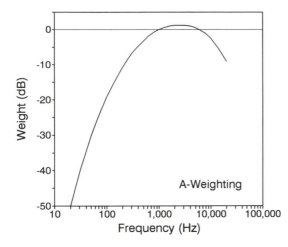

FIGURE 5.5. Weighting factors used to derive A-weighted sound levels (from Kinsler et al. 1982; Kryter 1985). Shows number of decibels to be added to ⅓-octave, octave, or other band levels before the band levels are integrated to obtain the overall A-weighted sound level.

ear to different frequencies (Fig. 5.5). With A-weighting, sound energy at frequencies below 1 kHz and above 6 kHz is deemphasized. To determine the sound level in dBA, sound power in the A-weighted spectrum is integrated over frequency. Thus, information about the frequency spectrum of airborne noise is not available in the single dBA number resulting from A-weighting, but different noises can be compared (Table 5.2). Such comparisons are meaningful if one is assessing the effects of the ambient noise on humans or animals with a simi-

TABLE 5.2. A-weighted sound levels for some common airborne sounds[a]

A-weighted level (dBA)		
re 20 μPa	re 1 μPa	Source of noise
110 - 120	136 - 146	Discotheque, rock-n-roll band
100 - 110	126 - 136	Jet flyby at altitude 300 m (1000 ft)
90 - 100	116 - 126	Power mower[b]; cockpit of light aircraft
80 - 90	106 - 116	Heavy truck at 64 km/h at 15 m; blender[b]
70 - 80	96 - 106	Car at 100 km/h at 7.6 m; clothes washer[b]
60 - 70	86 - 96	Vacuum cleaner[b]; air conditioner at 6 m
50 - 60	76 - 86	Light traffic at 30 m
40 - 50	66 - 76	Quiet residential—daytime
30 - 40	56 - 66	Quiet residential—nighttime
20 - 30	46 - 56	Wilderness area

[a] From Kinsler et al. (1982).
[b] Measured at operator's position.

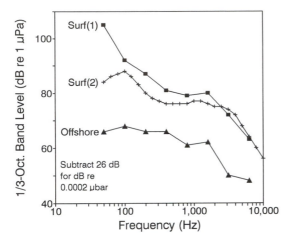

FIGURE 5.6. Airborne ambient noise measured near seacoasts, on a ⅓-octave basis. From Malme and Smith (1988), based on BBN (1960) for surf (1) and offshore, and Abrahamson (1974) for surf (2). Expressed in dB re 1 µPa for consistency with underwater sound levels; subtract 26 dB to convert to dB re 0.0002 µbar (=dB re 20 µPa).

lar range of best hearing sensitivity. dBA data are less relevant to animals that are most sensitive to different frequencies.

Few data are available on airborne sound levels in marine areas, but wave and surf noises are important contributors. Fig. 5.6 shows ⅓-octave band levels measured near beaches. The A-weighted levels corresponding to the three noise spectra in Fig. 5.6 are as follows:

Surf (BBN 1960)	90 dBA re 1 µPa	64 dBA re 20 µPa
Surf (Abrahamson 1974)	87 dBA re 1 µPa	61 dBA re 20 µPa
Offshore (BBN 1960)	72 dBA re 1 µPa	46 dBA re 20 µPa

Comparison with Table 5.2 indicates that surf noise was comparable in level to vacuum cleaner noise as received at the operator's position, whereas the lower noise level offshore was comparable to quiet residential noise during daytime.

Airborne sounds from ships, boats, helicopters, and industrial sites can contribute significantly to the airborne ambient noise to which marine mammals are exposed when at the surface or hauled-out (Section 2.3 in Brueggeman et al. 1990). However, aside from the data summarized in Fig. 5.6, we are unaware of data on overall ambient noise levels in coastal and marine areas far from specific sources of man-made noise. Characteristics of airborne noise from aircraft are discussed in Section 6.2.1. Propagation of airborne sounds is discussed in Sections 4.6 and 4.7.

CHAPTER 6

MAN-MADE NOISE[1]

6.1 Introduction

Most man-made noises that could affect marine mammals arise
from a few general types of activities in and near the sea: transportation, dredging, construction, hydrocarbon and mineral exploration and
recovery, geophysical surveys, sonars, explosions, and ocean science
studies. Two or more of these sources may contribute to the total
noise at any one place and time.

The sound source is the initial element in the source-path-receiver
model used to estimate the range to which a sound may be detected.
Three interrelated parameters used to describe a source are its level,
frequency, and temporal pattern (Section 2.3). Source level refers to
the amount of radiated sound at a particular frequency and distance,
usually 1 m. It is usually expressed in dB re 1 µPa-m (=dB re 1 µPa
at 1 m). Sources are categorized as "transient" if their duration is
brief, such as pulses from airguns, sonars, or explosions; or "continuous" if they persist for long times, such as sounds of an oil drilling
platform. Except for frequency-specific tones, noise measurements
usually are presented as spectrum levels, which depict sound level per
unit frequency, in dB re 1 µPa²/Hz. However, noise levels also can be
determined for bands of frequencies; levels in ⅓-octave bands are commonly presented (Section 2.2.4). The bandwidth of a ⅓-octave band is
23% of its center frequency. Because ⅓-octave bands considered here
always exceed 1 Hz in width (i.e., center frequency ≥5 Hz), ⅓-octave
levels exceed spectrum levels. Spectra of transient sources are often
determined from short segments of sound recorded when their source
levels are highest. Noise from continuous sources may be averaged
over a longer time period. Terminology is described in more detail in
Chapter 2 and the Glossary.

---

[1] By Charles R. Greene, Jr., and Sue E. Moore, Greeneridge Sciences Inc.

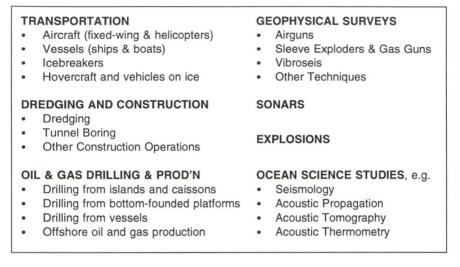

TRANSPORTATION	GEOPHYSICAL SURVEYS
• Aircraft (fixed-wing & helicopters)	• Airguns
• Vessels (ships & boats)	• Sleeve Exploders & Gas Guns
• Icebreakers	• Vibroseis
• Hovercraft and vehicles on ice	• Other Techniques
DREDGING AND CONSTRUCTION	**SONARS**
• Dredging	
• Tunnel Boring	**EXPLOSIONS**
• Other Construction Operations	
OIL & GAS DRILLING & PROD'N	**OCEAN SCIENCE STUDIES**, e.g.
• Drilling from islands and caissons	• Seismology
• Drilling from bottom-founded platforms	• Acoustic Propagation
• Drilling from vessels	• Acoustic Tomography
• Offshore oil and gas production	• Acoustic Thermometry

FIGURE 6.1. General types of man-made sounds in the ocean.

Source levels are rarely measured at the reference distance (e.g., 1 m). "Near-field" measurements are not very useful (Section 2.3.2). Instead, more distant measurements of received sound level are converted to an *estimated* source level by assuming or measuring the acoustic propagation loss from 1 m to the actual measurement distance. Such adjustments may be in error because they often rely on simplifying assumptions about the propagation process (Chapter 4). The importance of specifying the assumptions used to derive source level estimates cannot be overstated.

This chapter provides an extensive summary of the characteristics of underwater sounds associated with human activities. The sources can be divided into seven general types (Fig. 6.1). Studies to date have not focused equally on all sources, nor have they been conducted in all geographic regions. However, if source levels are known, they can be used to predict zones of acoustic influence around any site where sound propagation and ambient noise conditions are known.

6.2 Transportation

6.2.1 Helicopters and Fixed-Wing Aircraft

Introduction.—Hubbard (1995) and M. Smith (1989) give comprehensive reviews of aircraft noise generation, measurement, effects

on people, and control. Airborne sounds from aircraft are directly relevant to marine mammals that haul out on land or ice, and perhaps
to any marine mammal at the surface. However, the complex process
of air-to-water transmission (Section 4.7) affects the characteristics of
aircraft sound received by marine mammals below the surface. The
level of underwater sound from any type of aircraft depends on receiver depth and the altitude, aspect, and strength of the noise source.

Underwater sounds from passing aircraft are necessarily measured far beyond the 1-m distance for which underwater source levels
are normally determined. Indeed, the concept of a 1-m source level for
underwater noise from an aircraft is not very meaningful. When
dealing with aircraft sound, an altitude of 300 m is the usual reference distance for in-air measurements and predictions, and the same
convention is appropriate for underwater sound from aircraft. It is
impossible to isolate the concepts of source level and propagation loss
when considering underwater noise from aircraft. Hence, this subsection necessarily contains information about the received levels of
aircraft noise as a function of aircraft altitude, water depth, and
hydrophone depth.

The angle at which a line from the aircraft to the receiver inter-
sects the water's surface is important. At angles >13° from the vertical, much of the incident sound is reflected and does not penetrate into
the water. This is especially true with calm seas, deep water, or
shallow water with a nonreflective bottom (Section 4.7). Some airborne sound penetrates water at angles >13° from the vertical when
rough seas provide water surfaces at suitable angles (Lubard and
Hurdle 1976). However, the acoustic wavelengths of the low-frequency
sounds that dominate helicopter noise (<50 Hz, λ>6.7 m in air, λ>30 m
in water) are much longer than typical ocean wave heights. Hence,
the sea surface is effectively flat for acoustic purposes at these low frequencies.

Water depth and bottom conditions strongly influence the propagation and levels of underwater noise from passing aircraft. Lateral
propagation is better in shallow than in deep water, especially when
the bottom is reflective. Many reflected paths are possible in shallow
water. As a result, the 13° critical angle may not limit air-to-water
sound transmission to the same extent in shallow as in deep water.
The time during which an airborne source passing overhead can be
received underwater is lengthened in shallow water by multiple reflections (Section 4.7).

Frequency Composition of Aircraft Sounds.—Aircraft are powered by either reciprocating or turbine engines. Either engine type can drive either propellers or helicopter rotors, and turbine engines can also be turbojets or turbofans that do not drive propellers or rotors. We give only limited attention to jet (i.e., turbojet or turbofan) aircraft here, although naval jets often operate at low altitudes in coastal and offshore areas, and there are major coastal airports near which jet transport aircraft often fly at low altitudes.

Reciprocating engine sounds are dominated by the cylinder firing rate, which causes a harmonic family of tones in the sound spectrum. The fundamental frequency of this family is

$$f \text{ (Hz)} = \text{(rpm/60)} \times \text{(no. cyl.)} / \text{(no. revolutions/firing/cyl.)} \qquad (6.1)$$

Four-cycle engines turn twice per cylinder firing. Thus, a 4-cycle, 6-cylinder reciprocating engine turning at 2400 rpm produces a tone at 120 Hz, with harmonics at 240 Hz, 360 Hz, and so on. (*Harmonics* are tones at integer multiples of the fundamental frequency.)

Turbine engine sounds are characterized by the whine of the blades within different stages of the engine; tones occur at frequencies from several hundred hertz to well above 1 kHz. For example, the power turbines of the Bell 212 helicopter turn at 33,000 rpm (550 Hz) and the turbine *blade-rate tone* is the number of blades x 550.

The primary sources of sound from aircraft, aside from those powered by turbojet or turbofan engines, are their propellers or rotors. The rotating blades produce tones with fundamental frequencies that depend on the rotation rate and number of blades:

$$f \text{ (Hz)} = \text{(no. blades)} \times \text{(rpm/60)} \qquad (6.2)$$

For example, a three-bladed propeller turning at 3000 rpm results in a tone at 150 Hz. A two-bladed helicopter rotor turning at 330 rpm results in a tone at 11 Hz. A helicopter tail rotor with two blades turning at 1650 rpm results in a tone at 55 Hz. Harmonics are likely in each case. The larger the number of blades, the higher the fundamental frequency for a given rotation rate.

Dominant tones in noise spectra from helicopters and fixed-wing aircraft generally are below 500 Hz (e.g., Fig. 6.2). In general, the dominant tones from aircraft are harmonics of the blade rates of the propellers or the main and tailrotors. However, other tones associated with the engines and other rotating parts may also be present, leading to a potentially large number of tones at many frequencies. Table 6.1

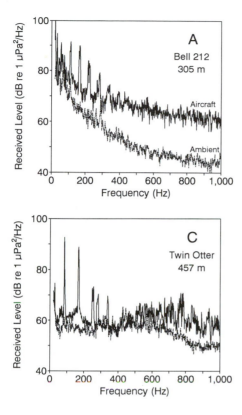

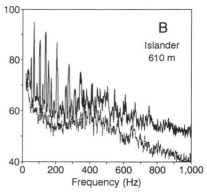

FIGURE 6.2. Aircraft noise spectra: received levels of underwater sound during flyovers by *(A)* Bell 212 helicopter and *(B-C)* two fixed-wing aircraft at altitudes of 305-610 m. Tones occur at frequencies related to piston firing rate (B) and propeller or rotor blade rate (A-C). The lower (dashed) spectrum is ambient noise before or after the overflight. Reanalyzed from recordings of Greene (1985a); analysis bandwidth 1.7 Hz, averaged over 8.5 s.

lists the dominant frequencies and corresponding mechanical sources for several aircraft types.

Because of doppler shift effects, the frequencies of the tones received at a stationary site diminish when an aircraft passes overhead (Fig. 6.3). The apparent frequency is increased while the aircraft approaches and is reduced while it moves away.

Levels and Durations of Aircraft Sounds.—Levels and durations of sounds received underwater from a passing aircraft depend on the altitude and aspect of the aircraft, receiver depth, and water depth. In general, the peak received level in the water as an aircraft passes directly overhead decreases with increasing altitude (Table 6.2). Received level also diminishes with increasing receiver depth when the aircraft is directly overhead (Urick 1972). However, when the aircraft is not directly overhead, aircraft noise can be stronger at midwater than at shallow depths.

TABLE 6.1. Aircraft noise: characteristics and frequencies of dominant tones for various helicopters and fixed-wing aircraft used offshore[a]

A. HELICOPTERS Model	Main rotor speed (rpm)	No. rotor blades (main/ tail)	Tones (Hz)
Bell 212	324	2/2	10.8 + harmonics
Bell 214ST	354 (calc.)	2/2	11.8 + harmonics
Sikorsky 61	203	5/5	68 and 102

B. FIXED WING AIRCRAFT Model	Type	No. blades/ propeller	Tones (Hz) Propeller	Engine
Britten Norman Islander	Piston	2	68 - 74	102
de Havilland Twin Otter	Turboprop	3	82 - 84	
Grumman Turbo Goose	Turboprop	3	100	
Lockheed P-3	Turboprop	4	68	

[a] Sources: Urick (1972), Moore et al. (1984), Greene (1985a), Richardson et al. (1990a:87*ff*).

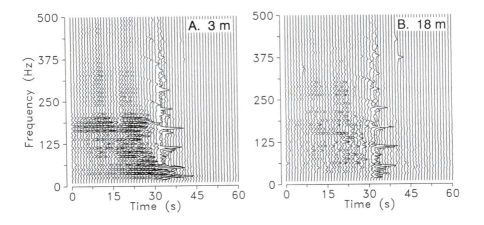

FIGURE 6.3. Helicopter noise spectra: received levels of underwater sound at depths *(A)* 3 m and *(B)* 18 m during overflights by Bell 212 helicopter at 150 m altitude. Helicopter was flying toward the hydrophones prior to time 30 s, overhead at 30 s, and away thereafter; water depth ~170 m. Note doppler shift in tone frequencies as helicopter flies over. Reanalyzed from recordings of Richardson et al. (1990a:90).

TABLE 6.2. Aircraft noise: estimated source levels for dominant tones or frequency bands, plus spectral density levels of broadband noise at selected frequencies[a]

Aircraft (frequency)	Aircraft altitude (m)	Received level (dB re 1 μPa)	Estimated source level (dB re 1 μPa-m)	Estimated source spectral density level, in dB re 1 (μPa-m)²/Hz at frequency (Hz)			
				1000	2000	4000	8000
Helicopter							
Bell 212	152	109	149	111	107	101	93
(22 Hz tone)	305	107	151				
	610	101	151				
Fixed Wing							
B-N Islander	152	101	142	102	97	91	75
(70 Hz tone)							
Twin Otter	457	107	147	105	98		
(82 Hz tone)	610	100	150				
P-3 Orion	76	124	162				
(56-80 Hz	152	121	162				
band)[b]	305	114	160				
(890-1120	76	112	150				
Hz band)	152	107	148	124[c]			

[a] Based on procedure of Young (1973) as applied to levels received 3-18 m underwater by Urick (1972) for P-3 and Greene (1985a) for others.
[b] Most energy in this band was from a tone at 68 Hz.
[c] Computed from the 148 dB source level for the ⅓-octave band at 890-1120 Hz.

The duration of audibility of a passing aircraft is quite variable. Sounds from approaching aircraft are detectable far longer in air than in water. For example, an approaching Bell 214ST helicopter (a noisy model) became audible in air over 4 min before it passed the hydrophones, but was detectable underwater only for 38 s at 3 m depth and 11 s at 18 m (Greene 1985a). Helicopters often radiate more sound forward than backward, and thus can be heard for longer as they approach than as they move away (Fig. 6.3). Aircraft tend to be audible for longer at shallow than at deep receiver depths (Urick 1972; Greene 1985a; Fig. 6.3). Duration of audibility also tends to increase with increasing aircraft altitude.

The source level of aircraft noise can be estimated based on levels received underwater by applying the procedure of Young (1973). Levels received underwater decrease with increasing aircraft altitude, but estimated source levels are essentially independent of altitude, as expected (Table 6.2). Large aircraft like the P-3 tend to be noisier than smaller ones like the Twin Otter or Islander (Table 6.2). Helicopters are generally ~10 dB noisier than fixed-wing aircraft of similar size. Helicopters tend to produce a larger number of tones and higher broadband levels.

Noise levels in ⅓-octave bands may be especially useful in interpreting noise effects on animals. C.I. Malme has used measured data to derive expected overall and ⅓-octave levels at the water's surface directly below aircraft at altitude 300 m under standard temperature, humidity, and pressure conditions (Fig. 6.4). Nominal "source" levels at 1 m would be ~50 dB higher (20 log 300). Levels are about 5-15 dB higher during takeoff and climb than during cruise or approach. For propeller-driven aircraft (Fig. 6.4B), the twin peaks in the 60- to 170- Hz range represent the fundamental and second harmonic frequencies of the propeller blade-rate tones (*cf.* Table 6.1).

Jet aircraft produce widely varying sound levels, depending on aircraft type, phase of flight, and other factors. Many high performance military jets are extremely noisy, especially when using afterburners (e.g., F-4C twin-turbojet fighter in Fig. 6.4C). Older jet transport aircraft are noisier than those with newer-generation engines, for example Boeing 727 versus 737-300 (Fig. 6.4C). Given the lack of rotors and propellers, sounds from jets do not include prominent tones at low frequencies; broadband noise extends across a wide frequency range. Blade-rate tones account for the high-frequency squealing in jet sounds; the low-frequency roar is the jet mixing noise from the engine exhaust. The tones and jet mixing noise are directional (Smith 1989). A listener standing at the departure end of a runway hears the screaming tones as the aircraft approaches and the low-frequency exhaust roar as the aircraft passes over and departs. The high-frequency tones are rapidly absorbed in the atmosphere. Hence, a high-flying jet seems silent during approach and only the low-frequency rumble is heard from the after aspect of the aircraft.

Sonic Booms.—An aircraft flying supersonically produces a sharp, low-frequency pressure pulse at the surface. The received waveform is nominally N-shaped, representing an initial rapid pressure increase corresponding to a bow shock wave, relaxation, and an

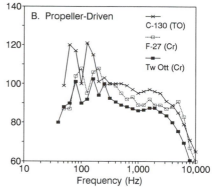

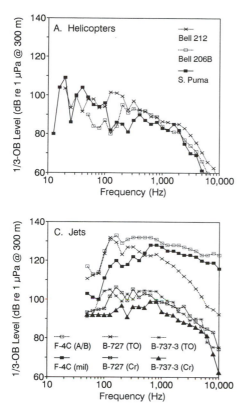

FIGURE 6.4. Aircraft noise spectra: estimated ⅓-octave levels at water's surface from aircraft flying overhead at 300 m altitude. ***TO***=takeoff or climb, ***Cr***=cruise, ***A/B***=afterburners, ***mil***=maximum without A/B. Calculated by C.I. Malme from data of Greene (1985a), Brueggeman et al. (1990), and BBN archives. Richardson and Malme (1993:652) give comparable data for more aircraft types.

abrupt return to ambient pressure corresponding to a tail shock wave. Sonic booms contain energy across a wide range of frequencies, but most is below 100 Hz. For typical high-altitude (6-30 km) cruise conditions, the peak in-air overpressures at the surface are on the order of 1-3 lb/ft^2, or 154-164 dB re 1 μPa, and the duration is usually 100-300 ms. A supersonic transport of mass 180 tonnes flying at Mach 2.7 and at relatively low altitude (7.6 km) would produce an overpressure of 215 Pa or 167 dB re 1 μPa, with duration 50 ms. If it were flying at 30 km altitude, corresponding values would be 77 Pa or 158 dB re 1 μPa, with duration 180 ms (Hubbard 1995). Hubbard describes sonic boom generation, propagation, and measurements.

During supersonic flights over water, little of the sonic boom energy reaching the surface propagates into the water. For a calm sea and level flight at speeds below Mach 4.4, the sonic boom incident angle is >13°, and no sound energy propagates into the water (Section 4.7). However, a type of surface sound wave is produced; its pressure diminishes rapidly with increasing depth. Pressures in the sea may momentarily exceed spectrum level ambient noise by as much as 50 dB down to depths of "a few hundred feet" between 0.5 and a few hundred hertz (Cook et al. 1972). Cook et al. (1972) and Sparrow (1995) provide more information about sonic booms as received underwater.

Summary.—The sounds from helicopters and propeller-driven aircraft contain many tones related to the rotor or propeller blade rate, with most energy at frequencies below 500 Hz. Helicopters tend to be noisier than similar-sized fixed-wing aircraft, large aircraft tend to be noisier than smaller ones, and aircraft on takeoff or climb tend to be noisier than those during cruise or especially approach.

The amount of aircraft noise entering the water depends primarily on aircraft altitude and the resultant "26° cone" modeled by Snell's law and secondarily on sea surface conditions. Underwater sounds from aircraft are strongest just below the surface directly under the aircraft. When the aircraft is overhead, levels decrease with increasing aircraft altitude or increasing receiver depth. The level and frequency content of aircraft sounds propagating in water are strongly affected by water depth and bottom conditions. The lateral distance at which aircraft noise becomes undetectable varies with local ambient noise conditions, water depth, and bottom reflectivity, but is generally less than the corresponding distance in the air. Hence, underwater noise from a passing aircraft is generally brief in duration, especially when compared with the duration of audibility in the air. An aircraft whose closest point of approach is far from overhead may be audible in air but inaudible or only weakly audible underwater.

6.2.2 Boats and Ships

Vessels ranging from the smallest boats to the largest supertankers all produce underwater sound. Vessels are major contributors to the overall background noise in the sea (Chapter 5), given their large numbers, wide distribution, and mobility. Here we discuss the characteristics of noise from individual vessels. Sound levels and frequency characteristics are roughly related to ship size and speed, but there is significant individual variation among vessels of similar classes.

The primary sources of sounds from all vessel classes are propeller cavitation, propeller singing, and propulsion or other machinery. *Propeller cavitation* noise results from two types of vortex cavitation, tip-vortex and hub-vortex, and two types of blade surface cavitation, back and face. Propeller cavitation is usually the dominant noise source (Ross 1976). *Propeller singing* arises when vortex shedding frequencies reinforce a resonant vibrational frequency of a propeller blade. The result is a strong tone between 100 and 1000 Hz. Propeller singing is exacerbated if a propeller is damaged or if propellers on a multiple-propeller vessel operate asynchronously. Cavitation bubbles absorb vibrational energy, so singing commonly ceases when cavitation is strong. Unlike propeller cavitation and singing, which originate outside the hull of a vessel, noise from *propulsion machinery* originates inside and reaches the water via the vessel hull. Sources include rotating shafts, gear reduction transmissions, reciprocating parts, gear teeth, fluid flow turbulence, and mechanical friction. *Other sources* include auxiliaries (pumps, nonpropulsion engines, generators, ventilators, compressors), flow noise from water dragging along the hull, and bubbles breaking in the wake. Ross (1976) provides a comprehensive review of vessel noise.

Vessel noise, like aircraft noise, is a combination of narrowband "tonal" sounds at specific frequencies and "broadband" sounds with energy spread continuously over a range of frequencies. Levels and frequencies of both tonal and broadband sounds tend to be related to vessel size, but are also strongly affected by vessel design and speed. Large vessels create stronger and lower-frequency sounds because of their greater power, large drafts, and slower-turning engines and propellers. They also have large hull areas that efficiently couple the machinery sound to the water. For medium to large vessels, tones dominate up to ~50 Hz. These tones are related to propeller blade rate and secondarily to rates of engine cylinder firing and shaft rotation. Broadband components, caused primarily by propeller cavitation and flow noise, may extend to 100 kHz, peaking at 50-150 Hz (Ross 1976). Auxiliary machinery such as pumps and compressors can produce tones at frequencies up to several kilohertz. Small vessels typically have small propellers with high rotation rates. The small propellers result in cavitation noise at higher frequencies, and the high rotation rates result in blade-rate tones at relatively high frequencies.

Medium- and high-speed diesel engines, which are built with simple connecting rods, are very noisy; their noise may overshadow propeller cavitation (D. Ross, personal communication). Slow-speed diesel engines (<250 rpm) have articulated connecting rods and are relatively quiet. The latter are used for most large tankers, freighters, and container ships. Hence, cavitation noise dominates the radiated noise from these large modern ships.

There are many published data on vessel noise, including the book by Ross (1976) and specific measurements by Buck and Chalfant (1972), Scrimger and Heitmeyer (1991), and others. Most published data concern rather old vessels. However, a few data are available for modern supertankers, bulk carriers, and container ships (Cybulski 1977; Leggat et al. 1981; Thiele and Ødegaard 1983). Such vessels have been estimated to radiate noise 5-8 dB stronger than that from typical 1945-vintage ships (Ross 1976). Noise characteristics of modern military vessels are intensively studied but not published. Much effort has been given to quieting submarines and other naval vessels, but large ships operating at high speed are inevitably noisy.

Boats.—Small boats equipped with outboard engines are common in coastal waters, but there are few published measurements of their sounds (Young and Miller 1960; Stewart et al. 1982; Moore et al. 1984). Large outboard engines can produce overall free-field source levels on the order of 175 dB re 1 µPa-m. Noise levels associated with larger boats with inboard or outdrive engines are very dependent on their operating status. Table 6.3 shows some estimated source levels at 1 m; received levels at range 50 m would be about 34 dB lower. The dominant frequencies are higher for outboards than for somewhat larger boats (Fig. 6.5A). Spectra from boats in this class contain strong tones at frequencies up to several hundred hertz (Fig. 6.6A).

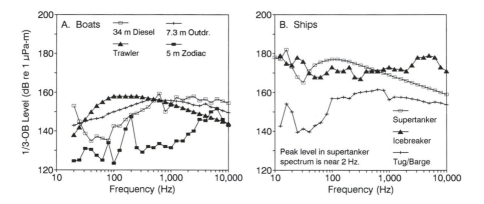

FIGURE 6.5. Estimated ⅓-octave source levels of underwater noise (at 1 m) for examples of *(A)* boats and *(B)* ships. Icebreaker noise was from *Robert Lemeur* pushing on ice at full power (7.2 MW) and zero speed (Brueggeman et al. 1992a,b). "Supertanker" is a composite based mainly on Cybulski (1977). Other data in (A) and (B) from Malme et al. (1989) and Richardson and Malme (1993).

TABLE 6.3. Estimated source levels (1 m) of noise components from small vessels, including small tugs and crewboats. Data do not span all frequencies where boat noise is expected, and thus understate broadband source levels

Vessel (length)	Frequency (Hz)		Source level (dB re 1 µPa-m)	Description
MS *Sparton*[a] (25 m)	37,	tone	166	Tug pulling empty barge
Arctic Fox[b]	1000,	⅓-oct.	170	Tug pulling loaded barge
" "	1000,	⅓-oct.	164	Tug pulling empty barge
" "	5000,	⅓-oct.	161	Tug pulling loaded barge
" "	5000,	⅓-oct.	145	Tug pulling empty barge
Twin diesel[c] (34 m)	630,	⅓-oct.	159	
Trawlers[c]	100,	⅓-oct.	158	Same level: 100, 125, 160, 200, 250 ⅓-oct.
Imperial Adgo[d] (16 m)	90,	tone	156	Crewboat, 2nd harmonic of prop blade rate
Outboard drive[c] (7 m, 2 x 80 hp)	630,	⅓-oct.	156	Same level: 400, 500, 630 & 800 Hz ⅓-oct.
MV *Sequel*[d] (12 m)	250 to 1000		151	Fishing boat, 7 knots
Zodiac[c] (5 m, 25 hp)	6300,	⅓-oct.	152	Outboard engine

[a] Buck and Chalfant (1972)   [b] Miles et al. (1987)
[c] Malme et al. (1989)   [d] Greene (1985a)

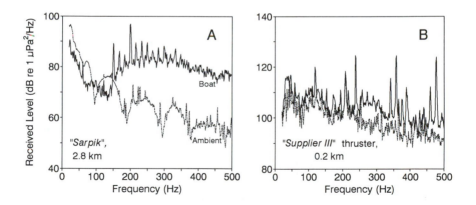

FIGURE 6.6. Received underwater sound spectra for two diesel-powered boats: *(A) Imperial Sarpik* at range 2.8 km, and *(B) Canmar Supplier III* with 336 kW (450 hp) bow thrusters at 0.2 km. The dotted spectrum is ambient noise before or after boat measurement. Note the different vertical scales in (A) and (B). Reanalyzed from recordings of Greene (1985a); analysis bandwidth 1.7 Hz.

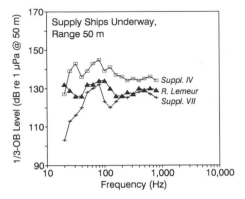

FIGURE 6.7. Received ⅓-octave levels of underwater sound from three supply ships underway at 18.5 km/h (*Canmar Supplier VII*) or 22 km/h (*Canmar Supplier IV* and *Robert Lemeur*). Respective full-power levels are 4.0, 5.4, and 7.2 MW (5280-9600 bhp). From Greene (1985a).

Small Ships.—Support and supply ships (lengths roughly 55-85 m) are generally diesel-powered with two propellers. These ships have larger slower-rotating propellers than the smaller vessels just discussed. Typical small-ship propellers have four blades, diameter 3 m, and turn at ~160 rpm. The fundamental blade-rate tone is therefore around 10-11 Hz. Often the propellers are in nozzles (cowlings). These protect the propellers, help to direct the thrust, and improve maneuverability. Nozzles tend to reduce radiated noise at some aspects and frequencies.

Greene (1987a) determined ⅓-octave sound levels for three supply ships underway at cruising speed (Fig. 6.7). Radiated sound levels were higher for a ship lacking nozzles around the propellers (*Canmar Supplier IV*) than for a larger, more powerful vessel with nozzles (*Robert Lemeur*). Brueggeman et al. (1990:2-19*ff*) also found *Supplier IV* to be noisy relative to *Lemeur*.

Supply ships commonly have hydraulic- or electric-powered bow thrusters to help maneuver. A bow thruster may create a strong harmonic family of tones with a rather high fundamental frequency corresponding to the high rotation rate of the thrusters (Greene 1985a, 1987a; Brueggeman et al. 1990). For example, the received noise spectrum in Fig. 6.6B includes a harmonic family of tones with fundamental frequency 118 Hz (see also Fig. 3.3A). These sounds were generated by a transverse bow thruster. The first nine harmonics were prominent, extending to 1064 Hz. In another case, noise increased by 11 dB when bow thrusters began operating (Fig. 6.8).

Few data on 1-m source levels are available for this class of vessels. However, data on broadband received levels versus range give a good indication of the relative levels for various vessels (Fig. 6.9). In

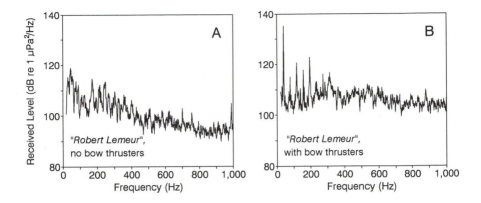

FIGURE 6.8. Received underwater sound spectra from supply ship *Robert Lemeur* before and during bow thruster operation; range 0.56 km. Broadband (20-1000 Hz) levels were 130 dB and 141 dB, respectively. Reanalyzed from recordings of Greene (1987a); analysis bandwidth 1.7 Hz.

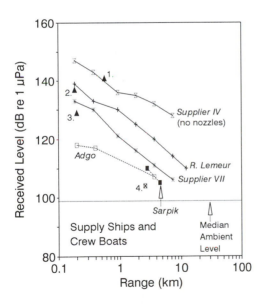

FIGURE 6.9. Vessel noise versus range: received underwater sound levels at 20-1000 Hz for selected diesel powered crew boats (squares) and small ships (other symbols) in relation to range. Single-range measurements: 1, *Robert Lemeur* bow-thrusters (not underway); 2, *Canmar Supplier III* bowthrusters; 3, *Canmar Supplier VIII*; 4, *Sequel*. All data except (1) are for vessels underway. Data from Greene (1985a, 1987a).

general, the larger vessels radiated higher overall noise levels. An exception is the aforementioned *Canmar Supplier IV*, which lacked propeller nozzles and was noisier than *Robert Lemeur*, a larger ship with nozzles. Broadband source levels for most small ships are ~170-180 dB re 1 µPa. Hall et al. (1994) give additional data.

Commercial Vessels and Supertankers.—Large commercial vessels and supertankers have powerful engines and large, slow-turning propellers (~80-110 rpm). These vessels produce high sound levels, mainly at low frequencies.

Several authors have reported noise data for commercial vessels (e.g., Table 6.4). For example, Ross (1976) reviewed measurements for the supertanker *Chevron London*. Tones with a fundamental frequency of 6.8 Hz were evident in noise measured 139-463 km away. The strongest elements were at 40-70 Hz; source levels were ~190 dB re 1 µPa-m. Leggat et al. (1981), based on Cybulski (1977), reported source level spectra (2-80 Hz) for *Mostoles* and *World Dignity*, two fully laden supertankers underway in deep water (Fig. 6.10). Noise levels were highest at the lowest frequencies measured, near 2 Hz. Strong broadband components caused by propeller cavitation were centered at 40-50 Hz for *Mostoles*, which had a propeller 6.3 m in diameter, and near 100 Hz for *World Dignity*, with a 9-m propeller. Figure

TABLE 6.4. Sounds from large commercial ships underway: fundamental frequency, estimated source level of that tone, and measured spectrum level of broadband noise at the specified frequency[a]

Vessel name	Ship length (m)	Source level of dominant tone		Source spectrum level (dB re 1 µPa²/Hz at 1 m)
		Freq. (Hz)	(dB re 1 µPa at 1 m)	
MS *Thor I* (freighter)	135	41.0	172	
SS *F.S. Bryant* (tanker)	135	428.0	169	
SS *Houston* (tanker)	179	60.0	180	
SS *Hawaiian E.* (container ship)	219	33.0	181	
K. Maru (bulk carrier)	-	28.0	180	173 @ 100 Hz
		36.0	180	
Chevron London (supertanker)	340	6.8	190	
Mostoles (supertanker)	266	7.6	187[b]	158 @ 40-50 Hz
World Dignity (supertanker)	337	7.2	185[b]	161 @ 100 Hz
MS *Jutlandia* (container ship)	274	7.7	181	
Third harmonic:		23.0	198	
Fifth harmonic:		38.3	186	

[a] Data from Buck and Chalfant (1972), Ross (1976), and Thiele and Ødegaard (1983).
[b] Actual levels of tones are several dB lower than suggested by Fig. 6.10; levels are estimated from spectrum graphs by adding 10 log (analysis bandwidth)—here 10 log (0.32) = -5 dB (Section 2.2.3).

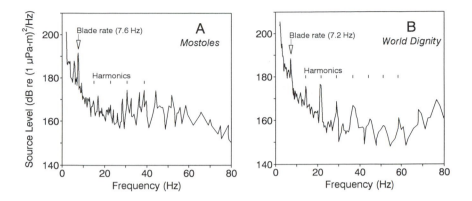

FIGURE 6.10. Low-frequency source level spectra for supertankers: *(A) Mostoles*, 103 ktons, 266 m long, 12.6 knots, 16.8 MW; and *(B) World Dignity*, 271 ktons, 337 m, 17.7 kt, 28.3 MW. From Leggat et al. (1981), based on Cybulski (1977); analysis bandwidth 0.32 Hz.

6.5B shows Malme's estimate of the ⅓-octave source level spectrum at ≥10 Hz for a generic supertanker, based on these and other data. Broadband source levels of supertanker noise can exceed 205 dB re 1 µPa-m if components down to ~2 Hz are included. Low-frequency noise levels from large container ships can also be high, as exemplified by MS *Jutlandia* in Table 6.4 (data of Thiele and Ødegaard 1983).

In general, all vessels produce noise in the same ways. Propeller cavitation produces most of the broadband noise, with dominant tones arising from the propeller blade rate. Propellers create more noise if damaged, operating asynchronously, or operating without nozzles. Propulsion and auxiliary machinery can also radiate significant noise. Radiated noise is roughly related to ship size, speed, and mode of operation. Large ships tend to be noisier than small ones, and ships underway with a full load (or towing or pushing a load) produce more noise than unladen vessels. Noise also increases with ship speed.

6.2.3 Icebreaking

Icebreaking produces stronger and more variable sounds than would normally be produced by a ship of that size and power. Typically, the icebreaker rams forward into the ice until momentum is lost, followed by backing astern in preparation for another run at the ice. Strong cavitation sounds occur when the ship reverses direction from astern to forward, and when it is stopped by the ice after ramming.

When the ice is thin, continuous forward progress may be possible. Even then, more power is required than when the same ship is underway in open water, and more noise is generated.

The effect of icebreaking on radiated ship noise has been measured by recording sounds from the same icebreaking supply ships underway at a standard distance in open water and in ice (Greene 1987a). During icebreaking, received sound levels in the 20- to 1000-Hz band increased by 14 dB near *Supplier VII* (4.0 MW; Fig. 6.11) and by ~12-13 dB near *Robert Lemeur* (7.2 MW; Fig. 6.12). The difference decreased as range increased (Fig. 6.12), indicating more rapid attenuation of sound below heavy ice. Even so, icebreaking caused substantial increases in noise levels out to at least 5 km.

The increases in noise level during icebreaking vary over time (Thiele 1988:40ff; Malme et al. 1989). For example, noise levels increased when *Robert Lemeur* pushed on ice (Fig. 6.13). This was caused by propeller cavitation, which produced some energy up to >5 kHz. The icebreaking sounds were detectable >50 km away. In general, spectra of icebreaker noise are wide (e.g., Fig. 6.5B) and highly variable over time (e.g., Richardson and Malme 1993:643).

Physical crushing of ice contributes little to the overall increase in noise during icebreaking. Thiele (1984, 1988) placed accelerometers in the bow of the icebreaker *John A. MacDonald* to sense icebreaking

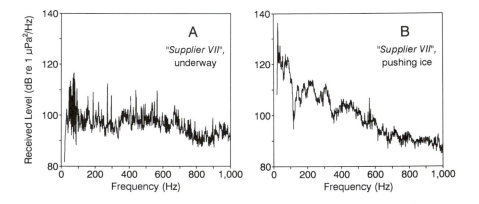

FIGURE 6.11. Icebreaker noise spectra: received underwater sound pressure spectra for icebreaking supply vessel *Canmar Supplier VII (A)* underway in open water and *(B)* icebreaking. Broadband (20-1000 Hz) received levels 130 dB and 144 dB, respectively (range 0.37 km). Reanalyzed from data of Greene (1987a); analysis bandwidth 1.7 Hz.

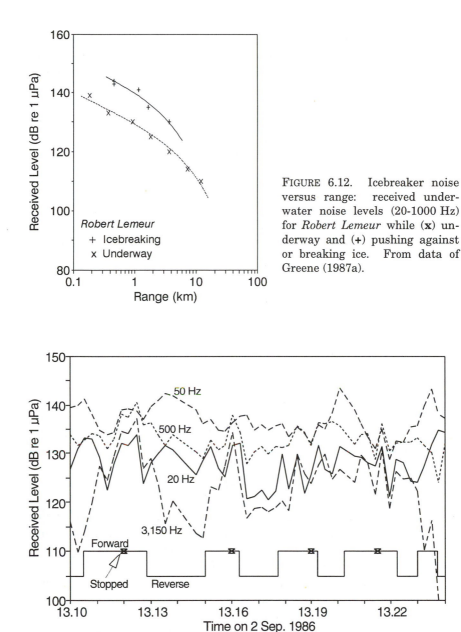

FIGURE 6.12. Icebreaker noise versus range: received underwater noise levels (20-1000 Hz) for *Robert Lemeur* while (**x**) underway and (**+**) pushing against or breaking ice. From data of Greene (1987a).

FIGURE 6.13. Icebreaker noise versus time: 14-minute time sequence of received underwater noise levels in ⅓-octave bands centered at 20, 50, 500, and 3150 Hz. Travel direction of icebreaker *Robert Lemeur* (forward or reverse) is shown at bottom, with times when ship was stopped by ice. Each measurement is a 16.5-s average at range 0.46 km. Data of Greene (1987a), from Malme et al. (1989:App. B).

vibration, and in the stern to sense propeller vibration. Underwater noise received at a distant location was clearly correlated with propeller cavitation but not with icebreaking vibration. Thus, the increased noise during icebreaking is due mainly to the propellers.

Noise levels during icebreaking are usually highest during the full astern phase (Table 6.5). The increases range from 5 to 10 dB. However, exceptions occur, and the phase(s) with peak sound levels may depend on frequency (Fig. 6.13).

Thiele (1988) described icebreaking noise from the *John A. Mac-Donald* in two types of ice. In Baffin Bay in an area of 1-m ice floes, 50-80% ice coverage, the ship ran ahead essentially unhindered by ice. In Lancaster Sound, there was 100% shore-fast ice, and the ship made only slow progress by backing and ramming. Comparative levels for ⅓-octave bands were as follows:

Location	Condition	Power, MW	⅓-OB center freq., Hz	Source level, dB re 1 μPa-m
Baffin Bay	Ahead	5.5	31.5	177
" "	Astern	—	50	~187
Lancaster S.	Ahead	10.0	50	172
" "	Astern	"	50	181

As usual, source level was higher during movement astern than ahead. It is not known why the estimated source levels were higher in the lighter ice condition (Baffin Bay). The low-frequency underwater sounds of backing and ramming in Lancaster Sound were occasionally audible 55 km away. Thiele found several strong tones below 20 Hz, including one at 2.4 Hz. These infrasonic tones were the fundamentals and harmonics of the propeller shaft and blade rates.

Hall et al. (1994) give measurements and estimated source levels for the icebreaking supply ships *Kalvik*, *Ikaluk*, and *Canmar Supplier II* breaking ice at a Beaufort Sea drillsite. They estimated the broadband (10-10,000 Hz) source levels to be 181-183, 184 and 174 dB re 1 μPa-m for the three ships, respectively.

In summary, the alternating periods of ramming and backing that are common during icebreaking cause variations in radiated noise levels. Icebreakers pushing ice radiate noise ~10-15 dB stronger than when underway in open water, primarily due to strong propeller cavitation. There are tones at frequencies related to the propeller blade rate below 200 Hz, including some strong tones below 20 Hz, and lesser components extending beyond 5 kHz. On a ⅓-octave basis, levels can be high even at frequencies above 5 kHz. The duration of

TABLE 6.5. Estimated source levels (at 1 m) for icebreaker noise. Source levels for strong tones from MV *Arctic* are listed under "Broadband" because the dB reference units there are correct. For MV *John A. MacDonald* the ⅓-octaves with strongest source levels were centered at 50 Hz for all three operating conditions[a]

Description	Frequencies (Hz)	Source levels Broadband (dB re 1 µPa-m)	Spectrum (dB re (1 µPa-m)²/Hz)
MS Voima (max. 10.2 MW)			
icebreaking full astern	broadband	190	
icebreaking full ahead	broadband	180-185	162 @ 100 Hz
open water, 50-60% pwr	broadband	177	
MV Arctic (max. 11.0 MW)			
icebreaking ahead	10-1000	184	
icebreaking astern	10-1000	191	
icebreaking ahead	Tones @ 53, 205	Tones 171	
icebreaking astern	Tone @ 79	Tone 177	
MV John A. MacDonald (max. 11.2 MW)			
idle	⅓ octave		160 @ 50 Hz
icebreaking ahead	⅓ octave		172 @ 50 Hz
icebreaking astern	⅓ octave		181 @ 50 Hz

[a] Data from Thiele (1981, 1988) and LGL and Greeneridge (1986).

a single episode of strong cavitation noise is generally about one minute, followed by several minutes of less intense noise as the icebreaker repositions itself. However, increased noise levels can also occur at times during repositioning, primarily because of intermittent propeller cavitation while moving astern and reversing direction. Measured noise levels are often 7-8 dB higher for icebreakers going astern than when moving ahead. When present, nozzles around the propellers significantly reduce radiated propeller noise during icebreaking.

6.2.4 Hovercraft and Other Vehicles

Hovercraft ride on a self-generated air cushion and can operate over open water or ice. Tracked vehicles, large-tired rolligons, trucks, and ordinary construction equipment often operate on shore-fast ice. Noise generated on ice is transmitted into the water directly below, but it does not propagate well laterally. The following is a brief summary of the few published measurements from such sources, excluding on-ice seismic profiling noise, which is covered in Section 6.5.3.

Hovercraft produce strong in-air sounds, but few data on their underwater sounds are available. Slaney (1975) measured underwater noise from a Bell Voyageur hovercraft during a "flypast". At a receiver depth of 1.8 m, lateral range 46 m, received levels in ⅓-octave bands centered at 80-630 Hz were ~110 dB re 1 µPa; the 50- to 2000-Hz band level was 121 dB.

Small snowmobiles have high-speed two-cycle engines. These are noisy in air and create sounds at higher frequencies than larger, slower machinery. The amount of sound passing through ice into the water below is expected to vary greatly depending on snow, ice, and temperature conditions. The spectrum of snowmobile sound as received under the ice includes much energy near 1-1.25 kHz, but levels vary widely: spectrum levels ~90 dB re 1 $\mu Pa^2/Hz$ at range 148 m in one study, versus only 55-60 dB at range ~200 m in another (Holliday et al. 1980, 1984).

Several authors have described underwater sounds near various types of heavy vehicles and machinery operating on ice. Results are difficult to compare because of differences in sources and measurement techniques. Holliday et al. (1984) described sounds from several large moving vehicles. Cummings et al. (1981b) reported that the strongest received spectrum level for a Caterpillar tractor operating on ice at range 3.7 km was 66 dB re 1 $\mu Pa^2/Hz$ at ~800 Hz, with an "overall" level of 77 dB re 1 µPa. de Heering and White (1984) reported that, at 125-600 Hz, underwater noise levels from a stationary tracked vehicle were ~5-10 dB stronger with the vehicle standing on bare ice than on snow. However, when the tracked vehicle was traveling, noise levels on snow-covered versus bare ice were similar in the 125- to 4000-Hz band; above 4 kHz the snow attenuated the sound. Greene (1983) measured sound levels associated with road-building on ice, including underwater sounds from a pump used to flood the future roadbed. The strongest tone, at 86 Hz, was 97 dB re 1 µPa at range 0.37 km in water 10 m deep.

In summary, hovercraft and vehicles on ice can transmit significant noise into the water. For on-ice sources, levels are affected by ice condition (temperature, snow cover) and are generally much lower than noise levels generated by vessels in water. Snow absorbs sound. Running vehicles standing on ice blanketed by snow transmit less noise to water than the same vehicles standing on bare ice. Water depth also affects sound transmission from sources on ice. However, factors affecting underwater noise levels from sources on ice have not been studied extensively.

6.3 *Marine Dredging and Construction*

Marine dredging, tunnel boring, and various construction activities in and near the sea can create underwater sounds. Most studies of these sounds have dealt with construction of offshore oil industry facilities in the Arctic. Offshore drilling in shallow arctic waters is often done from man-made islands or caissons placed on the bottom or on subsea berms. Man-made islands and subsea berms can be built either by dredges operating in the open-water season or by on-ice activities in winter. Underwater explosions are sometimes involved in marine construction; their sounds are described in Section 6.7.

6.3.1 Dredging
Marine dredging is common in coastal waters. Dredges are used to deepen channels and harbors, to create land or submerged platforms, and for subsea mining. Received levels of dredging sound can exceed ambient levels out to considerable distances (Fig. 6.14). Underwater noise from three types of dredges has been recorded in the

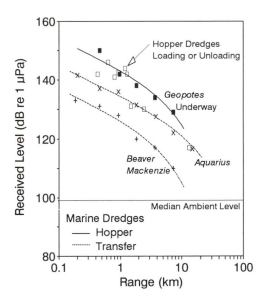

FIGURE 6.14. Dredge noise versus range: received underwater sound levels (20-1000 Hz) of hopper dredges (squares) and transfer dredges (**x**, **+**) in relation to range. All were operating in the Beaufort Sea. Hydrophone depths 9-18 m. From data of Greene (1985a, 1987b).

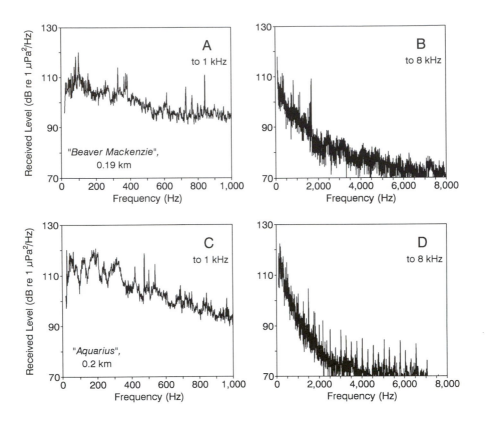

FIGURE 6.15. Received spectrum levels of transfer dredge noise for frequencies 20-1000 Hz (left) and 20-8000 Hz (right). *(A,B) Beaver Mackenzie* dredging at range 0.19 km; *(C,D) Aquarius* dredging at 0.2 km. Reanalyzed from recordings of Greene (1987b); analysis bandwidth 1.7 Hz (left) and 3.4 Hz (right).

Beaufort Sea: cutter-suction transfer dredges, hopper dredges, and clamshell dredges. *Transfer dredges* are moored or anchored ships that extend suction pipes to the seafloor and discharge pipes to a barge or discharge site. A cutter head loosens gravel, which is pumped as a slurry through a pipe to the discharge site. A *hopper dredge* is a ship that moves over a dredging site, fills its hoppers, and then travels to the construction or discharge site to offload the material either by pumping it out as a slurry or by dumping the load through gates in the bottom of the ship. A *clamshell dredge* pulls up large scoops of gravel within opposing buckets that clamp together; barges are often used to transfer this dredged material to another site.

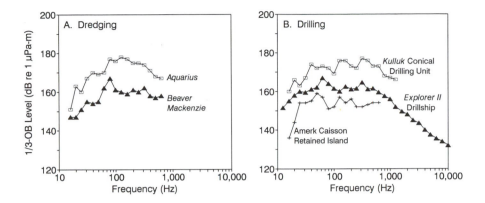

FIGURE 6.16. Estimated ⅓-octave source levels of underwater noise (at 1 m) for *(A)* marine dredging and *(B)* offshore drilling. From Malme et al. (1989) based on data of Greene (1987b) and Miles et al. (1987).

Greene (1985a, 1987b) found that two cutter-suction transfer dredges produced quite different sound levels, and that hopper dredges were at least as noisy as the noisier of the two suction dredges (Fig. 6.14). Broadband (20-1000 Hz) underwater sounds from these dredges would normally diminish below the typical broadband ambient noise level (about 100 dB re 1 μPa) within 25 km of the dredges. However, some dredges emit strong tones, and these would be detectable at ranges >25 km in some situations.

The strongest underwater sounds from cutter-suction transfer dredges were primarily at low frequencies (Fig. 6.15). However, high-frequency tones were also present and conspicuous against the lower levels of broadband dredge and ambient noise found at high frequencies. Above 30 Hz, source levels for *Aquarius* were comparable to those for a large tanker. However, the tanker was much noisier below 30 Hz (Fig. 6.16A versus 6.5B).

Underwater noise levels from hopper dredges fluctuated with operating status (Greene 1985a, 1987b). The highest levels occurred during loading. At all times, low-frequency energy predominated.

Sounds from a clamshell dredge were quite variable, depending on the phase of the operation (Miles et al. 1986, 1987). Computed source levels in the ⅓ octave of strongest noise, centered at 250 Hz, varied from 150 to 162 dB re 1 μPa-m. The strongest sound was from the winch motor that pulled the loaded clamshell back to the surface. This noise, with a broadband source level of ~167 dB re 1 μPa-m, included many harmonics of a 125-Hz fundamental tone. A short transient "clank" sound was associated with the closing of the clam-shell, but this sound contained little acoustic energy. Noise from the tug and barge used to transfer the dredged material (Fig. 6.5B) was stronger than that produced by the clamshell dredge itself.

In summary, dredges can be strong sources of continuous noise in nearshore regions. Dredge noises are strongest at low frequencies. Because of the rapid attenuation of low frequencies in shallow water, dredge noise normally is undetectable underwater at ranges beyond 20-25 km. Tones may appear in the spectra of dredge noise, even at frequencies above 6 kHz. Although noise levels from powerful ships can exceed those from dredging, single ships usually do not produce strong noise in one area for a prolonged period. In contrast, dredging often continues in one area for days or weeks at a time.

6.3.2 Tunnel Boring

Large boring machines with rotating cutter heads can be used to drill tunnels for undersea roads, railways, and sewage outfalls. Mal-me and Krumhansl (1993) measured sounds in the water above a 50-head Robbins machine boring a tunnel 8 m in diameter. When boring was underway, the sounds were predominantly broadband in charac-ter, strongest below 10 Hz, with diminishing energy at increasing fre-quencies up to at least 500 Hz. When received in shallow water, there also were strong components at 30-100 Hz because of resonance effects related to water depth.

6.3.3 Other Construction Operations

Greene (1983) measured noise under shore-fast ice during winter construction of an artificial island near Prudhoe Bay, Alaska. Roads were built on the sea ice and trucks hauled gravel to a site in water 12 m deep. At distances ≥3.6 km, there was no evidence of noise com-ponents above 1000 Hz, and little energy below 1000 Hz. Construc-tion-related sounds did not propagate well in shallow water under the ice during winter.

Sounds from various onshore activities propagate into nearshore waters. Coupling may or may not be very good, depending on source depth and ground material. Land-based explosions can couple into deep water and travel as "T-phase" waves, a phenomenon used to monitor underground nuclear explosions and earthquakes.

6.4 Oil and Gas Drilling and Production

Offshore drilling is usually done from man-made islands or platforms, or from drillships accompanied by support vessels. When recoverable deposits are found, further marine construction may precede production. These offshore activities produce underwater noise. Also, they require aircraft and vessel support that may further ensonify broad areas. Thus, offshore drilling and production involves various activities that produce a composite underwater noise field.

Several extensive studies of underwater noise associated with offshore oil and gas exploration have been conducted. Gales (1982) measured noise near platforms and man-made islands where drilling or production were occurring. Recordings were made off Santa Barbara, California; in Cook Inlet, Alaska; and in the Atlantic off New Jersey. Gales presents the only comprehensive work to date on spectral characteristics of underwater noise from drilling and production operations in temperate waters. In the Arctic, noise levels, spectral characteristics, and propagation were measured near drillsites of several types in the Canadian Beaufort Sea (Greene 1985a, 1987b), Alaskan Beaufort Sea (Miles et al. 1986, 1987; Greene 1987a), and Chukchi Sea (Brueggeman et al. 1990, 1992a,b). Other studies that have provided data on drilling noise in the Alaskan Beaufort Sea include Malme and Mlawski (1979) and the several recent (1990-1994) reports by J.D. Hall, M.L. Gallagher and K.D. Brewer.

6.4.1 Drilling from Islands and Caissons
Offshore drilling is done from three types of facilities: **(1)** natural, man-made and caisson islands; **(2)** platforms standing on legs; and **(3)** drilling vessels, including semisubmersibles and drillships. The facility used depends on water depth, oceanography, ice cover, and other factors.

Drilling from Islands and Ice Pads.—Underwater noise levels from drillsites on natural and artificial islands are low. Noise is transmitted very poorly from the drillrig machinery through land into the water. Drilling noise from icebound islands is generally confined to low frequencies and has a low source level. It would be audible at range 10 km only during unusually quiet periods; the usual audible range would be ~2 km. Under open-water conditions, drilling sounds from islands may be detectable somewhat farther away, but the levels are still relatively low.

Noises associated with drilling rigs operating on two icebound gravel islands, one natural and one man-made, were recorded in March under the sea ice near Prudhoe Bay, Alaska (Malme and Mlawski 1979). Most noise was below 200 Hz. Broadband noise decayed to ambient levels within ~1.5 km. Low-frequency tones were measurable to ~9.5 km under low ambient noise conditions, but were essentially undetectable beyond ~1.5 km with high ambient noise.

In very shallow arctic water, winter drilling is sometimes done from pads of ice resting on the bottom. Water is pumped to the surface, where it freezes and gradually thickens the ice until the ice undersurface contacts the bottom. Noise does not propagate far from these rigs. Noise from a rotary-table drillrig on one ice pad was primarily below 350 Hz. In water 6-7 m deep, the noise attenuated rapidly from ~125 dB at range 130 m to ~85 dB (and barely detectable) at 2 km (ice cover 2 m; 31 log R loss rate; Richardson et al. 1990a). Cummings et al. (1981b), working in even shallower water, reported an overall received level of only 86 dB re 1 µPa at 480 m from a rig drilling on ice. There were many tones at 10-160 Hz.

Noise measurements have also been made in early autumn with partially open water near two man-made islands off Prudhoe Bay in water 12-15 m deep: Davis et al. (1985) re Seal I.; Johnson et al. (1986) re Sandpiper I. Noise levels at distances as close as 450 m were quite low, comparable to median ambient levels expected for sea state one with no shipping (Section 5.2.1). Underwater sounds from Seal Island, when it was manned but inactive, were not detectable 2.3 km away, even though power generators were in use (Davis et al. 1985). During well-logging[2], the only additional sound evident underwater was a 468-Hz tone detectable up to 5 km away. Sound propagation from the logging equipment appeared to involve the air as well as the water, as levels were 4-5 dB higher at 3 m than at 9 m depth at ranges 500-700 m.

Drilling on an artificial island (Sandpiper I.) produced notable underwater sound, but its level was low (Figs. 6.17A and 6.17B). Median broadband (20-1000 Hz) levels at range 0.5 km were 8-10 dB higher with drilling. The most obvious components were tones at 20 and 40 Hz, attributed to power generation (Figs. 6.17A and 6.17B). The 20-Hz tone was 6-11 dB higher during drilling, and the 40-Hz

---

[2] Drilling operations include *tripping* (extracting or lowering the drillstring), *cleaning*, and *well-logging* (lowering instruments on a cable down the hole).

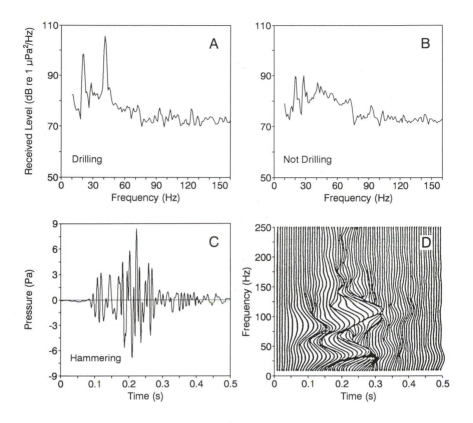

FIGURE 6.17. Underwater noise near Sandpiper artificial island, Alaskan Beaufort Sea, *(A)* with versus *(B)* without drilling, and *(C,D)* in the presence of hammering. Range 0.5 km for received spectrum levels in (A, B), and 1 km for (C, D). Analysis bandwidth 1.7 Hz in (A, B). Reanalyzed from recordings of Johnson et al. (1986).

tone was 15-24 dB higher then. These tones often were weakly detectable at range 0.5 km without drilling, and at 3.7 km with drilling. There was rapid attenuation (24-30 dB) from 0.5 to 3.7 km, no doubt partly because of the shallow water. The effective source level of the 40-Hz tone was low: ~145 dB re 1 µPa-m (Miles et al. 1987).

Impulsive hammering sounds associated with installation of a conductor pipe on Sandpiper I. were as high as 131-135 dB re 1 µPa at range 1 km when pipe depth was >20 m below the island. In contrast, broadband drilling noise at this distance was only ~100-106 dB. During hammering, blows occurred about every 3 s, signal duration was 0.2 s, and the transient signals had strongest components at 30-40 Hz and ~100 Hz (Figs. 6.17C and 6.17D). Similarly, Moore et al.

(1984) reported that received levels for transient pipe-driving bangs recorded 1 km from a man-made island near Prudhoe Bay were 25-35 dB above ambient levels in the 50- to 200-Hz band. Such sounds might be received underwater as far as 10-15 km from the source—farther than drilling sound.

Drilling from Caissons.—Caissons have often been used for offshore drilling in the Beaufort Sea. Three types of caissons have been used, each likely to have different sound transmission properties: **(1)** Ring caissons—steel ring-shaped structures that are floated into place, ballasted down onto the bottom or onto a subsea berm, and then filled with sand or gravel. The drillrig and support facilities are set up on this sand or gravel as on a conventional island. **(2)** Self-contained floating concrete rigs like Glomar's *CIDS* (Concrete Island Drilling System) and BeauDril's *Molikpaq*—floated into place and ballasted down onto a subsea berm. **(3)** A section of a ship with a drillrig mounted on it, like Canmar's *SSDC* (Steel-Sided Drilling Caisson)—ballasted down with water onto a subsea berm or ancillary support structure. Richardson and Malme (1993:648) include photographs.

Underwater sounds from drilling on the three types of caissons probably differ in level, but few data exist. Ring-retained caissons may be the quietest. The gravel or sand should dampen vibrations from rig machinery, as on conventional islands. There might be some differences because of the near-vertical caisson walls. In the absence of ice, these are exposed directly to the water and may radiate sound levels intermediate between those from drillships and from shallow-sloping sand or gravel islands. An important feature of caissons is the presence of standby vessels during open-water conditions and, in the Arctic, into the freeze-up period. Such vessels contribute significant sound to the water, as they do around floating drillrigs (Section 6.4.3).

Greene (1985a, 1987b) measured underwater sounds during diverse activities at three ring-caisson sites. The 20- to 1000-Hz band levels at range 1.8 km were 113-126 dB re 1 μPa. At all sites, received sound levels varied with activities of the surrounding support vessels. Estimated ⅓-octave source levels (20-1000 Hz) were much higher than those for drilling on artificial islands, but lower than those for drillships (Fig. 6.16B; *cf.* Section 6.4.3).

Sounds from the *Glomar CIDS* concrete drilling caisson were measured by Hall and Francine (1990, 1991). In the absence of drilling, radiated levels of underwater sound were low, at least at frequencies above 30 Hz. The "overall" received level was 109 dB re 1 μPa at

278 m, excluding any infrasonic components. When *CIDS* was drilling in early winter, radiated sound levels above 30 Hz were again relatively low (~89 dB at 1.4 km). However, when infrasonic components were included, the received level was 112 dB at 1.4 km; more than 99% of the sound energy received was below 20 Hz. Levels at ranges 222-259 m were 121-124 dB, depending on aspect. There were strong infrasonic tones from 1.375 to 1.5 Hz, corresponding to the rotation rate of the drilling turntable. The maximum detection distance for the infrasonic tones was not determined. Such tones would probably attenuate rapidly in water shallow enough for use of a bottom-founded caisson. Hall and Francine estimated that the source levels for *CIDS* were low, even when the infrasonic tones were included. However, actual source levels probably were higher than estimated because propagation loss close to *CIDS* was not modeled realistically.

Sounds from Canmar's *SSDC* were measured during drilling operations in water 15 m deep with 100% ice cover (Gallagher et al. 1992b). During drilling, vertical axis accelerometer signals from the drillrig floor included weak tones at the rotary table turning rate (90 rpm, or 1.5 Hz) and at the drive motor rate (14.6 Hz). There was also a broad spectral maximum at 6.2-8.7 Hz, attributed to a pinion gear. None of these infrasonic acceleration peaks appeared in the hydroacoustic data presented. At range 115 m, the strongest underwater tone was at 5 Hz (119 dB re 1 μPa). Other tones appeared at 20, 60, 150, and 450 Hz. At range 715 m, the 5-Hz tone was apparently not detectable, but weak tones were present at 150-600 Hz. The broadband (20-1000 Hz) received level at 215-315 m was 116-117 dB re 1 μPa, higher than the 109 dB reported for *CIDS* at range 278 m.

Summary.—Underwater noise associated with drilling from natural barrier islands or man-made islands is generally weak, and is inaudible at ranges beyond a few kilometers. Drilling noise from caisson-retained islands (CRI or ring caissons) is much stronger. At least during open-water conditions, noise is conducted more directly into the water at CRI sites than at island drillsites. Noise associated with drilling activities at both island and CRI sites varies considerably with ongoing operations. The highest documented levels were transient pulses from hammering to install conductor pipe. No data are available on characteristics of drilling noise from icebound CRI sites.

Data from a self-contained concrete drilling caisson indicate that it was relatively quiet at frequencies above 10-20 Hz. However, there was a strong tone near 1.4 Hz attributed to the rotary drilling table.

The *SSDC* drilling caisson was apparently several decibels noisier at sonic frequencies. However, it did not transmit infrasonic rotary table tones into the water.

6.4.2 *Drilling from Bottom-Founded Platforms*

Noise associated with conventional drilling platforms is relatively unstudied. Gales (1982) recorded noise from one drilling platform and three combined drilling/production platforms off California. Platform noise was so weak that it was nearly undetectable even alongside the platform during sea states ≥3. However, source level computations were not possible because of the close measurement ranges relative to the sizes of the platforms.

Although only stylized noise spectra were reported, the strongest tones from all four platforms were at very low frequencies, near 5 Hz. Received levels of these tones were 119-127 dB re 1 µPa at near-field measurement locations. The highest frequency tone was at 1.2 kHz. These near-field measurements are not directly comparable with results of other studies, but they suggest that conventional bottom-founded drilling platforms may not be very noisy.

6.4.3 *Drilling from Vessels*

Vessels used for offshore drilling include semisubmersibles and drillships. They can be either anchored firmly or dynamically positioned, and they are accompanied by supply vessels and, where needed, icebreakers. Drillships apparently are noisier than semisubmersibles. Semisubmersibles lack a large hull area. Their machinery is mounted on decks raised above the sea on risers supported by submerged flotation chambers. Sound and vibration paths to the water are through either the air or the risers, in contrast to the direct paths through the hull of a drillship.

Semisubmersibles.—Noise from semisubmersibles has been recorded by several researchers. Greene (1986) measured sounds from *SEDCO 708* drilling in water 114 m deep in the Bering Sea. Overall broadband levels did not exceed local ambient levels in corresponding bands beyond ~1 km, although weak tones were received as far as ~18 km away. Estimated source levels were as follows:

	Broadband		Tones		
Frequencies (Hz):	10-500	80-4000	60	181	301
Est. Source Levels: (dB re 1 µPa-m)	154	154	149	137	136

These are rather low source levels compared with those of many sources discussed earlier, even though support boats as well as the semisubmersible itself were present. There was substantial variability in both the sound levels and in the frequencies of tones received.

Gales (1982) measured noise from two diesel-powered semisubmersibles with unmuffled exhaust stacks. The strongest tones measured 13-15 m from the two vessels were at 29 and 70 Hz (each at 125 dB re 1 μPa). There were somewhat weaker (110-122 dB) infrasonic tones at 7-14 Hz. Source levels could not be estimated because the measurements were taken in the near field.

Drillships.—Noise levels are generally higher near drillships than near semisubmersibles or caissons. The drillship hull contains the rig generators, drilling machinery, and the rig itself. The hull is well coupled to the water. The drilling machinery no doubt contributes to the level of sound radiated from the vessel, but no infrasonic tones have been reported.

Greene (1987b) measured noise from two drillships (*Canmar Explorer I* and *II*). These are converted Liberty freighters with ice strengthening. Levels were notably higher during drilling than during well-logging (Fig. 6.18). Close to *Explorer II*, noise levels seemed lower at bow and stern aspects than at beam aspects (Greene 1987a). Noise from well-cleaning was comparable to that from drilling and

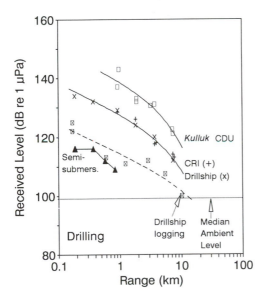

FIGURE 6.18. Drilling noise versus range: received broadband levels versus range for underwater noise from four types of offshore drilling plus well-logging. Bandwidth 20-1000 Hz for *Kulluk* conical drilling unit (CDU), caisson retained island (CRI), drillship *Explorer II* drilling, and drillship *Explorer I* logging; 20-500 Hz for semisubmersible *SEDCO 708* drilling. CRI's fitted curve (not shown) was almost the same as that for the drillship. From data of Greene (1986, 1987b).

somewhat stronger than that from tripping.   Footnote [2] in Section
6.4.1, earlier, defines these drilling terms.

Miles et al. (1987) estimated source levels of drilling sounds from
Explorer II based on their 1986 measurements. They compared their
results with Greene's data for the same ship in earlier years, and concluded that the ship's noise changes from year to year, probably because of changes in operating machinery. Brueggeman et al. (1990)
found that a sister vessel, *Explorer III*, emitted slightly stronger noise
when dredging a glory hole and progressively weaker sounds while
drilling, cementing, and tripping.

Drillship spectra often contain prominent tones, generally up to
600 Hz. *Explorer II*'s spectrum was dominated by strong tones at 254
and 277 Hz. These were attributable to turbochargers on the diesel-
electric generators. These tones changed frequency with the generator
load and disappeared with light loads, as expected. Thus, measurements taken at different times may show different spectra, depending
on electric load and number of generators operating. It is not known
whether these drillships emit strong tones at infrasonic frequencies.

Greene (1987b) measured sounds from the ice-strengthened "Conical Drilling Unit" (CDU) *Kulluk*. *Kulluk* is a specialized floating platform designed for arctic waters. *Kulluk* was by far the strongest of
the drillship sound sources; the 20- to 1000-Hz broadband level was
several decibels higher than that for *Explorer II* drilling at corresponding ranges (Fig. 6.18). The estimated source level was also higher
across a wide range of frequencies (Fig. 6.16B). Brewer et al. (1993)
and Hall et al. (1994) reported data from *Kulluk* operating in another
area. The broadband source levels (10-10,000 Hz) during drilling and
tripping were estimated to be 191 and 179 dB re 1 µPa-m, respectively, based on measurements at depth 20 m in water ~30 m deep
(Hall et al. 1994). Received levels at depth 10 m were notably less
than those at 20 m.

Summary.—Offshore drilling is conducted from natural, man-
made, or caisson-retained islands, from platforms, or from specially
designed vessels. In general, more sound is radiated underwater
during drilling operations from drillships than from semisubmersibles.
In contrast, noise from drilling on islands radiates very poorly to
water, making such operations relatively quiet. Noise levels from
drilling platforms and certain types of caissons have not been well
documented, but are apparently intermediate between those from
vessels and islands. Drilling operations often produce noise that

includes strong tonal components at low frequencies, including infra-sonic frequencies in at least some cases.

6.4.4 Offshore Oil and Gas Production

Offshore oil and gas production is usually carried out from bot-tom-standing metal platforms or from islands. Underwater noise from platforms standing on metal legs would be expected to be relatively weak because of the small surface area in contact with the water and the placement of machinery on decks well above the water. Sounds from production on islands are also likely to be strongly attenuated, as documented for drilling on natural and artificial islands (Section 6.4.1).

Noises from 11 production platforms and a man-made island were summarized by Gales (1982). His measurements were in the near field and were not suitable for source level estimates. The platforms were bottom-standing steel structures with multiple steel legs. The strongest tones from four production platforms were at very low fre-quencies, between ~4.5 and 38 Hz, when measured at ranges 9-61 m. Two platforms powered by gas turbines produced more tones than did two that had at least partial shore power. Two platforms had peak sound spectrum levels at 50-200 Hz or 100-500 Hz, whereas sound levels fell with increasing frequency near the other two platforms.

In contrast, noise levels were very low near the man-made Rincon production island, made of sand protected by outer rock in water 14 m deep (Gales 1982). The major source of underwater noise was a sub-merged pump, which was not run continuously. Tones at 30-120 Hz had received levels of only 89-94 dB when measured only 34 m from the island. The author rated production noise from the man-made island as "very quiet" relative to that from metal-legged production platforms. Gales surmised that the low noise levels from the produc-tion equipment were probably the result of an onshore power supply, poor conduction of sound through the rock and fill island, and poor conduction of low-frequency sound in shallow water.

These results are generally consistent with the expectations. However, more data on noise around these and other types of produc-tion platforms and islands are needed before a quantitative analysis of production sounds will be possible.

6.5 *Marine Geophysical Surveys*

Marine geophysical surveys are conducted to study geological processes and to locate geological structures of types often associated with petroleum deposits.   Marine geophysical surveys use high-energy sources of sound or vibration to create seismic waves in the earth's crust beneath the sea. High-energy, low-frequency sounds, usually in the form of short-duration pulses, are created along survey grids. Subsurface geologic structures are characterized by receiving and processing the sequence of refracted and reflected signals. Sound pulses from marine seismic surveys are often detectable in the water tens or even hundreds of kilometers from the source (Greene and Richardson 1988; Bowles et al. 1994). Useful reviews of marine seismic survey technology can be found in Kramer et al. (1968), Lugg (1979), and Johnston and Cain (1981).   Standard calibration procedures are described in Fricke et al. (1985) and in Johnston et al. (1988).

This section reviews the underwater noises from nonexplosive seismic survey sources in widespread use by the geophysical industry: airguns, sleeve exploders, gas guns, and Vibroseis®. Several other nonexplosive sources are mentioned in Section 6.5.4. In the past, explosive charges were the standard sources for marine seismic exploration, and in some countries explosives are still used for this purpose (Wright 1985). Noise pulses from underwater explosions are described in Section 6.7.

The seismic survey literature often refers to peak-to-peak (p-p) pressures in bar-meters (P_a). These can be converted to source levels in dB re 1 µPa-m$_{p-p}$ as follows:

$$L_s \text{ (dB re 1 µPa-m)}_{p-p} = 20 \log (P_a) + 220 \qquad (6.3)$$

"Peak-to-peak" values from equation (6.3) are ~6 dB higher than "zero-to-peak" values. A small airgun (0.16 L) could have a source level of 1.2 bar-m$_{p-p}$, equivalent to 222 dB re 1 µPa-m$_{p-p}$ or 216 dB zero-to-peak.   Corresponding figures for a 65-L array of airguns might be ~110 bar-m$_{p-p}$, 261 dB$_{p-p}$, and 255 dB$_{0-p}$.

It is difficult to compare any of these values with levels from continuous sources, which are normally expressed on a "root-mean-square" (rms) pressure basis. For an ideal sinusoid, the rms level is 9 dB lower than the p-p value and 3 dB lower than the 0-p value. However, seismic and other impulses are not ideal sinusoids, so any simple conversion formula is approximate.

6.5.1 Airguns

Airgun arrays are now the most common energy sources for marine geophysical surveys. Airguns function by suddenly venting high-pressure air into the water. This produces an air-filled cavity that expands violently, then contracts, and re-expands; sound is created with each oscillation. Although a single airgun is sometimes used, seismic surveys are usually conducted by towing an array of airguns (Table 6.6) at depth 4-8 m behind a small ship (Barger and Hamblen 1980; Hoff and Chmelik 1982). To study deep structures, large arrays with 12-70 airguns are used. In other applications, only a few airguns may be used. The guns are typically fired once every several seconds. A long cable containing many hydrophones is towed behind the airgun array to receive the reflected signals from beneath the seafloor.

TABLE 6.6. Characteristics of some marine seismic energy sources[a]

Source description	P_c(MPa)[b]	V_c(L)	d (m)	P_a (bar-m)	dB re 1 μPa-m
Airgun Arrays					
GSC 7900	-	129.5	-	174	259
ARCO 4000	12.9	65.6	10	~110	255
GECO Array 3100 + 1640	13.8	77.7	7.6	82.4	252
GSI Array 4000 pnu-con	13.8	66.8	6.1	80.0	252
GECO Array 3100	13.8	50.8	7.6	76.3	252
SSL Array 4440	13.8	72.8	8.5	73.4	251
GSI Array Jonsson 2000	13.8	32.8	6.1	55.0	249
GECO Array 1985 + 1640	13.8	59.4	7.6	49.4	248
Western Array 1050	31.0	17.2	6.1	42.0	246
GECO Array 1985	13.8	32.5	7.6	41.9	246
SSL Array 1460	13.8	23.9	7.6	25.3	242
Western Array 555	31.0	9.1	6.1	25.2	242
GECO 594 Subarray	13.8	9.7	8.2	11.9	235
Single Airguns					
Small airgun	13.8	0.16	9.1	1.2	216
Mid sized airgun	13.8	4.92	9.1	3.4	225
Large airgun	13.8	32.8	9.1	8.0	232

[a] From Johnston and Cain (1981) except for ARCO 4000 (Greene 1985b), GSC 7900 (Parrott 1991), and single airguns (Lugg 1979).
[b] P_c = pressure within guns before release, in MPa; V_c = total volume of guns, in liters; d = depth of guns below the surface, in meters; P_a = source strength (acoustic pressure at reference distance 1 m, in bar-meters peak-to-peak; applies to downward propagation); dB value is zero-to-peak (add ~6 dB for peak-to-peak).

Peak levels of sound pulses from airgun arrays are much higher than the continuous sound levels from any ship or industrial source. Broadband source levels of 248-255 dB re 1 µPa-m, zero-to-peak, are typical of a full-scale array (Barger and Hamblen 1980; Johnston and Cain 1981; Greene 1985b). The most powerful airgun arrays have source levels as high as 259 dB_{0-p} (174 bar-m) and total gun volumes as large as 130 L or 7900 in^3 (Parrott 1991). Smaller arrays often have source levels of about 235-246 dB re 1 $µPa-m_{0-p}$ (12-42 bar-m; Table 6.6). Characteristics of the sound pulses depend on array design, including airgun sizes, number, spacing, and air pressure (Kramer et al. 1968; Barger and Hamblen 1980). Those references, and the source levels just quoted, refer to downward propagation.

Of greater interest are the levels and characteristics of the sound pulses that propagate horizontally in the water. Airgun arrays are designed to direct a high proportion of the sound energy downward. The effective source level for horizontal propagation is generally less than that for vertical propagation, and depends on array geometry and aspect relative to the long axis of the array. With an elongated array whose long axis is in line with the tow direction, sound levels directly ahead of and behind the seismic ship may be at least 10 dB less than levels directed downward or to the side (Fig. 6.19). Malme et al.

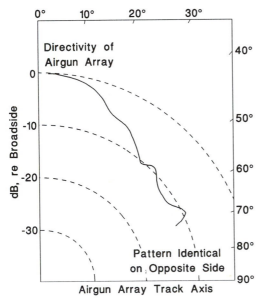

FIGURE 6.19. Measured horizontal directivity pattern of peak pressure from a 65.5-L array of airguns, relative to broadside output. The 40 airguns were in two parallel lines of 20. From Malme et al. (1983).

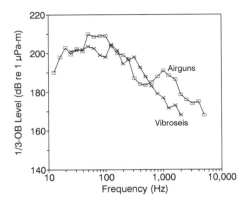

FIGURE 6.20. Estimated ⅓-octave source levels (at 1 m) for horizontal propagation of two types of seismic survey signals: airgun array pulses from a 32-gun 28.7-L array on *Western Polaris* (end-fire, averaged over pulse duration), and Vibroseis signals. Data from Malme et al. (1989). Estimates for Vibroseis are subject to considerable uncertainty (see Section 6.5.3).

(1984) noted that levels at bow or stern aspect from such an array may be no higher than those from a single airgun. However, with other array layouts, levels at bow and stern aspect may exceed those to the side (Duncan 1985).

Despite the downward "focusing" effect of the array, strong sound pulses are projected horizontally into the water in certain directions, and these can be detected many kilometers away (e.g., Malme et al. 1983; Greene and Richardson 1988; Hall et al. 1994). Figure 6.20 shows the estimated ⅓-octave source-level spectrum for horizontally propagating pulses off the ends of a 28.7-L airgun array whose sounds were measured by Miles et al. (1987). These levels are averaged over the duration of the pulse—a procedure that gives levels ~10 dB lower than the peak levels. Even at "end-fire" aspect and averaging over pulse duration, estimated source levels were near 210 dB re 1 µPa-m in several ⅓-octave bands, and 217 dB overall (Malme et al. 1989). Higher levels would be expected to the side or from larger arrays.

Signals from airguns originate as short, sharp pulses, typically emitted every 10-15 s, although shorter or longer intervals are sometimes used. For deep surveys, most emitted energy is at 10-120 Hz, but the pulses contain some energy up to 500-1000 Hz (Fig. 6.21). The latter components are weak when compared to the low-frequency energy but strong when compared to ambient noise levels. As pulses propagate horizontally in shallow water, low frequencies attenuate rapidly, leaving only the higher-frequency energy (Fig. 6.21B versus 6.21C).

During horizontal propagation, initially-short pulses become elongated during multiple reflections between surface and bottom. The primary pulse is several milliseconds long when emitted, but can be ≥¼-½ s in duration after traveling a few kilometers in shallow water.

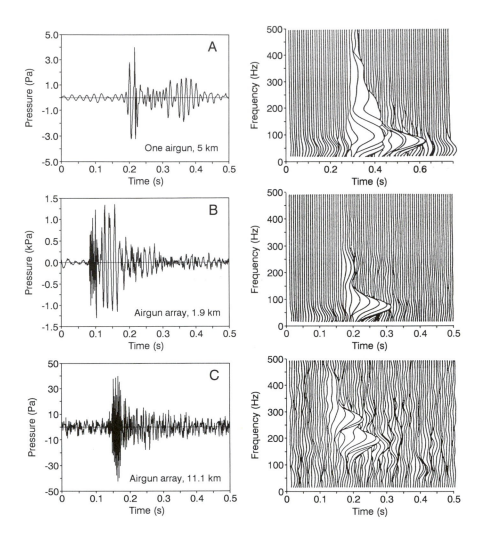

FIGURE 6.21. Airgun pulse characteristics: pressure waveforms (left) and waterfall spectrograms (right) for *(A)* a pulse from a single 40-in³ (0.66-L) airgun received underwater at 5 km range, and for pulses from a 28-L airgun array at *(B)* 1.9 km and *(C)* 11.1 km. Note the differing vertical scales for the three waveforms. Adapted from Greene and Richardson (1988).

The elongated pulse also tends to develop a particular pattern of frequencies as it propagates. In shallow water, it often develops a downward sweep in frequency (Fig. 6.21). The sweep can be from ~200-400 Hz near the leading edge of the pulse to ~100-200 Hz at the

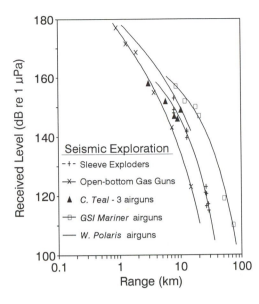

FIGURE 6.22. Seismic survey noise versus range in continental shelf waters, with best-fit regression curves. Adapted from Greene and Richardson (1988).

end (Greene 1985a). This downward "chirp" results from geometrical dispersion of sounds undergoing multiple reflections between surface and bottom in shallow water (Section 4.4). In deeper water with upward refraction of sound rays, as often occurs in ice-covered waters, the combination of multiply-refracted, surface-reflected sound rays forms a frequency upsweep (Officer 1958; Richardson et al. 1987b:340).

In some areas, low-frequency energy may travel long distances through bottom sediments, re-entering the water far from the source. Sound speed is generally faster in the bottom than in water. Hence, at a distant receiver there may be an initial low-frequency pulse, resulting from the bottom-traveling energy, followed an instant later by a higher-frequency pulse resulting from the water-traveling energy.

Received levels of seismic pulses diminish with increasing range in a manner similar to other underwater sounds, at least beyond the near field (Fig. 6.22). The decrease often can be described by spherical or cylindrical spreading loss (i.e., 20 or 10 log range) plus a linear function of range for losses due to absorption and scattering (Greene and Richardson 1988). Their linear coefficients for airgun levels ranged from -0.61 dB/km for water 20-110 m deep to -0.97 dB/km for water <20 m deep. In water ~25-50 m deep, airgun arrays are often audible to ranges of 50-75 km. Detection ranges can exceed 100 km during quiet times with efficient propagation, or in deeper water.

Differences in sound attenuation rate can have a strong effect on the received levels. Malme et al. (1986a) describe differences for pulses traveling upslope, downslope, and parallel to shore. With sand or rock bottoms, seismic pulses traveling upslope are attenuated fastest. Also, received levels from a single airgun decreased by 15 log R but those from an airgun array decreased by 25 log R in the same area (Malme et al. 1986a). This difference may have been due to surface reflections that depend on array aspect (see Grachev 1983).

Received levels of airgun pulses are lower just below the surface than at deeper depths. In one case, received levels at ranges 9-17 km were 1-4 dB less at 9 m depth than at 18 m (Greene 1985a). Similarly, pulses from a three-airgun array at ranges 3-10.4 km averaged ~7 dB less at depth 3 m than at 9-18 m (Greene and Richardson 1988). This phenomenon is caused by surface interference—the Lloyd mirror effect (Section 4.5.2; Urick 1983:131).

In summary, airgun arrays (and some other seismic sources) produce noise pulses with very high peak levels. However, the short duration of each pulse limits the total energy. With increased distance from the source, received pulses from airgun arrays generally decrease in level but increase in duration. Beyond a few kilometers, the elongated pulses are "chirp"-like: in shallow water, higher frequencies tend to arrive first. Levels can vary dramatically with horizontal aspect; the strongest levels are abeam the long axis of the array and the weakest are in line with that axis. Pulses traveling upslope along rock or sand bottoms are attenuated faster than those radiated alongshore or downslope. Pulses from an airgun array may attenuate more rapidly than those from a single gun, depending on array aspect. However, received levels from arrays are normally higher than those from a single airgun because of the stronger source level of the array. Received levels at a specific range are generally several decibels lower near the surface than at deeper depths (e.g., at 3 m versus 9-18 m).

6.5.2 Sleeve Exploders and Gas Guns

Although airguns are the most widely used sources for geophysical surveys, arrays of sleeve exploders and open-bottom gas guns are sometimes used. These devices are charged with a mixture of oxygen and propane, which is exploded to produce the sound pulse. Although the arrays direct as much energy as possible downward, strong sound pulses propagate horizontally, even in shallow water.

The resulting pulsed signals are quite similar to those from a small array of airguns in terms of source level and pulse characteristics. Pulses from sleeve exploders and gas guns, like those from airguns, become elongated and "chirp"-like with increasing horizontal range (Fig. 3.2; Greene and Richardson 1988). Received levels from a 12-sleeve array operating in shallow water were 148-153 dB re 1 μPa_{0-p} at 8 km and 115-117 dB at 25-29 km. Received levels for open-bottom gas guns operating in even shallower water ranged from 177 dB at 0.9 km to 123 dB at 14.8 km. Best-fit equations for transmission loss within these ranges (Fig. 6.22) included a 10 log R cylindrical spreading loss term plus a linear term with coefficients -1.39 dB/km for water 15-30 m deep (sleeve exploders) and -2.33 dB/km for water 9-11 m deep (gas guns).

In summary, sleeve exploders and open-bottom gas guns produce high-energy pulses with levels and propagation characteristics similar to those of airgun signals. As with airgun signals, received levels generally decrease, and signal duration increases, with increasing range. In shallow water, higher frequencies (~200 Hz) usually arrive before lower frequencies (~70 Hz) at ranges of several kilometers. This results in a downward sweeping "chirp"-like sound.

6.5.3 Vibroseis®

Vibroseis is a method of seismic profiling on shore-fast ice, usually over shallow water. The ice is energized by vibrating it with powerful hydraulically-driven pads mounted beneath a line of trucks. A typical Vibroseis signal sweeps from 10 to 70 Hz but harmonics extend to ~1.5 kHz. Vibroseis signals are transient but not impulsive: each sweep lasts 5-20 s and there are 10 sweeps before the trucks move 70-100 m along the shot line to the next station. Most energy is beamed downward, but some is detectable in the water to the side of the Vibroseis convoy.

Effective source levels for horizontal propagation are uncertain. For horizontal beam-aspect propagation from a four-vibrator array, Holliday et al. (1984) estimated a source level of 187 dB re 1 µPa-m at 50 Hz during a sweep from 10 to 65 Hz. Cummings et al. (1981b) cited a corresponding source level of 185 dB in the overall frequency band to 2 kHz. Allowing for rapid attenuation due to the surface-source and shallow water (Section 4.5.2), Malme et al. (1989) derived considerably higher estimates of the ⅓-octave source level spectrum from the same data (Fig. 6.20). Holliday et al. (1984) reported a level

20 dB lower for endfire (ahead or behind) aspects. Downward radiation was thought to be stronger.

Propagation losses for underwater Vibroseis noise generally increased with frequency and were larger in shallower water for a given frequency. Losses ranged from 22.5 dB/km at 10 Hz to 31.2 dB/km at 60 Hz (Holliday et al. 1984). The linear relationship to distance indicates that much of the attenuation was due to absorption into the bottom and overlying ice cover, and to scattering due to local boundary roughness (Chapter 4; Urick 1983). However, interpretation is confounded by the fact that parts of some propagation paths may have been through the air, ice, and bottom as well as the water. Under these conditions, Holliday et al. (1984) estimated that in-water Vibroseis sounds would diminish to the ambient noise level (about 70 dB) at distances of 3.5-5 km. Thus, the underwater area ensonified by seismic surveying is smaller for a Vibroseis rig operating on ice above shallow water than for an array of airguns, sleeve exploders, or gas guns operating in open water (*cf.* Fig. 6.22).

6.5.4 Other Techniques

Many other devices are sometimes used as sources of energy for seismic surveys. Some, such as arrays of water guns, can produce quite strong low-frequency noise pulses (Table 6.7). Many other devices produce weaker pulsed signals, often at higher frequencies (Kramer et al. 1968; Lugg 1979). Although some of these sources have been used for many years, we are not aware of any measurements documenting lateral sound transmission from them. However, the characteristics of the initial energy discharge have been reported (e.g., Kramer et al. 1968; Malme et al. 1986a).

Water guns produce pulses by creating a large void in the water similar to a cavitation bubble, after which the void collapses. An initial low-amplitude pulse associated with release of high-pressure water is followed by a major pulse that occurs with the collapse of the water cavity. Relative to comparably sized airguns, the spectrum of water gun pulses has a higher proportion of energy above 200 Hz. This occurs because there is no significant gas-filled bubble, and thus little low-frequency bubble-pulse energy (Hutchinson and Detrick 1984). As a result, water guns are often used for high-resolution seismic profiling.

The pressure waveform from spark sources has a characteristic double peak. The spark discharge forms a steam bubble and initial

TABLE 6.7. Representative seismic energy sources, method of energy generation, and estimated source level[a]

Source	Method	Size	Source level (dB re 1 μPa-m)$_{peak}$	Dominant frequencies
EXPLOSIVES				
TNT	Chemical	0.5 kg	267	Broadband
		14 kg	278	"
Black Powder	Chemical	0.5 kg	246	"
NON EXPLOSIVE				
Airgun(s)	Compressed air discharged into piston assembly	4.9 L	225[b]	
		33 L	232	<120 Hz
		66 L array	255	
Sleeve Exploder	Ignition of gas mixture in a rubber sleeve	1 sleeve	217[b]	
Vibroseis	Continuously driven piston; variable frequency waveform		210	10-70 Hz
		4 units	187[c]	
Water Gun(s)	High-pressure water to solenoid-triggered piston	0.9 L	217[b]	
		24 L array	245	
Sparker	Electric discharge of a capacitor bank across electrodes	30 kilojoules	221	
Boomer	Electric discharge of a capacitor across two metallic plates	500 joules	212	

[a] Vibroseis source level of Holliday et al. (1984) was based on lateral measurements; other source levels were based on total energy. Most other data from Johnston and Cain (1981) and Malme et al. (1984:A-7).
[b] Usually employed in arrays with higher total source level.
[c] Holliday et al. (1984).

pressure pulse; the bubble then collapses to produce a large secondary pulse. The second large peak is followed by a number of smaller pulses from bubble-pulse oscillations. Pulse characteristics vary with power and operating depth.

Echosounders and side-scan sonars operating at moderate to extremely high frequencies (3-500 kHz) are widely used to survey the seafloor. These devices, which are often used simultaneously with one of the previously mentioned sources for subbottom profiling, are discussed in the next section.

6.6 Sonars

There are two basic types of sonars: passive and active. Passive sonars only listen to incoming sounds and are not of concern here. Active sonars are used for many purposes involving detection of objects underwater. Most ships and boats have simple depth-finding sonars (fathometers). Other commercially available sonars are used to find fish, to measure currents, and to survey plankton and the ocean floor. Many military sonars are designed to search for, locate, and classify submarines. Other military sonars detect obstacles, including the bottom, ice floes overhead, and objects ahead. Sonars are used in weapons like mines and torpedoes to find targets and to actuate explosives. In addition to vessel- and weapon-mounted sonar systems, sonars can be fixed to the ocean bottom, suspended or towed from vessels or helicopters, or built into sonobuoys dropped and controlled from aircraft.

In concept, the simplest active sonars emit omnidirectional pulses ("pings") and time the arrival of echoes. One-half the round-trip travel time multiplied by the sound speed yields the distance to the reflector, or sonar target. A more complicated sonar emits an omnidirectional ping and then rapidly scans a steered receiving beam to provide directional as well as range information. More advanced sonars use multiple preformed beams, listening for echoes from several directions simultaneously and providing efficient detection of both direction and range. Some sonars have a transmit pulse that is scanned through a range of azimuths at a selected depression angle while multiple preformed beams in azimuth and elevation/depression receive the echoes.

Another kind of sonar transmits sound continuously, and the frequency varies during the transmission. With these CTFM sonars (Continuous Transmission Frequency Modulation), range is derived from the difference between the transmitted and received frequencies. These sonars can also scan in azimuth and elevation. Sonars may use coded waveforms that permit continuous transmission and enhance detection for given transmit signal power levels.

Sonar frequencies range from a few hundred hertz for long-range search sonars to several hundred kilohertz for sonars used in mine-hunting, accurate mapping and profiling, and plankton surveys. High-frequency sonars emit sounds with short wavelengths, permitting smaller transducers and higher resolution but have shorter range because of higher absorption losses (Section 4.5.1). Low-frequency sonars permit useful performance over longer ranges, but require large transducers and have lower resolution; targets have to be larger and fine details are not discernible. The optimum frequency depends on the task. Submarines are large, reflect sounds with long wavelengths, and need to be detected at long range; sonars operating at low and moderate frequencies can be used. Fish are small and will be detected only with shorter wavelengths.

Pulse power levels from sonars can be high. However, average power output from a pulsed sonar is much lower than peak levels during emission of pulses. Source levels of commercially available bottom-profiling sonars, during emission of a pulse, are often 210-230 dB re 1 µPa-m on the axis of the beam (Table 6.8). In general, pulse durations can range from tens of microseconds to a second or more, depending on sonar type and transmission mode.

Characteristics of military sonars are rarely published, but it can be assumed that some have substantially higher power output. Watkins et al. (1985a) described submarine sonar signals at 3.25-8.4 kHz in pulses 0.145-0.45 s long, usually in sequences of 4-20 or more pulses at rates of ~1-5 pulses/min. *Jane's Underwater Warfare Systems*

TABLE 6.8. General characteristics of certain active sonars[a]

Sonar Type	Frequency (kHz)	Duration (ms)	Source Level[b] (dB re 1 µPa-m)
Depth sounders	12+		180+
Bottom profilers	0.4-30	0.1-160	200-230
Side scan	50-500	0.01-0.1	220-230
Navigation (transponders)	7-60	3-40	180-200
Military			
Search and surveillance	2-57	4-1000	230+
Mine and obstacle avoidance	25-500	1-30	220+
Weapon-mounted	15-200		200+
Underwater telephone [not a sonar]	5-11	Continuous	180-200

[a] Based mainly on information in Watts (1994) and manufacturers' literature.
[b] Root mean square pressure.

1994-95 (Watts 1994) provides data on some military sonars, but specific characteristics of the powerful active sonars on military surface ships and submarines are not available.

Underwater acoustic telephones—known in the U.S. Navy as "Gertrude", UQC, or UCS—are used to communicate with nearby submarines. These systems are not sonars, but are mentioned for completeness. U.S. and Russian systems operate at 8-11 kHz and 5-8 kHz, respectively, with source levels of ~180-200 dB re 1 μPa.

6.7 Explosions

6.7.1 Uses of Marine Explosives

With the possible exception of underwater volcanic eruptions and major earthquakes, man-made underwater explosions are the strongest point sources of sound in the sea. Pressure pulses from high explosives are the one type of "noise" known to be able to cause physical injury or death to marine mammals (Section 9.10.2).

For many decades, explosives have been used routinely underwater. Depth charges, mines, torpedoes, and bombs have been discharged underwater in very large numbers during wartime and training. During infrequent tests to confirm the resistance of military ships to underwater explosions, up to 4500 kg of high explosive are detonated (U.S. Navy 1993). Underwater demolition is a common military and civilian application, typically involving 10-1000 kg of high explosive per blast. In extreme cases, underwater demolition blasts have employed up to 1,250,000 kg of high explosive (Thomson 1958).

Smaller charges are widely used. Thousands of 0.9-kg Mk 61 "SUS" (underwater signaling) charges have been used as acoustical signal sources in ocean science studies to measure sound transmission loss and bottom characteristics. In the past, similar charges were widely used to detect submarines via explosive echo-ranging. Very large numbers of "seal bombs", each containing a few grams of explosive, have been used by tuna fishermen to direct the movements of dolphins associated with tuna (Cassano et al. 1990). Other fishermen often use them in attempts to discourage seals from entering fishing gear (Shaughnessy et al. 1981; Mate and Harvey 1987).

Until the mid-1960s, explosives were the main energy source during marine seismic surveys for hydrocarbon deposits below nearshore waters (Fitch and Young 1948). Charges were fired either close to the surface or below the sea-floor. These placements minimized bubble-pulse oscillation (Section 6.7.2). Typical charges were 14-23 kg of high explosive. Off California, because of concerns about damage to fish and other marine life, high-explosive charges were replaced by black powder after 1951 (Jakosky and Jakosky 1956; Lugg 1979). Black powder has a much slower burn rate (called *deflagration*—speed 0.03-0.3 m/s) than does dynamite or TNT (4.6-9.1 km/s). The rate of initial pressure increase is much less steep during deflagration, and fewer fish are killed. Elsewhere, high explosives were used for seismic exploration through the 1960s. By the 1970s, single-point explosive charges had been largely replaced by airgun arrays and other "low-energy" sources (Lugg 1979; Section 6.5). However, explosives are still used occasionally during seismic surveys in shallow areas (Wright 1985). Sometimes ropelike line charges are used. These lengthen the pressure rise time, distribute the blast over space, and reduce local effects.

6.7.2 Characteristics of Marine Explosions

Even small (~½ kg) explosions are sometimes detectable thousands of kilometers away via the SOFAR channel. World War II aviators downed in deep water dropped such small charges into the SOFAR channel and were rescued based on localization of signals received at diverse locations (Urick 1983). Depth charges (91-136 kg) detonated in the SOFAR channel off Australia were detected near Bermuda, halfway around the earth (Section 4.3; Shockley et al. 1982).

The underwater pressure signature of a detonating explosion is composed of the initial shock pulse followed by a succession of oscillating bubble pulses if the explosion is sufficiently deep not to vent through the surface (Fig. 6.23; Staal 1985; Urick 1983). Properties of the initial pressure shock wave are often represented by the semi-empirical equations of A.B. Arons et al., summarized in Urick (1983).

When high explosive detonates underwater, pressure rises within a microsecond or so to a maximum pressure defined empirically as

$$P_{peak} = 5.24 \times 10^{13}(W^{1/3}/R)^{1.13} \; \mu Pa \tag{6.4}$$

where W is charge weight in kg and R is distance from explosion in m (from Urick 1983, adapted to metric units). The instantaneous pressure at time t after the onset of the shock wavefront, P(t), is given by

$$P(t) = P_{peak} \; e^{-t/tc} \tag{6.5}$$

$$t_c = 92.5 \; W^{1/3}(W^{1/3}/R)^{-0.22} \; \mu s \tag{6.6}$$

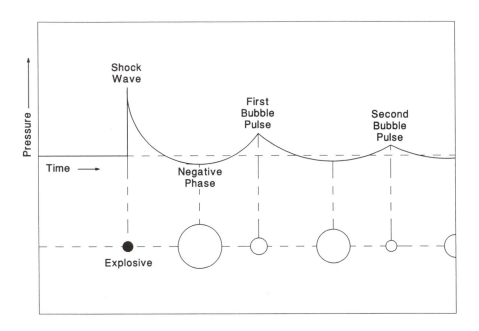

FIGURE 6.23. Underwater explosion bubble and pressure time history. From Staal (1985).

These equations apply close to the explosion point if it is remote from the surface, bottom, or other boundaries.

The rise time of the pulse is extremely brief relative to that from an airgun array or other nonexplosive seismic sources. The rapidity of the pressure increase is related to the extent of biological injury. The time constant given by equation (6.6), representing the time required for pressure to drop exponentially to 37% of its initial value, is also short.

Equations (6.4-6.6) are derived from explosion shock theory and are confirmed by experiments. However, they are not applicable at long ranges. Shock theory assumes that the pressure wave, initially exponential, distorts because of the pressure dependence of the sound speed (Rogers 1977). Gaspin (1983) derived a limiting range R_0 for the applicability of equations (6.4-6.6), here revised for metric units:

$$R_0 = 4.76W^{1/3} \text{ meters} \tag{6.7}$$

(W in kg). For example, with charge weight 1000 kg, the limiting range is only 47.6 m. For longer ranges, Rogers applies weak-shock

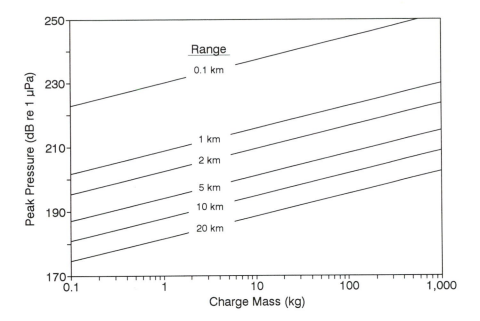

FIGURE 6.24. Dependence of peak pressure from underwater explosion on charge mass and range. Based on equation (6.8).

theory to derive equations for the peak pressure P_m and the time constant τ of an exponential pressure wave:

$$P_m(R) = P_0 \{[1+2(R_0/L_0) \ln(R/R_0)]^{1/2}-1\} / [(R/L_0) \ln(R/R_0)] \qquad (6.8)$$

$$\tau(R) = t_0[1+2(R_0/L_0) \ln(R/R_0)]^{1/2} \qquad (6.9)$$

for

$$L_0 = (\rho_0 c_0^3 t_0) / (P_0 \beta) \qquad (6.10)$$

where $\rho_0 = 1026$ kg/m^3 (water density), $c_0 = 1500$ m/s (sound speed), $\beta = 3.5$, and P_0 and t_0 are computed from equations (6.4, 6.6) for range R_0. Figure 6.24 graphs the peak pressure as estimated from equation (6.8) versus charge weight for various ranges.

Arons (1948) presented equations describing the bubble pulse parts of the waveform (Fig. 6.23) in terms of charge weight and depth as well as type of explosive. The time between the shock pulse and the first bubble pulse is

$$T = 0.48 \, K \, W^{1/3}[d + 10]^{-5/6} \text{ seconds} \qquad (6.11)$$

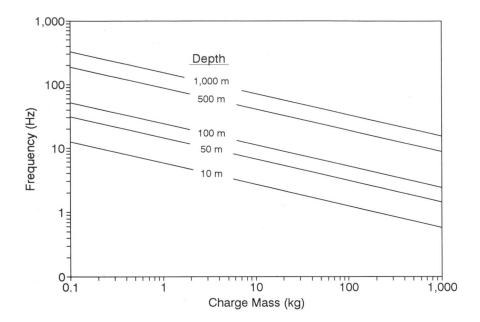

FIGURE 6.25. Dependence of first bubble-pulse frequency from underwater explosion on charge mass and charge depth. Based on $1/T$ as calculated from equation (6.11).

where W is charge weight in kg and d is charge depth in m (from Urick 1983, revised to metric units). K depends slightly on the type of explosive and is 4.36 for TNT. The reciprocal of T, in hertz, is the first bubble-pulse frequency, for which there is a broad peak in the sound energy density spectrum. This frequency decreases as charge size increases and as charge depth decreases (Fig. 6.25). Weston (1960) presents equations for the pressure energy density spectrum of the total waveform, which varies as $W^{4/3}$.

The shock front always travels more slowly than the acoustic wave immediately following it, causing the shock front to be overtaken continuously during propagation (Rogers 1977). When reflecting boundaries are considered, as in shallow water, the aspects of acoustic propagation are important (see Chapter 4 and Section 6.5). When charge depth is shallow, source characteristics may be modified by bubble migration toward or to the surface, by surface cavitation, and by surface reflection cancellation.

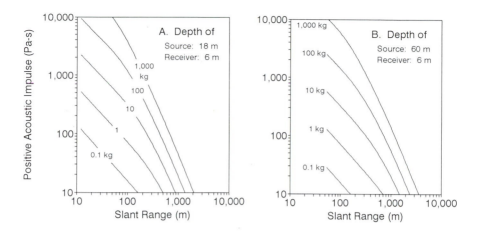

FIGURE 6.26. Dependence of positive impulse from an underwater explosion on charge mass (0.1 to 1000 kg) and slant range for two depth combinations. Based on equation (6.13).

Research on blast damage to animals has determined that, with high explosives, the positive acoustic *impulse* is closely correlated with organ damage (Section 10.6.3). The positive impulse is computed from the integral of the initial positive pressure pulse [equation (6.5)] over time, with units pascal-seconds (Pa·s). Gaspin (1983) evaluates the integral over a time Δt, where Δt is the difference in travel times for the surface-reflected blast and the directly-received blast to arrive at the receiver. The reflected blast signal cancels out any further positive portions of the directly-received blast.

$$\Delta t = \{ \, [\, (d + S)^2 + H^2]^{0.5} - R \} \, / \, c_0 \tag{6.12}$$

where d is the charge depth in m, S is the receiver depth in m, H is the horizontal distance between the charge and receiver in m, R is the slant range between the charge and the receiver in m, and c_0 is the sound speed in m/s. The positive impulse (Fig. 6.26) is given by

$$I = P_{peak} \, t_c \, (1 - e^{-\Delta t / t_c}) \tag{6.13}$$

where P_{peak} is given by equation (6.4) for $R < R_0$ or equation (6.8) for $R > R_0$,

R_0 is given by equation (6.7), and

t_c is given by equation (6.6) or (6.9), also depending on the value of R relative to R_0.

Note that, to obtain impulse I in pascal-seconds, the peak pressure given by equation (6.4) in micropascals must be converted to pascals, and the time constant given by equation (6.6) in microseconds must be converted to seconds.

A proceedings volume entitled *Effects of Explosives Use in the Marine Environment* presents much more information about explosions and their effects on marine life (G.D. Greene et al. 1985).

6.8 Ocean Science Studies

Some ocean science studies use acoustical energy to probe the characteristics of water masses and the bottom. Among the strongest sources are those used for ocean bottom surveys. These employ airguns and other sources used by the seismic survey industry, side scan and other sonars, and occasionally explosions (Sections 6.5-6.7). In addition, acoustic energy is used to investigate sound transmission loss and the properties of oceanic water masses (acoustic oceanography). Sound sources used in the last two of these types of studies are described here.

Since World War II, oceanographers and underwater acousticians have used 0.9-kg high-explosive devices to study sound propagation and bottom characteristics around the world (Section 3.5.3). SUS charges typically detonate at depths of 18 or 244 m. Based on equations in the preceding subsection, the peak pressure at range 1 km is 208 dB re 1 µPa, and the bubble-pulse frequencies at depths 18 and 244 m are 8 and 50 Hz, respectively. The estimated impulse at 1 km is 7.1 Pa·s. These devices continue to be used. Sometimes they are used to trigger larger detonations.

Sound projectors ("underwater loudspeakers") are widely used in sound transmission and acoustical oceanography studies. The latter studies include acoustic tomography, which examines the structure (sound speed, density, salinity, temperature) of ocean sections by acoustics. Tomographic studies use arrays of receivers and sometimes multiple transmitters. Source levels range from ~165 dB re 1 µPa for short-range tests to 190-220 dB for long-range experiments. Many of these studies have been done over the past 20 years. Signal frequencies, characteristics, and durations vary widely depending on objectives. Most long-range tests are at 50-200 Hz, given the rapid attenuation of high-frequency sounds in the sea (Section 4.5.1). A recent 2600-km trans-Arctic test was at 20 Hz (Mikhalevsky et al. 1994).

Acoustic thermometry studies are specialized long-range propagation tests to study long-term trends in sound speed and thus ocean temperature. The Heard Island Feasibility Test occurred in early 1991 (Section 4.3; Baggeroer and Munk 1992; Munk et al. 1994). Acoustical signals of three types, centered at 57 Hz, were projected into the SOFAR channel at depth 175 m, generally for ½-1 h every 3 h over a 7.3-day period. When the source level was at its maximum, five sources in a vertical array produced an effective source level (for horizontal propagation) of ~220-221 dB re 1 µPa-m. At these times, received levels were 160 dB or more at distances out to 1 km, 137 dB at range 72 km and depth 80 m, and 120 dB or more at ranges out to at least 100-1000 km, depending on receiver depth (Bowles et al. 1991, 1994). The signals were detected via hydrophones up to halfway around the world (~17,500 km range), including Bermuda and the west coast of the U.S.A.

A follow-on project titled Acoustic Thermometry of Ocean Climate (ATOC) is planned to monitor temperature trends in the Pacific Ocean (ARPA and NMFS 1994; ARPA 1995). Projectors are to be installed off Kauai (Hawaii) and central California for reception at various sites in the North Pacific and as far away as New Zealand. Coded signals centered near 75 Hz (bandwidth 35 Hz) are to be projected, initially at an overall source level of ~195 dB re 1 µPa-m for 20 min every 4 h on every fourth day. The omnidirectional sources will be in the SOFAR channel at 850-980 m depth, so received levels near the surface above the projectors should be below 140 dB re 1 µPa. At long horizontal ranges (100+ km), received levels will be much lower (<120 dB) but more uniform over the depth range 100 to 2500 m. After 1996, ATOC may expand to other ocean basins and continue for 10+ years.

6.9 Comparison of Noise Sources

The potential effects of man-made noise on marine mammals will depend partly on whether the sounds are transient or continuous. An animal's response to a pulsed or intermittent sound with a particular peak level may be quite different than its response to a continuous sound at the same level (Section 9.8.3). Hence, our summary of noise sources is organized into two categories depending on whether the source is transient or continuous (Table 6.9).

Among the transient sources, explosions produce by far the highest peak pressures: 267 dB re 1 µPa-m for even a small ½-kg charge.

TABLE 6.9. Summary and comparison of source levels for selected sources of man-made underwater noise. Most data are taken from the 1/3-octave band level summaries of Malme et al. (1989)[a]

Sound source	Broadband (45-7070 Hz)	Source levels, dB re 1 µPa-m 1/3-octave band center frequencies						Highest level 1/3-octave band		Strong infra-sonics?
		50	100	200	500	1000	2000	Freq.	Level	
TRANSIENT										
Aircraft Flyover[b]										
C-130 (4 turboprop)	175	149	* 150	151	150	145	146	63	170	No
Bell 212 helicopter	162	* 154	155	151	145	142	142	16	159	Yes
B-N Islander (2 prop.)	157	143	* 150	145	140	133	131	63	152	No
Twin Otter (2 turboprop)	156	134	140	* 141	141	136	133	160	151	No
Icebreaking, R. Lemeur	193	177	183	180	180	176	179	100	183	Yes
Seismic Survey										
Air gun array (32 guns)	216	210	209	199	184	191	178	50	210	Yes
Vibroseis on ice	210	203	198	* 194	188	177	168	125	204	Yes
Sonar, military search	230+	0	0	0	0	0	*	[2-5k]	230+	No
Explosions, 60 m depth										
0.5 kg TNT	peak 267	*						21		Yes
2 kg TNT	" 271	*						13		Yes
20 kg TNT	" 279	*						6		Yes
Ocean Acoustics Studies										
Heard Island Test	220	217	* 0	0	0	0	0	50+63	217	No
ATOC	195	0	* 0	0	0	0	0	80	192	No

CONTINUOUS

Vessels Underway

								Freq (Hz)		Detectable
Tug and barge, 18 km/h	171	143	157	161 *	156	157	157	630	162	Yes
5-m Zodiac	156	128	148	132	132	138 *		6300	152	No
Supply ship (*Kigoriak*)	181	162	170	166	164	159		100	174	Yes
Large tanker	186	174	177 *	176	172	169	166	100+125	177	Yes

Snowmobile

								Freq (Hz)		Detectable
(224-7070 Hz)	130	-	-	114	118 *	122		1600	124[c]	No

Drillships

								Freq (Hz)		Detectable
Kulluk (45-1780 Hz)	185	174	172	176 *	176	168	-	400	177[c]	No?
Canmar Explorer II	174	162 *	162	161	162	156	148	63	167	No?

Dredging

								Freq (Hz)		Detectable
Aquarius (45-890 Hz)	185	170	177 *	171	-	-		160	178[c]	No?
Beaver Mackenzie (45-890 Hz)	172	154	167	159	158	-	-	100	167[c]	No?

[a] Note that some sources also emit strong sounds at frequencies below 45 Hz, not considered here. * denotes that strongest 1/3-octave band was in this range but was one of those not explicitly tabulated.

[b] Aircraft flyover source levels were computed by Malme et al. (1989) for a standard altitude of 1000 ft (305 m). For consistency with other sound sources, those values were changed to a reference range of 1 m by adding 50 dB.

[c] Data are incomplete but the frequency bands not analyzed apparently contained little energy, with the possible exception of infrasonic frequencies for some sources.

The most powerful sonars and the highest-energy nonexplosive sources used during seismic surveys also produce high peak pressures. However, because of the short durations of the noise pulses from all of these sources, average received levels may be lower than those from some sources of longer-duration sounds such as a passing supertanker or icebreaker, or an ocean-acoustics research source. Even the strongest sources of continuous sound, such as supertankers, emit sounds whose peak levels are much lower than those from strong transient sources. However, the peak and average levels are similar in the case of a continuous source.

Most studies of man-made noise have not considered frequencies below 10-20 Hz. However, ships, icebreakers, and some drilling platforms are known to emit strong infrasonic tones. In some cases, such as a supertanker or some bottom-founded drilling platforms, a high proportion of the emitted energy may be at infrasonic frequencies. The inconsistent availability of acoustic data from low frequencies is a significant data gap. It is not known how many marine mammals can detect infrasounds. Some of the baleen whales are the marine mammals most likely to do so (Section 8.6). At least in deep water, where infrasounds sometimes propagate well, infrasonic components of man-made sound could be important to marine mammals. However, in shallow continental shelf waters, low-frequency sounds usually attenuate rapidly. Given this, plus the often-high ambient noise levels at low frequencies, strong infrasounds in nearshore areas may often be undetectable far from their sources even if marine mammals can hear at those frequencies.

CHAPTER 7

MARINE MAMMAL SOUNDS[1]

Marine mammals create sounds to communicate about the presence of danger, food, a conspecific, or other animal; and about their own position, identity, and territorial or reproductive status. In addition, odontocete cetaceans use echolocation sounds to detect, localize, and characterize underwater objects (Au 1993), including obstacles, prey, and one another.

Male pinnipeds that compete for females and territory on land use airborne calls and visual displays during courtship and aggressive encounters (E.H. Miller 1991). Mothers and pups vocalize in air and underwater to maintain contact. Pinnipeds and cetaceans that mate in the water apparently use underwater calls to coordinate mating (Ray et al. 1969; Silber 1986; Watkins et al. 1987; Riedman 1990).

As a group, marine mammals produce many kinds of sounds with variable physical properties. Many species produce a large number of different sounds and combinations of sounds, as may different individuals within a species. Calls of only a few species have been studied in detail. The full acoustic repertoire of some species is difficult to document, partly because the calls often do not fall into obvious categories.

Many studies have attempted to correlate the occurrence of specific kinds of sounds with specific behaviors or situations (e.g., Watkins 1981b; Clark 1983; Hoelzel and Osborne 1986). However, for free-ranging marine mammals, these relationships are known only for a few species. The specific function(s) of most sounds made by most species are unknown.

This chapter summarizes the types of sounds produced by various marine mammals. The sounds of particular species are summarized in tables, with some of the main references. However, brief notations in a table cannot adequately summarize the complexity and variability of most marine mammal sounds. For some groups of species, particu-

---

[1] By Denis H. Thomson and W. John Richardson, LGL Ltd.

larly odontocetes, the text discusses the general categories of sounds produced by the group. For other groups, the text discusses the calls of individual species. This chapter does not cite every reference on marine mammal sounds. Instead, it is an overview of available data, and a starting point for more specific literature searches

7.1 Baleen Whale Sounds

Much research has been conducted on the sounds produced by several species of baleen whales. Much has been learned about the acoustical characteristics and, to a limited extent, the functions of sounds produced by fin whales, humpback whales, and southern right whales. Gray and bowhead whale sounds are also well documented, but little is known about their functions. The sounds of blue, minke, and Bryde's whales have been described, but their functions are largely unknown. There are few data on the sounds made by the remaining three species: sei, northern right, and pygmy right whales. T.J. Thompson et al. (1979) and Watkins and Wartzok (1985) summarize the early literature.

There is no standard nomenclature for baleen whale sounds. Similar sounds are often given different names by different authors. The names of sounds listed in Table 7.1 are those used by the authors cited, mostly based on subjective aural interpretation. Different authors may use the same word to refer to dissimilar sound types.

It is difficult to study the context and functions of baleen whale sounds. Unlike other marine mammals, baleen whales are rarely held in captivity. It has rarely been possible to associate specific baleen whale sounds with specific animals whose activities were under observation. However, this can be done using hydrophone arrays that localize calling whales (Sections 3.2.4 and 3.6.1).

7.1.1 Bowhead Whale
Most calls emitted by bowhead whales are tonal frequency-modulated (FM) sounds at 50-400 Hz (Clark and Johnson 1984; Würsig and Clark 1993). Most single-note tones last ~1 s, but they may be as short as 0.4 s or as long as 3.7 s (Ljungblad et al. 1982c; Würsig et al. 1985b; see also Fig. 3.3B). Most of these sounds have little or no energy above 400 Hz, but a few extend to 1200 Hz. FM upsweeps and downsweeps seem to exhibit limited directionality, with sounds being somewhat stronger in front of the animal than behind (Clark et al.

1986). Bowheads, like other whales, also produce various nonvocal slap and blow sounds (Würsig et al. 1989; Würsig and Clark 1993).

Clark et al. (1986) and Cummings and Holliday (1987) estimated that source levels of simple moans range from ~128 to 178 dB re 1 μPa-m (broadband basis). Some other bowhead sounds have estimated source levels as high as 185-189 dB (Table 7.1). Some of this variation is real, but some represents uncertainty in estimates of propagation loss between the source and measurement locations. Hydrophone arrays have shown that a few calling bowheads are detectable up to 20 km away, although most localizable whales are ≤10 km away (Cummings and Holliday 1985; Davis et al. 1985; Clark et al. 1986; LGL and Greeneridge 1987).

There is little firm evidence of associations between specific sounds and behaviors for bowhead whales (Würsig and Clark 1993). High-pitched sounds and pulsatile sounds sometimes are proportionally more common near socializing bowheads than near other bowheads (Würsig et al. 1982, 1985b; Richardson et al. 1995). Clark (in Würsig et al. 1985b) speculated that bowheads, like southern right whales, may use an FM upsweep as a contact call. Würsig et al. (1985a) recorded bowhead calls as a mother and calf rejoined. Ellison et al. (1987) speculated that reverberations of calls might provide bowheads with information about ice conditions and assist in navigation.

Bowhead whales "sing" during spring migration through ice leads around northern Alaska (Ljungblad et al. 1982c; Cummings and Holliday 1987; Würsig and Clark 1993). Most songs consist of one to three themes composed of repeated phrases; phrases consist of one to five notes. In comparison with calls, song notes tend to be longer, cover a broader frequency range, and show more FM and AM variation (Würsig and Clark 1993). Typical songs last ~1 min, but song bouts may last from several minutes to hours. Within a given spring season, songs of different bowheads are generally similar, but different from the songs sung in other years. Cummings and Holliday (1987) found that, in general, only one bowhead of the number within range of the hydrophone could be heard singing at a time. When it stopped singing, another often began. Songs have not been noted during summer or autumn (Würsig and Clark 1993). There is no information about the age or sex class(es) of the singing bowheads, or about the function of their songs.

TABLE 7.1. Characteristics of underwater sounds produced by baleen whales

Species of whale	Signal type	Frequency range (Hz)	Dominant frequencies (Hz)	Source level (dB re 1 μPa at 1 m)	References
Bowhead	tonal moans	25-900	100-400	128-178	Ljungblad et al. 1982c; Cummings & Holliday 1987; Clark et al. 1986
	pulsive	25-3500	—	152-185	Clark & Johnson 1984; Würsig et al. 1985b; Cummings & Holliday 1987
	song	20-500	<4000	158-189	Ljungblad et al. 1982c; Cummings & Holliday 1987; Würsig & Clark 1993
S. right	tonal	30-1250	160-500	—	Cummings et al. 1972; Clark 1982, 1983
	pulsive	30-2200	50-500	172-187	"
				181-186	C. Clark (in Würsig et al. 1982)
N. right	moans	<400	—	—	Watkins & Schevill 1972; T. Thompson et al. 1979; Spero 1981
Pygmy right	thumps in pairs	to 300+	135-60	165-179	Dawbin & Cato 1992
Gray	moans	20-1200	20-200, 700-1200	185	Cummings et al. 1968; Fish et al. 1974; Swartz & Cummings 1978
	pulse modulated	80-1800	225-600	—	Dahlheim et al. 1984; S. Moore & Ljungblad 1984
	FM up-down sweep	100-350	300	—	"
	pulses	100-2000	300-825	—	
	clicks (calves only)	100-20,000	3400-4000	—	Fish et al. 1974; Norris et al. 1977

Species	Sound type				References
Humpback	song components	30–8000	120–4000	144–174	T. Thompson et al. 1979; K. Payne & Payne 1985
	shrieks	—	750–1800	179–181	P. Thompson et al. 1986
	horn blasts	—	410–420	181–185	"
	moans	20–1800	35–360	175	"
	grunts	25–1900+	—	190	"
	pulse trains	25–1250	25–80	179–181	Beamish 1979
	underwater blows	100–2000	—	158	P. Thompson et al. 1986
	fluke & flipper slap	30–1200	—	183–192	Winn et al. 1970a; Beamish 1979
	clicks	2000–8200	—	—	
Fin	moans, down-sweeps	14–118	20	160–186	Watkins 1981b; Watkins et al. 1987; Edds 1988; Cummings & Thompson 1994
	constant call	20–40	—	—	Edds 1988
	moans, tones, upsweeps	30–750	—	155–165	Watkins 1981b; Cummings et al. 1986; Edds 1988
	rumble	10–30	—	—	Watkins 1981b; Edds 1988
	whistles?, chirps?[a]	1500–5000	1500–2500	—	T. Thompson et al. 1979
	clicks?	16,000–28,000	—	—	"
Blue	moans	12–390	16–25	188	Cummings & Thompson 1971a, 1994; Edds 1982; Stafford et al. 1994
	clicks?	6000–8000 / 21,000–31,000	6000–8000 / 25,000	130, 159	Beamish & Mitchell 1971; Beamish 1979
Bryde's	moans	70–245	124–132	152–174	Cummings et al. 1986
	pulsed moans	100–930	165–900	—	Edds et al. 1993
	discrete pulses	700–950	700–900	—	"

(Table continues)

TABLE 7.1. Continued

Species of whale	Signal type	Frequency range (Hz)	Dominant frequencies (Hz)	Source level (dB re 1 µPa at 1 m)	References
Sei	FM sweeps	1500-3500	—	—	T. Thompson et al. 1979; Knowlton et al. 1991
Minke	down sweeps	60-130	—	165	Schevill & Watkins 1972
	moans, grunts	60-140	60-140	151-175	" ; Winn & Perkins 1976
	ratchet	850-6000	850	—	Winn & Perkins 1976
	clicks	3300-20,000	<12,000	151	Beamish & Mitchell 1973; Winn & Perkins 1976
	thump trains	100-2000	100-200	—	Winn & Perkins 1976

[a] ? denotes infrequently recorded and/or questionable correlation of sound with species.

7.1.2 Right Whales

Southern right whales use an "up" sound, a simple tonal FM up-sweep at 50-200 Hz and lasting ½-1½ s, for long-distance contact and to help bring groups together (Clark 1983). Calling ceases after groups join. A mother-calf pair that became separated beyond under-water visual range (75 m) both made "up" sounds and rejoined. A "down" call may be used to maintain acoustic but not physical contact. It is a low-frequency tonal FM downsweep of ½- to 1½-s duration at 100-200 Hz. Source levels of right whale calls have been estimated as 172-187 dB re 1 µPa-m (Table 7.1).

Other sounds include tones, high-frequency tonal FM sweeps, complex amplitude-modulated pulsatile sounds, mixtures of amplitude and frequency modulation, noisy broadband blows, and impulsive slaps, all with major energy at 50-1000 Hz (Clark 1982, 1983). The types of sounds produced are related to the activity, size, and sexual composition of the right whale group (Clark 1983). As the activity level of a group increases, the numbers of sounds increase and there is a change in the kinds of sounds (Clark 1983). Resting whales make few calls but do make some long blow sounds.

Northern right whales produce calls similar to those of southern right whales, but few data are available (Watkins and Schevill 1972; T.J. Thompson et al. 1979). Those summering in the Bay of Fundy use low-frequency sounds as contact calls (Spero 1981).

Pygmy right whales, which occur in the Southern Hemisphere, are not closely related to other right whales (McLeod et al. 1993). A juvenile produced thumplike sounds in pairs ½ s apart. Each thump was 140-225 ms long and consisted of a frequency downsweep from an initial 90-135 Hz to ~60 Hz (Table 7.1; Dawbin and Cato 1992). Source levels were ~165-179 dB re 1 µPa-m peak-to-peak (i.e., peak level ~159-173 dB).

7.1.3 Gray Whale

The most common sounds made by the gray whale are knocks and pulses with frequencies from <100 Hz to 2 kHz and most energy at 327-825 Hz. A series of 2-30 pulses lasts an average of 1.8 s (Dahlheim et al. 1984; Dahlheim 1987). The source level for knocks was ~142 dB re 1 µPa-m (Cummings et al. 1968)—a rather low level. S.E. Moore and Ljungblad (1984) found that these knocks were the most common sounds recorded in the presence of feeding whales in summer. Bogoslovskaya (1986) believed that, in summer, gray whales feed in stable groups and that individuals within the group keep in acoustic contact when separated by distances >800 m.

The rate of sound production in gray whales may be related to the general level of social activity (Dahlheim 1987). Gray whales are relatively silent when dispersed in small groups on the summer feeding grounds, slightly more vocal when migrating, and most vocal when concentrated on their winter breeding/calving grounds (Dahlheim 1987). They make seven distinct types of sounds there, but the significance of these sounds to the species is unknown (Dahlheim 1987).

7.1.4 Humpback Whale

Humpback whales produce three kinds of sounds: **(1)** "songs" that are produced in late fall, winter, and spring by solitary individuals, **(2)** sounds made by whales within groups on the winter grounds, and **(3)** sounds made while on the summer feeding grounds.

Humpback whales produce stereotyped songs associated with reproduction (Tyack 1981; Tyack and Whitehead 1983; Helweg et al. 1992). Humpback song is complex, with many sound types. Song components range from $\leq$20 Hz to 4 kHz, and occasionally to 8 kHz. Estimated source levels average 155 dB re 1 μPa-m and range from 144 to 174 dB (T.J. Thompson et al. 1979; K. Payne and Payne 1985). Song can be detected by hydrophone at distances up to at least 13-15 km (H.E. Winn et al. 1975; Helweg et al. 1992). Songs last as long as 30 min in bouts up to 22 h long (R. Payne 1970; Winn et al. 1970a; Payne and McVay 1971).

Songs have been recorded on low-latitude wintering grounds in the North Atlantic, North Pacific, South Pacific, and Indian oceans; along some migration routes; and—much less often—during late summer or autumn on northern feeding grounds (L.K. Winn and Winn 1985; Mattila et al. 1987; McSweeney et al. 1989). At any one time, songs are similar within each of these large areas, but differ markedly between areas (H.E. Winn et al. 1981; Cato 1991; Jenkins et al. 1995). Over several years, the song in a given area gradually changes (Guinee et al. 1983; R. Payne and Guinee 1983; K. Payne and Payne 1985; Cato 1991).

Almost all humpback songs are produced by solitary males, generally 5-6 km apart (Tyack 1981). Singers seem to avoid one another, but may pursue or be joined by silent whales, at which time singing often ceases (Tyack 1981; *cf.* Helweg et al. 1992). Song is probably a reproductive display by males (Tyack and Whitehead 1983).

During winter, humpback whales within groups produce sounds very different from those of solitary animals. Group or "social" sounds are often associated with agonistic behavior among males competing for dominance and proximity to females (Tyack 1983; Silber 1986). The sounds extend from 50 Hz to ≥10 kHz, with most energy below 3 kHz (Silber 1986). These sounds, or the associated impact noises, can elicit reactions from humpbacks up to 9 km away (Tyack and Whitehead 1983).

Humpbacks are less vocal when on high-latitude feeding grounds in summer than when on their lower-latitude winter ranges. In southeast Alaska, their sounds are at ~20-2000 Hz, have median durations of 0.2-0.8 s, and estimated source levels of 175-192 dB re 1 µPa-m (P.O. Thompson et al. 1986). Calls are made while feeding. Some researchers speculate that they serve for prey manipulation and as assembly calls, and probably not to coordinate feeding (Nilson et al. 1989; see also Martin et al. 1993).

7.1.5 Fin Whale

The most common fin whale sound is a 20-Hz sound about 1 s in duration. In spring, summer, and fall these sounds occur in series of one to five pulses, but in winter they occur in repeated stereotyped patterns in most ice-free oceanic waters (Watkins 1981b; Watkins et al. 1987). The typical "20-Hz" sound sweeps downward from ~23 Hz to ~18 Hz over 1 s (Watkins 1981b). The usual bandwidth is 3-4 Hz (R. Payne and Webb 1971). The frequency sweep of Pacific fin whales is greater than that of Atlantic fin whales (P.O. Thompson et al. 1992). Most 20-Hz sounds have source levels of ~160-186 dB re 1 µPa-m, with extremes of 200 dB and ≤140 dB (Patterson and Hamilton 1964; Northrop et al. 1968, 1971; Watkins 1981b; Watkins et al. 1987; Cummings and Thompson 1994).

Fin whales primarily emit the 20-Hz signals during their reproductive season from autumn to early spring. Watkins et al. (1987) believe that the repetitive stereotyped 20-Hz signals are an acoustic display associated with reproduction.

Calls at 20 Hz, believed to be from fin whales, have been detected up to 185 km away (Cummings and Thompson 1971a). Payne and Webb (1971) suggested that fin whale calls might sometimes be detectable at much greater ranges. This has recently been confirmed by SOSUS (D. Mellinger, personal communication). However, in the upper 50 m of the water column, practical detection distances are

8-10 km in shallow water and 25 km in deep water (Watkins 1981b). In apparent response to faint received sounds from fin whales 20-25 km away, one fin whale reacted by swimming toward the group (Watkins 1981b). Watkins believes that most fin whale responses to singers are at distances <15 km.

Fin whales also produce sounds at frequencies up to 150 Hz, including 34- to 75-Hz tones, a 129- to 150-Hz tone preceding 20-Hz sounds, and generally downsweeping pulses in the range 118 to 14 Hz (Watkins 1981b; Cummings et al. 1986; Edds 1988). Sounds recorded by Cummings et al. (1986) were heard only when the whales were at depth, not during breathing at the surface. Watkins (1981b) heard these sounds mostly during interactions of two or more whales. Because of their relatively low source levels (155-165 dB), Watkins speculated that these sounds are used to communicate with nearby whales. Fin whales >15-20 km from one another apparently do not emit these higher-frequency sounds (Watkins 1981b).

A low-frequency broadband rumble with energy concentrated at 30 Hz may signify surprise, for example, in response to a close encounter with a ship, and may also be associated with agonistic behavior between whales (Watkins 1981b; Edds 1988). In general, the significance of the presumed short-distance sounds is not well known.

Fin whales that are moving and feeding also produce hydrodynamic and mechanical sounds, mostly at low frequencies (Watkins and Wartzok 1985). Jaw motions during feeding may produce strong sound pulses (Brodie 1993).

7.1.6 Blue, Bryde's, Sei, and Minke Whales

Blue whales produce lengthy, strong, low-frequency moans. Many are infrasonic by human standards. Blue whales off Chile produced low-frequency moans at 12.5-200 Hz, with durations up to 36 s, and overall source levels up to 188 dB re 1 µPa-m (Cummings and Thompson 1971a). A short, 390-Hz pulse was also produced during the moan. Each sound was uttered as a three-part sequence. P.O. Thompson et al. (1987) recorded low-frequency (<110 Hz) sounds from a group of blue whales in the Gulf of Mexico. Many sounds were stereotyped doublets. Edds (1982) recorded narrowband moans sweeping from 20 to 18 Hz and lasting ~16 s. Military hydrophone systems (SOSUS) are now providing many new data on these prolonged low-frequency moans by blue whales in both the North Atlantic and North Pacific (Gagnon and Clark 1993; Cummings and Thompson 1994;

Stafford et al. 1994). Functions of these sounds are unknown, but could involve long-distance communication. Some blue whale calls have been detected by SOSUS at distances >1000 km (D. Mellinger, personal communication).

Bryde's whales in the Gulf of California produce short moans with a mean frequency near 124 Hz (range 70-245 Hz; Cummings et al. 1986). Source levels could have been ~152-174 dB re 1 µPa-m. They also produce short pulsed moans, mainly at 165-500 Hz, and calves may produce discrete pulses at 700-900 Hz (Edds et al. 1993).

Sei whale calls apparently have been recorded only once or twice, off eastern Canada (T.J. Thompson et al. 1979; Knowlton et al. 1991). Recorded sounds consisted of two phrases of 0.5- to 0.8-s duration spaced 0.4-1 s apart. Each phrase consisted of 10-20 FM sweeps in the 1.5- to 3.5-kHz range.

Minke whales produce sounds described as downsweeps, up-sweeps, grunts, clicks, thump trains, and ratchets (Winn and Perkins 1976; T.J. Thompson et al. 1979). Thump trains may contain individual signature information. They lasted over 1 min and were composed of 50- to 70-ms thumps, with most energy at 100-200 Hz. Minke whales in coastal waters may have individual home ranges (Dorsey 1983; Edds and Macfarlane 1987). Minke whales might use sounds with identification information to maintain spacing.

7.1.7 High-Frequency Sounds and "Echolocation"

High-frequency clicks have been recorded near blue, fin, and minke whales, and lower-frequency clicks or pulses have been reported from Bryde's, sei, and humpback whales (Table 7.1). Some of the reported clicks may have been from distant odontocetes, or recording or analysis artifacts. Although there has been speculation about the possibility of echolocation in baleen whales, there is no evidence that they echolocate in the manner of toothed whales (Norris 1981; Watkins 1981b; Watkins and Wartzok 1985; *cf.* Section 7.2.4). If baleen whales produce high-frequency clicks, they do so infrequently.

Reverberations of low-frequency whale calls from large objects might provide whales with information about their physical environment. This could include ice characteristics (Ellison et al. 1987) or the presence of islands. However, we have not seen any evidence that whales have or use this capability.

7.2 Toothed Whale Sounds and Echolocation Signals

Odontocete sounds can be classified into three general categories: tonal whistles, pulsed sounds of very short duration used in echolocation, and less distinct pulsed sounds such as cries, grunts, and barks (Table 7.2).

Many odontocetes are very social. They sometimes form stable groups of various sizes, and individuals within these groups interact continually. Social interactions include mating and sexual activity, play, dominance interactions, and maternal behavior (Herman and Tavolga 1980; Tyack 1986a). Many species are very vocal when in groups and especially when interacting.

Many data on odontocete sounds have been obtained from captive animals. Caution is necessary in interpreting data on waveforms, frequencies, and source levels of sounds recorded in captivity. Sounds recorded in the wild and in captivity may differ because of real differences in the sounds emitted by captive versus free-ranging animals, or because of recording artifacts (Cummings et al. 1975; Watkins 1980b).

7.2.1 Kinds of Toothed Whale Sounds

In this section, we discuss whistles and pulsed sounds other than echolocation pulses. Various odontocete species produce whistle vocalizations, pulsed sounds, or both (Table 7.2). In general, whistling species are very social and assemble in herds of dozens to thousands of individuals (Tyack 1986a). Non-whistling species are generally found alone or in small groups (Herman and Tavolga 1980). There are at least two notable exceptions to this apparent relationship. (1) Sperm whales are quite social but mainly produce clicks (Watkins and Schevill 1977a; Watkins et al. 1985a,b). (2) Killer whales form very stable groups but usually use pulsed sounds to communicate; however, they do produce whistles (Ford and Fisher 1982). The harbor porpoise, which travels singly or in small groups, produces relatively low-frequency clicks (2 kHz) and other pulsed sounds (Busnel and Dziedzic 1966a). Dall's porpoise, which travels in small groups, also utters rather low-frequency clicks (0.04-12 kHz) and apparently does not whistle often (Evans 1973; Awbrey et al. 1979).

Whistles.—Most odontocete whistles are narrowband sounds—sometimes tones. Whistles typically have most of their energy below 20 kHz (Table 7.2). In oceanic and coastal dolphins there is a strong negative correlation between maximum whistle frequency and body size (Wang Ding et al. 1995). They suggest that frequencies of river dolphin whistles may tend to be lower for better propagation in rivers.

A large variety of whistles can be produced. The frequency pattern can be unmodulated, trilled, ascending, descending, ascending-descending, descending-ascending, or slowly wavering. A whistle can consist of one of these sound patterns, given once or repeated, or a series of sounds of several types. Over the duration of a whistle, the amplitudes of the ascending and descending portions can vary. Whistles can be continuous or have a variable number of breaks and segments within one whistle. For any one species, initial, final, maximum, and minimum frequencies may vary, as can the duration and level. The bottlenose dolphin can combine basic kinds of whistles into more complex phrases (Dreher and Evans 1964). Taruski (1979) has shown that the whistles of the long-finned pilot whale form a continuum in which no mutually exclusive types could be recognized.

Narrowband low-frequency calls, mainly at 300-900 Hz, have been recorded from bottlenose dolphins off eastern Australia (Schultz et al. in press). These sounds, unlike most odontocete calls, overlap in frequency with many low-frequency industrial sounds (*cf.* Chapter 6).

Clicks and Pulsed Sounds.—Most vocalizations recorded in the presence of sperm whales are clicks. Sperm whale clicks have a frequency range from <100 Hz to 30 kHz with most energy at 2-4 kHz and 10-16 kHz. Clicks are repeated at rates of 1-90 per second (Watkins and Schevill 1977b; Watkins et al. 1985a). Source levels of sperm whale clicks can be near 180 dB re 1 μPa-m (Watkins 1980a). Dunn (1969) reported a source level of 173 dB in a ⅓-octave band centered at 1 kHz. Levenson (1974) recorded source levels of 163-175 dB (mean 171 ± s.d. 3 dB) for 13 discrete sperm whale sounds.

Most (70 to 95%) killer whale social sounds are pulsed (Ford and Fisher 1982). These calls have been described as "screams" (Schevill and Watkins 1966) or as "harsh and metallic" (Steiner et al. 1979). Pulsed calls are very complex with energy at 500 Hz to 25 kHz and pulse repetition rates up to 5000 per second (Schevill and Watkins 1966; Ford and Fisher 1982). The pulse repetition rate for pulsed calls and echolocation clicks differs. Pulse repetition rate for echolocation clicks is 6 to 18 clicks/s (Schevill and Watkins 1966). Durations of pulsed calls range from 0.05 to 10 s, but most are 0.5-1.5 s long (Ford and Fisher 1982).

TABLE 7.2. Characteristics of underwater sounds produced by toothed whales, excluding known or suspected echolocation sounds. Asterisk (*) denotes species whose echolocation sounds are summarized in Table 7.3

Species	Signal type	Frequency range (kHz)	Dominant frequencies (kHz)	Source level (dB re 1 µPa at 1 m)	References
Physeteridae					
Sperm whale	clicks	0.1-30	2-4, 10-16	160-180	Backus & Schevill 1966; Levenson 1974; Watkins 1980a
Pygmy sperm w.*	clicks	60-200	120	—	Santoro et al. 1989
Ziphiidae					
Northern bottle-nose whale*	whistles	3-16	—	—	Winn et al. 1970b
	clicks	0.5-26+	—	—	"
Blainville's beaked whale	short whistles/ chirps	<1-6	—	—	D. Caldwell & Caldwell 1971a
Hubb's beaked whale	pulses	0.3-2, 0.3-80+	0.3-2	—	Buerki et al. 1989; Lynn & Reiss 1992
	whistles	2.6-10.7	—	—	
Monodontidae					
Beluga*	whistles	0.26-20	2-5.9	—	Schevill & Lawrence 1949; Sjare & Smith 1986a,b
	pulsed tones	0.4-12	1-8	—	"
	noisy vocalizations	0.5-16	4.2-8.3	—	"
Narwhal*	pulsed tones	0.5-5	—	—	Ford & Fisher 1978
	whistles	0.3-18	0.3-10	—	"

Delphinidae

Irrawaddy dolphin*

Killer whale*	whistles	1.5-18	6-12	—	Steiner et al. 1979; Ford & Fisher 1983; Morton et al. 1986
	pulsed calls	0.5-25	1-6	160	Schevill & Watkins 1966; Awbrey et al. 1982; Ford & Fisher 1983; S. Moore et al. 1988
False killer whale*	whistles	—	4-9.5	—	Busnel & Dziedzic 1968; Kamminga & van Velden 1987
Pygmy killer whale	growls, blats	—	—	—	Pryor et al. 1965
Long-finned pilot whale*	whistles	1-8	1.6-6.7[a]	—	Busnel & Dziedzic 1966a; Taruski 1979; Steiner 1981
	clicks	1-18	—	—	
Short-finned pilot whale*	whistles	0.5-20+	2-14	180	M. Caldwell & Caldwell 1969; Fish & Turl 1976
Risso's dolphin*	whistles	—	3.5-4.5	—	D. Caldwell et al. 1969
	rasp/pulse burst	0.1-8+?[b]	2-5	—	Watkins 1967b
Rough-toothed dolphin*	whistles	—	4-7	—	Busnel & Dziedzic 1966b
Tucuxi (*Sotalia*)*	whistles	3.6-23.9	7.1-18.5[a]	—	Wang Ding et al. 1995
Indo-Pacific humpback d.	whistles	1.2-16+	—	—	Schultz & Corkeron 1994

(Table continues)

TABLE 7.2. Continued

Species	Signal type	Frequency range (Hz)	Dominant frequencies (Hz)	Source level (dB re 1 µPa at 1 m)	References
Atlantic white-sided dolphin	whistles	—	6-15[a]	—	Steiner 1981
Pacific white-sided dolphin*	whistles	2-20+	4-12	—	M. Caldwell & Caldwell 1971
Dusky dolphin	whistles	1.0-27.3	6.4-19.2[a]	—	Wang Ding et al. 1995
White-beaked d.*	squeals	—	8-12	—	Watkins & Schevill 1972
Peale's dolphin	pulsed sounds (buzz)	0.3, 4-5	0.3	low	Schevill & Watkins 1971a
	clicks	to 12	to 5	low	"
	clicks	to 2	1		"
Fraser's dolphin	whistles	7.6-13.4	—	—	Leatherwood et al. 1993
Common dolphin*	whistles	—	2-18	—	M. Caldwell & Caldwell 1968; S. Moore & Ridgway 1995
	chirps	—	8-14	—	M. Caldwell & Caldwell 1968
	barks	—	<0.5-3	—	"
Bottlenose dolphin*	whistles	0.8-24	3.5-14.5[a]	125-173	Lilly & Miller 1961; Tyack 1985; M. Caldwell et al. 1990; Schultz & Corkeron 1994; Wang Ding et al. 1995
	low-freq. narrowband	<2	0.3-0.9	—	Schultz et al. in press

	rasp, grate, mew, bark, yelp	—	—	—	Wood 1953
Pantropical spotted d.	whistles	3.1-21.4	6.7-17.8[a]	—	Wang Ding et al. 1995
Atlantic spotted dolphin*	whistles	5.0-19.8	6.7-17.9[a]	—	M. Caldwell et al. 1973b; Steiner 1981; Wang Ding et al. 1995
	clicks	1-8	—	—	D. Caldwell & Caldwell 1971b
	squawks, barks, growls	0.1-3	—	—	" ; M. Caldwell et al. 1973
	chirps	4-8	—	—	M. Caldwell et al. 1973b
Striped d.	whistles	6-24+	8-12.5	—	Busnel et al. 1968
Spinner dolphin*	whistles (= squeals?)	1-22.5	6.8-16.9[a]	109-125?	Watkins & Schevill 1974; Steiner 1981; Norris et al. 1994; Wang Ding et al. 1995
	pulse bursts	very wide	5-60	108-115	Watkins & Schevill 1974; Norris et al. 1994
	screams	—	—	—	Norris et al. 1994
Clymene d.	whistles	6.3-19.2	—	—	Mullin et al. 1994a
Northern right whale dolphin*	whistles	?-16+	—	—	Leatherwood & Walker 1979
	tones	1-4	1.8, 3	—	"
Hector's d.*					
Commerson's d.*	pulsed "cry"	<10	0.2-5	—	Watkins & Schevill 1980; Dziedzic & De Buffrenil 1989
	clicks	—	6	—	Dziedzic & De Buffrenil 1989

(Table continues)

TABLE 7.2. Continued

Species	Signal type	Frequency range (Hz)	Dominant frequencies (Hz)	Source level (dB re 1 µPa at 1 m)	References
Heaviside's d.	pulsed sounds	0.8-5[c]	0.8-4.5[c]	—	Watkins et al. 1977
Phocoenidae					
Dall's porpoise*	clicks	0.04-12	—	120-148	Evans 1973; Evans & Awbrey 1984
Harbor porp.*	clicks	2	—	100	Busnel & Dziedzic 1966a; Schevill et al. 1969
Vaquita*					
Finless porp.*	clicks	1.6-2.2	2	—	Pilleri et al. 1980
River Dolphins					
Boutu*	squeals	<1-12+	1-2	—	M. Caldwell & Caldwell 1970
	whistles	0.2-5.2	1.8-3.8[a]	—	Wang Ding et al. 1995
Indus susu*	clicks	0.8-16	—	low	Andersen & Pilleri 1970; Pilleri et al. 1971
Baiji*	whistles	3-18.4	6	156	Jing Xianying et al. 1981; Xiao Youfu & Jing Rongcai 1989
Franciscana*					

[a] Dominant frequency range estimated as "mean minimum frequency minus 1 s.d" to "mean maximum frequency plus 1 s.d." (Steiner 1981; Wang Ding et al. 1995).
[b] ? denotes questionable data.
[c] Equipment capable of recording to 10 kHz only; congeners produce clicks with maximum energy at >100 kHz.

Killer whales are very gregarious and social groups (pods) of some populations are stable for many years. Hoelzel and Osborne (1986) identified 38 discrete call types from three pods resident in the Puget Sound area of western North America. Each resident pod tends to have a characteristic dialect (Ford and Fisher 1982, 1983). Several resident pods can be part of a clan that frequently socializes or travels together and shares many discrete types of calls (Ford 1991). There does not appear to be any sharing of calls among clans (Ford 1991). Similarly, S.E. Moore et al. (1988) documented many discrete types of pulsed calls off Iceland and Norway; there was little evidence of shared call types between those areas. Calls of Antarctic killer whales tend to be at higher frequencies (Awbrey et al. 1982).

7.2.2 Possible Functions of Toothed Whale Sounds

Most toothed whales are gregarious. Depending on the species, they often travel and feed in groups of three to thousands. There is increasing evidence that certain odontocete sounds serve an individual-identification function (e.g., Sayigh et al. 1993b). When feeding, odontocetes often cooperate to maximize feeding opportunities, for example, by herding prey. There is evidence that this coordination is mediated by acoustic contact.

Research on the functions of odontocete sounds is continuing. Some sound types tend to be produced under specific behavioral or seasonal circumstances (e.g., Jacobs et al. 1993). In the following discussion, comments about functions of various sounds are based on reports of general associations between specific sounds and behaviors—often not replicated. This discussion is, therefore, speculative. Echolocation is discussed later (Section 7.2.4).

Signature Calls.—Some researchers have identified seemingly-unique calls produced by specific individual odontocetes. These "signature calls" are believed to identify the sender. Most odontocete signature calls are whistles. However, sperm whales may use click sounds for individual identification (Watkins and Schevill 1977a). The pulsed sounds of each killer whale pod are also distinguishable (Ford and Fisher 1982, 1983; Ford 1991). Although some individual odontocetes produce distinguishable calls, for most species little is known about the functions, the degree of uniqueness, or its persistence over time. Therefore, much of the following discussion is highly speculative.

In many odontocete species, whistles may serve as identification calls and for other forms of communication (D.K. Caldwell and Caldwell 1977; Tyack 1986b). M.C. Caldwell and Caldwell (1965) found that 90% of the whistles from each bottlenose dolphin were signature calls, although in some situations the percentage is lower (Janik et al. 1994). The bottlenose dolphin can recognize the signature calls of other individuals within its group, as well as those of some individuals of other species (M.C. Caldwell et al. 1971, 1973a, 1990).

Whistles may also function in other forms of communication provided that the receivers recognize the identity of the sender. Whistles of a captured male Atlantic spotted dolphin elicited flight reactions from members of his own herd (Herman and Tavolga 1980). However, when played back to conspecifics in another area, the same whistles caused approach and investigation. Bottlenose dolphins mimic each other's signature whistles (M.C. Caldwell and Caldwell 1972; Tyack 1986b). These whistles may be used as contact calls to establish or maintain contact between individuals, including mother-calf pairs (Tyack 1987; Sayigh et al. 1990; Smolker et al. 1993). Signature whistles used by mother-calf pairs can remain stable for up to 12 years (Sayigh et al. 1990).

Whistles that could be signature whistles have been recorded from bottlenose, common, and dusky dolphins, Atlantic and Pacific white-sided dolphins, Atlantic and pantropical spotted dolphins, spinner dolphin, long-finned pilot whale, tucuxi, and boutu (M.C. Caldwell and Caldwell 1965, 1968, 1971; M.C. Caldwell et al. 1973b, 1990; Steiner 1981; Wang Ding et al. 1995). Bel'kovich and Shchekotov (1992) have recorded individual signals from belugas. Several other species are also known to whistle (Table 7.2), but it is not known whether their whistles are signature calls.

Sperm whales emit stereotyped click sequences called "codas" over periods lasting up to several hours. Some codas ("signature codas") may be used for individual identification (Watkins and Schevill 1977b; Adler-Fenchel 1980; Watkins et al. 1985b). The internal pulse structure of each click may also differ among individuals (Norris 1969). Slow clicks with an interclick interval of ~6 s and frequencies <4 kHz may convey some information about the sex and reproductive status of the sender (Weilgart and Whitehead 1988). Production of these slow clicks appears to be restricted to maturing or mature males.

Coordination of Activity.—Off Hawaii, spinner dolphins feed in large schools dispersed over distances up to 3 km (Norris and Dohl 1980). These schools move and reverse course together, and all members dive and surface within 1-2 min of each other. Thus, movements are coordinated but not fully synchronized. Norris and Dohl (1980) speculate that spinner dolphins use acoustic communication to pass information across the school. Norris et al. (1994) provide further information. Similarly, foraging killer whales are often dispersed over distances of 2 km. Vocalizations may be important in coordinating foraging and other activities (Hoelzel and Osborne 1986; Ford 1989).

In the South Atlantic, dusky dolphins forage in groups of 6-15 individuals, with 20 to 30 such groups spread over an area of 100 km^2 (Würsig and Würsig 1980). They speculate that the observed spacing of ~1 km between groups is maintained by listening for the vocalizations of other groups. When feeding, the dolphins often leap into the air. The Würsigs speculate that vocalizations and noise associated with leaping attract dolphin groups from ½-1 km distance, and that groups >1 km away use visual cues such as the sight of leaping dolphins and of seabirds attracted to the food concentration.

In the North Atlantic, the complexity of long-finned pilot whale whistles was positively correlated with complexity of overt behavior as follows: simple whistles were associated with whales milling or resting on the surface; complex whistles were associated with presumed feeding; and greater numbers of most whistle types were produced when whales were dispersed or when more than one group was present (Taruski 1979; Weilgart and Whitehead 1990).

Sperm whale clicks may function to maintain herd integrity during foraging in darkness at great depths or when the pod is scattered at the surface (Watkins and Schevill 1977a,b; Watkins et al. 1985a; Whitehead and Weilgart 1990). Clicks are heard most frequently when sperm whales are exhibiting diving/foraging behavior (Whitehead and Weilgart 1991). These may be echolocation clicks used in feeding, contact calls, or both. Animals sometimes regroup just prior to surfacing, or surface independently several kilometers apart but then swim in the same direction. Sequences of clicks at rates of 1-3 clicks/s, produced for periods of 30 s to 5 min, were associated with these activities (Watkins et al. 1985a). Lone sperm whales are generally silent (Watkins 1980a). Shared codas, similar to the signature codas mentioned earlier, may be used by several whales and may serve a communication function when the whales are at the surface (K.E. Moore et al. 1993; Weilgart and Whitehead 1993).

Hector's dolphins may also use echolocation clicks as calls in social situations (Dawon 1991).

7.2.3 *Directionality and Effective Range*
of Toothed Whale Sounds

Ranges at which toothed whale sounds are audible depend on the source level, directionality, and frequency of the sounds; on sea state and other factors affecting propagation and ambient noise (Chapters 4 and 5); and on hearing sensitivity (Chapter 8).

All echolocation clicks appear to be directional (Section 7.2.4). There have been few studies on directionality of other sounds. Sounds of the harbor porpoise, spinner dolphin, and sperm whale are probably omnidirectional (Møhl and Andersen 1973; Watkins and Schevill 1974; Watkins 1980a). The common dolphin apparently produces directional sounds, but echolocation clicks may have been the dominant sounds recorded (Fish and Turl 1976).

Reported source levels of non-echolocation sounds from toothed whales range up to at least 160-180 dB re 1 µPa-m for a few species (Table 7.2). Watkins (1980a) has detected sperm whale sounds at distances of 10 km and he estimates that sounds made in deep water can be detected with a hydrophone at 15 km (Watkins and Moore 1982). However, sperm whales apparently can vary the levels of their sounds. At some times they were barely audible via hydrophones only a few hundred meters away (Watkins 1980a).

At least some of the non-echolocation sounds emitted by certain other odontocetes are quite weak and would not be detectable beyond a few tens or hundreds of meters. Pulsed sounds emitted by Peale's dolphin, a South American species, had very low source levels—only ~80 dB re 1 µPa-m. These sounds, which were at a relatively low frequency (1 to 5 kHz), were not detectable at ranges exceeding 10-20 m (Schevill and Watkins 1971a). Similarly, the low-frequency (2 kHz) click of the harbor porpoise has a source level of only 100 dB re 1 µPa-m, and thus would be audible only over short distances (Møhl and Andersen 1973).

Spinner dolphins and boutu (Amazon river dolphin) have also been said to produce weak calls. However, at times both species emit strong calls (B. Würsig, personal observation). Burst-pulse calls from spinner dolphins have been recorded at ranges up to 1.6 km (Norris et al. 1994:184). In general, reported source levels must be treated cautiously, given their variability and the estimation difficulties in both captive and free-ranging animals (Section 3.6.1).

The ranges at which odontocete sounds can be detected with a suitable hydrophone are relevant in predicting the ranges at which those sounds could be detected by conspecifics. Odontocetes generally have good hearing sensitivity within the frequency ranges of their calls (Chapter 8). Hence, their detection ranges—like those of a sensitive hydrophone—will normally be limited by ambient noise. Fish and Turl (1976) recorded sounds of common and bottlenose dolphins, short-finned pilot whales, and northern right whale dolphins 200-1000 m from the animals. Pilot whale whistles were audible via hydrophones 400-1600 m away (Busnel and Dziedzic 1966a; Taruski 1979). While foraging, belugas may remain in acoustic contact over ranges of 300-500 m (Bel'kovich and Shchekotov 1992).

Echolocation signals, although often at high amplitude (see following section), are generally at high frequencies where there is rapid volume absorption of sound. At 50 and 100 kHz, for example, absorption losses of ~12 and 36 dB/km, respectively (Section 4.5.1), are added to normal spreading losses of 10-20 log (range in m). Echolocation signals from northern right whale dolphins were detected by hydrophone at a distance of 730 m (Leatherwood and Walker 1979). Evans and Dreher (1962) detected bottlenose dolphin echolocation signals at 450 m, with whistles audible at ~370 m. These distances are minima, given the strong directionality of echolocation pulses and the uncertain orientations of the calling animals relative to the hydrophone.

In summary, there are insufficient data to determine the ranges at which most odontocete sounds can be detected. A few observations indicate that many calls may only be detectable within a few hundred meters, and perhaps up to a maximum of ~1 km. However, sperm whales, pilot whales, and presumably some other species with relatively strong calls are detectable at distances >1 km. Some species whose sounds apparently have low source levels may be detectable only within a few tens of meters.

7.2.4 Echolocation by Toothed Whales

Echolocation has been demonstrated in several species of odontocetes (Table 7.3). Numerous other species produce clicks of types used in echolocation but have not been proven to echolocate (Table 7.3). There is no proof that sperm whales echolocate, but they probably do (Mullins et al. 1988).

Echolocating odontocetes produce directional forward-projecting pulsed sounds of high intensity and frequency. Each pulse is very brief, typically 50-200 µs in duration (Au 1993:134). In most but not all cases, pulses are spaced so an echo from the target is received

TABLE 7.3. Frequencies and peak-to-peak source levels of odontocete echolocation clicks for species with demonstrated echolocation abilities and for similar clicks by other species.

Echolocation Demonstrated

Species	Frequency (kHz)	Source level (dB re 1 µPa at 1 m)	Reference
Beluga	40-60, 100-120	206-225	Au et al. 1985, 1987; Au 1993
Killer whale	12-25	180	Diercks et al. 1971
False killer whale	25-30; 95-130	220-228	Kamminga & van Velden 1987; Thomas & Turl 1990
Short-finned pilot whale	30-60	180	Evans 1973
Tucuxi (*Sotalia*)	80-100	high	D. Caldwell & Caldwell 1970; Norris et al. 1972; Kamminga et al. 1993
Pacific white-sided dolphin	60-80	180	Evans 1973
Common dolphin	23-67	—	Dziedzic 1978, in Au 1993
Bottlenose dolphin	110-130	218-228	Au et al. 1974; Au 1993
Atlantic spotted dolphin	—	—	D. Caldwell & Caldwell 1971b
Commerson's dolphin	116-134	160	Kamminga & Wiersma 1981; Shochi et al. 1982; Evans et al. 1988; Dziedzic & De Buffrenil 1989; Au 1993
Dall's porpoise	135-149	165-175	Evans & Awbrey 1984; Hatakeyama & Soeda 1990; Hatakeyama et al. 1994
Harbor porpoise	110-150	135-177	Busnel et al. 1965; Møhl & Andersen 1973; Kamminga & Wiersma 1981; Akamatsu et al. 1994
Boutu	85-105	—	Diercks et al. 1971; Evans 1973; Kamminga et al. 1993

Echolocation-Type Clicks

	clicks		
Pygmy sperm whale		—	D. Caldwell et al. 1966; D. Caldwell & Caldwell 1987
Bottlenose whale	8-12	—	Winn et al. 1970b
Narwhal	40	218	Møhl et al. 1990
Irrawaddy dolphin	50-75	—	Kamminga et al. 1983
Long-finned pilot whale	6-11	—	McLeod 1986
Risso's dolphin	65	~120	Au 1993
Rough-toothed dolphin	5-32	—	Norris & Evans 1967
White-beaked dolphin	to 325	≤207	Mitson 1990
Spinner dolphin	low-65+	—	Watkins & Schevill 1974; Norris et al. 1994
N. right whale dolphin	1-40+?	170 rms	Fish & Turl 1976
Hector's dolphin	112-135	150-163	Dawson 1988; Dawson & Thorpe 1990; Au 1993
Heaviside's dolphin	2-5[a]	—	Watkins et al. 1977
Vaquita	128-139	—	Silber 1991
Finless porpoise	~128	—	Kamminga et al. 1986; Kamminga 1988
Indus susu	15-100	—	Herald et al. 1969; Pilleri et al. 1971
Baiji	20-120	156	Xiao Youfu & Jing Rongcai 1989
Franciscana	0.3-3, 10-16, 18-24+	—	Busnel et al. 1974

[a] Equipment capable of recording to 10 kHz only.

before the next pulse is emitted (Au 1993). For example, bottlenose dolphin clicks are typically ~50 ms apart when scanning a target at 20 m range, and 150 ms apart for a target at 100 m (Au 1993:116). In at least the few well-studied species, pulse duration, frequency, inter-click interval, and source level are adjusted by the animal for optimal performance under the prevailing conditions of ambient noise, reverb-eration, distance to target, and target characteristics. The echoloca-tion capabilities of the bottlenose dolphin, beluga whale, and false killer whale are well documented; abilities of other species are much less well studied. Au (1993) provides an excellent review.

   Directionality of Echolocation Signals.—Echolocation clicks are projected from an odontocete's head in a highly directional beam. However, the beam does not have sharply defined edges. Intensity decreases with increasing angular distance off-center. Beamwidth is commonly expressed as the angle within which the level is within 3 dB of that at the center of the beam.

   In the bottlenose dolphin, the 3-dB beamwidth is 10-11.7° at an angle 5° above the body axis (Au et al. 1978, 1986; Au 1980). In the beluga, the 3-dB beamwidth is only 6.5°, also tilted 5° upward (Au et al. 1987). In the baiji, the 3-dB beamwidth is 13° horizontally and 9° vertically, tilted 7.5° upward (Xiao Youfu and Jing Rongcai 1989). In the false killer whale, beamwidth is similar to that of the bottlenose dolphin, but the beam is aimed a few degrees below the body axis (Au et al. 1993). Directional echolocation beams have also been noted in many other species, including the pygmy sperm whale and killer whale; the rough-toothed, spinner, Commerson's, and northern right whale dolphins; the tucuxi and boutu; and the harbor porpoise (Norris and Evans 1967; D.K. Caldwell and Caldwell 1970, 1987; Norris et al. 1972; Watkins and Schevill 1974; Møhl and Andersen 1979; Leather-wood and Walker 1979; Shochi et al. 1982). High-frequency energy is especially strongly concentrated in the center of the beam; lower-frequency components are distributed more broadly (Schevill and Watkins 1966; Watkins 1980b).

   The effective source level for a highly directional transmitting beam is much higher than that for an omnidirectional beam of the same total power. The increase in intensity level due to directionality is 25-27 dB in the bottlenose dolphin and 32 dB in the beluga (Au et al. 1986, 1987). Such extreme directionality helps provide a good target localization ability and strong echo returns from targets. The directionality causes difficulties in characterizing echolocation clicks produced in the wild. The high-frequency components and maximum levels can be detected only when the beam is directed at the hydrophone. However, the orientation of the animal with respect to the receiver is usually unknown.

Source Levels of Echolocation Clicks.—Echolocation clicks have the highest source levels of any recorded marine mammal sounds, ranging up to 220-230 dB re 1 µPa-m in medium-sized odontocetes. In captive bottlenose dolphins, average source levels are ~220 to 222 dB re 1 µPa-m, with a maximum of 230 dB (Au et al. 1974; Au 1993). In a captive beluga, the source level varied from 206 to 218 dB re 1 µPa-m during a click train. The level increased by ~5 dB as range to the target increased, and from 204 to 222 dB when ambient noise increased. The strongest beluga click was ~225 dB (Au et al. 1985, 1987; Au 1993). Similarly, source levels of false killer whale clicks ranged up to 228 dB (Thomas and Turl 1990).

Source levels of echolocation clicks recorded from these species under controlled experimental conditions are considerably higher than those reported for most other species (Table 7.3). Most of the latter low values were measured under less than ideal conditions in the wild. However, echolocation-type clicks with level 218 dB re 1 µPa-m have been recorded in the wild from the narwhal (Møhl et al. 1990). That level may not represent the maximum capability of the narwhal.

Although these source levels are high relative to those of many man-made sounds, the pulses are extremely brief and apply only to a narrow range of directions in front of the animal. Also, source levels of echolocation clicks are normally quoted as peak-to-peak values as determined from the highest-amplitude portion of the waveform. These are ~6 dB higher than "peak" levels and ~15 db higher than the rms pressure averaged over the short duration of a typical pulse (Au 1993:6, 129). When these factors are taken into account, the overall energy content and acoustic power of odontocete pulses are not very high when compared to some man-made sources. Nonetheless, odontocetes usually seem to avoid directing strong echolocation pulses at nearby conspecifics (e.g., Norris et al. 1994:255).

Some small odontocetes—e.g. harbor and Dall's porpoises; Commerson's and Hector's dolphins—produce pulses with comparatively low peak levels (e.g., 150-177 dB re 1 µPa-m; Table 7.3). However, their pulses are longer than those of some larger odontocetes. As a result, these pulses contain more energy than would similar-level pulses from larger animals such as the bottlenose dolphin, beluga, or false killer whale, whose pulses are shorter (Au 1993:133*ff*).

Sound Frequencies Used in Echolocation.—Most species in which echolocation is demonstrated or suspected emit clicks at very high frequencies—well above the upper limit of human hearing (Table 7.3). With low ambient noise or during confinement in small tanks, bottlenose dolphins, belugas, and false killer whales often emit echolocation pulses in the 20- to 60-kHz range (Evans 1973; Au et al. 1985; Kamminga and van Velden 1987; Thomas et al. 1988c). However, with higher ambient noise levels or more distant targets, they emit stronger pulses at 100-130 kHz (Au et al. 1974, 1982, 1985; Thomas and Turl 1990). Apparently, "weak" pulses can be emitted in either frequency range but, at least in these three species, the strongest pulses are always >100 kHz (Au 1993).

Pulses from porpoises and some small dolphins (e.g., Commerson's, Hector's) are at very high frequencies: 120-150 kHz (Table 7.3).

The echolocation sounds of the killer whale are at unusually low frequencies, with most energy below 25 kHz (Diercks et al. 1971; Wood and Evans 1980). Despite this, most killer whales can hear sounds up to frequencies far above 35 kHz, consistent with other odontocetes (Au 1993:33; Bain et al. 1993).

Repetition Rate in Echolocation.—Two or three general types of echolocation click trains are emitted by odontocetes. **(1)** "Orientation clicks" with relatively long interclick intervals are used to scan the environment. **(2)** "Discrimination clicks", often at briefer intervals, are used to obtain detailed information about a target (Airapet'yants et al. 1973; Popper 1980a). The interclick interval, and thus the click repetition rate, is normally a function of the range being scanned. **(3)** Some types of click trains may be "nonfunctional collateral acoustic behavior", or part of the pulse production process (Au et al. 1987).

In the bottlenose dolphin, the interclick interval is generally greater than the two-way acoustic travel time (Au et al. 1974, 1982; Turl and Penner 1989). The brief lag between receipt of the echo from one click and emission of the next click can range from 7 to 50 ms (Au 1980; Au et al. 1982). The interclick interval increases with increasing distance to the target, from 10-25 ms at 1 m range to ~175-190 ms at 120 m (Au et al. 1974, 1982; Au 1980, 1993). In contrast, the two-way travel time for a sound pulse is ~1.3 ms at 1 m range and ~160 ms at 120 m. Click duration is 50-80 μs (Au 1993).

In the beluga, the interclick interval often is less than the two-way travel time, at least for targets at distances >40 m (Turl et al. 1987; Turl and Penner 1989). The beluga's echolocation performance is superior to that of the bottlenose dolphin in several respects. One possible reason is that shorter interclick intervals allow the beluga to process more information per unit time (Turl et al. 1987). Also, the beluga has better abilities to detect echo pulses amidst ambient noise.

Echolocation Ranges.—With a 7.62-cm sphere as target, maximum detection range (50% correct response) for a trained bottlenose dolphin under controlled conditions was 113 m (Au and Snyder 1980). Under similar conditions, a trained beluga had good echolocation abilities at distances up to at least 80 m (Au et al. 1987). The range detection threshold for a false killer whale was 119 m (Thomas and Turl 1990). Untrained bottlenose dolphins in open water may have detected a very large target 360 m away (Evans and Dreher 1962).

Many echolocation experiments have been conducted in small tanks where background noise and echolocation signals differ from those in typical natural conditions. Such results cannot be used to estimate maximum detection ranges. Also, most tests are done with small- or moderate-sized targets; larger targets presumably are detectable farther away. Maximum distances at which echolocation pulses can be heard by a second animal or by hydrophone (one-way travel; Section 7.2.3) are much greater than the maximum target distance at which the emitting animal can detect echoes (two-way travel).

Echolocation Functions.—Echolocation has been demonstrated in various odontocete species, and similar pulses have been recorded from some other odontocetes (Table 7.3). Further work may show that all dolphins and porpoises can echolocate. In most cases, echolocation has been demonstrated through the use of trained animals. Dolphins use echolocation not only to locate targets, but also to detect subtle differences in targets (Au 1993). The degree to which this ability is used in nature, especially for prey capture, is largely unknown.

Odontocetes echolocate for obstacle avoidance (P.W.B. Moore 1980). Evans and Dreher (1962) performed a simple field experiment demonstrating scouting and obstacle avoidance by wild bottlenose dolphins. A penetrable barrier that was a good acoustic reflector was strung across a channel routinely used by dolphins. Five dolphins approached the barrier, but at a distance of 360 m they turned away. They later made sonar runs (detected with a hydrophone) toward the barrier, rejoined the group, and ultimately passed the barrier.

Entrapment of marine mammals in fishing gear has become a worldwide problem (Perrin et al. 1994). Theoretical calculations and empirical observations show that at least some odontocetes can detect nets by echolocation. Dall's and harbor porpoises, bottlenose and Pacific white-sided dolphins, belugas, and false killer whales could all detect nylon monofilament gillnets through echolocation (Hatakeyama et al. 1994). If one animal broke through the net without getting entangled, other dolphins could detect the hole and swim through it. At least five of these six species produce echolocation clicks at up to 120+ kHz (Table 7.3). Clicks of the sixth species, the Pacific white-sided dolphin, have been reported at 60-80 kHz, and higher frequency clicks may have been present. Detection ranges for monofilament drift nets should range from a few meters to 30+ m (Au 1994; Hatakeyama et al. 1994). A key factor is the frequency of the echolocation clicks in relation to the size of the mesh, ropes, and other parts of the nets.

Even with an ability to detect nets by echolocation, many odontocetes become trapped. To date, efforts to make nets more reflective have not been very successful (Dawson 1994). However, some tests are showing promise. Modifications to make gillnets more detectable by echolocation or by "passive" listening (Section 9.12) may reduce but not eliminate mortality (Silber et al. 1994; Goodson et al. 1994).

Echolocation is not used to the exclusion of other senses. Captive boutus (Amazon River dolphins) appeared to use "passive" listening and vision to investigate their surroundings and to feed. Echolocation was also used, especially when visibility was poor, but vision was the preferred sensory modality (M.C. Caldwell et al. 1966). They speculated that young animals may have to learn how to echolocate.

Dolphins often use echolocation pulses in social contexts, even though they usually avoid exposing nearby conspecifics to strong pulses. Strong click-trains are sometimes directed at other cetacean species or humans (Norris et al. 1994).

Prey Stunning?—Bel'kovich and Yablokov (1963) and Norris and Møhl (1983) suggested that strong "echolocation" signals may be used to stun prey at close ranges. The threshold causing disorientation in 50% of very small experimental fish was 236 dB re 1 μPa (Zagaeski 1987). The maximum known source levels of echolocation pulses are in the 225-230 dB range (Table 7.3; Au 1993). Dolphins apparently do use echolocation-type clicks to disorient schools of fish, to extricate individual fish from a school, and even to break up a school (Hult 1982; Norris and Møhl 1983; Marten et al. 1989). Some sounds suspected as being used for prey debilitation are longer, lower-frequency pulses or "jaw claps" (Overstrom 1983; Norris et al. 1994:280*ff*). Odontocetes may use strong sound pulses as an aid in feeding, but the extent to which they are used to debilitate prey remains unknown.

7.3 Phocid Seal Sounds

Phocid (hair) seals are diverse in habits and habitats. Several northern and Antarctic species spend most or all of their time in the water or hauled out on ice. Species that haul out on land include harbor, spotted, gray, monk, and elephant seals. Most phocid seal calls seem to be associated with mating, mother-pup interactions, and territoriality. Underwater calls may be less important for species that perform these activities on land.

Some phocid species produce strong underwater sounds that may propagate for great distances (Ray et al. 1969; Watkins and Ray 1977; Thomas et al. 1983b). Others produce faint and infrequent sounds (Schevill et al. 1963). Underwater sounds of several species, including bearded, gray, harbor, harp, ribbon, spotted, ringed, Weddell, leopard, and crabeater seals, are thought to be associated with reproduction and territoriality; they are heard mainly in the mating season (Ray et al. 1969; Terhune and Ronald 1976a; Watkins and Ray 1977; Beier and Wartzok 1979; Thomas and DeMaster 1982; Stirling et al. 1983; K. Green and Burton 1988a,b; Asselin et al. 1993; Hanggi and Schusterman 1994). Phocids probably hear underwater sounds at frequencies up to ~60 kHz (Section 8.2.2). Calls between 90 Hz and 16 kHz have been reported (Table 7.4), but for some species other high-frequency sounds might have been missed. The acoustic source level has been estimated for at least five phocid species (Table 7.4). However, it is difficult to determine the range to a seal calling underwater, especially under ice, so reliable estimates of source levels are rare.

7.3.1 Ringed Seal and Bearded Seal
The ringed seal and bearded seal spend much of their time in the water, and calls presumed to be associated with territoriality and courtship are produced underwater. Because most relevant behaviors occur under water or under ice, it has not been possible to associate specific behaviors and call types. These seals haul out on the ice in spring, but their in-air vocal behavior has not been studied. The underwater calls of ringed and bearded seals are quite different.

TABLE 7.4. Characteristics of underwater sounds produced by pinnipeds and sirenians[a]

Species	Signal type	Frequency range (kHz)	Dominant frequencies (kHz)	Source level (dB re 1 µPa at 1 m)	References
Phocids[a]					
Bearded seal	song	0.02-6	1-2	178	Ray et al. 1969; Stirling et al. 1983; Cummings et al. 1983
Ribbon seal	frequency sweeps	0.1-7.1	—	160	Watkins & Ray 1977
Hooded seal	grunt	—	0.2-0.4	—	Terhune & Ronald 1973
	snort	—	0.1-1	—	"
	buzz (click)	to 6	1.2	—	"
Harp seal	15 sound types	<0.1-16+	0.1-3	130-140	Møhl et al. 1975; Watkins & Schevill 1979b; Terhune & Ronald 1986; Terhune 1994
	clicks	—	30	131-164	Møhl et al. 1975
Ringed seal	barks, clicks, yelps	0.4-16	<5	95-130	Stirling 1973; Cummings et al. 1984
Harbor seal & Spotted seal	social sounds	0.5-3.5	—	—	Beier & Wartzok 1979
	clicks	8-150+	12-40	—	Schevill et al. 1963; Cummings & Fish 1971; Renouf et al. 1980; Noseworthy et al. 1989
	roar	0.4-4	0.4-0.8	—	Hanggi & Schusterman 1992, 1994
	bubbly growl	<0.1-0.4	<0.1-0.25	—	"
	grunt, groan	<0.1-4	—	—	"
	creak	0.7-4	0.7-2	—	"

Species	Sound				References
Gray seal	clicks, hiss	0-30, 0-40	—	—	Schevill et al. 1963; Oliver 1978
	6 call types	0.1-5	0.1-3	—	Asselin et al. 1993
	knocks	to 16	to 10	—	"
Weddell seal	34+ call types	0.1-12.8	—	153-193	Thomas & Kuechle 1982; Thomas et al. 1983b; Thomas & Stirling 1983
Ross seal	pulses	0.25-1	—	—	Watkins & Ray 1985
	siren	4→1→4	—	—	"
Leopard seal	pulses (trills)	0.1-5.9	—	—	Ray 1970; Stirling & Siniff 1979; Rogers et al. 1995
	thump, blast, roar, etc.	0.04-7	—	—	Rogers et al. 1995
	ultrasonic	up to 164	50-60	low	Thomas et al. 1983a
Crabeater seal	groan	<0.1-8+	0.1-1.5	high	Stirling & Siniff 1979
Otariids[a]					
Calif sea lion	barks	<8	<3.5	—	Schusterman et al. 1967
	whinny	<1-3	—	—	"
	clicks	—	0.5-4	—	"
	buzzing	<1-4	<1	—	"
N. sea lion	clicks, growls	—	—	—	Poulter 1968
N. fur seal	clicks, bleats	—	—	—	Poulter 1968
Juan Fernández fur seal	clicks	0.1-0.2	0.1-0.2	—	Norris & Watkins 1971

(Table continues)

TABLE 7.4. Continued

Species	Signal type	Frequency range (Hz)	Dominant frequencies (Hz)	Source level (dB re 1 μPa at 1 m)	References
Walrus	bell tone	—	0.4-1.2	—	Schevill et al. 1966; Ray & Watkins 1975; Stirling et al. 1983
	clicks, taps, knocks	0.1-10	<2	—	
	rasps	0.2-0.6	0.4-0.6	—	Schevill et al. 1966
	grunts	≤1	≤1	—	Stirling et al. 1983
Sirenians					
W. Ind. manatee	squeaky	0.6-16	0.6-5	low	Schevill & Watkins 1965
Amaz. manatee	squeaks, pulses	6-16	6-16	—	Evans & Herald 1970
Dugong	chirp-squeak[b]	3-8	—	low	Nair & Lal Mohan 1975
	sound 1[b?]	1-2	—	—	Marsh et al. 1978
	chirp[b?]	2-4	—	—	"
	all sounds	1-8	—	—	Nietschmann 1984, in Nishiwaki & Marsh 1985

[a] Underwater sounds of monk and elephant seals, and of most southern otariids, have not been documented.
[b] Recorded in air.

Bearded seals produce distinctive trills whose dominant feature is a series of prolonged frequency downsweeps (Ray et al. 1969; Ouellet 1979). Bearded seals from various arctic areas appear to have identifiable geographic dialects (Cleator et al. 1987, 1989). In Alaskan waters, the trill generally starts at ~2.5 kHz, after which there is a short warbling upsweep to 3 kHz (Ray et al. 1969). The center frequency then descends, with modulations, to <1 kHz. Below 1 kHz the downsweep may be interrupted by an upsweep to ~2 kHz, after which the downsweep is resumed. There may be several downsweeps and upsweeps during a call. The call ends with the conclusion of the downsweep and, after a pause of up to 30 s, a 3-s pure-tone moan descending from 500 to 200 Hz. Overall call duration is highly variable, but usually at least 1 min (Ray et al. 1969).

Bearded seal sounds are a dominant component of the ambient noise in many arctic areas during spring (e.g., Thiele 1988). The song is thought to be a territorial advertisement call or a mating call by the male (Ray et al. 1969; Budelsky 1993). Cummings et al. (1983) estimated source levels of up to 178 dB re 1 µPa-m. Parts of some calls may be detectable 25+ km away (Cleator et al. 1989).

Ringed seal sounds are less complex and much lower in source level. Ringed seal sounds include 4-kHz clicks, rub sounds with peak energy at 0.5-2 kHz and durations of 0.08-0.3 s, squeaks that are shorter in duration and higher in frequency, "quacking barks" at 0.4-1.5 kHz and durations of 0.03-0.12 s, yelps, and growls (Schevill et al. 1963; Stirling 1973; Cummings et al. 1984). Ringed seal calls appear to have most energy below 5 kHz. Ringed seals may produce sounds at higher frequencies, given that their most sensitive band of hearing extends up to 45 kHz (Terhune and Ronald 1975b; Section 8.2.2) and that most studies used equipment unsuitable for frequencies >15 kHz. Source levels of ringed seal vocalizations, 95-130 dB re 1 µPa-m "peak source spectrum level", are low compared to those of most other marine mammals;[2] maximum detection range may be only ~1 km (Cummings et al. 1984).

No ringed seal calls associated solely with the reproductive season have been reported, but relative frequencies (Hz) of barks and yelps differ between seasons (Stirling 1973). The number of calls increases

---

[2] The source spectrum levels (1-Hz band) reported by Cummings et al. (1984) are not directly comparable to broadband source levels, which would be higher by an unknown amount.

markedly at the onset of the breeding season in April and then decreases in late spring (Stirling et al. 1983; Cummings et al. 1984).
Functions of sounds produced under the ice are unknown.

7.3.2 Ribbon Seal, Harp Seal, and Hooded Seal

Ribbon seals haul out and breed on the pack ice at or near the ice
edge in the Bering Sea; much of their social behavior occurs in the
water (Watkins and Ray 1977). They produce downward frequency
sweeps and puffing sounds (Watkins and Ray 1977). The downsweep
does not waver, exhibits several harmonics, varies in duration, and
varies in start and end frequency. Long sweeps last 4-4.7 s and sweep
from ~7100-3500 Hz down to 2000 Hz. Medium-length sweeps last
1.3-1.8 s and sweep from ~5300-2000 Hz down to 100 Hz. Short
sweeps last <1 s and sweep from ~2000-1750 Hz down to 300 Hz.
Source levels may be near 160 dB re 1 µPa-m (Watkins and Ray
1977). In addition to the downsweeps, a broadband "puff" lasted <1 s
with energy below 5 kHz (Watkins and Ray 1977).

Harp seals are numerous in the northwest and northeast Atlantic.
They aggregate into large herds near the ice edge in March. They
may use underwater sound to find the main herd and, on a finer scale,
to locate mates (Terhune and Ronald 1986). They are very vocal at
this time of year (Møhl et al. 1975). Those authors identified 16 types
of harp seal sounds during the breeding season; Terhune (1994) provided further data on those and three more call types. Most sounds
have maximum source levels of ~135-140 dB re 1 µPa-m (Watkins and
Schevill 1979b; Terhune and Ronald 1986). Under quiet conditions, a
strong harp seal sound might be detectable by another harp seal at a
distance of 2 km (Terhune and Ronald 1986). A vocalizing herd could
be detected with hydrophones at 30-60 km (Watkins and Schevill
1979b; Terhune and Ronald 1986).

Harp seals also produce clicks with source levels up to ~164 dB re
1 µPa-m (Møhl et al. 1975). Given the reduced hearing sensitivity of
seals to brief clicks relative to longer-duration sounds (Section 8.2.4),
clicks may not be detectable more than 1 km away (Terhune 1989b).
Airborne calls of harp seals have also been described (Terhune and
Ronald 1970; E.H. Miller and Murray 1995).

Hooded seals make three distinct types of sounds, with most energy at 0.1-1.2 kHz (Terhune and Ronald 1973). Two call types are low-
frequency pulses, similar to those of harbor seals. The third type is a
buzz similar to click trains emitted by gray seals. Males, females, and

young all produce clicks (Terhune and Ronald 1973). They also vocalize in air when hauled out on the ice.

7.3.3 Harbor and Spotted Seals

Harbor and spotted seals spend much time hauled out on land.
Many social interactions and calls occur on land as well as in water.

Spotted seals in captivity were relatively silent during most of the
year (Beier and Wartzok 1979). A male vocalized 2.5 times as much
as a female. The rate of underwater vocalization increased 1-2 weeks
before mating, was high on the first day of attempted mating, and
remained high for two weeks after mating. Underwater sounds produced by the mating pair included growls, drums, snorts, chirps,
barks, and a "creaky door" sound, with frequencies 500-3500 Hz and
durations 19-400 ms (Beier and Wartzok 1979).

In-air vocal activity of captive male *harbor seals* was high within
a group, but males were silent when alone or with pups (Ralls et al.
1985). Rate of vocalization in captive males increased as they reached
sexual maturity, and sexually mature males were more vocal than
females. The male's reproductive display includes repeated trains of
relatively low-frequency (<4 kHz) 20-ms underwater pulses produced
by long episodes of underwater bubble blowing, roars, grunts, and
creaks (Hanggi and Schusterman 1992, 1994). These were typically
preceded by fore-flipper slaps on the water surface, which produced
strong click sounds (Noseworthy et al. 1989). In the wild, in-air vocalizations coupled with visual signals are used to establish dominance
and to defend individual space on the haul-out site (Sullivan 1982).
These displays are typically initiated when animals are one body
length apart, and are usually of short duration (Sullivan 1982).

Calls of the harbor seal pup are transmitted simultaneously in-air
and underwater when the pup's head is in air (Renouf 1984). Airborne and underwater calls are individually distinct and are used by
the mother to recognize and maintain contact with her pup (Renouf
and Perry 1983; Perry and Renouf 1985, 1988). The fundamental frequency of the airborne calls is 350 Hz (Ralls et al. 1985). Underwater
calls are similar; however, the lower harmonics are absent and there
is a shift to higher frequencies.

7.3.4 Gray Seal

The gray seal breeds on land or ice, but agonistic behaviors are
not very intense (Bonner 1981a). There are no boundary displays and

fighting is minimal (Cameron 1967; Bonner 1981a). Vocalizations are important in establishing and maintaining the mother-pup bond (Fogden 1971).

Underwater, the gray seal utters hisses at 0-40 kHz, isolated clicks, and—less frequently—clusters of clicks at 0-30 kHz (Schevill et al. 1963; Oliver 1978). Asselin et al. (1993) have characterized seven types of underwater calls recorded during the breeding season. Except for "knocks", these calls were predominantly below 1-3 kHz.

7.3.5 Elephant Seals

Northern elephant seals mate on land. Threat displays and fighting are used to establish dominance among males, much as in otariid (eared) seals. In-air calls made by aggressive males include **(1)** snoring, which is a low-intensity threat, **(2)** a snort (0.2-0.6 kHz) made by a dominant male when approached by a subdominant male, and **(3)** a clap threat (<2.5 kHz), which may contain signature information at the individual level (Sandegren 1976; Shipley et al. 1981, 1986). Le Boeuf and Peterson (1969) believed that there were regional dialects in the clap threat calls, but that these are now disappearing (Le Boeuf and Petrinovich 1974; Shipley et al. 1981). In-air calls are accompanied by surface vibrations that can elicit reactions from conspecifics (Shipley et al. 1992).

In-air sounds made by females include a <0.7-kHz belch roar used in aggressive situations and a 0.5- to 1-kHz bark used to attract the pup (Bartholomew and Collias 1962). Pups use a <1.4-kHz call to maintain contact with the mother and to signify a need for attention (Bartholomew and Collias 1962). Mother and pup vocalizations are individually distinct (Insley 1989) and the female recognizes her own pup's call (Petrinovich 1974).

Underwater sounds of the elephant seal were recorded by Poulter (1968). He describes them as musical and sounding like a bell, cymbal, or guitar strings; no further details were provided.

7.3.6 Monk Seals

The Hawaiian and Mediterranean monk seals are endangered species, and the Caribbean monk seal is apparently extinct. Mating occurs in the water and whelping occurs on shore. Sounds made in air by Hawaiian monk seals were described by E.H. Miller and Job (1992). In-air sounds include **(1)** a soft liquid bubble at 100-400 Hz, **(2)** a loud, brief guttural expiration below 800 Hz during short-distance agonistic encounters, **(3)** a roar, also to 800 Hz, for long-distance threat, and **(4)** a belch cough made by males when patrolling (Miller and Job 1992). Females and pups communicate by calling to one another (Miller and Job 1992). Other workers have described a bellowing call ("grunting bawl") uttered when a mother is defending her pup from an intruder, when a nonreceptive female is approached by a male, or when a seal drives another from the beach (Kenyon and Rice 1959; Kenyon 1981). On land, courting male monk seals may utter a bellow and snort when approaching a female. When in the water, courting males may utter a coughing snort in air. Underwater sounds have not been reported, insofar as we know.

7.3.7 Antarctic Seals

Weddell seals are very vocal underwater and produce as many as 34 call types at 0.1-12.8 kHz (Thomas et al. 1983b). Estimated source levels range from 153 to 193 dB re 1 µPa-m (Thomas and Kuechle 1982). The calls are directional, with the strongest energy beamed downward (Schevill and Watkins 1971b). Calls may be longer when other seals are calling (Terhune et al. 1994b). Seals from different areas share some calls, but some call characteristics vary with location on both a large scale (Thomas and Stirling 1983; Thomas et al. 1988b) and a small scale (Morrice et al. 1994). Calling rate is lowest during the southern winter and peaks in spring (K. Green and Burton 1988a). They (1988b) hypothesized that Weddell seals "sing" from the period of pupping to the end of mating in October/November. During the breeding season, Weddell seals also produce several types of in-air sounds similar to some of their underwater sounds (Terhune et al. 1993, 1994a).

Leopard seals emit at least four types of underwater calls at 0.1-5.9 kHz, and similar in-air calls (Stirling and Siniff 1979). These calls are rapid pulses, interpreted by humans as trills. Another study identified 12 call types, with several types of trills at ~0.2-3.7 kHz being common (Rogers et al. 1995). A third study identified nine call types, with some geographic variation (Thomas and Golladay 1995); they described some calls as sounding "like strumming a comb" and as "soft and lyrical". A captive leopard seal also emitted various weak ultrasonic sounds, most with peak energy at 50-60 kHz but with some energy up to 164 kHz (Thomas et al. 1983a).

Crabeater seals produce low-frequency underwater groans with harmonics to >8 kHz and high source levels (Stirling and Siniff 1979).

Both crabeater and leopard seals are especially vociferous during the breeding season and between 19:00 and 06:00 hours (Thomas and DeMaster 1982).

Ross seals make a siren sound sweeping down from 4 to 0.1 kHz and then back up to 4 kHz (Watkins and Ray 1985). Less often they utter a pulsed sequence. Ross seals also make these sounds in air.

7.3.8 Echolocation by Phocids?

Both harbor and spotted seals emit faint clicks with most energy at 7-16 kHz (Renouf et al. 1980; Renouf and Davis 1982). They suggested that the harbor seal echolocates, based on its ability to catch live fish in a dark tank. As noted above, a leopard seal produced various ultrasonic sounds (Thomas et al. 1983a). However, the predominant view is that echolocation by seals has not been demonstrated unequivocally (Scronce and Ridgway 1980; Schusterman 1981a; Wartzok et al. 1984). Prey capture by seals in dark water may depend on listening for prey noises (Moulton 1960) rather than echolocation.

7.4 Eared Seal Sounds

Sea lions and fur seals defend territories, mate, and give birth on traditional terrestrial rookeries. In-air vocalizations are parts of the displays used to establish and defend territories, attract females, and establish and maintain the mother-pup bond. California sea lions also use underwater calls to establish territoriality and dominance. The underwater sounds of other species have not been studied extensively.

7.4.1 Underwater Sounds

California sea lions, when underwater, most commonly produce bark sounds. Barks made when the seal is in the water, with its head above the surface, are transmitted into the water and have similar acoustic characteristics in water and air (Schevill et al. 1963). Most of the energy is at frequencies <2 kHz. These barks are accompanied by clicks that are also audible in air and water. When submerged, their sounds include barks, whinny and buzzing sounds, and click trains (Schusterman et al. 1966). All sounds have most of their energy below 4 kHz and are associated with social situations (Schusterman et al. 1966, 1967). Barks are used in aggressive situations and may be territorial and dominance displays (Schusterman and Balliet 1969).

Northern sea lions are said to produce clicks, growls, snorts, and bleats (Poulter 1968). *South American, Australian,* and *New Zealand sea lions* all bark and produce clicks underwater (Poulter 1968). These sounds are also made in air.

Northern fur seals produce underwater clicks and bleating sounds (Poulter 1968; Cummings and Fish 1971). Schevill et al. (1963) attempted to record sounds from a captive fur seal but were unable to find purely underwater sounds. *Juan Fernández fur seals* produced low-frequency clicks (Norris and Watkins 1971).

Poulter (1963, 1966) and Shaver and Poulter (1967) suggested that California sea lions may have echolocation abilities, but this was rebutted by Evans and Haugen (1963) and Schevill (1968a). Further evidence for the lack of active sonar in this species was provided by Gentry (1967), P.W.B. Moore (1975), and P.W.B. Moore and Au (1975).

7.4.2 Airborne Sounds

California sea lions haul out to breed in late spring and summer. Males defend territories, discontinuously, for a period of four months. Bulls on territories bark incessantly (Peterson and Bartholomew 1967). The rate of vocalization of a territorial male increases if an intruder approaches. Males also bark during courtship. Females with pups bark at intruders. Females also squeal, belch, and growl. For several hours after birth, mother and pup conduct vocal interchanges that last ~15-20 min (Peterson and Bartholomew 1967). Later, mother and pup are able to recognize one another by their calls (Trillmich 1981). The male barks have most energy at <1 kHz, female belches and growls are at 0.25-4 kHz, the female pup-attraction call is at 1-2 kHz with harmonics to 5 kHz, and the pup's bleat is at 0.25-6 kHz (Peterson and Bartholomew 1969).

Northern sea lion males remain on their terrestrial breeding territories in June and July and defend them with threat displays that include airborne vocalizations and some fighting. Threat displays include a roar and hiss (Schusterman 1981b). Females defend a birthing territory with vocal and visual signals. Vocal exchanges between mother and pup begin soon after birth and may be significant in maintaining the mother-pup bond (Schusterman 1981b).

Australian sea lion females are very aggressive in defending their young, emitting broadband roars and hisses (Stirling 1972). Females emit low-frequency pup-attraction calls. Pups emit higher-frequency female-attraction calls. Stirling also illustrates bark and threat calls from adult males.

Northern fur seal males fight to establish breeding territories but use visual and vocal displays to maintain their well-defined territories and to court females. Their calls are described as trumpeted roars, low roars, puffs, and clicklike vocalizations (Peterson 1968). Females and pups use individually distinct "bawls" to rejoin after separation (Peterson 1968; Insley 1989).

Southern fur seals, consisting of eight species of the genus *Arctocephalus* (Appendix 1), are very vocal when on land (Bonner 1981b). All species use similar sounds. A whimper or bark is the most common call and is associated with sexual arousal, affirmation of territory, social status, and recognition. A puff sound is a challenge; a low-pitched growl is a low-intensity threat; whines or moans are used by females as pup-attraction calls; and bawls are used by pups for cow attraction (Bonner 1981b). Stirling and Warneke (1971) gave more details, and reviewed what was then known about the occurrence of each call type in various *Arctocephalus* species. Later descriptions of in-air sounds from this group include Norris and Watkins (1971) for the Juan Fernández fur seal, Stirling (1971) for the Western Australian (= New Zealand) fur seal, and Trillmich and Majluf (1981) for the South American fur seal.

7.5 *Walrus Sounds*

Walruses produce at least four types of underwater sounds: clicks, rasps, a bell-like tone, and grunts (Schevill et al. 1966; Ray and Watkins 1975; Stirling et al. 1983). Base frequencies of most sounds are about 400-1200 Hz. The bell tone is preceded by a click and often includes tones at two different frequencies produced in sequence (Ray and Watkins 1975).

Only males make the bell tone (Schevill et al. 1966). Ray and Watkins (1975) interpreted stereotyped click sequences in combination with bell tones as a display song. In the Atlantic walrus, Stirling et al. (1987) found that the sounds of an individual walrus were consistent with one another, and different from those of other individuals.

Walruses are very vocal on land or sea ice. In-air roars, grunts, and guttural sounds are associated with agonistic behavior (E.H. Miller 1985). Calves use barks as distress calls, and possibly to inform the mother of the calf's location (see also Kastelein et al. 1995b). In older animals, barks are often used as a gesture of submission. Barks may be important in maintaining herd organization and in coordinating behavior (Miller 1985). Most airborne sounds have fundamental frequencies below 0.5 kHz, with most energy at <2 kHz. Whistles at 1-2 kHz also occur; they seem to be related to breeding (Verboom and Kastelein 1995).

7.6 Sea Otter Sounds

Sea otters spend much time in the water, but underwater sounds have not been studied. Airborne sounds of adults include whines, whistles, deep-throated growls, soft cooing sounds, chuckles, and snarls (Kenyon 1981). When stressed, otters may utter harsh screams (Kenyon 1981). They may produce a highly audible and visible display of vigorous kicking and splashing while patrolling their territories (Calkins and Lent 1975).

Maternal care occurs at sea and airborne vocalizations are important in maintaining mother-pup contact (Sandegren et al. 1973). When the mother dives for food, the pup vocalizes until she reappears. If the mother cannot locate her pup immediately on surfacing, she vocalizes and the pup responds. The pup also vocalizes in the presence of the mother, leading to nursing, grooming, or comforting. Most of the energy in mother and pup calls is at 3-5 kHz, but there are higher harmonics. Sandegren et al. (1973) recorded these sounds from a distance of 50 m in air and said that the sounds can be heard by humans at long distances, even over the sound of heavy surf.

7.7 Sirenian Sounds

7.7.1 Manatees
Manatees spend all of their lives in water, but little is known about the importance of acoustic communication. Underwater sounds of the Florida (=West Indies) manatee included high-pitched squeals, chirp-squeaks, and screams (Hartman 1979). Manatees were usually very quiet and made sounds only under conditions of fear, aggravation, protest, and male sexual arousal. Even when undisturbed, calves made sounds and these were usually answered by the mother (Hartman 1979). Mothers and calves that become separated apparently use acoustic communication to rejoin (Reynolds and Odell 1991:41).

Underwater calls of Florida manatees generally had fundamental tones at 2.5-5 kHz, but some were as low as 0.6 kHz (Schevill and Watkins 1965). The sounds were weak—only 10-12 dB above ambient at distance 3-4 m (Schevill and Watkins 1965). Duration was short, usually 0.15-0.5 s. Steel and Morris (1982) found that this species produced 10 types of sounds of short duration (0.06-0.4 s) and with average frequencies 1-12 kHz. Rapid amplitude and frequency modulation were common. Adult female sounds were lower in frequency than adult male sounds.

Sounds of an Amazonian manatee were similar to those of the Florida manatee, but at higher frequencies: fundamental at 6-8 kHz; strongest components at 12-16 kHz (Evans and Herald 1970). Some squeaks were accompanied by pulses.

7.7.2 Dugongs

Dugongs produce sounds at 1-8 kHz (Nishiwaki and Marsh 1985). Sounds are described as whistles, chirps, and chirp-squeaks, similar to those of manatees (Nair and Lal Mohan 1975; Marsh et al. 1978). Little calling occurred during feeding (Anderson 1982).

7.8 Summary

Underwater sounds of *baleen whales* (Section 7.1) are primarily at frequencies below 1 kHz and have durations from ~½ s to over 1 s and sometimes much longer. Some have fundamental frequencies as low as 20 Hz. Thus, the dominant frequencies in baleen whale sounds overlap broadly with those in many industrial sounds (*cf.* Chapter 6). Many baleen whale sounds are uncomplicated tonal moans or sounds described onomatopoetically as knocks, pulses, ratchets, thumps, and trumpetlike. Humpback whale sounds are more complex, and include extended songs. Bowhead whales also sing. Sounds with frequencies above 1 kHz are produced by humpbacks and some other species. Source levels of most baleen whale sounds are 150-190 dB re 1 μPa-m, apparently with much within-species variation.

Some *odontocete whales* communicate underwater with whistles at frequencies below 20 kHz; most of their energy is typically near 10 kHz (Section 7.2). Source levels for whistles may be 100-180 dB re 1 μPa-m. The killer whale produces whistles but most of its sounds are pulsed and at 1-6 kHz; source levels range up to 160 dB re 1 μPa. Most calls by the sperm whale and the phocoenid porpoises are clicks, some of which may be used for communication. Most odontocete sounds are detectable to humans with hydrophones at distances within no more than 1 km. However, some sperm whale clicks propagate well to longer distances. Most components of odontocete social sounds are above the low-frequency range where most man-made sounds are concentrated. However, there is broad overlap with the frequencies of many man-made sonars (*cf.* Section 6.6).

The echolocation capabilities of the odontocetes that have been studied are very well developed (Section 7.2.4). Echolocation pulses are generally at high frequencies—30 to 130 kHz or higher. However, killer whale echolocation signals have most energy at 12-25 kHz. The echolocation signals are projected forward of the animal in a narrow beam extending several degrees on either side of the animal's center-line. Peak-to-peak source levels in medium-sized odontocetes can be as high as 220-230 dB re 1 µPa-m, but the energy content is relatively low because the pulses are short and directional. The effective range in these species may be up to 100-350 m, depending on the target and environment. Source levels in some small species are lower, but pulse durations are longer. Specific functions of echolocation sounds in nature are little known.

Among *pinnipeds* that mate and pup on land, males typically use airborne calls as well as visual displays to establish and defend territories, to compete with other males for access to females, and for mating. Airborne calls are also used to establish and maintain the mother-pup bond. Underwater vocalizations appear to be limited to barks and clicks at frequencies ranging from <1 to 4 kHz (Section 7.3). In contrast, pinnipeds that mate in the water are often quite vocal during the breeding season. Most underwater sounds have frequencies from <1 to 10 kHz. Source levels reportedly range from ~95 to ~193 dB re 1 µPa-m, but few source level data are available.

All pinnipeds, the sea otter, apparently the manatee, and at least some cetaceans use sound to establish and maintain the mother-offspring bond. The calls appear to be especially useful when mother and pup are attempting to reunite after a separation.

Evidence for associations between specific underwater sounds and functions is, for most species, weak or nonexistent. Many marine mammals are gregarious, often coordinate activities, and often have to find one another in a visually limited environment. It is assumed but only occasionally demonstrated that these phenomena are mediated, in part, by calls. (1) Some sounds appear to be used for long-distance communication associated with reproduction, territoriality, feeding, and maintenance of group structure. (2) Over short distances, sounds may be used in social interactions involving aggression, dominance, individual identification, and mother-pup contact.

Sounds of many species of marine mammals have been described in varying levels of detail, but the source levels, directionality, maximum detection distances, and functions of most sound types are unknown or poorly documented. Many source level data were obtained from captive animals and it is unknown whether these data are representative of source levels in free-ranging animals. It is not possible to estimate maximum detection distances of sounds for which these data are lacking, nor to evaluate the severity of masking by man-made sounds.

CHAPTER 8

MARINE MAMMAL HEARING[1]

8.1 Introduction

We need to understand marine mammal hearing abilities in order to assess their abilities to detect man-made sounds, and to detect communication, echolocation, or other sounds of interest in the presence of natural and man-made noise.

The hearing ability of any mammal, marine or otherwise, is a complex function of at least six specific abilities and processes:

(1) *Absolute threshold:* The level of sound that is barely audible in the absence of significant ambient noise is the absolute hearing threshold. More precisely, it is the lowest sound level that is detected during a specified percentage of experimental trials. A statistical definition is necessary because, even for a single animal, the minimum detectable sound level varies over time. Also, threshold varies with frequency (Hz). The graph relating threshold to frequency is the *audiogram* (see Figs. 8.1-8.3, later in this chapter). The *best frequency* is the one with the lowest threshold, that is, the best sensitivity. The best frequency varies among species. Some species are more sensitive than others at their respective best frequencies.

(2) *Individual variation:* The auditory sensitivity of different individuals varies. Published audiograms for most marine mammal species are based on data from only one or two individuals. Animal-to-animal variation is to be expected.

(3) *Motivation:* Even in a quiet environment, sensitivity of a particular animal—as measured by standard psychoacoustical methods—varies depending on motivation. As a result, it is necessary to use a statistical definition of absolute threshold, as noted in (1).

(4) *Masking*: One of the main auditory tasks of any animal is to detect sound signals in the presence of background noise. Natural

---

[1] By W. John Richardson, LGL Ltd.

ambient noise includes contributions from waves, precipitation, other animals and—in some areas—ice (Chapter 5). Background noise can also include sounds from distant human activities (Chapter 6). In animals that are highly dependent on sound, the ability to recognize sound signals amidst noise is important in communicating, detecting predators, locating prey, and—in toothed whales—echolocation. The signal-to-noise (S/N) ratio required to detect a pure-tone sound signal in the presence of background noise is called the *critical ratio*. Critical ratios vary with frequency.

(5) *Localization:* Sound source localization is the ability to determine the direction from which a sound is arriving. Localization is important in detecting and responding appropriately to predators, prey, and other sound sources. Good sound localization ability is also related to good ability to detect a sound signal in the presence of background noise. When a sound signal arrives from a very different direction than does the dominant component of the background noise, the signal may be detectable even if the background noise is stronger. However, if they arrive from similar directions, the signal will normally need to be at least as strong as the noise at similar frequencies in order to be detected.

(6) *Frequency and intensity discrimination:* The ability to discriminate sounds of different frequencies and levels is no doubt important to marine mammals in distinguishing various types of sounds made by conspecifics, and in distinguishing sound signals from background noise.

Hearing abilities have been studied in some toothed whales, hair seals, and eared seals. A few data are available for sirenians (manatees). Direct measurements of the hearing sensitivity of baleen whales, walruses, and sea otters are lacking. Most of the available data on underwater hearing deal with frequencies of 1 kHz or above, and many relate to frequencies above 20 kHz.

Little information is available about underwater hearing at frequencies below 1 kHz, where many man-made sounds have their dominant components. However, several studies of low-frequency hearing are under way (e.g., Gerstein et al. 1993; Thomas et al. 1993; Kastak and Schusterman 1995; W. Au, personal communication). The few data on low-frequency hearing now available suggest that in marine mammals, as in other animals, sensitivity deteriorates with decreasing frequency below the "best" frequency. This is probably, in part, an adaptation to the typically high levels of natural background noise at low frequencies (Chapter 5). However, it is not known how closely baleen whales follow this trend. They emit low-frequency sounds. That, plus the anatomy of their auditory organs (Ketten 1991, 1992, 1994), suggests that baleen whales have good low frequency hearing.

Marine mammal hearing has been reviewed by several authors, notably Popper (1980a,b), Fobes and Smock (1981), Schusterman (1981a), Ridgway (1983), Watkins and Wartzok (1985), C.S. Johnson (1986), Nachtigall (1986), Moore and Schusterman (1987), and Au (1993). Bullock and Gurevich (1979) reviewed earlier Russian literature. R.R. Fay (1988) tabulated and graphed most pre-1988 data, and compared them with audiometric data from other vertebrates.

This review includes recent results not available to earlier reviewers and emphasizes topics relevant to questions about effects of man-made noise on marine mammals. These include sensitivity as a function of frequency, frequency and intensity discrimination, sound localization abilities, and masking. Some other fundamental aspects of hearing that are not directly related to our concerns are not discussed here. Omitted topics include the anatomical and physiological bases of sound detection, neural processing of auditory data, and temporal discrimination of closely spaced sounds.

8.2 Audiograms: Frequency Range and Sensitivity

Sensitivities of marine mammals to sounds of different frequencies are shown by audiograms, which are normally obtained by behavioral tests on captive, trained animals. However, electrophysiological methods also can be used to obtain data on hearing sensitivity in relation to frequency (Section 3.6.2). Some workers restrict the term audiogram to data obtained by behavioral methods; others use the term more loosely and refer to *electrophysiological audiograms* and *behavioral audiograms*. Behavioral methods can determine absolute sound levels that are both detectable and effective in eliciting specific behavioral responses. In contrast, electrophysiological or *auditory evoked potential (AEP)* methods produce data about the relative sensitivity of some part of the sensory or nervous system to various sounds. We emphasize results from behavioral testing methods, but electrophysiological (AEP) studies are also mentioned.

In most marine mammal species tested for hearing abilities, only one or two individuals have been studied. Thus, little is known about intraspecific variability. The most extensive data on individual variation are from the bottlenose dolphin and beluga: **(1)** Seeley et al. (1976) used a neurophysiological method to determine the high-frequency audiograms (5-200 kHz) of five dolphins. Results from four individuals were similar to one another and to other data for this species. However, one elderly animal had much poorer sensitivity. Ridgway and Carder (1993) subsequently found that high-frequency hearing loss is common in elderly captive dolphins. **(2)** Behavioral audiograms of six belugas have been reported; results were quite consistent (White et al. 1978; Awbrey et al. 1988; C.S. Johnson et al. 1989). AEP data from two more belugas were similar, but suggested that the range of best sensitivity might be narrower than suggested by the behavioral audiograms (Popov and Supin 1990).

Terhune (1981) suggested that enough data were available to talk of general odontocete (toothed whale), phocid (hair seal), and otariid (eared seal) hearing abilities. Such generalizations must be treated cautiously, as few individuals or species have been studied in detail, and there is evidence of some intra- and interspecific differences in hearing abilities. However, available data show reasonably consistent patterns of hearing sensitivity within each of three groups: small and medium-sized odontocetes, phocinids, and otariids:

8.2.1 Toothed Whales

Behavioral Audiograms.—Behavioral audiograms have been reported for seven species of small- to moderate-sized toothed whales (Fig. 8.1). A partial audiogram is available for an eighth species, Risso's dolphin (Nachtigall et al. 1995). These species include representatives of the oceanic dolphin, river dolphin, porpoise, and monodont groups, but not of the sperm or beaked whales. All eight species hear sounds over a wide range of frequencies (Fig. 8.1).

Hearing extends at least as low as 40-75 Hz in the beluga and bottlenose dolphin, the two species whose sensitivities at low frequencies have been reported in detail (Johnson 1967; Awbrey et al. 1988; C.S. Johnson et al. 1989). However, their sensitivity at these low frequencies seems quite poor (Fig. 8.1). Preliminary data indicate that the thresholds of a Pacific white-sided dolphin also deteriorate at low frequencies (Thomas et al. 1993; J.A. Thomas, personal communication). Although these odontocetes usually seem rather insensitive to low-frequency sounds, they may be more sensitive to some combination of low-frequency particle motion and pressure fluctuations when in the near-field of the acoustic source (Turl 1993).

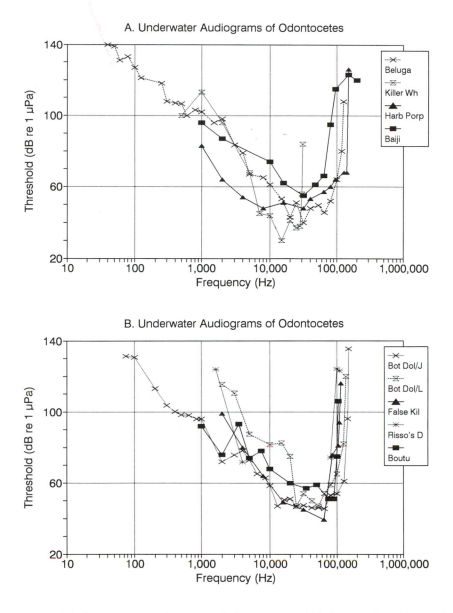

FIGURE 8.1. Underwater audiograms of odontocetes: **(A)** beluga (*n*=6—White et al. 1978; Awbrey et al. 1988; C.S. Johnson et al. 1989); killer whale (Hall and Johnson 1972), but see text; harbor porpoise (Andersen 1970a); Chinese river dolphin or baiji (Ding Wang et al. 1992); **(B)** bottlenose dolphin (Johnson 1967; Ljungblad et al. 1982b); false killer whale (Thomas et al. 1988a); Risso's dolphin (Nachtigall et al. 1995); Amazon river dolphin or boutu (Jacobs and Hall 1972). *n*=1 except where noted.

In contrast, the high-frequency hearing abilities of most small- to medium-sized odontocetes are exceptionally good. This is related to their use of high-frequency sound for echolocation. The hearing range extends up to 80-150 kHz in at least some individuals of all eight of the species tested. One killer whale whose hearing abilities have been reported in detail (Fig. 8.1A) differed from other odontocetes in that its upper hearing limit was only ~31 kHz (Hall and Johnson 1972). However, this was apparently an individual with impaired hearing. New data from other killer whales show upper frequency limits near 120 kHz (Bain et al. 1993; Bain and Dahlheim in Au 1993:33).

Within the range of "middle" frequencies where odontocetes have their best sensitivity, their hearing is very acute. When there was little background noise, the killer whale tested by Hall and Johnson (1972) could detect a 15-kHz signal of ~30 dB re 1 µPa, a very low value. The minimum thresholds were ~39-55 dB for six additional odontocete species shown in Fig. 8.1. Overall, the frequencies at which these seven species had best sensitivity ranged from ~8 to 90 kHz (Fig. 8.1). The best sensitivity of the Risso's dolphin could not be determined (Nachtigall et al. 1995).

Within the frequency range of optimum hearing sensitivity, variations in threshold of a few decibels may be artifacts. Artifacts can be caused by spatial variations in background noise and sound exposure level in test tanks, by the discrete frequencies and discrete intensity steps used during testing, and by changes in physiological condition or motivation within the sometimes lengthy testing period.

Below the frequency range of optimum sensitivity, thresholds increase gradually with decreasing frequency. However, estimated auditory thresholds for many species may be inaccurate, and possibly too high, for frequencies below 1-10 kHz. The relatively small sizes of the tanks used for most hearing tests cause complications, including echoes, standing waves, elevated noise levels, and nearby pressure release boundaries (Cummings et al. 1975). Such problems were suspected to have affected the results in several studies: Hall and Johnson (1972) on killer whale; Jacobs and Hall (1972) on boutu; Awbrey et al. (1988) on beluga; Ding Wang et al. (1992) on Chinese river dolphin; and Ljungblad et al. (1982b) on bottlenose dolphin. Some of the differences between the reported audiograms for two bottlenose dolphins (Fig. 8.1B) may be attributable to tank problems, combined with unusual test methods (Au 1993:33), in the last of these studies.

The limited and questionable data on hearing sensitivity of marine mammals at low frequencies (<1000 Hz) are a particular concern in the context of this book. Much of the man-made noise in the sea is at low frequencies (Chapter 6). More data are needed.

Electrophysiological Audiograms.—Auditory evoked potential (AEP) methods have been applied to several species of oceanic and river dolphins, porpoises, and a sperm whale calf. These results are based on neural responses received by electrodes implanted in the animal's brain or, in more recent studies, applied outside the skull. Audiograms based on AEPs have been obtained for some species whose behavioral audiograms have not been determined. These include dolphins of the genera *Stenella* and *Sotalia* (Bullock et al. 1968; Popov and Supin 1990), and the sperm whale calf (Carder and Ridgway 1990).

The shapes of electrophysiological audiograms are similar to those obtained behaviorally. In harbor porpoises, however, the lowest (best) threshold determined by AEP methods was at a much higher frequency than that determined behaviorally (~125-130 kHz versus 8-32 kHz—Voronov and Stosman 1983; Popov et al. 1986; Bibikov 1992; *cf.* Andersen 1970a). Also, AEP methods suggest that the harbor porpoise and boutu have two frequency ranges of best sensitivity and W-shaped audiograms (Popov and Supin 1990). Behavioral audiograms for these species have the conventional U-shape (Figs. 8.1A and 8.1B).

Electrophysiological methods provide data on the relative sensitivity of some part of the nervous system to different sounds, but do not provide data directly comparable to behavioral audiograms (Popper 1980a). However, AEP methods hold promise for examining the hearing abilities of marine mammals, potentially including beached or entrapped baleen whales or other animals difficult to hold in captivity (Ridgway and Carder 1983; Carder and Ridgway 1990; Dolphin 1995; Szymanski et al. 1995). AEP data can be obtained noninvasively with external electrodes.

8.2.2 Pinnipeds

Underwater Hearing.—Underwater audiograms have been obtained with behavioral methods for four species of *hair (phocid) seals*, including one monachid (monk seal) and three phocinid species (harbor, ringed, and harp seals) (Fig. 8.2A). Another phocinid, the gray seal, has been studied using AEPs (Ridgway and Joyce 1975). Behavioral audiograms have also been obtained for two species of

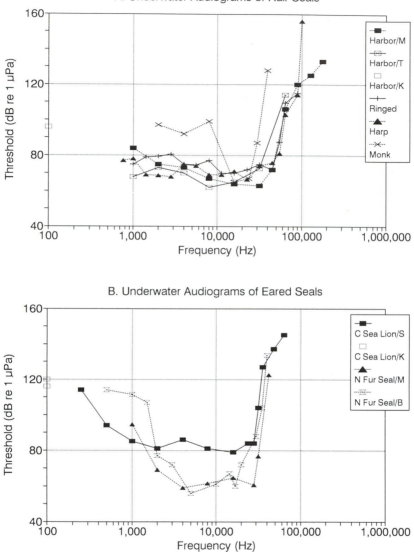

FIGURE 8.2. Underwater audiograms of pinnipeds: *(A) Hair seals*—harbor seal (Møhl 1968a; Kastak and Schusterman 1995; Terhune and Turnbull 1995); ringed seal (Terhune and Ronald 1975a, *n*=2); harp seal (Terhune and Ronald 1972); monk seal (Thomas et al. 1990b); *(B) Eared seals* (otariids)—California sea lion (Schusterman et al. 1972; Kastak and Schusterman 1995, *n*=2); northern fur seals (Moore and Schusterman 1987, *n*=2; Babushina et al. 1991). *n*=1 except where noted.

eared seals: the California sea lion and northern fur seal. In comparison with odontocetes, pinnipeds tend to have lower best frequencies, lower high-frequency cutoffs, and poorer sensitivity at the best frequency. However, some pinnipeds—especially phocinids—may have better sensitivity at low frequencies (≤1 kHz) than do odontocetes (Fig. 8.2A versus 8.1).

Phocinid seals have essentially flat audiograms from 1 kHz to ~30-50 kHz, with thresholds between 60 and 85 dB re 1 µPa (Møhl 1968a; Terhune and Ronald 1972, 1975a; Terhune 1981, 1989a; Terhune and Turnbull 1995; Fig. 8.2A). At frequencies below 760 Hz, the only data are for one harbor seal, whose 100-Hz threshold was 96 dB re 1 µPa (Kastak and Schusterman 1995). Some phocinids can detect underwater sound at very high frequencies if it is sufficiently intense—up to 180 kHz in the case of a harbor seal. However, above 60 kHz sensitivity is poor (Fig. 8.2A) and different frequencies cannot be discriminated (Møhl 1968a,b). The functional high-frequency limit is thus around 60 kHz for the species tested (Schusterman 1981a).

The three phocinid species for which more than one individual has been tested (ringed, harbor, and gray seals) show some intraspecific variability (Terhune and Ronald 1974, 1975a; Ridgway and Joyce 1975; Terhune 1988, 1989a). However, variation among audiograms of different phocinid species may be no greater than that among individual humans (Fletcher 1940; Terhune 1981).

Monachid seals include the Antarctic seals—Weddell, leopard, Ross, and crabeater seals—plus monk and elephant seals (see Appendix 1). Thomas et al. (1990b) found that a Hawaiian monk seal had a narrower range of best frequencies (12-28 kHz) than do the phocinids (Fig. 8.2A). Outside that narrow range its hearing was less sensitive than that of phocinids, and the high-frequency cutoff was lower—near 30 kHz. As noted by Thomas et al., it would be interesting to know if these results from one seal are characteristic of all monk seals, or of other monachid species that are more vocal than the monk seal.

The underwater hearing abilities of *eared (otariid) seals* are, in some respects, intermediate between those of phocinids and the one monk seal. The high-frequency cutoff is 36-40 kHz (Schusterman 1981a)—lower than for phocinids but slightly higher than for the one monk seal (Fig. 8.2). Sensitivity at low frequencies also seems intermediate, judging from the 100- and 1000-Hz data and the slopes of the audiograms at the lowest frequencies measured (Fig. 8.2). Sensitivity in the range of best hearing does not seem to differ substantially among the otariids, phocinids, and monachids (Fig. 8.2). Fur seal hearing is most sensitive, ~60 dB re 1 μPa, between 4 and 17-28 kHz (Moore and Schusterman 1987; Babushina et al. 1991), whereas the sea lion apparently is most sensitive, ~80 dB, at 2 and 16 kHz (Schusterman et al. 1972). The threshold of the California sea lion deteriorates from ~85 dB at 1 kHz to 116-120 dB at 100 Hz (Schusterman et al. 1972; Kastak and Schusterman 1995).

In-Air Hearing.—As amphibious animals, pinnipeds need to respond to airborne as well as underwater sound. In-air sensitivities have been determined behaviorally for northern fur seals, a California sea lion, harbor seals, and a harp seal (Fig. 8.3).[2] Also, relative thresholds of in-air hearing at different frequencies have been determined by the AEP method for California sea lions and a harbor seal (Bullock et al. 1971) and for two gray seals (Ridgway and Joyce 1975). Walruses react to airborne sounds at 0.25 to 8 kHz, but absolute thresholds were not determined (Kastelein et al. 1993).

In air, otariids apparently have slightly greater sensitivity and a higher high-frequency cutoff than do phocinids (Fig. 8.3; also Bullock et al. 1971). The cutoff frequencies of otariid hearing are similar in air (32-36 kHz) and water (36-40 kHz; Schusterman 1981a). In contrast, the in-air cutoffs of the harbor and gray seals are ~20 kHz, considerably lower than their underwater cutoffs around 60 kHz (Fig. 8.3; Ridgway and Joyce 1975). Based on behavioral experiments, some otariids and harbor seals seem most sensitive near 2 kHz and 8-16 kHz, and less sensitive at the intermediate 4 kHz frequency (Fig. 8.3).

In-air sensitivity of pinnipeds deteriorates as frequency decreases below 2 kHz. The most extensive behavioral data now available are from a harbor seal and a northern fur seal, extending down to 100 Hz in each case (Fig. 8.3). The harbor seal data may be confounded by high background noise at frequencies below 1 kHz (Terhune 1991). However, similar 100 Hz thresholds have been obtained for another harbor seal and a California sea lion (Fig. 8.3; Kastak and Schusterman 1995). AEP results from the harbor seal, gray seal, and California sea lion show similar trends (Bullock et al. 1971; Ridgway and Joyce 1975).

---

[2] Data from another California sea lion (Schusterman 1974) are now considered to be artifactual, and the reliability of the harp seal data for 1-8 kHz is uncertain (Watkins and Wartzok 1985; Moore and Schusterman 1987).

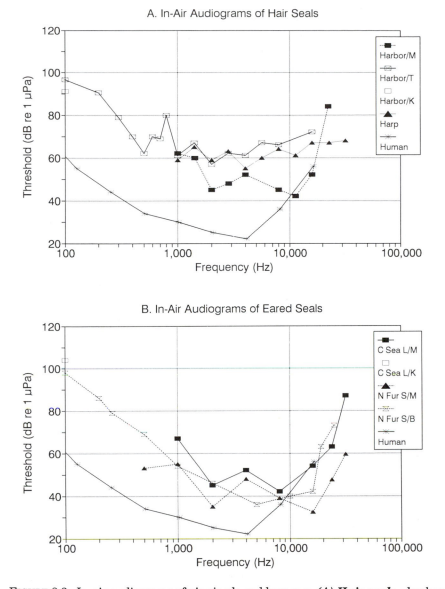

FIGURE 8.3. In-air audiograms of pinnipeds and humans: *(A) Hair seals*—harbor seal (Møhl 1968a; Kastak and Schusterman 1995; Terhune and Turnbull 1995); harp seal (Terhune and Ronald 1971); *(B) Eared seals*—California sea lion (Moore and Schusterman 1987; Kastak and Schusterman 1995); northern fur seals (Moore and Schusterman 1987, $n=2$; Babushina et al. 1991). Human data ($n=9$) from Sivian and White (1933) via R.R. Fay (1988). $n=1$ except where noted. Note use of standard "underwater" scale (dB re 1 µPa), which equals standard "in-air" scale (dB re 0.0002 µbar) plus 26 dB.

Pinnipeds all appear to be considerably less sensitive to airborne sounds below 10 kHz than are humans (Fig. 8.3). Pinniped auditory systems are adapted to hear underwater as well as airborne sound, probably compromising their in-air sensitivity.

The relative sensitivities of in-air and underwater hearing are difficult to compare. In this section, we have expressed hearing thresholds in dB relative to 1 µPa for in-air hearing as well as underwater hearing. In-air hearing thresholds are usually expressed in dB relative to 0.0002 dynes/cm^2 or its equivalent, dB re 0.0002 µbar (see Table 2.1 in Section 2.2). To convert from the latter units to dB re 1 µPa, one adds 26 dB. However, even when underwater and in-air thresholds are expressed in the same units, such as dB re 1 µPa, they are not directly comparable because acoustic impedance differs between air and water. To allow direct comparisons, it is necessary to convert the threshold values from pressure units (which are affected by the impedance) into intensity levels, in dB re 1 µW/cm^2 (Wainwright 1958; Terhune 1991). When this is done, otariids and especially phocinids are found to be more sensitive to sounds in water than in air (Møhl 1968a; Moore and Schusterman 1987; Terhune 1989a, 1991; Kastak and Schusterman 1995).

8.2.3 Sirenians

A *West Indian manatee*'s hearing sensitivity has been determined recently by behavioral testing (Gerstein et al. 1993). It heard sounds from 15 Hz to 46 kHz, with best sensitivity at 6-20 kHz. Sensitivity was good at the best frequency: 48-50 dB re 1 µPa. Below 3 kHz the manatee was reportedly more sensitive than any other marine mammal studied to date, and hearing extended down into the infrasonic range (15 Hz). Sensitivity at 10-32 kHz was also unexpectedly good, given that manatee calls are below 10-12 kHz (Section 7.7.1). The full audiogram is not yet available.

Some AEP data are also available. A West Indian manatee seemed most sensitive around 1-1.5 kHz, notably less sensitive at 4 kHz, and even less so at 8 kHz. However, there may have been some sensitivity up to 35 kHz (Bullock et al. 1982).

In an *Amazonian manatee*, AEPs showed that sensitivity was similar from 5 to 20 kHz. Sensitivity deteriorated above 20 kHz, but with some response up to 50 kHz (Klishin et al. 1990; Popov and Supin 1990). Another individual—a small immature—apparently had some hearing ability at frequencies as low as 200 Hz (Bullock et al. 1980).

The anatomy of the manatee hearing apparatus has been studied (e.g., Fischer 1988; Ketten et al. 1992). The latter authors found evidence of a "low-frequency" ear with a narrow frequency range, poor sensitivity, and poor localization ability. However, the preliminary data of Gerstein et al. (1993) suggest that manatees may hear better than suggested by this anatomical evidence.

Ketten et al. speculated that *dugongs* may have more sensitive hearing than manatees. However, we do not know of any specific data on dugong hearing.

8.2.4 Effects of Sound Duration and Repetition

In terrestrial mammals, signal duration influences the hearing threshold when the signal is shorter than 0.1-1 s (Clack 1966; R.R. Fay 1988). With shorter signals, threshold increases with decreasing duration. With longer signals, threshold is not affected by duration. Because many marine mammals produce brief click sounds, most notably the echolocation clicks of odontocetes, it is important to know whether their sensitivity to such sounds is affected by click duration. This information is also important in interpreting audiograms. Most behavioral audiograms for marine mammals have been obtained using pure tones played to the test animals for at least ½ s. As indicated below, these signals were long enough to avoid the complicating effects of short signal duration on threshold.

Johnson (1968a) investigated the effect of signal duration on detection of tones by a bottlenose dolphin. Tone pulses longer than 0.1 to 0.2 s elicited similar thresholds regardless of pulse duration. With shorter pulses, thresholds increased as pulse duration decreased. The threshold for high-frequency (20-100 kHz) single clicks of 0.2 ms duration was ~10-20 dB poorer (i.e., higher) than for sounds longer than 0.1 to 0.2 s (Johnson 1968a).

Johnson (1991) obtained similar results for the beluga. At pulse durations <0.1 s, thresholds for single tone pulses at 60 kHz increased as pulse duration diminished. As expected, thresholds for a series of brief pulses 10 ms apart were lower than those for single pulses of corresponding length. Thresholds for the series of pulses, like those for single pulses, increased as pulse duration diminished. Thresholds were lower for constant-frequency tone pulses than for frequency- or period-modulated tone pulses with pulse durations >0.1 ms, but the reverse for very short (0.025 ms) pulses (Johnson 1992).

Likewise, evoked potentials recorded in the cerebrum of the bottlenose dolphin increased in amplitude as tone duration increased (Bullock and Ridgway 1972). Also, evoked potentials recorded at most locations in the auditory cortex of the harbor porpoise increased in amplitude and decreased in threshold as tone duration increased (Popov et al. 1986).

In a Chinese river dolphin (baiji), the pulse duration effect extended to longer pulses. Thresholds were higher for ½-s than for 5-s pulses across a wide frequency range (10-96 kHz). Thresholds continued to increase as pulse duration diminished to 20 ms (Ding Wang et al. 1992).

Terhune (1988, 1989b) has done signal duration experiments on a harbor seal. At most frequencies tested, thresholds to tone pulses of various durations were similar as long as the duration was at least 50 ms, but thresholds increased as duration decreased from 50 ms. Thresholds for brief tone pulses or broadband clicks were 30-40 dB higher than the threshold for a prolonged pure tone at the most sensitive frequency (Terhune 1988, 1989b).

Thus, short-duration signals, such as echolocation clicks or other brief sounds, have higher thresholds than indicated on standard audiograms. However, Bullock and Ridgway (1972) found locations in the midbrain of the bottlenose dolphin that seemed specialized for processing very brief (<2 ms), rapid-onset, rapidly repeated, high-frequency (>30 kHz) clicks. These are all characteristics of odontocete echolocation signals. Given the importance of echolocation to toothed whales, their neural processing is no doubt highly adapted for detecting and integrating successive echoes (Au 1990, 1992; Johnson 1991).

Pinnipeds seem less responsive to click stimuli than are odontocetes (Bullock et al. 1971). However, even in pinnipeds, the repetition rate of tone pulses affects threshold. With pulses 0.05 s long, the average thresholds of a harbor seal in both water and air decreased (improved) by ~5 dB as pulse rate increased from 1 to 10 pulses per second (Turnbull and Terhune 1993). They note that the magnitude of this effect is similar in the harbor seal and humans.

8.3 *Frequency and Intensity Discrimination*

The abilities to discriminate frequencies and intensities are probably related to the ability to detect sound signals amidst background noise. Good frequency and intensity discrimination seem associated with good abilities to detect sounds partially masked by noise (Section 8.5). These discrimination abilities are doubtless also important in distinguishing and interpreting various types of calls, and in recognizing individual animals from their calls.

8.3.1 Frequency Discrimination

Frequency-modulated (FM) tones evoke greater neural responses than pure tones in odontocetes (Bullock et al. 1968; Ridgway 1980) and to a lesser degree in pinnipeds (Bullock et al. 1971). FM tonal whistles are important social signals for many odontocetes and some pinnipeds (Section 7.2.1). The greater response of odontocetes than of pinnipeds to FM signals may be related in part to the finer frequency discrimination abilities of odontocetes:

The frequency difference required to perceive two tones as being at separate frequencies, or a single tone as being constant in frequency versus frequency modulated, is the *difference limen* or *DL* (Herman and Arbeit 1972; Jacobs 1972). DL is computed by subtracting the frequency (F, in Hz) of the reference tone from that of the tone just perceivable as being different. In mammals, DL generally increases with frequency. To facilitate comparisons, the relative DL or *Weber ratio* is calculated as DL/F. When multiplied by 100, this gives DL as a percentage of base frequency (100·DL/F).

Toothed Whales.—Odontocetes have good frequency discrimination capabilities. Anatomical evidence is consistent with the hypothesis that the inner ears of dolphins are specialized to detect and discriminate high-frequency sounds (Wever et al. 1971a,b,c, 1972; Ketten and Wartzok 1990; Ketten 1994).

Psychophysical tests show that the bottlenose dolphin has excellent frequency discrimination throughout its hearing range with relative DLs of 0.21-0.81% from 2 to 130 kHz (R. Thompson and Herman 1975). Results from two individuals were similar (Fig. 8.4A). In both air and water, adult humans perform about as well as the bottlenose dolphin within the limited range of frequencies where both have been tested (Fig. 8.4A; Thompson and Herman 1975; Wier et al. 1977; Sinnott and Aslin 1985). Humans and bottlenose dolphins have the best frequency discrimination abilities of all the terrestrial and marine mammals that have been tested behaviorally (R.R. Fay 1988).

Russian workers have reported that harbor porpoises have even better frequency discrimination abilities than bottlenose dolphins, with very low relative DLs even above 150 kHz. These results have been

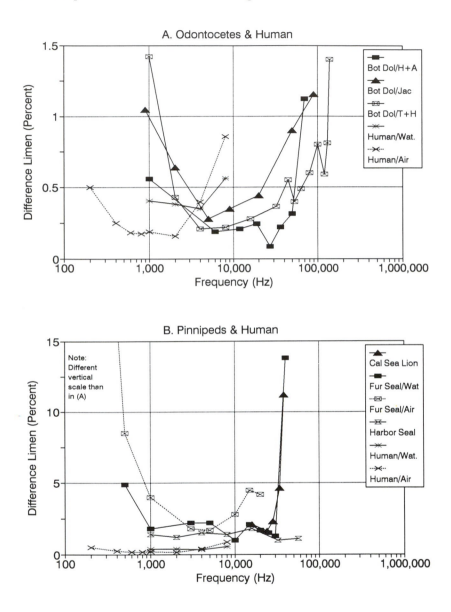

FIGURE 8.4. Frequency discrimination abilities of marine mammals and humans in water (solid lines) and air (dashed lines): *(A) Odontocetes*—bottlenose dolphin #1 (Herman and Arbeit 1972; Thompson and Herman 1975); bottlenose dolphin #2 (Jacobs 1972); human (in water, Thompson and Herman 1975; in air, Wier et al. 1977); *(B) Pinnipeds*—California sea lion (Schusterman and Moore 1978); northern fur seal (Babushina et al. 1991); harbor seal (Møhl 1967); human as in (A). Note the 10-fold difference in the vertical scales of (A) and (B).

questioned because of the methods used or the lack of information about methods (*cf.* Bullock and Gurevich 1979; Popper 1980a,b). More recently, Popov et al. (1986) reported that frequency shifts as small as 0.1% cause changes in evoked potential from the auditory cortex of the harbor porpoise, with the smallest frequency shift thresholds being at 120-125 kHz. These results are notable because of the small relative DL (0.1%) and the very high frequency where it was found. Replication using a behavioral testing method is desirable.

Pinnipeds.—Pinnipeds have less precise frequency discrimination abilities than do toothed whales (Fig. 8.4). The harbor seal's DLs in water are 1.0-1.8% from 1 to 57 kHz (Møhl 1967, 1968b). Neither harbor nor ringed seals seem able to discriminate frequencies above ~60 kHz (Møhl 1967; Terhune and Ronald 1976b). A California sea lion had relative DLs of ~2% at 16-28 kHz, but did not perform as well at 34-38 kHz (Schusterman and Moore 1978). A northern fur seal tested underwater had relative DLs of 1-2% at 1-30 kHz, with rapidly deteriorating DLs outside that frequency range (Babushina et al. 1991). When tested in air, the same fur seal had a narrower optimum frequency range (Fig. 8.4B).

A harbor seal was 1-5 dB more sensitive to descending-frequency than to ascending-frequency swept tones (Turnbull and Terhune 1994). If this is a general phenomenon in pinnipeds, it could be related to the types of calls they use. Calls of some pinniped species such as bearded, ribbon, harp, and Ross seals include prominent frequency sweeps (Section 7.3).

8.3.2 Intensity Discrimination

Intensity or level discrimination may be important in detecting sound signals in the presence of noise. Also, discrimination of intensities received by the two ears may be important in directional localization (Section 8.4). In humans, tones differing in level by as little as ~1 dB can be distinguished within the 200- to 8000-Hz range. Other terrestrial species that have been tested have poorer intensity discrimination abilities (R.R. Fay 1988).

Very few data are available on intensity discrimination by pinnipeds. The California sea lion can discriminate tones differing in level by as little as 3 dB at 16 kHz (Moore and Schusterman 1976).

Somewhat more information is available for toothed whales. Johnson (1971, 1986) suggested, from limited data, that a bottlenose dolphin detected level differences of 0.35 to 2.0 dB. Dubrovskiy (1990) found that bottlenose dolphins discriminated clicks differing by as little as 1-2 dB, depending on signal level. Bullock et al. (1968) reported that, in some dolphins, differences in evoked potential can occur with level differences as small as 1 dB. Similarly, Popov et al. (1986) found that, at 125 kHz, evoked potentials in the auditory cortex of the harbor porpoise differed when level changed by 3 dB at a low received level (40 dB re 1 µPa), and by as little as 0.5 dB at a higher level (60-80 dB). These data suggest that odontocetes have good intensity discrimination abilities, similar to those of humans. However, more tests at various intensities and frequencies, preferably using behavioral testing methods, would be useful.

8.4 *Directional Hearing and Source Localization*

The ability to localize sound sources is important in social interactions and in prey detection by echolocation or by normal listening. It is also important in detecting a signal of interest in the presence of man-made or other noise (Section 8.5.3; Kryter 1985:49, 76).

Humans and other terrestrial mammals listening in air can determine, with variable precision, the direction from which a given sound is arriving. The precision of localization depends on species, frequency, and other characteristics of the sound (Gourevitch 1980; R.R. Fay 1988). In air, humans and other mammals use differences in levels and arrival times of sounds reaching the two ears to determine the direction of a sound source. Intensity differences are most important at high frequencies and time/phase differences at lower frequencies.

The directional hearing ability of humans is much poorer underwater than in air (Feinstein 1966; Smith 1985). Sound speed is ~5x higher in water than in air, greatly reducing interaural time of arrival differences. Also, the path of sound to the middle and inner ear differs for humans in water as compared to humans in air. Bone conduction probably reduces the ability of terrestrial animals (like humans) to localize underwater sounds.

In whales, unlike humans, the auditory organs are largely isolated from the skull, enhancing directional hearing underwater (Dudok van Heel 1962; Fleischer 1980; Oelschläger 1986a,b). In pinnipeds the auditory organs are fused to the skull, suggesting a reduced underwater localization ability. However, pinnipeds have other adaptations for hearing in both water and air (Repenning 1972; Møhl and Ronald 1975; Ramprashad 1975; Terhune 1989a).

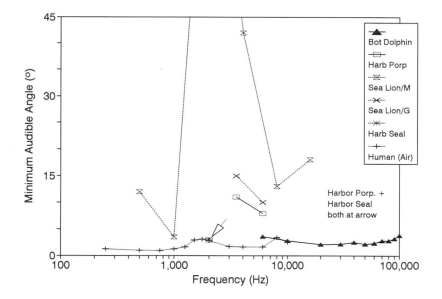

FIGURE 8.5. Azimuthal sound localization abilities for tones: marine mammals in water and human in air. See text for definition of Minimum Audible Angle. Adapted from R.R. Fay (1988:509), showing data of Renaud and Popper (1975) for bottlenose dolphin, Andersen (1970b) and [at arrow] Dudok van Heel (1962) for harbor porpoise, Moore and Au (1975) and Gentry (1967) for California sea lion, Møhl (1964) for harbor seal [at arrow], and Mills (1958) for human in air.

The *Minimum Audible Angle* (*MAA*) is normally defined as the smallest angle at which a sound source is recognizable as being off midline—off the animal's long axis. When two projectors on opposite sides of the midline are used to determine MAA, MAA normally is taken to be half the angle subtended at the animal by lines extending to the two projectors. However, the literature contains varying definitions of MAA in cases with no midline sound source.

8.4.1 Toothed Whales

Some toothed whales have good sound localization abilities. A bottlenose dolphin distinguished two pure-tone sources as close as 2° to 3° on either side of the midline with tones at 10 to 80 kHz (Renaud and Popper 1975). At 6 kHz and 90-100 kHz, MAA rose to 3-4° (Fig. 8.5). These MAAs were determined with the dolphin oriented toward the midpoint between two speakers. When the dolphin was turned 15° to the side, the MAA for tones at 40 kHz improved from ~2.5° to 1.5°

(Renaud and Popper 1975). At azimuth 30°, MAA deteriorated to 5°. Thus, MAA was optimal when tones arrived from 15° off-midline. This is consistent with evidence that the lower jaw, which is also angled relative to the midline, is important for sound reception in odontocetes (Norris and Harvey 1974; Popper 1980a). Localization ability of the one dolphin tested was similar to that of humans in air (Fig. 8.5; *cf.* Mills 1958). Humans have good localization abilities relative to other terrestrial mammals (R.R. Fay 1988).

The bottlenose dolphin's MAAs in the vertical and horizontal planes were similar (Renaud and Popper 1975). This was surprising because interaural intensity and time differences are absent in the vertical plane. Au (1993:51) discusses possible explanations.

Broadband clicks resembling echolocation clicks were spatially resolved with even greater precision than tones. The bottlenose dolphin had MAAs of 0.7-0.9° for clicks centered at 64 kHz (Renaud and Popper 1975). Clicks and other broadband sounds should be more easily localized than are the tones used in most tests. Clicks contain more acoustic information.

In these experiments, the dolphin's head was stationary. Head movement is expected to improve localization ability. Thus, free-ranging dolphins likely have even better localization abilities than these results indicate. Some tests have suggested that MAAs of dolphins can be <<1°, although doubts have been expressed about these reports (Bullock and Gurevich 1979:86; Popper 1980a).

Au and Moore (1984) studied the directional characteristics of a bottlenose dolphin's hearing at 30-120 kHz. The dolphin exhibited a cone of peak sensitivity centered about the animal's midline in the horizontal plane and directed 5-10° upward in the vertical plane. The angular width of the cone of sensitivity decreased as frequency increased, resulting in highly directional sensitivity at 120 kHz:

	30 kHz	60 kHz	120 kHz
Horizontal beamwidth*	59.1°	32.0°	13.7°
Vertical beamwidth*	30.4°	22.7°	17.0°
Directivity index (DI)	10.4 dB	15.3 dB	20.6 dB
* to the -3 dB points.			

The *Directivity Index* (*DI*) is a measure of the effectiveness of the acoustic receiver in limiting the effects of omnidirectional background noise. Echolocation sounds emitted by toothed whales are also highly directional (Section 7.2.4). In the bottlenose dolphin, the transmitting beam is slightly narrower than the receiving beam in both the horizontal and the vertical planes. Thus, DI for emitted signals exceeds DI for reception (Au et al. 1978; *cf.* Au and Moore 1984).

Evoked potential studies on bottlenose and river dolphins also show that their hearing is most sensitive when sounds arrive from the front (Popov and Supin 1990). Azimuthal variation in sensitivity increases with increasing frequency (Popov et al. 1992; Supin and Popov 1993). With high-frequency sounds, relative sound levels at the boutu's two ears depend on direction to the sound source. Interaural intensity differences apparently are involved in localization.

The MAA of the harbor porpoise to tones at rather low frequencies (2-6 kHz) was determined in two studies with unrestrained animals (Dudok van Heel 1959, 1962; Andersen 1970b). One porpoise did reasonably well at 2 kHz (MAA 3°), but the other's performance at 3.5-6 kHz (MAA 8-11°) was poorer than that of the bottlenose dolphin (Fig. 8.5). These harbor porpoises were not tested with clicks, which would probably be easier to localize, or at the high frequencies used for echolocation. Evoked potential data for this species show strong directional variation in hearing thresholds at 30-160 kHz; harbor porpoises were most sensitive to sounds arriving at angles within ~15-30° of straight ahead (Voronov and Stosman 1983).

8.4.2 Pinnipeds

Pinnipeds also have localization abilities, but they are less precise than those of bottlenose dolphins. The harbor seal can determine which of two underwater transducers is producing a 2-kHz tone when the sources are ~6° apart (i.e., MAA = 3°; Møhl 1964, 1968b). Another harbor seal distinguished clicks from two underwater sources ~9° apart (i.e., MAA = 4½°; Terhune 1974). In air, the MAA of this harbor seal for clicks was ~1½°, as determined by a different procedure. In air, localization ability was better for broadband than for narrowband noise, and very poor for pure tones.

Sound localization ability seems more variable and generally poorer for sea lions than for odontocetes and phocinid seals. Evoked potential tests on California sea lions revealed "only a weak directionality" of underwater hearing (Bullock et al. 1971). That species had an MAA of ~9° for low-frequency clicks (near 1 kHz; Moore 1975). With tones, the sea lion performed poorly at some frequencies and well at others (Fig. 8.5). At 1 kHz, the MAA for pulsed pure tones was quite good—4° (Moore and Au 1975). The poorer localization of short clicks than of longer tones contrasts with results from the bottlenose dolphin and (in air) the harbor seal, which localized clicks better than tones. Sea lions seem to have great difficulty in localizing tones near 2 kHz, but have some directional hearing ability at higher as well as lower frequencies (Gentry 1967; Moore and Au 1975; Fig. 8.5). They may localize based on interaural timing differences at low frequencies and intensity differences at higher frequencies (Moore and Au 1975).

8.4.3 Baleen Whales

Localization abilities of toothed whales and pinnipeds for sounds below 0.5-2 kHz are generally untested and may be less precise than at higher frequencies with shorter wavelengths. However, baleen whales have some ability to localize sounds at frequencies of a few hundreds or tens of hertz. Baleen whales sometimes swim toward distant calling conspecifics (Watkins 1981b; Tyack and Whitehead 1983) or toward sounds projected by underwater playback methods (Clark and Clark 1980; Dahlheim 1987). Also, some baleen whales swim directly away from a source of killer whale sounds (Cummings and Thompson 1971b; Malme et al. 1983) or industrial noise (Chapter 9). It is not known if these whales localized sound sources by the same psychophysical processes as used by odontocetes and pinnipeds. In some cases, the oriented movements by baleen whales were direct and had short response times. This suggests that they were not orienting solely by sequential comparison of intensities at different locations.

8.5 Auditory Masking

8.5.1 Critical Ratios

Hearing threshold audiograms (Figs. 8.1-8.3) represent the lowest levels of sound detectable in a quiet environment. However, the sea is usually noisy, even in the absence of man-made sounds. Background ambient noise often interferes with or *masks* the ability of an animal to detect a sound signal even when that signal is above the absolute hearing threshold.

Background noise levels are commonly measured on a *spectrum level* basis, representing the amount of noise energy at each frequency (per hertz). Spectrum levels are expressed in dB re $(1 \, \mu Pa)^2$ per Hz (Section 2.2). The amount by which a pure-tone signal must exceed the spectrum level background noise in order to be audible is termed the *Critical Ratio* (*CR*). CRs can be determined by presenting a pure tone to a test animal while background *white noise* is present (Fig. 8.6). White noise is broadband noise in which all frequencies in the noise spectrum are of equal level. In some tests, the white noise is limited to some range of frequencies above and below the test frequency. This has little effect on the results as long as the bandwidth of the white noise exceeds the masking bandwidth (Section 8.5.2). A CR of 20 dB at a particular frequency means that a tone at that frequency must have a level ≥100 dB re 1 µPa to be heard over white noise with a spectrum level of 80 dB re $(1 \text{ µPa})^2/\text{Hz}$.

Note that the background noise level used in estimating critical ratios is the level *per hertz*, not the overall background noise level. Animals often detect sound signals whose levels are similar to the overall noise level. The critical ratio is related to the width of the band within which background noise affects an animal's ability to detect a sound signal at a given frequency (Section 8.5.2).

Critical ratios tend to increase with increasing frequency, other than at quite low frequencies: ▸ In a bottlenose dolphin, a pure-tone signal at 6 kHz had to exceed spectrum level noise by 22 dB to be detected, whereas a 70-kHz tone had to exceed spectrum level noise by ~40 dB (Fig. 8.6A; Johnson 1968b). ▸ A beluga is the marine mammal whose CRs have been measured across the widest frequency range: 40 Hz to 115 kHz (C.S. Johnson et al. 1989). Below 2 kHz, its CRs in water were relatively constant, resembling those of humans in air (Fig. 8.6A versus 8.7). Above 2 kHz, CRs of the beluga increased with frequency. ▸ In a false killer whale, CRs were lower (better) in the 8- to 24-kHz range than for the bottlenose dolphin, beluga, or humans at those frequencies, and about as good as those of humans at their best frequencies (Thomas et al. 1990c; Fig. 8.6A versus 8.7). ▸ Similarly, in killer whales, CRs ranged from 20 dB at 10 kHz to 40 dB at 80 kHz (Bain et al. unpublished data, cited in Bain and Dahlheim 1994:244). ▸ Burdin et al. (1973) obtained evidence that, at 1-10 kHz, critical ratios of dolphins are also lower (better) than those of a human.

Underwater, critical ratios of two northern fur seals (averaged) ranged from a low of 19 dB at 4 kHz to 27 dB at 32 kHz (Fig. 8.6B). These values are a few decibels lower than CRs of the bottlenose dolphin at similar frequencies (Fig. 8.6A). In contrast, two ringed seals apparently had average CRs higher than those of all other marine mammals tested at corresponding frequencies (Fig. 8.6B).

Critical ratios are not greatly different for underwater and aerial hearing (Fig. 8.6 versus 8.7; Moore and Schusterman 1987; R.R. Fay

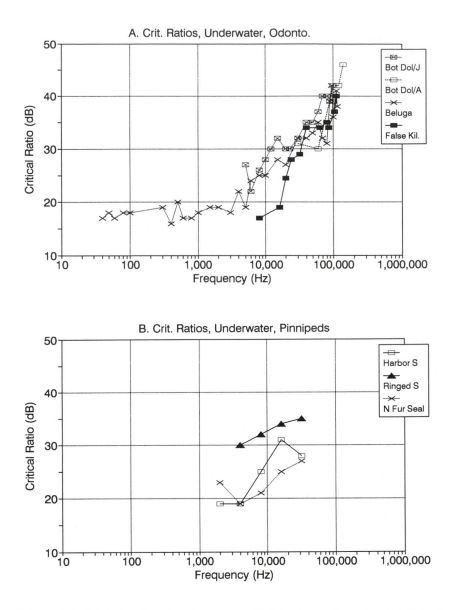

FIGURE 8.6. Critical ratios of marine mammals listening underwater: *(A) Odonto-cetes*—bottlenose dolphin (Johnson 1968b; Au and Moore 1990); beluga (C.S. Johnson et al. 1989); false killer whale (Thomas et al. 1990c); *(B) Pinnipeds*—harbor seal (Terhune and Turnbull 1995); ringed seal (Terhune and Ronald 1975b, *n*=2); northern fur seal (Moore and Schusterman 1987, *n*=2). *n*=1 except where noted.

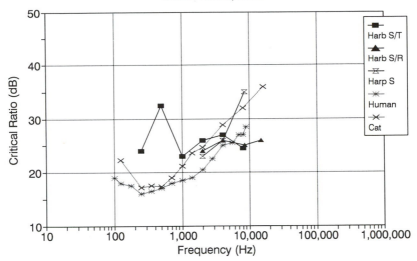

FIGURE 8.7. Critical ratios of pinnipeds and selected terrestrial mammals listening in air: harbor seal (Renouf 1980, *n*=2; Terhune and Turnbull 1995, *n*=1); harp seal (Terhune and Ronald 1971, *n*=1); human (Hawkins and Stevens 1950, *n*=4); cat (Watson 1963, *n*=4).

1988). CRs of one harbor seal measured in both water and air were similar in most respects (Turnbull and Terhune 1990, 1993). They note that this was to be expected, since "impedance mismatches and other outer and middle ear influences would alter the signal and noise levels similarly. Therefore, it would be expected that the critical ratios should not vary between the two media...".

Critical ratios of northern fur seals and a harbor seal, like those in humans and some other terrestrial mammals, may deteriorate at low frequencies (Figs. 8.6B and 8.7). In the one odontocete whose CRs have been determined at low frequencies, a beluga, there was no such deterioration (Fig. 8.6A).

8.5.2 Masking Bands

A pure tone is masked mainly by noise at frequencies near the frequency of the tone. Noise at frequencies outside this *masking band* has little influence on detection of the signal unless the noise level is very high (Spieth 1956; Kryter 1985:45*ff*). In humans and other terrestrial mammals, much effort has been devoted to determining the

A. Est. Mask. BW, Underwater, Odonto.

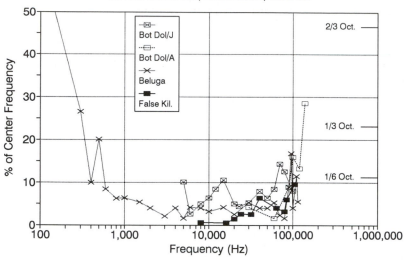

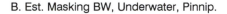

B. Est. Masking BW, Underwater, Pinnip.

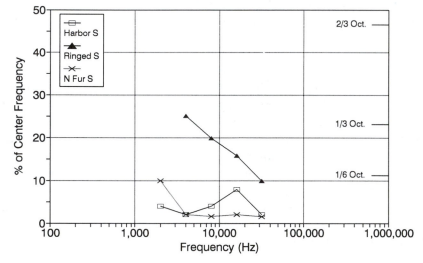

FIGURE 8.8. Estimated masking bandwidths of marine mammals listening underwater, expressed as percentages of center frequency and based on the equal-power assumption. *(A)* Odontocetes. *(B)* Pinnipeds. Sources same as for Fig. 8.6.

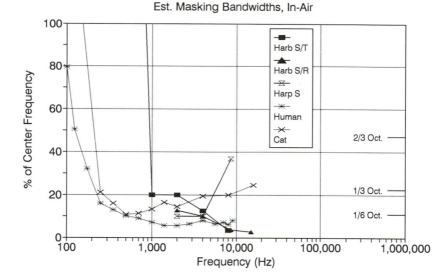

FIGURE 8.9. Estimated masking bandwidths of pinnipeds and selected terrestrial mammals listening in air, expressed as percentages of center frequency and based on the equal-power assumption. Note difference in vertical scale relative to Fig. 8.8. Sources same as for Fig. 8.7.

width of the masking band and its relationship to critical ratio (CR). Fletcher (1940) proposed the *equal-power method*. This assumes that signal power must equal or exceed total noise power in the masking band in order to be audible. If so, masking bandwidth (in Hz) is

$$BW = \text{antilog } CR/10 \qquad\qquad (8.1)$$

where CR is the minimum detectable level of a tonal signal in dB above the spectrum level of the noise. This equation gives the width of the band of white noise containing total power equal to that of the signal tone (Scharf 1970). For white noise, band level equals spectrum level plus 10 log (BW). Johnson (1968b), Terhune (1981), and others have used equation (8.1) to calculate masking bandwidths. Figures 8.8 and 8.9 show results of such calculations, expressed as a percentage of the center frequency of the masking band.

Based on available critical ratio data and the equal-power assumption, masking bands for marine mammals often appear to be <$\frac{1}{6}$ octave wide at intermediate frequencies; masking bandwidth is <11.6% of the center frequency (Figs. 8.8 and 8.9). However, at some intermediate frequencies, estimated masking bandwidth exceeded ⅓ octave for ringed seals listening underwater and a harp seal in air.

At low and very high frequencies, masking bands apparently widen, on a percentage of center frequency basis. This was so at low frequencies for a beluga in water (Fig. 8.8A) and a harbor seal in air (Fig. 8.9), and at high frequencies for a bottlenose dolphin in water (Fig. 8.8A). This phenomenon probably would be found in other species if they were tested at low and high frequencies. This effect is evident in many terrestrial mammals (Fig. 8.9; R.R. Fay 1988).

When attempting to calculate the maximum radius of audibility of marine mammal sounds or a specific man-made noise in the presence of background noise, it is often assumed that effective masking bands are ~⅓ octave wide (e.g., R. Payne and Webb 1971; Gales 1982; Miles et al. 1987). However, masking bandwidth may often be less than ⅓ octave (Fig. 8.8). If so, noise power in the masking band will be less than calculated from the ⅓ octave assumption, and the maximum radius of audibility may be greater than calculated. In contrast, at low frequencies, masking bandwidth may exceed ⅓ octave, as noted by Gales (1982). If so, noise power in the masking band will be higher than calculated from the ⅓ octave assumption, and maximum radius of audibility of low-frequency sound may be less than calculated. These arguments all depend on the validity of the critical ratio equal-power (hereafter *CR/EqP*) method—the assumption that a narrowband sound signal is masked when total noise power in the masking band equals or exceeds the power of the signal.

Masking bandwidth can be measured directly using tones or narrowband noise as the masking sound. The term *critical band* is used for such direct empirical measures (Scharf 1970). In terrestrial mammals, the equal-power assumption often provides only a rough estimate of the critical band (Zwicker et al. 1957; Scharf 1970; Kryter 1985). In humans, the critical band is ~2.5 times wider than the CR/EqP band at that frequency. This implies that humans can detect a signal a few dB below the band level of noise in the critical band, contrary to the equal-power assumption of Fletcher (1940).

Direct measurements of critical bandwidth have been obtained for a harbor seal and a bottlenose dolphin, and there are related evoked potential data from other bottlenose dolphins. For the harbor seal, directly measured critical bands in both air and water were narrower than those estimated from the CR/EqP method (Turnbull and Terhune 1990). Evoked potential data from dolphins also seem to show narrow critical bands at high frequencies (Supin and Popov 1990; Supin et al. 1993). In contrast, behavioral testing of a dolphin revealed very wide critical bands at 30-120 kHz: ~5.6 times wider than expected based on the CR/EqP method (Au and Moore 1990; Au 1993). The "2.5x" ratio between critical bandwidth and CR/EqP bandwidth, as found in humans, is not a general phenomenon (Au and Moore 1990; Turnbull and Terhune 1990). Based on the 5.6x ratio, the dolphin apparently detected high-frequency tonal sounds whose levels were ~7.5 dB less than the total noise level in the critical band (10 log 5.6 = 7.5)

Critical ratios of 20+ dB are not incompatible with negative or near-zero values of threshold signal/noise (S/N) ratios. CRs relate the level of a narrowband signal to the *spectrum* level of background noise ("per Hz") at frequencies near that of the signal. In contrast, negative or near-zero threshold S/N ratios, such as the -7.5 dB figure just mentioned, represent signal level relative to *total* noise level in a masking band tens, hundreds, or thousands of hertz wide.

Humans also detect signals such as tones and speech at negative S/N ratios (Miller et al. 1951; Scharf 1970). Structured signals such as human speech and echolocation click sequences of dolphins may be especially well detected because their frequency content and temporal features usually differ from those of the background noise. Redundancy and context can also facilitate detection of weak signals. These phenomena may help marine mammals detect weak sounds in the presence of natural or man-made noise.

Critical ratio data are valuable despite the uncertain relationships among CRs, critical bandwidths, and hearing thresholds. CR data help identify the frequencies that are least and most prone to masking. They also allow us to estimate the received level at which a narrowband sound will be just detectable given a specified level of broadband background noise. The masking effects of man-made noises containing strong tonal components are not as readily predicted using CR data. Behavioral and evoked potential data on masking of one pure tone by another are relevant in this situation (e.g., Johnson 1971; Turnbull and Terhune 1990; Supin and Popov 1990). However, few such data are available for masking by low-frequency tones, which are common components of industrial noise (Chapter 6).

8.5.3 Adaptations for Reduced Masking

Most masking studies present the signal and the masking noise from the same direction. The sound localization abilities of marine mammals suggest that, if signal and noise come from different directions, masking would not be as severe as critical ratio data suggest. The dominant background noise may be highly directional if it comes from a specific source such as a ship or industrial site. Even some natural sources of background noise, such as surf, ice, or wind-induced surface noise, may be strongly directional in the horizontal or vertical plane (Hamson 1985; Wilson et al. 1985). Directional hearing may significantly reduce the masking effects of these noises by improving the effective S/N ratio. In the cases of high-frequency hearing by the bottlenose dolphin, beluga, and killer whale, empirical evidence confirms that masking depends strongly on relative directions of arrival of sound signals and the masking noise (Zaitseva et al. 1975; Au and Moore 1984; Penner et al. 1986; Dubrovskiy 1990; Bain et al. 1993; Bain and Dahlheim 1994).

A study of directional masking at 80 kHz was done using an unrestrained bottlenose dolphin exposed to tones (Zaitseva et al. 1975). Tones were emitted directly ahead of the animal, and a source of white noise was moved to various positions around the dolphin. At 0° azimuthal separation the critical ratio was ~40.7 dB (Zaitseva et al. 1975). When the source of masking noise was moved to angles 7-180° from the source of tones, CR decreased progressively from ~35 dB to 11 dB. The reduction in masking is not as large with a stationary animal or at lower frequencies (Au and Moore 1984). However, the reduction may be even larger for clicks or other broadband sounds than for pure tones (Dubrovskiy 1990).

In general, the masking effect of background noise on dolphin echolocation is much reduced if the noise either comes from a direction other than that of the target or is omnidirectional. Tests with the noise source in line with the target are not representative of the most common echolocation tasks in the wild, where background noise will rarely come solely from the direction of the target. Thus directional hearing, coupled with the strongly directional nature of the echolocation pulses (Section 7.2.4), is an important adaptation to improve echolocation performance.

The beluga takes advantage of its directional sound emission and hearing capabilities while echolocating (Penner et al. 1986). When a noise source was placed in line between the whale and target, the whale bounced its echolocation beam off the water surface. This allowed the whale to concentrate its emitted pulses, and presumably its "receiving beam", in a direction slightly (~7°) different than that of the noise source. This allowed the beluga to detect the target when the noise level was too high to allow detection by conventional straight-line echolocation. No such capability was found in the bottlenose dolphin (Penner et al. 1986).

Toothed whales, and probably other marine mammals as well, have additional capabilities besides directional hearing that can facilitate detection of sounds in the presence of background noise. There is evidence that toothed whales can shift the dominant frequencies of their echolocation signals from a frequency range with much ambient noise toward frequencies with less noise (Au et al. 1974, 1985; Moore and Pawloski 1990; Thomas and Turl 1990; Romanenko and Kitain 1992). Some of these studies also showed that source levels of echolocation signals may increase when necessary to circumvent noise.

These data demonstrating adaptations for reduced masking pertain almost exclusively to the very high-frequency echolocation signals of toothed whales. There is less information about the existence of corresponding mechanisms at moderate or low frequencies, or in other types of marine mammals. Zaitseva et al. (1980) found that, for the bottlenose dolphin, the angular separation between a sound source and a masking noise source has little effect on the degree of masking when the sound frequency is 18 kHz, in contrast to the pronounced effect at higher frequencies.

Directional hearing has been demonstrated at frequencies as low as 0.5-2 kHz in several marine mammals (Section 8.4). This ability may be useful in reducing masking at these frequencies. In killer whales, directional effects on masking are evident for tonal signals at frequencies as low as 4 kHz (Bain and Dahlheim 1994). Masking was reduced by 7 dB at 90° azimuthal separation, and by 5-12 dB at 150° separation. Bain and Dahlheim also found some masking of tones at 8 and even 20 kHz by noise at 0.5-5 kHz. Masking was reduced for killer whale click trains and calls in comparison with tonal signals.

A rapid sequence of brief sounds is more detectable amidst background noise than is a single brief sound. This phenomenon is well known for echolocating dolphins (Johnson 1991; Au 1993). It also occurs during detection of short tone pulses by a harbor seal (Section 8.2.4; Turnbull and Terhune 1993). Animals can increase the effective range of echolocation signals or communication calls by emitting a closely spaced series of calls rather than a single brief sound.

Additional studies of masking are needed, including work on more species, sounds at low frequencies (<2 kHz), and directional masking.

Relationships between equal-power bandwidths computed from critical ratios, directly measured critical bandwidths, and threshold S/N ratios are especially in need of study. The demonstrated directional hearing abilities of some pinnipeds and baleen whales probably give them some improved capabilities, as demonstrated in toothed whales. Whether most marine mammals can adjust the frequencies and source levels of their various call types to increase communication range in the presence of noise has not been studied. Estimated source levels of some marine mammal sounds vary widely, suggesting that the animals might be able to tailor the source level to the circumstances. However, much of this apparent variation is undoubtedly an artifact of variation in propagation conditions between the source and measurement locations. It is not known how much real variation there is in the source levels of sounds from free-ranging marine mammals.

8.6 Baleen Whale Hearing

No psychoacoustical or electrophysiological work on the auditory sensitivity of any baleen whale has been reported. However, various species react behaviorally to calls from conspecifics and to certain man-made sounds (Chapter 9). Most of the man-made sounds that elicited reactions were at frequencies below 1 kHz. The reaction thresholds were usually rather high—well above the threshold for detection by instruments. It is not known whether weaker sounds were below the whales' detection thresholds, or were detected but too weak to elicit an overt behavioral response. We suspect the latter, given that reaction thresholds are quite variable, apparently depending on the perceived relevance or threat (Chapter 9). Gray whales detected killer whale sounds whose received levels were about equal to the broadband noise level (Malme et al. 1983). Field studies of the acoustic responsiveness of marine mammals can set an upper bound on the detection threshold (e.g., Dahlheim and Ljungblad 1990; Frankel et al. 1995). However, actual thresholds may be lower.

All evidence concerning the shape of the baleen whale audiogram is indirect: (1) Anatomical and paleontological evidence suggests that baleen whales are adapted to hear low frequencies (Fleischer 1976, 1978; J.C. Norris and Leatherwood 1981). The basilar membrane of the cochlea is much broader, thinner, and less rigidly supported than in odontocetes (Ketten 1991, 1992, 1994). (2) Fin whales react to 20-Hz calls from conspecifics (Watkins 1981b). (3) Observed reactions to airgun pulses and underwater playbacks of recorded man-made sounds show that gray, humpback and bowhead whales hear sounds with dominant components in the 50- to 500-Hz range (Chapter 9). **(4)** Humpback whales reacted to humpback sounds (400-550 Hz) at received levels as low as 102 dB re 1 µPa (Frankel et al. 1995). Bowheads fled from a distant, approaching boat when the broadband received noise level was as low as 90 dB re 1 µPa (Richardson and Greene 1993). **(5)** Humpback whales reacted to sonar signals at 3.1-3.6 kHz, beepers at 3.5 kHz, and "clinkers" emitting broadband pulses centered at 4 kHz (Lien et al. 1990, 1992; Maybaum 1993). Todd et al. (1992) suspected that whales reacted to "clinkers" (source levels 135-145 dB re 1 µPa) at distances up to 600 m, where the received level was presumably ~80-90 dB. **(6)** Watkins (1986) states that baleen whales often react to sounds at frequencies up to 28 kHz, but not to pingers and sonars at 36 kHz and above. **(7)** For each species, the frequency range of reasonably acute hearing presumably includes the frequency range of the calls. Most baleen whale sounds are concentrated at frequencies less than 1 kHz, but sounds up to 8 kHz are not uncommon (Section 7.1).

Thus, based on indirect evidence, at least some baleen whales are quite sensitive to frequencies below 1 kHz, but can hear sounds up to a considerably higher but unknown frequency.

Some or all baleen whales may hear sounds at frequencies well below those detectable by humans. The calls of most well-studied species include components at ≤50 Hz, and blue and fin whales commonly emit sounds with dominant components at ≤20 Hz (Section 7.1). These whales undoubtedly hear these types of sounds. Even if the range of sensitive hearing does not extend below 20-50 Hz, whales may hear strong infrasounds at considerably lower frequencies. In other mammals, the low-frequency portion of the audiogram slopes upward gradually as frequency decreases, typically by 20-40 dB per 10-fold reduction in frequency (R.R. Fay 1988). If hearing sensitivity is good at 50 Hz, strong infrasounds at 5 Hz might be detected.

Thresholds of most other marine mammals range between 40 and 70 dB re 1 µPa at the frequencies to which they are most sensitive (Figs. 8.1 and 8.2). If baleen whales have similar thresholds, but shifted to frequencies below 1 kHz, oceanic ambient noise rather than absolute detection threshold usually would limit detection. Even in quiet conditions (sea state 1) without any industrial activities nearby, average ambient noise levels in the ocean are above 75 dB re 1 µPa in all ⅓-octave bands below 1 kHz (Fig. 5.1B). Masking bandwidths may exceed ⅓ octave at low frequencies (Section 8.5.2), in which case ocean noise levels in masking bands would be even higher. Because average ambient noise levels tend to diminish with increasing frequency, baleen whales may not have evolved such acute hearing at low frequencies as have pinnipeds or especially toothed whales at their frequencies of best sensitivity.

Behavioral evidence indicates that baleen whales have directional hearing capabilities (Section 8.4.3), even though low-frequency long-wavelength sounds are probably most important for baleen whales. The baleen whale's ear is partially isolated from the skull. This may be important for accurate sound localization (Fleischer 1978). The relatively large distance between the ears of large whales may enhance their ability to localize sound cues (Gourevitch 1980). Norris (1981) suggested that baleen whales may be able to find prey concentrations by localizing the sounds produced by swimming fish. However, specific data are needed on all of these points.

We are not aware of any information, direct or indirect, on auditory masking in baleen whales. Critical ratio functions are similar among many vertebrates (R.R. Fay 1988; Figs. 8.6 and 8.7), and those of the baleen whales may be comparable. Baleen whales may also have lower critical ratios when signal and noise are angularly separated. Given the large size of baleen whales' heads, this directional effect may extend to lower frequencies than in other mammals.

Empirical measurements of auditory parameters are needed for baleen whales. It has not been practical to conduct psychoacoustical tests on baleen whales to obtain behavioral audiograms, or behavioral data on directional hearing or critical ratios. These tests are normally done on trained, captive animals. However, useful data on auditory parameters may be obtainable via evoked potential methods applied to beached or entrapped baleen whales (Ridgway and Carder 1983). Such data would have important limitations, but would be useful in assessing potential auditory capabilities of baleen whales.

8.7 *Summary and Comparisons*

The hearing abilities of a few species of toothed whales, hair seals, and eared seals have been studied in some detail. Data on the hearing abilities of manatees and walruses are limited, and hearing abilities of baleen whales and sea otters have not been studied directly. Hearing data are important in evaluating the abilities of marine mammals to detect various natural and man-made sounds. Hearing data are also needed to assess the effects that man-made sounds will have on detectability of natural sounds important to the animals.

Toothed whales are most sensitive to sounds above ~10 kHz. Their upper limits of sensitive hearing range from ~65 kHz to well above 100 kHz in most individuals. The sensitivity of many toothed whales to high-frequency sounds is related to their use of high-frequency sound pulses for echolocation and moderately high-frequency calls for communication. Low-frequency hearing has not been studied in many species, but bottlenose dolphins and belugas hear sounds at frequencies as low as 40-125 Hz. However, below ~10 kHz sensitivity deteriorates with decreasing frequency. Below 1 kHz, where most industrial noise energy is concentrated, sensitivity seems poor.

Sensitivity decreases as the duration of a *single* sound pulse decreases below ~0.1-0.2 s. However, toothed whales apparently have neural mechanisms specialized for processing *sequences* of short pulses, such as are used for echolocation. Toothed whales have good frequency and intensity discrimination abilities, as well as good directional localization capabilities.

Masking of sound signals by background noise has been studied under laboratory conditions in the bottlenose dolphin and beluga. Above ~2 kHz, critical ratios increase with increasing frequency, and are generally similar to those of the human at corresponding frequencies. At lower frequencies, critical ratios of the beluga (the only species studied) are unrelated to frequency. Critical bands in the bottlenose dolphin appear to be wider than predicted based on the equal-power assumption. This indicates that some odontocetes detect sounds weaker than the total background noise in the masking band. Most masking experiments have tested the ability of an animal to detect a sound signal in the presence of noise coming from the same direction. At very high frequencies (e.g., 80 kHz), masking is greatly reduced when the sound signal and masking noise arrive from different directions, or when the signal arrives from one direction but the noise is omnidirectional. This reduction in masking due to directional hearing is less evident at moderate frequencies (e.g., 18 kHz).

Baleen whale hearing has not been studied directly. However, there are indirect indications that they are sensitive to low- and moderate-frequency sounds. There are no specific data on sensitivity, frequency or intensity discrimination, or localization. However, gray

whales detect killer whale sounds whose received levels are about
equal to the broadband noise level, and several species seem able to
determine the direction of arrival of underwater sounds. The lack of
specific data on hearing abilities is a major limitation in evaluating
the effects of man-made noise on baleen whales. The data gaps are of
special concern because baleen whales apparently are more dependent
on low-frequency sounds than are other marine mammals; many
industrial sounds are concentrated at low frequencies.

Hair seals apparently can detect very high frequencies of underwater sound—up to 180 kHz in the harbor seal. However, the
upper limit of effective hearing is ~60 kHz, above which sensitivity is
poor and different frequencies cannot be discriminated. Underwater
sensitivity is about the same from 1 or 2 to 50 kHz. Within this range
of best underwater hearing, sensitivity is not as high as in toothed
whales. Sensitivity at low frequencies (e.g, 100 Hz) is better than in
odontocetes or eared seals. In-air hearing of phocinid seals is less
sensitive than underwater hearing, and the upper frequency limit is
lower (~20 kHz). The underwater hearing threshold of a harbor seal
increased as the duration of a sound decreased below ~50 ms, as in
other animals. Pinnipeds seem less specialized for processing click
sequences than are toothed whales. Their frequency discrimination
abilities also seem less precise. Harbor seals have reasonably good
directional localization abilities. Critical ratios are similar in water
and air, increase with increasing frequency (at least in water), and
probably are similar to those of other mammals.

Eared seals are similar to hair seals with regard to underwater
hearing sensitivity at moderate frequencies. However, their upper
frequency limit is lower—36-40 kHz versus 60 kHz. Sensitivity
decreases as frequency decreases below 2000 Hz, but strong sounds at
100 Hz can be heard. In-air hearing of eared seals is less sensitive
than underwater hearing, but the difference in capabilities between
air and water may be less pronounced than in hair seals. The upper
frequency cutoff in air is only slightly less than that in water (32-36
versus 36-40 kHz). Frequency discrimination and directional localization appear less precise than in toothed whales. Critical ratios of the
fur seal increase with increasing frequency, and are rather low (good)
relative to other mammals listening at corresponding frequencies.

Sirenian hearing has not been reported in detail. However, a
West Indian manatee was sensitive to frequencies ranging from infrasonic to ultrasonic (15 Hz-46 kHz). It was most sensitive at 6-20 kHz.

CHAPTER 9

DOCUMENTED DISTURBANCE REACTIONS[1]

9.1 Introduction

Many researchers have described behavioral reactions of marine mammals to human presence, boats, and aircraft. Although most of these data are anecdotal, they provide useful information about situations in which some species react strongly, react weakly or inconsistently, or do not react at all. No specific data on received sound levels are available for most of these incidents, but some reports mention the distances where reactions were or were not found.

During the past 15 years, several studies have been conducted specifically to determine the behavioral reactions of certain species of marine mammals to human activities. In most cases, received sound levels were measured or estimated. Some studies involved uncontrolled observations of animals exposed to boats, aircraft, seismic exploration, marine construction, offshore drilling, or simple human presence. Other studies included controlled tests of reactions to actual or simulated human activities. A few studies used both observational and experimental approaches to offset their differing limitations and advantages (see Section 3.6.3).

Almost all data on disturbance reactions, whether observational or experimental, have concerned short-term behavioral reactions. These studies often determined distances or received sound levels at which animals first reacted noticeably. Recognized reactions usually involved cessation of feeding, resting, or social interaction, and onset of alertness or avoidance. In pinnipeds, observed avoidance reactions commonly involved movement from haulout sites to water. In whales, avoidance may mean hasty diving, swimming away, or both. Various

---

[1] By W. John Richardson, LGL Ltd.

other changes in behavior have also been attributed to disturbance. In most studies, little or no information has been obtained about the duration of altered behavior after disturbance.

The significance of short-term behavioral responses to the long-term well-being of individuals and populations is rarely known. Most brief interruptions of normal behavior may have little effect on overall energy balance and reproductive performance. However, physiological reactions may occur even if no overt behavioral response is evident (e.g., MacArthur et al. 1979; Section 11.8.4). Uncertainties about physiological, long-term, and population consequences are common for all types of marine mammals and all sources of disturbance.

This chapter summarizes available data on reactions of marine mammals to noisy human activities: aircraft; ships, boats, icebreakers, and other vehicles; dredging and marine construction; offshore drilling and hydrocarbon production; marine geophysical (seismic) surveys; sonars; explosions; ocean science studies; purposeful scaring; and human presence in general. In many cases the only available data are anecdotal, and it is often uncertain whether observed reactions were attributable to noise or to other stimuli. Our emphasis is on underwater sounds, but for pinnipeds most data concern reactions of animals hauled out on land or ice to airborne sounds.

This chapter concludes by reviewing presently available data on tolerance, habituation, and sensitization. Behavioral habituation is the progressive waning of responses to stimuli that are learned to lack significance to the animal (Thorpe 1963). In contrast, sensitization refers to increasing responsiveness over time. The implications of the short-term behavioral reactions described in this chapter to the long-term welfare of marine mammals are discussed in Sections 11.5-11.7.

9.2 Reactions to Aircraft

Many observations of marine mammal reactions to aircraft, or lack of reactions, have been reported. In many cases, airborne or waterborne noise from aircraft was the apparent stimulus. However, vision was probably involved in some cases. Variable responses to aircraft are partly a result of differences in aircraft type, altitude, and flight pattern (e.g., straight versus circling). These factors can affect the spectral properties, temporal properties, and level of noise received by animals (Section 6.2.1).

Effects of sonic booms from supersonic aircraft and rocket launches are special cases because of their high levels and sudden onsets (Cummings 1993). Effects on some pinnipeds have been studied (Section 9.2.1), but we are not aware of any specific data for cetaceans.

9.2.1 Pinnipeds

There has been little systematic study of the reactions of pinnipeds to aircraft overflights, but many opportunistic observations have been reported. Most were anecdotal and received sound levels were rarely measured.

In general, pinnipeds hauled out for pupping or molting are the most responsive to aircraft. They react to aircraft sound by becoming alert and often by rushing or (when on ice) slipping into the water. The following paragraphs review the available evidence by species. In very few of these cases was it determined that the reaction was specifically to aircraft noise as opposed to visual cues.

Harbor seals often temporarily leave pupping beaches when aircraft fly over, and do not always haul out at the same site when they return to land (B.W. Johnson 1977). Newborn pups are unable to follow their mothers into the water and permanent separation may result. Johnson (1977) estimated that low-flying aircraft may have been responsible for the deaths of more than 10% of ~2000 pups born on one Alaskan island in 1976. Aircraft flying below 120 m altitude nearly always caused seals to vacate the beaches, sometimes for 2+ hours. Responses to overflights at altitudes of 120-305 m varied. Aircraft were more disturbing on calm days, when at low altitudes, and after recent disturbances (sensitization). Helicopters and large aircraft were reportedly more disturbing than small aircraft.

Other studies of harbor seals have shown reactions to aircraft, but not the mortality noted by Johnson (1977). In Glacier Bay, Alaska, harbor seals usually reacted strongly to small aircraft at altitudes below ~61 m; overflights above 76 m elicited only minor reactions (Hoover 1988). Harbor seals contaminated by oil often stayed on haulouts during low-altitude overflights (Frost and Lowry 1993).

In California, harbor seals reacted with alert posture and often with rapid movement, especially when the aircraft was visible (Bowles and Stewart 1980). Seals rushed into the water in response to some sonic booms and to a few of the overflights by light aircraft, jets above 244 m, and helicopters below 305 m. Sometimes the seals did not return to land until the next day, although they more commonly returned the same day. Similar observations have been obtained during rocket launches (Stewart 1993; Stewart et al. 1993). Likewise, Osborn (1985), also working in California, found that aircraft flying below 150 m altitude over harbor seals caused alert reactions and, in 2 of 11 cases, rapid movement into the water.

Harbor seals can habituate to frequent overflights. Many aircraft using Vancouver International Airport fly low over a haulout site. These seals show little or no reaction (M. Bigg, in S.R. Johnson et al. 1989:53).

Spotted seals pup on the ice in the Bering Sea in spring, and haul out on beaches in summer; they seem very sensitive to aircraft. Spotted seals on ice react at considerable distances by "erratically racing across floes and eventually diving off" (Burns and Harbo, in Cowles et al. 1981). This might result in mother-pup separation. Spotted seals on beaches move into the water when a survey aircraft flies over at altitudes up to 305-760 m or more, and at lateral distances up to 1 km (Frost and Lowry 1990; Frost et al. 1993; Rugh et al. 1993). This occurs despite frequent exposure to aircraft at low altitude. However, spotted seals apparently accommodated to the extent that they returned to the beaches quickly after the aircraft departed.

Ringed seals and *bearded seals* hauled out on the ice often dive when approached by a low-flying aircraft or helicopter (e.g., Burns and Harbo 1972; Burns and Frost 1979; Alliston 1981), but do not always do so (e.g., Burns et al. 1982). Specific details on range and altitude effects are lacking. For bearded seals, helicopters may be more disturbing than fixed-wing aircraft (Burns and Frost 1979).

Reactions of ringed seals concealed in subnivean lairs (below snow on ice) varied with aircraft altitude and lateral distance (Kelly et al. 1986). Radio-telemetry showed that some seals left the ice when a helicopter was at an altitude ≤305 m and within 2 km lateral distance. The noise received in a subnivean lair is reduced by snow (Cummings and Holliday 1983). Counts of ringed seal calls in water suggested that seal abundance in one area subjected to low-flying aircraft and other disturbances was similar to that in less disturbed areas (Calvert and Stirling 1985).

Northern elephant seals and *California sea lions* at San Miguel Island, California, seemed less responsive than harbor seals (Bowles and Stewart 1980). Jets above altitude 305 m produced no reaction; those below 305 m usually caused limited movement but no major reaction. Light aircraft flying directly overhead at altitudes ≤150-

180 m often elicited alert reactions and, in sea lions, movement (B.S. Stewart, personal communication, 1994). Helicopters above 305 m usually caused no observable response; those below 305 m always caused the pinnipeds to raise their heads, often caused some movement, and occasionally caused "rushes" by some animals into the water. Helicopters that are turning or hovering sometimes caused mass movements even at ranges ≥1.6 km and altitudes ≥300 m if winds were calm or blowing from the helicopter toward the pinnipeds (B.S. Stewart, pers. comm., 1994). Sonic booms caused a startle reaction involving some movement into the water, and noise from a distant exploding rocket caused most sea lions (but not elephant seals) to stampede (Stewart et al. 1993). Bowles and Stewart (1980) suspected that disturbance-induced stampedes or mother-pup separations may cause increased mortality. However, observations during actual sonic booms and tests with a carbide cannon simulating sonic booms (Section 9.12) provided no evidence of mortality.

Northern sea lions on haulouts exhibit variable reactions to aircraft (Calkins 1979). Approaching aircraft usually frighten some or all animals into the water. Immatures and pregnant females are more likely to enter the water than are territorial males and females with small pups. Withrow et al. (1985) saw 1000+ animals stampede off a beach in response to a Bell 205 helicopter >1.6 km away.

Northern fur seals on the Pribilof Islands sometimes stampede from rookeries and haulouts in response to low-level overflights; stampedes are especially likely after July and among nonbreeding fur seals (R.L. Gentry, in Herter and Koski 1988). Fur seals usually seem startled by sonic booms, and sometimes stampede into the water (A. Antonelis, in S.R. Johnson et al. 1989). However, stampedes do not always occur after overflights or sonic booms, and mortality apparently has not been noted (S.R. Johnson et al. 1989).

Walrus responses to overflights of terrestrial haulout sites vary with range, aircraft type, flight pattern, age, sex, and group size. Some Atlantic walruses approached by a small (Bell 206) helicopter raised their heads when the helicopter was over 2½ km away (Salter 1978, 1979). Some oriented toward or rushed into the water when the helicopter came within 1.3 km at altitude <150 m. DeHavilland Otter aircraft (piston engine) caused escape reactions by walruses at horizontal ranges <1 km during overflights at altitudes as high as 1000-1500 m (Salter 1979). Adult females, calves, and immatures were more likely than adult males to enter the water during disturbance.

Walrus reactions seem quite variable (Fay et al. 1984). Small herds may be more easily alarmed than large ones (Banfield et al. 1955). Some walruses exposed to repeated aircraft disturbance at haulout sites close to airstrips seem more tolerant of aircraft noise (i.e., partially habituated; D.G. Roseneau, in Malme et al. 1989). S.R. Johnson et al. (1989) summarized these and other similar accounts of the variable reactions of walruses to aircraft.

Severe disturbance may cause stampedes into the water by all walruses at a haulout site. Loughrey (1959) described calves crushed to death by stampeding walruses. Tomilin and Kibal'chich (in Fay 1981) reported that an overflight at 150 m by a medium-sized aircraft (IL-14) caused a stampede in which 21 calves were crushed and two fetuses aborted. D. Fisher, in S.R. Johnson et al. (1989), described a stampede in response to a low-flying aircraft; 2 or 3 of 4000-5000 animals were killed. Ovsyanikov et al. (1994) reported that an over-flight at altitude 800 m resulted in the deaths of 102 walruses of all sex and age classes at Wrangel Island. Many traumatized walruses left the rookery but may have died later. Ovsyanikov et al. concluded that "More efficient protection of walrus rookeries in Russia is an urgent need."

Brueggeman et al. (1990:3-52) stated that ~12% of 34 walrus groups observed in open waters of the Chukchi Sea and 38% of 229 groups on pack ice reacted to a Twin Otter survey aircraft, usually near 305 m altitude. Groups in the water reacted by creating a no-ticeable splash when diving; those on the ice "escaped" into the water. Fay et al. (1984) observed that walruses hauled out on open pack ice in July left the ice when a helicopter approached within 400-600 m flying upwind, or 1000-1800 m flying downwind.

In *summary*, pinnipeds hauled out on land or ice react to the air-borne sound and/or sight of aircraft by becoming alert and, in many cases, by rushing into the water. They tend to react most strongly if the aircraft is flying low, passes nearly overhead, and causes abrupt changes in sounds. Helicopters may be more disturbing than fixed-wing aircraft, but the lack of data on sound exposure levels makes this difficult to evaluate. Responsiveness can vary according to stage of the breeding cycle. Partial habituation probably occurs under some conditions. However, repeated exposure of harbor seals to aircraft may result in increased rather than reduced responsiveness. Stam-pedes triggered by aircraft sometimes increase pup mortality due to crushing or increased rates of pup abandonment, but direct mortality has rarely been documented.

These observations almost all relate to pinnipeds on land or ice. There are few specific data on reactions of pinnipeds in water to either airborne or waterborne sounds from aircraft. During aerial surveys, seals in open water often dive when overflown by an aircraft at low altitude. However, some ringed seals surfaced within 20-30 m of ice pans only a few minutes after a Bell 212 helicopter had landed and shut down no more than 40 m from the ice edge (C.R. Greene, personal observations). Walruses in the water occasionally dive hastily when an aircraft passes overhead at 305 m altitude (Brueggeman et al. 1990). More definitive statements cannot be made because behavior before and after disturbances, and reactions to high-altitude flights, cannot be observed from the disturbing aircraft.

9.2.2 Toothed Whales

Reactions of toothed whales to aircraft have been reported less often than reactions of pinnipeds. This perhaps indicates that the airborne sounds (and visual stimuli) from an aircraft are less relevant to toothed whales and other marine mammals in the water than to pinnipeds hauled out on land or ice. Cetaceans reacting to aircraft may dive, slap the water with flukes or flippers, or swim away from the aircraft track. Their activity during the overflight sometimes seems to influence whether or not their behavior is disturbed. Insofar as we know, there are no data on received sound levels that do and do not elicit disturbance reactions by toothed whales.

Belugas did not react to an aircraft of unspecified type flying at 500 m, but when it was at 150-200 m they dove for longer periods, had shorter surface intervals, and sometimes swam away (Bel'kovich 1960; Kleinenberg et al. 1964). Feeding belugas were reportedly less prone to disturbance, whereas lone animals dove even when the aircraft was at 500 m. Singles and small groups often dove under ice floes when the aircraft descended. At least some of these observations off Russia were in deep water. Belugas in offshore waters near Alaska in spring have variable reactions to a turbine helicopter or fixed-wing aircraft (Richardson et al. 1991a). Some show no overt response even if the aircraft is within 100-200 m. Others look upward, dive abruptly, or turn sharply away when it flies over at altitudes up to 460 m.

Belugas in shallow summering areas also react to aircraft, often by swimming away or diving (Fraker 1978; Fraker and Fraker 1979;

Finley 1982; Finley et al. 1982; Gales 1982; Caron and Smith 1990). Belugas in the St. Lawrence estuary dove suddenly when jet fighters and a Bell 206 helicopter flew overhead at "low" and 305 m altitude, respectively (Macfarlane 1981; Sergeant and Hoek 1988). When Inupiat hunters concluded that low-flying aircraft were preventing belugas from entering an Alaskan bay, the timing of aircraft traffic was adjusted to reduce the suspected interference (Burns and Seaman 1985).

Narwhals dove hastily as a Bell 206 helicopter approached at altitudes below 244 m and, to a lesser degree, at 305 m (Kingsley et al. 1994). Also, some narwhal groups dived 0.5-1 km ahead of a small fixed-wing aircraft (Partenavia Observer) approaching at 305 m altitude, apparently in response to the aircraft (Born et al. 1994).

Data on reactions of other species of toothed whales to aircraft are meager. Some *sperm whales* showed no obvious reaction to a helicopter at very low altitude unless they were in its downwash (R. Clarke 1956). Similar observations have been obtained for subadult male sperm whales off New Zealand (B. Würsig, pers. obs.). Gambell (1968) mentions that sperm whales seemed unaware of a Cessna 310 observation aircraft, usually at 150 m altitude. Mullin et al. (1991) reported that some sperm whales remained at the surface when a Twin Otter flew over at 150-230 m altitude, but others dove immediately. Mullin et al. found that dwarf and pygmy sperm whales usually dove. *Beaked whales* seem especially sensitive to aircraft overflights, usually diving immediately and sometimes remaining submerged for long periods thereafter (CeTAP 1982; Dohl et al. 1983; Mullin et al. 1991).

Dall's *porpoises* often dove, moved erratically, or rolled to look upward when a Bell 205 helicopter flew over at 215-365 m (Withrow et al. 1985). About 8-9% of Dall's and harbor porpoises changed direction suddenly or dove hastily when overflown by a Twin Otter aircraft at 60 m altitude; only ~2% of the *delphinids* showed such reactions (G.A. Green et al. 1992). Dolphins also did not seem to react to a Bell 204 helicopter at 366-549 m altitude (D. Au and Perryman 1982; R.P. Hewitt 1985 and pers. comm.). Mullin et al. (1991) noted that bottlenose and most other dolphins generally did not react to a survey aircraft unless its shadow passed over them, whereupon they dove suddenly. However, spinner dolphins sometimes seemed more sensitive, diving when the aircraft circled overhead. Hawaiian spinner dolphins resting in nearshore bays dive abruptly in response to a small Cessna 172 aircraft at 300 m altitude (B. Würsig, pers. obs.).

9.2.3 Baleen Whales

Bowhead whales reacted to a circling piston-engined aircraft frequently when it was at ≤305 m altitude, infrequently when it was at 457 m, and rarely when it was at ≥610 m (Richardson et al. 1985b,c). The most common reactions to the Britten-Norman Islander aircraft were a hasty dive, a turn away from the aircraft, or dispersal away from the area being circled. These reactions were most common when whales were in shallow water, where the aircraft sound level received underwater is often higher than in deep water (Section 4.7). When the Islander aircraft circled the same whales at 305 m altitude as well as 457 or 610 m, intervals between successive respirations averaged less when the aircraft was at the lower altitude. Relative roles of sound and visual stimuli in eliciting the reactions were unknown.

The responsiveness of bowheads to aircraft is variable, apparently depending on behavioral state and habitat. Bowheads in shallow water and resting bowheads seem most responsive. Bowheads actively feeding, socializing, or mating seem less so (Richardson and Malme 1993). Repeated low-altitude (150 m) overflights during aerial photogrammetry studies of feeding bowheads sometimes elicit abrupt turns and hasty dives. However, the photographed individuals are often found in the same areas on subsequent days (Koski et al. 1988). Thus, overflights do not displace many (if any) bowheads from feeding areas.

Fewer data on reactions of bowheads to aircraft have been collected during spring and especially winter. Responsiveness in spring is similar to that in summer-autumn (Marquette et al. 1982; Richardson et al. 1991a). In winter, bowheads often dove during low-altitude (150-250 m) overflights by a large P-3 patrol aircraft (Ljungblad 1986).

Bowheads react similarly to helicopters and fixed-wing aircraft. Helicopters often elicit no overt reaction, but sometimes result in an abrupt turn or hasty dive. This occurs during both spring (Dahlheim 1981; Richardson et al. 1991a) and summer (Berzin and Doroshenko 1981; Richardson et al. 1985c).

Right whales often seem to tolerate a light single-engine aircraft circling overhead. Watkins and Schevill (1976, 1979a) observed feeding behavior of northern right whales by circling 50-300 m overhead in a light aircraft. Some disturbance may occur when the aircraft is below 150 m (Watkins and Moore 1983). Payne et al. (1983) state that southern right whales off Argentina rarely reacted strongly to a light aircraft circling at 65-150 m. A few, probably <2%, swam rapidly or dove as the aircraft came overhead. However, most did not show such a clear startle reaction, and reactions were brief. Off Australia, southern right whales showed no overt response to single overflights by a light aircraft but dives by adults were longer and surfacings shorter when the aircraft circled at 150 m (Ling and Needham [1990]).

Payne et al. (1983) noted that single southern right whales were more likely to react than were socializing groups, consistent with results from bowheads. Likewise, northern right whales in small groups (≤3 whales) often dove during overflights but larger groups usually did not (Fairfield 1990). Southern right whales may be strongly disturbed by helicopters at low altitude (Best 1981; Ling and Needham [1990], R. Payne, pers. comm.).

Gray whale reactions to aircraft also are variable. On the Alaskan summering grounds, mother-calf pairs seemed particularly sensitive to a small turboprop survey aircraft at 335+ m altitude. The adult usually moved over the calf, or the calf swam under the adult (Ljungblad et al. 1983; J.T. Clarke et al. 1989). A mating group of gray whales did not react immediately to the arrival of a survey aircraft at 366 m altitude, but dispersed after it had circled at 670 m for 11 min (Clarke et al. 1989). Migrating gray whales rarely showed detectable reactions to a straight-line overflight by a Twin Otter at 60 m altitude (G.A. Green et al. 1992).

Migrating gray whales react to underwater playbacks of recorded underwater sounds from a Bell 212 helicopter (Malme et al. 1983, 1984). There were significant course changes and some whales slowed down in response to an average of three simulated passes per minute. Received broadband sound levels eliciting minor avoidance reactions by 10, 50, and 90% of the whales were 115, 120, and >127 dB re 1 µPa. These tests did not determine if gray whales would respond to noise from a single overflight, and excluded the strong low-frequency components of Bell 212 noise. However, the playbacks showed that gray whales respond to helicopter noise itself; vision was not involved.

SRA (1988) stated that migrating gray whales never reacted overtly to a Bell 212 helicopter at >425 m altitude, occasionally reacted when it was at 305-365 m, and usually reacted when it was below 250 m. Reactions consisted of abrupt turns, dives, or both.

In the calving lagoons of Baja California, gray whales herded into shallow water by a helicopter hovering at very low altitude "churned the water with flukes and fins until their wakes became swirling cauldrons of foam", especially when sensitized by repeated herding (Walker 1949). Mothers occasionally "shielded" calves with their bodies, as observed in summer (Ljungblad et al. 1983). Harassment by low-flying (≤75 m) aircraft "causes the animals to dive and occasionally leads to separation of mother and young" (Withrow 1983).

Humpback whale reactions to aircraft have been mentioned by several authors, but we know of no published systematic studies. Some humpbacks were disturbed by overflights at 305 m altitude but others showed no apparent response to flights at 152 m (Shallenberger 1978). Responses to a small aircraft depended on group size and composition; whales in large groups showed little or no response but some all-adult groups exhibited avoidance (Herman et al. 1980). Authors reporting no obvious reaction included Friedl and Thompson (1981), who detected no reaction to a P-3 patrol aircraft at 150-350 m, and Kaufman and Wood (1981).

Helicopter disturbance to humpbacks off Hawaii is a concern (Tinney 1988; Atkins and Swartz 1989). Helicopters and fixed-wing aircraft are prohibited from approaching within a slant range of 1000 ft (305 m) from humpbacks near Hawaii (NMFS 1987). Humpback reactions to aircraft have been studied recently at Kauai (C. Clark, M. Smultea and B. Würsig, pers. comm., 1994).

Less information is available about reactions of *other species* of baleen whales to aircraft. Minke whales usually responded to an H-52 turbine helicopter at 230 m altitude by changing course, rolling onto the side, or slowly diving (Leatherwood et al. 1982). Other "fright" reactions were seen occasionally. I.W.C. (1990) mentions that minke whales off Norway were disturbed by a helicopter. A few minke and fin whales off Alaska reacted to a turbine survey aircraft by diving briefly (Ljungblad et al. 1982a). Watkins (1981b) was able to observe the behavior of fin whales from a light aircraft circling at 50-300 m, but he implies that engine noise or the aircraft shadow sometimes caused reactions. Bird (1983) and Bauer and Herman (1986) listed other related cases.

In *summary*, data on reactions of baleen whales to aircraft are meager and largely anecdotal. Only Malme et al. (1984) provided data on reactions of whales to aircraft sound isolated from other stimuli. Theirs was also the only study to determine whale reactions versus received sound level. Whales often react to aircraft overflights by hasty dives, turns, or other changes in behavior. Responsiveness depends on the activities and situations of the whales. Whales actively engaged in feeding or social behavior often seem rather insensitive. Whales in confined waters, or those with calves, sometimes seem more responsive. Most of these generalizations also seem to apply to tooth-ed whales—at least to belugas. There is no indication that single or occasional aircraft overflights cause long-term displacement of whales.

9.2.4 Sirenians and Polar Bears

Manatees were more disturbed by survey aircraft noise from a Bell 47G helicopter than from a Cessna 172 fixed-wing aircraft (Rath-bun 1988). However, the helicopter was flown lower and slower (20-160 versus 160 m; 0-20 versus 130 km/h), so interpretation is difficult.

Polar bears often run away from aircraft passing at low altitudes (e.g., altitude <200 m and lateral distance <400 m). Helicopters are often used to scare bears away from human facilities (Shideler 1993). Most polar bears in snow dens continue to occupy their dens after close approaches by helicopters or other aircraft (Amstrup 1993). Snow greatly attenuates helicopter noise (Blix and Lentfer 1992).

9.3 Reactions to Ships and Boats

Disturbance of marine mammals by ships and boats is of much interest because of their substantial noise levels, large numbers, wide-spread distribution, and mobility. Many authors have commented on reactions or lack of reactions by marine mammals, especially ceta-ceans, to ships and boats. However, without controlled tests, it is often uncertain how much the observed behavior differed from that expected in the absence of a vessel. The few studies involving repeat-ed observations or controlled experiments are most valuable.

Many reactions to ships or boats are presumably reactions to noise. Reactions often are at long distances and often follow changes in engine and propeller speed (see below). Also, Schevill (1968b) found that a largely silenced motorboat could move among cetaceans without disturbing them. However, visual or other cues often cannot be ruled out, and are no doubt involved in some cases.

9.3.1 Pinnipeds

Few authors have described responses of pinnipeds to boats or ships. Most published information is anecdotal.

Walruses observed by Salter (1979) showed no detectable response when outboard motorboats approached the terrestrial haulout site to distances of 1.8-7.7 km. Similarly, Brooks (in Fay 1981) said that wal-ruses appeared not to be disturbed by the sound of outboard engines

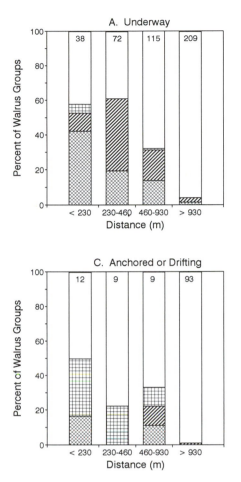

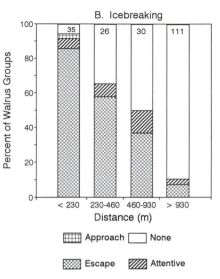

FIGURE 9.1. Percentage of walrus groups showing various reactions to icebreaker at four distances with ship *(A)* underway in open water, *(B)* icebreaking, *(C)* anchored or drifting. Walruses were hauled out on ice pans in the Chukchi Sea, 1989-1991. Sample sizes are numbers of walrus groups seen at each distance. Compiled from Brueggeman et al. (1990, 1991, 1992b).

at distances >400 m. High-frequency noise from outboards may be more disturbing than low-frequency noise from diesel engines (Fay et al. 1984). In one area of Alaska, walruses hauled out on land seemed more tolerant of passing outboard motorboats when those walruses were not hunted than in years with hunting from boats (D.G. Roseneau, in Malme et al. 1989).

For walruses hauled out on ice, reaction probability and type depend strongly on distance (Fig. 9.1A). Reaction distance also depends on ship speed, and may be influenced by the sight and possibly the smell of the ship as well as its sound (Fay et al. 1984). Walruses reacted at greater distances when a ship approached traveling downwind than when it was traveling upwind (Fay and Kelly 1982;

Fay et al. 1984). Sound and smell are both detectable farther away in the downwind direction. However, walruses sometimes do not react until the ship is well inside the distance where it first becomes audible to humans.

Walrus reactions to ships include waking up, head-raises, and entering the water. Females with young seem more wary than adult males. Walruses in open water are less responsive than those on ice pans, usually showing little reaction unless the ship is about to run over them (Fay et al. 1984). Fay et al. speculated that vessel disturbance may lead to increased calf predation and abandonment. Calves were often the last walruses to leave ice pans as a ship approached, and a polar bear killed one calf as walruses left the ice.

Northern fur seals are quite tame when first encountered by a ship, but avoid it if it engages in seal hunting (H. Kajimura, in S.R. Johnson et al. 1989:48). Kajimura suspected that, once sensitized in this way, fur seals showed avoidance at distances up to a mile. *South African (Cape) fur seals* are attracted to fishing vessels to feed, and are sometimes sucked into propeller nozzles, killing the seal and damaging the propeller (Wickens 1994).

Sea lions in the water tolerate close and frequent approaches by vessels, and sometimes congregate around fishing vessels. Sea lions hauled out on land are more responsive (Peterson and Bartholomew 1967:18), but rarely react unless a boat approaches within 100-200 m (Bowles and Stewart 1980; B.S. Stewart, pers. comm., 1994). Reactions to nearby boats are most common if motor noise varies in level. Visual cues probably are also involved.

Harbor seals that give birth on tidal flats in Holland often move into the water in response to boats (Reijnders 1981; Brasseur 1993; Mees and Reijnders 1994). This may reduce pup survival (Bonner 1982). In California, small boats that approach within ~100 m often displace harbor seals from haulouts; less severe disturbance can cause alert reactions without departure (Bowles and Stewart 1980; Allen et al. 1984; Osborn 1985). After leaving a haulout in response to a boat, some seals return within 1 h; others remain absent for 3+ h. Reactions to canoes and kayaks are at least as great as those to motorboats (Allen et al. 1984; Osborn 1985; Swift and Morgan 1993). In Glacier Bay, Alaska, harbor seals hauled out on ice floes move into the water when vessels approach within 100-300 m depending on vessel type (Calambokidis et al. 1983). Small boats with quiet engines, little human motion on board, and slow, constant speeds elicit the least reaction (Hoover 1988). Elsewhere in Alaska, harbor seals in the presence of many fishing vessels pay little attention to boats 200+ m away, become alert at 150-200 m, and vacate the haulout site when boats come within ~60 m (J. Burns, in S.R. Johnson et al. 1989:55).

In places with many boats, harbor seals may habituate (S.R. Johnson et al. 1989). In England, some harbor and *gray seals* permit close approach by tour boats that repeatedly visit haulout locations (Bonner 1982). Bonner suggested that seals habituate to sounds from specific tour vessels.

Harp seal calling rate may have decreased after a trawler and seal hunters came within 2 km of a whelping area (Terhune et al. 1979). It was not certain whether (1) some seals moved away or (2) all remained but vocalized less often. However, harp and *hooded seals* return to traditional breeding and molting areas off Newfoundland each year despite centuries of disturbance by vessels and seal hunting (Brodie 1981a,b). *Ringed seals*, in most cases hauled out on ice pans, often showed short-term escape reactions when a ship came within ¼-½ km (Brueggeman et al. 1992a).

In general, evidence about reactions of seals to vessels is meager. The limited data, plus the responses of seals to other noisy human activities, suggest that seals often show considerable tolerance of vessels. It is not known whether these animals are truly unaffected or are subject to stress. This uncertainty applies to many human activities and all marine mammals, and is discussed in Sections 11.6.5 and 11.8.4.

9.3.2 Toothed Whales

Many odontocetes show considerable tolerance of vessel traffic. However, they sometimes react at long distances if confined by ice or shallow water, or if previously harassed by vessels.

Beluga reactions to vessels range from great tolerance to extreme sensitivity, apparently depending on whale activities and experience, habitat, boat type, and boat behavior. Belugas that are hunted from power boats in traditional estuarine concentration areas return each summer even though hunting causes short-term displacement and may change local distribution (e.g., Fraker 1980; Brodie 1981a,b; Reeves and Mitchell 1981; Seaman and Burns 1981; Burns and Seaman 1985; Caron and Smith 1990). Belugas return annually even if seriously overhunted (Finley 1982; Finley et al. 1982). Part of the

West Hudson Bay population returned to the port of Churchill annually despite a harvest of ~500 whales per summer (Sergeant 1981).

Likewise, belugas are rather tolerant of the frequent passages by larger vessels traveling in consistent directions in summering areas such as the St. Lawrence River, Cook Inlet, and Beaufort Sea (Fraker 1977b; Macfarlane 1981; Sergeant 1981, 1986; Burns and Seaman 1985; Pippard 1985). However, belugas often flee from fast and erratically moving small boats. Some also disperse when small ships approach, occasionally at distances up to 2.4 km (Fraker 1977a, 1978). Call types, rates, and frequencies may change during boat approaches, possibly to increase call detectability (Lesage et al. 1993).

In the St. Lawrence estuary, numbers of belugas in one area diminished during a several-year period when boat activity increased (Caron and Sergeant 1988). It is not known whether the additional vessels caused the decline in use by belugas. In the short term, reactions of these belugas to boats ranged from approach to strong avoidance. The frequency and intensity of disturbance varied with the number and speeds of the boats, the activity and ages of the whales, and location (Blane 1990; Blane and Jaakson 1994). Belugas were strongly disturbed when boats approached at speeds higher than idle, and especially when two boats approached from opposite directions. Young belugas were less likely than adults to react. In comparison with belugas engaged in other activities, feeding or traveling belugas were less likely to react to boats but, when they did react, responses were stronger. Blane (1990) concluded that continued use of some areas with much boat traffic by feeding and traveling belugas reflected the value of these areas to the whales, and should not be interpreted as meaning that the whales were undisturbed.

There is evidence of some long-term and seasonal habituation of St. Lawrence belugas to boats: (1) In recent years, avoidance responses to "unobtrusive" approaches have become less frequent, and cases of belugas approaching boats ("interactive behavior") have become more common. (2) Interactive behavior is more common late than early in the summer field season (E.M. Lynas, in Blane 1990). A similar "curious whale" phenomenon is well known in wintering gray whales (Section 9.3.3).

In Bristol Bay, Alaska, belugas feed amidst hundreds of salmon fishing boats (Frost et al. 1984). Feeding belugas were not easily displaced even when purposefully harassed by motorboats (Fish and Vania 1971). However, in another study, belugas in a river stopped feeding and swam downriver in response to motorboats even when the received noise level was low. Belugas were more responsive to outboard motorboats than to other vessels (Stewart et al. 1982). Habituation to noise from fishing boats was presumably a factor. The higher frequencies in outboard engine noise (Section 6.2.2) were probably also significant. Beluga hearing sensitivity improves with increasing frequency (Section 8.2.1).

In contrast, belugas react strongly and at extraordinarily long ranges to noise from ships and icebreakers in deep channels of the Canadian high arctic during spring. Data from two different research teams and several years show that belugas typically swim rapidly away when a ship approaches within 35-50 km (LGL and Greeneridge 1986; Cosens and Dueck 1988; Finley et al. 1990). These distances may approximate those where belugas first hear the higher-frequency components (e.g., 5 kHz) of the ship noise (Cosens and Dueck 1993). Pod integrity, surfacing/dive behavior, and call types also change. Belugas travel up to 80 km from the ship track (e.g., Fig. 9.2), and typically remain away for 1-2 days (Finley et al. 1990).

Narwhals, when in the same situation, tend to exhibit "freeze/silent" behavior rather than the "flight/alarm call" behavior of belugas. However, some narwhals also moved long distances away (Fig. 9.2). The differing responses of these belugas and narwhals to ships are similar to their respective responses to killer whales (Finley et al. 1990).

These strong reactions at long ranges are unique in the literature on disturbance to marine mammals. Possible reasons for the acute responsiveness are the partial confinement of whales by heavy ice, scarcity of ships in the high arctic in spring, and good sound propagation conditions (LGL and Greeneridge 1986). Belugas in the Beaufort Sea may also be more sensitive to ship noise when the whales are in open water leads amidst ice during spring than at other times (Norton Fraker and Fraker 1982; Burns and Seaman 1985).

Dolphins of many species often tolerate or even approach vessels, but at times members of the same species show avoidance. Reactions to boats often appear related to the dolphins' activity: resting dolphins tend to avoid boats, foraging dolphins ignore them, and socializing dolphins may approach (B. Würsig, pers. obs.). Dolphins can reduce the energetic cost of travel by "riding" the bow and stern waves of vessels (Williams et al. 1992). Attraction of some species to vessels can bias ship-based surveys of odontocetes (e.g., Bouchet et al. 1985).

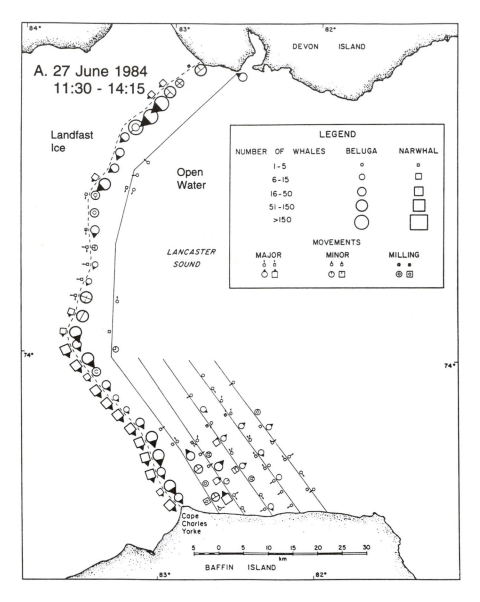

FIGURE 9.2. Long-distance effects of ships on belugas and narwhals in the Canadian high arctic. Maps show distribution and movements of belugas (circles) and narwhals (squares) **(A)** before approach and **(B)** after approach of two ships—"LSL" and "ARC". Based on aerial surveys along landfast ice edge (dashed line) and over open water (continuous transect lines). The two ships reached the ice

(Caption continues)

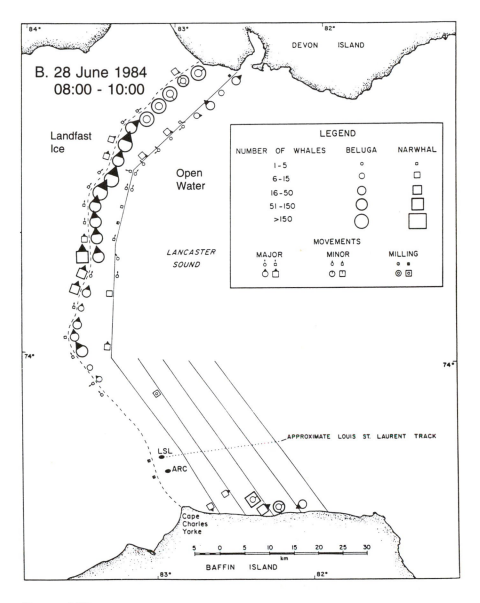

FIGURE 9.2B

edge 2 h before and 1 h after survey (B). "Major" versus "minor" movements mean >75% versus 25-75% of the whales moved in the indicated predominant direction. From G.W. Miller and R.A. Davis, in LGL and Greeneridge (1986).

Bottlenose dolphins reside in many channels used by vessels ranging in size from large tankers down to pleasure and sport-fishing boats (e.g., Barham et al. 1980; Shane 1980; Acevedo 1991; Fertl 1994). This species commonly approaches boats, sometimes swimming in their bow and stern waves (Shane et al. 1986) or feeding on prey made more accessible by human fishing activities (e.g., Corkeron et al. 1990). In Mexico, bottlenose dolphins exposed to frequent boat traffic showed little reaction unless a boat came within ~5 m (Acevedo 1991). Although this species shows much tolerance of boats, boats often cause altered behavior. Shane (1990) found that altered behavior was least common when dolphins were actively socializing.

In some situations, dolphins tend to avoid vessels, and this too can bias boat-based surveys. Bottlenose dolphins often were seen near a 7.3 m boat, but individuals that had been captured and released for research purposes seemed to be sensitized: they fled when the capture boat was 400+ m away (Irvine et al. 1981). In Wales, resident bottlenose dolphins tended to avoid an area of heavy boat activity (P.G.H. Evans, in Moscrop 1993:67). Black (Chilean) dolphins were generally timid near boats, but sometimes approached them (Crovetto and Medina 1991). In the tropical Pacific, pelagic dolphins (mainly *Stenella* spp.) showed avoidance up to 5-12 km from approaching ships, with strong avoidance at 2-5 km (Norris et al. 1978; D. Au and Perryman 1982; Hewitt 1985). These dolphins probably had been sensitized by previous harassment during tuna seining; seiners set nets around dolphins to catch the associated tuna (Norris et al. 1978; Pryor and Norris 1978). In the Gulf of Mexico, most *Stenella* approached survey vessels and many bow-rode; however, striped dolphins tended to show avoidance (Würsig and Lynn in press).

Killer whales are subject to intense boat-based whalewatching in some areas (Duffus and Dearden 1993). Off British Columbia, they rarely showed obvious avoidance to boats within 400 m. However, detailed analysis showed subtle tendencies to swim faster, especially when more than one boat was nearby, and to move toward less confined waters (Kruse 1991). Swimming speeds when boats were within 400 m were not obviously related to boat size or engine type.

Reactions of *other large delphinids* to boats vary within species from avoidance to bow-riding (P.G.H. Evans 1987:286; Baird and Stacey 1991a,b; Stacey and Baird 1991; Würsig and Lynn in press). Melon-headed whales sometimes approached a survey vessel and bow-rode, but at other times avoided the vessel (Mullin et al. 1994).

In some parts of the world, various delphinid species have been hunted by drive fisheries, in which boats are used to herd a pod of animals into a bay or other confined area where they can be killed. These hunts are based on the animals' tendency to swim away from a group of boats advancing in a coordinated and noisy manner (e.g., Kasuya 1985; Bloch et al. 1990; Kishiro and Kasuya 1993).

River dolphins in Peru—boutu and riverine tucuxi—moved away from boats, but resumed pre-disturbance activities within a few minutes (Leatherwood et al. 1991). Ganges river dolphins in Nepal seemed unaffected by rowboats and canoes, but avoided areas used by motorized ferries (Smith 1993).

Harbor porpoises are often seen from boats, but tend to change behavior and move away (Flaherty 1981; Taylor and Dawson 1984). Avoidance may occur up to 1-1½ km from a ship (Barlow 1988; Palka 1993), but is stronger within 400 m (Polacheck and Thorpe 1990). The *vaquita* (Gulf of California harbor porpoise) tends to surface for briefer periods when a boat is nearby, often breathing only one or two times per surfacing when near a boat (Silber et al. 1988). In contrast, *Dall's porpoises* often approach vessels (Withrow et al. 1985) or seem to ignore them (Watkins et al. 1981).

Sperm whales, when chased by catcher boats, often change direction, disperse into smaller subgroups, and travel long distances underwater (Gambell 1968; Lockyer 1977). Reactions to less threatening vessels are weaker and variable, often involving course changes and shallow dives (Gaskin 1964; Reeves 1992). Various researchers have found that a small motorized or sailing vessel, operated nonaggressively, can be used near sperm whales without disturbing them appreciably (Papastavrou et al. 1989). However, startle reactions have been seen during some attempts to approach close to sperm whales (Whitehead et al. 1990).

Off New Zealand, some sperm whales start to avoid outboard-powered whalewatching vessels up to 2 km away; behavioral changes include altered surfacing-respiration-dive patterns and more erratic surface movements (J. McGibbon, in Cawthorn 1992). Near those boats, surface times tended to be reduced, with fewer blows per surfacing, shorter intervals between successive blows, and increased frequency of dives without raised flukes (Gordon et al. 1992). However, many individual sperm whales tolerate the boats and remain in the area despite repeated boat encounters (Gordon et al. 1992; B. Würsig, pers. obs.).   Gordon et al. found that calling behavior was little affected by boats.

In the Gulf of Mexico, pygmy sperm whales, dwarf sperm whales, and *beaked whales* tended to orient away from survey vessels (Würsig and Lynn in press).   Sorensen et al. (1984) found evidence that densities of "squid-eating cetaceans" may be reduced within several kilometers of vessels off the U.S. east coast.   However, northern bottlenose whales frequently approach stationary or slow-moving ships.   They may circle a vessel for >1 h (Reeves et al. 1994).

Collisions between boats and toothed whales seem uncommon. Bottlenose dolphins in the Gulf of Mexico are occasionally injured or killed by boat propellers (Reynolds 1985; Fertl 1994), as are Chinese river dolphins (baiji) in the Yangtze River (Zhou Kaiya and Zhang Xingduan 1991).   Sperm whales have been struck and killed by ships (Slijper 1962).

In *summary*, toothed whales sometimes show no avoidance reaction to vessels, or even approach them.   However, avoidance can occur, especially in response to vessels of types used to chase or hunt the animals.   This may cause temporary displacement, but we know of no clear evidence that toothed whales have abandoned significant parts of their range because of vessel traffic.   Reactions can vary greatly even within a species, as in belugas.   It is not known whether toothed whales exposed to recurring vessel disturbance are stressed or otherwise affected in a negative but inconspicuous way (see Chapter 11).

9.3.3 Baleen Whales

There have been specific studies of the reactions of gray, humpback, and bowhead whales to vessels, and limited information is available for some other species.   The widely used photo-identification method (Hammond et al. 1990) depends on the fact that slow-moving boats often can approach whales without seriously disturbing them.

Watkins (1986) summarized reactions of baleen whales to boats based on his experience with several species near Cape Cod.   Most weak vessel sounds seemed to be ignored.   Whales that had been exposed repeatedly to whalewatching vessels sometimes approached those vessels.   On the other hand, whales often moved away in response to strong or rapidly changing vessel noise.   Avoidance was especially strong when a boat approached directly (Watkins 1986). These phenomena were also mentioned by Beach and Weinrich (1989) and have been documented in more detailed studies of various species.

One indication that the reactions were to noise and not some other stimulus is that whales exhibited little reaction to a silenced boat (Schevill 1968b).

In the 19th century, when auxiliary steam engines were added to commercial whaling vessels, whalers found that bowhead whales were more readily approached under sail than with the engine running (Lubbock 1937:401). Also, when commercial whaling switched from steam-powered vessels to noisier diesel-powered catcher boats, whales were more frightened. Steam-powered vessels often could approach whales slowly, but diesel vessels had to pursue whales at high speed (Tønnessen and Johnsen 1982:688). Whales that had been hunted recently were more difficult to approach (Ash 1962:8)—an example of sensitization.

Gray Whale.—The gray whale winters and reproduces in lagoons along the coast of Baja California and migrates north to the Bering and Chukchi seas off Alaska for the summer. Reactions to vessels have been studied in winter and to some extent during migration. Little information is available for the summering grounds (Bird 1983; Bauer and Herman 1986:23-29).

Vessels in gray whale breeding lagoons can cause short-term escape reactions, particularly when boats move fast or erratically (Reeves 1977; Swartz and Cummings 1978; Swartz and Jones 1978, 1981). There is little response to slow-moving or anchored vessels. The proportion of incidents in which the whales flee whalewatching vessels decreases as the winter progresses, suggesting habituation. Jones and Swartz (1984, 1986) found no evidence that whales left a lagoon when whalewatching vessels were present. In fact, some gray whales are attracted to quiet, idling, or slow-moving boats, especially in late winter (Norris et al. 1983; Withrow 1983; Bryant et al. 1984; Dahlheim et al. 1984; Jones and Swartz 1984, 1986). This "curious whale" behavior has become more prevalent in recent years.

Some whales are attracted specifically to noise from idling out-board engines (Swartz and Cummings 1978; Dahlheim et al. 1981, 1984). No avoidance was evident during underwater playbacks of recorded outboard engine noise, and some whales approached the projector (Dahlheim 1987). With actual boats or playbacks of outboard noise, call rate increased and call structure changed. Average received levels of calls also increased, perhaps indicating that source levels of calls increased with boat noise. Dahlheim concluded that gray whales were not seriously disturbed by noise from small boats, but that calling behavior changed to reduce masking by boat noise.

Long-term effects of vessel traffic in the wintering lagoons are questionable, but there is evidence of abandonment of certain areas. Gray whales formerly wintered in San Diego Bay, but no longer do so (Rice and Wolman 1971; Reeves 1977). Ship disturbance may have been one of several factors involved. Shipping and other disturbance associated with an evaporative salt works in Guerrero Negro Lagoon apparently caused gray whales to abandon that lagoon for a few years. The whales returned after shipping decreased (Gard 1974; Reeves 1977; Bryant et al. 1984). Gray whales continued to use a less confined bay nearby even with heavy ship traffic, but tended to avoid the actual shipping channel (Withrow 1983). It is not known whether gray whales that tolerate such human activities suffer any stress or other negative effects (Chapter 11).

During migration, Wyrick (1954) noted that gray whales changed course at a distance of 200-300 m in order to move around a vessel in their paths. The fastest-moving whale recorded by Sumich (1983) was near a boat; fast-moving whales breathed and used energy more rapidly than slower whales. Some mother-calf pairs seemed especially responsive (Tilt 1985:21). With increasing numbers of whalewatching boats, migrating gray whales changed course more often (Bursk 1983; Bursk, in Atkins and Swartz 1989:11). Nonetheless, ships often come very close to migrating gray whales; some do not seem to react until the ship is within 15-30 m (Schulberg et al. 1989). Many collisions have been reported, often killing the gray whale (Shallenberger 1978; Patten et al. 1980; Schulberg et al. 1989).

Some migrating gray whales disturbed by vessels tend to exhale underwater and to expose their blowholes only to inhale, thereby making themselves difficult to see (Hubbs and Hubbs 1967; Bursk 1983). Similar "snorkeling" behavior has been seen when gray whales were exposed to killer whales or their sounds (Hubbs 1965; Cummings and Thompson 1971b), or to nearby explosions (Gilmore 1978).

Migrating gray whales commonly remain close to shore, but there have been many sightings far off southern California in recent decades (Rice 1965; Dohl and Guess 1979; Graham 1989; Schulberg et al. 1989). This might mean that whales migrating nearshore have been displaced offshore by ships and other human activity (Rice 1965; Wolfson 1977). However, it is also possible that the offshore route was always used but was overlooked earlier; or that a shift occurred for reasons unrelated to disturbance, such as the recent population increase (Rice 1965; Dohl and Guess 1979; Graham 1989). This question is unresolved.

Little information is available about reactions of summering gray whales to vessels. Hatler and Darling (1974) showed that a few gray whales return annually to a summer feeding area with frequent boat traffic. In the main summering area off eastern Russia, gray whales have, until recently, been hunted from a catcher boat. Zimushko and Ivashin (1980) reported that, during whaling, frightened gray whales appeared at the surface without seeming to blow. This is reminiscent of the "snorkeling" by gray whales disturbed during migration. Bogoslovskaya et al. (1981) stated that summering gray whales moved away if a vessel was within 350-550 m or if it pursued feeding whales, but "pay no attention" to a more distant vessel. A case of a "curious" gray whale has been reported from the Bering Sea (M. Dahlheim, in Jones and Swartz 1984:351).

The eastern Pacific gray whale population has recovered from overhunting (Buckland et al. 1993) even though much of its nearshore range is heavily used by vessels and other human activities. This indicates much tolerance of noisy human activities (Cowles et al. 1981; S.E. Moore and Clarke in press) despite the various reactions noted above. Malme et al. (1989:5-9) described the heavy vessel traffic encountered by some gray whales migrating through Unimak Pass, a "chokepoint" for both ships and whales moving between the Pacific Ocean and Bering Sea.

Humpback Whale.—Concern has been expressed about vessel disturbance of humpback whales wintering off Hawaii and summering off southeast Alaska. There was evidence of decreased abundance along the coast of Oahu since the 1940s and 1950s, coincident with drastic increases in human activity including shipping. However, no direct causal link was established (K.S. Norris and Reeves 1978). The main concern is the long-term cumulative effect of many vessels, tourists, and aircraft (Shallenberger 1978). Reactions to boat approaches are variable, ranging from approach to avoidance (Payne 1978a; Salden 1993). On rare occasions humpbacks "charge" toward the boat and "scream" underwater, apparently as a threat (Payne 1978a). Humpback density may be inversely related to the daily amount of boat traffic and to the local amount of human activity (Herman 1979; Kaufman and Wood 1981). The latter authors stated that behavior sometimes was affected when boats came within about 275 m. A study of the songs of humpback whales approached by boats (T.F. Norris 1994) indicated that durations of some song elements were altered, but most measures of song characteristics were unaffected.

A systematic study of short-term reactions of Hawaiian humpbacks to vessels, mostly small boats, was done by Bauer (1986) and Bauer and Herman (1986). Measures of respiration, diving, swimming speed, social exchange, and aerial behaviors (breaching, head lunging) were correlated with vessel numbers, proximity, speed, and direction changes. Results differed among categories of whales (e.g., singers, other singletons, mothers, calves). Overall, humpbacks attempted to avoid vessels and sometimes directed threats toward them. Behaviors indicative of avoidance included increased frequencies of surfacings without blows and of dives initiated without raised flukes. The various effects often occurred when vessels were ½-1 km away. Smaller pods and pods containing a calf were more affected than were larger pods (Bauer et al. 1993). Bauer and Herman (1986) concluded that reactions to vessels probably are stressful to humpbacks, but that the biological significance of this assumed stress is unknown.

Another study of short-term effects found that, when a boat approached within ½ mile, humpbacks showed significant changes in several variables: reduced proportion of time at surface, longer dives, altered directions (avoidance), and reduced speeds after the boat departed (M.L. Green and Green 1990). Effects persisted 20+ min after the boat departed. Green (1990) found that humpbacks moved out of a favored area (radius 2 km) on days when parasail boats operated.

Some longer-term Hawaiian studies suggest that mother-calf pairs became proportionately less frequent close to shore when recreational boating was increasing (Glockner-Ferrari and Ferrari 1985, 1990; Salden 1988). Whether the link with boats was causal is not proven; varying survey procedures complicated interpretation, and there was some conflicting evidence (Forestell et al. 1991).

Tinney (1988) and HWRT (1991) provide recent reviews of disturbance effects on humpbacks near Hawaii. Vessels are prohibited from approaching within 100 yards (91 m) of any humpback whale off Hawaii, and within 300 yards (274 m) of those in designated cow/calf areas (NMFS 1987). The population seems to be increasing despite exposure to human activities, so long-term negative effects are not apparent at the population level (Bauer et al. 1993). However, this population is still much below its estimated pre-whaling size (HWRT 1991).

On the southeast Alaska summering grounds, observations during the 1970s suggested that, when boats and cruise ships approached within a few kilometers, humpback whales tended to move away, to exhibit "threat" behaviors such as aerial displays, or to change their respiration and diving cycles (Jurasz and Jurasz 1979a; Dean et al. 1985). Whales seemed especially responsive to rapidly moving vessels and to abrupt changes in vessel speed. Sounds from the noisier ships dominated the ambient sound "out to a range of up to six miles in some measurements" (Malme et al. 1981; Miles and Malme 1983). In 1978, humpbacks left Glacier Bay unusually early. Whether this was caused by increased vessel activity (Jurasz and Jurasz 1979a), reduced food availability (Bryant et al. 1981), or something else was the subject of controversy (Marine Mammal Commission 1979/80).

A subsequent detailed study confirmed that humpbacks often move away when vessels are within several kilometers (Baker et al. 1982, 1983; Baker and Herman 1989). Baker et al. hypothesized that humpbacks have two avoidance strategies: **(1)** Vertical avoidance when vessels are within 2 km, i.e., increased dive durations, decreased blow intervals, and decreased swimming speeds. **(2)** Horizontal avoidance when vessels are 2-4 km away, i.e., decreased dive durations, longer blow intervals, and greater speeds. Baker et al. also found indications that approaching vessels triggered some aerial behaviors— breaching, flipper and tail slapping—as suggested by Jurasz and Jurasz (1979a). Although vessels caused short-term changes in behavior, including avoidance, some specific humpbacks remained for several weeks in areas often used by vessels, and returned to the area in later years (Baker et al. 1988, 1992).

Reactions of humpbacks to vessels vary considerably. Some humpbacks show little or no reaction when vessels are well within the several-kilometer "zone of influence" noted above. For example, Watkins et al. (1981) reported that passage of a tanker within 800 m did not disrupt feeding humpbacks. Humpbacks seem less likely to react overtly when actively feeding than when resting or engaged in other activities (Krieger and Wing 1984, 1986). Also, variations in sound propagation affect the radius of influence (Watkins and Goebel 1984).

There are strong local and annual differences in prey availability off southeast Alaska, and humpbacks concentrate where prey is concentrated (Bryant et al. 1981; Krieger and Wing 1986; Dolphin 1987). Some year-to-year changes in humpback distribution are consistent with changes in prey availability. Feeding humpbacks undoubtedly can be displaced temporarily by vessels. However, the roles of disturbance and changing prey availability in affecting longer-term changes in humpback distribution off southeast Alaska are unresolved (Dean et al. 1985; Krieger and Wing 1986; Baker and Herman 1989). In any case, restrictions have been placed on numbers and activities of vessels entering Glacier Bay (Baker et al. 1988).

Humpback whales of other populations also avoid some boats that approach closely (e.g., ANPWS 1991; Helweg et al. 1991; Goodyear 1993). In winter, mothers with newborn calves seem most sensitive (Clapham and Mattila 1993). Among migrating humpbacks off eastern Australia, females are more responsive than males to biopsy darting (M.R. Brown et al. 1994). The most extensive data are from summer feeding grounds off Cape Cod. Humpbacks remain there for extended periods and return annually, despite exposure to many ships, fishing vessels, and whalewatching boats (Beach and Weinrich 1989; Clapham et al. 1993). Humpbacks that are approached slowly and steadily, following established guidelines for whalewatching, show no "adverse reactions". However, those approached within <30 m, or via aggressive boat maneuvers, show various changes in behavior (Schilling et al. 1989). Watkins (1986) noted that humpbacks in this area have become less responsive to vessels since whalewatching became common, but they still tend to be silent when near boats. Recently, some humpbacks, mainly young animals, have begun to approach slow-moving whalewatch vessels (Watkins 1986; Belt et al. 1989). Some occur in busy shipping lanes, and some are struck by vessels (HWRT 1991; Swingle et al. 1993; Wiley et al. 1995).

Bowhead Whale.—In the Beaufort Sea, oil industry personnel on ships see bowheads (Ward and Pessah 1988), sometimes within a few hundred meters. However, more detailed studies show that some bowheads begin to avoid approaching diesel-powered vessels 4 km or more away—too far away to be observed from the vessel (Richardson et al. 1985b,c; Koski and Johnson 1987). Avoidance usually involves altered headings, fast swimming speeds, and short surfacings with few blows per surfacing. Richardson and Malme (1993) provide a more detailed review. Only a few bowheads (~1%) show scars from collisions with vessel propellers (George et al. 1994).

The first reaction to an approaching vessel is usually to try to outswim it. When an overtaking vessel is within a few hundred meters, bowheads often turn and swim perpendicularly away from the boat's track, but other whales remain on course. Bowheads can be displaced by as much as a few kilometers while fleeing. They cease fleeing when the vessel is a few kilometers past. Some individually recognizable bowheads return to feeding locations within 1 day after being displaced by boats (Koski and Johnson 1987). Whether they would return after repeated disturbance is not known. Noise levels that elicit fleeing are sometimes low. In one test with a 13-m diesel-powered boat, the received level near fleeing bowheads (range 4 km) was only ~84 dB re 1 µPa in the dominant ⅓-octave band, or ~6 dB above ambient in that band.

Bowheads are more tolerant of vessels moving slowly or in directions other than toward the whales (Richardson and Finley 1989; Wartzok et al. 1989). This is also true in other whale species (e.g., Watkins 1986; Edds and Macfarlane 1987; Atkins and Swartz 1989). Even so, subtle effects on surfacing and blow cycles were noted once when diesel engines began idling 3-4 km away (Richardson et al. 1985b,c). However, Wartzok et al. (1989:207) found that bowheads >500 m to the side of or behind a small ship seemed unaffected, and that bowheads often approached within 100-500 m when the ship was not maneuvering toward the whales. Some of these bowheads tolerated received broadband noise levels up to 110-115 dB re 1 µPa, in contrast to the strong avoidance noted above in response to lower but increasing noise levels from an approaching boat. Bowheads actively engaged in social interactions or mating may be less responsive to boats (Wartzok et al. 1989).

One radio-tagged bowhead was repeatedly approached by a small ship on several days (Wartzok et al. 1989:209). Approximate dive times were reduced on each of three days when the ship was within 500 m for 1½-2½ h. Dive patterns were apparently normal on the three days following days of ship disturbance, and the whale remained in the general area where the ship was operating.

Bowheads in the Beaufort Sea are more difficult to approach closely with outboards than with unmotorized boats (Hobbs and Goebel 1982; Goodyear et al. 1987). Besides being noisier, outboards are used during the continuing autumn hunt for these bowheads.

Few data are available about reactions of bowheads to vessels in other seasons and regions. In the northern Bering Sea during late autumn, whales moved away if a vessel approached within 400-600 m (Kibal'chich et al. 1986). However, any whales reacting at longer ranges might not have been seen. The bowheads that occupy the eastern Canadian Arctic avoided steam-powered whaling ships in the 19th century (Lubbock 1937:401). They seem very responsive to motorboats (Degerbøl and Freuchen 1935; Richardson and Finley 1989) even though they have not been hunted intensively since 1911.

In general, bowheads react strongly and rather consistently to approaching vessels of a wide variety of types and sizes. Bowheads interrupt their normal behavior and swim rapidly away. Surfacing, respiration, and diving cycles are affected. The fleeing response often subsides by the time the vessel has moved a few kilometers away. After single disturbance incidents, at least some bowheads return to their original locations. Vessels moving slowly and in directions not toward the whales usually do not elicit such strong reactions.

Right Whales.—Northern right whales, like bowheads, are often approachable in a slowly moving boat, but move away from vessels that approach more rapidly (Watkins 1986; Goodyear 1989, 1993; M.W. Brown et al. 1991). Right whales seen from whalewatching vessels tend to be oriented away when first seen, but not when last seen (S. Kraus, in Atkins and Swartz 1989:17). They are consistently silent when disturbed by boats (Watkins 1986). When mating or feeding, they often seem oblivious to close passage of small vessels, provided there is no abrupt change in course or engine speed (Goodyear 1989; Mayo and Marx 1990; Gaskin 1991; RWRT 1991:10).

Behavioral reactions of right whales to distant but approaching ships are poorly documented. Ships strike many right whales and kill some (Brownell et al. 1986; Kraus 1990; RWRT 1991; Kenney and Kraus 1993). Thus, these slow-moving whales are not very successful in avoiding collisions—a major source of mortality. A vessel speed limit of ≤9 km/h may reduce collisions (Slay et al. 1993).

Southern right whales off Argentina showed variable responses to small outboard-powered boats (Cummings et al. 1972; Payne et al. 1983). Some whales allowed the boat to approach to "touching distance" and some whales approached stationary boats. However, other whales avoided boats. Close approaches were possible only when the boat moved slowly. Similar observations have been reported for right whales wintering off South Africa (Donnelly 1969; Saayman and Tayler 1973). In Argentina, there is concern about reactions of right whales to boats engaged in commercial and especially individual whalewatching trips (Garciarena 1988).

In Australia, some mother-calf pairs allow close approach by small boats (Chittleborough 1956; Robinson 1979). However, Robinson noted that a mother "adopted a low profile", reminiscent of the inconspicuous behavior of some disturbed gray whales. When vessels pass offshore from one nearshore calving area, right whale mothers are said to interpose themselves between the vessel offshore and the calf inshore (R. Ulmann, Warrnambool, Victoria, pers. comm., 1991).

Rorquals.—Many workers have commented briefly on the reactions of rorquals to ships, but there have been few detailed studies. Gunther (1949) stated that fin whales "usually moved off gently" as a ship approached but were less responsive when feeding. Feeding blue whales may also be rather unresponsive to passing ships (R. Sears et al., in Mansfield 1983:42). During prolonged high-speed chases by ships, the breathing rates of rorquals increase (Lockyer 1981).

Reactions of *fin, blue*, and *minke whales* summering in the St. Lawrence estuary to ships and whalewatch boats were assessed in 1973-1975 (Mitchell and Ghanimé 1982), 1979 (Edds and Macfarlane 1987), and 1980 (Macfarlane [1981]). In 1973-1975, whales moved away during about 15% of 232 vessel-whale encounters. In other cases the whales remained, but most changed direction abruptly or dove to avoid close approach by the vessel. In 1979, fin whales also avoided most vessels by slight changes in heading or by increasing the duration and speed of underwater travel, at distances ≥1 km. The most marked reactions by fin and blue whales in 1979-1980 occurred when boats made fast erratic approaches and/or sudden changes in speed or direction. A slow approach, even in a large boat, usually caused little reaction. Surfacing and respiration patterns were not always noticeably affected, but some surfacing sequences near boats were erratic or short. Low-frequency vessel noise often masked fin whale social sounds, and higher-frequency outboard noise masked minke whale sounds. Fin whales continued to call in the presence of vessel noise (Edds 1988).

Off New England, fin whales show reduced durations of surfacings and dives, and fewer blows per surfacing, when whalewatch and other boats are nearby (Young 1989; Stone et al. 1992). The same trends are seen when fin whales are chased (Ray et al. 1978). In recent years, fin whales off Cape Cod have shown less tendency to avoid vessels than they did before about 1976 (Watkins 1986). This may represent habituation to the development of the whalewatch industry. Watkins (1981a) and Watkins et al. (1981) found that fin whales ignored observation boats that remained >100 m away, and showed little response to slowly approaching boats if they maintained a steady speed, but avoided boats whose speed or course changed rapidly, or whose propellers were reversed. Fin whales tend to be silent when ships are near (Watkins 1986).

Minke whales are sometimes difficult to approach closely (Macfarlane [1981]), even though they often approach and even swim under vessels (Winn and Perkins 1976; Leatherwood et al. 1982). The frequency of ship-seeking by minke whales may have diminished recently off Cape Cod (Watkins 1986). The occurrence of ship-seeking versus ship-avoidance is often discussed in relation to sightability of minke whales during ship-based censuses (Horwood 1981; Butterworth and Best 1982; Butterworth et al. 1982; Joyce et al. 1989; Borchers and Haw 1990). Overall, when vessels are underway, minke whales generally do not approach and sometimes avoid. However, ship-seeking sometimes occurs when vessels are stationary or moving slowly (I.W.C. 1982:734; Tillman and Donovan 1986).

Bryde's whales showed little response to a boat approaching slowly at steady speed (Watkins 1981a). Bryde's whales, like several other species, are easier to approach when they are feeding (Gallardo et al. 1983). Ship-seeking has been reported (Cummings et al. 1986).

Sei whales, according to Gunther (1949), tended to be more difficult to approach with a ship than were fin whales: "They took more erratic courses...; when they reappeared after sounding they were usually far away and moving in any direction but the direction in which the ship was heading." Sei whales may be less responsive to ships when feeding than at some other times (Lockyer 1981).

Summary.—When baleen whales receive low-level sounds from distant or stationary vessels, the sounds often seem to be ignored. Some whales approach the sources of these sounds. When vessels approach whales slowly and nonaggressively, whales often exhibit slow and inconspicuous avoidance maneuvers. In response to strong or rapidly changing vessel noise, baleen whales often interrupt their normal behavior and swim rapidly away. Avoidance is especially strong when a boat heads directly toward the whale. Some baleen whales travel several kilometers from their original location in response to a straight-line pass by a vessel through that site. Avoidance reactions are not always effective in preventing collisions, injury, and mortality, especially for right whales.

9.3.4 Sirenians, Sea Otters, and Polar Bears

In Florida, more *West Indian manatees* are killed by collisions with boats than by any other known cause (O'Shea et al. 1985; Ackerman et al. 1989). Propeller cuts are common, but many boat-killed manatees die from impact trauma without cuts (Beck et al. 1982; Wright et al. 1991). Manatees apparently can hear the sound frequencies emitted by outboard engines, but their ability to localize the direction of the boat is uncertain (Section 8.2.3). Manatees often attempt to avoid oncoming boats by diving, turning, or swimming away, but the reaction is usually slow and does not begin until the boat is within ≤50-100 m (Hartman 1979; Weigle et al. 1993). Some manatees may habituate to boats, increasing the collision risk (Curtin and Tyson 1993). However, there is evidence of reduced use of some areas with chronic boat disturbance (Provancha and Provancha 1988). Winter aggregations in favored warm-water habitats can be dispersed by human activity. Prolonged displacement into colder water may have serious effects, possibly including some mortality (Hartman 1979; Kochman et al. 1985).

In Queensland, *dugongs* in shallow (<2 m) water sometimes swim rapidly in response to motorboats up to 1 km away. Dugongs tend to head for deeper water even if this brings them closer to the boat's path (Preen 1992). Dugongs in deeper water are less responsive. They dive several seconds before the boat arrives, and resurface several seconds after it has passed. Dugongs tend to avoid areas of heavy boat activity. In Western Australia, Anderson (1982) observed reactions of dugongs to a boat that passed through a feeding area at two speeds. During an approach at 15 km/h, dugongs began swimming away at range 150 m, and they were displaced by ~500 m. An hour later they returned to the feeding area. In contrast, when approached at 50 km/h, dugongs showed little reaction.

Sea otters often allow close approaches by boats, but sometimes avoid heavily disturbed areas. Riedman (1983) noted that some rafting sea otters exhibited mild interest in a boat passing a few hundred meters away, but were not alarmed. Garshelis and Garshelis (1984) reported that sea otters tend to avoid southern Alaskan waters with frequent boat traffic, but reoccupy those areas in seasons when boats are less frequent. Also in Alaska, ~15% of the sea otters along boat survey transects were not detected because they moved away from the approaching boat (Udevitz et al. 1995). Some sea otters on shore moved into the water during the approach of a small powerboat traveling parallel to and 100 m from shore (Garrott et al. 1993).

Polar bears appear to be little affected by shipping (Fay et al. 1984:353). Some bears walk, run, or swim away, but these reactions are brief and local, and other bears show no reaction or approach the vessel (Brueggeman et al. 1991:3-29; Rowlett et al. 1993).

9.4 Reactions to Icebreaking

There is little information about the effects of icebreaking ships on most species of marine mammals. Concern arose because of proposals, now dormant, to ship oil and gas from the Canadian Arctic in large icebreaking ships (Peterson 1981). Several smaller oil industry icebreakers have been used routinely in the Beaufort and Chukchi seas to extend the offshore drilling season. Many icebreakers and ice-strengthened cargo ships are used on Russia's northern sea route (Armstrong 1984; Barr and Wilson 1985; Brigham 1985) and elsewhere in the Arctic and Antarctic. Besides causing strong underwater noise (Section 6.2.3), icebreakers might have nonacoustic effects: crushing of animals, ice entrapment of some that follow the icebreaker track, and disruption of ice habitat. Nonacoustic effects are reviewed by Richardson et al. (1989:315).

Ice type strongly influences the types of marine mammals present and the nature of icebreaker operations. Some species prefer loose ice at the edges of pack ice fields whereas others prefer close pack ice. Only a few seal species plus the polar bear occupy landfast ice. In loose pack ice, ship speed and noise may be similar to those in open water. In heavier pack ice or thick landfast ice, ship speed will be reduced, power levels higher, and propeller cavitation greater; ship noise will be higher and more variable (Section 6.2.3).

The *walrus* is the pinniped whose reactions to icebreakers are best known. Fay et al. (1984) compared their reactions to icebreaking versus ships in open water. Reactions to icebreaking tended to occur at longer distances. Walruses on the ice became alert when the ship was 2+ km away. Females and young entered the water and swam away when the ship was ½-1 km away. Males did so at 0.1-0.3 km away. However, Fay et al. also noted that some walruses, ringed seals, and bearded seals scrambled *onto* ice when a ship breaking ice headed toward them.

During another study, of 202 walrus groups seen on ice floes during icebreaking, 32% dove into the water, and an additional 6% became alert while on the ice (Brueggeman et al. 1990, 1991, 1992b). The probability of an escape reaction increased sharply with diminishing distance from the icebreaker, and for each distance category was higher during icebreaking than other ship operations (see Fig. 9.1 in Section 9.3.1). Aerial surveys suggested that walruses hauling out on ice floes may have tended to avoid the area within ~10-15 km of the icebreaker (Brueggeman et al. 1990). Some underwater sounds from the icebreaker were potentially detectable at midwater depth well beyond 25 km away, but the detection range for walruses near the water's surface or hauled out on ice was uncertain.

When *ringed* and *bearded seals* on pack ice were approached by an icebreaker breaking ice, many dove into the water when the ship came within 0.93 km (½ n.mi.). Seals tended to be less sensitive when the same ship was underway in open water (Brueggeman et al. 19-92a). Similarly, Kanik et al. (1980) found that most ringed and *harp seals* 1-2 km from an icebreaker remained on the ice; seals closer to the icebreaker often dove into the water. Ringed seals have been seen feeding among overturned ice floes close behind icebreakers (Brewer et al. 1993). In general, care must be taken in interpreting observations from the icebreaker itself. Any animals that react at a long distance may avoid the ship without being observed. Also, animals that show no avoidance may be undisturbed, but alternatively may be disturbed but have no avenue of escape in the ice.

In areas of stable landfast ice, ambient sound levels are sometimes low (Section 5.2.2), so icebreaking could increase the noise level dramatically. Ringed seals occupy arctic fast ice, maintaining breathing holes through the winter. Their mobility is severely limited by the need for access to breathing holes. Alliston (1980, 1981) determined the numbers and distributions of seals during spring at study sites in the Beaufort Sea and Labrador where icebreakers had traveled through the landfast ice the previous winter. There was no indication of reduced seal numbers in areas that had been subject to icebreaking. Indeed, ringed seals may have preferentially established breathing holes in ship tracks.

Whales do not occur in landfast ice, but icebreaking in fast ice during spring can disturb *narwhals* and especially *belugas* near ice edges many kilometers away (Section 9.3.2). These species were affected by icebreakers traveling either in open water or through fast ice. After initially being displaced in response to relatively low levels of noise from the approaching ship (94-105 dB re 1 μPa in the 20- to 1000-Hz band), the whales sometimes returned 1-2 days later when icebreaker noise levels were still as high as 120 dB in that band (Finley et al. 1990). Not surprisingly, icebreaker-based observers (e.g.,

Kanik et al. 1980) apparently have not noticed these strong reactions of belugas and narwhals to icebreakers. Observations from separate platforms—e.g., aircraft or ice edge—are necessary to study reactions at such long distances.

It has been speculated that narwhals or belugas might follow icebreakers into ice-covered areas and become trapped by refreezing ice. No evidence of this was noted by LGL and Greeneridge (1986). However, Thomas et al. (1981) observed *killer whales* accompanying icebreakers into the Antarctic ice.

Reactions of *baleen whales* to icebreaking are largely unknown. In the Beaufort Sea, migrating bowhead whales apparently avoided an icebreaker-supported drillsite by 25+ km during the autumn of 1992. There was intensive icebreaking around the drillsite almost daily (Brewer et al. 1993). However, migrating bowheads also avoided a nearby drillsite in another autumn with little icebreaking (LGL and Greeneridge 1987). Thus, the relative roles of icebreaker noise, drilling noise, and the ice itself in diverting bowheads around these drillsites are uncertain.

As noted earlier, *polar bears* show either no or very limited reactions to ships and icebreakers (Section 9.3.4).

The few available data on reactions of marine mammals to icebreaking have involved animals that encounter icebreakers infrequently. Studies of the acoustic and other effects of repeated icebreaker traffic would be necessary to assess long-term effects.

9.5 Reactions to Other Vehicles

9.5.1 On-Ice Vehicle Traffic

Vehicle traffic on ice, which is largely confined to landfast ice, may disturb seals and polar bears occupying this habitat. *Ringed seal* numbers apparently declined near a snowmobile track on landfast ice (Bradley 1970). Whether this was caused by disturbance, hunting, or both is unclear. However, Calvert and Stirling (1985) found no clear evidence of reduced numbers of ringed seals in areas subject to traffic and hunting. During a more detailed study, passing snowmobiles elicited variable reactions from ringed seals hauled out in subnivean (under snow) lairs on the ice (Burns et al. 1982; Kelly et al. 1986, 1988). One seal remained in its lair during passes within ½ km. Other seals left their lairs in response to snowmobiles up to 2.8 km away. These seals could not have seen the snowmobiles, and presumably responded to airborne sound. Most if not all seals later returned.

J.E. Green and Johnson (1983) found no evidence that intensive on-ice traffic and construction in winter affected the average density of ringed seals within ~13 km as compared with the density elsewhere in the region. However, densities of seal holes were lower within a few kilometers of the construction than they were slightly farther away. Thus, some localized displacement of seals probably occurred.

Polar bears sometimes emerge from dens on ice or shorelines when on-ice vehicle traffic passes within a few hundred meters. Some dens may be abandoned, which could lead to reduced cub survival. However, other bears continue to occupy dens when wheeled or tracked vehicles pass—sometimes repeatedly—within a few hundred meters (Amstrup 1993).

Reactions of marine mammals in the water to noise from vehicles on ice have not been studied. Sound is often transmitted efficiently through sea ice into water.

9.5.2 Hovercraft

Hovercraft can be used over water, ice, or land. Except for one study of gray whales, little information is available about reactions of marine mammals to hovercraft.

Reactions of migrating *gray whales* to large military hovercraft were studied by SRA (1988) and Schulberg et al. (1989, 1991). When an LCAC hovercraft (Landing Craft, Air Cushion) approached within a few hundred meters, spacing between migrating whales sometimes decreased and whales occasionally turned, stopped traveling for a few minutes, or dove abruptly. Schulberg et al. (1991) observed gray whales from a circling aircraft during a series of 27 controlled LCAC passbys. Reaction distances tended to be shorter when the LCAC was "on air cushion" than when floating, probably because of reduced transmission of noise into the water when "on cushion". (Specific noise levels were not reported.) Reaction distance to an approaching LCAC "on cushion" averaged 296 m (n=23, max.=600 m). Gray whales always reacted to a hovercraft approaching from the front (±50°), but generally did not react if it approached from the rear. Approaches from the rear may reduce disturbance but, in the absence of whale avoidance, increase the risk of collision. Although sighting conditions were good during all trials, and the LCAC crew knew that whales were nearby, the crew saw the whale(s) during only 11 of 27 approaches, at distances 0 to 600 m (mean 233 m). Gray whales that reacted resumed normal behavior after an average of 6.9 min.

Toothed whales react in variable ways to hovercraft. Dolphins tended to remain farther away than did gray whales, but a group of pilot whales showed no reaction to an LCAC <100 m away (Schulberg et al. 1989). Belugas reportedly left an area through which a hovercraft had passed, and did not return for at least 8 h (Fraker 1977a).

Reactions of *seals* to hovercraft are also little known. A ringed seal remained on the ice in its lair when a hovercraft passed ~2½ km away (Kelly et al. 1988). However, harbor seals hauled out near an airport were more responsive to occasional hovercraft passes than to frequent aircraft overflights (M. Bigg, in S.R. Johnson et al. 1989:53).

9.5.3 Hydrofoils and Jet Skis

Hydrofoils, like hovercraft, are high-speed vessels, generally powered by gas-turbine engines. These are quite noisy, at least in air. Military hydrofoils have struck at least two *gray whales* off California, killing one; another hydrofoil struck a whale off Venezuela (Hudnall 1978; Shallenberger 1978). Noise from large hydrofoils operating near Hawaii apparently caused *humpbacks* to respond in some unspecified manner (Shallenberger 1978; Tinney 1988). Also, some *spinner dolphins* attempting to bow-ride were injured or killed (Hudnall 1978).

Jet skis are very small motorized "personal watercraft" propelled by water jets. There has been much concern about jet ski disturbance to humpback whales in Hawaii (Tinney 1988). We have not seen any detailed data on whale reactions to jet skis, but their noise, high speeds, and erratic motions are likely to disturb whales.

9.6 Reactions to Dredging and Construction

Dredges are major sources of underwater noise in some nearshore areas (Section 6.3; Greene 1987b). Marine dredges are used to deepen ship channels, to construct artificial islands, and for other offshore construction projects. Aside from one study on bowhead whales and ongoing work on northern right whales, the effects of dredging and other construction operations on most types of marine mammals have received little or no study.

9.6.1 Dredging

Belugas in the Mackenzie estuary showed less reaction to stationary dredges than to moving barges despite similarities in their sounds (Ford 1977; Fraker 1977a,b). Belugas approached as close as 400 m from stationary dredges. Fraker (1977a) concluded that passage of belugas along a shoreline was temporarily blocked by a dredging operation involving frequent barge traffic, but not by dredging with little barge traffic. *Spinner dolphins* reduced their use of a Hawaiian bay after the start of a noisy construction project for a water pipeline (Shallenberger 1978).

Bowhead whales were seen near the construction site of an artificial island in the Beaufort Sea over a 2-week period in August 1980. Aerial surveys detected bowhead whales within 800 m of the site, and industry personnel reported some closer approaches (Richardson et al. 1985a,b,c, 1990b). A suction dredge and other vessels were active at that construction site when bowheads were seen nearby. Dredge sounds were well above ambient levels up to several kilometers away (e.g., 120 dB re 1 µPa at range 1.2 km; Fig. 6.14). Smaller numbers of bowheads were seen near other construction sites at distances where they were exposed to considerable underwater noise from suction and hopper dredges (112-117 dB: Richardson et al. 1985c, 1990b).

There has been one experimental study of bowhead reactions to dredge noise. On 3 days, recorded underwater noise from a suction dredge was projected into the water near bowhead whales (Richardson et al. 1990b). Estimated broadband received levels of the noise near the whales ranged from <113 to 131 dB re 1 µPa, or from <11 to 30 dB above ambient levels. Sample sizes were small and low-frequency (<50 Hz) components of the dredge sound were underrepresented because of projector limitations. However, the more distant whales— those exposed to the least noise—exhibited weak and inconspicuous avoidance. Those exposed to stronger sounds (122-131 dB, or 21-30 dB above ambient) exhibited more conspicuous avoidance. They stopped feeding and moved from within 0.8 km of the sound projector to locations >2 km away.

During these playbacks, the noise level was increased gradually over 10 min, so the reactions were not startle reactions in the usual sense. However, the gradual onset of dredge noise over 10 min did not fully represent the time course of noise exposure for a traveling whale approaching a dredge or vice versa, or especially for a stationary whale near a stationary dredge.

Bowheads behaved normally in some areas ensonified by actual dredging even though other bowheads showed avoidance at similar noise levels during playbacks. This may mean that whales habituate to steady dredge noise even if they are disturbed when they first encounter it. On the other hand, bowhead numbers in the general area of construction and drilling in the Beaufort Sea were apparently reduced after the first few years of intensive offshore exploration (Richardson et al. 1987a). It is not known whether this distributional change was a long-term effect of industrial activities or was caused by another factor such as food availability (Thomson et al. 1986; Bradstreet et al. 1987; Ward and Pessah 1988).

Northern right whales wintering in nearshore waters along the southeast coast of the U.S.A. have, in recent years, been exposed to intensive dredging of ship channels by hopper dredges (RWRT 1991; Slay et al. 1993). Such dredges are noisy (Fig. 6.14). Right whales, like bowheads, apparently show some tolerance of this noise. However, we have seen no data on behavioral reactions to the dredges, nor on dredge effects on numbers present. Dredges also pose a collision hazard to right whales (Section 9.3.3; Best 1984).

Gray whales provide the best documented case of a long-term change in baleen whale distribution as a result of industrial activities, including dredging. Gray whales were virtually absent from a lagoon in Baja California during several years with much shipping (Bryant et al. 1984; Section 9.3.3). Bryant et al. suggested that "the constant dredging operation necessary to keep the channel open...may have been the main source of disturbance". Gray whales reoccupied the lagoon after shipping subsided.

9.6.2 Other Construction Operations

Construction equipment operated on small artificial islands seemed to have little effect on *belugas*. They were seen "within a few feet" of an artificial island during quiet periods, and moved farther away but did not leave the area when construction equipment was in use (Fraker 1977a). Sounds produced on islands are attenuated greatly at the air-water and bottom-water interfaces (Section 6.4.1).

Three studies of *ringed seals* hauled out on the ice in the Beaufort Sea during spring suggest that construction of artificial islands can cause local displacement, but overall effects seem negligible: **(1)** Kingsley (1986) stated, without details, that seal densities were no lower adjacent to artificial islands than elsewhere in the eastern Beaufort

Sea. **(2)** J.E. Green and Johnson (1983) found that some seals apparently had been displaced from the area within a few kilometers of an artificial island constructed in winter by over-ice truck transport of fill (Section 9.5.1). **(3)** Frost and Lowry (1988) and Frost et al. (1988) found that seal densities within 3.7 km of artificial islands were lower than 3.7-7.4 km away. The effect was strongest near active islands: 50-70% reduction within 3.7 km. However, on a broader scale, densities were higher, not lower, within the region with artificial islands. Overall, effects of island construction and operation on ringed seals seem insignificant.

Harbor seals that haul out in Kachemak Bay, Alaska, continued to haul out during construction of hydroelectric facilities ~1.6 km away (D. Roseneau and D. Trugden, in S.R. Johnson et al. 1989:54).

Northern fur seals hauled out on St. George Island, Bering Sea, showed little reaction to onshore quarrying operations (Gentry et al. 1990). The strongest overt response was assumption of an alert posture (raised head) when heavy equipment was operating as close as ~100 m away or when underground blasting occurred 0.6-2 km away. There was no evidence of displacement.

We are not aware of specific data on reactions of *sirenians, sea otters*, or *polar bears* to dredge or construction noise. However, they often approach existing man-made facilities such as, respectively, power plants (Shane 1984), docks, and artificial islands (Stirling 1988b). Also, manatees often use previously dredged basins (Shane 1983; Provancha and Provancha 1988).

9.7 Reactions to Offshore Drilling and Production

Anecdotal accounts have been published about sightings of various marine mammals, mostly cetaceans, near offshore drilling and oil or gas production sites. A few controlled playback studies and comprehensive monitoring programs have also been done, mainly on baleen whales. Cetaceans are often seen within the areas ensonified by drill-rigs and perhaps within the smaller areas ensonified by production platforms. However, noise from drillsites sometimes elicits avoidance or other reactions, at least by baleen whales.

9.7.1 Reactions to Offshore Drilling
Pinnipeds.—Reactions of most pinnipeds to drilling and related activities have not been studied extensively. *Ringed seals* are often

seen near drillships drilling in the Arctic during summer and autumn (Ward and Pessah 1986; Brueggeman et al. 1991:A-8; Gallagher et al. 1992a; Brewer et al. 1993; Hall et al. 1994). In spring, some ringed and *bearded seals* approached and dove within 50 m of an underwater sound projector broadcasting steady low-frequency (<350 Hz) drilling sound (Richardson et al. 1990a, 1991a). At that distance, the received sound level at depths greater than a few meters was ~130 dB re 1 µPa. These observations demonstrate some tolerance of drilling noise by seals. However, it is uncertain whether seal numbers and behavior near drillships or playback sites differed from those that would occur without drilling. In spring, densities of ringed seals were reduced within 3.7 km of artificial islands, on some of which drilling was under way (Frost and Lowry 1988).

Reactions of *walruses* to icebreaker-supported drillships were summarized in Section 9.4 and Fig. 9.1. The dominant influence was apparently icebreaking noise rather than drilling *per se*.

Toothed Whales.—*Belugas* have often been seen near drillsites, and additional data on reactions to drilling sounds have been obtained via underwater playbacks. Belugas were seen regularly within 100-150 m of "operational" artificial islands (Fraker 1977a,b; Fraker and Fraker 1979). However, belugas swimming along an ice lead in spring changed course when they came within 1 km of a stationary drillship, and exhibited more active avoidance when support vessels were moving near the drillship (Norton Fraker and Fraker 1982).

These and other observations (Section 9.3.2) suggest that belugas may be especially responsive when in leads during spring. However, this was not evident during playbacks of steady low-frequency (<350 Hz) drilling noise into leads north of Alaska in spring (Richardson et al. 1990a, 1991a). Migrating belugas showed no overt reactions until they were within 200-400 m, even though the noise was detectable by hydrophones up to 5 km away. Within 200-400 m, some belugas diverted or hesitated for a few minutes, but then continued within 50-200 m of the operating projector. Belugas may have been unable to hear the low-frequency drilling sounds until they came within ~200-400 m, given their poor hearing sensitivity below 1 kHz (Section 8.2.1).

Reactions of belugas to underwater playbacks of sounds from a semisubmersible drillship—*SEDCO 708*—have also been tested in the field and in captivity. During tests in an Alaskan river (Stewart et al. 1983), belugas within 1.5 km usually swam faster in the same direction as they had been moving before the playback, and respiration rates sometimes increased. During two tests, belugas swimming toward the noise source did not react overtly until they were within 50-75 m and 300-500 m. Reactions included rapid swimming and, in one case, reversal of direction. However, most belugas passed close to the projector where received sound levels must have been high. Reactions to drillrig noise were less severe than those to motorboat noise (*cf.* Stewart et al. 1982).

Captive belugas sometimes showed brief avoidance responses when startled by the onset of a playback of actual or simulated *SEDCO 708* sound, excluding the lowest-frequency components (Thomas et al. 1990a). This avoidance lasted only ~30 s. Belugas often swam within 1 m of the projector, where received levels were at least 153 dB re 1 µPa. Group structure was not affected. Surfacing-respiration-dive cycles were not strongly affected, but dives tended to be shorter. Plasma catecholamine levels were normal 8-40 min after playbacks ceased, indicating that the animals were not stressed. Thomas et al. concluded that they could not detect any short-term behavioral or physiological effects despite the high level of sound exposure. However, they recommended caution in extrapolating these results to wild belugas around oil platforms.

These results may be another example of the degree to which belugas can adapt to repeated or ongoing man-made noise when it is not associated with negative consequences. In some other situations, strong avoidance can occur in response to weak sounds (Section 9.3.2).

Bottlenose dolphin distribution near oil production platforms in the Gulf of Mexico was summarized by Mullin et al. (1989). They mention evidence of a disassociation (possibly artifactual) in one depth stratum, and of attraction to platforms in a deeper stratum. The latter may be related to prey concentrations near platforms. No data were given about typical distances of dolphins from platforms.

Other toothed whales apparently also show considerable tolerance of drillrigs. Kapel (1979) reported many long-finned pilot whales within visual range of drillships and their support vessels off West Greenland. Sorensen et al. (1984) saw several species—mainly common, Risso's, bottlenose, and *Stenella* dolphins—within 18 km of drillrigs off New Jersey, but gave no further information about distances. Sightings per unit effort were similar with and without rigs.

Baleen Whales.—Kapel (1979) reported numerous baleen whales —mainly fin, minke, and humpback whales—within visual range of drillsite vessels off West Greenland. More detailed data have been obtained subsequently from systematic playback and monitoring studies of bowhead, gray, and (to a limited degree) humpback whales.

Bowhead whales whose behavior seemed normal have often been seen within 10-20 km of drillships operating in open water during summer. On two occasions bowheads were only 8 and 4 km away during drilling (Richardson et al. 1985a,c, 1990b). Also, industry personnel reported to us 10 sightings at distances ~0.2-5 km from drillships, and saw others at unstated distances (Ward and Pessah 1988). Broadband sound levels 4 and 10 km from one of the drillships approached by bowheads, *Canmar Explorer II*, were 118 and 109 dB re 1 µPa, respectively. These levels were 20 and 11 dB above the average background level (Fig. 6.18; Greene 1985a, 1987b).

Although bowheads were observed well within the ensonified zones around active drillships, playbacks of drillship noise to a small number of bowheads demonstrated some avoidance. Our playbacks of *Explorer II* drillship noise (excluding components below ~50 Hz) showed that some bowheads reacted to broadband received levels near 94-118 dB re 1 µPa—no higher than the levels tolerated by bowheads seen a few kilometers from actual drillships (Richardson et al. 1985a,c, 1990b). The playback results of Wartzok et al. (1989) seem consistent: the one observed case of strong avoidance of *Kulluk* drilling noise was at a broadband received level ≥120 dB.

Two explanations may account for the seemingly different reactions of summering bowheads to playbacks versus actual dredging (Section 9.6.1) and drilling: habituation and variable sensitivity. Bowheads may react to the onset of industrial noise (over several minutes) during a brief playback, but habituate when that sound level continues for a long period near an actual drillship or dredge. However, playbacks also showed that responsiveness varies among individuals and days. Thus, whales seen near actual drillships may have been some of the less responsive individuals—those remaining after the more responsive animals had moved out of the area. Both habituation and variable sensitivity may have been involved.

Taken together, results of drillship and dredge noise playbacks indicated that a typical summering bowhead does not react overtly unless broadband received sound levels are ~115 dB re 1 µPa, or ~20 dB above the ambient level. Based on noise within the dominant ⅓-octave band, the reaction criteria are ~110 dB re 1 µPa or ~30 dB above ambient in that band (Richardson et al. 1990b). Received industrial noise levels diminish to 20 or 30 dB above the ambient noise level (radius of responsiveness) well before they diminish to the ambient level (radius of presumed audibility). Hence, the radius of responsiveness around a drillsite is apparently much smaller than the radius of audibility.

Calling rates of bowheads seemed lower during drillship noise playbacks than before or after playbacks (Richardson et al. 1985c, 1990b; Wartzok et al. 1989). However, elevated background noise during playbacks tends to mask the fainter calls. It is uncertain whether bowhead call rate actually declined in the presence of drilling noise.

In autumn, bowheads migrating west past active drillships and support vessels were monitored in the Alaskan Beaufort Sea during 1986 and 1991-1993. In 1986 and 1993, most bowheads apparently avoided the area within 10 km of the drillship (LGL and Greeneridge 1987; Hall et al. 1994). They passed either north (offshore) or south (inshore) of the drillsite. In 1986 and probably 1993 as well, some bowheads apparently began to divert around the drillsite when still 20+ km away. At radius 10 km, the underwater sound field was dominated by industrial noise in both years. In 1986, noise at 10 km radius, where most if not all bowheads apparently reacted, averaged 114 dB broadband and 104 dB in the two ⅓-octave bands with strongest noise (Greene 1987a). This suggests that autumn-migrating bowheads may be slightly more responsive than summering bowheads. Only about half of the latter reacted to 115 dB (broadband) or 110 dB (dominant ⅓ octave). One contributing factor may have been the greater variability of the drillsite noise in autumn, in part resulting from the variable activities of icebreakers and other support vessels.

In 1991-1992, aerial surveys in the same area showed that most autumn-migrating bowheads remained 20+ km seaward of the single drillships operating in those years. It is uncertain whether the offshore routes represented drillsite avoidance or a normal response to the heavier ice in 1991 and 1992 (Gallagher et al. 1992a; Brewer et al. 1993). The lack of data on tracks of individual bowheads as they approached the drillsites in 1991-1993 makes it difficult to interpret the distributional data from those years.

In spring, bowheads migrating through leads north of Alaska have been exposed to playbacks of recorded drilling platform sounds (Richardson et al. 1991a). Sound components above 50 Hz were projected into the leads, and were detectable by hydrophones (and presumably by bowheads) up to 4-10 km away. The behavior of some

TABLE 9.1. Behavioral reactions of spring-migrating bowhead whales versus distance from noise source and received noise level (dB re 1 µPa), based on playback of recorded drilling noise into a lead through heavy ice, 13 May 1990 [a]

| | | Received level (L_r) | | L_r : Ambient ratio | |
| | | Broad- | Dominant | Broad- | Dominant |
Reaction criterion	Distance (km)	band	⅓ octave	band	⅓ octave
Possible subtle behavior changes [b]	4	101 dB	95 dB	12 dB	14 dB
Increased turning frequency [b]	2	114	108	25	27
Strong behavior changes [b]	1	124	118	35	37
Typical closest point of approach	0.2	131	125	42	44

[a] From Richardson et al. (1991a), with updated sound-level estimates from C.R. Greene and J. Hanna (in prep.). Broadband refers to 20-1000 Hz.
[b] Many of these whales continued to approach the sound projector.

approaching whales was altered subtly when they were still 1-2 km or possibly 2-4 km from the projector, but many bowheads approached within a few hundred meters. Whales within 1 km showed significant changes in several measures of behavior. Some whales made small-scale diversions in migration routes in order to pass at least a few hundred meters to the side of the noise source.

The spring migration was not blocked even on a day when the only available lead passed within 200 m of the operating projector. However, bowheads approaching the projector on that day showed clear behavioral changes, diversion to the far side of the lead, and attempts to divert under the ice (Table 9.1). Received sound levels at distances where reactions began (2-4 km) were similar to the reaction thresholds noted in summer and autumn. However, when no alternative route was available, bowheads continued to migrate through areas with higher sound levels (Table 9.1).

Thus, in spring, as in summer and autumn, bowheads often tolerated drilling sounds whose received levels were well above the ambient level. However, when the received level became high enough, avoidance reactions occurred.

Gray whales migrating along the California coast have been studied when exposed to underwater playbacks of noise from four drilling or production facilities (Table 9.2; Malme et al. 1983, 1984). Migrat-

TABLE 9.2. Received broadband sound levels (dB re 1 µPa) at which various percentages of migrating gray whales reacted to simulated sources of industrial noise, level 100 m from the actual source, and range (m) from the actual source at which 50% avoidance is expected [a]

Sound source	Levels for various percent avoidance			Actual level at 100 m	Actual range (m) for 50% avoidance
	10%	50%	90%		
CONTINUOUS SOURCES					
Drillship [b]	110 dB	117 dB	122 dB	136 dB	1100 m
Semisubmersible [b]	115	120	>128	101	11
Drilling Platform [b]	114	117	>128	89	4
Production Platform [b]	120	123	>129	109	20
TRANSIENT SOURCES					
Helicopter (B-212) [c]	115	120	>127	103	-
Airgun (1.6 L) [d]	164	170	>180	180	400

[a] From Malme et al. (1984:9-6).
[b] Underwater playback of recorded continuous noise.
[c] Underwater playback simulating average of three helicopter passes per minute.
[d] Single 100-in^3 airgun operating at 4500 psi (30 MPa) fired once every 10 s.

ing gray whales showed statistically significant responses to all noise types. The usual reactions were reduced swimming speeds and slight seaward or shoreward diversions to avoid the sound projectors.

Received noise levels at which gray whales reacted were similar among the four sources of continuous noise (Table 9.2), and similar to the received levels of drillship and dredge sound to which bowheads react. However, the source levels for these facilities varied widely, as indicated by the "Level at 100 m" column of Table 9.2. Hence, the distances from the actual industrial sites at which reactions would be expected varied widely, from 4-20 m for the relatively quiet platforms and semisubmersible to 1.1 km for the noisier drillship. These predicted radii of response off California are lower than would be expected in the Bering and Beaufort seas, where sound attenuates less rapidly with increasing distance (Miles et al. 1987).

The predicted response distances for migrating gray whales, especially for the quieter sources, are only first approximations. The sound playback experiments could not fully duplicate the near-field sound fields close to large industrial sources. Also, whales probably would react to visual cues as well as to sound when very close to an actual industrial site.

Malme et al. (1986b, 1988) attempted similar playback tests with gray whales summering in the northern Bering Sea. They used the same recording of drillship sounds as had been used with migrating gray whales and summering bowheads. There was no clear evidence of disturbance when broadband received noise levels were 103-110 dB re 1 µPa, but there was possible avoidance at 108-119 dB in another trial. Surfacing-respiration-dive cycles apparently changed during exposure to drillship noise. Malme et al. concluded that the more extensive data from migrating gray whales were probably reasonably applicable to summering animals as well. A few gray whales have been seen within several kilometers of actual drillships in the Chukchi Sea (Brueggeman et al. 1991, 1992a).

Drillship sounds have also been projected into a Mexican wintering lagoon (Dahlheim 1987). During prolonged (6-8 h) playbacks, gray whales tended to move away from the sound projector and to reduce their calling rates. These results were in contrast to the reactions to outboard engine noise—a common sound in the lagoons (*cf.* Section 9.3.3). With drilling sound, gray whales also altered some call characteristics, and received levels of calls tended to be higher. In these two respects, the results were similar to those with outboard engine noise, and were interpreted as adaptations to reduce masking (Dahlheim 1987). Numbers of gray whales in the lagoon were unusually low after a month of drillship and other playbacks; total playback duration was 120 h in 6- to 8-h blocks (Jones et al. 1994). Whale numbers returned to normal the following winter. Jones et al. concluded that the playbacks were the most likely cause of the whales' early departure in 1984.

Humpback whales were studied by Malme et al. (1985) when they were exposed to playbacks of drillship noise ($n=2$ trials) and of semi-submersible, drilling platform, and production platform noise ($n=1$ trial of each). No clear avoidance responses were evident at broadband received levels up to 116 dB re 1 µPa.

In *summary*, cetaceans apparently avoid stationary industrial activities such as dredging, drilling and production when the received sounds are strong, but not when the sounds are barely detectable. Besides avoidance, other behavioral effects (e.g., changes in surfacing-respiration-dive cycles) are sometimes seen as well. Whales seem most responsive when the sound level is increasing or when a noise source first starts up, as during a brief playback experiment or when migrating whales are swimming toward a noise source. Although limited, the data suggest that stationary industrial activities producing continuous noise result in less dramatic reactions by cetaceans than do moving sound sources, particularly ships. Some cetaceans may partially habituate to continuous noise.

Some cetaceans enter areas that are strongly ensonified by stationary industrial operations. The radius of avoidance around industrial sites seems considerably smaller than the radius of audibility, assuming that mammals can usually hear sounds whose levels exceed the background level in the corresponding band. Whether there is any reduction in utilization of areas that are ensonified but beyond the radius of demonstrated avoidance usually cannot be determined from presently available evidence. The sizes of zones of influence are discussed in more detail in Chapter 10.

Sirenians, Sea Otters, and Polar Bears.—We have seen no data on reactions of *sirenians* to drilling.

Sea otters were observed by Riedman (1983, 1984) during underwater playbacks of drillship, semisubmersible, and production platform sounds. She reported no evidence of any changes in behavior or in use of the ensonified area during playbacks. However, sea otters observable at the surface probably were receiving little underwater noise (Section 4.5.2), and underwater sound would be inaudible to an otter with its head above the surface. Some sea otters continued to dive and feed below the surface in a normal manner during playbacks. These animals would have been exposed to the industrial noise. Most of the foraging otters observed by Riedman (1983) were 400+ m away from the projector site. All of those observed by Riedman (1984) were at least 1.2 km away. At 1.2 km, received sound levels in the dominant ⅓-octave band were usually 10+ dB above the ambient noise level (Malme et al. 1983:5-37; 1984:5-24).

Polar bears often approach stationary drillships and drillsites on caissons and artificial islands when ice is present nearby (Stirling 1988b). Bears are attracted by food odors and perhaps by seals utilizing rig-induced cracks in the ice. Any acoustic or vibration effects from drillrigs on artificial islands are probably confined to a short radius (Blix and Lentfer 1992; Amstrup 1993).

9.7.2 Offshore Oil and Gas Production

Oil production platforms have been in place off California for many years. *Gray whales* regularly migrate through the area (Brownell 1971), but we have seen no detailed data on distances of closest approach or possible noise disturbance. Oil industry personnel report seeing pinnipeds and whales near platforms, and that the animals approach more closely during low-noise periods (Gales 1982; McCarty 1982). Playbacks of recorded production platform noise indicate that gray whales react if received levels exceed ~123 dB re 1 µPa—similar to the levels of drilling noise that elicit avoidance (Table 9.2).

Personnel from production platforms in Cook Inlet, Alaska, report that *belugas* are seen within 9 m of some rigs, and that steady noise is nondisturbing to belugas (Gales 1982; McCarty 1982). Flare booms attract belugas, possibly because flares attract salmon. Pilot whales, killer whales, a minke whale, and unidentified dolphins were also reported near Cook Inlet platforms. Personnel on production platforms in Bass Strait, Australia, also see cetaceans near platforms (R. Nash, BHP Petroleum, pers. comm., 1991).

Sea lions were said to be common around production platforms off California and in Cook Inlet (Gales 1982; McCarty 1982).

In general, there are few published data on underwater noise levels near production platforms (Section 6.4.4) and on the marine mammals near those facilities. However, underwater noise levels may often be low, steady, and not very disturbing. Stronger reactions would be expected when sound levels are elevated by support vessels or other noisy activities.

9.8 *Reactions to Seismic Exploration*

Marine geophysical exploration by acoustic means, hereafter called seismic exploration, employs underwater sounds whose peak source levels greatly exceed those of other activities discussed above (Section 6.5). However, most seismic exploration sounds are short, discontinuous pulses, separated by quiet periods. (Vibroseis is an exception.) In past decades, high explosives were commonly used as energy sources for marine seismic exploration, and explosives are occasionally still used in some areas. However, arrays of airguns, gas exploders, and vibrators (Vibroseis) are the dominant sources nowadays. These produce waterborne sounds with broadband source levels of 220-255 dB re 1 µPa-m (Section 6.5). These levels are high, but less so than levels associated with kilogram-quantities of high explosive (Section 6.7). Much of the seismic energy from array sources is directed downward. Even so, the effective source level for horizontal propagation in the water is high. Underwater sound pulses from airgun arrays and similar sources are often audible many tens of kilometers away (Section 6.5).

This section summarizes the reactions of marine mammals to noise from nonexplosive seismic exploration. Behavioral and blast effects of explosives, whether used for seismic exploration or other purposes, are discussed later (Section 9.10). McCauley (1994) reviews effects of nonexplosive seismic exploration on fish and other animals.

Readers are cautioned that levels of pulsed underwater sounds from seismic exploration (and from sonars and explosions) are measured in different ways by different researchers. The resulting data are not always directly comparable (Section 6.5; Greene 1995).

9.8.1 Pinnipeds

Open-Water Seismic Exploration.—We are not aware of any detailed data on reactions of seals to noise from seismic exploration in open water. An air gun caused an initial startle reaction among *South African fur seals*, but was ineffective in scaring them away from fishing gear (Anonymous 1975a). *Gray seals* exposed to noise from airguns reportedly did not react strongly (J. Parsons, in G.D. Greene et al. 1985:283). However, no details were given and it is unclear whether the seals were in water or air.

Seals in both water and air sometimes tolerate strong noise pulses from nonexplosive and explosive scaring devices (Sections 9.10.1 and 9.12), especially if attracted to the area for feeding or reproduction. Thus, we might expect seals to be rather tolerant of, or habituate to, repeated underwater sounds from distant seismic sources, at least when the animals are strongly attracted to an area. Whether these seals would suffer any deleterious effects such as stress is unknown. Reactions of pinnipeds to seismic vessels at close ranges are unknown and not predictable from "scaring device" observations. Close to a seismic ship there is the further factor of disturbance by the ship itself (Section 9.3.1).

On-Ice Seismic Exploration.—More specific information is available about reactions of *ringed seals* to Vibroseis®—a common method of seismic exploration in areas covered by landfast ice during winter (Section 6.5.3). Measurable underwater or airborne noise is detectable in ringed seal lairs up to ~2-6 km from the Vibroseis source (Holliday et al. 1984). Most of the energy is at low frequencies. The hearing sensitivity of ringed seals has not been determined below 1 kHz, but probably diminishes at lower frequencies (Section 8.2.2).

Early studies suggested that ringed seal densities may be reduced in parts of the Alaskan Beaufort Sea where there was Vibroseis during the preceding winter (Burns et al. 1981). It was unknown whether this effect, if real, resulted from seismic noise itself or the on-ice vehicle traffic and human activity associated with Vibroseis.

Subsequent surveys did not show reduced densities in areas with Vibroseis (Kelly et al. 1988). Over half of the seal holes within 150 m of seismic lines remained in use, but holes ≤150 m from seismic lines were more likely to be abandoned than were holes farther away (Burns et al. 1982). They concluded that "some localized displacement of ringed seals occurs in immediate proximity to seismic lines but, overall, displacement...is insignificant...". Radio tagging showed that, although one seal left its subnivean lair when a single Vibroseis source was within 644 m, other seals used sites within 19-700 m of actual Vibroseis lines after seismic surveys were completed (Kelly et al. 1986, 1988). Rates and types of ringed seal calls were similar before and after exposure to playbacks of Vibroseis sound. Some seals called during playbacks (Cummings et al. 1984).

Overall, Vibroseis operations in winter can displace some ringed seals. However, this effect is very localized. Effects on the distribution and numbers of seals on landfast ice seem minimal.

9.8.2 Toothed Whales

Seismic operators sometimes see dolphins near operating airguns (Duncan 1985). However, aside from a few noteworthy observations of sperm whales, we are not aware of any systematic data on behavior of odontocetes exposed to seismic noise. This is surprising, given the wide occurrence of both odontocetes and marine seismic surveys.

Most energy from airgun arrays and other "high-energy" sources is below 100 Hz—below the frequencies of the calls and optimum hearing of odontocetes (Sections 7.2 and 8.2.1). Thus, they may be rather insensitive to these sound pulses. However, even at distances of many kilometers, overall received levels of airgun pulses are often ≥130 dB re 1 μPa, and thus potentially audible to toothed whales (*cf.* Fig. 8.1). Also, these pulses often include energy up to 200-500 Hz, where odontocete hearing is better than at ≤100 Hz. Thus, despite the apparently poor low-frequency hearing of odontocetes, airgun pulses may often be audible to them out to a radius of 10-100 km (Section 10.4.3).

In the case of *sperm whales*, behavioral reactions to seismic pulses may occur at long ranges. Sperm whales in the Gulf of Mexico apparently moved away, possibly by 50+ km, when seismic surveys began (Mate et al. 1994). Also, sperm whales in the southern Indian Ocean ceased calling during some (but not all) times when seismic pulses were received from an airgun array >300 km away (Bowles et al. 1994); received pulse levels were 10-15 dB above ambient levels. These data are limited, but show that reactions of sperm whales and other odontocetes to seismic pulses deserve detailed study.

Seismic and geotechnical surveys often include bottom-profiling via sonars and other sources operating in the kilohertz range (Section 6.5.4). Again, reactions of odontocetes are unknown. However, the higher the frequency, the more likely that reactions would occur. Some odontocetes, particularly sperm whales, react to sonar pulses and other acoustic "pings" (Section 9.9).

9.8.3 Baleen Whales

The behavior of some species of baleen whales has been observed opportunistically in the presence of noise from distant seismic exploration. Also, reactions of gray, bowhead, and humpback whales to airgun noise have been studied via controlled experiments.

Gray Whale.—Ljungblad et al. (1982a) saw 36 gray whales behaving normally in the Chukchi Sea during exposure to sounds from airguns 36-68 km away. Behaviors included nursing by a mother-calf pair 42 km from the ship and bottom feeding by most other animals.

Gray whales migrating along the California coast reacted to strong pulses from a single airgun and a full-scale array (Malme et al. 1983, 1984). By some measures, clear behavioral effects were evident when received levels were ≥160 dB re 1 μPa, corresponding to ranges <5 km from a 65.5-L (4000-in^3) array of 20 airguns and <1 km from a single 1.64-L (100-in^3) airgun (Fig. 9.3). Gray whales that reacted generally slowed, turned away from the noise source, and increased their respiration rates. Some moved, apparently intentionally, into a "sound shadow" created by topography. Northbound mothers and calves may have been especially responsive. Reactions to a full-scale airgun array were most pronounced when the whales were to the side of the array's long axis—the direction in which most energy was radiated (Fig. 6.19). In the test area, effective ranges for 10%, 50%, and 90% probability of avoidance were ~3.6, 2.5, and 1.2 km broadside from the airgun array, where received noise levels were 164, 170, and 180 dB (Malme et al. 1984). Less consistent or dramatic reactions were suspected at received levels of 140-160 dB, farther away.

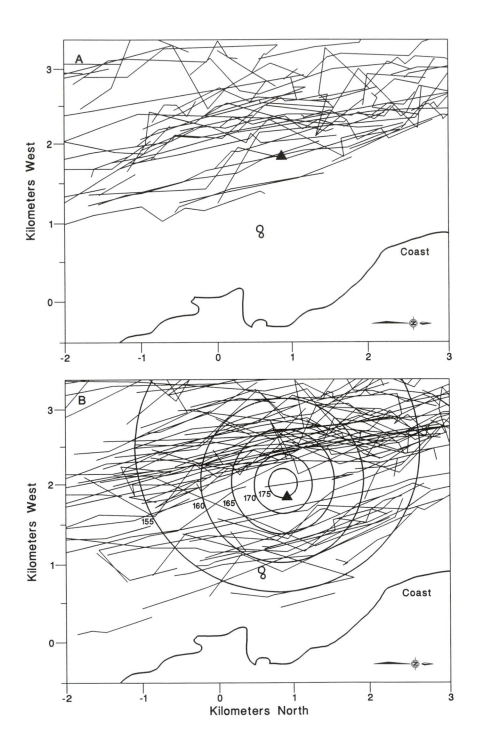

The tests on migrating gray whales showed that an operating seismic vessel passing nearby can affect migration temporarily. The threshold for distinct reactions to seismic pulses, ~170 dB average pulse level, was ~50 dB higher than that for continuous industrial noises (Table 9.2). Humans are also more sensitive to continuous than to pulsed noise with equivalent peak level (Fidell et al. 1970).

Reactions of gray whales summering in the Bering Sea to a single 1.64-L airgun with source level 226 dB re 1 μPa-m were tested by Malme et al. (1986b, 1988). Received levels eliciting avoidance by 10% and 50% of the whales were ~163 and 173 dB, respectively. Although results from summering and migrating whales were similar, the summer data were less precise because of lower sample size and other complications. Sound propagation conditions at the Bering Sea test site were better than off California. Hence, expected radii of responsiveness were higher in the Bering Sea. When exposed to seismic pulses, summering gray whales also had significantly shorter surfacings and dives, with fewer breaths per surfacing and longer intervals between successive breaths. These subtle effects may have persisted for >1 h after the airgun ceased firing.

Bowhead Whale.—Behavior of bowheads exposed to seismic pulses has been observed in the Beaufort Sea during summer and autumn. There have been both opportunistic observations near operating seismic ships (e.g., Reeves et al. 1984; Richardson et al. 1986) and controlled tests with single airguns and airgun arrays (Richardson et al. 1986; Ljungblad et al. 1988). When a seismic vessel approaches within a few kilometers, most bowheads show strong avoidance and changes in surfacing, respiration, and dive patterns. Bowheads exposed to pulses from vessels more than ~7½ km away rarely show avoidance. However, their surfacing, respiration, and dive cycles tend to be altered in the same manner as those of whales closer to the vessels (Fig. 9.4). The following is a condensation of a more detailed review by Richardson and Malme (1993).

On five occasions, reactions of bowhead groups were observed as an operating seismic vessel was directed toward and past the whales

← FIGURE 9.3. Swimming tracks of gray whales migrating south along the California coast *(A)* under control conditions and *(B)* while a 1.64-L airgun was firing. Triangle shows location of anchored boat. (B) includes estimated received level contours for average airgun pulse level; note avoidance of the area near the airgun. Redrawn from maps of Malme and Miles (1985) and P. Tyack (pers. comm., 1994).

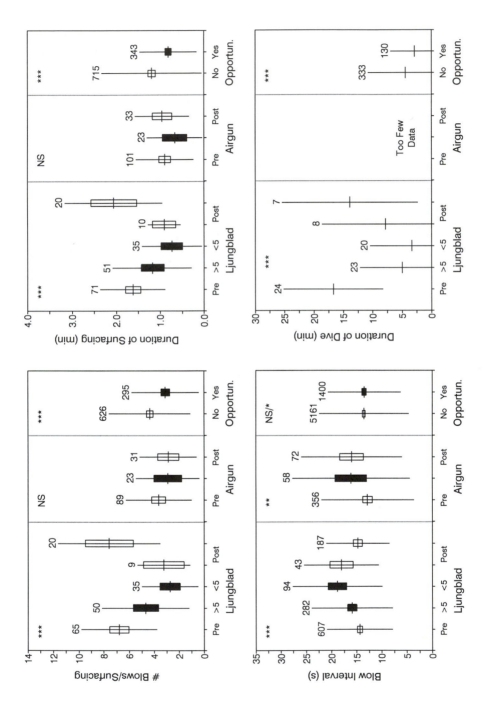

FIGURE 9.4. Surfacing, respiration, and dive behavior of bowhead whales observed in the presence and absence of seismic pulses (calves excluded). Black boxes highlight situations with seismic noise. For each variable, the *left* section shows pooled data from four experiments when bowheads were approached by seismic vessels during autumn; results are shown, in sequence, for the pre-experiment phase (no seismic source within 10 km); two experimental phases, approaching ship 5-10 km and <5 km away; and two postexperiment phases, <30 and 30-60 min after the experiment (recalculated from Ljungblad et al. 1988:Table 2). The *center* section shows pooled data from three experiments when summering bowheads were exposed to noise from a single 0.66-L airgun 3-5 km away; behavior was observed before, during, and after the airgun fired (Richardson et al. 1986). The *right* section compares data from undisturbed summering bowheads versus those receiving pulses from seismic ships 6-99 km away (Richard-son et al. 1986). Mean, ±1 s.d. (vertical line), ±95% confidence limits (wide bar), and sample size are shown. NS means $P > 0.1$; *, **, and *** mean $P \leq 0.05$, 0.01, and 0.001, respectively. NS/* means NS or * depending on how the test was done. Tests based on one-way ANOVA for Ljungblad and airgun data, and methods described by Richardson et al. (1986) for opportunistic data.

(Richardson et al. 1986; Ljungblad et al. 1988). Initial behavioral changes were detected up to 8.2 km away, at received noise levels of 142-157 dB re 1 µPa. All bowheads were moving away by the time an airgun array was within 3-7.2 km (4 cases), or by the time a vessel with a single airgun came within 1¼ km. Received levels at the distances where active avoidance became evident were 152-178 dB. Bowheads swam rapidly away once active avoidance began. Some whales were displaced by several kilometers, and behavior was altered for up to 1 h in four tests by Ljungblad et al. (1988) and at least 2.4 h in a test by Richardson et al. (1986). There were also strong tendencies for reduced surfacing and dive durations, fewer blows per surfacing, and longer intervals between successive blows during ship approaches. These effects were strongest at ranges <5 km, but were evident at 5-10 km (Fig. 9.4).

Five additional tests with one 0.66-L (40-in³) airgun showed that summering bowheads usually continued normal activities when the airgun began firing 3-5 km away. Peak pulse levels were ≥118-133 dB re 1 µPa (Richardson et al. 1986). Bowheads oriented away from the airgun during two of five tests. In those cases there was no boat or compressor noise, so the whales apparently determined the approximate direction of arrival of the airgun pulses. Surfacing and respiration variables did not change much during airgun tests, but trends were consistent with those during tests with actual seismic boats.

Bowheads more than 6-8 km from seismic vessels rarely show overt avoidance, but may be affected subtly. Richardson et al. (1986) summarized opportunistic observations on 21 occasions when summering bowheads received noise pulses of 107 to 158+ dB re 1 µPa from seismic ships 6-99 km away. General activities and call types were indistinguishable from those without seismic noise. There was no detectable avoidance, and calling rate was reduced little if at all. However, on average, these bowheads had shorter surfacings and dives, with fewer blows per surfacing and longer intervals between successive blows, than did bowheads not exposed to man-made noise (Fig. 9.4). These trends probably were an actual seismic effect. They were consistent with trends during seismic tests closer to bowheads (see above) and summering gray whales (Malme et al. 1988). These changes in surfacing-respiration-dive behavior were seen up to 54-73 km from a seismic vessel. There, received pulse levels varied from <125 dB to ≥133 dB re 1 µPa.

Several other studies have also provided opportunistic data on bowheads near seismic ships. Bowheads usually continued normal activities when exposed to pulses from ships several kilometers or more away (Reeves et al. 1984; Richardson and Malme 1993). Subtle reactions were sometimes suspected, but it was usually uncertain whether any given behavior was related to seismic noise. In one case, bowheads swam rapidly away from an approaching seismic vessel 24 km away (Koski and Johnson 1987). Surfacings and dives were short, with few blows per surfacing and slightly longer than average blow intervals—the same pattern noted above. This apparent response is the longest-distance avoidance of a seismic vessel noticed to date for any baleen whale.

Thus, most bowheads usually show strong avoidance when an operating seismic vessel is within 6-8 km, and there probably are some effects at greater distances. In three studies of bowheads and one of gray whales, surfacing-dive cycles have been unusually quick in the presence of seismic noise, with fewer breaths per surfacing and longer intervals between breaths (Richardson et al. 1986; Koski and Johnson 1987; Ljungblad et al. 1988; Malme et al. 1988). This pattern was evident among bowheads 6-73 km from seismic vessels as well as during controlled tests at closer ranges. Besides these subtle effects, strong avoidance may occur infrequently at distances of 20+ km (Koski and Johnson 1987), although active avoidance usually does not begin unless the seismic ship is closer than 8 km.

Although bowheads react strongly to seismic ships within several kilometers, bowheads—like gray whales—often tolerate the strong seismic pulses received at somewhat greater distances. In both species, received noise levels when the whales begin to flee are 150-180 dB re 1 µPa. This is much higher than their "avoidance thresholds" for continuous sounds (e.g., from vessels, dredging, drilling, or oil production). Bowheads often show no overt reactions to noise pulses from ships 6-25 km away. Even at 25 km, these pulses seem strong and obtrusive to humans listening via hydrophones or sonobuoys.

On the longer term, there is also some tolerance of ongoing exposure to seismic noise. For example, summering bowheads were seen regularly for several weeks in an area where a seismic ship was working (Richardson et al. 1986, 1987a). We also saw many bowheads in areas where there had been much seismic work in previous summers. However, it is not known whether the same individuals remained in or returned to these areas of exposure.

Inupiat whalers suggest that, since seismic work began off northern Alaska, the autumn bowhead migration has tended to be farther offshore. Aerial surveys conducted in the relevant area since 1982 provide no evidence of such a trend (Moore and Clarke 1992). However, the question remains open because of sampling limitations. Whether or not there has been local displacement, bowheads still migrate west through the Beaufort Sea each autumn, even though seismic work occurred there annually for many years, often during part of the autumn migration period (G.W. Miller et al. 1991).

Humpback Whale.—Humpback reactions to seismic noise have been studied in less detail than those of gray and bowhead whales. Malme et al. (1985) studied movements of humpbacks summering in southeast Alaska when exposed to pulses from a 1.64-L airgun. No persistent avoidance was found, but the results were confounded by whale movements independent of any airgun effect. During three of seven tests, some humpbacks seemed startled when the airgun was first turned on at ranges up to 3.2 km, but these responses did not persist. Sound levels received by "startled" whales were 150-169 dB re 1 µPa. Malme et al. concluded that subtle effects may have occurred, but that there was no clear evidence of avoidance at exposure levels up to 172 dB re 1 µPa effective pulse pressure level. In the test areas, this level was obtained at ranges of 140 to 260 m from the airgun.

Fin and Blue Whales.—Off Oregon, fin and blue whales have been reported to continue calling in the presence of noise pulses from airguns (McDonald et al. 1993).

Summary.—Baleen whales seem quite tolerant of low- and moderate-level noise pulses from distant seismic surveys. They usually continue their normal activities when exposed to pulses with received levels as high as 150 dB re 1 μPa, and sometimes even higher. Such levels are 50+ dB above typical ambient noise levels. However, lower received levels can have subtle effects on surfacing and respiration patterns. Bowhead and gray whales often show strong avoidance several kilometers from an airgun array, at received levels 150-180 dB. Bowheads sometimes swim a few kilometers away, and normal activities can be disrupted for an hour or more.

These short-term observations provide no information about long-term effects on baleen whales. It is not known whether impulsive noises affect reproduction rate or distribution and habitat use in later days or years. Gray and bowhead whale populations continue to use areas and general migration corridors where they have been exposed to intermittent seismic work for many years. However, it is not known **(1)** whether the same individuals return to areas of previous seismic exposure, **(2)** whether seismic work has caused local changes in distribution or migration routes, or **(3)** whether whales that tolerate strong seismic pulses are stressed (see Sections 11.5-11.8).

9.8.4 Sirenians, Sea Otters, and Polar Bears

We have seen no data on reactions of *sirenians* to seismic noise.

Behavior of *sea otters* along the California coast was monitored by Riedman (1983, 1984) while they were exposed to noise pulses from a full-scale array of airguns (67 L) and a single airgun. No disturbance reactions by otters were evident when the full-scale seismic ship passed as close as 1.85 and 0.9 km. Feeding otters continued to dive and feed successfully at these times. No apparent reactions were evident among otters that were rafting, grooming, swimming, mating, or interacting with pups (Riedman 1983). Otters also did not respond noticeably to the single 1.6-L airgun (Riedman 1983, 1984). However, some rafting otters exhibited interest in the boat towing the airgun. The results suggest that sea otters are less responsive to marine seis-

mic pulses than are baleen whales. However, Riedman (1983) cautioned that there are no data on reactions of otters >400 m offshore.

Polar bears are unlikely to be affected by seismic noise in the
water. When they swim, their heads are normally above or at the surface, where underwater noise is undetectable or weak owing to pressure release effects.

On-ice seismic work in winter is more likely to disturb polar
bears. A female bear with cubs reportedly abandoned her den prematurely when a seismic crew operated on the ice nearby (J. Lentfer, in
Trasky 1976). Another female with cubs left her den prematurely
while a Vibroseis crew operated 1.9-2.5 km away (Amstrup 1993).
Those cubs survived, but premature departure from dens is correlated
with reduced cub survival (Amstrup 1993). Sound and vibration from
Vibroseis were not detectable in simulated bear dens more than a few
hundred meters away (Blix and Lentfer 1992). It is unclear whether
this would be true for actual dens.

9.9 Reactions to Sonars

Ships and larger boats routinely use fathometers, and powerful
side-looking sonars are common on many military, fishing, and bot-
tom-survey vessels (Section 6.6). Sounds from these sources must
often be audible to marine mammals and apparently cause disturbance in some situations.

Reeves (1992) summarized the use of active sonars in commercial
whaling after World War II. Catcher boats sometimes used sonar to
track whales underwater. This often caused strong avoidance by
baleen whales (Ash 1962). A whale scarer that emitted "ultrasonic"
pulses reportedly tended to scare baleen whales to the surface (Reeves
1992).

Wintering *humpback whales* responded to 3.3-kHz sonar pulses
by moving away, and to 3.1- to 3.6-kHz sonar sweeps by increased
swimming speeds and track linearity (Maybaum 1990, 1993). No consistent effect on dive cycles or underwater calling was evident. Humpbacks showed no obvious responses to acoustic pingers operating at 27-
30 kHz (P. Harcourt and S. Hobbs, in Goodyear 1993), and neither
humpbacks nor northern right whales reacted to sonic tags at 50 kHz
(Goodyear 1993). Watkins (1986) states that humpback, fin, and right
whales often react to sounds at frequencies from 15 Hz to 28 kHz, but
not to pingers and sonars at 36 kHz and above.

Lockyer (1977) describes use of a 24-kHz scanning sonar on a catcher boat to study *sperm whale* behavior. Whalers rarely used sonar to follow sperm whales as it tended to scatter them.

Sperm whales usually cease emitting pulsed sounds when exposed to a short sequence of noise pulses from acoustic pingers emitting ~1 pulse per second at 6-13 kHz (Watkins and Schevill 1975). Source levels of these pulses were low, ~110-130 dB re 1 μPa-m. The duration of the whales' silent period decreased with increasing pinger-to-whale distance. In contrast, sperm whales usually do not cease calling or otherwise react to continual pulsing from echosounders, e.g., at 12 kHz (Backus and Schevill 1966; Watkins 1977). One whale adapted its click intervals to match the timing of the echosounder pulses. Higher-frequency pulses (30-60 kHz) cause no obvious reaction, even if transmitted from a tag on the whale's back (Watkins et al. 1985a, 1993; Papastavrou et al. 1989). It is uncertain how this relates to evidence that 60-kHz pulses were faintly audible to a sperm whale calf; its best hearing was at 5-20 kHz (Carder and Ridgway 1990).

Sperm whales exposed to strong pulses from submarine sonars in the eastern Caribbean became silent, interrupted their activities, and moved away (Watkins et al. 1985a, 1993). Some of the submarine sonar signals that elicited reactions were at 3.25-8.4 kHz in pulses 0.145-0.45 s long, usually in sequences of 4-20 or more pulses at rates of ~1-5 pulses/min. However, sperm whales exposed to frequent and strong military sonar signals in the Mediterranean Sea continued calling (J. Gordon, pers. comm., 1994). Some mass strandings of *beaked whales* occur when there are naval maneuvers offshore, but no causal link has been proven (Simmonds and Lopez-Jurado 1991).

Dall's porpoises showed avoidance reactions in response to several types of pulsed sounds at 20-143 kHz (Hatakeyama et al. 1995). Free-ranging animals strongly avoided various 20- to 50-kHz pulsed signals at ranges of 100-700 m. Based on this work and on tests with captive Dall's porpoises, Hatakeyama et al. estimated the reaction thresholds for pulses at 20-100 kHz as ~116-130 dB re 1 μPa, but higher for pulses shorter than 1 ms or for pulses at >100 kHz.

Delphinids sometimes react to sonars, but data are very limited. Captive false killer whales showed some avoidance when first exposed to pulse sequences at 24-115 kHz and received levels above ~170 dB re 1 μPa. There was little or no reaction at lower received levels, and responses diminished with repeated exposure (Akamatsu et al. 1993). Echosounders are among the noisemaking methods used during the

Faroese drive fishery for long-finned pilot whales (Bloch et al. 1990). Some tuna fishermen in the Eastern Tropical Pacific found that pelagic dolphins were alarmed by sonar (F. Awbrey, pers. comm., 1995).

Some *harp seals* seemed to alter their swimming patterns when they encountered the beam of an echosounder, nominally at 200 kHz (Terhune 1976). However, there was significant energy at lower frequencies that would be audible to a harp seal. Behavior of *ringed* and *Weddell seals* did not seem to be affected by 60-69 kHz acoustic pingers attached to the seals (Wartzok et al. 1992a,b).

We have not seen specific data concerning sonar effects on other species of cetaceans or pinnipeds, or on sirenians, sea otters, or polar bears. Most of these animals presumably can hear sonars emitting energy below 20 kHz. This will include most sonars designed to detect objects at long distances (Section 6.6). Many short-range echosounders and other sonars operate mainly at higher frequencies. Some of them must be audible to the many odontocetes, seals, and perhaps other species whose underwater hearing extends above 20 kHz (Section 8.2).

High-power sonars emit sufficient energy to cause concern about possible hearing damage and nonauditory physical effects on human divers nearby (Smith 1985; Section 10.6.4). Recently, unofficial accounts have been circulating concerning negative diver reactions at very long distances from a specialized high-power low-frequency military sonar. For marine mammals, no information on this topic is available, at least in the open literature.

The disturbance and physical effects of sonars on marine mammals deserve more study, given the wide use of sonars, the high power of some units, and the paucity of relevant data.

9.10 Reactions to Explosions

Pressure pulses from explosions have higher peak levels than those from any other man-made source, and very rapid rise-times. At close distances, explosives also produce shock waves, which propagate in a different manner than acoustical energy. Shock waves from high explosives can cause severe physical injury and death. Underwater explosions are common during marine construction and demolition, and during military operations in both peace and war. In addition, underwater explosions were the standard energy source for marine seismic exploration in past decades. In some countries, explosives are still used for certain seismic programs.

This section discusses behavioral reactions (Section 9.10.1) and then physical damage (Section 9.10.2). Models that predict "safe" and lethal distances are summarized in Section 10.6.3.

9.10.1 Behavioral Reactions

Data on the behavioral responses of marine mammals to explosions are limited for pinnipeds, cetaceans, and polar bears, and to our knowledge nonexistent for sirenians and sea otters.

Pinnipeds.—Small explosives are often used in attempts to prevent pinnipeds from feeding around fishing gear (e.g., Mate and Harvey 1987). "Seal bombs" are firecracker-like explosives with up to a few grams of explosive, fused to explode a few meters below the surface. Source levels are ~200 dB re 1 µPa, maximum fast Sound Pressure Level (Awbrey and Thomas 1987), and ~220 dB re 1 µPa, peak (Myrick et al. 1990b). In contrast, shellcrackers fired from shotguns and smaller pyrotechnics fired from pistols can explode above, at, or below the surface, with widely varying effective source levels. On the U.S. west coast, these devices initially startle seals and sea lions, and often induce them to move away from feeding areas temporarily (Mate and Harvey 1987). However, avoidance wanes after repeated exposure. Thereafter, some animals tolerate quite high levels of underwater sound pulses in order to prey on fish.

Similarly, South African fur seals that feed around fishing vessels generally dove or fled when firecrackers with 2-11 g of explosive detonated underwater, but returned within a few minutes (Anonymous 1972; Shaughnessy et al. 1981). Charges had to be thrown repeatedly to discourage feeding (Anonymous 1976).

Northern fur seals breeding on land showed no visible reaction to large but muffled underground blasts from quarries 0.6-2 km away (Gentry et al. 1990). Some nonbreeding males within ~300 m looked up in response to the strongest blasts. South American fur seals and sea lions may also be quite unresponsive to blasting (R. Harcourt, in Gentry et al. 1990). Gray seals exposed to noise from Aquaflex linear explosives reportedly did not react strongly (J. Parsons, in G.D. Greene et al. 1985:283).

Thus, pinnipeds seem quite tolerant of noise pulses from explosions. It is not known whether hearing damage or other injuries occurred during any of these situations. Close exposure to blasts from seal bombs might cause hearing damage or other injuries (Section 9.10.2).

Toothed Whales.—During the 1950s, small explosive charges were dropped into an Alaskan river in attempts to scare belugas away from salmon. Success was limited (Fish and Vania 1971; Frost et al. 1984). Small explosive charges were "not always effective" in moving bottlenose dolphins away from sites in the Gulf of Mexico where larger demolition blasts were about to occur (Klima et al. 1988). Odontocetes may be attracted to fish killed by explosions, and thus attracted rather than repelled by "scare" charges. Hence, scare charges are now not used in the Gulf of Mexico platform removal program (G.R. Gitschlag, pers. comm., 1994). Captive false killer whales showed no obvious reaction to single noise pulses from small (10 g) charges; the received level was ~185 dB re 1 µPa (Akamatsu et al. 1993). Jefferson and Curry (1994) review several additional studies that found limited or no effects on killer whales and other odontocetes.

"Seal bombs" have been used extensively to influence movements of pelagic dolphins, mainly *Stenella*, during purse-seining for yellowfin tuna associated with dolphins (Glass 1989; Cassano et al. 1990; Myrick et al. 1990a,b). Seal bombs were often used to prevent dolphins from escaping before the net was fully set. After the net was set, bombs were sometimes used to direct fleeing dolphins toward a part of the net where they could escape. In 1989, seal bombs were used in at least 40% of all sets around dolphins by U.S. purse-seiners who were monitored (Cassano et al. 1990). At that time, U.S. law prohibited use of bombs with >2.59 g of explosive. However, infractions were common: the small ("Class C") seal bombs were often used in clusters, and larger bombs with up to 5.76 g of explosive were also widely used. It was common for 10-50 bombs to be used during a net set, and 200-600 were used in some sets (Cassano et al. 1990). In 1990, the U.S.A. banned the use of seal bombs in this fishery because of concern about blast effects on dolphins (Section 9.10.2). Various other countries have taken similar action, but some infractions occur.

Baleen Whales.—Few data have been published on baleen whale behavior near explosions. *Gray whales* exposed to noise from seismic exploration via explosives "were seemingly unaffected and in fact were not even frightened from the area" (Fitch and Young 1948). Seismic charges in use then usually consisted of 9-36 kg of high explosives. However, Gilmore (1978) believed that similar underwater blasts within a few kilometers of the gray whale migration corridor sometimes interrupted migration or elicited "snorkeling" behavior (see Section 9.3.3).

Dynamite blasts near Bermuda did not interrupt *humpback whale* song (Payne 1970, 1978b; Payne and McVay 1971). Recently, humpbacks in a Newfoundland inlet have been exposed repeatedly to large explosions in subbottom rock (Lien et al. 1993b). Charge size was usually 200-2000 kg. Humpbacks were common within 10 km of the blast site. Whales ~2 km from blasts showed no sudden dives, abrupt movements, or other obvious reactions. During blasts, received noise levels at range 1.85 km were ~150 dB re 1 µPa/Hz at 350 Hz. It is not known whether the nonresponsive whales had habituated before observations began, or if any of them had suffered hearing damage. However, at least two humpbacks were injured and probably killed by the blasts (Section 9.10.2).

In general, some baleen whales show no strong behavioral reaction to noise pulses from distant explosions. They also show considerable tolerance of similar noise pulses from nonexplosive seismic exploration (Section 9.8.3). However, strong seismic pulses elicit active avoidance, suggesting that explosives may sometimes do so as well.

Sirenians, Sea Otters, and Polar Bears.—Polar bears sometimes can be scared away by shellcrackers or other pyrotechnics. However, habituation is rapid if pyrotechnics are used repeatedly without reinforcement by other techniques (Shideler 1993).

9.10.2 Blast Damage

Section 10.6.3 summarizes models that have been developed to predict "safe" and lethal distances based on factors such as charge size and depth, and animal size and depth. Those models are based mainly on data from terrestrial mammals held underwater (Yelverton et al. 1973; Yelverton 1981). In general, damage tends to occur at boundaries between tissues of different densities. Gas-containing organs, especially the lungs and gastrointestinal tract, are especially susceptible to damage. The auditory system is also relatively susceptible because it is adapted to respond to pressure changes. However, specific data on blast damage to marine mammals, and especially to their auditory systems, are very limited.

Pinnipeds.—Explosive charges in the kilogram (or larger) range sometimes kill pinnipeds. Fitch and Young (1948) reported that, on at least three occasions, California sea lions were killed by explosives being used for seismic exploration. Charge sizes and distances were not given. Northern fur seals within 23 m of an 11.4-kg dynamite charge were killed consistently (H. Hanson, in Trasky 1976). Reiter

(1981) reports without further details that "there was evidence of [fur] seals...killed from concussion in the immediate area of demolition" when a grounded ship was broken up by ~454 kg of explosives. Harbor seals were killed by a large underground nuclear test below one of the Aleutian Islands (Fuller and Kirkwood 1977). However, various otariids (and odontocetes) that were within 5 km of a 1,250,000 kg conventional explosion in a reef reportedly were still "swimming in the area" after the blast (Thomson 1958).

Pinnipeds undoubtedly can be injured by explosions, but we have seen few confirmed reports of this. Bohne et al. (1985, 1986) found that the inner ears of 5 of 11 Weddell seals showed evidence of damage consistent with exposure to high noise levels. Numerous explosive charges had been detonated nearby, but there was no proven causal link. We have seen no reports of injury to pinnipeds from seal bombs, but at close range they probably cause injuries (see below).

Toothed Whales.—Specific reports of dolphin injuries from seal bombs are lacking (Cassano et al. 1990). However, Myrick et al. (1990a,b) concluded that a Class-C charge could cause injury when detonated within 1-3 m of a dolphin. The estimated safe standoff distance was beyond 4 m. These conclusions were based on tests with dolphin carcasses, fish, and inanimate targets, plus previous studies of explosive effects on other mammals. A similar charge killed a human diver when it exploded ~0.3 m from his head (Hirsch and Ommaya 1972).

Larger explosions can kill dolphins. Chinese river dolphins, Irrawaddy dolphins, and finless porpoises have been killed by explosions in rivers (Zhou Kaiya and Zhang Xingduan 1991; I.G. Baird et al. 1994). In the Gulf of Mexico, dolphins are often seen near obsolete oil industry platforms scheduled for explosive removal (Klima et al. 1988). Demolition blasts are delayed when dolphins are within 915 m, and no confirmed blast injuries or mortality have been reported.

Baleen Whales.—Two dead humpback whales with severe mechanical damage to the ears were found near a site of repeated subbottom blasting, including one 5000-kg blast (Ketten et al. 1993; Ketten 1995). Damage included round window rupture, ossicular chain disruption, tissue dissection, fluid leakage, and (in one whale) bilateral periotic fractures. No such damage was evident in humpbacks not exposed to blasts. The auditory damage was similar to that in humans exposed to severe blast injury. The two whales probably were killed by the blasts, but it is not known how close they were to the explosions.

Sirenians, Sea Otters, and Polar Bears.—Studies of sea otters done in association with nuclear tests provide the most detailed available data on susceptibility of any marine mammal to shock waves. A large underground test below Amchitka Island, Alaska, killed many sea otters along the coast (Fuller and Kirkwood 1977). These otters were killed by peak pressures of ~100-300 psi, equaling 70-210 N/cm^2 or 237-246 dB re 1 μPa, peak (R.L. Rausch, in Trasky 1976 and Westworth 1977).[2] The thoracic organs, central nervous system, and middle ear were most severely affected. Laboratory tests showed that several sea otters exposed to shock waves with peak pressure 103-251 N/cm^2 suffered unspecified damage but lived, whereas others exposed to 207-296 N/cm^2 died (Wright and Allton 1971). A pregnant sea otter exposed to 169 N/cm^2 also died.

These data may not be directly relevant for marine mammals close to conventional explosions, where pressure would increase more rapidly than the 50-ms rise time during the sea otter studies. As rise time becomes more rapid, more severe damage is expected with a given peak pressure.

Dugongs are sometimes killed during fishing with dynamite in Sri Lanka (Leatherwood and Reeves 1989). Heinsohn (1979) also noted that explosions could kill sirenians and, if carried out intensively, change local distribution patterns.

We are not aware of any specific data on the susceptibility of polar bears to blast damage.

Summary.—Few specific data are available about either the disturbance or blast injury effects of underwater explosions on marine mammals. Certain pinnipeds and toothed whales exhibit short-term avoidance reactions, and some avoidance is likely in other groups as well. However, various marine mammals show considerable tolerance of noise pulses from explosions, even when specifically used in attempts to scare mammals away. Nearby blasts can injure or kill marine mammals, but threshold levels for injury or death are not well established (see Section 10.6).

---

[2] 1 N/m^2 = 1 Pa, and 1 N/cm^2 = 10^4 Pa or 10^{10} μPa. Thus, L_r (in dB re 1 μPa, peak) = 20 log (10^{10}·L_r) in N/cm^2.

9.11 Reactions to Ocean Science Studies

Many studies of ocean and seafloor properties have been based on analysis of the properties of the refracted, reflected, or direct sound pulses from explosives and various nonexplosive sources. Reactions of marine mammals to pulses from explosives, other seismic sources, and sonars are discussed in preceding sections.

This section concerns marine mammal reactions to extended, but not continuous, broadcasts of low-frequency (LF) sounds. Acoustical oceanographers and other underwater acousticians often project strong nonexplosive LF sounds into the sea to study sound propagation and ocean properties affecting propagation (Section 6.8). This type of work has been done for many years. It has become controversial recently because of the possible effects on marine mammals (Cohen 1991; Herman 1994; Holing 1994; NRC/OSB 1994; Potter 1994). Few specific data are available on reactions of marine mammals to these sounds.

When LF sounds are used for ocean science research, they are usually projected into the deep sound channel, where propagation is efficient (Section 4.3). These LF sounds may be received hundreds or even thousands of kilometers away. Marine mammals with good LF hearing might hear the test sounds at long distances if they dive deep enough. At low and medium latitudes, channel depth is usually 600-1800 m (Munk 1990). Sound levels will be highest there. However, at long horizontal distances, some energy approaches much closer to the surface. Also, channel depth is ≤200 m in polar and subpolar areas, including parts of the North Pacific, Northwest Atlantic, and Southern Oceans where many cetaceans and pinnipeds occur. When acoustic tests are done there, foraging dives of many species could be deep enough to reach depths with maximum sound level.

Payne (1978b) mentioned that humpback whales near Bermuda continued to sing in their normal manner while exposed to very strong nonexplosive sounds within the frequency range of humpback songs. The specific levels and characteristics of the sounds received by the whales are unknown.

During the Heard Island Feasibility Test in the southern Indian Ocean (Section 6.8), reactions of marine mammals to an especially powerful source of LF sound were studied (Bowles et al. 1994; Munk et al. 1994). Sound at ~57 Hz was projected intermittently for 7.3 days, usually for periods of ½-1 h every 3 h. Overall source levels were initially 218-221 dB re 1 µPa-m, later diminishing to ~205 dB

(Birdsall et al. 1994). Source depth was ~175 m. Near the surface, the estimated received level from five projectors was ~160 dB at all distances within 1 km. At range 1 km, the estimated received level was ~160 dB at any depth. Received level remained above 120 dB out to a distance of ~100 km near the surface, and to distances beyond 1000 km at depths 50+ m (Bowles et al. 1991).

Sighting rates for medium- and large-sized whales—mainly pilot, beaked, and balaenopterid whales—were lower during than before transmissions. The transmitted sounds may have elicited avoidance by some whales of these types, especially beaked whales and especially in the area visible from the source vessel itself. Sperm and pilot whales ceased calling during the LF sound transmissions, and resumed calling within 36 h after transmissions ended. However, some large whales remained in the general area during transmissions. Overall, the evidence of avoidance was not conclusive: sample sizes were low, differences were not statistically significant, and whales probably reacted to the ships in addition to any reactions to the transmitted sounds (Bowles et al. 1994).

In contrast, hourglass dolphins and Antarctic fur seals did not avoid the source, and may have been attracted. During transmissions, several pods of dolphins approached the ship below which the source was suspended, and rode its bow wave in a seemingly normal manner. Sighting rates for dolphins were higher during the 7-day period of intermittent transmissions than during the preceding 5 days. Groups of dolphins and fur seals seen <1 km from the operating 57-Hz source were receiving levels near 160 dB re 1 μPa while they were near the surface, and higher levels when they dove, plus strong ship noise. A possible interpretation is that dolphins and fur seals were attracted to the source vessels and sounds, or at least showed no avoidance. Another possibility is that, when near the source, they reduced their exposure to strong LF sounds by spending more time at the surface, thereby becoming more conspicuous to the observers. Available data do not allow discrimination of these possible explanations.

Bottlenose dolphins in Florida showed no significant reaction to underwater playbacks of a sound signal used in some shorter-range ocean science studies: an M-code signal at 800-900 Hz (Tyack et al. 1993). Dolphins receiving levels above 120 dB re 1 μPa showed no significant reactions. This may exemplify a general low sensitivity of many odontocetes to low-frequency sounds. However, boats were very common in the study area. The M-code stimulus may have been unremarkable to dolphins that had habituated to highly variable background noise, including boat noise (Tyack et al. 1993).

In general, only limited data are available on the reactions of marine mammals to the strong low-frequency sounds used during some ocean acoustics research. At least a few of the odontocete and pinniped species show some tolerance of LF sounds. At low and moderate latitudes, where the sound channel is deep, the greatest concern is for deep-diving cetaceans and pinnipeds, and particularly for any of those that have acute LF hearing. Little is known about either the hearing sensitivity or behavioral responsiveness of most deep-diving species. However, ocean acoustics signals are often strong enough that even the odontocetes with rather insensitive LF hearing (Section 8.2.1) should be able to hear the sounds at ranges of many kilometers.

The U.S. Office of Naval Research has begun several studies of the effects of LF sounds on marine mammals. Also, marine mammal studies are to be done as part of the Acoustic Thermometry of Ocean Climate (ATOC) project, a planned North Pacific follow-on to the Heard Island test (Section 6.8; ARPA and NMFS 1994; ARPA 1995). These studies should provide important data on the effects of LF noise on marine mammals.

9.12 Purposeful Scaring via Noise

The presence of marine mammals is sometimes considered undesirable. Some species interfere with fishing or aquaculture and cause economic losses. Also, many mammals are injured or killed by entanglement in gear. Acoustic methods are often used in attempts to keep marine mammals away from fishing gear or from sites where large explosions are about to occur. There have also been attempts to use underwater sound to direct the movements of cetaceans that are at risk of entrapment in ice, confined waterways, or shallows. Jefferson and Curry (1994) reviewed much of the relevant literature, including many reports that are not mentioned here.

Electronic noisemaking devices of several types have been tested, mainly on pinnipeds. "Acoustic Harassment Devices" (AHDs) emitting strong tone pulses or pulsed frequency sweeps in the 11- to 17-kHz range have been used extensively in attempts to keep pinnipeds away from nets and aquaculture facilities (Mate and Harvey 1987; Rueggeberg and Booth 1989). Source levels were ~187-195 dB re 1 μPa-m. There was a substantial deterrent effect on harbor seals, but effectiveness declined slowly over time. Also, some large individuals habituated or were less sensitive, and foraged with modified techniques (Mate 1993). In the absence of other negative stimuli, some pinnipeds may ultimately be attracted by AHD sounds after learning their association with fish—the "dinner bell" effect. In California sea lions, there was an initial startle response but no deterrent effect thereafter.

Pure tones at 1-100 kHz seemed to have little if any scaring effect on a harbor seal (Anderson and Hawkins 1978).

Electronically synthesized "roar" sounds resembling aggressive polar bear calls (frequencies 100-600 Hz) have some deterrent effect on polar bears, but must be projected at high intensity (Wooldridge and Belton 1980). Sea otters were not repelled by a loud airborne warble tone near 1 kHz nor by air horns or narrowband pulses at 0.5 to 20 kHz underwater (Davis et al. 1987).

Small explosive charges and other *pyrotechnics* often have a short-term scaring effect on pinnipeds, odontocetes, and polar bears (Section 9.10.1). *Warning shots* can have a similar effect. These methods are used by fishing and aquaculture interests to deter pinnipeds (Shaughnessy et al. 1981; Mate and Harvey 1987; Rueggeberg and Booth 1989) and, less often, odontocetes (Jefferson and Curry 1994). Pyrotechnics and warning shots are also used to deter polar bears (Shideler 1993). However, some of these methods risk injuring or killing marine mammals or human bystanders, and are only partially effective in scaring marine mammals away from areas to which they are strongly attracted. Blasts or shots must often be repeated frequently to be effective even in the short term. That may cause rapid habituation and loss of long-term effectiveness. Also, in "fisheries-protection" applications, there can be concern that pyrotechnics may disturb fish (e.g., Shaughnessy 1985).

An *arc-discharge* device that created underwater noise pulses also had only limited value in scaring South African fur seals (Shaughnessy et al. 1981; Shaughnessy 1985). This device produced up to one pulse per 10 s with a rather low source level, 132 dB re 1 µPa-m.

Noise pulses of other types have been tested. Some were partially or temporarily effective in scaring marine mammals away, or at least in gaining their attention. Other tests have shown little scaring effect, especially with pinnipeds attracted to food concentrations or breeding sites. A "Seal Scram" electronic device that emits random underwater sound pulses reportedly has some effect on North Atlantic phocid seals but not on South African fur seals (Wickens et al. 1992a).

An air gun was ineffective in scaring South African fur seals away from fishing gear (Anonymous 1975a). When exposed to intense pulses of airborne noise from a carbide pest control cannon simulating sonic booms, breeding northern elephant seals rarely showed reactions more severe than brief alert responses. Some California sea lions moved into the water temporarily, but there was no mortality of pups or adults (Stewart 1981, 1982).

In Japan, noise pulses obtained by striking an iron pipe held in the water have been used to help drive false killer whales and other dolphins into hunting areas (Kasuya 1985; Akamatsu et al. 1993). Captive false killer whales also showed some avoidance upon initial exposure to pulse sequences of this type (0.2-5.2 kHz) if the received level was above ~170 dB re 1 μPa. These reactions resembled those to higher-frequency sonarlike pulses (Section 9.9). Bottlenose dolphins off Tunisia fled when similar "bang pipes" were tested there (Mhenni 1993). Bang pipes were not effective in deterring killer whales from fishing gear in Alaska (M. Dahlheim, in Jefferson and Curry 1994).

Dall's porpoises react to sequences of ultrasonic pulses at received levels of ~116-130 dB re 1 μPa (Section 9.9). When alarm devices emitting these types of pulses at source levels near 185 dB re 1 μPa-m were attached to gillnets, there was a slight reduction in the bycatch of porpoises (Hatakeyama et al. 1995).

Harbor porpoises also become entangled in gillnets. Fewer porpoises were caught in nets equipped with alarms whose dominant noise components were near 2-2½ kHz than were caught in control nets (Lien et al. 1993a, 1995). However, the effect may have been at least partly attributable to weaker high-frequency components, possibly at 17.5 kHz or above (Kastelein et al. 1995a). Source levels of these alarms were low—only 115-119 dB re 1 μPa-m.

Humpback whales are less likely to collide with cod traps equipped with beepers emitting weak pulses at 3.5 kHz or "alarms" emitting broadband pulses centered at 4 kHz (Lien et al. 1990, 1992). These devices produce relatively weak sounds: 135-145 dB re 1 μPa-m at 4 kHz for "alarms". These sounds may have no strong scaring effect themselves; humpback and minke whales tend to be seen *closer* to nets with than to nets without operating alarms (Todd et al. 1992). However, there is apparently a short-range deterrent effect either to the alarms *per se* or to the cod trap after the alarms alert whales to the presence of the gear.

In general, considerable work has been done to develop and test pulse-emitting alarm devices designed to reduce cetacean by-catch in fishing gear. Some results are promising. However, alarms are not 100% effective, and there are logistical, habituation, and other problems. In some cases, alarms may be counterproductive through scaring fish or attracting mammals (dinner bell effect; Dawson 1994).

Recorded killer whale calls, when played back underwater, initially scared South African fur seals away, but they quickly returned (Anonymous 1975a,b; Shaughnessy et al. 1981). The killer whale calls had been recorded elsewhere. It was suspected that calls from the local population might be more effective. Likewise, killer whale playbacks initially induced a harbor seal to haul out of the water, but habituation occurred and the seal ceased hauling out (Anderson and Hawkins 1978). Sea otters were repelled by either aerial or underwater playback of killer whale calls (Davis et al. 1987).

Dall's porpoises off Japan may have departed in response to playbacks of killer whale calls (Hatakeyama et al. 1995).

Belugas attracted into an Alaskan river by salmon concentrations showed strong avoidance during underwater playbacks of killer whale calls at source level 170 dB re 1 µPa-m (Fish and Vania 1971). They concluded that belugas could be prevented from entering the river (~3 km wide) by one projector on each side. However, the beluga deterrent program was abandoned after 1978 (Frost et al. 1984).

Migrating gray whales also showed immediate and dramatic avoidance reactions to playbacks of killer whale calls (Cummings and Thompson 1971b; Malme et al. 1983). In both studies, the reactions were more pronounced than those to playbacks of recorded tones, random noise, or industrial sounds. The killer whale calls had been recorded near the migration route of the gray whales. Likewise, gray whales in a wintering lagoon showed stronger reactions to playbacks of killer whale calls than to other sounds (Dahlheim 1987). In contrast, southern right whales showed little reaction to playbacks of killer whale calls from distant locations (Cummings et al. 1972, 1974).

In *summary*, acoustic methods have had variable but often only limited and temporary success in scaring marine mammals. Small explosions and gunfire have some effect, but they are potentially injurious if used indiscriminately. Playbacks of calls from the local population of killer whales may sometimes be effective. However, habituation will probably limit the long-term effectiveness of any scaring measure. Habituation may be reduced by using scaring measures sparingly, irregularly, and in combinations, and by occasional reinforcement with more threatening stimuli. Most tests have been on animals attracted to food concentrations. In some other situations, marine mammals might be more easily scared. In many jurisdictions, attempts to scare marine mammals are prohibited or restricted. Scaring should be attempted only where justifiable and in compliance with local regulations.

9.13 Reactions to Human Presence

The disturbance effects of human presence are difficult to separate from reactions to vehicles, boats, aircraft, and presence of various types of machinery. Furthermore, it is generally impossible to determine from uncontrolled observations whether animals are reacting to sounds from humans or to the sight, movement, or smell of humans or their appurtenances. We summarize data on reactions of marine mammals to humans, excluding many cases attributable to aircraft, boats, or other equipment. Most observations are anecdotal.

Harbor seals hauled out on shore can be disturbed by passing hikers, recreational vehicles and small boats. This has been noted in many areas, including the western U.S.A. and Alaska, eastern Canada, and western Europe (e.g., Johnson 1977; Bowles and Stewart 1980; Reijnders 1981; Renouf et al. 1981; Allen et al. 1984; Osborn 1985; Brasseur 1993; Suryan 1993; Swift and Morgan 1993). Similar observations have been reported for *gray seals* (Bonner 1978; Renouf et al. 1981). Harbor seals spent more time scanning and less time "sleeping" in areas with human disturbance and occasional hunting (Terhune 1985). In the absence of hunting or active harassment, habituation probably occurs (Awbrey 1980; Bonner 1982; Thompson 1992; Brasseur 1993). Indeed, harbor seals often haul out on manmade structures.

When some adult gray seals are killed at breeding colonies, some of the other females are deterred from coming ashore, or desert their pups, or are deterred from returning in later years. Collectively, these disturbance effects cause decreased pup production (Harwood and Greenwood 1985).

Harp seals hauled out on the ice for whelping were affected temporarily by the presence of tourists (Kovacs and Innes 1990). Females spent less time with their pups when tourists were present. When with pups, females spent more time alert and aggressive, defending the pups against human approach, and less time nursing. Pup behavior was also affected by tourists on the ice. Normal behavior usually resumed within 1 h after tourists left (Kovacs and Innes 1990).

Hawaiian monk seals that whelp on remote beaches are often driven into the water by passing humans, and may avoid beaches where they have been disturbed often (Kenyon 1972). Pups disturbed by tagging subsequently hauled out farther away from the first haul-out site as compared with untagged seals (Henderson and Johanos 1988). Recurring human activity in critical habitats results in population decline, and reduced human activity can lead to population growth (Gerrodette and Gilmartin 1990).

Northern elephant seals on beaches show little reaction to humans during the breeding season, but during molting often depart in response to the sight or smell of humans. If disturbance is not frequent, seals usually return within 1 day (Stewart 1982 and pers. comm., 1994).

Sea lions and *fur seals*, in contrast, may abandon some haulout sites at least partly because of human harassment (Peterson and Bartholomew 1967; Calkins 1979; C. Fowler, in S.R. Johnson et al. 1989: 48). People walking near or in California sea lion and northern fur seal rookeries and haulouts can cause major short-term disturbance. Weekly disturbance of California sea lions caused many females and pups to relocate (Stewart 1982). Lewis (1987) found that 22 of 23 stampedes of northern sea lions from a whelping beach were caused by human disturbance during pup censuses. Few pups were killed but the subsequent behavior of some animals seemed altered, including reduced mother-pup contact. When disturbance forces female South African fur seals to flee into the sea, some pups are deserted and die. There is also disruption of mating activities, leading to reduced pup production the next year (Wickens et al. 1992b).

Responsiveness of sea lions to humans varies with breeding status and prior experience. Territorial males and females with young pups often are less responsive (Peterson and Bartholomew 1967; Stirling 1972). "California" sea lions in the relatively undisturbed Galapagos are less responsive to humans than are those in California. Similarly, Australian sea lions at breeding and whelping sites are usually afraid of humans, but those at a nature reserve apparently habituated to humans (Stirling 1972). At locations other than breeding and whelping areas, habituation seems more common; sea lions often haul out on man-made structures, often close to humans.

Walruses that have hauled out are sensitive to close approaches on foot, especially if approached from upwind when scent may prompt fleeing (Loughrey 1959). Walruses may not return to land for 3-4 days after being displaced (Mansfield and St. Aubin 1991). Walruses may have abandoned some traditional terrestrial haulout sites after establishment of settlements nearby (Salter 1979). However, hunting was probably a factor in those cases. Frost et al. (1982:525) also mention evidence that "regular human disturbance has prevented the long-term use" of three haulout sites in Alaska.

Odontocetes are presumably less susceptible to disturbance by human presence than are pinnipeds that haul out on land. In several areas, small numbers of dolphins have become habituated to humans, and regularly approach them (Connor and Smolker 1985; Lockyer and Morris 1986; Shane et al. 1986; Lockyer 1990; Pryor et al. 1990; Domning 1991). The highly variable responses of odontocetes to boats, depending largely on the past experiences of those animals with similar boats, were summarized in Section 9.3.2. Belugas show short-term localized displacement when harassed, but persist in using traditional summering grounds even when hunted intensively (Finley et al. 1982).

Mysticetes often tolerate close approaches by human swimmers and by humans in slow-moving boats (Payne 1972; Jones and Swartz 1984; Tinney 1988). However, they can be disturbed by humans or quiet boats that appear abruptly at close quarters. Gray whales summering close to shore may move away when persons appear or move on the shore (Sauer 1963). Inupiat whalers hunting from the ice-edge find that bowhead whales are alarmed by the sight or sound of humans or human activities (Carroll and Smithhisler 1980).

Sea otters often seem quite tolerant of boats or humans nearby (e.g., Calkins 1979), but sometimes avoid heavily disturbed areas (Section 9.3.4). Riedman (1984) noted that some sea otters dove in alarm and swam away in response to a sudden strong noise combined with sight of her at a distance of 150 m. *Polar bears* may either approach or avoid humans, but they are not significantly disturbed by simple human proximity (Stirling 1988b; Amstrup 1993; Shideler 1993).

9.14 Tolerance, Habituation, and Sensitization

Tolerance refers to the occurrence of marine mammals in areas where they are exposed to human activities or man-made noise. Behavioral habituation is a more specific phenomenon involving the progressive waning of responses to stimuli that are learned to lack significance to the animal (Thorpe 1963). Tolerance no doubt develops as a result of habituation in many cases. However, progressive waning of responses by individually identified animals is rarely documented. Thus, only a few cases of tolerance have been demonstrated unequivocally to result from habituation. In this section, we first mention examples of general tolerance, and then mention cases where there is evidence that tolerance developed through habituation.

In contrast, sensitization refers to increasing responsiveness over time (Section 9.14.3).

9.14.1 Tolerance

Marine mammals are often seen in regions with much human activity. Thus, certain individuals or populations exhibit some tolerance of anthropogenic noise and other stimuli. This tolerance has rarely been studied specifically, but many relevant anecdotal or "common knowledge" observations can be found in the literature.

Baleen whales, for example, use shipping lanes in the St. Lawrence estuary and off Cape Cod each year despite frequent exposure to vessels (e.g., Mitchell and Ghanimé 1982; Beach and Weinrich 1989). Baleen whales also feed consistently in rich fishing grounds where large numbers of trawlers operate (Brodie 1981a,b). Gray whales continue to migrate through heavily traveled shipping lanes along the west coast of North America twice each year. Indeed, because of the nearly ubiquitous nature of ship noise in the ocean (Section 5.2.3), most deep water areas where whales occur are ensonified by ship noise to some extent. Gray whales are also exposed to seismic exploration and whalewatching boats during this migration (Miles 1984; Atkins and Swartz 1989). Bowhead whales continue to return to parts of the Canadian Beaufort Sea where there has been seismic exploration in previous years (Richardson et al. 1987a). Humpback whales off Newfoundland tolerated repeated exposure to strong noise pulses from nearby explosions (Lien et al. 1993b).

Odontocetes often tolerate repeated exposure to many vessels. Many dolphins actively approach boats.

Pinnipeds also exhibit much tolerance of some human activities. Some species often haul out on man-made structures where there is considerable human activity, including boat traffic, aircraft traffic, and human presence (e.g., Mate and Harvey 1987; S.R. Johnson et al. 1989; Thompson 1992). Marine mammals in captivity, presumably including both toothed whales and pinnipeds, are very tolerant of the explosions and flashes associated with fireworks displays (Awbrey 1980:244).

In some areas, manatees and sea otters tolerate much vessel traffic or other human activity.

Thus, many if not all marine mammals can tolerate some degree of chronic exposure to man-made noise. This is so even though the mammals may show short-term behavioral reactions and localized displacement when they are exposed to particularly strong disturbance. Most cases of tolerance may have developed via the habituation process, but more study would be needed to prove this.

Marine mammals may or may not be affected by the tolerated activities. Because of ecological or physiological requirements, many marine mammals may have no alternative but to occupy areas where they are chronically exposed to noise (Brodie 1981b; Blane 1990). Many authors have discussed the implications of masking of communication sounds by this noise. However, there is no documentation concerning the actual effects of masking in field situations. Likewise, it is not known whether marine mammals that are chronically exposed to human activity are subject to negative physiological effects (stress). These matters are discussed further in Chapter 11.

9.14.2 Habituation

Behavioral habituation refers to the gradual waning of responses when a repeated or ongoing stimulus lacks any significant consequences for the animal (Thorpe 1963). Habituation has rarely been demonstrated in a rigorous way during field studies of marine mammals, since this requires repeated observations of known individuals. However, as identified in preceding sections, apparent habituation has often been reported, based on comparisons of the behavior of (1) one group of animals at different times or (2) two or more groups of animals exposed to different amounts of human activity. Most cases of tolerance listed above may involve habituation even though the "gradual waning of responses" has not been observed directly. The following are some more specific examples.

Pinnipeds provide many examples of habituation. One is the apparent accommodation of harbor and gray seals to repeated approaches by tourboats as opposed to their lesser tolerance of some other vessels (Bonner 1982). Similarly, harbor seals living near a major airport have apparently become habituated to repeated aircraft overflights, given that harbor seals in other situations react strongly to aircraft (Johnson 1977; M. Bigg, in S.R. Johnson et al. 1989). Spotted seals continue to be displaced from their haulout beaches by each aircraft overflight, but they accommodate to the extent that they haul out again quickly (Frost and Lowry 1990). The effectiveness of acoustic methods for scaring pinnipeds away from fish concentrations wanes rapidly (Section 9.12).

In toothed whales, one example is the decline in avoidance responses of captive false killer whales upon repeated exposure to various strong pulsed sounds (Section 9.9). Further examples of apparent habituation are evident in belugas: their tolerance of boats in various areas versus their extreme sensitivity to the first icebreaker approach of the year in a remote area of the high arctic, and their declining responses to boats in the St. Lawrence estuary within and among years (Section 9.3.2). In some areas, wild dolphins have become very tolerant of humans and may actively approach them (Section 9.13). In contrast, Kruse (1991) found that the responses of killer whales to repeated boat disturbance did *not* diminish during the whalewatching season.

Several cases of apparent habituation have been reported in baleen whales. When wintering gray whales first enter the calving lagoons, they are comparatively wary of small boats. Later in winter they are less wary, and some individuals actively seek out motorboats (Section 9.3.3). Watkins (1986) suggested that, near Cape Cod, reactions of various species changed over the years as whalewatching became popular. Some species, particularly humpback and fin whales, are now less wary of boats. Dolphin (1987) reported that humpbacks off southeast Alaska initially reacted to an outboard motorboat used in his research, but soon accepted it. Malme et al. (1985) suggested that reactions of humpbacks to noise pulses from an airgun may have waned after the first exposure. Richardson et al. (1990b) found that some bowheads occurred near actual dredges and drillships producing continuous noise even though bowheads exhibited avoidance at the onset of about the same levels of drillship or dredge noise.

Many manatees exposed to boats and tourists are becoming tame, approaching boats and people (Curtin and Tyson 1993). This habituation may increase their vulnerability to collisions with boats.

Polar bears habituate to pyrotechnic scaring devices and warning shots if these are used repeatedly without reinforcement by other methods such as plastic bullets (Shideler 1993). Bears that are habituated to people may be especially dangerous, based on evidence from grizzly bears (Herrero and Fleck 1990).

These observations suggest that marine mammals, like other animals, tend over time to become less sensitive to those types of noise and disturbance to which they are repeatedly exposed. This reduction in responsiveness is not likely to occur if the animals are harmed or harassed severely when exposed to the noise or disturbance.

9.14.3 Sensitization

Increasing responsiveness to human activities over time has been reported in a few cases, as mentioned in previous sections:

- ▸ harbor seals were more responsive to aircraft after recent disturbance episodes (Section 9.2.1; B.W. Johnson 1977);
- ▸ gray whales reacted vigorously to repeated herding by helicopter (Walker 1949; Section 9.2.3);
- ▸ northern fur seals avoided ships that engaged in seal hunting (H. Kajimura, in S.R. Johnson et al. 1989:48; Section 9.3.1);
- ▸ bottlenose dolphins avoided a boat that had been used for earlier dolphin capture-and-release work (Irvine et al. 1981; Section 9.3.2);
- ▸ pelagic dolphins in the eastern tropical Pacific showed strong avoidance of approaching ships, probably because of previous experience with tuna seiners (Norris et al. 1978; Au and Perryman 1982; Hewitt 1985; Section 9.3.2);
- ▸ whales that had been hunted recently were more difficult to approach (Section 9.3.3; Ash 1962:8);
- ▸ harbor seals spent more time scanning and less time "sleeping" in areas with human disturbance and occasional hunting (Terhune 1985; Section 9.13).

These cases of heightened responsiveness all involved prior exposure to human activities that can be interpreted as severe and threatening. In this situation, some marine mammals apparently develop lower response thresholds and/or more dramatic response patterns. These cases of sensitization to severe disturbance contrast with habituation, when responses wane after repeated exposure to "benign" stimuli (Section 9.14.2).

9.15 Summary and Comparisons

Aircraft overflights at low altitude can cause pinnipeds hauled out on land or ice to escape into the water, occasionally leading to some mortality of young through abandonment or trampling. Toothed and baleen whales sometimes dive or turn away during overflights, but responsiveness seems to vary depending on the activity of the animals. Effects on cetaceans seem transient, and occasional overflights probably have no long-term consequences on cetaceans. The relative roles of sound and vision in eliciting reactions are unknown.

Ship and boat noises do not seem to have strong effects on pinnipeds that are in the water, but the data are very limited. Pinnipeds hauled out on land or ice often are more responsive to nearby vessels. Many toothed whales show some tolerance of vessels, but may react at distances of several kilometers or more when confined by ice or shallow water, or when they have learned to associate the vessel with harassment. Belugas near ice in spring sometimes react to noise from approaching ships at distances of 50 km or more. At some other times, belugas tolerate very high levels of human activity.

Baleen whales sometimes flee from approaching ships and boats, especially from vessels that are moving rapidly, directly toward the whales, or erratically. However, there is little evidence that baleen whales travel far or remain disturbed for long after a single vessel passes. Gray and possibly humpback and bowhead whales may have reduced their utilization of certain heavily disturbed areas. However, the continued presence of various whale species in some areas heavily traveled by ships indicates a considerable degree of tolerance to ship noise. Avoidance reactions are not always effective in avoiding collisions with vessels.

Sirenians usually do not react until boats are close, and collisions are common. Occasional vessel traffic has little effect on sea otters and polar bears.

Icebreaker noise effects have not been studied extensively. There is limited evidence that icebreaker traffic in winter does not reduce numbers of ringed seals present along the icebreaker tracks later in the spring. *Hovercraft* cause avoidance by some cetaceans and seals.

Stationary offshore activities (drilling, dredging, production) often seem to have less effect on cetacean behavior than do moving sound sources such as aircraft and ships. However, avoidance responses have been demonstrated when certain whales are exposed to high levels of these sounds either near actual oil industry operations or via underwater playbacks of recorded industrial noise. Responsiveness varies considerably. However, reactions have only been found when received noise levels were well above ambient levels. Thus, the few species of cetaceans studied apparently did not react overtly if they could barely hear the industrial noise; they only reacted when it was well above the ambient noise.

Fewer data are available concerning effects of noise from drilling, dredging, and production on pinnipeds, toothed whales, sea otters, and polar bears. These animals do, at least sometimes, tolerate considerable noise from such sources.

Seismic exploration noise is stronger than noise from other nonexplosive sources. Some ringed seals and polar bears may abandon areas where on-ice seismic techniques (Vibroseis) are used in winter. However, the effect is very localized. Other species of seals often tolerate strong noise pulses. However, specific effects on pinnipeds and odontocetes are poorly known.

Baleen whales often seem to behave normally when exposed to strong noise pulses from seismic vessels several kilometers or more away. However, most gray and bowhead whales swim away when a seismic vessel approaches within a few kilometers. Also, bowheads exposed to pulses from distant seismic vessels often exhibit subtle behavioral changes even if they remain in the area. Sea otters seem less responsive than baleen whales to marine seismic exploration.

Sonar and pinger pulses up to ~28 kHz often cause cessation of calling and avoidance in sperm whales, and avoidance in some baleen whales. There are indications of avoidance in Dall's porpoises and harp seals as well. Effects of sonars on other marine mammals are largely unreported. Sonar effects deserve additional study.

High explosives, when detonated underwater, produce shock waves and very sharp noise pulses. A few cases of mortality or injury to pinnipeds, dolphins, humpback whales, and sea otters have been reported. Nearby blasts cause short-term avoidance in some pinnipeds and odontocetes. However, they and some baleen whales often show little reaction to strong noise pulses from more distant explosions. The available data are largely anecdotal.

Ocean science studies often use strong low-frequency (<1000 Hz) sounds projected into the deep sound channel to study ocean properties. Some dolphins and pinnipeds may be rather insensitive to these sounds, but more data are needed. Baleen whales and the deep-diving odontocetes and pinnipeds are of special concern.

Acoustic scaring methods have had variable but often only limited and temporary success in scaring marine mammals away from places where their presence is undesirable. Habituation to the noise is common, especially when the animals are strongly attracted to a concentrated food source.

Overall, noise from human activities sometimes causes pronounced short-term behavioral reactions and temporary local displacement of certain marine mammals. Sometimes the effects are more subtle, and at other times no effects are detectable even in the presence of strong man-made noise. Some noisy activities, notably disturbance to pinnipeds at haulout sites, can cause limited mortality through stampedes or abandonment. The continued presence of various marine mammals in certain areas despite intense ship traffic and other human activities suggests that many marine mammals tolerate much human activity. However, some marine mammals may have no suitable alternative locations. It is not known whether marine mammals that tolerate chronic noise exposure are stressed or otherwise deleteriously affected.

CHAPTER 10

ZONES OF NOISE INFLUENCE[1]

10.1 Introduction

In assessing potential effects of man-made noise on marine mammals, it is important to estimate the radius within which acoustic effects are expected. There are at least four criteria for defining the radius or zone of influence. (1) The most extensive of these zones is the area within which the mammal might hear the noise—the *zone of audibility*. (2) The *zone of responsiveness* is the region within which the animal reacts behaviorally or physiologically. This zone can be smaller than the zone of audibility, as marine mammals often do not react overtly to noises that are faint but presumably audible (Chapter 9). (3) The *zone of masking* is the region within which noise is strong enough to interfere with detection of other sounds, such as communication or echolocation calls, prey sounds, or other natural environmental sounds. The zone of masking is highly variable in size (Section 10.5). (4) The *zone of hearing loss, discomfort, or injury* is the area near the noise source where, for explosions and possibly some other strong sources, the received sound level is high enough to cause discomfort or tissue damage to auditory or other systems.

This chapter discusses what is known about these four conceptual zones of noise influence on marine mammals, based largely on material in preceding chapters. The source level and spectral characteristics of a man-made noise (Chapter 6), together with its rate of attenuation with increasing distance (Chapter 4), determine its level and characteristics at various distances from the source. The level and spectral characteristics of the natural ambient noise (Chapter 5) determine the range at which a man-made noise diminishes below the natural background noise and becomes inaudible. Levels, spectral characteristics,

---

[1] By W. John Richardson, LGL Ltd., and Charles I. Malme, Bolt Beranek and Newman Inc.

and directionality of marine mammal sounds (Chapter 7) affect the distance to which they can be heard by conspecifics or, in the case of echolocation, the distance to which echoes from a given target can be detected. The functions of mammal sounds are important in evaluating effects of acoustic masking. Hearing abilities of marine mammals (Chapter 8) are obviously important in estimating zones of acoustic influence, as are the known reactions to man-made noise (Chapter 9).

It can be argued that a review of "zone of influence" concepts is premature. Many assumptions must be made in predicting radii of acoustic influence on marine mammals. Existing data are rarely adequate to allow precise predictions. Also, radii of influence for a given noise source and mammal will vary greatly with time, location, and other factors. Despite these problems, zone of influence estimates are already being used in attempts to "protect" marine mammals from some noisy human activities. Thus, a review of zone of influence concepts is warranted. At the least, it is useful in identifying data gaps.

10.2 Zone of Audibility

10.2.1 Limitation by Ambient Noise

Ambient noise often determines whether a listening animal can detect a specific sound, man-made or otherwise. This is usually true for sounds at frequencies where the animal has good hearing abilities. Outside that optimum frequency range, detectability may be determined by absolute hearing threshold, not ambient noise.

Masked Hearing Threshold.—If the received level of a man-made noise is much lower than that of the background noise, the man-made noise is not detectable and cannot affect the animal. To be undetectable, its received level must be well below the ambient level at all frequencies to which the animal is sensitive. We say "well below" because some animals detect sounds with levels slightly less than the ambient noise level in the corresponding frequency band (Section 8.5.3). Some mammals detect differences in level as small as 1 dB (Section 8.3.2). A man-made noise whose received level is 6 dB below the background noise level increases the total noise level to 1 dB above the background level [equation (2.9)]. This 1 dB increase might be detected by some mammals.

Weak and barely detectable sound signals may, however, provide little usable information. It is unlikely that man-made sounds with received levels slightly less than the background noise level in the corresponding band—that is, signal-to-noise ratio (SNR) <0 dB—would cause disturbance even if faintly audible. There is little information on this point. However, Malme et al. (1983) found that gray whales swimming toward a source of killer whale sounds first reacted when the received level of killer whale calls was similar to the ambient noise level (SNR ≈ 0 dB). Killer whales sometimes attack gray whales (Ljungblad and Moore 1983). If gray whales do not react to killer whale sounds unless SNR ≥0 dB, it is unlikely that they would react to man-made sounds with SNR <0 dB.

The two species of toothed whales whose hearing has been studied in most detail, bottlenose dolphins and belugas, have good hearing abilities for high-frequency echolocation sounds in the presence of noise. They detect some sounds with received levels several dB less than the background noise level in the corresponding critical band (Section 8.5.3; Turl et al. 1987). Thus, they probably hear quite faint signals from man-made sonars operating at high frequencies. However, their hearing sensitivity is much poorer at the low frequencies where many other man-made noises are concentrated (Section 8.2.1).

Critical ratio data (Section 8.5.1) provide some information about the level of man-made noise that would be barely detectable. The critical ratio is the difference, in dB, between the level of a tone that is barely detectable and the spectrum level (i.e., /Hz basis) of background white noise. White noise is noise with a flat spectrum—the same level at each frequency. Critical ratios measured under laboratory conditions have been reported for a few pinnipeds and toothed whales, but not for any baleen whales, sea otters, or sirenians.

Unfortunately, critical ratio data usually provide only rough guidance about the situations in which man-made noises would be detectable in the field. The spectrum of background ambient noise is rarely flat, and man-made noises are rarely limited to a single pure tone. Also, most measurements of critical ratios in marine mammals listening underwater are at ≥2 kHz (Fig. 8.6). A beluga is the only marine mammal whose critical ratios have been measured underwater at the low frequencies where many man-made noises are concentrated (C.S. Johnson et al. 1989).

In summary, mammals generally can barely detect a sound signal whose received level equals the level of background noise in the same ⅓-octave band. This "rule of thumb" applies, roughly, to a wide range of species, including humans, in the frequency range where they have good hearing capabilities (Section 8.5.2). However, some marine mammals probably hear sounds with levels a few dB less than that. For pinnipeds and especially toothed whales, hearing probably is not acute at the low frequencies where much man-made noise occurs.   For baleen whales, specific data on hearing sensitivity are lacking, but their hearing is probably acute at low frequencies (Section 8.6).

Masking at Low Frequencies.—In some terrestrial mammals, critical bandwidths widen (as a percentage of center frequency) at frequencies below 1 kHz, and greatly exceed ⅓ octave at ≤100 Hz (Fig. 8.9). If this is true in marine mammals, their ability to detect low-frequency man-made sounds would be poorer than implied by preceding paragraphs. Gales (1982) took account of this possibility when he estimated potential radii of audibility of industrial sounds at low frequencies.   He assumed that, below 450 Hz, the critical ratio might be a constant 20 dB, and thus critical bandwidth might be a constant 100 Hz [equation (8.1)] rather than ⅓ octave.

The only relevant data are for a beluga listening in water (C.S. Johnson et al. 1989) and for a harbor seal listening in air (Terhune 1991; Terhune and Turnbull 1995). In the beluga, critical ratios at 40-1000 Hz were roughly constant at ~17 dB (Fig. 8.6A), corresponding to a masking bandwidth of ~50 Hz [equation (8.1)].   Hence, estimated masking bandwidth as a percentage of center frequency increased with decreasing frequency, and exceeded ⅓ octave below ~300 Hz (Fig. 8.8). Similarly, in the harbor seal listening in air, masking bandwidth on a percentage basis became wider below 1000 Hz (Fig. 8.9). At present there are no similar data for other marine mammals, although several workers are actively studying low-frequency hearing.

Belugas apparently are specialized for high-frequency hearing and yet maintain narrow critical bands at frequencies as low as a few hundred hertz (Fig. 8.8).   Baleen whales, which are believed to be well adapted for low-frequency hearing, probably also have narrow critical bands at low frequencies. In the examples later in this chapter (Section 10.4), we assume that baleen whales can barely detect a low-frequency sound signal whose received level equals the level of background noise in the same ⅓-octave band. The validity of this assumption cannot be established with available data. This uncertainty has an important bearing on the accuracy of predicted radii of audibility when ambient noise is the factor limiting hearing.

Directional Hearing.—Animals often can localize the directions of arrival of sound signals (Section 8.4). They may also localize some directional components of ambient noise.   In either case, a sound signal may be detectable farther from its source than would be possible without a directional localization ability (Section 8.5.3). Directional hearing abilities at low as well as high frequencies are important: many man-made noises are concentrated at low frequencies (<1 kHz; Chapter 6), where directional hearing is difficult because of the long wavelengths.

Localization abilities of some toothed whales are good at high frequencies (≥10 kHz) and present at frequencies of a few kilohertz (Section 8.4.1). However, in the bottlenose dolphin, localization abilities may be effective in improving detectability only for sounds above 18 kHz (Zaitseva et al. 1980). Harbor seals can localize sounds at 2 kHz, but the effects of this ability on detectability of weak directional sounds are unknown. There are no behavioral data on localization abilities of toothed whales or phocid seals below 2 kHz. Sea lions have limited localization abilities at frequencies as low as 500 Hz. Localization abilities of baleen whales have not been tested formally, but may extend as low as a few hundred hertz (Section 8.4.3).

For pinnipeds and especially toothed whales, directional hearing probably increases detection distances for many directional sounds at kilohertz frequencies. However, it is doubtful whether directional hearing provides them with much advantage in hearing continuous low-frequency sounds. Impulsive or variable low-frequency sounds with rapid onsets or decays might be localizable to some extent. The apparent directional hearing abilities of baleen whales may assist them in detecting directional low-frequency sound. However, we know of no data, for any marine mammal, on the improvement in SNR achievable through directional hearing at the low frequencies of many man-made noises.

10.2.2 Limitation by Hearing Sensitivity

Hearing is sometimes limited by absolute hearing thresholds rather than ambient noise. This occurs at frequencies where the absolute threshold exceeds the background noise level near that frequency. Again, background noise within the critical band is important. As a first approximation, we assume that critical bands are ~⅓ octave wide.

Fig. 10.1 suggests that marine mammal hearing is sometimes limited by absolute hearing thresholds rather than ambient noise. The three species whose audiograms are shown represent the three major groups of marine mammals for which behavioral audiograms have been determined: toothed whales, eared seals, and hair seals.

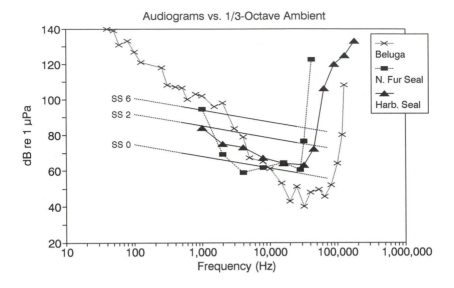

FIGURE 10.1. Underwater audiograms of a representative toothed whale, eared seal, and hair seal in relation to typical ⅓-octave ambient noise levels at three sea states (SS). Beluga data are averaged from White et al. (1978), Awbrey et al. (1988), and C.S. Johnson et al. (1989); northern fur seal data from Moore and Schusterman (1987); and harbor seal data from Møhl (1968a). Ambient noise estimates are from Fig. 5.1B, based on Knudsen et al. (1948).

The beluga has very sensitive hearing at high frequencies (10-100 kHz), but its thresholds increase steadily as frequency decreases below 10 kHz. At low frequencies, beluga hearing is apparently limited by hearing thresholds, not ambient noise (Fig. 10.1). At sea states (SS) 0, 2, and 6, the absolute threshold is above the typical ⅓-octave natural ambient noise level at frequencies below ~10, 3, and 2 kHz, respectively. In contrast, beluga hearing is limited by ambient noise from a few kilohertz up to ~100 kHz, where absolute thresholds are lower than typical ambient noise levels (Fig. 10.1).

Although the northern fur seal and harbor seal have poorer hearing sensitivity than the beluga at high frequencies, they have better underwater sensitivity than belugas below a few kilohertz (Fig. 10.1). Hence, pinnipeds may be noise-limited down to lower frequencies than are belugas. Under windy conditions (e.g., SS 6), the harbor seal is noise-limited down to well below 1 kHz, and probably as low as 100 Hz where the absolute threshold of one individual was 96 dB re 1 µPa

(Kastak and Schusterman 1995). Under SS 2 conditions, pinnipeds appear to be threshold-limited below ~1-1.5 kHz (Fig. 10.1).

The specific frequency ranges within which a given animal's hearing is threshold- versus noise-limited depend strongly on ambient noise conditions, which vary widely (Chapter 5). However, for many ambient noise conditions, the beluga may be threshold- rather than noise-limited at the low frequencies where many man-made sounds are concentrated. The situation is less clear-cut for some pinnipeds, which may be noise-limited even at frequencies as low as 1 kHz, at least under windy conditions.

This analysis assumes that critical bandwidth is ~⅓ octave. In the beluga, critical ratios are known down to 40 Hz, so more precise predictions are possible. The critical ratio is ~17 dB from 40 to 1000 Hz (Fig. 8.6; C.S. Johnson et al. 1989). Absolute thresholds decrease from ~140 dB at 40 Hz to 100 dB at 1000 Hz (Fig. 10.1). Thus, the beluga would be expected to be threshold-limited if the spectrum level of the ambient noise were <123 dB re 1 µPa/Hz at 40 Hz (140 minus 17 dB) or <83 dB/Hz at 1000 Hz. At these frequencies, ambient noise is almost always below these levels (Chapter 5; Urick 1983), so the beluga would be threshold-limited. In contrast, at 10 kHz, the beluga's absolute hearing threshold is ~60 dB and the critical ratio is ~25 dB. At 10 kHz, belugas would be threshold-limited only if the spectrum level of ambient noise were below ~35 dB/Hz, which is uncommon. Thus, critical ratio data confirm that beluga hearing is threshold-limited at frequencies below a few kilohertz, and noise-limited at higher frequencies.

When hearing is threshold-limited, the level of man-made noise falls below the hearing threshold before it reaches the ambient level (Fig. 10.2, case A). If the man-made noise is too faint to be heard, the animal will not be disturbed by it. This would be true even if the man-made noise were still above the background level, and thus detectable by instruments or by other species whose hearing at relevant frequencies is more sensitive. In this case, the maximum possible zone of potential noise influence would be smaller than that suggested by considering ambient noise alone.

In other situations, hearing will be limited by ambient noise. This will occur if ambient levels are high or if the species has sensitive hearing at the frequencies where the man-made noise is concentrated. In these cases, absolute hearing threshold will be lower than the typical level of ambient noise. The maximum radius of potential noise

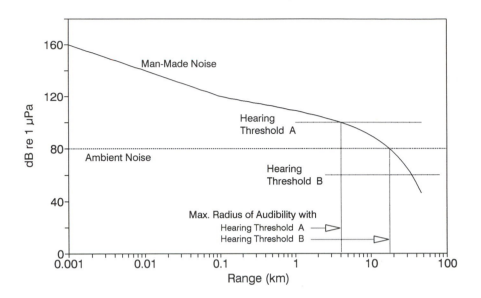

FIGURE 10.2. Schematic depiction of the maximum radius of audibility of a man-made noise when hearing threshold is *(A)* higher and *(B)* lower than ambient noise level in the critical band. Maximum radius of audibility is threshold-limited in *(A)* and ambient-limited in *(B)*.

influence will be determined by ambient noise level rather than absolute hearing threshold (Fig. 10.2, case B).

No data on hearing sensitivity are available for baleen whales. We assume that their auditory systems are very sensitive to low-frequency sounds (Section 8.6). If so, baleen whales, unlike toothed whales, are noise-limited at the low frequencies of many man-made noises. Thus, the maximum radius of influence of low-frequency man-made noise on baleen whales is likely to be that where the level of man-made noise diminishes below the ambient level (Fig. 10.2, case B). However, this is an assumption, not an established fact.

No similar analysis has been attempted for sirenians, sea otters, or polar bears. For sirenians, this analysis may be possible when new data on the manatee audiogram (Gerstein et al. 1993) are reported. However, in addition to the audiogram, data on ambient noise in the inshore waters occupied by manatees will be needed.

There is no information about the significance to marine mammals of the very low-frequency components of some man-made noises. Infrasounds are defined here as sounds at frequencies <20 Hz. The species most likely to hear infrasounds are the baleen whales. Some baleen whales emit, and presumably hear, sounds at frequencies ≤20 Hz (Section 7.1). Besides the lack of data on hearing sensitivity at low frequencies, only limited data are available on the source levels and propagation of man-made infrasounds, and on the levels of infrasonic ambient noise. Although source levels may be high (e.g., Cybulski 1977; Gales 1982; Hall and Francine 1990), infrasounds probably attenuate rapidly in most continental shelf waters.

10.2.3 Summary

The maximum possible radius of influence of a man-made noise on a marine mammal is the distance from the noise source at which the noise can barely be heard. This distance is determined by either the hearing sensitivity of the animal or the background noise level, depending on circumstances. Many man-made sounds are dominated by low-frequency components. Toothed whales and some pinnipeds are not highly sensitive to these low frequencies. Hence, for these animals, the maximum radius of audibility of many man-made sounds will be determined by the hearing sensitivity of the animals rather than the background noise level. The radius of audibility of higher-frequency man-made sounds (e.g., at 5-30 kHz) will normally be limited by background noise level, since toothed whales and many pinnipeds are more sensitive to high- than to low-frequency sounds. In contrast, baleen whales are assumed to be quite sensitive to low-frequency sounds. The maximum radius of audibility of low-frequency sounds to baleen whales is probably determined by background noise. Limitation by background noise rather than absolute threshold may extend into the infrasonic range in some species of baleen whales.

Because the maximum radius of audibility can depend on the hearing ability of the receiving animal, this radius may vary widely depending on the species and individual. If a man-made noise is at low frequencies, the maximum radius of audibility will be greater for a species with good versus poor low-frequency hearing (e.g., baleen whale versus beluga). Additional data on critical ratios and directional discrimination, especially at low frequencies, would be helpful.

Although the maximum radius of audibility is the maximum potential distance at which a man-made noise could affect marine mammals, man-made noises probably have few or no deleterious effects at such large distances. Many marine mammals tolerate levels of man-made noise well above the known or presumed auditory thresholds (Section 9.14).

10.3 Zone of Responsiveness

We define the "zone of responsiveness" to be the area around a source of man-made noise within which marine mammals of a given species show observable behavioral responses to that human activity. In this report, we consider only the reactions to noise. Noise is often the stimulus detectable farthest away from a human activity. However, reactions may be to another stimulus, such as visual appearance or perhaps odor, or to a combination of stimuli.

Studies summarized in Chapter 9 indicate that many marine mammals react overtly to man-made noises. Typically, there is no reaction when the source is beyond a given distance, and a reaction when the source is closer. The distance at which reactions become evident varies widely, even for a given species and a given human activity. Also, reactions often become stronger as the source becomes closer. Thus, the "zone of responsiveness" is a real phenomenon for many species and human activities, but its radius is a statistical phenomenon: a small percentage of the animals may react at a long distance, the majority may not react unless the human activity is somewhat closer, and a small percentage may not react unless it is closer still. For example, Malme et al. (1984) estimated the received levels of various industrial noises avoided by 10%, 50%, and 90% of the migrating gray whales, and the associated distances from the noise sources (Table 9.2 in Section 9.7.1).

Marine mammals often behave normally in areas where man-made noise is detectable by instruments (Chapter 9). Many of these mammals presumably hear the man-made noise, but some may not. For example, small toothed whales exposed to weak low-frequency noise may not hear it. For species whose hearing sensitivity is known (Chapter 8), analysis of existing data on tolerated sound levels might show whether sounds were "detectable but tolerated" or undetectable.

10.3.1 Behavioral Indicators of Disturbance

Avoidance reactions are the most obvious manifestations of disturbance. Avoidance responses can be strong or weak. For example, animals may swim rapidly and directly away from a noise source, or they may swim at a more normal speed with only a slight tendency to move away (Chapter 9). Migrating whales may avoid stationary sources on their original course by deflecting their course slightly, perhaps by ~30°, as they approach the source (Fig. 9.3; LGL and Greeneridge 1987). This allows them to pass well to the side of the industrial site without making a large change in course, and without a large increase in the length of their migration. Nonetheless, this change in course constitutes a form of avoidance. Pinnipeds hauled out on beaches or ice may stampede abruptly into the water, or may move less quickly, perhaps leaving a fraction of the individuals on the haul-out site (Chapter 9). All of these behaviors represent avoidance, but there is a gradation in the apparent severity of disturbance.

Avoidance reactions are not always directed away from the source of disturbance. Pinnipeds on a beach often move *toward* a boat or aircraft traveling on or over the water seaward of the haul-out site. Likewise, cetaceans in a shallow nearshore area sometimes flee into deeper water even if the disturbance source is offshore.

Other changes in behavior besides avoidance may indicate disturbance. Pinnipeds hauled out on land or ice often become alert in the presence of noise from an approaching aircraft or vessel (Chapter 9). This alert response may be the only visible manifestation of disturbance, or it may be followed by avoidance (movement into the water). Similarly, cetaceans may change their general activities in the presence of man-made noise. At the onset of man-made noise, cetaceans that are resting or socializing at the surface often dive or start to travel slowly. This travel is not necessarily oriented away from the noise source.

In cetaceans, mean durations of surfacings and dives, number of blows per surfacing, and intervals between successive blows often are affected by man-made noise. When bowheads and gray whales are exposed to man-made noise of various types, we often see unusually brief surfacings and dives, and fewer blows per surfacing (Richardson et al. 1985b, 1986, 1990b; Malme et al. 1988; Richardson and Malme 1993). In some cases, usually with distant noise sources, these changes in surfacing, respiration, and diving behavior occur without obvious avoidance. These changes in surfacing, respiration, and diving behavior can be quantified. They may be useful as indicators of stress in some situations without overt avoidance.

10.3.2 Possible Response Criteria

How should one attempt to measure or define circumstances when a marine mammal will respond to man-made noise? The most appropriate procedure may involve estimating the level of man-made noise that causes some specified proportion of the mammals to react in a defined way. Acoustic thresholds of this type have rarely been determined in the field. More commonly, field researchers have estimated the distance from the noise source at which responses first were noticed (Chapter 9).

Sound Level Criteria.—One possible response criterion is that, under defined conditions, a given species will probably react if the received sound level exceeds a specific level, for example 120 dB re 1 µPa in a stated bandwidth. If sufficient data are available, it may also be possible to specify what percentage of the animals react at various received noise levels (e.g., Table 9.2, from Malme et al. 1984).

It is not certain what frequency band should be considered when deriving response criteria. Malme et al. (1984) considered broad bands that included all frequencies with significant energy. However, mammalian hearing processes are affected primarily by sounds within the same ⅓-octave band (Chapter 8). A more appropriate response criterion might be the sound level in the ⅓-octave band containing the most intense noise, considering only the ⅓-octave bands within the frequency range where hearing abilities are good.

Response thresholds based on ⅓-octave bands are expected to be slightly lower than those based on broad bands. The sound level in a given ⅓-octave band cannot be greater, and is usually less, than that in any broader band containing that ⅓ octave (Section 2.2.4). For example, Richardson et al. (1990b) estimated the received levels of drilling and dredging sounds at which roughly half of the summering bowhead whales reacted upon initial exposure. The response threshold was ~115 dB re 1 µPa on a broadband (20-1000 Hz) basis, and ~110 dB in the ⅓-octave band where industrial noise was most prominent.

Signal-to-Noise Ratio Criteria.—A second possible response criterion is the signal-to-[ambient] noise ratio (SNR). SNR may be more important than the absolute level of man-made sound. Because of the logarithmic nature of sound levels measured in decibels (Chapter 2), SNR is calculated as the *difference* between the signal level (in dB) and the background noise level (in dB). Intuitively, a 110-dB man-made sound seems more likely to be disturbing when the ambient noise level in the corresponding band is 80-90 dB than when it is 100 dB or especially 110 dB (i.e., when SNR is 20-30 dB rather than 10 or 0 dB). At SNR = 0 dB, the man-made noise is probably nearly undetectable. Roughly half of the summering bowhead whales reacted upon initial exposure to drilling and dredging sounds whose broadband received levels were ~20 dB above the ambient noise level, or when the level in the most prominent ⅓-octave band was ~30 dB above the ambient level in that band (Richardson et al. 1990b).

Thus, we made rough estimates of the response thresholds that would apply to summering bowheads based on each of four procedures: broadband absolute levels and SNRs, and ⅓-octave absolute levels and SNRs. However, we could not determine which criterion was most appropriate. Sample sizes were too small, responses of different whales too variable, and various sound levels and SNRs too highly intercorrelated. We are not aware of any study of marine mammal disturbance that has determined which criterion is most appropriate.

In general, acoustic annoyance reactions in humans correlate better with the absolute level of an intruding sound signal than with its SNR (Robinson et al. 1963). However, when background noise level is not much less than the received level of the intruding signal, the threshold of annoyance is shifted upward (Spieth 1956; Pearsons 1966) and SNR is more relevant. Hence, the usual practice in determining human annoyance criteria involves psychoacoustic testing to determine sound levels that produce a quantifiable level of annoyance. Correction factors based on prevailing background noise levels may then be applied (Kryter 1985).

At this time, it is not possible to determine with any confidence whether marine mammal disturbance criteria should be based on broadband sound measurements, ⅓-octave data, or some other bandwidth. It is also not known whether absolute or relative (SNR) criteria should be used.

Distance or Altitude Criteria.—From a management or mitigation perspective, guidelines based on distance rather than received sound level or SNR may be the only practical ones. In some regions whalewatching vessels are subject to guidelines indicating that they should not approach closer than some fixed distance (Atkins and Swartz 1989). Permits issued to operators of seismic vessels sometimes indicate that they should shut down their airguns or other noise sources if whales are seen within a specified distance, or if monitoring to confirm the absence of whales within such a distance is temporarily impractical (Reeves et al. 1984). Section 1.3.3 mentions more examples of distance-based guidelines applied in several countries.

Distance criteria are relatively simple to specify, implement, and monitor for compliance. However, received sound level and distance are imperfectly correlated (Chapter 4). Thus, received sound level x km from a specific human activity may vary with time or location even if source level remains constant. Also, source level may vary over time, and there is additional variation in the levels emitted by different sources of a specific class (e.g., different seismic boats or different aircraft). If disturbance is actually a function of received sound level or SNR, distance criteria are less than ideal. However, guidelines based on sound levels or especially SNR would be more difficult to apply; sound levels are not as easily measured as is distance.

A partial solution may be to consider data that are as site-, activity-, and species-specific as possible when formulating distance criteria. For aircraft disturbance, rather than apply one altitude criterion to all situations, two or three different criteria might be developed for various combinations of habitat (e.g., coastal haul-out sites versus at sea), aircraft type, and species. In the case of whalewatching, different criteria might apply for different regions, small versus larger vessels, or mother-calf pairs versus other animals. By refining the distance criteria, some allowance can be made for regional variations in sound propagation conditions, and for species, regional, or other consistent variations in responsiveness of marine mammals.

10.3.3 Variations in Responsiveness

Marine mammals show wide within-species variations in responsiveness to man-made noise. They sometimes continue their normal activities when exposed to high levels of noise (e.g., from boats, seismic exploration, or industrial sites). At other times, members of the same species exhibit strong avoidance at much lower levels of man-made noise (Chapter 9). There are doubtless several reasons for this variation, some physical and some biological.

Physical Factors.—Variability and rate of change of the sound are important. Marine mammals often are more responsive to sounds with varying or increasing levels than to steady sounds (Chapter 9).

Sound propagation conditions account for some variation in the radius of noise influence. Even if the response threshold remains constant, in terms of threshold noise level or signal-to-noise ratio, variation in propagation loss rates will cause large differences in expected

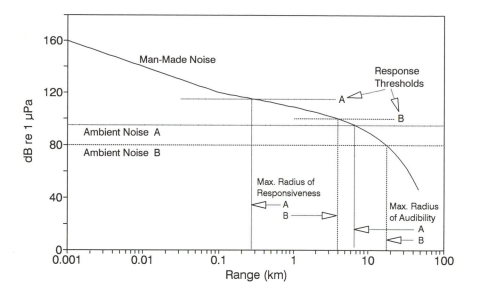

FIGURE 10.3. Schematic depiction of the effect of a 15-dB change in ambient noise level on maximum radii of audibility and responsiveness, assuming that animals respond when the level of man-made noise is at least 20 dB above the ambient noise level in the critical band.

reaction distances. Received sound levels will drop below any specified threshold at widely varying distances from the noise source. For example, variations in propagation seemed to affect the radius of influence of vessel noise on humpback whales (Watkins and Goebel 1984). Also, wind direction can affect the reaction distance for sea lions and elephant seals hauled out on land when a helicopter maneuvers nearby (Section 9.2.1) or for walruses hauled out on ice when a ship approaches (Section 9.3.1). These reactions occur at longer ranges when the wind blows from noise source toward the animals, presumably because following wind can enhance airborne propagation (Section 4.6.2).

Background noise levels may also affect apparent responsiveness to man-made noise if the response threshold is a given signal-to-noise ratio rather than an absolute sound level (Section 10.3.2; Fig. 10.3). Background noise can vary by ±10 or even ±20 dB from day to day. This variation causes drastic changes in the distances within which other sounds can be heard and within which they are 10, 20 or 30 dB above the ambient noise level (e.g., Fig. 10.3). If response threshold is a specific SNR, a 15-dB increase in background noise level will reduce the response distance severalfold (Fig. 10.3). Conversely, if the probability of reaction is determined by the absolute received level of man-made sound and not its SNR, the radius of responsiveness would not change when ambient level changes.

Thus, reaction distances are expected to vary because of changes in propagation conditions and perhaps in background noise levels. Improved propagation conditions or reduced background noise levels might double or triple the average reaction distance in some situations. Conversely, with poorer than average propagation or ambient noise conditions, reaction distance might be no more than half of the average value. Superficially, these changes in reaction distances seem to represent changes in responsiveness. In fact, these variations are due to physical factors, and are expected even if actual responsiveness, in terms of threshold noise level or SNR, remains constant.

Biological Factors.—*Activity* of the animals often seems important. In baleen whales, single whales that were resting quietly seemed more likely to be disturbed by human activities than were groups of whales engaged in active feeding, social interactions, or mating (Payne et al. 1983; Krieger and Wing 1984, 1986; Richardson et al. 1985b,c; Gaskin 1991). Similarly, bottlenose dolphins seemed least responsive to a small boat when they were socializing (Shane 1990).

Age and sex classes can vary in responsiveness. For example, when aircraft flew low over northern sea lions on a haulout site, immatures and pregnant females were more likely to enter the water than were territorial males and females with small pups (Calkins 1979). During flights over Atlantic walruses, adult females, calves, and immatures were more likely than adult males to enter the water (Salter 1979). In summering gray whales, mother-calf pairs seemed especially sensitive to aircraft (Ljungblad et al. 1983).

Habitat or physical situation of the animals can also be important. Walruses are more responsive to approaching boats when hauled out on ice than when in the water (Fay et al. 1984). Bowhead whales whose movements are partly restricted by shallow water or a shoreline sometimes seem more responsive to noise (Richardson et al. 1985b,c). Vessel traffic may have stronger influences on belugas when their movements are partly confined by ice (Section 9.3.2).

Habituation, the gradual waning of response when a stimulus is not associated with significant consequences, is responsible for much variation in responsiveness to man-made noise (Section 9.14.2). Conversely, *sensitization* may occur: animals that associate a specific sound with severe harassment may be especially responsive to that sound (Section 9.14.3). Available data on reaction thresholds to a given sound often pertain to initial exposure, or to animals whose history of exposure is not known.

Individual variation in the responsiveness of different animals is expected even after allowing for all physical and biological factors mentioned above. Inherent individual variability is not easily demonstrated in the field, where there is little or no control over either the external factors or the animals. However, hearing sensitivity of captive animals varies from time to time, presumably reflecting motivational and physiological changes (Terhune and Turnbull 1995). Some audiograms shown in Section 8.2 are averages; others are from single animals. Actual sensitivity varies above or below these values. There probably are similar variations in hearing sensitivity and behavioral responsiveness in the field.

Variation in responsiveness among different individuals, or for one individual at different times, may greatly affect the radius of responsiveness. Fig. 10.4 shows the theoretical effect of a 10- or 20-dB

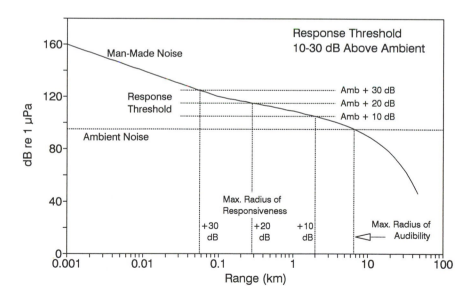

FIGURE 10.4. Schematic depiction of the effects of varying response threshold on maximum radius of responsiveness.

change in responsiveness. In the cases illustrated, the theoretical maximum radius of responsiveness ranges from ~0.06 to 2 km with response criteria ranging from SNR = 30 to SNR = 10 dB.

In general, several physical and biological factors are known or suspected to affect the responsiveness, actual or apparent, of a given species of marine mammal to man-made noise. As a result, maximum radius of responsiveness can vary widely among individuals or locations, and over time. Thus, radius of responsiveness, even for a specific type of man-made sound and a particular species, is a variable, not a constant. Field studies can provide some ability to predict the radius of responsiveness under specific conditions. However, even after intensive work of this type, there will undoubtedly be unexplained individual variation in the threshold and radius of responsiveness. Whenever a criterion of responsiveness is stated, there should be a statement about the situation to which it applies, the fraction of the animals expected to react, and the type of reaction expected.

10.4 *Estimating Radii of Audibility and Responsiveness*

Here we illustrate a method to predict the radii of audibility and responsiveness around human activities in coastal and offshore waters. As examples, we estimate these radii for various situations and mammal species that could be found off the California coast. We do not consider all possible combinations of species, human activities, and physical conditions that could occur there. However, we provide scenarios involving

- three major groups of marine mammals—baleen whales, toothed whales, and pinnipeds;
- five human activities—a relatively quiet oil production platform, a moderately noisy drillship, a noisy seismic exploration vessel, and two aircraft (helicopter and jet fighter);
- shallow and deep waters with differing ambient noise and propagation conditions, plus in-air propagation from passing aircraft.

Examples for four more areas with different physical conditions and species—the Beaufort Sea, Bering Sea, northwest Atlantic, and Gulf of Mexico—were described in Chapter 9 of Richardson et al. (1991b). Richardson and Würsig (in press) show some Beaufort Sea cases involving bowheads and belugas exposed to seismic and drillship noise.

To predict radii of noise influence around human activities, we consider

- source levels and characteristics of noise from each activity,
- attenuation of that noise as it propagates in water or air,
- ambient noise level, and
- hearing and response thresholds of the mammal in question.

If the necessary data are available or can be estimated, readers can apply the approach illustrated below to other species, locations, and human activities. The examples below highlight some of the important data gaps that exist, and illustrate the types of data that need to be acquired to predict radii of influence with reasonable accuracy.

10.4.1 Predicted Noise Exposure

Source Level Spectra.—Source or reference levels of the human activities considered here are shown, on a ⅓-octave basis, in Fig. 10.5. The ⅓-octave basis seems most consistent with the properties of mammalian hearing systems (Sections 8.5.2 and 10.2.1). Most of these source level spectra were derived by Malme et al. (1989) from field data of various authors. Chapter 6 provides more information and similar spectra for other sources.

For many human activities, no source level data are available above 5-20 kHz. Many marine mammals hear sounds extending up to much higher frequencies (Section 8.2). Hence, it has been necessary to extrapolate to higher frequencies based on the slope of the spectrum at the highest frequencies with data and, for cavitating and impulsive sources, on accepted power laws for these phenomena. However, when it is necessary to extrapolate over several octaves, estimates for the highest frequencies are very speculative. Fortunately, for most activities considered, ⅓-octave source levels diminish with increasing frequency. Also, high frequencies attenuate rapidly with increasing distance in both water and air. Hence, the questionable estimates at high frequencies are not a serious problem. The higher and better-defined source levels at lower frequencies are usually the key ones in estimating zones of influence.

For most sources considered, source level can be estimated at frequencies as low as 15-25 Hz. Source levels at lower frequencies are generally unknown but probably high for certain sources (Sections 6.2-6.5). The lack of data at very low frequencies is not believed to be a significant problem when assessing noise effects on pinnipeds or especially toothed whales, whose low-frequency hearing apparently is not

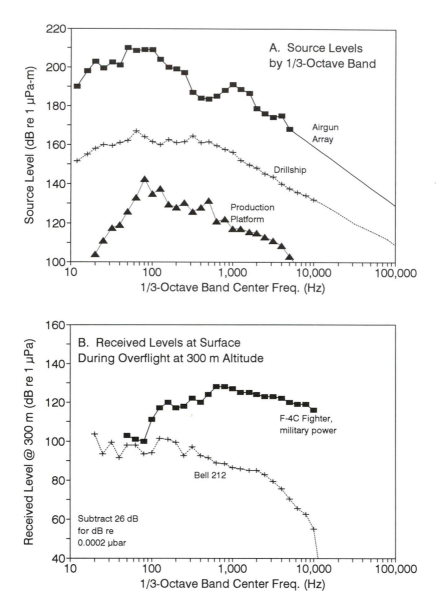

FIGURE 10.5. Estimated ⅓-octave source or reference levels for sounds from representative human activities. **(A)** Source levels, at nominal 1 m distance, for horizontal propagation of underwater sounds from airgun pulses (*Western Polaris*), drillship *Explorer II*, and production platform off California. **(B)** Airborne sounds from two aircraft at 300 m altitude: Bell 212 helicopter (cruising) and F-4C jet fighter (full power, no afterburners), as measured at surface under standard day conditions. Lines to right of highest-frequency datapoints are extrapolations.

acute. However, it is an important data gap for baleen whales if conditions are suitable for propagation of low-frequency sounds.

Transmission Loss, Underwater.—For each region of interest, TL must be measured or modeled to estimate received levels versus range; received level equals source level minus TL. For the California coast, TL estimates for nearshore waters ~50 m deep were based largely on the field measurements of Malme et al. (1983, 1984, 1986a). Weston/Smith propagation models (Section 4.4) were used to summarize these data and extend the frequency range covered. Weston/Smith models were also used to estimate propagation in deeper waters (~180 m) with a more rocky bottom. The models incorporated an equation (Thorp 1967) to predict absorption losses at high frequencies. In other situations, more complex models may be needed, for example, to deal with range-dependent propagation conditions or with interference phenomena at specific frequencies.

Transmission loss data and model estimates were organized by ⅓ octaves, matching the ⅓-octave source level spectra. A spreadsheet program was used, interpolating and extrapolating as necessary to allow for ⅓ octaves where TL data were missing. Each curve in Fig. 10.6 represents TL between range 1 m and the range specified at the left end of the curve. Similar TL graphs for other locations around North America are given in Appendix 3 of Richardson et al. (1991b).

Under the assumed conditions, propagation losses at ranges beyond ~0.1 km are less rapid in deep than in shallow water, especially at low frequencies (Fig. 10.6). Very high-frequency sounds always attenuate rapidly owing to volumetric absorption (Section 4.5.1).

Transmission loss estimates in Fig. 10.6 extend well beyond the frequencies and distances for which field data are available, and well beyond those to which simple TL models are normally applied. In general, our TL and received level estimates for frequencies below 100 Hz and above 5 kHz, and for ranges beyond 40 km, should be considered less reliable than those for intermediate frequencies and shorter ranges. In all cases, TL and received level predictions are valid only for the specific bottom types for which they were derived.

Transmission Loss, In-Air.—A TL model applicable to airborne sound is used to predict noise transmission from a passing aircraft to pinnipeds hauled out on shore. For California, we assumed spherical ($20 \log R$) spreading loss plus an additional atmospheric absorption term appropriate for an air temperature of 25°C and a relative humidity of 80% (Fig. 10.7).

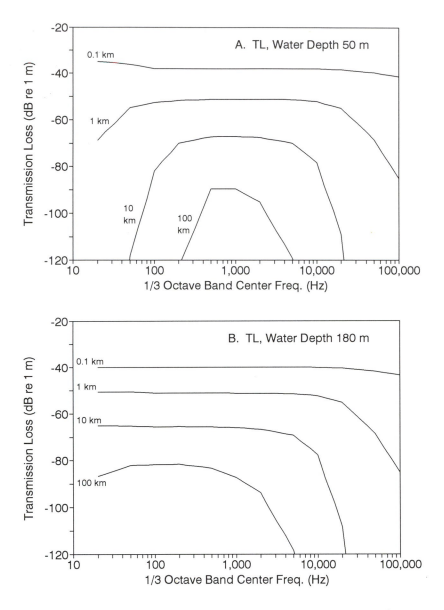

FIGURE 10.6. Estimated transmission loss spectra for underwater sound in water depths **(A)** 50 m and **(B)** 180 m off central California, showing expected TL between the sound source and ranges 0.1-100 km as a function of frequency. Based on Malme et al. (1986a) and Weston/Smith model extrapolations.

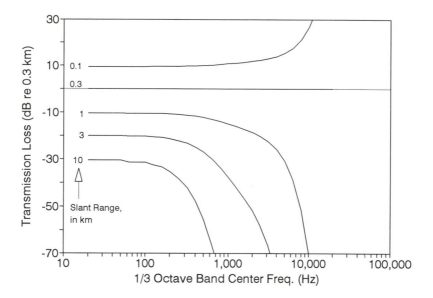

FIGURE 10.7. Estimated transmission loss spectra for airborne sound near a central California beach, relative to levels expected at surface below an aircraft at 300 m altitude, as a function of frequency. Assumes 25°C and 80% relative humidity.

Ambient Noise.—Measured or estimated ambient noise levels are needed to determine the maximum potential radius of audibility of a man-made noise. This is the distance at which its received level diminishes below the ambient level in the corresponding band, provided the receiving animal's hearing sensitivity is less than the ambient level (case B in Fig. 10.2). Ambient noise data are also needed to determine the radius of behavioral responsiveness if the mammals respond overtly when man-made noise exceeds the ambient level by a specified amount (e.g., 20 dB; Section 10.3.2). For these purposes, ambient noise data need to be expressed on a ⅓-octave basis.

Airborne ambient noise along the California coast is dominated by surf noise. Our examples (Figs. 10.8 and 10.9) show in-air noise levels from the surf and offshore zones, from BBN (1960) (Section 5.6).

Off California, ambient noise in nearshore waters is dominated by sounds from shrimp. Shrimp noise becomes stronger with decreasing depth. This noise extends from 500 Hz to above 20 kHz. Below 500 Hz, noise from coastal shipping has an important influence on ambient noise levels. Spectra reported by Malme et al. (1984) were used to estimate ambient noise in each ⅓-octave band on typical days (Fig.

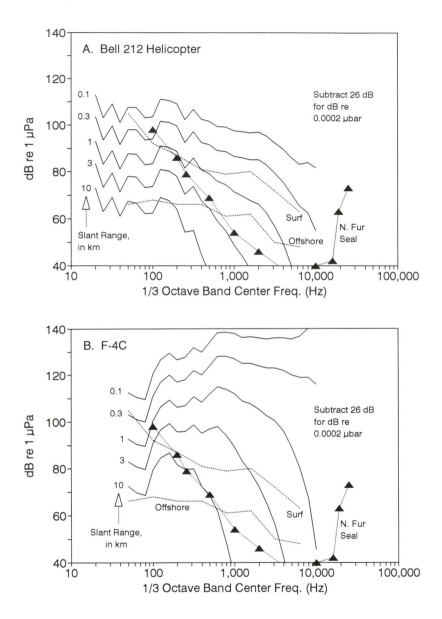

FIGURE 10.8. Predicted ⅓-octave received level spectra in the air at various slant ranges from *(A)* Bell 212 helicopter and *(B)* F-4C jet fighter. Dashed lines show typical airborne ambient noise spectra in the surf zone (top) and offshore (bottom), also on a ⅓-octave basis. Triangles show absolute in-air hearing thresholds of a northern fur seal, from Babushina et al. (1991).

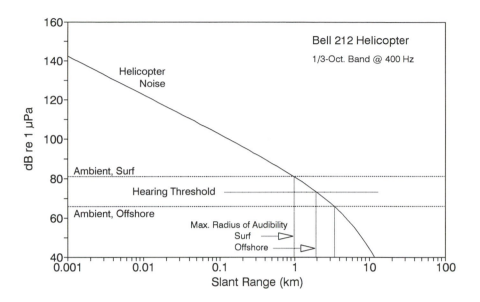

FIGURE 10.9. Predicted maximum radius of audibility of in-air sound from a Bell 212 helicopter, considering the ⅓-octave centered at 400 Hz. Horizontal lines show typical ambient noise levels in that band for the surf zone and offshore, and the absolute in-air hearing threshold of a northern fur seal near 400 Hz. Same data as at 400 Hz in Fig. 10.8A.

10.10A, later). In deeper water near the California shelf break, shrimp noise is not a major contributor; ship traffic and wind are the dominant factors. In the absence of site-specific data, our examples (e.g., Fig. 10.10B) use a deep water spectrum for Sea State 2 and moderate to heavy ship traffic, adapted from Urick (1983).

Predicted Noise Exposure.—By adding estimated TL spectra such as Fig. 10.6 or 10.7 to source level spectra such as Fig. 10.5, site- and range-specific received level spectra can be estimated for each source. Given the source and TL spectra, received level spectra can be calculated and graphed easily by a spreadsheet (Figs. 10.8-10.12). By including ambient noise spectra, one can identify the distances at which the received man-made noise levels drop below ambient noise levels at corresponding frequencies. Source, received, and ambient noise levels are all estimated on a comparable basis, by ⅓ octaves.

10.4.2 Hearing and Response Thresholds

Hearing thresholds of marine mammals are summarized in Section 8.2. These data are used in the following sections to judge whether radii of audibility for a given species and sound type are limited by their auditory thresholds or by ambient noise (Section 10.2.2; Fig 10.2).

For species whose hearing thresholds are unknown, including all baleen whales, an assumption is necessary about whether the animals are threshold- or ambient-limited. We assume that baleen whales have sensitive hearing at the low to moderate frequencies where most man-made noises are concentrated (Sections 8.6 and 10.2.2). Thus, we assume that these species are ambient-limited, at least in the range 20-1000 Hz. Hence, hearing threshold data are not essential to estimate radii of audibility of sounds at these frequencies. However, the lack of threshold data for infrasonic sounds (<20 Hz) is a significant data gap, as is the scarcity of data on infrasonic source levels, propagation, and ambient noise. Large vessels and some industrial activities are strong sources of infrasound.

Assumptions about behavioral response thresholds are based on data reviewed in Chapter 9 and concepts summarized in Section 10.3. For most species and human activities, the available data are meager or lacking, and extrapolations or other assumptions must be made.

10.4.3 Predicted Radii of Influence

Aircraft Overflights.—Received ⅓-octave spectra of in-air sound from two aircraft were predicted as a function of slant range (Fig. 10.8) by combining their estimated source level spectra (Fig. 10.5B) with the transmission loss estimates (Fig. 10.7). In-air ambient noise levels are shown in Fig. 10.8 for beaches subjected to surf and for quieter conditions offshore. These levels are compared with the in-air hearing thresholds of a northern fur seal.

In the surf zone, the high ambient noise levels are expected to prevent detection of helicopter noise at distances much beyond 1 km regardless of hearing sensitivity. The helicopter noise components that would be detectable farthest away would be those at about 125 to 500 Hz. They would exceed the corresponding ambient noise levels at ranges out to ~1 km (Fig. 10.8A). At and near 400 Hz, the fur seal's in-air hearing thresholds would permit detection of the helicopter noise at a radius of 2 km under quiet conditions. However, in the surf zone actual detection radius would be limited to ~1 km by the high ambient noise. These relationships can be seen more clearly in Fig. 10.9, depicting the situation at 400 Hz. After the frequency detectable to greatest range is identified by reference to a graph such as Fig. 10.8A, it is useful to replot the data for that frequency in "level versus range" format, as in Fig. 10.9.

Under quieter offshore conditions, helicopter noise would be detectable farther away. Components at 50-200 Hz might be detectable up to ~10 km away if the receiving animal had good in-air hearing sensitivity at low frequencies (Fig. 10.8A). However, in the northern fur seal, absolute hearing thresholds would limit the radius of detectability to about 2 km regardless of ambient noise levels (Figs. 10.8A and 10.9). Human hearing at low frequencies is more sensitive than that of the fur seal (Fig. 8.3). With low ambient noise, humans can sometimes hear a Bell 212 helicopter 10 km away.

A jet fighter operating at high power is much noisier than the Bell 212 helicopter at frequencies above 100 Hz (Fig. 10.5B). In the surf zone, the received level near 200 Hz is expected to exceed ambient surf noise as well as the fur seal in-air hearing threshold at ranges up to ~7 km (Fig. 10.8B). In offshore areas, jet noise in several ⅓-octave bands would exceed the corresponding ambient noise levels out to distances well beyond 10 km. However, the fur seal's hearing thresholds would limit detection to ~10 km.

For the fur seal, radii of responsiveness to aircraft noise cannot be estimated from acoustic data because acoustic response thresholds are uncertain. Section 9.2.1 summarizes available data on pinniped reactions to aircraft at different altitudes and lateral distances. Strong avoidance may occur only when aircraft approach well within the radius of audibility.

Drillship Noise.—Received ⅓-octave spectra of drillship sound as a function of distance (Fig. 10.10) were predicted by combining the source level spectrum of *Explorer II* (Fig. 10.5A) with the transmission loss estimates for nearshore and offshore waters along the California coast (Fig. 10.6). Attenuation was more rapid in the nearshore area, so maximum detection distance under typical ambient noise conditions is predicted to be ~25 km in the nearshore region but ~100 km near the shelf break (Figs. 10.10A,B). Assuming that baleen whales have sensitive hearing at low frequencies, they should hear the drillship at distances up to 25 km in nearshore areas, where the gray whale is common during migration, and up to 100 km near the shelf break, where the blue whale is common during summer and autumn.

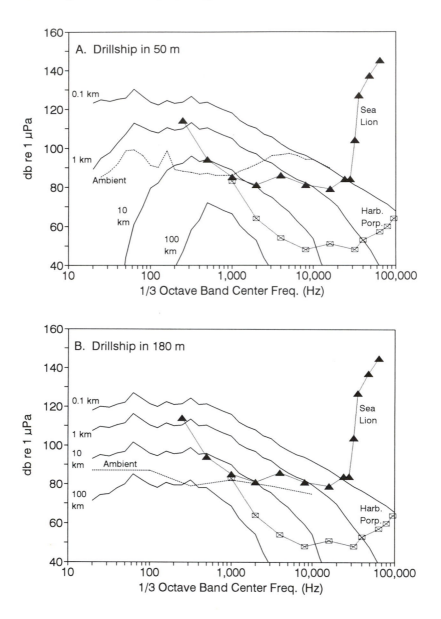

FIGURE 10.10. Predicted ⅓-octave received level spectra at various ranges from a drillship operating off the California coast *(A)* in nearshore waters and *(B)* near the shelf break. Dashed line shows a typical ambient noise spectrum, also on a ⅓-octave basis. Squares and triangles show, respectively, the absolute underwater hearing thresholds of harbor porpoise (Andersen 1970a) and California sea lion (Schusterman et al. 1972).

About 50% of the gray whales exhibit avoidance when the broadband received level of drillship sounds is 117 dB re 1 μPa (Malme et al. 1984, 1986b, 1988; Section 9.7.1), or ~106 dB in a ⅓-octave band. Received levels of drillship sounds are predicted to diminish below 106 dB in the strongest ⅓-octave band at a range of ~3 km in nearshore waters where gray whales occur (Fig. 10.10A) and ~6 km near the shelf break. It is not known whether response thresholds of blue whales, which often occur near the shelf break off California, are similar to those of gray whales.

The harbor porpoise is a common coastal species off California. Like other toothed whales, it has sensitive hearing at high frequencies, but below 4 kHz its sensitivity diminishes rapidly with diminishing frequency (Section 8.2.1). Nonetheless, its sensitivity at 2 kHz would be sufficient to detect noise from a drillship ~50 km away if ambient noise were low enough to allow this (Figs. 10.10A,B). However, under typical ambient noise conditions, the radius of detectability will be limited by ambient noise rather than absolute hearing sensitivity at frequencies ≥1 kHz (Figs. 10.10A,B). With typical ambient noise, the maximum radius of detectability may be ~12 km in nearshore waters and ~25 km near the shelf break. These predictions are speculative because hearing sensitivity of harbor porpoises below 1 kHz is unknown. The predictions assume that their hearing sensitivity deteriorates with diminishing frequency below 1 kHz, as in other small odontocetes (Section 8.2.1). There are no data on acoustic response thresholds of harbor or other porpoises to drillship sounds, so radii of responsiveness cannot be estimated.

The California sea lion has more sensitive underwater hearing at moderate to high frequencies (≥1 kHz) than at lower frequencies. However, its absolute sensitivity at high frequencies is considerably poorer than that of the harbor porpoise and other toothed whales (Section 8.2.2). Its underwater hearing sensitivity around 500-2000 Hz is apparently sensitive enough to detect noise from a drillship 10-15 km away in both nearshore and shelf-break waters (Fig. 10.10). However, the ambient noise level will often be high enough to prevent detection of the drillship that far away. Again, there are no data on acoustic response thresholds of California sea lions near drillships, so radii of responsiveness cannot be estimated.

Production Platform Noise.—The acoustic source levels of production platforms of types used off California are considerably lower than those of drillships (Fig. 10.5), although additional data on their levels are needed (Section 6.4.4). Consequently, received levels of platform sounds will diminish below the ambient noise level at considerably closer distances (Fig. 10.11). Under typical ambient noise conditions, low-frequency noise from a production platform might be detectable no more than ½ km away in nearshore waters and 2 km away near the shelf break. Given our usual assumptions about baleen whale hearing, these are the predicted radii of audibility for gray, blue, or other baleen whales.

For gray whales, the median response threshold to playbacks of production platform noise was 123 dB re 1 µPa on a broadband basis (Section 9.7.2; Malme et al. 1984) or ~117 dB on a ⅓-octave basis. The received level of production platform noise in the strongest ⅓ octave would diminish below 117 dB well within 100 m of the platform in both nearshore and shelf-break waters (Fig. 10.11). Hence, the predicted maximum radius of responsiveness of gray whales to production platform noise is <100 m. At such short distances, visual stimuli might be important as well.

For harbor porpoises, the predicted radius of audibility of production platform noise is limited by its low source level, the animals' poor hearing sensitivity at low frequencies, and the high ambient noise levels at moderate to high frequencies (Fig. 10.11). With typical ambient noise, porpoises are not expected to detect production platform noise at distances beyond 100 m, assuming that porpoise hearing deteriorates with diminishing frequency below 1 kHz. Response thresholds are unknown, but no reaction to the noise would be expected beyond the maximum radius of audibility (i.e., ≤100 m). Again, visual effects are a possibility at such close ranges.

The situation is similar for California sea lions. Predicted levels of production platform noise are below the hearing threshold, the ambient noise level, or both at all distances beyond 100 m. California sea lions have been reported to be common around production platforms off California (Gales 1982; McCarty 1982).

Seismic Pulses.—In contrast, noise pulses from airguns have very high source levels. Levels in some ⅓-octave bands are expected to remain above the typical ambient noise levels out to distances exceeding 100 km—especially in the deeper waters near the shelf break (Fig. 10.12). Baleen whales off California are expected to hear seismic pulses from seismic ships >100 km away. At these ranges, received seismic pulses are several tenths of a second long—long

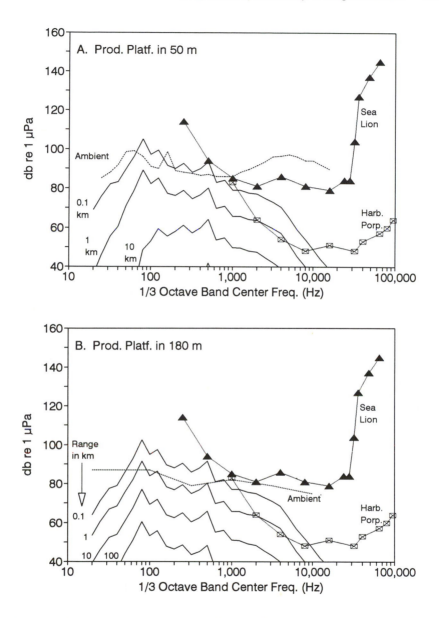

FIGURE 10.11. Predicted ⅓-octave received level spectra at various ranges from a production platform operating off the California coast (*A*) in nearshore waters and (*B*) near the shelf break. Presentation as in Fig. 10.10.

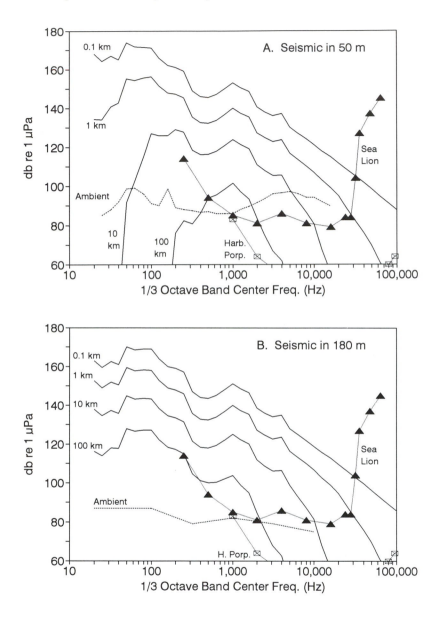

FIGURE 10.12. Predicted ⅓-octave received level spectra at various ranges from an array of airguns operating off the California coast *(A)* in nearshore waters and *(B)* near the shelf break. Presentation as in Fig. 10.10, except for altered vertical scale.

enough that the short pulse/higher threshold phenomenon (Section 8.2.4) is not expected.

Most migrating gray whales show pronounced avoidance when the broadband received level of seismic pulses is 164-180 dB re 1 µPa (Malme et al. 1984; Section 9.8.3). This is equivalent to ~156-172 dB in a ⅓-octave band. Received levels of seismic pulses off California are predicted to diminish below 156-172 dB (⅓-octave basis) at ~0.1-1 km from a seismic ship in nearshore waters, and 0.1-2 km from a ship near the shelf break (Fig. 10.12). Weaker reactions are likely at somewhat greater distances (Malme et al. 1983, 1984). Predicted avoidance distances are less than observed and predicted response radii of bowhead whales near seismic ships in the Beaufort Sea (Section 9.8.3; Richardson and Würsig in press). The difference is attributable to regional differences in sound propagation and to a slightly higher apparent response threshold for gray whales than for bowheads.

The seismic pulses are also expected to be strong enough to be detected by harbor porpoises and California sea lions at distances as great as 100 km from the seismic vessel (Fig. 10.12). At 500-800 Hz, components of the seismic sounds from a ship 100 km away are expected to exceed both the typical ambient noise levels and the absolute auditory thresholds of both species. (For harbor porpoises, this conclusion assumes that thresholds deteriorate steadily as frequency decreases below 1 kHz.) On days with higher-than-average ambient noise levels, the radius of audibility of seismic pulses in shallow waters could be <100 km for both harbor porpoises and sea lions.

Radii of responsiveness of harbor porpoises and sea lions to seismic pulses cannot be estimated. We know of no data on responses of harbor porpoises or other small toothed whales to seismic pulses. There are published observations, largely anecdotal, indicating that sea lions and some other pinnipeds may tolerate strong noise pulses (Section 9.10.1). However, these data are inadequate for estimation of response distances.

10.4.4 Limitations of Radius of Influence Estimates

The scenarios discussed above show that it is frequently difficult or impossible to estimate radii of audibility and responsiveness. Needed data are often lacking.

Source level spectra often do not include the full range of frequencies at which the species of interest have some hearing ability. These include low and infrasonic frequencies when baleen whales are of interest, and high and ultrasonic frequencies for pinnipeds and especially odontocetes. Also, source level estimates for 1 m range include various uncertainties: they usually are estimated from measurements at longer ranges; they often vary over time; and values for a given source often are assumed based on data from a "similar" source.

Transmission loss spectra are subject to uncertainty even when site-specific field measurements are available. They are especially uncertain when based on models incorporating assumed physical parameters. Uncertainties tend to be largest for long ranges, low frequencies, and shallow waters.

Ambient noise spectra are highly variable among locations and over time at a given location. Although much is known about underwater ambient noise, levels at a given site, time, and frequency are often difficult to predict. There are few data on airborne ambient noise in marine environments. Small changes in ambient noise can cause large differences in expected radii of influence (Fig. 10.3).

Hearing thresholds have been measured for only a few individual marine mammals of a few species. Data are lacking for baleen and beaked whales, the walrus, and the sea otter; and are meager for sperm whales, monachid seals, and sirenians (Section 8.2). For most species whose thresholds have been measured, data do not extend to low frequencies where levels of man-made noise are often highest.

Critical ratio and *critical bandwidth* data are also scarce, especially at low frequencies. These data are needed to determine whether it would be most appropriate to measure sounds in some bandwidth other than ⅓ octave.

Acoustic response thresholds have not been determined for many combinations of species and sound sources. Even when these data are available, it is not known what measure is most appropriate to marine mammals—absolute level or "signal-to-ambient noise ratio". Also, the most relevant measurement bandwidth is not known. A further complication is that response thresholds are quite variable among individuals and situations. Response thresholds also depend on the measure of response: low threshold for initial alert reaction versus higher threshold for active avoidance. *Reaction distance* data are more widely available than are data on acoustic response thresholds (Chapter 9). However, site-specific data on sound level versus range are rarely available. Hence, most conversions of reaction distances into estimated acoustic response thresholds are of unknown accuracy.

Nonacoustic stimuli, such as the sight of an aircraft or structure, may be partly responsible for eliciting some disturbance reactions.

Because of these data gaps and complications, prediction of detection and response radii usually requires across-species extrapolations and other assumptions. Even then, predictions are not always possible. However, as shown earlier, potential radii of audibility and responsiveness can sometimes be estimated roughly. These estimates are useful in designing studies to obtain needed data, and in identifying situations where it would be prudent to adopt mitigation measures to reduce disturbance.

10.5 Zone of Masking

Man-made noise can interfere with detection of acoustic signals such as communication calls, echolocation sounds, and environmental sounds important to marine mammals. If the noise is strong enough relative to the received signal, the signal will be "masked" and undetectable. At least in theory, a source of man-made noise is surrounded by a "zone of masking". However, the area where masking will occur is highly variable, even for a single marine mammal and a single type of man-made noise. The size of this zone depends on the many factors that affect the received levels of the background noise and the sound signal (e.g., Fig. 10.13).

10.5.1 Relative Distances and Levels of Signal and Masker

Any man-made noise strong enough to be audible, i.e., detectable above natural background noise, will increase the total background noise (natural plus man-made). This will interfere with an animal's ability to detect a sound signal if the signal is weak relative to total noise level. Thus, the maximum radius of audibility of a man-made noise is also the maximum theoretical radius where it might mask other sounds. However, only the most marginally detectable signals would be masked by the slight increase in background noise occurring at the maximum radius of masking. Stronger sound signals would be masked only if the listener were closer to the source of man-made noise (in Fig. 10.13, compare panel B with E, or panel C with F).

For a receiving animal close to a strong source of man-made noise, the noise level will be high and the animal will be able to hear only nearby animals whose calls have high received levels. For a receiving animal farther from the noise source, the man-made noise

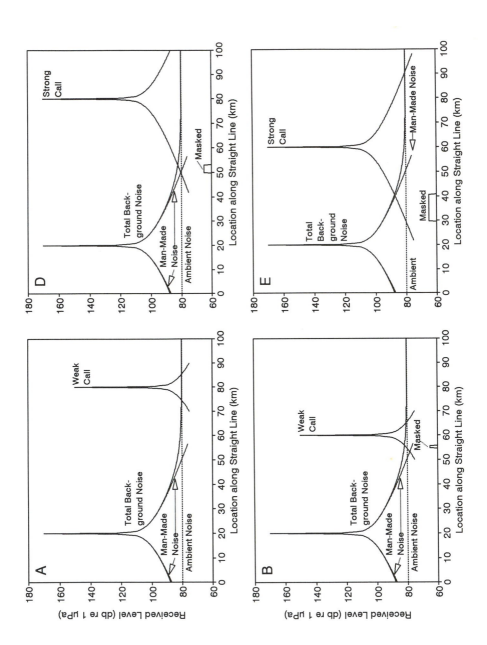

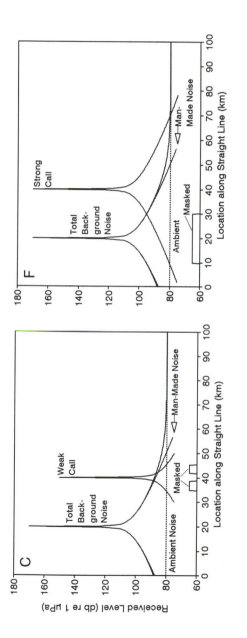

FIGURE 10.13. Schematic depiction of masking as influenced by source level of mammal calls (left versus right panels: 150 versus 170 dB re 1 μPa-m) and distance between noise source and calling animal (top, middle, and bottom panels show 60, 40, and 20 km). The call would be detectable at locations where it is the strongest sound. Locations designated "Masked" are places where the call is masked by man-made noise, i.e., where the call's received level is above the natural ambient level but below the total background noise level. At the "Masked" locations, the call would be detectable without but not with the man-made noise. It is assumed that the source of man-made noise, calling mammal, and listener are all located along a straight line. Man-made noise and ambient noise are the same in all panels, and are measured in the critical band surrounding the call frequency. Propagation loss for the man-made noise and mammal call are calculated from equation (4.7) with $R_1 = 1$ km and $\alpha + (A) = 0.5$ dB/km.

level will be lower and the animal will be able to hear weaker calls from more distant animals. The same arguments apply to detection of other environmental sounds. For practical purposes, the only relevant noise is that within the masking bandwidth, perhaps ⅓ octave wide, centered at the frequency of the signal (Section 8.5).

The main factors affecting detection of a sound signal in the presence of background noise (natural or man-made) are related as follows:

$$\text{SNR} = L_r - N_r \tag{10.1}$$

where SNR = signal-to-noise ratio (in dB) at receiving animal, considering components within the masking bandwidth;

L_r = received level of sound signal in the masking band; defined as $L_r = L_s - TL + G$;

N_r = noise level (natural + man-made) at receiver within masking band,

$$N_r = 10 \log (\text{alog } [N_{nat}/10] + \text{alog } [N_{mm}/10]); \tag{10.2}$$

L_s = source level of sound signal in the masking band;

TL = transmission loss from source to receiver;

G = gain factor—an adjustment for receiver properties, such as directional discrimination (see Section 10.5.2).

Some specific SNR, perhaps 0 dB, is required to detect a sound signal. An x dB increase in noise level (natural plus man-made), or an x db decrease in source level of the signal, will reduce SNR by x dB. This will reduce the radius within which mammal calls or other sounds will be detectable. The reduction will depend strongly on transmission loss rate if other factors, including source level of signal, are unchanged. For example, the expected reduction in detection distance when total noise level increases by 3-20 dB is as follows:

Increase in noise →	3 dB	6 dB	10 dB	20 dB
With spherical spreading	29%	50%	68%	90%
With cylindrical spreading [a]	50	75	90	99

[a] Propagation loss often is intermediate between spherical and cylindrical; cylindrical spreading does not occur near the source (Chapter 4).

Thus, large reductions in maximum potential radius of communication will result if noise levels increase by 10-20 dB while other factors remain unchanged. This is especially true if cylindrical spreading is occurring. Species that may communicate acoustically over long distances, such as some baleen whales, would be most seriously affected: **(1)** SNR is likely to be low, and **(2)** a given percentage reduction in communication radius translates into a large numerical reduction when range is large.

There is little information about the functions of most marine mammal calls, so it is difficult to predict the effects of a reduction in detection distance. Payne and Webb (1971) suggested that some baleen whales may use strong low-frequency calls to communicate over very long distances. We know of no specific evidence that whales respond to one another over ranges greater than ~20-25 km (Watkins 1981b). However, this may be largely a limitation of traditional observation methods. Continued work with the U.S. Navy's Integrated Undersea Surveillance System (Section 3.2.4) may show whether whales react to one another at distances longer than previously found. If so, they must respond to weak calls, and their communication would be susceptible to masking by man-made noise at similar frequencies.

Miles et al. (1987) examined the potential masking of bowhead whale calls based on measured sound propagation conditions in the Alaskan Beaufort Sea. They illustrated how the source level of the whale call (or other sound signal) greatly affects the severity of masking by man-made noise. Estimated source levels of bowhead calls vary widely (Section 7.1.1). A faint call (e.g., 140 dB re 1 µPa-m) can be masked even by a distant source of man-made noise, such as a 170 dB source 30 km away, unless the calling and listening whales are close together (<0.7 km in this case). However, if the source levels of calls and man-made noise are comparable, calls can be heard if the listening whale is closer to the calling whale than to the source of man-made noise (Figs. 10.13D-F). Many human activities have source levels similar to those of strong bowhead calls, ~170-180 dB re 1 µPa-m. A bowhead 20 km from such a source might hear strong calls from other whales within ~20 km; a whale 5 km from the source might hear strong calls from whales within ~5 km. This approximation would require modification for species whose calls are weaker or stronger than typical levels of man-made noise at similar frequencies. Also, it applies only within the distance where received levels of calls and man-made noise exceed the background noise level.

Distant sources of man-made noise are unlikely to mask short-distance acoustic communication. Noise from a distant source, if audible, is likely to be well below the received level of calls from a nearby mammal. Acoustic communication is more likely to be masked when a listening marine mammal is near a source of man-made noise and/or is listening to a distant conspecific. In these cases, the received level of man-made sounds might equal or exceed that of the mammal calls. The radius of masking by man-made noise is greater when the sound signal is a little above the natural background level than when it is much above that level. When the signal is barely detectable without man-made noise, even a weak man-made noise might raise the background noise (natural plus man-made) above the signal level and mask the signal. In that extreme case, the radius of masking might equal the radius of audibility of the man-made noise.

10.5.2 Adaptations for Reduced Masking

Besides the dependence on signal source level and on relative distances of the receiving animal from the signal and noise sources, there are other reasons why no single radius of masking can be defined. These include possible changes in call intensity or frequency in response to background noise conditions, directional hearing capabilities, and variations over time in received levels of interfering noise. Little is known about the roles of these processes in marine mammal hearing under field conditions, but they have the potential to greatly reduce masking effects (Section 8.5.3).

Source Levels.—Source levels of the calls of most marine mammals have not been studied in detail. However, in at least a few species, source levels vary widely (Chapter 7). Echolocating dolphins sometimes adjust source levels of echolocation pulses as a function of the background noise level, emitting more intense pulses when background noise is strong (Au et al. 1974; Au 1993). Most man-made sounds will not mask echolocation sounds because their frequencies usually differ. Man-made sonars whose frequencies do overlap with dolphin echolocation sounds usually emit pulsed sounds, which also would not mask most echolocation signals. However, communication calls often overlap in frequency with man-made noises. Masking of communication calls by man-made noise would be less common if mammals vary the source levels of their calls as a function of background noise, "intended" communication distance, or both.

Miles et al. (1987) provided an example of this in a theoretical analysis of masking of bowhead whale calls by industrial sources in the Beaufort Sea. Consider a receiving whale 12 km from a 170-dB industrial source. It would hear a calling whale only up to ~3.3 km away if the source level of the calls was 160 dB, but ~30 km away if the source level was 180 dB. Insofar as we know, adaptation of call strength to background noise level has been demonstrated only in toothed whales, and only for echolocation calls. However, gray whales may increase the levels of their calls when exposed to playbacks of motorboat noise (Dahlheim 1987).

Frequency Adaptation.—Some toothed whales seem able to adjust the frequencies of their echolocation calls, within limits, to avoid frequencies where background noise levels are high (Section 8.5.3). However, it is not known how much flexibility various marine mammals may have in adjusting the frequencies of communication calls. Most species either produce broadband calls containing energy at a variety of frequencies or, at different times, produce narrowband calls at varying frequencies. When communication at one frequency is masked by strong man-made noise, calls or call components at other frequencies may still be audible. Belugas may sometimes take advantage of this phenomenon by emitting communication calls dominated by frequencies subject to little noise interference (Lesage et al. 1993). It is not known how widespread or useful this capability may be.

Directional Hearing.—The directional hearing abilities of many marine mammals (Section 8.4) imply that the gain factor G in equation (10.1) may be positive. If so, the maximum masking potential of industrial noise would only occur when an animal attempts to listen to a signal arriving from the same direction as the man-made noise. There is some evidence that, in toothed whales, directional hearing is helpful in reducing masking at the high frequencies used for echolocation but not (or less so) at the moderate frequencies used for communication (Section 8.5.3). Larger animals with wider heads may tend to have better directional discrimination abilities for low- to moderate-frequency sounds. There is no direct evidence that the known directional hearing abilities of some marine mammals reduce masking at low frequencies. However, this probably occurs, at least in large whales.

Temporal Variations.—Levels of man-made noise often vary over time because of varying source levels and propagation conditions. Thus, masking by man-made noise may be intermittent, just as masking by natural ambient noise must depend strongly on daily variations in sea state and other factors affecting natural ambient noise. Animals for which faint sound signals are important must be adapted to periodic natural masking, and presumably can tolerate occasional masking by man-made sounds.

Summary.—Communication calls and other natural sounds important to marine mammals undoubtedly are masked by man-made and natural noise under some conditions. Some controlling factors are known from physical principles and auditory studies on captive toothed whales and pinnipeds. However, there is little specific information about the nature and effects of masking under field conditions, nor about adaptations that marine mammals may use to reduce masking. The few relevant data on masking have come largely from studies of high-frequency echolocation by toothed whales. However, echolocation is unlikely to be seriously masked by most man-made noises which, except for sonars, tend to be at lower frequencies. Lower-frequency man-made noises are more likely to affect detection of communication calls and other potentially important natural sounds, for example, surf or ice noise, prey noise, or killer whale sounds.

10.6 Zone of Hearing Loss, Discomfort, and Injury

In humans, prolonged or repeated exposure to high levels of airborne sound accelerates the normal process of gradual hearing deterioration with increasing age (Kryter 1985). This deterioration is a *permanent threshold shift (PTS)*. In addition, temporary increases in threshold occur during and shortly after exposure to high noise levels. This *temporary threshold shift (TTS)* can last from a few minutes to hours or days. In humans and terrestrial mammals, airborne sound levels that cause TTS after short exposure appear to be similar to those causing PTS after prolonged exposure. Given the difficulty of studies of long-term phenomena such as PTS, measured data on noise/TTS relationships are often used to predict sound levels that will, after long exposure, result in PTS.

Permanent hearing damage does not always develop gradually. In terrestrial mammals, brief exposure to extremely high sound levels, such as those from nearby explosions, can cause immediate onset of permanent hearing impairment (PTS) and nonauditory physiological and sensory effects. Explosions, if close enough and large enough, can also cause injury to nonauditory organs and death.

There are almost no published data concerning these types of effects on marine mammals. A few marine mammals killed by underwater explosions have been examined. As expected, their injuries often include damage to the auditory system (Section 9.10.2). Some marine mammals that survive nearby underwater or in-air explosions probably also sustain hearing damage, but available evidence is meager (Section 9.10.2). We have seen no reports demonstrating whether high levels of steady or impulse noise cause "discomfort" or nonauditory physiological effects in marine mammals. There are no published studies of TTS in marine mammals, although some data of this type may appear soon. Even for human divers, there are few available data on auditory and nonauditory effects of high-intensity underwater noise (P.F. Smith 1985; Hollien 1993). However, human divers often suffer hearing impairment, probably at least in part because of noise exposure (Hollien 1993).

Thus, this discussion of criteria and radii of hearing damage, discomfort, and injury is speculative. It is based largely on analogies with humans and other terrestrial mammals, often in air rather than underwater. The auditory and other systems of marine mammals have special adaptations for life in water, which is denser and much less compressible than air. Thus, the applicability of terrestrial mammal data to marine mammals is uncertain. Nonetheless, various extrapolations and models have been proposed to predict the radius of possible injury, auditory and otherwise, around underwater blasts. These approaches are summarized in Sections 10.6.2 and 10.6.3. It can be argued that these methods are too speculative to warrant detailed discussion. However, they are being used in some environmental impact assessments and to design mitigation measures (e.g., U.S. Navy 1993). Therefore, these models require discussion here.

10.6.1 Temporary Threshold Shift

In humans, exposure to strong airborne noise, even for a brief period, causes a temporary elevation of the hearing threshold: a temporary threshold shift or TTS (Kryter 1985). The magnitude of TTS depends on the level and duration of noise exposure, among other factors. In humans, exposure to continuous airborne noise with sound pressure level 90-100 dBA (re 20 µPa or re 0.0002 dynes/cm^2, the usual standard for airborne sound) will cause a TTS of a few decibels. This is roughly the level received by the operator of a lawn mower or inside a small aircraft (Table 5.2). In-air exposure to 110-120 dBA, as in a discotheque, will cause a TTS of 20 dB or more (Kryter 1985). Recovery of the normal auditory threshold following the end of exposure to strong noise is gradual. It can require minutes, hours, or days, depending on the degree of TTS. TTS also occurs in humans exposed to strong underwater noise (Smith 1985).

There are no published data on the occurrence of TTS in marine mammals, let alone about its quantitative relationships to noise exposure. TTS could have negative effects on the ability to hear and use natural sounds. To evaluate the importance of this temporary impairment, it would be necessary to consider the ways in which marine mammals use sound, and the consequences if access to this information were impaired. The scarcity of data on the functions of most marine mammal sounds, and on the importance of other natural sounds to marine mammals, makes it difficult to evaluate the significance of TTS. However, TTS might impair their abilities to communicate; to locate food or to navigate by echolocation; and to hear sounds from prey, predators, or other natural sources. These presumed negative effects of TTS are similar to those of masking (Section 10.5). Indeed, TTS and masking would both be expected when animals are exposed to strong man-made noise. However, TTS would persist for some time after noise exposure and masking ended.

It would be desirable to take advantage of any opportunities (field or laboratory) that may arise to test the hearing abilities of any marine mammal after exposure to strong noise. This might be done either by evoked potential techniques or, if the animal had previously been trained for audiometric measurements, by behavioral testing. If marine mammals exposed to strong noise exhibit TTS, this can be taken as an indication of potential susceptibility to long-term hearing impairment if exposed repeatedly or continuously to such sounds (Chappell 1980; Kryter 1985; NRC/OSB 1994).

10.6.2 Permanent Hearing Impairment

Continuous Man-Made Noise.—There are no data on noise levels that induce permanent hearing impairment in marine mammals. In humans, the normal process of hearing loss with increasing age can be accelerated by chronic exposure to workplace noise ~80 dB or more above the absolute hearing threshold (Kryter 1985).

If the "80 dB above threshold" value from humans listening in air also applies to marine mammals listening in water, very prolonged exposure to noise levels of ~120 dB re 1 µPa—80 dB above threshold at best frequency—might be required to induce permanent threshold shift (PTS) in belugas. The equivalent figure for fur seals might be ~140 dB, given their higher absolute threshold. Hearing damage thresholds from very prolonged exposure might be somewhat higher than 120 and 140 dB, respectively, for some other toothed whales and pinnipeds, given their higher absolute thresholds (Section 8.2). However, the validity of the "80 dB above threshold" criterion is unknown.

Some marine mammals tolerate, at least for a few hours, continuous sound at received levels above 120 dB re 1 µPa. However, others exhibit avoidance when the noise level reaches ~120 dB (Chapter 9; Section 10.3). It is doubtful that many marine mammals would remain for long in areas where received levels of continuous underwater noise are 140+ dB at frequencies to which the animals are most sensitive.

To be exposed continuously to a received level of 140 dB re 1 µPa, mammals would have to be quite close to most sources of continuous man-made noise. Received levels typically diminish by ~60 dB between the source and a radius of 1 km (Chapter 4). To obtain a received level of 140 dB at 1 km radius, the source level would have to be ~200 dB re 1 µPa-m. Few human activities emit continuous sounds at source levels ≥200 dB re 1 µPa-m (Chapter 6).

Prolonged exposure to noise levels above 120 dB is more likely. This could occur out to a radius of 10-20 km from strong sources of continuous noise. However, for most continuous sources operating at most sites, noise would diminish below 120 dB within 1-5 km, and sometimes well within 1 km (Miles et al. 1987).

The "80 dB above threshold" criterion for human PTS refers to exposure for ~8 h/day over ~10 years. Given the normal mobility of most marine mammals, we would not expect them to remain close to any one site long enough to be exposed to 140 dB for very long, even if the animal exhibited no avoidance reaction to this high noise level. Also, many of the strongest sources of nonimpulsive man-made noise (e.g., supertankers and icebreakers) are themselves mobile or discontinuous. Some species might remain within the larger "≥120 dB zone" for days or weeks, but few species would be expected to remain in an area with radius ≤10-20 km throughout a season or year. A seal using breathing holes near an icebound noise source might be one exception.

Another important factor in interpreting the analogies with humans is that toothed whales and pinnipeds whose hearing sensitivity has been measured are most sensitive at frequencies of at least several kilohertz. Most energy in the noise from many human activities is at lower frequencies (Chapter 6). Hearing sensitivity of various toothed whales and pinnipeds is known or suspected to be poorer at these frequencies, probably reducing the potential for auditory damage from prolonged exposure to low-frequency man-made noise (Kryter et al. 1966; Chappell 1980). This assumed mitigative factor may not apply to baleen whales, whose hearing sensitivity is expected to be good at low frequencies.

We hypothesize, therefore, that permanent hearing impairment caused by prolonged exposure to *continuous* man-made noise is not likely to occur in marine mammals, at least for sounds with source levels up to ~200 dB re 1 µPa-m. Direct evidence bearing on this hypothesis is obviously desirable, but will be very difficult to obtain. A long period must elapse before realistic sound levels are likely to have detectable effects. Also, ethical and legal considerations normally prevent experiments that might injure marine mammals. Indirect evidence based on studies of TTS would be more readily obtained.

We emphasize that the applicability of the "80 dB above threshold" criterion to marine mammals is unknown. A criterion based on human hearing in air may not apply to marine mammals in water. Indeed, it is not certain that it even applies to humans in water. There is evidence that the dynamic range of human hearing is less in water than in air (Hollien 1993). If so, the "80 dB above threshold" criterion for prolonged exposure may be too high. Conversely, the adaptations of marine mammals to the large changes in static pressure encountered during diving may provide greater resistance to the rapid pressure fluctuations that comprise a strong sound. If so, the "80 dB above threshold" criterion may be too low. This uncertainty seems unresolvable with the data now available.

Although it is doubtful that exposure to any strong, continuous source would persist long enough to cause PTS in a marine mammal, some continuous sources definitely cause behavioral reactions with potential negative consequences. With a 200 dB re 1 µPa-m source level, altered behavior or displacement could occur out to radii of 10 km or more, given that behavioral responses by cetaceans sometimes occur at received levels ≤120 dB re 1 µPa (Chapter 9 and Section 10.3.2).

Intermittent Noise.—Intermittent noise is noise that is discontinuous or widely variable in level, but not impulsive. In humans, the lower the daily duration of exposure to intermittent airborne noise, the higher the noise level that can be tolerated without risk of permanent hearing damage after several years of intermittent exposure. For airborne noise at frequencies to which the human ear is most sensitive

(~3 kHz), one widely accepted Damage Risk Criterion (DRC) is ~80 dB above threshold for 8 h of exposure per day. For narrowband sounds, such as tones or ⅓-octave bands, this DRC increases to 82 dB for 2 h of exposure per day, 88 dB for ½ h/day, 98 dB for 7 min/day, and 115 dB for ≤1½ min/day (Kryter et al. 1966). At frequencies other than 3 kHz, human hearing is less sensitive, and higher sound levels can be tolerated without risk of significantly elevated PTS.

Again, it is not known how closely the process of PTS in marine mammals, as caused by intermittent noise, may parallel that for humans listening in air. If the processes are similar, the DRC for ½-2 h of exposure per day may be only a few dB higher than that for 8 h/day. However, the DRC for noise lasting only a few minutes per day may be substantially higher. Thus, risk of hearing damage may not be much reduced if exposure is reduced from ~8 to ½-2 h/day, but might be notably reduced by restriction to a few minutes per day.

Human DRCs for repeated exposures to intermittent noise are based mainly on studies of Temporary Threshold Shift (TTS) after single short exposures. This indirect approach is based on epidemiological studies showing that TTS after short-term exposure is a useful indicator of PTS after long exposure (Kryter 1985). A similar indirect approach might be useful in determining DRCs for marine mammals exposed to intermittent noise.

In humans, a sound that is about 155 dB above the normal absolute threshold level is high enough to cause immediate damage and permanent threshold shift (Kryter 1985:272). If this applies to marine mammals, whose hearing thresholds are often 40-70 dB re 1 μPa (Section 8.2), then a received level of 195-225 dB re 1 μPa might cause immediate hearing damage. With continuous and intermittent sources, levels of this magnitude are restricted to the immediate vicinity of the strongest sources. Indeed, some of the strongest sources, such as supertankers and icebreakers, are not point sources. Although their nominal source levels exceed 195 dB, levels this high may not be present at any one location. In the case of a point source such as a powerful sound projector, animals close enough to be exposed to a level of 195-225 dB would necessarily be within a few meters or tens of meters of the source. In these situations, received level decreases about 6 dB per doubling of distance. Thus, the received level would be reduced to well below 195 dB if the animal moved only a short distance farther away. Many marine mammals would avoid such a noisy location, although it is not certain that all would do so (Chapter 9).

The greatest risk of immediate hearing damage might be if a powerful source were turned on suddenly at full power while a mammal was nearby. In the ATOC ocean acoustics project (Section 6.8), each transmission is to begin at low intensity and the sound level will then increase gradually ("ramp up") over several minutes before reaching a maximum of 195 dB re 1 µPa-m (ARPA and NMFS 1994; ARPA 1995). This approach is intended to give any deep-diving mammals near the source the opportunity to move away before they are exposed to the maximum source level. Whether most mammals would actually do so deserves more study. However, some bowhead whales start to move away as industrial noise from a nearby sound projector ramps up over several minutes (W.J. Richardson, personal observation).

Impulsive Noise.—Explosions, sonars, and several methods of seismic exploration produce brief noise pulses whose peak levels are much higher than those of most continuous or intermittent noises (Sections 6.5-6.7). Source levels of pulses from many sonars, airgun arrays, and other nonexplosive sources of pulsed sounds are 230-255 dB re 1 µPa-m. Sounds from high-frequency sonars attenuate rather quickly in seawater. However, received levels of low-frequency energy in the pulses from airgun arrays often exceed 160 dB re 1 µPa out to distances of 5-10 km, and can exceed 140 dB to distances of 15-30 km (Greene and Richardson 1988). Pulses from explosions can have even higher source levels and more rapid rise-times (Section 6.7).

There are no data on auditory damage in marine mammals relative to received levels of underwater noise pulses. Chappell (1980) discussed the available evidence concerning effects of sharp airborne pulses of sound on terrestrial mammals, and speculated about the relevance of these data to marine mammals.

Many studies of the effects of strong airborne noise pulses on human hearing have been done (Kryter 1985). Most were based on TTS, assuming that noise pulses causing substantial TTS have some risk of causing PTS. From these data, W.D. Ward (1968) developed human Damage Risk Criteria for airborne impulse noise. The basic criterion specifies the maximum permissible peak pressure during exposure to 100 impulses over an interval of at least 4 min on one day. The DRC diminishes by 2 dB for each doubling of pulse duration from

- ▸ 164 dB re 20 µPa (= 0.0002 dynes/cm^2) for very brief pulses (25 µs) to
- ▸ 152 dB for pulses 1.5 ms long (or longer if the pulses are simple positive pressure pulses), with a further decrease to

> ▸ 138 dB for prolonged (>200 ms) pulses with alternating positive and negative pressure peaks.

There are further provisions to

> ▸ adjust the DRC upward or downward by 5 dB per 10-fold change in number of pulses per day if that number is not 100, and to
> ▸ allow levels 5 dB higher if pulses arrive at a grazing rather than normal angle.

Thus, under no conditions should there be human exposure to a peak level >179 dB re 20 µPa—the DRC for 100 25-µs pulses (164 dB) plus 10 dB to allow for 1 rather than 100 pulses, plus another 5 dB to allow for grazing incidence. For a single long pulse at normal incidence, the DRC would be 148 dB. This is 138 dB plus the 10-dB single-pulse adjustment.

These human DRCs for airborne impulses are all in dB re 20 µPa. The human auditory threshold in these units is near 0 dB. Thus, these DRCs might also be taken as the number of dB by which the peak pressure must exceed threshold in order to produce some risk of hearing damage. Assuming that marine mammals have underwater thresholds of 40-70 dB re 1 µPa (Section 8.2), DRCs for marine mammals underwater (in dB re 1 µPa) might be on the order of 40-70 dB higher than DRCs for humans in air (in dB re 20 µPa).

If so, the DRC for a marine mammal exposed to 100 seismic pulses might be 178-208 dB re 1 µPa (Table 10.1). This allows for the fact that seismic pulses, as received ≥1 km horizontally from the source, have alternating positive and negative pressure peaks and total durations may be ≥200 ms. However, the duration of near-peak pressure is <200 ms, so hearing damage is unlikely unless peak pressure is several dB above 178-208 dB. For 10 elongated sonar pulses, the DRC might be 183-213 dB: 138 dB plus 5-dB adjustment for only 10 pulses plus 40- to 70-dB threshold. For a single brief explosive pulse, the range might be 214-244 dB: 164 dB plus 10-dB adjustment for single pulse plus 40- to 70-dB threshold (Table 10.1).

We emphasize that these values are all extremely speculative, given the unknown relevance of human in-air data to marine mammals underwater. As noted earlier, the dynamic range of human hearing may be narrower underwater than in air (Hollien 1993). One should not assume that marine mammals exposed to somewhat lower levels of pulsed underwater sound than those mentioned above would necessarily be "safe" or, on the contrary, that those exposed to somewhat

TABLE 10.1. Auditory Damage Risk Criteria for humans exposed to noise pulses in air (Ward 1968) and, by speculative inference, for marine mammals exposed to noise pulses in water[a]

Number of pulses	DRC for human in air (in dB re 20 µPa)	Speculative DRC (in dB re 1 µPa) for marine mammal listening in water with hearing threshold	
		40 dB re 1 µPa	70 dB re 1 µPa
100 long	138	178	208
10 long	143	183	213
1 long	148	188	218
1 short	174	214	244

[a] See text for explanation and qualifications.

higher levels would necessarily suffer auditory damage. The speculation in preceding paragraphs is useful not to identify "safe" levels and distances, but rather to identify situations worthy of concern, mitigative action, and further study. With these caveats, what are the implications for marine mammals near sources of strong noise pulses?

Animals directly below an *airgun array* could be exposed to levels near 178-208 dB re 1 µPa even at depths down to several hundred meters; the source levels of airgun arrays for downward propagation can be ≥250 dB (Section 6.5.1), and spherical spreading can be assumed to occur. However, the effective source level for horizontal propagation is lower by ~10-30 dB, depending on aspect. Animals would probably have to be within 1 km to the side of an airgun array to be exposed to 178 dB, and well within 100 m to receive 200 dB or more.

This speculation suggests that some marine mammals within 1 km horizontally from a seismic vessel might be subject to immediate hearing damage. However, this is based on DRCs from humans and an assumed 40-dB absolute hearing sensitivity (138 dB + 40 dB). A 40-dB absolute threshold has been found only in certain odontocetes and only at frequencies much higher than those of the dominant energy in seismic pulses (Section 8.2). When the main frequencies of impulse noise are below those of maximum auditory sensitivity, the damage risk is reduced, at least in terrestrial mammals (Price 1986). Absolute thresholds at low frequencies have not been measured in many species, but probably are well above 40 dB even in species adapted for low-frequency hearing. Ambient noise levels at low frequencies tend to exceed those in the kilohertz range, even when ship traffic noise is ignored (Section 5.2).[2] It is unlikely that marine mammals would have evolved low-frequency hearing so sensitive that it is always strongly masked by natural background noise levels. The 138-dB human DRC, if transferable to marine mammals, probably should be added to a low-frequency threshold well above 40 dB.

Thus, mammals probably would have to be well within 100 m of an airgun array to be susceptible to immediate hearing loss, with the possible exception of marine mammals directly below the array. We emphasize that this is an untested hypothesis needing study. It is based on unverified assumptions about the applicability of human Damage Risk Criteria to marine mammals in water, where energy conduction processes and auditory anatomy are quite different. Most baleen whales in the path of an oncoming seismic vessel would probably avoid the vessel by well over 100 m (Section 9.8.3), thus avoiding the possibility of hearing damage. It is not known whether other marine mammals would show avoidance or whether, if they did not, their hearing might be harmed.

Most seismic exploration programs involve many closely spaced "shots". We expect that extended or repeated exposure to seismic pulses is unlikely to cause permanent hearing damage in marine mammals, given the foregoing discussion of DRCs and

- ▸ the transitory nature of seismic exploration,
- ▸ the presumed ability of marine mammals to tolerate exposure to strong calls from themselves or other nearby mammals, and
- ▸ the avoidance responses that occur in at least some baleen whales when received levels of seismic pulses exceed ~170 dB re 1 µPa.

Again, this "evidence" is indirect and the conclusion is speculative.

Sharp noise pulses from underwater *explosions*, on the other hand, definitely can damage the hearing system (Section 9.10.2). High explosives produce strong noise pulses with sharper onsets (more rapid pressure increases) than are produced by nonexplosive sources of seismic pulses (Section 6.7.2; Staal 1985). When kilogram quantities of high explosives are detonated, source levels of the resulting pulses exceed those from any nonexplosive seismic source.

---

[2] Marine mammal hearing systems evolved before ship noise was a factor. Hence, ship noise should not be considered when discussing the ambient noise levels to which their hearing systems are adapted.

As noted above, extrapolations from human DRCs suggest that marine mammal auditory systems might be at risk from a single explosive pulse if the peak received level exceeded 214-244 dB (164 dB plus 10-dB allowance for single pulse plus thresholds of 40-70 dB; Table 10.1). As in the case of airgun pulses, actual thresholds are likely to be well above 40 dB at the low frequencies where most explosions have their dominant energy. If so, the human data might imply a minimum DRC of ~224 dB re 1 µPa (peak pressure). That level would be expected to occur at distances of about 189, 407, and 877 m, respectively, from the detonation points of 1-, 10-, and 100-kg charges of high explosive [equation (6.8) in Section 6.7.2]. It is not known whether these values based on human DRCs in air are valid for marine mammals underwater.

10.6.3 Explosion Injury Models

Several workers have used a different approach to develop procedures for estimating distances within which underwater explosions may cause death or obvious injuries to organs. These procedures are based mainly on studies of blast injury to terrestrial mammals held underwater (Yelverton et al. 1973; Yelverton 1981). The severity of these injuries seemed most closely related to the positive acoustic impulse received by the animal. Positive impulse is a measure of the mechanical impact produced by a short-duration pressure pulse, taking account of both its magnitude and its duration (Section 6.7.2). Explosion injury models are based on estimates of impulse at various ranges and depths around a blast of specified size and depth. These models have the merit of being based on actual tests of blast effects on mammals in water. However, the data used to develop the models were severely limited:

- based on submerged terrestrial, not marine, mammals;
- blast tests were conducted in shallow water;
- limited range of mammal sizes;
- considered only gross injuries evident upon simple necropsy.

Nonetheless, the resulting models are widely used in attempts to predict and mitigate explosion effects on marine mammals. As summarized in Section 9.10.2, data on blast injuries to marine mammals are extremely limited.

Yelverton et al. (1973) reported the impulse strengths that caused various levels of injury to dogs, rhesus monkeys, and sheep held underwater near blasts (Table 10.2). They looked for eardrum rupture

TABLE 10.2. Underwater blast damage criteria for medium-sized terrestrial mammals held underwater, expressed in three equivalent measures of impulse[a]

Criterion	bar·ms	psi·ms	Pa·s
High incidence of moderately severe blast injuries, including eardrum rupture. No mortality.	2.76	40	276
High incidence of slight blast injuries, including eardrum rupture.	1.38	20	138
Low incidence of trivial blast injuries; no eardrum ruptures.	0.69	10	69
Safe level. No injuries.	0.34	5	35

[a] Adapted from Yelverton et al. (1973).

and other macroscopic injuries to the auditory system, but did not take account of hearing damage that was undetectable during simple necropsies. Yelverton et al. used their data to develop a procedure for estimating "safe ranges" for marine mammals exposed to underwater blasts. These estimates did not depend on body mass. Hill (1978) and Wright (1982) describe variations of this method.

Subsequent analysis showed that the threshold for blast injuries in submerged terrestrial mammals depended on body size (Yelverton 1981). The upper limit for no injury ranged from 26 Pascal·seconds for rats (0.2 kg) to 210 Pa·s for sheep (45 kg), with higher values for 1% and 50% mortality (Fig. 10.14).

Goertner (1982) used the data for submerged terrestrial mammals to develop a computer program that estimates the maximum radius at

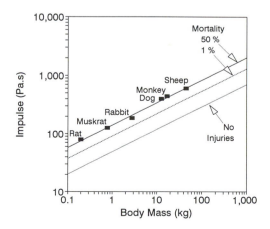

FIGURE 10.14. Three provisional Damage Risk Criteria for terrestrial mammals exposed to underwater blast, as a function of body mass (Yelverton 1981). Datapoints pertain to 50% mortality criterion. See Section 6.7.2 for method of calculating impulse based on charge size, distance, and other parameters.

which slight injuries might occur as a function of body size and depth in the water. Each prediction refers to a specific charge mass, charge depth, water depth, mammal depth, and mammal size. The model takes account of extensive physical data on attenuation of shock waves traveling through water, plus available data and models concerning blast effects on submerged terrestrial mammals with varying body-cavity sizes. In general, the impulse received from a given blast increases with charge depth and mammal depth, unless the mammal is close to and deeper than the charge. For a given impulse, injury potential is assumed to be inversely related to mammal size. However, water depth, bottom hardness, type of high explosive, and charge design (spherical or otherwise) all affect the received impulse and the resultant organ damage.

O'Keeffe and Young (1984) show representative results of calculations based on Goertner's model. For example, a 5.5-kg high-explosive charge at depth 1.5 m is predicted to cause slight injury to manatees at distances up to ~40 m in the case of adults and ~85 m for calves. Fig. 10.15 shows examples of "slight injury" ranges for much larger charges—545 and 4540 kg. A 4540-kg charge detonated 61 m deep is predicted to cause slight injury to marine mammals with masses of 10, 100, 1000, 10,000, and 100,000 kg at distances up to about 2300, 1900, 1400, 975, and 530 m, respectively, depending on their depth in the water. The accuracy of these predictions is unknown for many reasons, including the fact that most of these size categories are larger than any of the submerged terrestrial mammals for which data are available (Fig. 10.14). Also, those data concern gross internal injuries and eardrum rupture, not subtle auditory effects. O'Keeffe and Young suggested multiplying the calculated "slight injury" distances by at least a factor of two to provide an adequate margin of safety.

Simplified equations to predict "safe ranges" were given by Young (1991), based on the more detailed models noted above. These equations predict safe range for the worst combination of blast depth and mammal depth, and thus are presented as "conservative" estimates of safe range (Fig. 10.16). Young suggests using these equations for initial planning, but using the more detailed model (Goertner 1982) for more specific planning. All of these methods are based largely on the Yelverton et al. (1973) tests and injury criteria (Table 10.2).

Safe ranges for human divers exposed to underwater blasts have been estimated by intentionally exposing divers to distant blasts and from other evidence (Gaspin 1983). Safety criteria recommended for

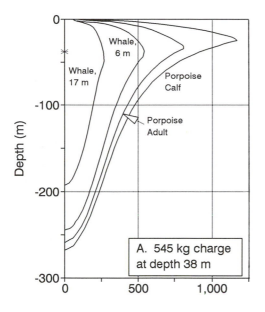

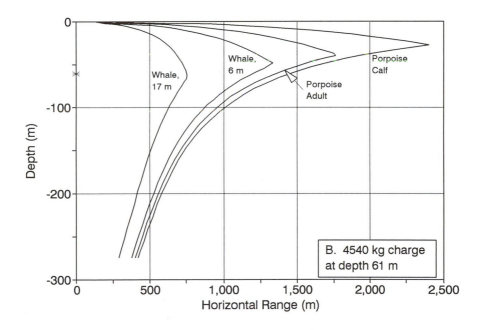

FIGURE 10.15. Predicted distances from underwater blasts at which slight lung or intestinal injuries would be expected in four sizes of marine mammals at different depths: *(A)* 545-kg high-explosive charge at 38 m depth; *(B)* 4540-kg charge at 61 m depth. Adapted from O'Keeffe and Young (1984), based on Goertner (1982).

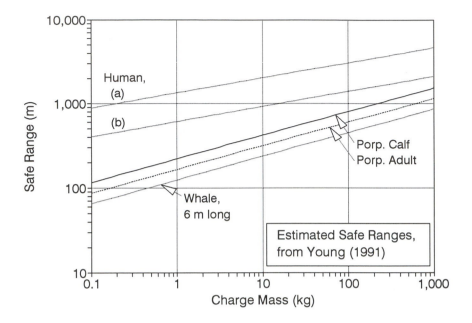

FIGURE 10.16. Estimated safe ranges for marine mammals of three sizes, and for human divers, versus size of underwater blast. Adapted to metric from equations of Young (1991), which are said to overestimate actual safe ranges in most situations. For marine mammals, given a charge mass of M (kg), safe range R in meters is predicted as $R = c \cdot M^{0.28}$, where $c = 220$ for calf dolphin or porpoise, 165 for adult dolphin or porpoise, and 124 for small whale. For a human diver, $R = c \cdot M^{0.18}$, where (a) $c = 1335$ for deep water with diver at 15 m depth and charge at 30 m depth, and (b) $c = 608$ for diver and charge on bottom in water 9 m deep.

humans are more stringent that those used in the Goertner (1982) and Young (1991) models for marine mammals. Humans are believed to be at no risk of injury if the impulse in the received shock wave and its bottom reflection totals ≤2 psi·ms (≤14 Pa·s) and the peak over-pressure is ≤100 psi (≤690 kPa or ≤237 dB re 1 µPa). Gaspin concluded that, under pressing military situations, it might be acceptable to risk exposing a human diver to an impulse of up to 10 psi·ms (69 Pa·s) provided that peak overpressure is ≤100 psi. In this case there would be some risk of minor injury (Table 10.2). On the basis of these criteria, Gaspin graphed the "safe" and "risk of minor injury" horizontal ranges for a human diver near a TNT blast as a function of charge size, swimmer depth, and water depth. Young (1991) gave simplified "safe range" equations for human divers in two situations (Fig. 10.16).

Shock waves created by different high explosives have slightly different peak pressure/time/distance/depth relationships. No single conversion factor can be used to convert an estimated safe range for TNT into a safe range for another type of explosive (Gaspin 1983:11).

In summary, there is little specific information about the susceptibility of marine mammals to underwater blasts (Section 9.10.2), and data for submerged terrestrial mammals are also limited, especially regarding blast-induced auditory damage. Marine mammals are presumably better adapted to pressure changes and other aspects of the aquatic medium. However, their auditory systems are also better adapted to transmit rapid pressure fluctuations in the water to the inner ear. Thus, it is not clear whether marine mammals are less, equally, or more vulnerable to blast injury than are terrestrial mammals. In the absence of specific marine mammal data, it can be argued that, at least for the smaller marine mammals, protection measures should be planned using the conservative human safety criteria of Gaspin (1983) and Young (1991) rather than the less conservative criteria that have been proposed for marine mammals.

Susceptibility to blast damage is believed to decrease with increasing mammal size. However, it has not been demonstrated that this trend in small- and medium-sized terrestrial mammals (Fig. 10.14) applies to marine mammals, nor that it can be extrapolated to large mammals, nor that it applies to auditory damage as well as gross injuries.

Most of these questions cannot be studied by direct experiments on marine mammals because of ethical and legal considerations. However, it would be useful to test the hearing abilities of any live marine mammal that is accessible after inadvertent exposure to an explosion, especially if the received impulse can be estimated. Auditory structures of any marine mammals killed by explosions should also be examined (Ketten 1995).

10.6.4 Discomfort Threshold and Nonauditory Effects

Intense sounds in air or water can produce discomfort and other nonauditory effects in humans. Human divers exposed to intense underwater noise (e.g., 190 db re 1 µPa) sometimes report discomfort, apparent rotation of the visual field, or dizziness (Smith 1985).

Little has been published about these nonauditory effects in terrestrial mammals, let alone marine mammals. However, nonauditory effects of strong underwater sounds apparently have military relevance. Respiratory cavities of various sizes can be induced to resonate in response to strong underwater sounds with appropriate wavelengths (Duykers and Percy 1978; ARPA 1995). This phenomenon has apparently been studied to evaluate the feasibility of using strong underwater sounds to deter human divers from approaching sites of military significance.

Recently, human divers have reported discomfort when exposed to sounds from a powerful low-frequency (LF) sonar at very long ranges. Physiological studies to investigate the basis for this discomfort are under way in the U.S.A. Some non-acoustic effects may be elicited by stimulation of Pacinian corpuscles (Woolley and Ellison 1993; ARPA 1995), which are mammalian sensory structures sensitive to LF vibration. Also, Crum and Yi Mao (1994) estimate that human divers and marine mammals exposed to LF sound at levels >210 dB re 1 µPa may be at risk from acoustically enhanced growth of gas bubbles in body fluids.

If some military sonar systems have significant nonauditory effects on humans, there is reason for concern about their effects on marine mammals. Results of ongoing research in this area should be made public to better define the implications for marine mammals.

Seismic exploration creates some of the most intense anthropogenic sounds for which detailed information is available. For example, the received level from a seismic vessel can be 160 dB out to 5-10 km, and 180 dB out to perhaps 1 km. Whales have been seen within a few kilometers of operating seismic vessels (Section 9.8.3). Whether seismic sound pulses cause any discomfort to marine animals is not known. It is probably important that seismic (and sonar) sounds are intermittent. Intermittent pulses with peak levels 160-180 dB are less likely to cause discomfort than would continuous 160- to 180-dB noise.

Human divers operating some types of underwater power tools, such as stud guns, are exposed to impulsive noise levels of ~210 dB re 1 µPa (J. Mittleman, in Smith 1985). They do not report discomfort or "noticeable effects on ears" even though received impulses exceed the 2 psi·ms (14 Pa·s) safe exposure limit cited in Section 10.6.3. However, the waveform of a stud gun impulse presumably differs from that of an explosion impulse, as does the waveform of a seismic pulse. The 14 Pa·s criterion was developed for explosions.

Disturbance effects are likely to cause most marine mammals to avoid any "zone of discomfort or nonauditory effects" that may exist. Ringed seals confined by fast ice are one species for which avoidance might be impractical, although radiotelemetry evidence suggests that even they have some ability to move (Kelly et al. 1986). Also, sudden onset of a source of intense sound near marine mammals might, until they move away, result in discomfort or nonauditory effects. However, we are not aware of any specific studies of the occurrence of these phenomena in marine mammals, nor on the levels and characteristics of sounds that might elicit them.

10.7 Summary

Predicted radii of audibility and responsiveness depend strongly on the source level and spectral characteristics of noise from the human activity, the rate of acoustic attenuation with distance, and the ambient noise level and its spectral characteristics. Attenuation and ambient noise, in turn, are affected by variables such as water depth, water and bottom properties, sea state, ice cover, and many others. Radii of audibility estimated in Section 10.4.3 assume "typical" ambient noise levels. Normal day-to-day variations in ambient noise are expected to cause drastic changes in the radius of audibility for all situations when hearing is "ambient-limited" (Section 10.2.1). Predicted radii of influence are also uncertain because of variability and uncertainties in biological phenomena like auditory sensitivity, detection of infrasounds, and behavioral response thresholds. Much caution is essential in interpreting estimated radii of influence such as those in Section 10.4.3. They are most useful when compared with one another, that is, in a relative sense. They are undoubtedly less useful as predictors of actual radii of audibility or responsiveness in specific circumstances.

10.7.1 Radii of Audibility
Despite the limitations of these predictions, it is clear that some man-made sounds will be audible much farther away than others. Strong acoustic sources like seismic exploration and icebreaking are probably audible 100 km or more away in many cases. This is especially true for baleen whales, assuming that their hearing is very sensitive to low-frequency sounds. However, low-frequency seismic pulses may be strong enough to be heard at distances of 100 km or more even by some toothed whales and pinnipeds, whose low-frequency hearing is apparently not very sensitive. At the other extreme, a bottom-founded oil production platform may not be audible to toothed

whales and pinnipeds more than a few hundred meters away, or to baleen whales more than a few kilometers away, at the most.

Available propagation loss and ambient noise data show that average radii of audibility must vary seasonally and among regions. Elevated levels of ambient noise caused by snapping shrimp or surf, for example, can cause significant reductions in typical radii of audibility. Day-to-day variability in ambient noise can affect the radius of audibility drastically.

Uncertainties about absolute hearing sensitivity are important data gaps in estimating radii of audibility. For baleen whales, no direct data on hearing sensitivity are available. We assume that they are quite sensitive to low-frequency sounds, but corroboration is needed. The lack of data on sensitivity of baleen whales to infrasounds (at <20 Hz) is an important data gap. Behavioral audiograms of several species of toothed whales and pinnipeds have been determined, but there are few data below ~1 kHz, where many man-made noises are strongest. The lack of behavioral audiograms for sirenians and sea otters prevents quantitative "zone of audibility" estimates for these animals. Work is in progress on the low-frequency thresholds of some odontocetes, pinnipeds, and the manatee.

Our estimates of radius of audibility assume that marine mammals can hear a sound whose level in one or more ⅓-octave bands exceeds the background noise level in the corresponding band. Masking bandwidths undoubtedly vary. Experimental data on masking exist for a few species of marine mammals, but most data concern the rather artificial case of pure tones masked by white noise. Also, the examples in Section 10.4.3 do not allow for the possibility that directional hearing extends the radius of audibility.

For all of these reasons, estimated radii of audibility are preliminary first approximations. Their greatest value may be in identifying phenomena needing further study.

10.7.2 Radii of Responsiveness

Many marine mammals tolerate man-made noise that is apparently audible but not unduly intense (Chapter 9). However, when the level is high enough, they often exhibit avoidance or other behavioral reactions. Thus, the radius of responsiveness is often much smaller than the radius of audibility. For example, seismic pulses are often detectable 100+ km away, but gray and bowhead whales usually show overt avoidance only to seismic vessels within a few kilometers.

Few studies have attempted to determine the threshold noise levels that elicit behavioral reactions. For many combinations of human activity and type of marine mammal, one can only quote the closest distances at which animals have been seen, without allowance for the unknown received noise levels. Even the distance data are lacking for many combinations of human activity and mammal type. Thus, the scarcity of measured noise levels at which marine mammals do and do not react to various man-made sounds is a significant data gap.

Even for a given species in a given area and season, there is wide variability in the responsiveness of different individuals to noise. Large sample sizes are needed to characterize response criteria statistically. "Radius of response" predictions in Section 10.4.3 are distances where we expect an average individual to react. Some may occur closer to the noise source; others may react strongly at greater distances. Among the factors affecting responsiveness are the animal's current activity and its past experience (if any) with that sound type.

This chapter considers only noise-elicited reactions. Some marine mammals may also react to visual or other cues, especially in cases of human activities that do not emit strong sounds.

10.7.3 Radii of Masking

Man-made noise can undoubtedly interfere with detection of calls, echolocation sounds, and environmental sounds at frequencies similar to the noise. However, the "radius of masking" will be highly variable, depending on many factors. These include the distances of the listener from the sources of the acoustic signal and masking noise, the levels of those two sources, transmission loss from each source to the listener, directional hearing abilities of the listener, relative directions from listener to the sources of the signal and noise, and whether the signal level or frequency is adjusted in response to the masking noise.

Available data on masking in marine mammals have come mainly from studies of high-frequency echolocation by toothed whales. Except for sonars, most sources of man-made noise are at lower frequencies, where masking is largely unstudied in marine mammals.

10.7.4 Radii of Hearing Loss, Discomfort, and Injury

Predicted radii of hearing loss, discomfort, and injury in marine mammals exposed to strong sounds are also highly speculative, given the scarcity of data. It is assumed that the hearing sensitivity of marine mammals, like that of other vertebrates, can be reduced at least temporarily by exposure to strong noise. However, there are no published data on sound levels, continuous or transient, necessary to cause either temporary or permanent hearing impairment. Approaches for adapting criteria developed for humans and other terrestrial mammals listening in air to marine mammals listening underwater have been discussed (Section 10.6.2). These approaches are extremely speculative, and could be seriously in error in either direction. It is also not known whether marine mammals experience nonauditory sensations or discomfort when exposed to very high levels of underwater sound, as do human divers in some situations.

Underwater explosions can kill or injure marine mammals. Existing methods for predicting "safe" ranges, based mainly on tests with submerged terrestrial mammals, are summarized in Section 10.6.3. However, existing methods give little attention to potential hearing damage. The more conservative criteria that have been proposed for human divers perhaps should be applied to marine mammals as well.

CHAPTER 11

SIGNIFICANCE OF RESPONSES AND NOISE IMPACTS[1]

11.1 Introduction

Marine mammals undoubtedly hear man-made noises from many sources. Cetaceans and manatees are exposed primarily to underwater sounds. Pinnipeds and sea otters are often exposed to airborne sounds as well. Most man-made sounds to which marine mammals are exposed are dominated by low frequencies, although there are exceptions such as ship sonars. The hearing systems of baleen whales are assumed to be adapted for detecting natural low-frequency sounds. Pinnipeds and especially toothed whales are better adapted for detecting higher-frequency sounds, but they can hear strong low-frequency sounds as well (Chapter 8). Data on the hearing abilities of manatees and sea otters are meager or lacking, preventing a meaningful assessment of their abilities to detect man-made sounds. Data for manatees may be available soon (cf. Gerstein et al. 1993).

The fact that marine mammals can detect man-made noise does not, in itself, show that marine mammals are affected deleteriously by the noise. Chapter 9 cites many examples of marine mammals that commonly occur close enough to noise sources to be well within the ensonified zone. In many of these cases, activities of animals within the ensonified zone seem unaffected by the noise.

However, there is rarely any definitive information about the numbers of mammals within the ensonified zone relative to numbers that would have been there if there were no man-made noise. Also, there is almost no information about the possibility that marine mammals occurring within an ensonified zone are "stressed" or otherwise affected in a way that might impair their long-term well-being or

[1] By W. John Richardson, LGL Ltd., and Bernd Würsig, Texas A & M University at Galveston.

reproductive success. For example, acoustic masking will reduce the ability of a marine mammal near a noise source to hear faint calls from distant conspecifics or other faint natural sounds. The consequences of masking are unclear, given the scarcity of data on the importance of various natural sounds to most marine mammals.

Overt behavioral reactions observable when marine mammals are exposed to man-made noise range from subtle to obvious. The more obvious reactions include pinnipeds stampeding into the water when disturbed by humans on foot or in aircraft or boats, and whales swimming at maximum speed away from an approaching ship. However, even in the most extreme cases, the duration of observable disturbance is usually short—on the order of minutes or a few hours. The longer-term implications of these short-term reactions are usually unknown. However, in the case of pinnipeds at breeding rookeries, recently born calves are sometimes killed or maimed during stampedes.

This chapter discusses these issues further, and includes a brief review of parallels between the reactions of marine and terrestrial mammals to man-made noise. In many ways, terrestrial mammals are easier to study. Some techniques useful in disturbance studies of terrestrial mammals may be relevant for future work on marine mammals, e.g., radio-telemetry of heart rate or other physiological variables. Telemetry has shown that, in some terrestrial species, heart rate changes in response to man-made noise even when there is no outward evidence of disturbance. Such findings in terrestrial mammals may be relevant in interpreting observations of marine mammals, or in designing future marine mammal studies.

The present chapter also includes brief comments on some ways in which negative effects of man-made noise can be reduced. This can often be done by effective facility designs and by regulations concerning methods or timing of operations. In addition, the adaptations of marine mammals to variability in the natural environment probably provide them with some capabilities useful in coping with man-made noise. These may include an ability to adjust call strength or frequency to reduce acoustic masking, and a tendency to move away from areas where stressors of various types are present.

11.2 Area Affected versus Habitat Available

A relevant factor in considering possible effects of a noisy human activity on marine mammals is the size of the zone of acoustic influence relative to the amount of suitable habitat available. Special concern would arise if a marine mammal population concentrates in one or a few areas whose dimensions are small relative to the potential radius of noise influence, and if a noisy human activity is expected to occur near a concentration point. Examples include pinnipeds hauling out in dense aggregations on favored beaches, cetaceans that concentrate in localized nearshore areas, and manatees that concentrate in warm-water discharges. The dimensions of these mammal concentrations are often smaller than the dimensions of the area ensonified by a single site of human activity, or by a single passing vessel or aircraft. In these cases, a significant proportion of a marine mammal population might be exposed to noise from a single noisy activity.

On the other hand, there may also be more potential for effective mitigation if a population is highly concentrated. It may be easier to adjust the locations and timing of human activities to minimize disturbance to the mammals if they concentrate in one area, or in a few small areas, than if they are broadly distributed.

In contrast, some species of marine mammals can be widely dispersed within offshore areas totalling 10^5-10^7 km^2. In these cases, only a small percentage of the population is likely to be within the radius of acoustic influence around a given human activity. For example, if the radius of responsiveness is 20 km (a relatively large value—see Chapter 10), the area of responsiveness is ~10^3 km^2 (πr^2). This is only 1% to 0.01% of 10^5-10^7 km^2. Thus, a single human activity is unlikely to cause disturbance *at any given time* to more than a small percentage of a widely dispersed population. Of course, it may at the same time affect another species with a more clumped distribution.

Even with widely dispersed populations, in some situations a large part of the population might be exposed to man-made noise:

1. If radius of responsiveness is 20 km, radii of audibility and masking may be ~100 km. This corresponds to an area of audibility or masking of 0.3×10^5 km^2, or 30% to 0.3% of 10^5-10^7 km^2. Thus, there are situations when a significant percentage of a dispersed population may be able to hear a single human activity even if only a small percentage are within its radius of responsiveness. In general, however, marine mammals that are exposed to faint noise from a distant human activity usually show no overt reactions to it (Chapter 9), and only the faintest natural sounds would be masked by weak man-made noise from a distant human activity (Section 10.5).

2. Although the number of animals in an ensonified area at one time may be small, a high percentage of the population may have to pass through that area at some time within a season. This would apply in the case of animals that migrate through a narrow passage whose waters might be ensonified by a stationary human activity, e.g., gray whales migrating through Unimak Pass in the Aleutian Islands in spring and autumn, or bowhead whales migrating through nearshore lead systems around northwest Alaska in spring. If the passage is narrow relative to the radius of responsiveness, much or all of the population might be affected.

3. A given population of marine mammals is likely to be exposed to noise from various human activities within its range, e.g., a ship in one place, fishing boats somewhere else, marine construction in a nearshore area, and elsewhere perhaps seismic exploration, oil drilling, military sonar, or ocean acoustics research. Although the proportion of the population exposed to noise from any one source may be small, the proportion exposed to at least one noise source may be much higher. There may be few or no parts of the range where man-made noise is absent. In large areas of the world's oceans, even when there is no nearby source of man-made noise, background noise levels below ~300 Hz are often dominated by distant shipping noise and are several decibels above "preindustrial" levels (Section 5.2.3). Little is known about cumulative noise effects on marine mammals (Section 11.7).

4. Although a marine mammal population may be spread over a large area, some parts of that area may be more important than others because of the presence of an important food source or breeding area. If the zone of influence of a noise source includes one or more key areas, a disproportionate percentage of the population might be affected.

Thus, there are circumstances in which significant numbers of marine mammals can be exposed to man-made noise even when the population is widely distributed.

11.3 Auditory Interference by Masking

The auditory masking process was described in Section 8.5, and the size of the "zone of masking" around a noise source was discussed in Section 10.5. Although masking has been studied in laboratory conditions in a few species of toothed whales and pinnipeds, it is difficult to extrapolate these results to practical field conditions. Experimental studies normally assess the effects of uniform "white noise" on audibility of pure-tone signals. White noise has the same level at each frequency across a broad band. In reality, background noise is not "white", and sound signals are rarely pure tones. It would be useful if additional laboratory work on masking could be done using sound signals and background noises more typical of those occurring in the field. It is difficult to work with low-frequency sounds (<1 kHz) in small tanks, but studies of masking need to extend down to the low frequencies where many man-made noises are concentrated. Two studies, on a beluga listening underwater and a harbor seal listening in air, have provided data on low-frequency masking (C.S. Johnson et al. 1989; Terhune 1991). More low-frequency data are needed.

Some marine mammals have hearing capabilities that apparently compensate, to an unknown degree, for masking (Sections 8.5.3 and 10.5.2). Most of the available data on compensatory mechanisms concern echolocation pulses and other high-frequency sounds. Additional studies of these compensatory abilities are needed, including lower frequencies where most man-made noises are concentrated, and including sea otters and manatees as well as toothed whales and pinnipeds. Unfortunately, masking processes in baleen whales are not amenable to laboratory study. This is a concern, as it is the baleen whales whose sounds overlap most with the frequencies of many man-made noises.

Another complication is that there are few data on the consequences if communication, echolocation, or ambient sounds are masked for various periods of time. Too little is known about the functions and importance of these natural sounds in the lives of even the best-studied species of marine mammals. Masking affects primarily the weaker sound signals received from distant sound sources. Masking noise must be strong to conceal strong signals from close sources. There is little information about the importance to marine mammals of hearing the weak sounds that are most subject to masking.

Masking is a natural phenomenon. Marine mammals must cope with it even in the absence of man-made noise, just as humans and other terrestrial animals cope with their inability to hear natural sounds from sources beyond certain distances. The maximum radius of audibility of airborne and waterborne sounds varies widely because of natural variations in background noise. The presence of man-made noise at some places and times will increase the variability in background noise levels, and make masking more common.

The consequences of elevated background noise levels, especially when these increases are temporary and local, are impossible to determine from available data. The ocean is naturally noisy and variable, and marine mammals must be well adapted to the natural range of ambient noise. Marine mammals probably can tolerate, with few or no negative effects, some increase in masking relative to natural levels. The limits of this tolerance cannot be determined until more is known about **(1)** the importance to marine mammals of faint sound signals from conspecifics (Chapter 7), predators, prey, and other natural sources; **(2)** signal detection abilities of marine mammals in the presence of background noise (Section 8.5), including directional hearing abilities at frequencies where masking is an issue (Section 8.4); and **(3)** abilities of marine mammals to adjust their call strengths and perhaps frequencies to minimize masking effects (Section 10.5.2).

Although further data are needed, localized or temporary increases in masking probably cause few problems for marine mammals, with the possible exception of populations highly concentrated in an ensonified area. However, a more extensive and continuous noise field could result if a number of noise sources were distributed through a major part of the range of a mammal population. In this "multiple/distributed source" case, masking might be more of a problem. Shipping is one human activity in this category (Møhl 1981). Large areas of the world's oceans have chronically elevated ambient noise levels below ~300 Hz owing to the cumulative effect of many ships (Section 5.2.3). The potential masking effects of this noise on baleen whale communication were pointed out almost 25 years ago (Payne and Webb 1971), but their biological significance remains largely unknown.

11.4 Behavioral Disruption

Most data on marine mammal disturbance, whether based on uncontrolled observations or experiments, concern short-term behavioral reactions. Various studies have determined the distance, or occasionally the received sound level, at which the animals first react. Reactions often include cessation of resting, feeding, or social interactions; increased alertness (in pinnipeds); changes in surfacing, respiration, or diving cycles (in cetaceans); and onset of avoidance (Section

10.3.1). Avoidance may mean departure from a haulout site (pinnipeds), hasty diving, swimming away, or some combination of these actions. In most studies, little or no information has been obtained about the duration of altered behavior after disturbance. Thus, available data almost all pertain to short-term changes in behavior, lasting minutes or hours. However, effects may persist for 1-2 days when pinnipeds are displaced from terrestrial haulout sites or High Arctic beluga whales flee from approaching ships (Sections 9.2.1 and 9.3.2).

11.4.1 Variations in Responsiveness

Marine mammals show wide within-species variations in responsiveness to man-made noise. They sometimes continue their normal activities in the presence of high levels of man-made noise. At other times, members of the same species exhibit strong avoidance at much lower noise levels. This apparent variability is partly attributable to variations in physical factors, specifically the characteristics of the man-made noise, its attenuation rate, and the background noise level (Section 10.3.3). However, the variability in responses is also partly attributable to real differences in the sensitivity of different individual animals, or of the same animal at different times. Some of these differences are associated with differences in activities (e.g., resting, feeding, socializing), age and sex differences, habitat effects, habituation or sensitization, and residual individual variation (Chapter 9; Section 10.3.3). Thus, the radius of responsiveness varies widely among individuals, locations, and times. No single criterion of disturbance will apply to all circumstances, even for a particular type of animal and a particular human activity.

This variability makes it difficult to define criteria of responsiveness and has led to seemingly conflicting evidence about sensitivity to some types of noise. Large sample sizes are needed to characterize variation in responsiveness. Careful attention must be given to the circumstances of each observation. Even when these are well defined, there will be individual variation in sensitivity.

11.4.2 Short-Term Behavioral Disruption and Displacement

Little is known about the consequences of short-term disruptions in the normal activities of marine mammals. This problem is largely a result of the scarcity of data on the importance of most natural activities of marine mammals. Without such data, it is difficult to assess the consequences of a disruption in natural activities.

The first reaction of pinnipeds hauled out on land or ice is often to raise the head and become alert (Chapter 9). When disturbance is mild, this may be the only overt reaction, in which case the consequences for the animals are presumably insignificant or nil. With more severe disturbance, pinnipeds commonly move into the water, often in a stampede. Some young can be trampled to death during stampedes (Section 9.2.1), and a walrus calf was reported killed by a polar bear as walruses left the ice in response to ship disturbance (Section 9.3.1; Fay et al. 1984). However, direct mortality during disturbance-induced stampedes seems uncommon. Some pinniped young may be permanently separated from their mothers during stampedes, and subsequently die of starvation (e.g., B.W. Johnson 1977) or predation. However, direct proof of this is difficult to obtain.

Pinnipeds normally move back and forth between the water and haulout sites on land or ice even in the absence of disturbance. When they move into the water as a result of disturbance, they typically return within a few hours or by the next day (Sections 9.2.1 and 9.3.1). Thus, a single displacement probably does not have severe consequences in most cases. Repeated disturbance and displacement is more likely to have important negative effects, especially at haulout sites used for breeding or pup-rearing.

In contrast to the many observations of reactions by pinnipeds hauled out on land or ice to airborne noise, there is little information about effects of man-made noise on pinnipeds in the water.

Cetaceans often change their general activity when exposed to man-made noise. Cetaceans that were at rest at the surface often become active, begin to dive and surface, and may swim away from the noise source (Chapter 9). Cetaceans that are actively engaged in feeding or especially socializing often seem to tolerate considerable disturbance before reacting. However, when exposed to sufficiently strong or threatening noise (perhaps supplemented by other sensory cues), feeding or socializing cetaceans often interrupt this normal activity and dive or swim away. The duration of behavioral disruption following the end of disturbance has rarely been determined.

Bowhead whales that flee from approaching boats, including seismic vessels, often resume their previous behavior within ½-1 h. However, altered behavior sometimes persists longer (Sections 9.3.3 and 9.8.3; Richardson et al. 1986). On two occasions, bowheads whose feeding was interrupted by boat disturbance swam several kilometers away but returned to the feeding area by the next day (Section 9.3.3).

It is not known how often bowhead whales have access to zooplankton in densities suitable for efficient feeding (Bradstreet et al. 1987; Richardson et al. 1987b). If good feeding conditions are infrequent, temporary displacements of this nature might have significant energetic consequences if repeated several times in a season (Section 11.6.4).

11.4.3 Social Disruption

Social disruption is another potentially important negative effect of disturbance. Aggregated animals may flee in different directions upon the approach of a fast-moving noisy vessel or aircraft. The duration of social disruption is rarely determined, but is often at least several hours for cetaceans engaged in cooperative feeding or sexual activity, and possibly a day or more in some cases (e.g., pinnipeds returning to a haulout site). The consequences of this disruption on individuals and the population are poorly understood. It may result in disruption of social ordering, sexual behavior, care of the young, and cooperative activities. It may also increase aggression when the social order is in flux. At least in pinnipeds, social disruption may cause the dominant males in these polygynous societies to lose control of reproductively receptive females. However, there is little direct information about most of these points. We can only assume that repeated social disruption is a disadvantage because it decreases or disrupts the activities that would have occurred naturally, and it may affect adversely a social ordering that took time and energy to become established. This disruption is likely to affect the efficiency of avoiding predators, finding food, mating, and caring for the young.

A common reaction of cetaceans exposed to noise is to cease or reduce calling. This has often been noticed in baleen whales (e.g., Watkins 1986) and sperm whales (Section 9.9). Assuming that many calls have communication functions, cessation of calling could indicate some social disruption. During the Heard Island ocean acoustics study, calling by sperm whales seemed to stop over a large area during the several-day period of noise emissions and for as much as 36 hours thereafter (Bowles et al. 1994); calling apparently also stopped upon exposure to rather weak noise pulses from a seismic vessel hundreds of kilometers away. In this case, the seemingly low response threshold and large radius of noise influence are reasons for concern. However, sperm and other whales do not always cease calling in response to boat or pulsed noise (Chapter 9). This variability, plus the meager data on functions of calling in sperm and other whales, makes it difficult to assess the social significance of these observations.

Separation of dependent young from their mothers is a potentially severe consequence of disturbance-induced social disruption. The possibility of mother-calf separation when pinnipeds stampede from a haulout site has already been mentioned. Concern has also been expressed about the possibility of mother-calf separation in cetaceans if they flee in different directions. This is unlikely to occur unless the whales are already separated by some distance before disturbance begins. In baleen whales, older (but still nursing) calves occasionally are separated from their mothers by a few hundred meters. However, at least for bowhead whales, present knowledge of reaction thresholds, sound propagation, and masking suggests that a mother and calf separated by up to 1 km would be able to communicate acoustically as they began reacting to an approaching ship, and presumably could rejoin (Koski et al. 1988). Consistent with this, Wartzok et al. (1989: 136, 213) reported two sightings of bowhead cows and calves separated by a few hundred meters that rejoined as a small ship approached.

In general, little is known about the biological significance of the short-term disturbance reactions discussed in Chapter 9. We suspect that isolated disturbance incidents usually have minimal or no lasting effects. Marine mammals cope with occasional disruption of their activities by predators, bad weather, unusual ice conditions (at high latitudes), and other natural phenomena. It is reasonable to suppose that they can also tolerate occasional brief periods of man-induced disturbance, e.g., by a single passing ship or aircraft. However, prolonged disturbance, as might occur if a stationary and noisy human activity were established near a marine mammal concentration area, likely is a more important concern. The long-term implications would depend in part on habituation. If the animals fail to habituate and, as a consequence, are excluded from an important concentration area or are subject to ongoing stress while in that area, there could be long-term effects on individuals and the population. Conversely, when habituation occurs, as it does for some marine mammals exposed to ongoing human activities, the consequences may be minimal.

11.5 *Habituation versus Continued Responsiveness*

Behavioral habituation is the gradual waning of responsiveness when a stimulus is not associated with any significant consequences.

Marine mammals are often seen in situations indicating that they are tolerating exposure to man-made noise (Section 9.14). In a few cases there is evidence—usually indirect or circumstantial—that the animals were more responsive to the noise when first exposed, but habituated during continued or repeated exposure.

We are not aware of any detailed studies of habituation in marine mammals. However, this phenomenon is well known in other types of animals (e.g., Chapter III in Thorpe 1963; Majors and Myrick 1990). Habituation, by definition, occurs only when there is repeated or continuous exposure to a stimulus not accompanied by anything that the animal perceives as threatening. Many man-made sounds, both waterborne and airborne, probably fall into this category. However, certain forms of disturbance may be encountered too rarely to allow habituation. Even if habituation to a given stimulus has developed in a marine mammal, it is not known how often the animal must be exposed to that type of disturbance in order to remain habituated to it. For example, if animals are exposed to disturbance repeatedly during one season of the year and become habituated, it is uncertain whether they would still be habituated the next year. The "curious-whale" phenomenon in wintering gray whales and St. Lawrence estuary belugas seems to involve both a long-term waning in responsiveness over the years and a shorter-term component within each year's tourist season (Section 9.3).

Animals are less likely to habituate to a highly variable sound than to a steady sound. They are unlikely to habituate to a sound associated with a threat, e.g., to motorboat noise if they are hunted or harassed from motorboats. A few observations suggest that some marine mammals discriminate between a threatening stimulus, such as noise from a boat used to capture dolphins, and an otherwise similar benign stimulus (Irvine et al. 1981). Indeed, responsiveness to repeated threatening stimuli can increase over time (Section 9.14.3).

11.6 Long-Term Effects

11.6.1 Mortality

There have been very few documented cases of direct mortality as a result of disturbance, and there is much evidence that most types of disturbance do not cause direct mortality. The best-documented cases of direct mortality caused by noise disturbance involve occasional trampling of young pinnipeds during stampedes from haulout sites, usually triggered by aircraft overflights (Section 9.2.1). Boats and people on land near whelping grounds can also trigger stampedes. Disturbance may also lead to increased mortality via abandonment of dependent pinniped pups by their mothers (B.W. Johnson 1977), and perhaps via increased predation on the young (Fay et al. 1984). Besides direct mortality of pups, pup production may be reduced if disturbance deters pregnant females from coming ashore, or from returning in later years (Harwood and Greenwood 1985).

Disturbance-induced displacement of manatees from warm-water discharges in Florida during cold winters may cause some mortality due to hypothermia (Hartman 1979; Kochman et al. 1985). However, this is probably less common than manatee mortality from direct collision with motorboats.

Ships and icebreakers occasionally injure or kill marine mammals by collision. Collision-induced mortality cannot be attributed directly to noise disturbance. Indeed, local displacement in response to the noise of an approaching vessel is a method for avoiding collision injuries or mortality. However, some whales react to the sound of an approaching boat by attempting to outrun it. This response is often ineffective, especially for slow-swimming species like bowhead and probably right whales. Because these animals react to noise in the way that they do, they are often closely approached by vessels and sometimes hit.

Although occasional mortality of a few individual animals as a result of disturbance is undesirable and often illegal, it is—from a biological perspective—the long-term population consequences of disturbance and mortality that are of most concern. For example, if disturbance causes long-term abandonment of part of the range where the population formerly concentrated, the carrying capacity of the environment for the population might be reduced. If many individuals continue to occur in an area subject to ongoing or intermittent disturbance, concern arises about the possibility that normal activities might be affected enough to reduce the reproductive rate via social disruption, effects on energy balance, or some other form of stress.

Explosions can, if large enough and close enough, kill any marine mammal. Some cases of pinniped, cetacean, and sea otter mortality from explosions have been reported (Section 9.10.2). This mortality is attributable to shock waves, not noise, but the two are related. For some local populations of river dolphins, deaths from explosions used for demolition and fishing may be common enough to be a significant source of mortality (Zhou Kaiya and Zhang Xingduan 1991; Baird et al. 1994). There has been much publicity about potential mortality from ship-shock tests (U.S. Navy 1993) and explosive removal of off-shore platforms (Klima et al. 1988). In contrast, we have seen very few data on marine mammal deaths from underwater explosions during past decades when these blasts were more frequent (Section 6.7.1) and when less attention was given to their environmental effects.

From a population perspective, marine mammals occupying the North Atlantic, parts of the Pacific, and various other waters are presently exposed to far fewer large underwater explosions than they were during World War II. The use of high explosives for marine seismic exploration has also largely ceased. There are no data on the frequency of explosion-induced deaths, injuries, and hearing-impairment among marine mammals during World War II and during periods of seismic exploration with explosives. Whatever the losses of individuals may have been, now-existing populations of marine mammals survived those periods.

11.6.2 Injury

Explosions can also injure marine mammals, and their hearing systems may be most susceptible (Sections 9.10.2 and 10.6). Available data on occurrence of gross injuries due to explosions are limited. Even less is known about inconspicuous auditory damage. Small charges are no longer widely used in the eastern Pacific tuna fishery, in which nets are set around dolphins (Section 9.10.1). However, in some areas "seal bombs" are still used to deter pinnipeds from fishing and aquaculture gear (Section 9.12). We know of no data on the frequency, severity, and consequences—individual and population—of hearing impairment from these small charges or from larger blasts.

The possibility of hearing damage from exposure to strong nonexplosive sounds is discussed in Section 10.6.2. Again, almost no data are available for marine mammals. Some elderly captive bottlenose dolphins have impaired high-frequency hearing (Seeley et al. 1976; Ridgway and Carder 1993). Whether noise exposure was involved in causing this hearing loss is unknown. Extrapolations based on data from humans and other terrestrial mammals listening in air suggest that marine mammals are unlikely to suffer hearing impairment from exposure to continuous man-made sounds. Hearing damage may be more likely upon close exposure to strong intermittent or impulsive sounds such as sonars or seismic exploration pulses. However, the relevance of guidelines based on terrestrial mammals is unknown, and there are no data for marine mammals (Section 10.6.2). Studies of Temporary Threshold Shift (TTS) upon exposure of marine mammals to strong noise would be useful as an indication of sound levels that might, after long exposure, cause permanent hearing impairment.

Pinniped stampedes caused by aircraft overflights or other human activities no doubt also injure animals, especially pups (Section 9.2.1).

11.6.3 Long-Term Displacement

Although certain marine mammals no longer occupy some areas that they used in earlier years, it is rarely known what role (if any) noise disturbance had in causing long-term abandonment of a part of the range. Habitat may become unsuitable for reasons other than elevated noise, e.g., local increases in hunting or by-catch, or changes (natural or man-related) in turbidity, water temperature, or food abundance. In an uncontrolled field situation where many factors change simultaneously, it is rarely possible to isolate the specific cause of any observed change in numbers of marine mammals. Indeed, it is uncommon to have a series of reliable counts long enough to quantify the numerical change, let alone determine its cause.

In baleen whales, a few cases of medium- or long-term displacement of animals from local areas have been ascribed, at least tentatively, to repeated disturbance. Underwater noise was presumably a major factor in some or all of these cases, although noise effects cannot be separated from those of other stimuli.

1. The best-documented case was the abandonment by gray whales of a calving lagoon in Baja California for several years, and their return after vessel traffic diminished (Section 9.3.3; Gard 1974; Reeves 1977; Bryant et al. 1984). Abandonment of San Diego Bay by gray whales was another possible case.

2. Humpback mothers and calves may now avoid some nearshore waters off Hawaii where human activities, largely recreational, are intense (Section 9.3.3; Glockner-Ferrari and Ferrari 1985, 1990; Salden 1988).

3. Reduced use of Glacier Bay, Alaska, by humpback whales has been suspected to be a consequence of vessel disturbance (Section 9.3.3; Jurasz and Jurasz 1979a; Dean et al. 1985). However, changes in prey abundance probably also influenced local distribution of humpbacks in that area (Bryant et al. 1981; Krieger and Wing 1986; Dolphin 1987).

4. Numbers of bowhead whales using an area ($\sim 10^4$ km^2) of intensive offshore oil exploration in the Canadian Beaufort Sea apparently diminished a few years after the onset of offshore drilling in 1976 (Richardson et al. 1985a, 1987a). Bowheads were numerous in the center of the main industrial area in 3 of 5 years from 1976 to 1980 versus 0 of 6 years from 1981 to 1986. During the mid-1980s, vessels working in and near the main industrial area included 5 drillships, 2 drilling caissons, 5-6 seagoing dredges, 9-10 helicopters, 3-4 seismic exploration ships, 4 icebreakers, ~ 10 supply ships, and other support vessels. Industrial activities in this area declined in the late 1980s. Unfortunately, funding for surveys also was curtailed then, so it is not known whether use of the area by bowheads increased after industrial operations declined.

   Whether the decline in bowhead use of the main industrial area was caused by disturbance, changing food availability, or other factors is unproven (Richardson et al. 1985a, 1987a; Duval 1986; Ford et al. 1987; Ward and Pessah 1988). Bowheads concentrate in areas where zooplankton is highly concentrated, and locations of zooplankton concentrations varied within and between years (Bradstreet et al. 1987).

5. Nishiwaki and Sasao (1977) suggested that reduced catches of minke and Baird's beaked whales off parts of Japan were caused by greatly increased ship traffic. However, their results were confounded by changes in harvest methods and effort, and in other types of potential disturbance. In our view, and that of Payne (1978b), the results do not prove that numbers of whales declined as a result of shipping. Indeed, the continued presence of beaked whales off the entrance to Tokyo Bay despite heavy ship traffic shows considerable tolerance of shipping.

It is noteworthy that all of these cases are controversial and open to alternative explanations. One common limitation is that systematic data were not collected in a sufficiently consistent fashion across the years. Also, long-term case studies of this nature generally lack both geographic replication and control data from undisturbed areas.

It may be misleading to compare the many reports of noise tolerance (Section 9.14) versus the few reports of probable long-term displacement by noise. Changes in utilization of an area may be slow and difficult to detect, given the long lifetimes of most marine mammals and the slow rate of change in habitat quality in many areas. The effects of man-made noise on marine mammals have been an issue for less than 25 years, and most research directed specifically at this topic has been done in the past 15 years. If marine mammals did react to noise from human activities by reduced use of certain areas, there would often be insufficient reliable and systematic information to document the trend. In contrast, it is easy to document cases where marine mammals remain in an ensonified area. Thus, cases of partial or even complete abandonment of disturbed areas may be more common than available evidence indicates.

If permanent displacement occurs, the consequences to the population are difficult to determine. In general, one can speculate that an area where the density of animals is low, and similar to the densities in many other areas, is unlikely to be critical either to individuals or to the population. However, this would not apply if the area were important to a small but important component of the population, e.g., mothers with calves, or for an important function, e.g., mating. Areas used consistently by many animals are likely important both to individuals and to the population. However, it is rarely known whether a particular location provides unique resources not available elsewhere. It is also rarely known whether other similar habitats to which displaced animals might move are already supporting as many marine mammals as they can. It should not be assumed, in the absence of specific information, that displaced animals will be able to fare as well in some other part of the population's range. On the other hand, it is also not justifiable to assume, without specific data, that displaced animals will be seriously harmed or will cease to reproduce. One of the many complications is that, for many marine mammals, the habitat on which they depend is "mobile", varying within and among years.

Very little research has been done on these questions, in part because of the difficulty of conducting the necessary types of long-term studies. This research would require study of the site tenacity, well-being, and reproductive success of known individuals, including some that remain in preferred undisturbed locations ("controls") and others that are displaced. This type of work is most likely to be practical on pinnipeds that haul out in areas that are consistent and amenable to study. If such animals are expected to be displaced by a planned human activity, it would be desirable to initiate long-term research on the fate and reproductive success of displaced individuals as compared with controls, including pre-disturbance work if possible. Replication of the observations in two or more similarly disturbed areas and two or more undisturbed but otherwise similar control areas would provide more power to detect and attribute effects than is typical in uncontrolled monitoring studies at single sites.

Designs for these types of studies are well known in theory (e.g., R.H. Green 1979). However, application of these designs to marine mammals is difficult because of problems involving logistics, necessary study duration, sample size, and pseudoreplication. Methods for conducting studies of medium- and long-term effects of disturbance on marine mammals need more thought and development.

11.6.4 Energetic Consequences

The energetic consequences of one or more disturbance-induced periods of interrupted feeding or rapid swimming, or both, have not been evaluated quantitatively. Subjectively, one would expect that a single such incident would have little effect on the energetic status of a marine mammal. However, repeated incidents of interrupted feeding and rapid swimming due to disturbance probably have negative effects on the well-being of individuals if disturbance occurs sufficiently often and for sufficiently long periods.

The frequency and duration of disturbance that might initiate negative effects are unknown, and would no doubt depend on the species, area, feeding requirements, and reproductive status of the mammals involved. Energetic consequences would be less severe in a region with abundant and widely distributed food than in an area where feeding is necessary but suitable food is less readily available. Animals subject to heavy natural energy drain, especially females in late pregnancy or lactation, probably would be most severely affected.

Energetic models that could be helpful in evaluating the energy cost of disturbance and displacement have been developed for other purposes (Huntley et al. 1987). For some species it may be possible to make reasonable estimates of the energy cost of x displacements averaging y km at average swimming speed z km/h, and of a w-hour interruption in feeding time. However, we suspect that there are few if any marine mammals for which food availability and foraging behavior are known well enough to allow meaningful predictions of energy intake by displaced versus undisplaced individuals. Thus, estimates of the net energetic effects of displacement probably are still beyond our prediction abilities. Even if this could be estimated, effects of a specified energy cost on individual reproductive output would be

404   Chapter 11. Significance of Responses & Noise Impacts

difficult to estimate. Energetic status is related to reproduction in at least some marine mammals (e.g., Boyd 1984; R.E.A. Stewart and Lavigne 1984; Lockyer 1986). However, available data are insufficient for quantitative predictions of disturbance effects on reproduction.

11.6.5 Tolerance and Stress

Many marine mammals occur in areas ensonified by man-made noise, often behaving in seemingly normal ways (Section 9.14). In some cases there is at least suggestive evidence of true habituation, i.e., diminished responsiveness after repeated or prolonged exposure to the noise. Animals that tolerate man-made noise are often presumed to be less affected by the noise than are others whose behavior is changed overtly, sometimes with displacement.

However, the presence of marine mammals in ensonified areas does not prove that the population, or even those individuals, are unaffected by the noise. It is rarely known how many individuals would have been present in the absence of noise, other factors being equal. The numbers in the ensonified area may be only a fraction of the numbers that would have been there without man-made noise. It is also not known whether masking of weak natural sounds by man-made noise causes any problems (Section 11.3).

Brodie (1981b) noted that marine mammals may stay in an area despite noise disturbance if no alternative areas meet the requirements of the animals. These animals might be stressed. The term "stress" means different things to different people. To Selye (1973), stress is the physiological response of the body to a demand made upon it by one or more external stimuli, the "stressors". To Broom and Johnson (1993:72), it is "an environmental effect on an individual which overtaxes its control systems and reduces its fitness or appears likely to do so". Stress often involves activation of the pituitary-adrenal axis. In response to external stimuli, the anterior pituitary releases more ACTH (adrenocorticotropic hormone), which in turn stimulates the adrenal cortex to release more adrenal corticoid hormones. These cause various more or less standard responses in different parts of the body—responses that may increase the animal's ability to cope with challenges. However, chronic activation of these physiological mechanisms may lead to harmful physiological effects (Selye 1973).

Many studies of terrestrial mammals, including humans, have looked for evidence that chronic noise exposure causes stress. Some studies have provided evidence of noise-induced stress, but the majority have been inconclusive or have shown no such evidence (for reviews, see Section 11.8.4; Kryter 1985:389*ff*; Majors and Myrick 1990). Marine mammals exhibit some of the same stress symptoms as found in terrestrial mammals, judging from the few species studied (e.g., C.A. Thomson and Geraci 1986; St. Aubin and Geraci 1988). However, there has been very little study of noise-induced stress in marine mammals. One exception was a study in which plasma catecholamines were measured in captive belugas before and after exposure to playbacks of recorded semisubmersible drillrig noise (Thomas et al. 1990a). Elevated levels of catecholamines are often found in stressed mammals. Thomas et al. found that noise exposure did not lead to elevated catecholamine levels in the blood. The general significance of this one study of belugas is unknown, especially in view of the short durations of noise exposure.

11.7 Cumulative Effects

The cumulative effect of all human activities—e.g., noise, pollution, habitat loss, collision mortality, by-catch, and hunting—is an obvious concern. Guidelines for Environmental Impact Assessments in some jurisdictions require that cumulative effects be considered (Spaling and Smit 1993). In the absence of specific data, this difficult task is usually handled subjectively, if at all. The cumulative effects on marine mammals of noise from multiple human activities have not been studied specifically, let alone the cumulative effects of noise plus nonacoustic phenomena. The following comments concern potential cumulative effects of multiple noise sources, not the broader issue of cumulative acoustic and nonacoustic effects.

The presence of multiple noise sources in an area might increase the severity of any deleterious noise effects resulting from single sources. Although the proportion of the population exposed to noise from one source may be small, the proportion exposed to at least one noise source may be much higher. If the animals are displaced from an area around some or all sources, the total amount of habitat affected will be greater than for any one source. Thus, a higher proportion of the population is likely to be affected as the number of sources increases.

If either the animals or the noise sources move, an individual animal would encounter a noise source more often. The consequences of increasingly frequent disturbance are uncertain but presumably negative. If the spacing of noise sources were on the same order as the radius of avoidance, the presence of several noise sources in an area might displace mammals from the entire area.

The long-term consequences of multiple noise sources are likely to depend partly on the degree of habituation to repeated noise exposure. Given the meager data on habituation in marine mammals, only qualitative predictions are possible. We expect that habituation would be most rapid and complete if the various noise sources emit similar sounds. Also, habituation to an array of stationary sources, such as offshore drilling or production rigs, is likely to be more complete than that to a similar number of equally noisy moving vessels.

The simultaneous presence of multiple noise sources will increase the amount of masking. The larger the number of noise sources in an area, the larger the percentage of the area that will be subject to a given severity of masking. Marine mammals must be able to cope with occasional masking, as masking is a natural phenomenon. However, consider a case where conspecifics can hear one another over distances of 10 km about 75% of the time in undisturbed conditions. These animals may be unable to coordinate their activities to the usual degree if there are enough noise sources to allow communication over 10 km only 10% of the time, and to allow communication with 75% success only within a radius of 2 km. Another concern is that, as the number of noise sources increases, the noise becomes less directional, making directional hearing (Section 8.4) less useful in discriminating sounds of interest from background noise.

As noted earlier, little is known about the importance of long-distance communication and the detection of other weak natural sounds by marine mammals. Thus, no specific assessment of the consequences of masking by multiple noise sources is possible.

Although effects of multiple noise sources on marine mammals have not been studied specifically, some relevant field observations have been mentioned earlier in this review. In some areas, both toothed and baleen whales remain in areas where many boats are present. Some pinnipeds persist in hauling out in areas with repeated boat traffic, aircraft overflights, or human presence. Thus, there is evidence of considerable tolerance of repeated exposure to noisy human activities that do not pose a direct threat (Section 9.14). Habituation is probably a major factor in these cases. However, there are also cases of seemingly reduced numbers of marine mammals in areas with many human activities (Section 11.6.3). It is difficult to obtain conclusive evidence about the occurrence, let alone the causes, of long-term displacements and population trends. The occurrence of long-term declines might be underestimated based on a simple tabulation of the number of studies reporting declines versus no *apparent* decline.

These comments deal with the cumulative effects of several different noise sources within the geographic range of a marine mammal population. Cumulative effects of acoustic and nonacoustic components of human activities are a further consideration. Nonacoustic effects are beyond the scope of this review. However, many of the reported reactions (or lack of apparent reactions), as summarized in Chapter 9, involve nonacoustic as well as acoustic effects. In uncontrolled field situations, it is difficult to isolate the specific stimuli to which marine mammals are responding.

11.8 Parallels in Terrestrial Mammals

Effects of noise disturbance on fish, birds, and terrestrial mammals, including humans, have been studied extensively in recent decades. In assessing effects of noise on marine mammals, the most meaningful comparisons may be with other mammals, particularly ungulates. Ungulates share a common ancestry with cetaceans, and a number of behavioral traits are similar in ungulates and cetaceans. Many terrestrial mammals are easier to study than are most marine mammals. Hence, the available data on reactions to noise are often more comprehensive for terrestrial mammals. Although these data cannot be extrapolated directly to marine mammals, a review of noise effects on terrestrial mammals could be helpful in interpreting the less detailed information from marine mammals. Work on terrestrial mammals is useful in suggesting hypotheses, study approaches, and ways of evaluating the results.

In this section we cite data on short- and longer-term reactions of terrestrial mammals to noise, plus data on physiological effects and habituation. This review is not comprehensive. We emphasize topics that seem most relevant to marine mammals. Useful reviews include Fletcher and Busnel (1978), Shank (1979), Sopuck et al. (1979), Dufour (1980), Kryter (1985), and Majors and Myrick (1990).

Although terrestrial mammals are often easier to study than marine mammals, some of the methodological problems are similar. In both groups, behavior, distribution, and physiological state are variable, and are affected by many factors besides disturbance. Furthermore, in both terrestrial and marine mammals, behavior, distribution, and physiology may be affected by research processes, e.g., presence of humans (Jordan and Burghardt 1986), overflights by survey aircraft (Bleich et al. 1994), or capture of the animals (M.W. Miller et al. 1991), thus confounding the research results. Direct measurements of noise exposure have been obtained even less often during disturbance studies on terrestrial mammals than for marine mammals. Much work has been done on developing acoustical measurement techniques for use in studies of noise and humans. In contrast, there has been little standardization of acoustical methods for use in studies of terrestrial or marine mammals. Hence, it is difficult to compare sound exposure in different studies.

11.8.1 Short-Term Reactions

Many authors describe the factors that affect "flight distances" or "reaction distances" of terrestrial mammals to various forms of disturbance. The concept of a flight or reaction distance in terrestrial mammals (Hediger 1934) is similar to the "radius of responsiveness" concept for marine mammals (Section 10.3). In terrestrial mammals, almost all results are presented in terms of distances rather than received sound levels. Reactions to acoustic, visual, or odor cues are rarely distinguished in terrestrial mammals. Even with this ambiguity, data from terrestrial mammals may be relevant here. Behavioral responses of animals to distant sources of disturbance may, in some cases, be similar regardless of the stimulus type(s) involved.

Short-term reactions of terrestrial mammals to disturbance, acoustic or otherwise, often begin with cessation of normal activities such as feeding or traveling. With mild disturbance, the reaction consists of an alert stance (sometimes oriented toward the source of disturbance), listening, watching, and sniffing (Reynolds 1974; Luz and Smith 1976; McLaren and Green 1985). Although this is a mild form of disturbance, it may—if prolonged—indicate significant interruption of important activities, e.g., feeding (Stockwell et al. 1991).

In more disruptive situations, the animal moves away slowly or bolts rapidly, fleeing the area. For example, over 80% of mountain goats *Oreamnos americanus* subjected to aircraft overflights responded by some form of behavioral change, and 33% displayed strong flight responses (Foster and Rahs 1983). Both auditory and visual cues were involved. Similar short-term flight reactions have been documented for other large mammals, including caribou *Rangifer tarandus* responding to aircraft and trucks (Calef et al. 1976; Cameron et al. 1979; Horejsi 1981; Harrington and Veitch 1991), deer *Odocoileus* spp. responding to snowmobiles (e.g., Dorrance et al. 1975; Richens and Lavigne 1978; Freddy et al. 1986), and muskoxen *Ovibos moschatus* responding to aircraft and snowmobiles (F.L. Miller and Gunn 1980; McLaren and Green 1985). Active fleeing generally lasts no more than a few minutes when the stimulus is brief, such as an aircraft passing overhead without circling. In most cases of short-term disturbance, previous behaviors are reestablished quickly.

Disturbance can displace terrestrial mammals from their original habitat by distances ranging from tens or hundreds of meters to a few kilometers. Sometimes they are displaced from preferred foraging habitat to less suitable areas (Ingold et al. 1993). In one area, radio-tagged bighorn sheep *Ovis canadensis* often move ≥1 km in response to a single aerial survey by helicopter (Bleich et al. 1990, 1994). Active fleeing is especially conspicuous, but sometimes the displacement comes about through a slight biasing of "normal" movement patterns so the net movement is away. For example, Edge and Marcum (1985) found that net movement of elk *Cervus elaphus* was gradually away from logging sites during weekdays and toward them during inactive weekend periods. Elk displaced by skiers returned within an average of 2 days (Cassirer et al. 1992). White-tailed deer *O. virginianus* displaced by snowmobiles returned within hours (Dorrance et al. 1975).

In marine mammals, parallels can be found with almost all of these phenomena (*cf.* Chapter 9).

11.8.2 Variations in Responsiveness

In terrestrial as well as marine mammals, reaction type and strength often vary with type and distance of disturbance source. For example, caribou in Labrador ran farther and longer in response to helicopter than to jet overflights (Harrington and Veitch 1991). Also, the lower the aircraft, the stronger the reaction by caribou (Calef et al. 1976). Marmots *Marmota marmota* reacted earlier and stayed in their burrows longer when approaching humans moved off their usual paths or were accompanied by dogs (Mainini et al. 1993). In mountain goats, the strength of reaction depended strongly on distance from aircraft and other disturbance sources (Foster and Rahs 1983).

Startle and flight reactions often occur when people approach quietly on foot, and may occur at greater distances than in response to noisy people or vehicles (Altmann 1958; Richens and Lavigne 1978; Eckstein et al. 1979; Freddy et al. 1986). This has also been seen in pinnipeds (Allen et al. 1984; Osborn 1985). Spinner dolphins, dusky dolphins, and southern right whales usually react more strongly to the sudden appearance of a swimmer or kayaker than to the approach of a noisy outboard vessel (B. Würsig, personal observation).

Disturbance responses of both terrestrial and marine mammals also vary widely depending on factors such as age, sex, season, breeding status, activity, and habitat (Cameron et al. 1995). In deer and elk, newborn fawns tend to "freeze" whereas older fawns more often flee. There is a corresponding change in the response of heart rate to disturbance. It often slows in young fawns but speeds up in older ones, i.e., bradycardia versus tachycardia (Jacobsen 1979; Espmark and Langvatn 1985).

In moose *Alces alces* and elk, variations in sensitivity are related to "a seasonally changing threshold of sensitivity due to reproductive and nutritional status; variations due to type of habitat; and variations due to the specific experience of the individual or group" (Altmann 1958). Moose mothers with newborn calves hide in dense cover or charge toward the intruder rather than run away. However, both run from intruders after the calf is about a month old. Moose bulls usually begin to flee when an intruder is far away, but during the rutting season the flight distance decreases almost to zero. The reaction distance of moose is largest during the hunting season (Altmann 1958). Other game species also tend to be more responsive at locations and times when they are hunted (e.g., Behrend and Lubeck 1968; Schultz and Bailey 1978).

Animals that are feeding or mating often are less responsive than some other animals (Altmann 1958; Bond 1971; Espmark 1972; MacArthur et al. 1982; Harrington and Veitch 1991). In elk, large herds are more likely to react to humans and traffic, possibly because the larger the herd, the greater the likelihood that it will contain an especially wary individual. If that individual flees, the rest of the herd follows (Czech 1991). Czech also found that elk tend to be less responsive when "hiding cover" is nearby.

Again, there are many parallels between terrestrial and marine mammals in the dependence of responsiveness on disturbance type and distance, season, habitat, and animal age, sex, breeding status, and activity (*cf.* Chapter 9).

11.8.3 Masking

Masking of communication calls and other sounds b noise has not been a major research topic in large ter1 mals. However, there have been studies of masking of tne airborne calls of birds and bats, and of the waterborne sounds important to fish. A few authors have emphasized the potential negative consequences of masking of natural sounds (Myrberg 1978). However, Busnel (1978) noted that some birds and fish live in naturally noisy environments, and apparently can hear the sounds important to them. Busnel suggested that masking or jamming of acoustic signals is difficult to accomplish, given the adaptations that animals have developed to reduce masking (e.g., Griffin et al. 1963; Busnel and Mebes 1975; Nachtigall and Moore 1988). Marine mammals have many of these same adaptations (Sections 8.5.3 and 10.5.2).

11.8.4 Physiological Effects and Stress

Physiological effects of noise on terrestrial mammals have been studied in the laboratory and, in a few cases, by heart rate telemetry or other means from free-ranging mammals. Many more data of this type are available for terrestrial than for marine mammals. The many human studies are reviewed by Kryter (1985:389*ff*), Berglund et al. (1990), and Duncan et al. (1993), and are not emphasized here.

Heart Rate.—This parameter is an indicator of disturbance in some terrestrial mammals. Depending on species and age, heart rate may decrease or increase during disturbance. The heart rate response often habituates upon repeated exposure (Section 11.8.5), although this is not always the case (*cf.* Moen et al. 1982). In bighorn sheep and white-tailed deer, heart rate sometimes goes up in response to vehicles or humans, even in cases with no overt change in behavior (MacArthur et al. 1982; Moen et al. 1982). This suggests that heart rate may be an especially sensitive indicator of disturbance. Heart rate is correlated, although not perfectly, with metabolic rate and the stress response, including cortisol release (MacArthur et al. 1982; Harlow et al. 1987a,b; Hargreaves and Hutson 1990). Heart rate can be monitored by telemetry and may be a useful indicator of stress, which is otherwise hard to measure in free-ranging mammals.

We are not aware of any study of marine mammals that has reported heart rate relative to disturbance. Advancements in telemetry and Time Depth Recorders (TDRs) make this approach feasible. However, the effects of diving on heart rate (e.g., D. Thompson and

Fedak 1993) may complicate use of heart rate as an indicator of disturbance in diving mammals.

Blood Pressure and Sleep Effects.—In humans, sudden noise from low-altitude military overflights elicits increases in blood pressure (Michalak et al. 1990). Some but not all studies suggest that humans chronically exposed to much noise tend to have high blood pressure (Berglund et al. 1990; Ising et al. 1990; Duncan et al. 1993).

In humans, prolonged or repeated noises can cause difficulties in falling asleep, changes in sleep patterns, and awakenings (Kryter 1985; Berglund et al. 1990; Öhrström et al. 1990). Aftereffects can include fatigue, mood changes, and impaired mental performance.

Noise effects on blood pressure and sleep do not seem to have been studied explicitly in terrestrial wildlife, and implications for marine mammals are unknown.

Endocrines and Reproduction.—In laboratory animals and humans, exposure to strong noise often results in significant increases in adrenal activity, including cortisol and/or catecholamine release, and related measures of stress (e.g., Ames 1978; Axelrod and Reisine 1984; Harlow et al. 1987a; Berglund et al. 1990; Majors and Myrick 1990). Low-altitude aircraft flights over various farm animals elicit cortisol release and may cause some sensitization; later exposure to even the weak noise from distant aircraft may elicit cortisol release (Ising et al. 1990).

In wild cougars *Felis concolor*, repeated disturbance reduced the proclivity of the adrenals to release cortisol upon further challenge. Similar dampening of adrenal function has been found in some other stressed mammals. It is not clear whether this represents enhanced or reduced ability to cope with further stress (Harlow et al. 1992).

Some studies suggest that strong noise can have negative effects on reproduction and rearing of young in laboratory animals (e.g., Bond 1971; M.C. Busnel and Molin 1978; Majors and Myrick 1990). In free-ranging caribou, calf survival was negatively and significantly correlated with frequency of exposure to low-level jet overflights during the calving, immediate postcalving, and insect harassment seasons (Harrington and Veitch 1992). This noteworthy and partly experimental study was made possible by satellite-linked radio collars. This work shows how important it may be to develop methods that can test the effects of repeated noise exposure on marine mammals.

Most studies in which noise caused adrenal activation and other physiological or reproductive effects involved intense sounds. There is often little or no apparent effect with weaker noise. Data from terrestrial mammals do not allow us to predict whether physiological responses would occur in marine mammals exposed to specific types, levels, and durations of man-made noise. However, the terrestrial studies are useful in suggesting the types of effects that might occur, and thus in designing studies of marine mammals.

11.8.5 Habituation, Sensitization, and Long-Term Effects

Long-term effects of noise on terrestrial mammals, like those on marine mammals, have been difficult to study. However, more data on the occurrence (or absence) of habituation and sensitization are available for terrestrial mammals, in part because of the wider use of radio-tags on terrestrial species.

Some workers found no evidence that terrestrial mammals habituate to repeated disturbance. For example, bighorn sheep that fled after helicopter overflights showed no tendency for reduced reactions to later flights (Bleich et al. 1994). In another study, the increased heart rate exhibited by bighorn sheep disturbed by humans did not diminish upon repeated disturbance; in some cases they became more sensitive (MacArthur et al. 1982). Likewise, in white-tailed deer disturbed by snowmobiles, Moen et al. (1982) found no evidence that the heart rate response diminished with repeated exposure. Mountain goats moved away when subjected to repeated human use of their area (Foster and Rahs 1983). They showed no habituation, and indeed seemed to become more sensitive to sounds.

However, most studies indicate that habituation occurs rapidly, often after only a few exposures. For example, muskoxen habituated to helicopter overflights after only four days of helicopter activity; responses that had at first been abrupt and strong waned to a brief interruption of normal activity (F.L. Miller and Gunn 1980). Marmots and bighorn sheep were less responsive to people on often-traveled trails or roads than to the less common situation of people off the trails (MacArthur et al. 1982; Ingold et al. 1993; Mainini et al. 1993). Dall sheep occupying areas near a road more readily crossed the road during their seasonal migration than did sheep from areas far from the road (Dalle-Molle and Van Horn 1991). Elk were more sensitive to skiers in a little-visited area than in an area with many humans (Cassirer et al. 1992). When not hunted, elk can become quite tolerant of humans (Schultz and Bailey 1978).

Similarly, white-tailed deer were less disturbed by snowmobiles in an area with much snowmobiling than in one with little snowmobiling (Dorrance et al. 1975). In another area, this species showed less tendency to run from snowmobiles in mid- to late winter than in early winter (Richens and Lavigne 1978). This is consistent with habituation, but the results may be at least partly explained by increased snow depth, reduced food availability, and deteriorating physical condition in late winter. Deer exposed to ongoing lumbering activities with chainsaw noise seemed relatively insensitive to snowmobiles, perhaps because of habituation to noise from small engines (Eckstein et al. 1979; Moen et al. 1982). In some areas, deer seem attracted by chainsaw noise, which they may learn to associate with increased availability of recently felled browse (Richens and Lavigne 1978). This effect parallels the "dinner bell" phenomenon in pinnipeds attracted to acoustic "scaring" devices employed near fishing gear or aquaculture facilities (Section 9.12; Mate and Harvey 1987).

Many studies have reported that domesticated and laboratory mammals habituate, at least partially, to ongoing noise exposure. Domesticated sheep acclimate to intermittent sounds unless they are extremely intense (Ames 1978). Both farm and wild animals exhibit brief startle reactions to sonic booms, but responses to subsequent sonic booms are usually reduced (Espmark 1972; Cottereau 1978). Elk, antelope, and bighorn sheep in pens habituated to most types of disturbance, although not low-altitude aircraft overflights; the heart rate response to high overflights habituated after about four passes (Bunch and Workman 1993). In captive red deer (elk) calves, the heart rate response to various disturbances (bradycardia) diminished to near zero after <10 exposures. However, subsequent exposure to a different stimulus evoked a strong response, showing that the habituation was specific to one disturbance type (Espmark and Langvatn 1985). Physiological reactions of dogs and monkeys to ongoing noise also tend to habituate (reviewed in Majors and Myrick 1990).

Many of these studies show that various terrestrial mammals exhibit considerable tolerance of noise and other human disturbances. Even when short-term displacement and other behavioral reactions occur, the animals usually do not totally abandon the area. For example, caribou in the Prudhoe Bay oil fields show many types of reactions to human activities. However, they continue to occupy the area, and their numbers have increased (Klein 1991). Even hunted animals usually either remain in the area or return after the hunting season.

However, it is rarely known whether numbers of animals present in chronically disturbed areas are as high as they would have been without disturbance. It is also rarely known whether mammals in disturbed areas are negatively affected by stress, or whether the same tolerance would occur in different situations (Klein 1991). In all of these respects, terrestrial and marine mammals are similar.

11.9 Methods by Which Marine Mammals May Mitigate Noise Effects

At least some marine mammals possess capabilities and behavioral traits that reduce their susceptibility to potential negative effects of man-made noise. These traits have presumably evolved to cope with natural variability and challenges in the environment. However, they can also assist marine mammals in coping with man-made noise.

11.9.1 Characteristics of Sounds Emitted

In at least two species of toothed whales, the bottlenose dolphin and beluga, source levels of *echolocation signals* may increase when the background noise level is high. Also, these species sometimes adjust the frequencies of their echolocation signals to avoid a frequency range where the background noise level is high (Au et al. 1974, 1985). A beluga has also been observed to direct its echolocation beam such that echolocation signals were bounced off the water's surface, providing angular separation between returning echoes and a point source of background noise (Penner et al. 1986). These observations indicate that the characteristics of the echolocation sounds of some toothed whales are modified in response to prevailing background noise to maximize the effectiveness of echolocation.

Some baleen and toothed whales may increase the source levels or alter the frequencies of their *communication sounds* to reduce masking. This has been noted in gray whales exposed to playbacks of boat and drilling noise, and in belugas exposed to boats (Dahlheim 1987; Lesage et al. 1993). Several other studies have shown changes in call types in the presence of man-made noise, but with no specific indication that these changes reduce masking (Chapter 9). In general, there is great variability in the source levels of calls by some species (e.g., bowhead whales—Clark et al. 1986; Cummings and Holliday 1987). Call frequencies also vary widely within species (Chapter 7). This variability suggests that call characteristics might be adjusted in relation to prevailing background noise conditions. However, variability in call characteristics presumably occurs, in part, to convey different information to receiving animals. We know little about the degree to which marine mammal calls can be modified without changing their meaning.

11.9.2 Hearing Abilities

The directional hearing abilities of certain marine mammals must often help them detect natural sounds in the presence of background noise (Sections 8.4 and 10.5.2). Directional hearing can help when the directional characteristics of the sound signal and background noise differ, e.g., signal is directional and background noise omnidirectional; signal and background noise both directional, but come from differing directions; signal omnidirectional but background noise directional.

Directional hearing will be most useful in detecting sounds of interest in the presence of background noise if sound frequency is high and the wavelength is commensurately short. In toothed whales, directional hearing is important in detecting high-frequency echolocation signals in the presence of noise (Zaitseva et al. 1975, 1980; Au and Moore 1984). However, some small- and medium-sized marine mammals have directional hearing at frequencies as low as 1-2 kHz (Section 8.4)—within the upper end of the frequency range where many man-made noises occur. It is not known how effective these directional capabilities in the 1- to 2-kHz range may be in detecting sound signals against background noise at those frequencies.

There is little information about the directional hearing abilities of baleen whales (Sections 8.4 and 8.6), whose low-frequency calls overlap broadly in frequency with the dominant low-frequency noise of many human activities. However, because of the large sizes of many baleen whales relative to acoustic wavelengths, baleen whales may have good localization abilities at low frequencies (<1 kHz). If so, their directional hearing may be an important pre-adaptation for coping with low-frequency noise from human activities.

11.9.3 Displacement

Displacement in response to man-made noise is normally assumed to be a negative effect. Normal behavior and social interactions are interrupted at least briefly, there is an energy cost (whether or not feeding was disrupted), and the location to which the animal is displaced may provide habitat that is less suitable.

However, displacement can have the benefit of removing the animal from a location where, had the animal remained, there might be more serious effects. By moving away, an animal will reduce masking by man-made noise. Displacement may also, after a brief period of active disturbance, reduce or avoid further behavioral disruption or physiological stress that might persist if the animal remained close to the noise source. In the case of extremely strong noise sources, such as a series of explosive discharges, displacement would remove the animal from an area where physical damage to the hearing system or other organs might otherwise occur during subsequent exposures (Section 10.6). Displacement from the path of an oncoming ship would reduce the possibility of collision, which might otherwise injure or kill the animal (Section 9.3.3).

Displacement from a preferred area is unlikely to be beneficial as compared with continued and undisturbed occupancy of the preferred area. However, it may be preferable for an animal to be displaced rather than to remain in an area where there is risk of physical injury or chronic behavioral or physiological effects. In this sense, displacement can be a mitigating measure initiated by the animal itself.

11.9.4 Habituation

If exposure to a particular type of man-made noise is not associated with any serious concomitant problems or risks, habituation may occur (Sections 9.14.2 and 11.5). If so, an animal that showed avoidance or other disturbance reactions during initial exposures to the noise may show weaker or no reactions during later exposures. This waning of responsiveness might allow the animal to continue to occupy its normal habitat and to continue its normal activities in the presence of some man-made noise. This could be beneficial to the animal, provided the noise has no serious residual effects via masking, stress, or some other mechanism not fully alleviated by habituation.

11.10 Methods by Which Humans Can Partially Mitigate Noise Effects

In many cases, noise impacts of human activities can be reduced or avoided by careful planning. Engineering aspects of noise control are outside the scope of this review. However, this section provides some general comments on noise-control approaches that have been used, or might be used, to reduce the effects of noise from some human activities on marine mammals. Noise reductions may be possible through (1) appropriate choice or design of equipment and facilities. Also, it may be possible to adjust (2) the seasonal or hourly timing of noisy activities, or (3) their locations, to avoid times and places when mammals are most congregated or sensitive. (4) Operational procedures sometimes can be adjusted to reduce the potential effects. These four approaches are discussed separately below. However, because they interact, they need to be considered together when choosing an optimum mitigation strategy.

11.10.1 Equipment Design

Noise control engineers, especially naval architects, devote much effort to reducing noise from ships (Chapter 10 in Ross 1976). Some approaches that are used to reduce noise emitted by military or passenger vessels might be applicable to other vessels for which noise reduction has not been a priority. It has been suggested that efforts to reduce ship noise should begin, on the assumption that this noise is harmful to some marine mammals (Holing 1994). Noise reduction would be most valuable for vessels that often operate in areas occupied by many noise-sensitive marine mammals. However, it is arguable whether there is now a compelling justification for costly and long-term efforts to implement noise standards for all oceangoing ships. More data are needed on (1) long-term effects of continued exposure to present levels of ship noise, (2) potential benefits of the modest reduction in noise emissions that might ultimately be achievable by affordable design changes for new vessels, and (3) possible increases in the risk of collisions between quieter ships and species such as right whales (see Section 9.3.3). Any benefits of reduced noise emissions would become evident slowly with the gradual retirement of noisier vessels.

Some types of offshore equipment are quieter than others with similar functions. When two or more types of equipment could fulfill the desired function in a region with many marine mammals, it may be possible to select the less noisy equipment. Many of the obvious examples concern the offshore oil industry, given that much attention has been focused on noise effects of that industry. However, some of the same principles could be applied to other noisy human activities.

For example, semisubmersible drillrigs seem less noisy than conventional-hull drillships, and bottom-founded platforms are probably quieter than either semisubmersibles or conventional drillships (Section 6.4). There are situations when more than one type of drilling platform is usable. If the area is important to marine mammals, relative noise emissions should be considered when deciding which type of platform to use. Similarly, in a noise-sensitive area with a steeply sloping bottom, it might be preferable to drill directionally from a quiet bottom-founded platform in shallow water (or onshore) than to use a noisier drillship farther offshore.

Few data have been reported concerning the relative noise emissions of various offshore oil production facilities. However, different types of platforms emit noise with varying levels and characteristics (Gales 1982). Islands or caissons may be quieter than platforms with metal legs. If oil production facilities are to be installed in an area where noise is a concern, it would be desirable to further investigate the noise emissions of various types of offshore production equipment.

Support vessels and aircraft operating around offshore drilling and production sites can contribute much of the total man-made noise in the area. This is especially true in the Arctic, where icebreaking—an especially noisy activity (Section 6.2.3)—is often necessary around drillships. In contrast, bottom-founded caissons generally do not require icebreaker support. Also, a caisson would probably emit less underwater noise than a drillship. If water depths are suitable for either system and the area is noise sensitive, acoustic effects should be taken into account in choosing which system to use.

Aside from the type of platform, the specific design of equipment may have an important influence on acoustic emissions. Often, much of the noise originates from power-generation equipment (Section 6.4). Gales (1982) found that platforms supplied with electrical power from shore tended to be quieter than those with generators. When generators must be used continuously, it might be possible to reduce their noise output by giving more attention to the designs of mountings and mufflers. Top-drive drillrigs may create less noise than rotary table rigs and may be preferable for noise control as well as other reasons.

In ocean acoustics studies, effects of strong low-frequency noise on marine mammals could be reduced by using projectors that can be operated at deep depths and in areas where mammals are uncommon. Operation at deep depths reduces noise exposure in near-surface waters, where most marine mammals spend much of their time. It could also be preferable to use sources designed for operation in deep ocean basins rather than sources that must be mounted along continental margins, where mammals are often more abundant.

11.10.2 Seasonal and Hourly Timing

It is sometimes possible to adjust the seasonal or hourly timing of noisy activities to avoid periods when mammals are most sensitive. For example, regulatory agencies have placed seasonal restrictions on some types of oil exploration operations in various areas. Off northern Alaska, the timing of on-ice seismic exploration has been restricted to avoid Vibroseis® operations (Section 6.5.3) during the spring when ringed seals are pupping. There and elsewhere, permits for open-water seismic operations with airgun arrays sometimes prohibit or discourage seismic surveys or offshore drilling during seasons when marine mammals of special concern, e.g., bowheads or right whales, are present. Discouragement may involve greater operational restrictions (Section 11.10.4) during seasons when the mammals are expected to be present.

It is sometimes possible to plan the timing of noisy activities such that there is little or no interference with either the human activity or the marine mammals. For example, blasting is sometimes necessary for marine demolition or construction, and it may need to be done near a coastal haulout site or some other concentration point for marine mammals. In such a situation, it would be desirable to blast during a season when the marine mammals are absent. In this way, careful planning may avoid interference with a human activity while also protecting marine mammals.

Marine mammal numbers in local areas sometimes follow regular hourly or tidal cycles. In these cases, a transient noisy or potentially injurious activity, such as demolition, could be scheduled for a time when the animals are likely to be absent or scarce. This approach could apply to some pinniped haulout sites, and to nearshore or estuarine areas that are occupied mainly at certain hours or tidal phases (e.g., Klinowska 1986; Norris et al. 1994).

11.10.3 Routing and Positioning

Aircraft and vessel traffic can sometimes be routed to avoid the most sensitive areas. This is practical when marine mammals concentrate at coastal haulout sites, or in specific nearshore or offshore areas with recurring feeding, socializing, or breeding concentrations.

Negative effects of aircraft on local sensitive areas can be reduced or avoided by maintaining an appropriate horizontal distance, minimum altitude, or both. Such restrictions are often included in lease offerings and permits for offshore industrial activities, and in guidelines applied to aircraft-based whalewatching. However, altitude restrictions may only be practical when clouds are absent or high. Both altitude and horizontal restrictions are impractical if marine mammal concentrations occur near essential landing sites.

In choosing sites for short-term tests or long-term operation of noisy equipment, marine mammal concentration areas should be taken into account. This applies, for example, to testing or long-term deployment of powerful active sonars or underwater sound projectors, and tests of the resistance of ships to underwater blasts.

It may be possible to locate some shore facilities to avoid coastal sites of special sensitivity. For example, there may be two or more possibilities for a harbor development, causeway, heliport, pipeline terminus, or other logistics base. If one of these is a concentration point for marine mammals, it will be desirable, from the marine mammal perspective, to select an alternative site for development.

11.10.4 Operational Procedures

In some countries, it has been required that underwater blasting and certain other noisy human activities include *visual monitoring* for the presence of marine mammals, and deferral of the activity when mammals are detected within a specified radius. For example, permits for marine seismic exploration in areas occupied by bowhead whales often contain a provision requiring shutdown if bowheads are seen close to seismic boats or if poor visibility prevents visual monitoring for whales. During the Heard Island ocean acoustics test, noise emissions were to be delayed when a cetacean was seen within 1 km of the source at a scheduled transmission time (Bowles et al. 1994).

When underwater explosions are planned, it is now common for a marine mammal (and sea turtle) monitoring program to be required, along with provision for delay when mammals are seen inside the estimated (Section 10.6.3) "safe radius". To allow reasonably effective visual monitoring, it may be specified that blast(s) be scheduled for daylight hours, and not near sunrise or sunset. Aerial- as well as vessel-based monitoring is required in some cases, including demolition of obsolete oil industry platforms in the Gulf of Mexico and ship-shock trials off California (U.S. Navy 1993).

Mitigation that depends on visual monitoring can be useful but has limitations. Not all of the mammals present are detected, even with well-trained and conscientious observers, good visibility, and low sea state; sightability deteriorates further under less ideal conditions

(Eberhardt et al. 1979). *Acoustical monitoring* could provide useful supplementary data, especially if positions of calling animals were determined by acoustical localization methods (Section 3.2.4).

Some other operational procedures, not depending on real-time monitoring, have been used or proposed:

Speed limit for boats: Speed limits have been adopted in certain areas occupied by toothed whales (e.g., Blane and Jaakson 1994), baleen whales (e.g., Slay et al. 1993), and Florida manatees (Reynolds and Odell 1991).

Minimize source level: When sounds are purposefully emitted, as during seismic exploration, sonar surveys, and ocean acoustics research, effects on marine mammals could be reduced by selecting a source level no higher than necessary.

Minimize duty cycle: When sound is emitted purposefully and intermittently, as in ocean acoustics research, effects on marine mammals could be reduced by transmitting as briefly and infrequently as feasible. For example, as compared with the Heard Island test, the ATOC project (Section 6.8) plans a lower duty cycle and source level, partly to reduce effects on marine mammals (ARPA and NMFS 1994; ARPA 1995).

Ramp-up: When sounds are projected during ocean acoustics or disturbance studies, projected sound level can be increased gradually. This approach provides animals that are very close to the source an opportunity to move farther away before exposure to the maximum projected level. Whether marine mammals actually do so needs study (Section 10.6.2).

Warning blasts: Before large explosions, small charges sometimes are detonated as a warning. Again, it is not certain that marine mammals consistently move away. Some mammals may approach rather than leave, if they have learned that explosions kill fish and thus provide a feeding opportunity—the "chumming" or "dinner bell" effect (Section 9.12). If warning charges are used, there should be monitoring to ensure that they are not counterproductive.

Staggered charges: Several limited-size blasts in sequence, rather than simultaneous blasts or one larger blast, often are used in underwater demolition. This reduces peak pressure and may also have engineering value (Booren 1985). Staggered charges are used in the Gulf of Mexico platform-removal program, with a stipulation that they be in rapid sequence to avoid "chumming".

The specific combination of mitigation measures that will provide the "best" combination of effectiveness and practicality will vary with type of noise, species of concern, and local circumstances. Some practical combination of the above approaches should provide significant mitigation in most situations. However, in some cases mitigation may be difficult, costly, or of limited effectiveness. Some known or potential effects of noise on marine mammals would not be easy to avoid without forgoing or significantly modifying the noisy human activity.

11.11 Role of Future Research

We expect that, for the foreseeable future, there will be continued concern about the effects of certain noise sources on marine mammals. Decisions will have to be made about the trade-offs between potential (but often poorly understood) effects of noise and disturbance on marine mammals versus the economic or other costs to forgo or mitigate noisy human activities. To support this decisionmaking, there will be a continuing need for more information about the short- and especially the long-term effects of various man-made noises.

Although further research is certainly needed, as summarized in Chapter 12, the research on any given question need not be open-ended. With appropriate research, sufficient data can be obtained to justify significant refinements in regulatory procedures. A case in point is the issue of noise from offshore oil industry activities and its effect on bowhead whales. Much research has been devoted to this issue (Richardson and Malme 1993). Many data gaps remain, but enough has been learned about noise effects on bowheads and some other baleen whales to allow important refinements in the restrictions and mitigation measures imposed on oil industry operations within the range of the bowhead whale. In some years, seismic work and offshore drilling were prohibited in the Alaskan Beaufort Sea during the autumn migration period of bowheads. Research documenting the nature of whale reactions to oil industry activities was one of the factors that justified refining the mitigation measures through greater emphasis on appropriate operational restrictions and monitoring, and less emphasis on seasonal restrictions (which, in the short arctic open-water season, had severe economic consequences for the oil industry).

Thus, research can provide the basis for implementing necessary and effective mitigation while, where warranted, allowing human activities to go ahead with as few restrictions as possible. Data needed to address some questions could, with sufficient funding, be obtained relatively quickly. The most appropriate research methodologies are better defined now than they were several years ago. Also, technological developments in such areas as Time-Depth Recorders, telemetry, acoustical localization, and data processing provide improved opportunities and efficiencies in gathering and analyzing necessary data. Thus, some questions are amenable to solution.

However, many questions remain difficult to address. Even for common species of marine mammals in accessible areas, effective research can be costly and time-consuming, and research permit requirements may cause significant complications (NRC/OSB 1994). Questions about noise effects on rare or difficult-to-observe species may best be approached by comparing limited data from those species with results of detailed studies on a common related species. If the two species react similarly, it may be justified to place some reliance on the detailed data from the commoner species, especially if the two species occupy similar niches. Even the limited data now available are sufficient to show similarities in the reactions of some species to different human activities, and in reactions of related species to a given human activity. Caution is needed in making generalizations and extrapolations among species, areas, and types of human activity. However, it is not necessary to treat every combination of species, region, and activity as an entirely new problem.

Questions about hearing abilities, which are normally addressed through tests on captive animals, remain intractable for baleen whales. Questions about potential hearing damage from strong sounds rarely can be addressed directly, for ethical reasons. Indirect approaches may provide some of the needed data. Possibilities include evoked potential techniques for auditory measurements (Section 3.6.2) and data on Temporary Threshold Shift as an indicator of sounds that might ultimately cause permanent hearing impairment (Section 10.6).

Questions about long-term and cumulative effects of noise on individuals and populations have been largely intractable up to this point. Methods for studies of these effects need further development. Some suggested approaches include, where feasible, use of marked animals, monitoring during pre-disturbance as well as disturbance periods, monitoring at control as well as disturbed sites, and replication at more than one disturbed site (Section 11.6.3).

CHAPTER 12

CONCLUSIONS AND DATA NEEDS[1]

Here we summarize the main conclusions from previous chapters, and we identify important data needs. Many data needs relating to particular species or human activities would become urgent only if there were plans to initiate that activity in an area important to marine mammals. Thus, the relative importances of many data needs depend on development plans. In most cases the type of needed research is self-evident. However, in some cases we give specific recommendations about high-priority research topics.

12.1 Sound Propagation

12.1.1 Present Knowledge
Sound levels, both underwater and in air, produced by animals, human activities, and other specific sources diminish with increasing distance from the source. However, the rate of transmission loss depends strongly on local conditions (Chapter 4). Consequently, a moderate-level source transmitting over an efficient path may produce the same received level at a given range as a stronger source transmitting through an area where sound is rapidly attenuated. Likewise, the radius of acoustic influence for a given industrial source can vary as much as 10-fold depending on local propagation conditions. Thus, a site-specific model of sound propagation is needed to predict received sound levels in relation to distance from a noise source.

In the relatively simple case of nonducted direct-path underwater transmission, or air-to-ground transmission for an aircraft, the rate of attenuation approximates "spherical spreading" ($20 \log_{10} R$) with an added absorption term αR:

$$L_r = L_s - 20 \log_{10} R - \alpha R - 60 \tag{12.1}$$

---

[1] By W. John Richardson, LGL Ltd.

Here L_r is the received level at range R km and L_s is the source level at range 1 m. L_r and L_s must be measured in decibels with the same reference, normally dB re 1 µPa underwater and dB re 20 µPa in air. α is the molecular absorption coefficient, which is frequency dependent. Underwater, the αR term is negligible at frequencies below a few kilohertz but it can be important at higher frequencies. In air, the αR term is significant even at lower frequencies. The "-60 dB" constant allows R to be expressed in kilometers rather than meters.

Even in the deep ocean or unbounded atmosphere, equation (12.1) is only a first approximation, given the effects of various modifying influences. In shallow waters or for airborne propagation near the ground, a more complex formulation is necessary. Modifying influences underwater include water depth, source and receiver depths, bottom slope, bottom composition, sea surface conditions, and vertical profiles of temperature and salinity. For very shallow water or ducted transmission beginning at distance R_1 from the source, equation (12.1) can be modified to assume cylindrical spreading (10 log R) beyond range R_1 plus an additional linear loss factor $(A)R$. The $(A)R$ term, in dB/km, represents "duct leakage" or other attenuation phenomena that are directly related to range:

$$L_r = L_s - 20 \log_{10} R_1 - 10 \log_{10} (R/R_1) - \alpha R - (A)R - 60 \qquad (12.2)$$

The transition range R_1 between spherical and cylindrical spreading depends on local conditions, but is often assumed (as a rough approximation) to equal the water depth or duct thickness.

More elaborate theoretical or semiempirical models for underwater and airborne sound propagation exist, usually with provision to incorporate parameters representing site-specific conditions. For underwater propagation, many of these models are designed for specialized applications and are not directly useful in predicting received levels of other man-made sounds. However, Parabolic Equation (PE) models are widely used, including some use in environmental impact assessments for noisy activities (ARPA 1995). In many cases, especially in shallow water, no standard theoretical model can adequately predict received levels at long distances; empirical site-specific data are then required.

Sound traveling from a source in air (aircraft) to a receiver underwater is a special case. Received level is affected by both in-air and underwater propagation, further complicated by the air-water interface. The received level underwater depends in a complex way on source altitude and lateral distance, receiver depth, water depth, and other variables. Considerable theoretical and limited empirical work on this problem has been published. Sections 6.2.1 and 12.3.1 summarize the characteristics of sounds from passing aircraft.

12.1.2 Data Needs and Recommended Research

Although sound propagation has been studied very intensively, site-specific models for underwater or airborne propagation are often lacking. *If it is necessary to make reliable predictions of received sound levels versus range, an adequate model is needed.* A theoretical or semiempirical model usually can be developed based on existing physical data or assumptions, but its accuracy will depend on the circumstances and available data.

Field measurements to support or verify the acoustic modeling are required in some situations. In the case of underwater propagation, field measurements will be needed if data on water mass and bottom properties are lacking, and if there is a requirement for high precision, for estimates of received levels at long ranges, or for estimates of propagation through shallow water. In the case of airborne propagation, field data may be needed if propagation near the ground is important, or if there is complex topography. *In these cases, site-specific data on physical conditions would be needed.*

12.2 Ambient Noise

12.2.1 Present Knowledge

Ambient noise is the residual background sound exclusive of components from sources of specific interest. It is important because it strongly affects the distances to which animal sounds, specific man-made sounds, and other sounds of interest can be detected by marine mammals or any receiver. As a first approximation, a sound signal is detectable only if its level is higher than that of the ambient noise at similar frequencies. As ambient noise level increases, sounds from a specific source disappear below the ambient level and become undetectable at progressively shorter ranges. Even within the range of detectability, variation in ambient noise greatly affects the prominence (signal-to-noise ratio) of sound signals.

Ambient noise levels at a given frequency and location typically vary by as much as 20 dB or more from one day to the next (Chapter 5). Hence, a given sound source may be detectable 10 times farther away on one day than on the next, and its signal-to- (ambient) noise ratio at each distance may change by 10-20 dB.

Above 500 Hz, ambient noise levels underwater are often dominated by wind and wave noise (Section 5.2.1). Ambient noise increases with increasing wind speed and wave height; wind speed is the direct influence. From ~500 Hz to at least 20 kHz, ambient levels on a "per Hz" or "spectrum level" basis decrease with increasing frequency, often at a rate of about -5 dB per doubling of frequency (i.e., per octave). On a ⅓-octave basis, ambient levels also tend to decrease with increasing frequency, but with a lesser slope of about -2 dB per octave or 0.67 dB per ⅓ octave. The reduced slope occurs because ⅓-octave bands become progressively wider with increasing frequency. At very high frequencies, above ~50 kHz, the ambient noise level increases with increasing frequency because of thermal noise related to molecular motion.

Below 500 Hz, especially in deep water, ambient noise underwater is often dominated by noise from distant shipping. Levels of ambient noise at low frequencies vary widely depending on the strength of the distant shipping component. In coastal areas, surf noise can be an important contributor and source of variation. Intermittent noises from volcanic and tectonic activity can also cause variation in low-frequency ambient noise, mainly below 100 Hz. Even at these low frequencies, ambient noise levels are related to wind speed when the shipping component is weak.

Precipitation, sea ice, and sounds from animals can also affect underwater ambient noise levels substantially. In addition, man-made sounds that come from unknown sources, or sources different from those of primary interest, are often considered to be part of the ambient noise. The importance of these contributions to ambient noise varies from day to day and, in some cases, with season.

In shallow water, the typical range of ambient noise levels is wider than that in deep water; the highest levels are higher and the lowest levels are lower (Section 5.4). Differing sound transmission conditions in shallow and deep water are partly responsible.

12.2.2 Data Needs and Recommended Research

Factors contributing to variability in ambient noise are known in a general way, but site-specific data on ambient noise levels at various places and times are often lacking. Variations in ambient noise have direct and large effects on the distance at which a given sound signal—e.g., man-made noise or marine mammal call—can be heard, and on its signal-to- (ambient) noise ratio at a given distance. *If these variables must be estimated accurately, site-specific data on ambient noise may be needed. This is especially true for shallow water areas where ambient noise is especially variable.*

Ambient noise data should be collected over a period long enough to be representative of the typical range of ambient noise conditions. Data should be collected at different seasons. Environmental data, including wind, wave, precipitation, and ice conditions, should be recorded concurrently to allow analysis of factors affecting ambient noise. Care must be taken to avoid system noise problems that can invalidate ambient noise measurements. Ambient noise statistics should be determined separately for all frequencies audible to all types of animals of concern. Both spectrum-level and ⅓-octave band-level statistics are helpful for interpreting the implications of ambient noise to marine mammals.

12.3 Man-Made Noise

12.3.1 Present Knowledge

The sounds emitted by a source are characterized by their source level, frequency composition, and temporal variation. Overall source levels of underwater sounds from human activities typically are 140-150 dB re 1 µPa at range 1 m for some weak sources, 160-170 dB for moderately strong sources, 180-200 dB for strong sources of continuous noise (icebreakers, large ships, ocean acoustics research), and 215-250 dB for very strong but transient sounds from seismic exploration and sonars. At distances >1 m, received levels diminish rapidly with increasing distance, as summarized in Chapter 4 and Section 12.1.1.

Noise levels from most human activities are highest at rather low frequencies—less than 500 Hz—when tones or conventional spectrum-level measurements are considered. On a ⅓-octave basis, the strongest sounds from many sources are also <500 Hz, but sometimes not as low in frequency as the peak spectrum levels or the strongest tones. Also, levels at low and high frequencies are often less divergent when measured in ⅓ octaves because ⅓-octave bands become wider with increasing frequency. Sources for which higher-frequency components (>500 Hz) are especially important include small boats, icebreaking and—in particular—many sonars.

Underwater sounds from *aircraft* are transient. Strong underwater sounds are detectable for roughly the period of time the aircraft is within a 26° cone above the receiver (Section 6.2.1). The zone of strong ensonification is enlarged in rough seas and in shallow water. Usually, an aircraft can be heard in air well before and after the brief period while it passes overhead and is heard underwater. Sound pressure in the water directly below an aircraft is greatest at the surface and diminishes with increasing receiver depth. However, the opposite can be true when the aircraft is not directly overhead. Near the surface or in shallow water, peak received level diminishes with increasing aircraft altitude, but duration of audibility may increase with increasing altitude. In deep water, well away from the surface, peak received level is nearly independent of aircraft altitude.

The main sources of sound from propeller-driven aircraft and helicopters are their propellers or rotors. Rotating blades produce tones with fundamental frequencies determined by the rotation rate and number of blades. The fundamental is usually <100 Hz. Harmonics are common at integer multiples of the fundamental, but most energy is at <500 Hz. Noise from jets varies widely depending on engine type, power setting, and aspect.

Ship noise levels are roughly related to ship size, speed, and mode of operation (Section 6.2.2). Large ships tend to emit more sound than small ones, and ships underway with a full load (or towing/pushing a load) are noisier than unladen vessels. Noise increases with speed, whether loaded or unloaded. The state of maintenance strongly influences radiated sound level. Ships with old auxiliary machinery, e.g., generators and compressors, tend to radiate more noise than newer or well maintained vessels. Source levels in the strongest ⅓-octave band range from 150-160 dB re 1 μPa-m for outboards and other small boats to at least 185-200 dB for supertankers and large container ships.

Propeller cavitation produces much of the broadband noise from ships and boats, and propeller singing can produce strong tones at the propeller blade rate and some of its harmonics. Propellers create considerably higher noise levels if damaged, not operating synchronously, or operating without nozzles. The dominant frequency tends to increase with decreasing vessel size. For medium to large ships, the fundamental blade-rate tone is below 15 Hz; most of the energy is below 100 Hz, with some energy to 500 Hz. Noise from smaller boats tends to be concentrated at higher frequencies. Small boats with outboard engines emit considerable noise over a wide frequency range, from ~100 Hz to several kilohertz.

Icebreaking produces strong sounds in high-latitude areas where man-made noise may be otherwise weak or absent. Icebreakers pushing ice radiate noise ~10-15 dB stronger than that when not pushing ice. During icebreaking, alternating periods of ice ramming and backing cause pronounced variations in radiated noise levels and spectra. The highest noise levels are due primarily to strong propeller cavitation, especially when backing up. There are tones at harmonic frequencies of the propeller blade-rate below 200 Hz, and lesser components extending beyond 5 kHz. The duration of a single episode of strong cavitation noise is generally ~1 min. When present, nozzles around the propellers reduce radiated propeller noise, especially during icebreaking.

Marine dredging and some *marine construction* operations introduce strong sounds of varying characteristics into the water, largely at low frequencies (Section 6.3). Estimated source levels of two dredges were 167 and 178 dB re 1 µPa-m in their strongest ⅓-octave bands. Because dredges operate in shallow water where low-frequency sounds attenuate rapidly, most components of dredge noise normally are undetectable underwater at ranges beyond 20-25 km. Tones often appear in dredge spectra, usually below 1 kHz but sometimes at higher frequencies. Dredging may continue in one area for days or weeks at a time.

Construction noise varies widely in level and characteristics. Construction of artificial islands in winter, including construction of an ice road, was relatively quiet underwater. Such activities are most likely in shallow water, through which low-frequency sounds do not propagate well. A large tunnel-boring machine introduced low-frequency sound, mainly <100 Hz, into water above the tunnel.

Offshore drilling produces widely varying underwater sounds, depending on the type of drilling platform (Section 6.4). Drilling from natural barrier islands or man-made islands generally produces only low-intensity underwater sounds, inaudible beyond ~1 km. Drilling noise from a self-contained concrete caisson was also weak at the frequencies usually considered, but there was a strong infrasonic tone near 1.4 Hz. Drilling noise from conventional metal-legged platforms is not very intense, and is strongest at very low frequencies (5 Hz). Drilling noise levels from semisubmersibles are also not especially high—e.g., 154 dB re 1 µPa-m in the 10- to 500-Hz band. Drilling noise from a caisson retained island was somewhat stronger—estimated as almost 160 dB re 1 μPa-m in the strongest ⅓-octave band. Drillships produce higher levels of underwater noise than do other types of drilling platforms, with estimated ⅓-octave source levels up to 167 and 177 dB re 1 μPa-m in the cases of two drilling vessels.

Drilling noise usually includes prominent tones at frequencies below ~300 Hz. In a few cases where infrasounds were studied, the strongest tones were at or below 5 Hz. Besides the strong dependence of noise level on type of drilling platform, noise from a particular platform varies over time.

Underwater noise from *offshore hydrocarbon production* has not been studied extensively. Metal-legged production platforms seem to radiate more underwater noise than do islands (Section 6.4.4). Platforms powered by gas turbines produce more noise than those with shore power. The strongest spectrum levels and tones are below 500 Hz.

Airgun arrays are now used for most marine seismic exploration (Section 6.5.1). They emit underwater pulses with peak levels much higher than levels from any source summarized above, but lasting only a fraction of a second. The pulse-to-pulse interval is typically 10-15 s, but can be less. Most energy in the pulses is below 100 Hz. However, in shallow water, the lowest-frequency energy is often attenuated rapidly, so the dominant energy at horizontal ranges beyond a few kilometers is often at 100-250 Hz. With increased distance from the source, received pulses decrease in level but increase to ¼-½ s in duration. In shallow water, the elongated pulses received at ranges beyond a few kilometers sound "chirp"-like, with higher frequencies usually arriving before lower frequencies.

Overall source levels of noise pulses from airgun arrays are very high, e.g., peak level 240-250 dB re 1 μPa-m. However, most energy is directed downward, and the short duration of each pulse limits the total energy. The effective source level for horizontal propagation can be 220-230 dB perpendicular to the array's long axis, but as much as 20 dB lower along the array axis. Pulses from seismic arrays are often detectable in the water 100+ km from the survey ship, and received levels within a few kilometers typically exceed 160 dB re 1 μPa. As with any low-frequency underwater sound from an underwater source, the received signals are generally lower by 1 to 7 dB near the surface (depth 3 m) than at deeper (≥9 m) depths.

Arrays of sleeve exploders, gas guns, and water guns also generate sound pulses underwater and are used for marine seismic exploration (Sections 6.5.2 and 6.5.4). They sound similar to airguns.

Vibroseis® is a technique used for on-ice seismic exploration in the Arctic (Section 6.5.3). The fundamental frequency of the energy sweeps from 10 to 70 Hz over several seconds, with harmonics extending up to ~1.5 kHz. Widely varying effective source levels have been reported. One study indicated that Vibroseis sounds in water below ice would diminish to the ambient noise level at range 3½-5 km.

Sonars emit transient sounds, often intense, that vary widely in power, frequency, and other characteristics. Frequencies range from hundreds of hertz for some long-range search sonars to hundreds of kilohertz for short-range high-resolution mapping, mine-hunting, or plankton surveys. Many commercial sonars have peak source levels of 210-230 dB re 1 μPa-m; military sonars are often more powerful. Sonar sounds differ from most other man-made sounds in that they are mainly at moderate and high frequencies.

Underwater explosions produce the strongest man-made pulses of underwater energy, often detectable hundreds or thousands of kilometers away (Section 6.7.2). High explosives produce pulses with a very rapid onset (shock waves), which change to conventional acoustic pulses as they propagate. The pressure versus time properties of pulses from high explosives are well known at short ranges, but harder to predict after many bottom and surface reflections.

Ocean science studies use sounds from airguns, sonars, or explosives (see above) or from underwater projectors to assess characteristics of water masses and of the bottom. Source levels from projectors range from ~165 dB re 1 μPa-m for short ranges to 190-220 dB for long-range tests. Long-range tests are generally at 50-200 Hz.

12.3.2 Data Needs and Recommended Research

Sounds emitted by many specific human activities have been measured. Extrapolations to similar unstudied sources are often possible. However, there can be considerable variation among individual sources of a given category. *When there is serious concern about the acoustic effects of a type of sound source not previously studied, e.g., a different class of ship or drillrig, data on the source level of its sounds, and on their spectral and temporal characteristics, are needed.*

Underwater sounds from many man-made sources have not been measured at frequencies below 10 to 20 Hz. Some sources—e.g., large ships, some drillrigs, production platforms—are known to emit strong sounds below 10-20 Hz. At least some baleen whales probably have good hearing sensitivity below 20 Hz. *When effects on baleen whales are a concern, data on radiated noise at low frequencies are needed.*

The preceding points apply to all types of sound sources. However, for some categories of sources, especially few data are available:

Underwater noises from marine dredging and construction have been studied in the Arctic but less so elsewhere. *Widely varying equipment and techniques are used in different circumstances, so noise characteristics will vary. This could be a major data need if extensive construction were planned in an area important to marine mammals.*

Underwater sounds from most types of drilling structures have been reported, but available data are often incomplete and quite variable. It would be desirable to obtain longer series of measurements for most types of platforms. For conventional metal-legged drilling platforms, underwater noise spectra have been determined but source levels could not be measured.

Available data on sounds from oil production platforms are very limited. Source levels seem low but cannot be determined quantitatively from available data.

Characteristics of underwater noise propagating horizontally from some sound sources used for shallow geotechnical surveys, e.g., sparkers, water guns, and side-scan sonars, have not been reported in the open literature insofar as we know. Measurements are needed of their signal characteristics versus horizontal range.

Very few data are available in the open literature on the characteristics of the sounds from military sonars. *Given the high source levels of some military sonars, and the large numbers of units deployed, this is a major data need.*

Airborne noise from many offshore human activities has not been described. *In-air data could be needed if these activities were planned near important haulout sites.*

12.4 Marine Mammal Sounds

12.4.1 Present Knowledge

Marine mammal sounds apparently have two basic functions: communication and echolocation. (1) All marine mammals emit sounds that are known or suspected to be used for intraspecific communication underwater, in air, or both. Call types used for communication are very diverse. For example, bottlenose dolphin sounds are mainly whistles, sperm whale sounds are generally click trains, and killer whales often emit other kinds of pulsed sounds. Baleen whales mainly utter low-frequency sounds. Pinniped sounds are highly variable. **(2)** Odontocetes are the only marine mammals in which echolocation has been proven to exist. All proven cases of echolocation involve click sounds.

Evidence for associations between specific underwater sounds and specific functions is, for most species, weak or nonexistent. Many marine mammals are gregarious, often coordinate activities, and often have to find one another in a visually limited environment. It is assumed but only occasionally demonstrated that these phenomena are mediated, in part, by calls. Some sounds seem to be used for long-distance communication. In whales, sounds produced while individuals are far enough apart to be out of visual contact may be associated with announcement of reproductive intentions, establishment of territory or spacing between animals, coordination of foraging and other activities, and maintenance or establishment of group structure. Over short distances, sounds may be used in social interactions involving aggression between individuals and establishment of dominance, for individual identification, and for establishment and maintenance of the mother-pup bond.

Underwater sounds of *baleen whales* (Section 7.1) are primarily at frequencies below 1 kHz and have durations from ~½ s to over 1 s, and sometimes much longer. Some have fundamental frequencies as low as 20 Hz. Thus, the dominant frequencies in baleen whale sounds overlap broadly with the dominant frequencies in many man-made sounds. Many baleen whale sounds are uncomplicated tonal moans or sounds that have been described as knocks, pulses, ratchets, thumps, and trumpet-like. Humpback and bowhead whale sounds are more complex and include extended songs. Source levels of most baleen whale sounds are 150-190 dB re 1 µPa-m, apparently with much within-species variation.

Some *odontocete (toothed) whales* apparently communicate underwater with whistles at frequencies below 20 kHz; most of their energy is typically near 10 kHz (Section 7.2). Source levels for whistles may be 100-180 dB re 1 µPa-m. The killer whale produces whistles but most sounds are pulsed sounds at 1-6 kHz; source levels are up to 160 dB re 1 µPa-m. Most calls by the sperm whale and the phocoenid porpoises are clicks, some of which may be used for communication. Most odontocete sounds are detectable to humans with hydrophones at distances out to no more than 1 km. However, sperm whale clicks may propagate out to 10+ km. Most components of odontocete social sounds are above the low-frequency range where many industrial sounds are concentrated.

The echolocation capabilities of the odontocetes that have been studied are well developed (Section 7.2.4). Echolocation pulses are generally at high frequencies—30 to 100 kHz or higher. However, killer whale echolocation signals have most energy at 12-25 kHz. Echolocation signals are projected forward in a narrow beam extending several degrees on either side of the animal's centerline. Peak source levels can be >210 dB re 1 µPa-m. The effective range of odontocete sonar may be up to 350 m, depending on species, ambient noise level, size and reflectivity of target, etc. Although the capabilities of echolocation systems have been studied in detail in a few species held in captivity, specific functions of echolocation in nature are not well demonstrated.

Pinnipeds that mate and breed on land use airborne vocalizations and visual displays to establish and defend territories, compete with other males for access to females, mate, and establish and maintain the mother-pup bond. Underwater vocalizations seem limited to barks and clicks at frequencies from <1 to 4 kHz (Section 7.3). In contrast, pinnipeds that mate in the water are often quite vocal during the breeding season. Most underwater sounds are at frequencies from <1 to 10 kHz. Source levels for five phocid species are reported as ~95-178 dB re 1 µPa-m.

All pinnipeds, the sea otter, perhaps the manatee, and at least some cetaceans use sound to maintain the mother-offspring bond. The calls appear to be especially useful when mother and pup are attempting to reunite after a separation.

12.4.2 Data Needs and Recommended Research

Sounds of many species of marine mammals have been described in varying levels of detail, but source levels, directionality, and maximum detection distances of most sound types are unknown or poorly documented (Chapter 7). Many source level data have come from captive animals and may not be representative of free-ranging animals. *For species in which data of these types are lacking, it is not possible to estimate the maximum detection distances of the sounds either in natural conditions or in the presence of man-made noise.* The species responsible for a specific call often is not known with certainty, making it difficult to interpret acoustic monitoring data.

Functions of most so-called communication calls are unknown or understood in only a rudimentary way. This limits assessments of the consequences if the sounds become inaudible because of masking by man-made noise. *Information about the distances over which marine mammals may need to communicate acoustically is a major data need in evaluating the effects of masking* (see also NRC/OSB 1994:42).

Uses of echolocation by free-ranging odontocetes are not well documented (Section 7.2.4). This would be a major data need if a human activity involving strong noise at high frequencies were planned to continue for a prolonged period in an area important to odontocetes. High-frequency sonars and echosounders are the main concern.

12.5 Marine Mammal Hearing

12.5.1 Present Knowledge

Toothed whales are most sensitive to sounds above ~10 kHz (Section 8.2.1). The reported upper limits of sensitive hearing range from near 80 kHz in the false killer whale to well above 100 kHz in some species. The sensitivity of many toothed whales to very high-frequency sounds is related to their use of very high-frequency sound pulses for echolocation and moderately high-frequency sounds for other functions, including communication. Low-frequency hearing has not been studied in many species, but at least the bottlenose dolphin and beluga hear sounds as low as 40-125 Hz. However, below ~10 kHz, sensitivity deteriorates with decreasing frequency. Below 1 kHz, where most man-made noise energy is concentrated, sensitivity appears to be poor, but data are scarce.

At least in the bottlenose dolphin, sensitivity decreases as the duration of a single sound pulse decreases below about 0.1-0.2 s. However, toothed whales apparently have neural mechanisms specialized for processing sequences of short pulses, such as are used for echolocation (Section 8.2.4). Toothed whales have good frequency and intensity discrimination abilities, as well as good directional localization capabilities (Sections 8.3 and 8.4).

Masking of sound signals by background noise has been studied under laboratory conditions in three odontocete species (Section 8.5). Above ~2 kHz, critical ratios increase with increasing frequency, and are similar to those of humans at corresponding frequencies. At lower frequencies, critical ratios of the one odontocete studied (beluga) are constant across frequency. Critical bands in the bottlenose dolphin seem wider than predicted based on the equal-power assumption. At very high frequencies (e.g., 80 kHz), masking is greatly reduced when the sound signal and masking noise arrive from different directions, or when the signal arrives from one direction but the noise is omnidirectional. This reduction in masking due to directional hearing is less evident at moderate frequencies, e.g., 18 kHz.

Baleen whales apparently are sensitive to low- and moderate-frequency sounds, probably with some variation among species (Section 8.6). There are no specific data on sensitivity, frequency or intensity discrimination, or localization abilities. However, gray whales can detect killer whale sounds at levels close to the broadband noise level, and several species seemingly can determine the direction of arrival of some underwater sounds.

Hair (phocid) seals have, in most cases, an effective upper frequency limit near 60 kHz, above which sensitivity is poor and different frequencies are not discriminated (Section 8.2.2). Underwater sensitivity is about the same from 1 or 2 kHz to 50 kHz. Within this range of best underwater hearing, sensitivity is not as high as in toothed whales. Sensitivity at low frequencies (<760 Hz) has not yet been reported in detail. Also, a monk seal had more limited hearing abilities than did other phocids. In-air hearing of phocid seals is less sensitive than underwater hearing, and the upper frequency limit is lower (~20 kHz). The underwater hearing threshold of a harbor seal increased as the duration of a sound decreased below about 50 ms, as in other animals. Pinnipeds seem less specialized for processing click sequences than are toothed whales. Their frequency discrimination abilities also seem less precise (Section 8.3.1). Harbor seals have reasonably good directional localization abilities (Section 8.4.2). Critical ratios increase with increasing frequency (at least in water), are similar in water and air, and probably are similar to those of other mammals (Section 8.5.1).

Eared seals are similar to hair seals with regard to underwater hearing sensitivity at moderate frequencies. However, their upper frequency limit is lower—near 36-40 kHz versus 60 kHz (Section 8.2.2). At least in the California sea lion, sensitivity decreases as frequency decreases from 2000 to 250 Hz, but high-level sounds at 100-250 Hz are audible. In-air hearing of eared seals is less sensitive than underwater hearing, but the difference in capabilities between air and water is less pronounced than in phocids. The upper frequency cutoff in air is only slightly less than that in water (32-36 versus 36-40 kHz). Frequency discrimination and directional localization seem less precise than in toothed whales (Sections 8.3.1 and 8.4.2). Critical ratios of the fur seal increase with increasing frequency, and are rather low (i.e., good) in comparison with other mammals listening at corresponding frequencies (Section 8.5.1).

Manatees may hear underwater sounds across a wide frequency range, from 15 Hz to 46 kHz, with best sensitivity at 6-20 kHz.

12.5.2 Data Needs and Recommended Research

Data on absolute hearing sensitivity versus frequency are needed to evaluate abilities of marine mammals to hear specific natural or man-made sounds. Such data are lacking for all baleen whales; for sperm, beaked, and other large toothed whales; and for sea otters (Section 8.2). Valuable data on absolute thresholds are available for several species of smaller toothed whales and pinnipeds. However, in most species these data do not extend below 1 kHz, where many man-made noises are concentrated. *Information about the absolute threshold for a species and frequency band of concern would be a data need if a substantial number of animals are to be exposed to man-made noise for a prolonged period. The data need would be more important if corresponding data were not available for any closely related species.* For species whose hearing cannot be studied in captivity, evoked potential methods applied to beached or entrapped animals may be useful (NRC/OSB 1994:48).

Data on noise masking under field conditions, compensatory mechanisms, and consequences of interrupted acoustic communication are needed (Section 8.5). Available data on masking are limited to a few species of odontocetes and pinnipeds, and mainly to detection of pure tones against a white noise background. (White noise has the same level at each frequency.) In practical field situations, the sound signals of interest often are not tones, and the background noise—natural or man-made—is rarely white noise. Data are lacking on the effectiveness of directional hearing and other compensatory processes in allowing detection of sound signals against a strong noise background, especially at the low frequencies where most man-made noises are concentrated.

No aspect of baleen whale hearing has been studied directly. There are no specific data on sensitivity, frequency or intensity discrim-

*ination, or localization abilities (Section 8.6). This is a major data
need when evaluating the effects of man-made noise on baleen whale
hearing and behavioral responsiveness.* This data need is of special
concern because baleen whales apparently are more dependent on low-
frequency sounds than are other marine mammals, and many man-
made sounds are concentrated at these low frequencies. No practical
method has been developed to conduct psychoacoustic tests on any
baleen whale. *Data on the sensitivity of baleen whales to infrasounds
(at <20 Hz) are needed, given their assumed sensitivity to slightly higher frequencies and the evidence of strong infrasonic components (<20
Hz) in certain industrial noises.*

12.6 Disturbance Reactions

12.6.1 Present Knowledge

Aircraft overflights at low altitude can cause pinnipeds hauled out
on land or ice to escape into the water, occasionally leading to some
mortality of young through abandonment or trampling (Section 9.2.1).
Some toothed and baleen whales dive or turn away during overflights,
with sensitivity depending on animal activity. For cetaceans, effects
seem transient and occasional overflights probably have no long-term
consequences (Sections 9.2.2 and 9.2.3). Relative roles of sound and
vision in eliciting reactions to aircraft are unknown.

Ship and boat noise does not seem to have strong effects on pinnipeds in the water, but the data are limited. However, pinnipeds hauled out on land or ice often are quite responsive to nearby vessels (Section 9.3.1). Many toothed whales show some tolerance of vessels, but
may react at distances of several kilometers or more when confined by
ice or shallow water, or when they have learned to associate the vessel
with harassment. Belugas near ice in spring sometimes react to noise
from approaching ships at distances of ≥50 km. In some other areas,
belugas tolerate very high levels of human activity (Section 9.3.2).

Baleen whales sometimes flee from approaching ships and boats,
especially from vessels that are moving rapidly, directly toward the
whales, or erratically. However, there is little evidence that baleen
whales travel far or remain disturbed for long after a single vessel
pass. Gray and possibly humpback and bowhead whales may have
reduced their use of some heavily disturbed areas. However, the continued presence of whales in some areas heavily traveled by ships
indicates considerable tolerance of ship noise (Section 9.3.3).

Sirenians show some avoidance of approaching boats, but the response is often too late and too slow to avoid being struck.

Icebreaker noise effects on marine mammals have not been studied extensively. Walruses and seals hauled out on ice often move into the water as an icebreaker approaches, although the opposite reaction (scrambling onto ice) has also been seen (Section 9.4). Icebreaker traffic in winter does not seem to reduce numbers of ringed seals present along the icebreaker tracks later in the spring.

Hovercraft elicit brief reactions from some gray whales, notably those approached from the front. Odontocete reactions are variable.

Stationary offshore activities, including drilling, dredging, and hydrocarbon production, seem to have less effect on cetacean behavior than do moving sound sources such as aircraft and ships. However, avoidance responses have been noted when some whales are exposed to high levels of these sounds either near actual oil industry operations or via underwater playbacks of recorded sounds (Sections 9.6 and 9.7). Responsiveness varies considerably. However, reactions have been found mainly when received noise levels were well above ambient levels. The few species of cetaceans studied apparently did not react overtly if they could barely hear the industrial noise. Even so, noise from a drillship and its supporting vessels may cause most migrating bowhead whales to avoid the drillsite by a radius of ~10-20 km.

Fewer (or no) specific data are available on effects of noise from drilling, dredging, production, and other stationary activities on pinnipeds, toothed whales, sea otters, and sirenians. However, they sometimes exhibit considerable tolerance of such operations.

Seismic exploration noise has higher peak levels than noise from any of the previously-discussed sources, but it is impulsive (airguns) or transient (Vibroseis). Some ringed seals abandon areas where the on-ice Vibroseis method is used in winter. However, the effect is very localized. Other species of seals often tolerate strong impulsive noises to which they have become accustomed (Section 9.8.1).

Odontocete reactions to seismic exploration have received little study (Section 9.8.2). Even though small odontocetes have poor hearing sensitivity at low frequencies, seismic pulses are strong enough to be heard by dolphins many kilometers away. Recent work suggests that sperm whales may become silent or show avoidance upon exposure to noise pulses from a distant seismic vessel.

Gray and bowhead whales often are observed behaving normally, insofar as can be determined, in the presence of strong noise pulses from seismic vessels several kilometers or more away. However, most gray and bowhead whales interrupt their prior activities and swim away when a full-scale seismic vessel emitting noise pulses approaches within a few kilometers (Section 9.8.3). Also, bowheads exposed to noise pulses from more distant seismic vessels often exhibit subtle behavioral changes consistent with those seen when the whales are actively avoiding a closer seismic vessel. Thus, whales exposed to noise from distant seismic ships may not be totally unaffected even if they remain in the area and continue their normal activities.

Sea otters seem less sensitive than baleen whales to marine seismic exploration (Section 9.8.4).

Sonars and similar pulsed sources may elicit quieting or avoidance by sperm and humpback whales (Section 9.9). However, there is little specific information on reactions versus type and level of sonar signal. We are not aware of any data on reactions of pinnipeds, sirenians, or sea otters to sonars. Sonar effects on marine mammals deserve study.

High explosives, when detonated underwater, produce not only a very sharp noise pulse, but also shock waves that can do physical damage to nearby animals (Section 9.10). Mortality of pinnipeds, dolphins, sea otters and possibly humpback whales exposed to explosions has been documented. Pinnipeds and cetaceans often seem to habituate to noise pulses from more distant explosions.

Reactions to low-frequency sounds from *ocean science studies* have not yet been studied extensively. During the Heard Island Feasibility Test, there were indications of avoidance or quieting by baleen whales and the larger odontocetes. In contrast, dolphins and fur seals seemed more conspicuous during the test. The biological significance of all these observations is uncertain (Section 9.11).

Purposeful acoustic scaring has variable but often only limited and temporary success in scaring marine mammals away from sites with abundant prey (Section 9.12). Pinnipeds will tolerate much man-made noise to gain access to food. However, acoustic "alarms" on fishing gear show promise for reducing the by-catch of some cetacean species.

Overall, noise from human activities sometimes causes pronounced short-term behavioral reactions and temporary local displacement of whales and hauled-out pinnipeds. Sometimes the effects are more subtle, and at other times no effects are detectable even with strong man-made noise. Overflights of pinnipeds at haulout sites can cause limited mortality through stampedes or abandonment. The continued presence of various marine mammals in certain areas despite much human activity, sometimes for decades, suggests that many marine mammals are quite tolerant of noise and other human activities (Section 9.14). However, there may be no suitable alternative locations for some marine mammals.

12.6.2 Data Needs and Recommended Research

General Issues.—It is often uncertain whether behavioral reactions of marine mammals to human activities are attributable to noise, visual cues, or a combination of cues. This doubt applies to most data on reactions to aircraft, and some data on reactions to ships and various other human activities. *This distinction may be a major data need when mitigative measures are being designed. The most appropriate mitigative measure(s) may depend on the specific cue(s) to which animals react.* Noise playback experiments provide a method for testing reactions to man-made noise in isolation from other cues.

The extent to which sound playback tests can be used in evaluating marine mammal reactions to noisy human activities needs further study. Playbacks have advantages, but practical playback equipment cannot precisely reproduce the sounds emitted by a strong noise source. There may be differences in source level and thus steepness of the received level versus distance gradient. There may also be differences in spectral composition, source depth, and near-field effects. Also, playbacks do not reproduce any associated nonacoustic cues.

Any possible long-term effects of man-made noise on marine mammal individuals and populations are, for the most part, unknown. This is a major data need, since it is the long-term effects on distribution and reproductive success that are most important. It is unclear whether the presence or absence of strong short-term behavioral reactions is a good indicator of long-term consequences. If human activities are regulated based on apparent short-term sensitivity (or lack of sensitivity) of marine mammals, and if short- and long-term effects are not well correlated, then the regulatory actions may be unnecessary or ineffective. *Research that can provide insight into long-term effects of noise on any species of marine mammal is a high priority.* Useful approaches may include studies of stress as assessed by telemetry of physiological parameters, site fidelity of known individuals to ensonified areas, and long-term displacement of individuals and populations. To be useful, most types of studies of long-term effects must be conducted in a consistent way over prolonged periods.

Specific data on habituation of marine mammals to man-made noise are needed (Section 9.14.2; NRC/OSB 1994:43). It is not known whether marine mammals that tolerate chronic noise exposure are stressed or otherwise harmed. Behavioral habituation is a process that might allow marine mammals to adapt to ongoing or repeated exposure to more-or-less innocuous man-made noises.   A better understanding of habituation in marine mammals is needed to allow more reliable predictions about the likely long-term effects of repeated or ongoing noise exposure.

Specific Sound Sources.—Some mortality of pinnipeds hauled out on land or ice has been reported or suspected as a result of aircraft overflights and ship approaches (Sections 9.2.1 and 9.3.1). Mortality has been attributed to stampede-induced injuries and pup abandonment. This mortality is a direct and negative impact on individuals and populations, but its extent is unclear. Many pinnipeds apparently habituate to such disturbances. Better data on reactions to aircraft and surface vessels are desirable for any situation in which a major pinniped haulout site is to be subjected to repeated close approaches by aircraft or vessels.

Effects of ship noise on marine mammals, and especially baleen whales, need more study. The strong low-frequency sounds of large ships, combined with their large numbers and mobility, result in a high potential for disturbance and masking effects, especially on baleen whales. Reactions of some species to ships may be more severe than is evident from casual ship-based observations, as the more responsive individuals are unlikely to be seen from ships.

Icebreaker effects on marine mammals have received only limited field study (Section 9.4). The strong and variable underwater noise from icebreakers is one reason for concern, along with the known sensitivity of belugas and narwhals to icebreaker noise. *Data on reactions of most other high-latitude species to icebreakers would be needed if plans for icebreaking tankers were revitalized, or if icebreaking in support of industrial or other operations were expanded.*

Short-term behavioral reactions of some species of marine mammals to various stationary offshore operations, e.g., marine construction, drilling and oil production, have been reported. In other cases, tolerance of these operations has been noted (Sections 9.6 and 9.7). It is not known how extensively these data can be extrapolated to related but untested species, or to noise from similar but untested industrial operations. Too few combinations of species and offshore activities have been studied to allow confident judgments about the generality of the results that have been obtained (see also NRC/OSB 1994:45).

Information is needed about reactions of odontocetes and pinnipeds to underwater noise from airgun arrays and other noise sources used for seismic exploration in open water (Sections 9.8.1 and 9.8.2). Also, there are no data for manatees. Marine seismic exploration is of widespread occurrence, and the peak levels of noise pulses from seismic sources are very high.

Data on reactions of mysticetes, odontocetes, and pinnipeds to sonars are needed. Many sonars emit very strong sound pulses. Unlike most other man-made noises, sonar signals often are at frequencies within the ranges of most sensitive hearing for many odontocetes and pinnipeds.

Data on effects of the strong, intermittent, low-frequency sounds used in some ocean science studies are needed. Because of the low frequencies used for long-range tests, and (at low to moderate latitudes) the placement of the noise source in the deep sound channel, the greatest concerns are about effects on baleen whales, the larger odontocetes, and deep-diving pinnipeds (see also NRC/OSB 1994:46).

12.7 Zones of Noise Influence

12.7.1 Present Knowledge

The *zone of audibility* around a source of man-made noise is the area within which a marine mammal can hear the noise (Section 10.2). This can be predicted, at least roughly, if the following data are available for each important frequency in the man-made noise: source level of man-made noise, site-specific transmission loss rate, ambient noise level, and absolute auditory threshold of the mammal of concern.

Strong acoustic sources like open-water seismic exploration and icebreaking are probably audible 100 km or more away in many cases (Section 10.4.3). This is especially true for baleen whales, assuming that their hearing is very sensitive to low-frequency sounds. However, low-frequency seismic pulses may be strong enough to be heard at 100 km or more even by some toothed whales and pinnipeds. At the other extreme, some bottom-founded oil production platforms are unlikely to be audible to toothed whales and pinnipeds more than a few hundred meters away, or to baleen whales more than a few kilometers away.

Propagation and ambient noise data show that the average radius of audibility around a particular type of noise source will vary among regions and days. Even for a specific human activity in a specific area, there is no single threshold distance within which animals will consistently detect the noise and beyond which they will not do so. Relationships between detectability and distance are probabilistic. Estimated radii of audibility are first approximations, useful mainly in identifying situations requiring more study.

The *zone of responsiveness* around a noise source is the area within which the animal would react to the noise. This zone is expected to be considerably smaller than the zone of audibility (Section 10.3). For example, seismic pulses can be detectable 100 km or more away, but baleen whales usually show no overt avoidance unless the seismic vessel is within a few kilometers.

Radius of responsiveness can be estimated from the types of data needed to estimate radius of audibility (see above) plus one more variable, the "behavioral response threshold". Even for a given species, area, and season, there is wide variation in the responsiveness of different individuals to noise (Section 10.3.3). Response criteria are probabilistic, and large sample sizes are needed to characterize them. "Radius of response" predictions in Section 10.4 are distances where we expect an average mammal to react. Factors affecting responsiveness include the current activity of the animal and its past experience, if any, with that type of sound.

The *zone of masking* around a noise source is the area within which its noise level is high enough to interfere with detection of other sounds of interest to a marine mammal, e.g., communication calls from conspecifics, echolocation signals, prey sounds, or other natural environmental sounds (Section 10.5). Any man-made noise strong enough to be audible increases the total background noise—natural plus man-made. This could interfere with an animal's ability to detect a sound signal if the signal were weak relative to total background noise level. Thus, the maximum radius of audibility of a man-made noise is also the maximum radius where it might impair detection of other sounds.

Only the weakest and most marginally detectable signals would be masked by the slight increase in background noise occurring at the maximum radius of masking. Stronger sound signals would be masked only if the listening animal were closer to the source of man-made noise. Dramatic reductions in the maximum potential radius of communication will result if noise levels increase by 10-20 dB while other factors remain unchanged. Factors affecting the "radius of masking" will include distance of the listener from the sources of the signal and masking noise, levels of those two sources, transmission loss from each source to listener, directional hearing abilities, relative directions from listener to the sources of signal and masker, and whether signal level or frequency is adjusted in response to the masking sound.

The *zone of hearing loss, discomfort, and injury* around a noise source is the relatively small area where, with a strong source, the received level of sound (and attendant acceleration and displacement) is high enough to cause physical discomfort or damage to the auditory or other systems (Section 10.6).

Leaving aside explosions, marine mammals are unlikely to suffer permanent hearing damage owing to noise from most human activities. This assumption is based mainly on extrapolations from terrestrial mammals (Section 10.6.2). This speculative approach suggests that underwater noise pulses from airgun arrays and similar sources might cause hearing damage to the few mammals that remain within ~100 m of these sources. Powerful sonars also might damage marine mammal hearing, especially in cases of sonars operating at frequencies to which marine mammal auditory systems are most sensitive.

It is not known whether marine mammals experience nonauditory sensations or discomfort when exposed to very high levels of underwater sound, as do human divers in some situations.

Shock waves from explosions are the one type of "noise" that definitely can cause hearing damage, and other physical injuries, to marine mammals. Models have been developed to predict the "safe range" in relation to charge size and the depths of the water, charge, and mammal (Section 10.6.3). These models are based mainly on data concerning gross blast damage to submerged terrestrial mammals and give little attention to subtle hearing damage. In the absence of those data, the more conservative criteria that have been proposed for human divers perhaps should be applied to marine mammals as well.

12.7.2 Data Needs and Recommended Research

Many assumptions must be made in predicting radii of audibility and responsiveness, partly because of data gaps and partly because of the wide variability in the quantitative factors involved in the predictions. Thus, much caution is necessary in interpreting these predictions.   They are probably most useful in a relative sense, and less useful as predictors of actual radii of audibility or responsiveness in specific circumstances.

Data on absolute hearing thresholds, especially at low frequencies, are needed; the lack of these data prevents meaningful estimates of radii of audibility for many species and situations, and requires bold extrapolations in other cases (Sections 8.2 and 12.5.2; see also NRC/ OSB 1994:47).   For baleen whales, large toothed whales, and sea otters, no direct data on hearing sensitivity are available.   For most pinnipeds and small toothed whales, there are no data on sensitivity at frequencies below about 1 kHz, where many man-made noises are strongest.

Our estimates of radii of audibility are based on unverified assumptions about detection of sounds in the presence of background noise (Section 10.2.1).   We assumed that marine mammals can hear a sound whose received level exceeds the background noise level in the corresponding frequency band, and that the effective filter bandwidth is ⅓ octave.   However, masking bandwidths and the minimum detectable signal-to-noise ratio undoubtedly vary.

Radii of masking cannot be predicted precisely, given the data needs noted in the previous paragraph and Section 10.5.   *Data on masking processes in various species, taking account of noise conditions that would be encountered in practical field situations, are needed.* Also, the scarcity of data on the functions of most marine mammal sounds makes it impossible to predict the biological effects of a reduction in maximum acoustic range.

Radii of responsiveness of cetaceans and pinnipeds to human activities are often reported in terms of distance but less commonly in terms of received sound level.   This limits our ability to generalize to situations where source levels or propagation loss are different.   For manatees and sea otters, even fewer data are available on behavioral responses to human activities. *Data on response thresholds, presented in acoustic terms, are needed* (Section 12.6.2).

Radii of responsiveness predicted in Section 10.4 consider only the acoustic aspects of human activities.   Some marine mammals may also react to visual or other stimuli.   This may be most likely with human activities whose acoustic effects are limited to short ranges.   Studies that distinguish the contributions of acoustic versus other cues to disturbance reactions are desirable.

Radii of auditory damage are speculative because there are no data on the levels of sounds or blast impulses that cause permanent hearing damage or temporary threshold shifts in marine mammals (Section 10.6). It is not known how closely the data from terrestrial mammals apply to marine mammals. We believe that exposure to most man-made noises is unlikely to cause hearing damage in marine mammals. Explosions are an obvious exception, and close exposure to seismic survey gear and sonars may also cause damage. *This interpretation needs confirmation, and damage thresholds should be quantified.* However, legal and ethical restrictions prevent direct tests of this type on marine mammals.

Studies of Temporary Threshold Shift (TTS) in marine mammals are a major data need. Sounds that cause TTS after short-term exposure may cause permanent auditory damage if continued for long periods. Thus, studies of TTS provide an indirect method to estimate the sound levels that might cause permanent hearing damage. Also, the conditions under which TTS occurs are of direct interest because TTS would affect the animals' ability to detect calls, echolocation sounds, and other important ambient sounds (see also NRC/OSB 1994:50). Any opportunities to test the hearing of any marine mammal after exposure to strong noise should be followed up. This might be done by evoked potential techniques or, if the animal had previously been trained for audiometric measurements, by behavioral testing.

12.8 *Significance of Responses and Impacts*

Marine mammals undoubtedly hear man-made noises from many sources. Cetaceans and manatees are exposed mainly to underwater sounds. Pinnipeds and sea otters are often subjected to airborne as well as underwater sounds. Most man-made sounds to which marine mammals are exposed are concentrated at low frequencies, but there are exceptions (e.g., sonars). Hearing systems of baleen whales are assumed to be adapted for detecting low-frequency sounds. Pinnipeds and especially toothed whales are better adapted for detecting higher-frequency sounds, but can hear strong sounds at low frequencies.

The fact that marine mammals can detect man-made noise does not, in itself, show that they are affected deleteriously by the noise. Many types of marine mammals commonly occur close enough to noise sources to be well within the ensonified zone. In many cases, activities of animals within the ensonified zone seem unaffected by the noise. However, when marine mammals are found within a zone ensonified by man-made noise, there are rarely any definite data on the numbers present relative to numbers that would have been there if there were no man-made noise. Also, there are almost no data on the possibility that marine mammals occurring within an ensonified zone are stressed or otherwise affected in a way that might impair their long-term well-being, or their reproductive success.

Special concern arises when a significant proportion of a marine mammal population is concentrated in the area ensonified by a noisy activity (Section 11.2). However, effective mitigative measures may be practical in these cases, since a minor change in siting of facilities or in seasonal timing of operations may greatly reduce the noise exposure. In contrast, marine mammals at sea sometimes are thinly distributed within large areas, and only a small percentage of the population is likely to be within the radius of acoustic influence around a given human activity. There are, however, circumstances in which many marine mammals can be exposed to man-made noise even when the population is widely distributed.

Masking is a natural and highly variable phenomenon to which marine mammals must be well adapted (Section 11.3). Marine mammals undoubtedly can tolerate some increase in masking relative to natural levels. The limits of this tolerance are unknown. The significance of acoustic masking in field conditions cannot be determined until more is known about (1) the functional importance to marine mammals of faint sound signals from conspecifics, predators, prey, and other natural sources; (2) signal detection abilities of marine mammals in the presence of background noise, including directional hearing abilities at frequencies where masking is an issue; and (3) abilities of marine mammals to adjust the strengths and perhaps frequencies of emitted sounds to minimize masking effects. More tests on masking should be done with sound signals and background noises typical of those occurring in field conditions, including low-frequency sounds.

Marine mammals show wide within-species variations in behavioral response thresholds when exposed to man-made noise. Thus, the radius of responsiveness varies widely among individuals and locations, and over time. No single criterion of disturbance will apply to all circumstances, even for a particular type of animal and human activity (Section 10.3.3).

Although there is little definite information about the long-term effects of short-term disturbance reactions, one can speculate that isolated disturbance incidents usually have minimal or no lasting effects. Marine mammals cope with disruptions by predators, bad weather, unusual ice conditions (at high latitudes), and other natural phenomena, and no doubt can also tolerate occasional brief periods of man-induced disturbance (Section 11.4).

The energetic consequences of most single disturbance incidents probably are insignificant, but there has been no specific work on this topic. Recurrent incidents of interrupted feeding and rapid swimming, if sufficiently frequent, can be assumed to have negative effects on the well-being of individuals. Relationships between disturbance frequency and severity of energetic effect have not been studied. Energetic modeling studies emphasizing disturbance effects could be of some value (Section 11.6.4).

Prolonged or repeated disturbance, as might occur if a stationary and noisy human activity were established near a marine mammal concentration area, is a more important concern than isolated short-term disturbance. The long-term implications of ongoing disturbance would depend in part on the degree to which the marine mammals habituate (Section 11.5). A better understanding of habituation by marine mammals to man-made noises is needed. We need repeated observations of the reactions of known individual animals. This work should be done with free-ranging animals that are individually recognizable via natural or artificial marks. Radio telemetry will often be helpful in maintaining contact with known individuals and in providing physiological data related to stress.

There are a few reports of probable or possible long-term displacement of marine mammals from ensonified areas (Section 11.6.3). It is rarely possible to identify the specific cause of an apparent long-term displacement; even the occurrence of displacement can be difficult to detect. The consequences of long-term displacement from ensonified areas are generally unknown. Meaningful studies of this question will be very difficult. Long-term work on the well-being and reproductive success of known individuals would be needed, including data from some animals that remain in preferred undisturbed areas and others that are displaced.

Cumulative effects of multiple noise sources should be considered in impact assessments (Section 11.7). Although the proportion of a marine mammal population exposed to noise from any one source may be small, the proportion exposed to at least one noise source may be much higher. The presence of multiple noise sources is expected to cause more frequent masking, behavioral disruption, and short-term displacement. These effects may be partly mitigated by habituation. Cumulative effects from nonacoustic as well as acoustic components of human activities are also a concern.

Reactions of marine mammals to man-made noise are in many ways similar to those of certain terrestrial mammals, especially ungulates (Section 11.8). Noise effects on some phenomena, e.g., physiological stress, are better known in terrestrial than in marine mammals. Some procedures known to be useful in terrestrial studies, e.g., telemetry to assess habituation and physiological effects, should be valuable in studies of marine mammals as well. Studies of disturbance effects on terrestrial mammals should be considered when designing and interpreting studies of marine mammal disturbance.

Marine mammals possess a number of characteristics that apparently pre-adapt them to cope with limited exposure to man-made noise (Section 11.9). These traits include certain attributes of their calls and hearing processes, the use of short-term avoidance reactions to reduce exposure to strong noise, and habituation. Within limits, these traits assist marine mammals in coping with man-made noise.

Noise impacts of human activities often can be reduced by careful planning (Section 11.10). Noise reductions may be possible by appropriate choice or design of equipment. Seasonal timing of activities often can be adjusted to avoid periods when marine mammals are present or most sensitive. The most sensitive areas often could be avoided when selecting sites for noisy human activities. Finally, operational procedures for some noisy activities could be adjusted to reduce acoustic and other disturbance to marine mammals.

Some practical combination of these measures should provide significant mitigation in most situations. However, in some cases, noise effects on marine mammals may not be avoidable without forgoing or significantly modifying the noisy human activity. Continued research will be needed to support informed decisionmaking about these matters. Well-focused research on noise effects should allow gradual refinement of regulatory actions to provide adequate protection for marine mammals while not unnecessarily restricting human activities.

LITERATURE CITED[1]

Abrahamson, A. 1974. Correlation of actual and analytical helicopter aural detection criteria. Tech. Rep. 74-102A. U.S. Army Air Mobility Res. & Dev. Lab., Fort Eustis, VA. 135 p. NTIS AD-B002067.[1]

Acevedo, A. 1991. Interactions between boats and bottlenose dolphins, *Tursiops truncatus*, in the entrance to Ensenada de la Paz, Mexico. *Aquat. Mamm.* 17 (3):120-124.

Ackerman, B.B., S.D. Wright, R.K. Frohlich and B.L. Weigle. 1989. Trends in manatee mortality in Florida. p. 1 *In*: Abstr. 8th Bienn. Conf. Biol. Mar. Mamm., Pacific Grove, CA, Dec. 1989. 81 p.

Acoustical Society of America. 1981. San Diego workshop on the interaction between man-made noise and vibration and arctic marine wildlife, Feb. 1980. Rep. from Acoust. Soc. Am., Washington, DC, for Alaska Eskimo Whaling Comm., Barrow, AK. 84 p.

Adler-Fenchel, H.S. 1980. Acoustically derived estimate of the size distribution for a sample of sperm whales (*Physeter catodon*) in the western North Atlantic. *Can. J. Fish. Aquat. Sci.* 37(12):2358-2361.

Airapet'yants, É.Sh., V.A. Voronov, Yu.V. Ivanenko, M.P. Ivanov, D.L. Ordovskii, B.F. Sergeev and V.I. Chilingiris. 1973. The physiology of the sonar system of Black Sea dolphins. *J. Evol. Biochem. Physiol.* 9(4):364-369.

Akal, T. and J.M. Berkson (eds.). 1986. Ocean seismo-acoustics, low frequency underwater acoustics. Plenum, New York. 915 p.

Akamatsu, T., Y. Hatakeyama and N. Takatsu. 1993. Effects of pulse sounds on escape behavior of false killer whales. *Nippon Suisan Gakkaishi* 59(8):1297-1303.

Akamatsu, T., Y. Hatakeyama, T. Kojima and H. Soeda. 1994. Echolocation rates of two harbor porpoises (*Phocoena phocoena*). *Mar. Mamm. Sci.* 10(4):401-411.

Allen, S.G., D.G. Ainley, G.W. Page and C.A. Ribic. 1984. The effect of disturbance on harbor seal haul out patterns at Bolinas Lagoon, California. *Fish. Bull.* 82(3):493-500.

Alliston, W.G. 1980. The distribution of ringed seals in relation to winter ice-breaking activities near McKinley Bay, N.W.T., January-June 1980. Rep. from LGL Ltd., Toronto, Ont., for Dome Petrol. Ltd., Calgary, Alb. 52 p.

---

[1] Many limited-circulation reports prepared for the U.S. government, and some others as well, are available on paper or microfiche from the U.S. National Technical Information Service, 5285 Port Royal Rd., Springfield, VA 22161, U.S.A. (telephone 703-487-4600; fax 703-321-8547). NTIS catalog numbers are included here when known.

Alliston, W.G. 1981. The distribution of ringed seals in relation to winter ice-breaking activities in Lake Melville, Labrador. Rep. from LGL Ltd., St. John's, Newf., for Arctic Pilot Proj., Petro-Canada, Calgary, Alb. 13 p.

Altmann, M. 1958. The flight distance in free-ranging big game. *J. Wildl. Manage.* 22(2):207-209.

Amato, I. 1993. A sub surveillance network becomes a window on whales. *Science* 261(5121):549-550.

Ames, D.R. 1978. Physiological responses to auditory stimuli. p. 23-45 *In*: J.L. Fletcher and R.G. Busnel (eds.), Effects of noise on wildlife. Academic Press, New York. 305 p.

Amstrup, S.C. 1993. Human disturbances of denning polar bears in Alaska. *Arctic* 46(3):246-250.

Andersen, S. 1970a. Auditory sensitivity of the harbour porpoise *Phocoena phocoena*. *Invest. Cetacea* 2:255-259.

Andersen, S. 1970b. Directional hearing in the harbour porpoise *Phocoena phocoena*. *Invest. Cetacea* 2:260-263.

Andersen, S. and G. Pilleri. 1970. Audible sound production in captive *Platanista gangetica*. *Invest. Cetacea* 2:83-86.

Anderson, P.K. 1982. Studies of dugongs at Shark Bay, Western Australia. II. Surface and subsurface observations. *Austral. Wildl. Res.* 9(1):85-99.

Anderson, S.S. and A.D. Hawkins. 1978. Scaring seals by sound. *Mamm. Rev.* 8 (1-2):19-24.

Anonymous. 1972. Crackers a deterrent for seals. *S. Afr. Ship. News Fish. Ind. Rev.* 27(11):47, 49.

Anonymous. 1975a. Phantom killer whales. *S. Afr. Ship. News Fish. Ind. Rev.* 30(7):50-53.

Anonymous. 1975b. Pressure mounts on seal problem; killer whale results inconclusive. *S. Afr. Ship. News Fish. Ind. Rev.* 30(10):47.

Anonymous. 1976. No more crackers. *S. Afr. Ship. News Fish. Ind. Rev.* 31(10): 45.

ANPWS. 1991. Australia. Progress report on cetacean research, May 1989 to May 1990. *Rep. Int. Whal. Comm.* 41:223-229.

ANSI. 1971. American national standard methods for the measurement of sound pressure levels. ANSI S1.13-1971 (R1976). Am. Natl. Standards Inst., New York. 34 p.

ANSI. 1978. Method for the calculation of the absorption of sound by the atmosphere. ANSI S1.26-1978. Am. Inst. Phys. for Acoust. Soc. Am., New York. 28 p.

ANSI. 1986. American national standard methods for measurement of impulse noise. ANSI S12.7-1986. Standards Secretariat, Acoust. Soc. Am., New York. 15 p.

ANSI. 1994. American national standard acoustical terminology. ANSI S1.1-1994. Standards Secretariat, Acoust. Soc. Am., New York. 56 p.

Armstrong, T. 1984. The Northern Sea Route, 1983. *Polar Rec.* 22(137):173-182.

Arons, A.B. 1948. Secondary pressure pulses due to gas globe oscillation in underwater explosions. II. Selection of adiabatic parameters in the theory of oscillation. *J. Acoust. Soc. Am.* 20(3):277-282.

ARPA. 1995. Final Environmental Impact Statement/Environmental Impact Report for the California Acoustic Thermometry of Ocean Climate project and its associated Marine Mammal Research Program. U.S. Advanced Res. Proj. Agency, Arlington, VA. 2 vol., var. pag.

ARPA and NMFS. 1994. Draft Environmental Impact Statement for the Kauai Acoustic Thermometry of Ocean Climate Project and its associated Marine Mammal Research Program. Advanced Research Projects Agency, Arlington, VA, and U.S. Natl. Mar. Fish. Serv., Silver Spring, MD. 2 vol., var. pag.

Ash, C. 1962. Whaler's eye. Macmillan, New York. 245 p.

Asselin, S., M.O. Hammill and C. Barrette. 1993. Underwater vocalizations of ice breeding grey seals. *Can. J. Zool.* 71(11):2211-2219.

Atkins, N. and S.L. Swartz (eds.). 1989. Proceedings of the workshop to review and evaluate whale watching programs and management needs/November 14-16, 1988, Monterey, CA. Cent. Mar. Conserv., Washington, DC. 53 p.

Au, D. and W. Perryman. 1982. Movement and speed of dolphin schools responding to an approaching ship. *Fish. Bull.* 80(2):371-379.

Au, W.W.L. 1980. Echolocation signals of the Atlantic bottlenose dolphin (*Tursiops truncatus*) in open waters. p. 251-282 *In*: R.-G. Busnel and J.F. Fish (eds.), Animal sonar systems. Plenum, New York. 1135 p.

Au, W.W.L. 1990. Target detection in noise by echolocating dolphins. p. 203-216 *In*: J.A. Thomas and R.A. Kastelein (eds.), Sensory abilities of cetaceans/ Laboratory and field evidence. Plenum, New York. 710 p.

Au, W.W.L. 1992. Target sonar discrimination cues. p. 357-376 *In*: J.A. Thomas, R.A. Kastelein and A.Ya. Supin (eds.), Marine mammal sensory systems. Plenum, New York. 773 p.

Au, W.W.L. 1993. The sonar of dolphins. Springer-Verlag, New York. 277 p.

Au, W.W.L. 1994. Sonar detection of gillnets by dolphins: Theoretical predictions. *Rep. Int. Whal. Comm. (Spec. Issue)* 15:565-571.

Au, W.W.L. and P.W.B. Moore. 1984. Receiving beam patterns and directivity indices of the Atlantic bottlenose dolphin *Tursiops truncatus*. *J. Acoust. Soc. Am.* 75(1):255-262.

Au, W.W.L. and P.W.B. Moore. 1990. Critical ratio and critical bandwidth for the Atlantic bottlenose dolphin. *J. Acoust. Soc. Am.* 88(3):1635-1638.

Au, W.W.L. and K.J. Snyder. 1980. Long-range target detection in open waters by an echolocating Atlantic bottlenose dolphin (*Tursiops truncatus*). *J. Acoust. Soc. Am.* 68(4):1077-1084.

Au, W.W.L., R.W. Floyd, R.H. Penner and A.E. Murchison. 1974. Measurement of echolocation signals of the Atlantic bottlenose dolphin, *Tursiops truncatus* Montagu, in open waters. *J. Acoust. Soc. Am.* 56(4):1280-1290.

Au, W.W.L., R.W. Floyd and J.E. Haun. 1978. Propagation of Atlantic bottlenose dolphin echolocation signals. *J. Acoust. Soc. Am.* 64(2):411-422.

Au, W.W.L., R.H. Penner and J. Kadane. 1982. Acoustic behavior of echolocating Atlantic bottlenose dolphins. *J. Acoust. Soc. Am.* 71(5):1269-1275.

Au, W.W.L., D.A. Carder, R.H. Penner and B.L. Scronce. 1985. Demonstration of adaptation in beluga whale echolocation signals. *J. Acoust. Soc. Am.* 77(2): 726-730.

Au, W.W.L., P.W.B. Moore and D. Pawloski. 1986. Echolocation transmitting beam of the Atlantic bottlenose dolphin. *J. Acoust. Soc. Am.* 80(2):688-691.

Au, W.W.L., R.H. Penner and C.W. Turl. 1987. Propagation of beluga echolocation signals. *J. Acoust. Soc. Am.* 82(3):807-813.

Au, W.W.L., J.L. Pawloski, T.W. Cranford, R.C. Gisner and P.E. Nachtigall. 1993. Transmission beam pattern of a false killer whale. *J. Acoust. Soc. Am.* 93(4, Pt. 2):2358-2359.

Awbrey, F.T. 1980. Sound spectra on San Miguel Island, 1979-1980. p. 229-246 *In*: J.R. Jehl, Jr., and C.F. Cooper (eds.), Potential effects of space shuttle sonic booms on the biota and geology of the California Channel Islands: Research reports. Tech. Rep. 80-1. Rep. from Cent. Mar. Stud., San Diego State Univ., and Hubbs/Sea World Res. Inst., San Diego, CA, for U.S. Air Force, Space Div. 246 p.

Awbrey, F.T. and J.A. Thomas. 1987. Measurements of sound propagation from several acoustic harassment devices. p. 85-104 *In*: B.R. Mate and J.T. Harvey (eds.), Acoustical deterrents in marine mammal conflicts with fisheries. ORESU-W-86-001. Oregon State Univ. Sea Grant Coll. Program, Corvallis, OR. 116 p.

Awbrey, F.T., J.C. Norris, A.B. Hubbard and W.E. Evans. 1979. The bioacoustics of the Dall porpoise-salmon drift net interaction. HSWRI Tech. Rep. 79-120. Rep. from Hubbs/Sea World Res. Inst., San Diego, CA, for U.S. Natl. Mar. Fish. Serv., Seattle, WA. 41 p.

Awbrey, F.T., J.A. Thomas, W.E. Evans and S. Leatherwood. 1982. Ross Sea killer whale vocalizations: Preliminary description and comparison with those of some Northern Hemisphere killer whales. *Rep. Int. Whal. Comm.* 32:667-670.

Awbrey, F.T., J.A. Thomas and R.A. Kastelein. 1988. Low-frequency underwater hearing sensitivity in belugas, *Delphinapterus leucas*. *J. Acoust. Soc. Am.* 84(6):2273-2275.

Axelrod, J. and T.D. Reisine. 1984. Stress hormones: Their interaction and regulation. *Science* 224(4648):452-459.

Babushina, Ye.S., G.L. Zaslavskii and L.I. Yurkevich. 1991. Air and underwater hearing characteristics of the northern fur seal: Audiograms, frequency and differential thresholds. *Biophysics* 36(5):909-913.

Backus, R.H. and W.E. Schevill. 1966. *Physeter* clicks. p. 510-528 *In*: K.S. Norris (ed.), Whales, dolphins, and porpoises. Univ. Calif. Press, Berkeley. 789 p.

Baggeroer, A. and W. Munk. 1992. The Heard Island Feasibility Test. *Phys. Today* 45(9):22-30.

Bain, D.E. and M.E. Dahlheim. 1994. Effects of masking noise on detection thresholds of killer whales. p. 243-256 *In*: T.R. Loughlin (ed.), Marine mammals and the *Exxon Valdez*. Academic Press, San Diego, CA. 395 p.

Bain, D.E., B. Kriete and M.E. Dahlheim. 1993. Hearing abilities of killer whales (*Orcinus orca*). *J. Acoust. Soc. Am.* 94(3, Pt. 2):1829.

Baird, I.G., B. Mounsouphom and P.J. Stacey. 1994. Preliminary surveys of Irrawaddy dolphins (*Orcaella brevirostris*) in Lao PDR and northeastern Cambodia. *Rep. Int. Whal. Comm.* 44:367-369.

Baird, R.W. and P.J. Stacey. 1991a. Status of Risso's dolphin, *Grampus griseus*, in Canada. *Can. Field-Nat.* 105(2):233-242.

Baird, R.W. and P.J. Stacey. 1991b. Status of the northern right whale dolphin, *Lissodelphis borealis*, in Canada. *Can. Field-Nat.* 105(2):243-250.

Baker, C.S. and L.M. Herman. 1989. Behavioral responses of summering humpback whales to vessel traffic: Experimental and opportunistic observations. NPS-NR-TRS-89-01. Rep. from Kewalo Basin Mar. Mamm. Lab., Univ. Hawaii, Honolulu, HI, for U.S. Natl. Park Serv., Anchorage, AK. 50 p. NTIS PB90-198409.

Baker, C.S., L.M. Herman, B.G. Bays and W.F. Stifel. 1982. The impact of vessel traffic on the behavior of humpback whales in southeast Alaska. Rep. from Kewalo Basin Mar. Mamm. Lab., Honolulu, HI, for U.S. Natl. Mar. Fish. Serv., Seattle, WA. 78 p.

Baker, C.S., L.M. Herman, B.G. Bays and G.B. Bauer. 1983. The impact of vessel traffic on the behavior of humpback whales in southeast Alaska: 1982 season. Rep. from Kewalo Basin Mar. Mamm. Lab., Honolulu, HI, for U.S. Natl. Mar. Mamm. Lab., Seattle, WA. 30 p. + fig., tables.

Baker, C.S., A. Perry and G. Vequist. 1988. Conservation update/Humpback whales of Glacier Bay, Alaska. *Whalewatcher, J. Am. Cetac. Soc.* 22(3):13-17.

Baker, C.S., J.M. Straley and A. Perry. 1992. Population characteristics of individually identified humpback whales in southeastern Alaska: Summer and fall 1986. *Fish. Bull.* 90(3):429-437.

Banfield, A.W.F., D.R. Flook, J.P. Kelsall and A.G. Loughrey. 1955. An aerial survey technique for northern big game. *Trans. N. Am. Wildl. Conf.* 20:519-532.

Barger, J.E. and W.R. Hamblen. 1980. The air gun impulsive underwater transducer. *J. Acoust. Soc. Am.* 68(4):1038-1045.

Barger, J.E. and D. Sachs. 1975. Transmission of sound through the scaled ocean surface. BBN Rep. 3103a. Rep. from Bolt Beranek & Newman Inc., Cambridge, MA, for Adv. Res. Proj. Agency, Arlington, VA. 76 p.

Barham, E.G., J.C. Sweeney, S. Leatherwood, R.K. Beggs and C.L. Barham. 1980. Aerial census of the bottlenose dolphin, *Tursiops truncatus*, in a region of the Texas coast. *Fish. Bull.* 77(3):585-595.

Barlow, J. 1988. Harbor porpoise, *Phocoena phocoena*, abundance estimation for California, Oregon, and Washington: I. Ship surveys. *Fish. Bull.* 86(3):417-432.

Barr, W. and E.A. Wilson. 1985. The shipping crisis in the Soviet eastern arctic at the close of the 1983 navigation season. *Arctic* 38(1):1-17.

Bartholomew, G.A. and N.E. Collias. 1962. The role of vocalization in the social behaviour of the northern elephant seal. *Anim. Behav.* 10(1):7-14.

Bauer, G.B. 1986. The behavior of humpback whales in Hawaii and modifications of behavior induced by human interventions. Ph.D. Thesis, Univ. Hawaii, Honolulu. 314 p.

Bauer, G.B. and L.M. Herman. 1986. Effects of vessel traffic on the behavior of humpback whales in Hawaii. Rep. from Kewalo Basin Mar. Mamm. Lab., Univ. Hawaii, Honolulu, for U.S. Natl. Mar. Fish. Serv., Honolulu, HI. 151 p.

Bauer, G.B., J.R. Mobley and L.M. Herman. 1993. Responses of wintering humpback whales to vessel traffic. *J. Acoust. Soc. Am.* 94(3, Pt. 2):1848.

BBN. 1960. Investigation of acoustic signalling over water in fog. BBN Rep. 674. Rep. from Bolt Beranek & Newman Inc., Cambridge, MA, for U.S. Coast Guard, Washington, DC. Var. pag.

Beach, D.W. and M.T. Weinrich. 1989. Watching the whales: Is an educational adventure for humans turning out to be another threat for endangered species? *Oceanus* 32(1):84-88.

Beamish, P. 1979. Behavior and significance of entrapped baleen whales. p. 291-309 *In*: H.E. Winn and B.L. Olla (eds.), Behavior of marine animals, vol. 3: Cetaceans. Plenum, New York. 438 p.

Beamish, P. and E. Mitchell. 1971. Ultrasonic sounds recorded in the presence of a blue whale *Balaenoptera musculus*. *Deep-Sea Res.* 18(8):803-809.

Beamish, P. and E. Mitchell. 1973. Short pulse length audio frequency sounds recorded in the presence of a minke whale (*Balaenoptera acutorostrata*). *Deep-Sea Res.* 20(4):375-386.

Beck, C.A., R.K. Bonde and G.B. Rathbun. 1982. Analyses of propeller wounds on manatees in Florida. *J. Wildl. Manage.* 46(2):531-535.

Beecher, M.D. 1988. Spectrographic analysis of animal vocalizations: Implications of the "uncertainty principle". *Bioacoustics* 1(2/3):187-208.

Behrend, D.F. and R.A. Lubeck. 1968. Summer flight behavior of white-tailed deer in two Adirondack forests. *J. Wildl. Manage.* 32(3):615-618.

Beier, J.C. and D. Wartzok. 1979. Mating behaviour of captive spotted seals (*Phoca largha*). *Anim. Behav.* 27(3):772-781.

Bel'kovich, V.M. 1960. Some biological observations on the white whale from the aircraft. *Zool. Zh.* 39(9):1414-1422 (Transl. NOO-T-403. U.S. Naval Oceanogr. Off., Washington, DC. 14 p. NTIS AD-693583).

Bel'kovich, V.M. and M.N. Shchekotov. 1992. Individual signals of belugas associated with hunting behavior in the White Sea. p. 439-447 *In*: J.A. Thomas, R.A. Kastelein and A.Ya. Supin (eds.), Marine mammal sensory systems. Plenum, New York. 773 p.

Bel'kovich, V.M. and A.V. Yablokov. 1963. Marine mammals 'share experience' with designers. *Nauka Zhizn'* 30(5):61-64.

Belt, C.R., M.T. Weinrich and M.R. Schilling. 1989. Behavioral development of humpback whales in the southern Gulf of Maine. p. 6 *In*: Abstr. 8th Bienn. Conf. Biol. Mar. Mamm., Pacific Grove, CA, Dec. 1989. 81 p.

Beranek, L.L. 1988. Acoustical measurements, rev. ed. Am. Inst. Phys., New York. 841 p.

Berglund, B., T. Lindvall and S. Nordin. 1990. Adverse effects of aircraft noise. *Environ. Int.* 16(4-6):315-338.

Berzin, A.A. and N.V. Doroshenko. 1981. Right whales of the Okhotsk Sea. *Rep. Int. Whal. Comm.* 31:451-455.

Best, P.B. 1981. The status of right whales (*Eubalaena glacialis*) off South Africa, 1969-1979. *Invest. Rep. Sea Fish. Inst. S. Afr.* 123. 44 p.

Best, P.B. 1984. Two right whale calves die in accidents. *Afr. Wildl.* 38(6):243.

Bibikov, N.G. 1992. Auditory brainstem responses in the harbor porpoise (*Phocoena phocoena*). p. 197-211 *In*: J.A. Thomas, R.A. Kastelein and A.Ya. Supin (eds.), Marine mammal sensory systems. Plenum, New York. 773 p.

Bird, J.E. 1983. The California gray whale (*Eschrictius* [sic] *robustus*): A review of the literature on migratory and behavioral characteristics. Appendix A *In*: C.I. Malme, P.R. Miles, C.W. Clark, P. Tyack and J.E. Bird, Investigations of the potential effects of underwater noise from petroleum industry activities on migrating gray whale behavior. BBN Rep. 5366. Rep. from Bolt Beranek & Newman Inc., Cambridge, MA, for U.S. Minerals Manage. Serv., Anchorage, AK. Var. pag. NTIS PB86-174174.

Birdsall, T.G., K. Metzger and M.A. Dzieciuch. 1994. The Heard Island papers/Signals, signal processing, and general results. *J. Acoust. Soc. Am.* 96(4): 2343-2352.

Blane, J.M. 1990. Avoidance and interactive behaviour of the St. Lawrence beluga whale (*Delphinapterus leucas*) in response to recreational boating. M.A. Thesis, Dep. Geogr., Univ. Toronto, Toronto, Ont. 59 p.

Blane, J.M. and R. Jaakson. 1994. The impact of ecotourism boats on the St Lawrence beluga whales. *Environ. Conserv.* 21(3):267-269.

Bleich, V.C., R.T. Bowyer, A.M. Pauli, R.L. Vernoy and R.W. Anthes. 1990. Responses of mountain sheep to helicopter surveys. *Calif. Fish & Game* 76 (4):197-204.

Bleich, V.C., R.T. Bowyer, A.M. Pauli, M.C. Nicholson and R.W. Anthes. 1994. Mountain sheep *Ovis canadensis* and helicopter surveys: Ramifications for the conservation of large mammals. *Biol. Conserv.* 70(1):1-7.

Blix, A.S. and J.W. Lentfer. 1992. Noise and vibration levels in artificial polar bear dens as related to selected petroleum exploration and developmental activities. *Arctic* 45(1):20-24.

Bloch, D., G. Desportes, K. Hoydal and P. Jean. 1990. Pilot whaling in the Faroe Islands July 1986-July 1988. *N. Atl. Stud.* 2(1-2):36-44.

Bogoslovskaya, L.S. 1986. On the social behaviour of gray whales off Chukotka and Koryaka. *Rep. Int. Whal. Comm. (Spec. Issue)* 8:243-251.

Bogoslovskaya, L.S., L.M. Votrogov and T.N. Semenova. 1981. Feeding habits of the gray whale off Chukotka. *Rep. Int. Whal. Comm.* 31:507-510.

Bohne, B.A. J.A. Thomas, E.R. Yohe and S.H. Stone. 1985. Examination of potential hearing damage in Weddell seals (*Leptonychotes weddelli*) in McMurdo Sound, Antarctica. *Antarct. J. U.S.* 20:174-176.

Bohne, B.A., D.G. Bozzay and J.A. Thomas. 1986. Evaluation of inner ear pathology in Weddell seals. *Antarct. J. U.S.* 21:208.

Bond, J. 1971. Noise/Its effect on the physiology and behavior of animals. *Agric. Sci. Rev.* 9(4):1-10.

Bonner, W.N. 1978. Man's impact on seals. *Mamm. Rev.* 8(1):3-13.

Bonner, W.N. 1981a. Grey seal *Halichoerus grypus* Fabricius, 1791. p. 111-144 *In*: S.H. Ridgway and R.J. Harrison (eds.), Handbook of marine mammals, vol. 2. Academic Press, London. 359 p.

Bonner, W.N. 1981b. Southern fur seals *Arctocephalus* (Geoffroy Saint-Hilaire and Cuvier, 1826). p. 161-208 *In*: S.H. Ridgway and R.J. Harrison, (eds.), Handbook of marine mammals, vol. 1. Academic Press, London. 235 p.

Bonner, W.N. 1982. Seals and man/A study of interactions. Univ. Wash. Press, Seattle, WA. 170 p.

Bonner, W.N. 1990. The natural history of seals. Facts on File, New York. 196 p.

Booren, R.T. 1985. Mitigation measures for controlling the side-effects of explosives use in water. p. 312-323 *In*: Proc. Workshop on Effects of Explosives Use in the Marine Environment, Jan. 1985, Halifax, N.S. Tech. Rep. 5. Can. Oil & Gas Lands Admin. Environ. Prot. Branch, Ottawa, Ont. 398 p.

Borchers, D.L. and M.D. Haw. 1990. Determination of minke whale response to a transiting survey vessel from visual tracking of sightings. *Rep. Int. Whal. Comm.* 40:257-269.

Born, E.W., M.P. Heide-Jørgensen, F. Larsen and A.R. Martin. 1994. Abundance and stock composition of narwhals (*Monodon monoceros*) in Inglefield Bredning (NW Greenland). *Medd. Grønl., Biosci.* 39:51-68.

Bouchet, G.C., J. Turnock and D.E. Withrow. 1985. Response of Dall's porpoise (*Phocoenoides dalli*) to survey vessels and the effect of movement on population estimates. In: Abstr. 6th Bienn. Conf. Biol. Mar. Mamm., Vancouver, B.C., Nov. 1985. [86 p.]

Bowles, A. and B.S. Stewart. 1980. Disturbances to the pinnipeds and birds of San Miguel Island, 1979-1980. p. 99-137 *In*: J.R. Jehl, Jr., and C.F. Cooper (eds.), Potential effects of space shuttle sonic booms on the biota and geology of the California Channel Islands: Research reports. Tech. Rep. 80-1. Rep. from Cent. Mar. Stud., San Diego State Univ., and Hubbs/Sea World Res. Inst., San Diego, CA, for U.S. Air Force, Space Div. 246 p.

Bowles, A.E., M. Smultea, B. Würsig, D. DeMaster and D. Palka. 1991. Biological survey effort and findings from the Heard Island Feasibility Test 19 January - 3 February, 1991. Rep. from Hubbs/Sea World Res. Inst., San Diego, CA, for Off. Prot. Resour., U.S. Natl. Mar. Fish. Serv., Silver Spring, MD. 102 p. Draft rep., 28 Oct. 1991.

Bowles, A.E., M. Smultea, B. Würsig, D.P. DeMaster and D. Palka. 1994. Relative abundance and behavior of marine mammals exposed to transmissions from the Heard Island Feasibility Test. *J. Acoust. Soc. Am.* 96(4):2469-2484.

Boyd, I.L. 1984. The relationship between body condition and the timing of implantation in pregnant grey seals (*Halichoerus grypus*). *J. Zool.* 203(1):113-123.

Bradley, J.M. 1970. Ringed seal avoidance behaviour in response to Eskimo hunting in northern Foxe Basin. M.A. Thesis, Dep. Geogr., McGill Univ., Montreal.

Bradstreet, M.S.W., D.H. Thomson and D.B. Fissel. 1987. Zooplankton and bowhead whale feeding in the Canadian Beaufort Sea, 1986. Sect. 1 *In*: Bowhead whale food availability characteristics in the southern Beaufort Sea: 1985 and 1986. Environ. Stud. 50. Indian & Northern Affairs Canada, Ottawa, Ont. 204 p.

Brasseur, S.M.J.M. 1993. Tolerance of harbour seals to human related disturbance sources during haulout. p. 32 *In*: Abstr. 10th Bienn. Conf. Biol. Mar. Mamm., Galveston, TX, Nov. 1993. 130 p.

Brekhovskikh, L.M. 1960. Waves in layered media. Academic Press, New York. 561 p.

Brewer, K.D., M.L. Gallagher, P.R. Regos, P.E. Isert and J.D. Hall. 1993. ARCO Alaska, Inc. Kuvlum #1 exploration prospect/Site specific monitoring program final report. Rep. from Coastal & Offshore Pacific Corp., Walnut Creek, CA, for ARCO Alaska Inc., Anchorage, AK. 80 p.

Brigham, L.W. 1985. New developments in Soviet nuclear arctic ships. *U.S. Naval Inst. Proc.* 111(12):131-133.

Brodie, P.F. 1981a. Marine mammals in the ecosystem of the Canadian east coast. 10 p. *In*: Proc. Offshore Environment in the 80s, December 2-4, 1980, St. John's, Newfoundland.

Brodie, P.F. 1981b. Energetic and behavioural considerations with respect to marine mammals and disturbance from underwater noise. p. 287-290 *In*: N.M. Peterson (ed.), The question of sound from icebreaker operations: The proceedings of a workshop. Arctic Pilot Proj., Petro-Canada, Calgary, Alb. 350 p.

Brodie, P.F. 1993. Noise generated by the jaw actions of feeding fin whales. *Can. J. Zool.* 71(12):2546-2550.

Broom, D.M. and K.G. Johnson. 1993. Stress and animal welfare. Chapman & Hall, London. 211 p.

Brown, M.W., S.D. Kraus and D.E. Gaskin. 1991. Reaction of North Atlantic right whales (*Eubalaena glacialis*) to skin biopsy sampling for genetic and pollutant analysis. *Rep. Int. Whal. Comm. (Spec. Issue)* 13:81-89.

Brown, M.R., P.J. Corkeron, P.T. Hale, K.W. Schultz and M.M. Bryden. 1994. Behavioral responses of east Australian humpback whales *Megaptera novaeangliae* to biopsy sampling. *Mar. Mamm. Sci.* 10(4):391-400.

Brownell, R.L., Jr. 1971. Whales, dolphins and oil pollution. p. 255-276 *In*: D. Straughan (ed.), Biological and oceanographical survey of the Santa Barbara Channel oil spill 1969-1970, vol. I. Biology and bacteriology. Allan Hancock Foundation, Univ. Southern Calif., Los Angeles. 426 p.

Brownell, R.L., Jr., P.B. Best and J.H. Prescott (eds.). 1986. Report of the workshop on the status of right whales. *Rep. Int. Whal. Comm. (Spec. Issue)* 10:1-33.

Browning, D.G. and R.H. Mellen. 1986. Attenuation of low-frequency sound in the sea: recent results. p. 403-410 *In*: H.M. Merklinger (ed.), Progress in underwater acoustics. Plenum, New York. 839 p.

Brueggeman, J.J., C.I. Malme, R.A. Grotefendt, D.P. Volsen, J.J. Burns, D.G. Chapman, D.K. Ljungblad and G.A. Green. 1990. Shell Western E & P Inc. 1989 walrus monitoring program: The Klondike, Burger, and Popcorn prospects in the Chukchi Sea. Rep. from EBASCO Environmental, Bellevue, WA, for Shell Western E & P Inc., Houston, TX. Var. pag.

Brueggeman, J.J., D.P. Volsen, R.A. Grotefendt, G.A. Green, J.J. Burns and D.K. Ljungblad. 1991. Shell Western E & P Inc. 1990 walrus monitoring program/The Popcorn, Burger and Crackerjack prospects in the Chukchi Sea. Rep. from EBASCO Environmental, Bellevue, WA, for Shell Western E & P Inc., Houston, TX. Var. pag.

Brueggeman, J.J., G.A. Green, R.A. Grotefendt, M.A. Smultea, D.P. Volsen, R.A. Rowlett, C.C. Swanson, C.I. Malme, R. Mlawski and J.J. Burns. 1992a. 1991 marine mammal monitoring program (seals and whales) Crackerjack and Diamond prospects Chukchi Sea. Rep. from EBASCO Environmental, Bellevue, WA, for Shell Western E & P Inc. and Chevron U.S.A. Inc. Var. pag.

Brueggeman, J.J., R.A. Grotefendt, M.A. Smultea, G.A. Green, R.A. Rowlett, C.C. Swanson, D.P. Volsen, C.E. Bowlby, C.I. Malme, R. Mlawski and J.J. Burns. 1992b. 1991 marine mammal monitoring program (walrus and polar bear) Crackerjack and Diamond prospects Chukchi Sea. Rep. from EBASCO Environmental, Bellevue, WA, for Shell Western E & P Inc. and Chevron U.S.A. Inc. Var. pag.

Bryant, P.J., G. Nichols, T.B. Bryant and K. Miller. 1981. Krill availability and the distribution of humpback whales in southeastern Alaska. *J. Mammal.* 62 (2):427-430.

Bryant, P.J., C.M. Lafferty and S.K. Lafferty. 1984. Reoccupation of Laguna Guerrero Negro, Baja California, Mexico, by gray whales. p. 375-387 *In*: M.L. Jones, S.L. Swartz and S. Leatherwood (eds.), The gray whale *Eschrichtius robustus*. Academic Press, Orlando, FL. 600 p.

Buck, B.M. and D.A. Chalfant. 1972. Deep water narrowband radiated noise measurement of merchant ships. Delco TR72-28. Rep. from Delco Electronics, Santa Barbara, CA, for U.S. Navy Off. Naval Res., Arlington, VA. 30 p.

Buck, B.M. and C.R. Greene. 1979. Source level measurements of an arctic sea ice pressure ridge. *J. Acoust. Soc. Am.* 66(Suppl. 1):S25-S26.

Buck, B.M. and J.H. Wilson. 1986. Nearfield noise measurements from an arctic pressure ridge. *J. Acoust. Soc. Am.* 80(1):256-264.

Buckland, S.T., J.M. Breiwick, K.L. Cattanach and J.L. Laake. 1993. Estimated population size of the California gray whale. *Mar. Mamm. Sci.* 9(3):235-249.

Budelsky, R.A. 1993. Sex and the single male: Bearded seal mating strategies off Pt. Barrow, Alaska. p. 33 *In*: Abstr. 10th Bienn. Conf. Biol. Mar. Mamm., Galveston, TX, Nov. 1993. 130 p.

Buerki, C.B., T.W. Cranford, K.M. Langan and K.L. Marten. 1989. Acoustic recordings from two stranded beaked whales in captivity. p. 10 *In*: Abstr. 8th Bienn. Conf. Biol. Mar. Mamm., Pacific Grove, CA, Dec. 1989. 81 p.

Bullock, T.H. and V.S. Gurevich. 1979. Soviet literature on the nervous system and psychobiology of Cetacea. *Int. Rev. Neurobiol.* 21:47-127.

Bullock, T.H. and S.H. Ridgway. 1972. Evoked potentials in the central auditory system of alert porpoises to their own and artificial sounds. *J. Neurobiol.* 3(1):79-99.

Bullock, T.H., A.D. Grinnell, E. Ikezono, K. Kameda, Y. Katsuki, M. Nomoto, O. Sato, N. Suga and K. Yanagisawa. 1968. Electrophysiological studies of central auditory mechanisms in cetaceans. *Z. Vergl. Physiol.* 59:117-156.

Bullock, T.H., S.H. Ridgway and N. Suga. 1971. Acoustically evoked potentials in midbrain auditory structures in sea lions (Pinnipedia). *Z. Vergl. Physiol.* 74: 372-387.

Bullock, T.H., D.P. Domning and R.C. Best. 1980. Evoked brain potentials demonstrate hearing in a manatee (*Trichechus inunguis*). *J. Mammal.* 61(1):130-133.

Bullock, T.H., T.J. O'Shea and M.C. McClune. 1982. Auditory evoked potentials in the West Indian manatee (Sirenia: *Trichechus manatus*). *J. Comp. Physiol. A* 148(4):547-554.

Bunch, T.D. and G.W. Workman. 1993. Sonic boom/animal stress project report on elk, antelope, and Rocky Mountain bighorn sheep. *J. Acoust. Soc. Am.* 93 (4, Pt. 2):2378.

Burdic, W.S. 1984. Underwater acoustic system analysis. Prentice-Hall, Englewood Cliffs, NJ. 445 p.

Burdin, V.I., V.I. Markov, A.M. Reznik, V.M. Skornyakov and A.G. Chupakov. 1973. Ability of *Tursiops truncatus* Ponticus Barabasch to distinguish a useful signal against a noise background. p. 162-168 *In*: K.K. Chapskii and V.E. Sokolov (eds.), Morphology and ecology of marine mammals. Wiley, New York. 232 p.

Burns, J.J. and K.J. Frost. 1979. Natural history and ecology of the bearded seal, *Erignathus barbatus*. Environ. Assess. Alaskan Cont. Shelf, Final Rep. Princ. Invest., NOAA, Juneau, AK 19:311-392. 565 p. NTIS PB 85-200939.

Burns, J.J. and S.J. Harbo, Jr. 1972. An aerial census of ringed seals, northern coast of Alaska. *Arctic* 25(4):279-290.

Burns, J.J. and G.A. Seaman. 1985. Investigations of belukha whales in coastal waters of western and northern Alaska. II. Biology and ecology. Rep. from Alaska Dep. Fish & Game, Fairbanks, AK, for U.S. Natl. Oceanic & Atmos. Admin. (R.U. 612, Contr. No. NA 81 RAC 00049). 129 p.

Burns, J.J., B.P. Kelly and K.J. Frost. 1981. Executive summary: Studies of ringed seals in the Beaufort Sea during winter. Rep. from Alaska Dep. Fish & Game, Fairbanks, AK, for Outer Cont. Shelf Environ. Assess. Program, NOAA. 21 p.

Burns, J.J., B.P. Kelly, L.D. Aumiller, K.J. Frost and S. Hills. 1982. Studies of ringed seals in the Alaskan Beaufort Sea during winter: Impacts of seismic exploration. Rep. from Alaska Dep. Fish & Game, Fairbanks, AK, for Outer Cont. Shelf Environ. Assess. Program, NOAA. 57 p.

Bursk, M.K. 1983. Effects of boats on migrating gray whales. Manuscript, San Diego State Univ., CA. 25 p.

Busnel, M.C. and D. Molin. 1978. Preliminary results of the effects of noise on gestating female mice and their pups. p. 209-248 *In*: J.L. Fletcher and R.G. Busnel (eds.), Effects of noise on wildlife. Academic Press, New York. 305 p.

Busnel, R.-G. 1978. Introduction. p. 7-22 *In*: J.L. Fletcher and R.G. Busnel (eds.), Effects of noise on wildlife. Academic Press, New York. 305 p.

Busnel, R.-G. and A. Dziedzic. 1966a. Acoustic signals of the pilot whale *Globicephala melaena* and of the porpoises *Delphinus delphis* and *Phocoena phocoena*. p. 607-646 *In*: K.S. Norris (ed.), Whales, dolphins, and porpoises. Univ. Calif. Press, Berkeley. 789 p.

Busnel, R.-G., and A. Dziedzic. 1966b. Caractéristiques physiques de certains signaux acoustiques du delphididé *Steno bredanensis*, Lesson. *C.R. Acad. Sci. Paris, Sér. D* 262:143-146.

Busnel, R.-G. and A. Dziedzic. 1968. Caractéristiques physiques des signaux acoustiques de *Pseudorca crassidens* Owen (Cetace Odontocete). *Mammalia* 32(1):1-5.

Busnel, R.-G. and H.-D. Mebes. 1975. Hearing and communication in birds: The cocktail-party-effect in intraspecific communication of *Agapornis roseicollis* (Aves, Psittacidae). *Life Sci.* 17(10):1567-1569.

Busnel, R.G., A. Dziedzic and S. Andersen. 1965. Rôle de l'impédance d'une cible dans le seuil de sa détection par le système sonar du marsouin *P. phocaena*. *C.R. Séances Soc. Biol.* 159:69-74.

Busnel, R.-G., G. Pilleri and F.C. Fraser. 1968. Notes concernant le dauphin *Stenella styx* Gray 1846. *Mammalia* 32:192-203.

Busnel, R.-G., A. Dziedzic and G. Alcuri. 1974. Études préliminaires de signaux acoustiques du *Pontoporia blainvillei* Gervais et d'Orbigny (Cetacea, Platanistidae). *Mammalia* 38(3):449-459.

Butterworth, D.S. and P.B. Best. 1982. Report of the Southern Hemisphere minke whale assessment cruise, 1980/81. *Rep. Int. Whal. Comm.* 32:835-874.

Butterworth, D.S., P.B. Best and M. Basson. 1982. Results of analysis of sighting experiments carried out during the 1980/81 Southern Hemisphere minke whale assessment cruise. *Rep. Int. Whal. Comm.* 32:819-834.

Calambokidis, J., G.H. Steiger and L.E. Healey. 1983. Behavior of harbor seals and their reaction to vessels in Glacier Bay Alaska. p. 16 *In*: Abstr. 5th Bienn. Conf. Biol. Mar. Mamm., Boston, MA, Nov. 1983. 112 p.

Caldwell, D.K. and M.C. Caldwell. 1970. Echolocation-type signals by two dolphins, genus *Sotalia*. *Q. J. Florida Acad. Sci.* 33(2):124-131.

Caldwell, D.K. and M.C. Caldwell. 1971a. Sounds produced by two rare cetaceans stranded in Florida. *Cetology* 4:1-6.

Caldwell, D.K. and M.C. Caldwell. 1971b. Underwater pulsed sounds produced by captive spotted dolphins, *Stenella plagiodon*. *Cetology* 1:1-7.

Caldwell, D.K. and M.C. Caldwell. 1977. Cetaceans. p. 794-808 *In*: T.A. Sebeok (ed.), How animals communicate. Indiana Univ. Press, Bloomington. 1128 p.

Caldwell, D.K. and M.C. Caldwell. 1985. Manatees *Trichechus manatus* Linnaeus, 1758; *Trichechus senegalensis* Link, 1795 and *Trichechus inunguis* (Natterer, 1883). p. 33-66 *In*: S.H. Ridgway and R. Harrison (eds.), Handbook of marine mammals, vol. 3. Academic Press, London. 362 p.

Caldwell, D.K. and M.C. Caldwell. 1987. Underwater echolocation-type clicks by captive stranded pygmy sperm whales, *Kogia breviceps*. p. 8 *In*: Abstr. 7th Bienn. Conf. Biol. Mar. Mamm., Miami, FL, Dec. 1987. 88 p.

Caldwell, D.K., J.H. Prescott and M.C. Caldwell. 1966. Production of pulsed sounds by the pigmy sperm whale, *Kogia breviceps. Bull. S. Calif. Acad. Sci.* 65(4):245-248.

Caldwell, D.K., M.C. Caldwell and J.F. Miller. 1969. Three brief narrow-band sound emissions by a captive male Risso's dolphin, *Grampus griseus.* Los Angeles County Mus. Nat. Hist. Found. Tech Rep. 5. 6 p. NTIS AD-693157.

Caldwell, M.C. and D.K. Caldwell. 1965. Individualized whistle contours in bottlenosed dolphins (*Tursiops truncatus*). *Nature (London)* 207(4995):434-435.

Caldwell, M.C. and D.K. Caldwell. 1968. Vocalization of naive captive dolphins in small groups. *Science* 159(3819):1121-1123.

Caldwell, M.C. and D.K. Caldwell. 1969. Simultaneous but different narrow-band sound emissions by a captive eastern Pacific pilot whale, *Globicephala scammoni. Mammalia* 33:505-508 + plates.

Caldwell, M.C. and D.K. Caldwell. 1970. Further studies on audible vocalizations of the Amazon freshwater dolphin, *Inia geoffrensis. Los Angeles County Mus. Contrib. Sci.* 187:1-5.

Caldwell, M.C. and D.K. Caldwell. 1971. Statistical evidence for individual signature whistles in Pacific whitesided dolphins, *Lagenorhynchus obliquidens. Cetology* 3:1-9.

Caldwell, M.C. and D.K. Caldwell. 1972. Vocal mimicry in the whistle mode by an Atlantic bottlenosed dolphin. *Cetology* 9:1-8.

Caldwell, M.C., D.K. Caldwell and W.E. Evans. 1966. Sounds and behavior of captive Amazon freshwater dolphins, *Inia geoffrensis. Los Angeles County Mus. Contrib. Sci.* 108:1-24.

Caldwell, M.C., N.R. Hall and D.K. Caldwell. 1971. Ability of an Atlantic bottlenosed dolphin to discriminate between, and potentially identify to individual, the whistles of another species, the spotted dolphin. *Cetology* 6:1-6.

Caldwell, M.C., D.K. Caldwell and N.R. Hall. 1973a. Ability of an Atlantic bottlenosed dolphin (*Tursiops truncatus*) to discriminate between, and potentially identify to individual, the whistles of another species, the common dolphin (*Delphinus delphis*). *Cetology* 14:1-7.

Caldwell, M.C., D.K. Caldwell and J.F. Miller. 1973b. Statistical evidence for individual signature whistles in the spotted dolphin, *Stenella plagiodon. Cetology* 16:1-21.

Caldwell, M.C., D.K. Caldwell and P.L. Tyack. 1990. Review of the signature-whistle hypothesis for the Atlantic bottlenose dolphin. p. 199-234 *In:* S. Leatherwood and R.R. Reeves (eds.), The bottlenose dolphin. Academic Press, San Diego, CA. 653 p.

Calef, G.W., E.A. DeBock and G.M. Lortie. 1976. The reaction of barren-ground caribou to aircraft. *Arctic* 29(4):201-212.

Calkins, D.G. 1979 [publ. 1983]. Marine mammals of Lower Cook Inlet and the potential for impact from outer continental shelf oil and gas exploration, development, and transport. Environ. Assess. Alaskan Cont. Shelf, Final Rep. Princ. Invest., NOAA, Juneau, AK 20:171-263. 650 p. NTIS PB85-201226.

Calkins, D. and P.C. Lent. 1975. Territoriality and mating behavior in Prince William Sound sea otters. *J. Mammal.* 56(2):528-529.

Calvert, W. and I. Stirling. 1985. Winter distribution of ringed seals (*Phoca hispida*) in the Barrow Strait area, Northwest Territories, determined by underwater vocalizations. *Can. J. Fish. Aquat. Sci.* 42(7):1238-1243.

Cameron, A.W. 1967. Breeding behavior in a colony of western Atlantic gray seals. *Can. J. Zool.* 45(2):161-173.

Cameron, R.D., K.R. Whitten, W.T. Smith and D.D. Roby. 1979. Caribou distribution and group composition associated with construction of the Trans-Alaska pipeline. *Can. Field-Nat.* 93(2):155-162.

Cameron, R.D., E.A. Lenart, D.J. Reed, K.R. Whitten and W.T. Smith. 1995. Abundance and movements of caribou in the oilfield complex near Prudhoe Bay, Alaska. *Rangifer* 15(1):3-7.

Carder, D.A. and S.H. Ridgway. 1990. Auditory brainstem response in a neonatal sperm whale, Physeter spp. J. Acoust. Soc. Am. 88(Suppl. 1):S4.

Carder, D.A. and S.H. Ridgway. 1994. A portable system for physiological assessment of hearing in marine animals. *J. Acoust. Soc. Am.* 96(5, Pt. 2):3316.

Caron, L.M.J. and D.E. Sergeant. 1988. Yearly variation in the frequency of passage of beluga whales (*Delphinapterus leucas*) at the mouth of the Saguenay River, Québec, over the past decade. *Naturaliste Can.* 115(2):111-116.

Caron, L.M.J. and T.G. Smith. 1990. Philopatry and site tenacity of belugas, *Delphinapterus leucas*, hunted by the Inuit at the Nastapoka Estuary, eastern Hudson Bay. *Can. Bull. Fish. Aquat. Sci.* 224:69-79.

Carroll, G.M. and J.R. Smithhisler. 1980. Observations of bowhead whales during spring migration. *Mar. Fish. Rev.* 42(9-10):80-85.

Cassano, E.R., A.C. Myrick, Jr., C.B. Glick, R.C. Holland and C.E. Lennert. 1990. The use of seal bombs on dolphin in the yellowfin tuna purse-seine fishery. Admin. Rep. LJ-90-09. U.S. Natl. Mar. Fish. Serv., La Jolla, CA. 31 p.

Cassirer, E.F., D.J. Freddy and E.D. Ables. 1992. Elk responses to disturbance by cross-country skiers in Yellowstone National Park. *Wildl. Soc. Bull.* 20(4):375-381.

Cato, D.H. 1991. Songs of humpback whales: The Australian perspective. *Mem. Queensl. Mus.* 30(2):277-290.

Cato, D.H. 1992. The biological contribution to the ambient noise in waters near Australia. *Acoust. Austral.* 20(3):76-80.

Cawthorn, M.W. 1992. New Zealand. Progress report on cetacean research, April 1990 to April 1991. *Rep. Int. Whal. Comm.* 42:357-360.

CeTAP. 1982. Characterization of marine mammals and turtles in the Mid- and North Atlantic areas of the U.S. Outer Continental Shelf. Rep. from Grad. School of Oceanogr., Univ. Rhode Island, Kingston, RI, for U.S. Bur. Land Manage., Washington, DC. 570 p. NTIS PB83-215855.

Chapman, D.M.F. and P.D. Ward. 1990. The normal-mode theory of air-to-water sound transmission in the ocean. *J. Acoust. Soc. Am.* 87(2):601-618.

Chappell, M.A. 1980. Possible physiological effects of space shuttle sonic booms on marine mammals. p. 195-228 *In*: J.R. Jehl, Jr., and C.F. Cooper (eds.), Potential effects of space shuttle sonic booms on the biota and geology of the

California Channel Islands: Research reports. Tech. Rep. 80-1. Rep. from Cent. Mar. Stud., San Diego State Univ., and Hubbs/Sea World Res. Inst., San Diego, CA, for U.S. Air Force, Space Div. 246 p.

Chittleborough, R.G. 1956. Southern right whale in Australian waters. *J. Mammal.* 37(3):456-457.

Clack, T.D. 1966. Effect of signal duration on the auditory sensitivity of humans and monkeys (*Macaca mulatta*). *J. Acoust. Soc. Am.* 40(5):1140-1146.

Clapham, P.J. and D.K. Mattila. 1993. Reactions of humpback whales to skin biopsy sampling on a West Indies breeding ground. *Mar. Mamm. Sci.* 9(4): 382-391.

Clapham, P.J., L.S. Baraff, C.A. Carlson, M.A. Christian, D.K. Mattila, C.A. Mayo, M.A. Murphy and S. Pittman. 1993. Seasonal occurrence and annual return of humpback whales, *Megaptera novaeangliae*, in the southern Gulf of Maine. *Can. J. Zool.* 71(2):440-443.

Clark, C.W. 1980. A real-time direction finding device for determining the bearing to the underwater sounds of southern right whales, *Eubalaena australis*. *J. Acoust. Soc. Am.* 68(2):508-511.

Clark, C.W. 1982. The acoustic repertoire of the southern right whale, a quantitative analysis. *Anim. Behav.* 30(4):1060-1071.

Clark, C.W. 1983. Acoustic communication and behavior of the southern right whale (*Eubalaena australis*). p. 163-198 *In*: R. Payne (ed.), Communication and behavior of whales. AAAS Sel. Symp. 76. Westview Press, Boulder, CO. 643 p.

Clark, C.W. and J.M. Clark. 1980. Sound playback experiments with southern right whales (*Eubalaena australis*). *Science* 207:663-665.

Clark, C.W. and W.T. Ellison. 1988. Numbers and distributions of bowhead whales, *Balaena mysticetus*, based on the 1985 acoustic study off Pt. Barrow, Alaska. *Rep. Int. Whal. Comm.* 38:365-370.

Clark, C.W. and J.H. Johnson. 1984. The sounds of the bowhead whale, *Balaena mysticetus*, during the spring migrations of 1979 and 1980. *Can. J. Zool.* 62 (7):1436-1441.

Clark, C.W., W.T. Ellison and K. Beeman. 1986. An acoustic study of bowhead whales *Balaena mysticetus*, off Point Barrow, Alaska during the 1984 spring migration. Rep. from Marine Acoustics, Clinton, MA, for North Slope Borough Dep. Wildl. Manage., Barrow, AK. 145 p.

Clark, C.W., C.J. Gagnon and D.K. Mellinger. 1993. Whales '93: The application of the Navy IUSS for low-frequency marine mammal research. p. 3 *In*: Abstr. 10th Bienn. Conf. Biol. Mar. Mamm., Galveston, TX, Nov. 1993. 130 p.

Clarke, J.T., S.E. Moore and D.K. Ljungblad. 1989. Observations on gray whale (*Eschrichtius robustus*) utilization patterns in the northeastern Chukchi Sea, July-October 1982-1987. *Can. J. Zool.* 67(11):2646-2654.

Clarke, R. 1956. Marking whales from a helicopter. *Norsk Hvalfangst-Tid.* 45(6): 311-318.

Cleator, H., I. Stirling and T.G. Smith. 1987. Geographical variation in the repertoire of the bearded seal. p. 11 *In*: Abstr. 7th Bienn. Conf. Biol. Mar. Mamm., Miami, FL, Dec. 1987. 88 p.

Cleator, H.J., I. Stirling and T.G. Smith. 1989. Underwater vocalizations of the bearded seal (*Erignathus barbatus*). *Can. J. Zool.* 67(8):1900-1910.

Cohen, J. 1991. Was underwater "shot" harmful to the whales? *Science* 252 (5008):912-914.

Connor, R.C. and R.S. Smolker. 1985. Habituated dolphins (*Tursiops* sp.) in Western Australia. *J. Mammal.* 66(2):398-400.

Cook, J.C., T. Goforth and R.K. Cook. 1972. Seismic and underwater responses to sonic boom. *J. Acoust. Soc. Am.* 51(2, Pt. 3):729-741.

Corkeron, P.J., M.M. Bryden and K.E. Hedstrom. 1990. Feeding by bottlenose dolphins in association with trawling operations in Moreton Bay, Australia. p. 329-336 *In*: S. Leatherwood and R.R. Reeves (eds.), The bottlenose dolphin. Academic Press, San Diego, CA. 653 p.

Cosens, S.E. and L.P. Dueck. 1988. Responses of migrating narwhal and beluga to icebreaker traffic at the Admiralty Inlet ice-edge, N.W.T. in 1986. p. 39-54 *In*: W.M. Sackinger et al. (eds.), Port and ocean engineering under arctic conditions, vol. II. Geophys. Inst., Univ. Alaska, Fairbanks. 111 p.

Cosens, S.E. and L.P. Dueck. 1993. Icebreaker noise in Lancaster Sound, N.W.T., Canada: Implications for marine mammal behavior. *Mar. Mamm. Sci.* 9(3): 285-300.

Costa, D.P. 1993. The secret life of marine mammals/Novel tools for studying their behavior and biology at sea. *Oceanography* 6(3):120-128.

Cottereau, P. 1978. Effect of sonic boom from aircraft on wildlife and animal husbandry. p. 63-79 *In*: J.L. Fletcher and R.G. Busnel (eds.), Effects of noise on wildlife. Academic Press, New York. 305 p.

Cowles, C.J., D.J. Hansen and J.D. Hubbard. 1981. Types of potential effects of offshore oil and gas development on marine mammals and endangered species of the northern Bering, Chukchi, and Beaufort Seas. Tech. Pap. 9, Alaska Outer Cont. Shelf Off., U.S. Bureau of Land Management, Anchorage, AK. 23 p. NTIS PB83-146142.

Crovetto, A. and G. Medina. 1991. Comportement du dauphin chilien (*Cephalorhynchus eutropia* Gray, 1846) dans les eaux du sud du Chili. *Mammalia* 55 (3):329-338.

Crum, L.A. and Yi Mao. 1994. Acoustically enhanced bubble growth at low frequencies and its implications for human diver and marine mammal safety. *J. Acoust. Soc. Am.* 96(5, Pt. 2):3252.

Cummings, W.C. 1993. Sonic booms and marine mammals: Informational status and recommendations. Rep. from Oceanographic Consultants, San Diego, CA, for NASA Langley Res. Cent., Hampton, VA. 64 p. NTIS N94-28198.

Cummings, W.C. and J.F. Fish. 1971. A synopsis of marine animal underwater sounds in eight geographic areas. U.S. Naval Undersea Res. & Dev. Cent. 97 p. NTIS AD-A068875.

Cummings, W.C. and D.V. Holliday. 1983. Preliminary measurements of sound attenuation by snow over a model seal lair. *J. Acoust. Soc. Am.* 74(Suppl. 1): S55.

Cummings, W.C. and D.V. Holliday. 1985. Passive acoustic location of bowhead whales in a population census off Point Barrow, Alaska. *J. Acoust. Soc. Am.* 78(4):1163-1169.

Cummings, W.C. and D.V. Holliday. 1987. Sounds and source levels from bowhead whales off Pt. Barrow, Alaska. *J. Acoust. Soc. Am.* 82(3):814-821.

Cummings, W.C. and P.O. Thompson. 1971a. Underwater sounds from the blue whale, *Balaenoptera musculus. J. Acoust. Soc. Am.* 50(4, Pt. 2):1193-1198.

Cummings, W.C. and P.O. Thompson. 1971b. Gray whales, *Eschrichtius robustus*, avoid the underwater sounds of killer whales, *Orcinus orca. Fish. Bull.* 69(3): 525-530.

Cummings, W.C. and P.O. Thompson. 1994. Characteristics and seasons of blue and finback whale sounds along the U.S. west coast as recorded at SOSUS stations. *J. Acoust. Soc. Am.* 95(5, Pt. 2):2853.

Cummings, W.C., P.O. Thompson and R. Cook. 1968. Underwater sounds of migrating gray whales, *Eschrichtius glaucus* (Cope). *J. Acoust. Soc. Am.* 44 (5):1278-1281.

Cummings, W.C., J.F. Fish and P.O. Thompson. 1972. Sound production and other behavior of southern right whales, *Eubalena* [sic] *glacialis. Trans. San Diego Soc. Nat. Hist.* 17(1):1-13.

Cummings, W.C., P.O. Thompson and J.F. Fish. 1974. Behavior of southern right whales: R/V *Hero* cruise 72-3. *Antarct. J. U.S.* 9(2):33-38.

Cummings, W.C., J.M. Holzmann and P.O. Thompson. 1975. Underwater sound pressure minima in bioacoustic test tanks. Rep. NUC TP 450. U.S. Naval Undersea Cent., San Diego, CA. 40 p. NTIS AD-A032768.

Cummings, W.C., D.V. Holliday, B.J. Graham and W.T. Ellison. 1981a. Underwater sound measurements from the Prudhoe region, Alaska, September-October 1980. T-81-SD-013-U. Rep. from Tracor Appl. Sci., San Diego, CA, for the Alaska Eskimo Whal. Comm., Barrow, AK. 104 p.

Cummings, W.C., D.V. Holliday and B.J. Graham. 1981b [publ. 1983]. Measurements and localization of underwater sounds from the Prudhoe region, Alaska, March, 1981. Environ. Assess. Alaskan Cont. Shelf, Final Rep. Princ. Invest., NOAA, Juneau, AK 19:393-444. 565 p. NTIS PB85-200939.

Cummings, W.C., D.V. Holliday, W.T. Ellison and B.J. Graham. 1983. Technical feasibility of passive acoustic location of bowhead whales in population studies off Point Barrow, Alaska. T-83-06-002. Rep. from Tracor Appl. Sci., San Diego, CA, for North Slope Borough, Barrow, AK. 169 p.

Cummings, W.C., D.V. Holliday and B.J. Lee. 1984 [publ. 1986]. Potential impacts of man-made noise on ringed seals: Vocalizations and reactions. Outer Cont. Shelf Environ. Assess. Program, Final Rep. Princ. Invest., NOAA, Anchorage, AK 37:95-230. 693 p. OCS Study MMS 86-0021; NTIS PB87-107546.

Cummings, W.C., P.O. Thompson and S.J. Ha. 1986. Sounds from Bryde, *Balaenoptera edeni*, and finback, *B. physalus*, whales in the Gulf of California. *Fish. Bull.* 84(2):359-370.

Curtin, K. and S.L. Tyson. 1993. Potential impacts of eco-tourism on manatees in Florida. p. 39 *In*: Abstr. 10th Bienn. Conf. Biol. Mar. Mamm., Galveston, TX, Nov. 1993. 130 p.

Cybulski, J. 1977. Probable origin of measured supertanker radiated noise spectra. p. 15C-1 to 15C-8 *In*: Oceans '77 Conference Record, Inst. Electr. Electron. Eng., New York. Var. pag.

Czech, B. 1991. Elk behavior in response to human disturbance at Mount St. Helens National Volcanic Monument. *Appl. Anim. Behav. Sci.* 29(1-4):269-277.

Dahlheim, M.E. 1981. Comments on bowhead acoustics. p. 64 *In*: San Diego workshop on the interaction between man-made noise and vibration and arctic marine wildlife, Feb. 1980. Rep. from Acoust. Soc. Am., Washington, DC, for Alaska Eskimo Whaling Comm., Barrow, AK. 84 p.

Dahlheim, M.E. 1987. Bio-acoustics of the gray whale (*Eschrichtius robustus*). Ph.D. Thesis, Univ. British Columbia, Vancouver, B.C. 315 p.

Dahlheim, M.E. and D.K. Ljungblad. 1990. Preliminary hearing study on gray whales (*Eschrichtius robustus*) in the field. p. 335-346 *In*: J.A. Thomas and R.A. Kastelein (eds.), Sensory abilities of cetaceans/Laboratory and field evidence. Plenum, New York. 710 p.

Dahlheim, M.E., J.D. Schempp, S.L. Swartz and M.L. Jones. 1981. Attraction of gray whales, *Eschrichtius robustus*, to underwater outboard engine noise in Laguna San Ignacio, Baja California Sur, Mexico. *J. Acoust. Soc. Am.* 70(Suppl. 1):S83-S84.

Dahlheim, M.E., H.D. Fisher and J.D. Schempp. 1984. Sound production by the gray whale and ambient noise levels in Laguna San Ignacio, Baja California Sur, Mexico. p. 511-541 *In*: M.L. Jones, S.L. Swartz and S. Leatherwood (eds.), The gray whale *Eschrichtius robustus*. Academic Press, Orlando, FL. 600 p.

Dalle-Molle, J. and J. Van Horn. 1991. Observations of vehicle traffic interfering with migration of Dall's sheep, *Ovis dalli dalli*, in Denali National Park, Alaska. *Can. Field-Nat.* 105(3):409-411.

Davis, L.I. 1964. Biological acoustics and the use of the sound spectrograph. *Southwest. Nat.* 9(3):118-145.

Davis, R.A., C.R. Greene and P.L. McLaren. 1985. Studies of the potential for drilling activities on Seal Island to influence fall migration of bowhead whales through Alaskan nearshore waters. Rep. from LGL Ltd., King City, Ont., for Shell Western E&P Inc., Anchorage, AK. 70 p.

Davis, R.W., F.W. Awbrey and T.M. Williams. 1987. Using sounds to control the movements of sea otters. *J. Acoust. Soc. Am.* 82(Suppl. 1):S99.

Dawbin, W.H. and D.H. Cato. 1992. Sounds of a pygmy right whale (*Caperea marginata*). *Mar. Mamm. Sci.* 8(3):213-219.

Dawson, S.M. 1988. The high frequency sounds of free-ranging Hector's dolphins, *Cephalorhynchus hectori*. *Rep. Int. Whal. Comm. (Spec. Issue)* 9:339-344.

Dawson, S.M. 1991. Clicks and communication: The behavioural and social contexts of Hector's dolphin vocalizations. *Ethology* 88(4):265-276.

Dawson, S.M. 1994. The potential for reducing entanglement of dolphins and porpoises with acoustic modifications to gillnets. *Rep. Int. Whal. Comm. (Spec. Issue)* 15:573-578.

Dawson, S.M. and C.W. Thorpe. 1990. A quantitative analysis of the sounds of Hector's dolphin. *Ethology* 86(2):131-145.

Dean, F.C., C.M. Jurasz, V.P. Palmer, C.H. Curby and D.L. Thomas. 1985. Analysis of humpback whale (*Megaptera novaeangliae*) blow interval data/Glacier Bay, Alaska, 1976-1979. Rep. from Univ. Alaska, Fairbanks, for U.S. Natl. Park Serv., Anchorage, AK. 224 p. (vol. 1) + diagrams (vol. 2).

Defran, R.H. and K. Pryor. 1980. The behavior and training of cetaceans in captivity. p. 319-362 *In*: L.M. Herman (ed.), Cetacean behavior: Mechanisms and functions. Wiley, New York. 463 p.

Degerbøl, M. and P. Freuchen. 1935. Mammals. Rep. 5th Thule Exped. 1921-24, vol. 2(4-5). Gyldendalske Boghandel, Nordisk Forlag, Copenhagen. 278 p.

de Heering, P. and B.F. White. 1984. Under ice measurements of the noise produced by a helicopter and a tracked vehicle. *J. Acoust. Soc. Am.* 75(3):1005-1007.

Diercks, K.J., R.T. Trochta, C.F. Greenlaw and W.E. Evans. 1971. Recording and analysis of dolphin echolocation signals. *J. Acoust. Soc. Am.* 49(6, Pt. 1): 1729-1732.

Diercks, K.J., R.T. Trochta and W.E. Evans. 1973. Delphinid sonar: Measurement and analysis. *J. Acoust. Soc. Am.* 54(1):200-204.

Ding Wang, Kexiong Wang, Youfu Xiao and Gang Sheng. 1992. Auditory sensitivity of a Chinese river dolphin, *Lipotes vexillifer*. p. 213-221 *In*: J.A. Thomas, R.A. Kastelein and A.Ya. Supin (eds.), Marine mammal sensory systems. Plenum, New York. 773 p.

Dohl, T.P. and R. Guess. 1979. Evidence for increasing offshore migration of the California gray whale, *Eschrichtius robustus* in southern California, 1975 through 1978. p. 13 *In*: Abstr. 3rd Bienn. Conf. Biol. Mar. Mamm., Seattle, WA, Oct. 1979. 64 p.

Dohl, T.P., R.C. Guess, M.L. Duman and R.C. Helm. 1983. Cetaceans of central and northern California, 1980-1983: Status, abundance, and distribution. Rep. from Cent. Coastal Mar. Stud., Univ. Calif., Santa Cruz, for U.S. Minerals Manage. Serv., Los Angeles, CA. 284 p. NTIS PB85-183861.

Dolphin, W.F. 1987. Ventilation and dive patterns of humpback whales, *Megaptera novaeangliae*, on their Alaskan feeding grounds. *Can. J. Zool.* 65(1): 83-90.

Dolphin, W.F. 1995. Steady-state auditory-evoked potentials in three cetacean species elicited using amplitude-modulated stimuli. *In*: R.A. Kastelein, J.A. Thomas and P.E. Nachtigall (eds.), Sensory systems of aquatic mammals. De Spil Publ., Woerden, Netherlands. (in press).

Domning, D.P. 1991. A former dolphin-human fishing cooperative in Australia. *Mar. Mamm. Sci.* 7(1):94-96.

Donnelly, B.G. 1969. Further observations on the southern right whale, *Eubalaena australis*, in South African waters. *J. Reprod. Fertil.*(Suppl. 6):347-352.

Dorrance, M.J., P.J. Savage and D.E. Huff. 1975. Effects of snowmobiles on white-tailed deer. *J. Wildl. Manage.* 39(3):563-569.

Dorsey, E.M. 1983. Exclusive adjoining ranges in individually identified minke whales (*Balaenoptera acutorostrata*) in Washington state. *Can. J. Zool.* 61(1): 174-181.

Dreher, J.J. and W.E. Evans. 1964. Cetacean communication. p. 373-393 *In*: W.N. Tavolga (ed.), Marine bio-acoustics. Pergamon, Oxford, U.K. 413 p.

D'Spain, G.L., W.S. Hodgkiss and G.L. Edmonds. 1991. The simultaneous measurement of infrasonic acoustic particle velocity and acoustic pressure in the ocean by freely drifting Swallow floats. *IEEE J. Oceanic Eng.* 16(2):195-207.

Dubrovskiy, N.A. 1990. On the two auditory subsystems in dolphins. p. 233-254 *In*: J.A. Thomas and R.A. Kastelein (eds.), Sensory abilities of cetaceans/ Laboratory and field evidence. Plenum, New York. 710 p.

Dudok van Heel, W.H. 1959. Audio-direction finding in the porpoise (*Phocaena phocaena*). *Nature (London)* 183(4667):1063.

Dudok van Heel, W.H. 1962. Sound and cetacea. *Neth. J. Sea Res.* 1(4):407-507.

Duffus, D.A. and P. Dearden. 1993. Recreational use, valuation, and management, of killer whales (*Orcinus orca*) on Canada's Pacific coast. *Environ. Conserv.* 20(2):149-156.

Dufour, P.A. 1980. Effects of noise on wildlife and other animals/Review of research since 1971. Rep. from Informatics Inc., Rockville, MD, for U.S. Environ. Prot. Agency, Washington, DC. 97 p. NTIS PB82-139973.

Duncan, P.M. 1985. Seismic sources in a marine environment. p. 56-88 *In*: Proc. Workshop on Effects of Explosives Use in the Marine Environment, Jan. 1985, Halifax, N.S. Tech. Rep. 5. Can. Oil & Gas Lands Admin. Environ. Prot. Branch, Ottawa, Ont. 398 p.

Duncan, R.C., C.E. Easterly, J. Griffith and T.E. Aldrich. 1993. The effect of chronic environmental noise on the rate of hypertension: A meta-analysis. *Environ. Int.* 19(4):359-369.

Dunn, J.L. 1969. Airborne measurements of the acoustic characteristics of a sperm whale. *J. Acoust. Soc. Am.* 46(4):1052-1054.

Duval, W.S. (ed.). 1986. Distribution, abundance, and age segregation of bowhead whales in the southeast Beaufort Sea, August - September 1985. Rep. 057. Environ. Stud. Revolv. Funds, Can. Oil & Gas Lands Admin., Ottawa, Ont. 117 p.

Duykers, L.R.B. and J.L. Percy. 1978. Lung resonance characteristics of submerged mammals. *J. Acoust. Soc. Am.* 64(Suppl. 1):S97.

Dziedzic, A. and V. De Buffrenil. 1989. Acoustic signals of the Commerson's dolphin, *Cephalorhynchus commersonii*, in the Kerguelen Islands. *J. Mammal.* 70(2):449-452.

Eberhardt, L.L., D.G. Chapman and J.R. Gilbert. 1979. A review of marine mammal census methods. *Wildl. Monogr.* 63. 46 p.

Eckstein, R.G., T.F. O'Brien, O.J. Rongstad and J.G. Bollinger. 1979. Snowmobile effects on movements of white-tailed deer: A case-study. *Environ. Conserv.* 6(1):45-51.

Edds, P.L. 1982. Vocalizations of the blue whale, *Balaenoptera musculus*, in the St. Lawrence River. *J. Mammal.* 63(2):345-347.

Edds, P.L. 1988. Characteristics of finback *Balaenoptera physalus* vocalizations in the St. Lawrence Estuary. *Bioacoustics* 1(2/3):131-149.

Edds, P.L. and J.A.F. Macfarlane. 1987. Occurrence and general behavior of balaenopterid cetaceans summering in the St. Lawrence Estuary, Canada. *Can. J. Zool.* 65(6):1363-1376.

Edds, P.L., D.K. Odell and B.R. Tershy. 1993. Vocalizations of a captive juvenile and free-ranging adult-calf pairs of Bryde's whales, *Balaenoptera edeni*. *Mar. Mamm. Sci.* 9(3):269-284.

Edge, W.D. and C.L. Marcum. 1985. Movements of elk in relation to logging disturbances. *J. Wildl. Manage.* 49(4):926-930.

Ellison, W.T. and K.S. Weixel. 1994. Considerations for designing underwater acoustical playback experiments. *J. Acoust. Soc. Am.* 96(5, Pt. 2):3316-3317.

Ellison, W.T., C.W. Clark and G.C. Bishop. 1987. Potential use of surface reverberation by bowhead whales, *Balaena mysticetus*, in under-ice navigation: Preliminary considerations. *Rep. Int. Whal. Comm.* 37:329-332.

Embleton, T.F.W., J.E. Piercy and N. Olson. 1976. Outdoor sound propagation over ground of finite impedance. *J. Acoust. Soc. Am.* 59(2):267-277.

Espmark, Y. 1972. Behaviour reactions of reindeer exposed to sonic booms. *Brit. Deer Soc. J.* 2(7):800-802.

Espmark, Y. and R. Langvatn. 1985. Development and habituation of cardiac and behavioral responses in young red deer calves (*Cervus elaphus*) exposed to alarm stimuli. *J. Mammal.* 66(4):702-711.

Evans, P.G.H. 1987. The natural history of whales & dolphins. Facts on File, New York. 343 p.

Evans, W.E. 1973. Echolocation by marine delphinids and one species of freshwater dolphin. *J. Acoust. Soc. Am.* 54(1):191-199.

Evans, W.E. and F.T. Awbrey. 1984. High frequency pulses of Commerson's dolphin and Dall's porpoise. *Am. Zool.* 24(3):2A.

Evans, W.E. and J.J. Dreher. 1962. Observations on scouting behavior and associated sound production by the Pacific bottlenosed porpoise (*Tursiops gilli* Dall). *Bull. S. Calif. Acad. Sci.* 61(4):217-226.

Evans, W.E and R.M. Haugen. 1963. An experimental study of the echolocation ability of a California sea lion, *Zalophus californianus* (Lesson). *Bull. S. Calif. Acad. Sci.* 62(4):165-175.

Evans, W.E. and E.S. Herald. 1970. Underwater calls of a captive Amazon manatee, *Trichechus inunguis*. *J. Mammal.* 51(4):820-823.

Evans, W.E., F.T. Awbrey and H. Hackbarth. 1988. High frequency pulses produced by free-ranging Commerson's dolphin (*Cephalorhynchus commersonii*) compared to those of phocoenids. *Rep. Int. Whal. Comm. (Spec. Issue)* 9:173-181.

Everest, F.A., R.W. Young and M.W. Johnson. 1948. Acoustical characteristics of noise produced by snapping shrimp. *J. Acoust. Soc. Am.* 20(2):137-142.

Fairfield, C.P. 1990. Comparison of abundance estimation techniques for the western North Atlantic right whale (*Eubalaena glacialis*). *Rep. Int. Whal. Comm. (Spec. Issue)* 12:119-126.

Fay, F.H. 1981. Modern populations, migrations, demography, trophics, and historical status of the Pacific walrus. Environ. Assess. Alaskan Cont. Shelf, Annu. Rep. Princ. Invest., NOAA, Boulder, CO, 1981(I):191-234. 620 p.

Fay, F.H. and B.P. Kelly. 1982. Herd composition and response to disturbance of walruses in the Chukchi Sea. Cruise report, K/S ENTUZIAST, 25 July-23 August 1982. NOAA-OCSEAP/R.U. 611. Outer Cont. Shelf Environ. Assess. Program, NOAA, Juneau, AK. 13 p.

Fay, F.H., B.P. Kelly, P.H. Gehnrich, J.L. Sease and A.A. Hoover. 1984 [publ. 1986]. Modern populations, migrations, demography, trophics, and historical status of the Pacific walrus. Outer Cont. Shelf Environ. Assess. Program, Final Rep. Princ. Invest., NOAA, Anchorage, AK 37:231-376. 693 p. OCS Study MMS 86-0021; NTIS PB87-107546.

Fay, R.R. 1988. Hearing in vertebrates: A psychophysics databook. Hill-Fay Associates, Winnetka, IL. 621 p.

Feinstein, S.H. 1966. Human hearing under water: Are things as bad as they seem? *J. Acoust. Soc. Am.* 40(6):1561-1562.

Fertl, D. 1994. Occurrence patterns and behavior of bottlenose dolphins (*Tursiops truncatus*) in the Galveston Ship Channel, Texas. *Texas J. Sci.* 46(4):299-317.

Fidell, S., K.S. Pearsons, M. Grignetti and D.M. Green. 1970. The noisiness of impulsive sounds. *J. Acoust. Soc. Am.* 48(6, Pt. 1):1304-1310.

Finley, K.J. 1982. The estuarine habit of the beluga or white whale *Delphinapterus leucas*. *Cetus* 4(2):4-5

Finley, K.J., G.W. Miller, M. Allard, R.A. Davis and C.R. Evans. 1982. The belugas (*Delphinapterus leucas*) of northern Quebec: Distribution, abundance, stock identity, catch history and management. *Can. Tech. Rep. Fish. Aquat. Sci.* 1123. 57 p.

Finley, K.J., G.W. Miller, R.A. Davis and C.R. Greene. 1990. Reactions of belugas, *Delphinapterus leucas*, and narwhals, *Monodon monoceros*, to ice-breaking ships in the Canadian high arctic. *Can. Bull. Fish. Aquat. Sci.* 224:97-117.

Fischer, M.S. 1988. Zur Anatomie des Gehörorganes der Seekuh (*Trichechus manatus* L.), (Mammalia: Sirenia). *Z. Säugetierk.* 53(6):365-379.

Fish, J.F. and C.W. Turl. 1976. Acoustic source levels of four species of small whales. NUC TP 547. U.S. Naval Undersea Cent., San Diego, CA. 14 p. NTIS AD-A037620.

Fish, J.F. and J.S. Vania. 1971. Killer whale, *Orcinus orca*, sounds repel white whales, *Delphinapterus leucas*. *Fish. Bull.* 69(3):531-535.

Fish, J.F., J.L. Sumich and G.L. Lingle. 1974. Sounds produced by the gray whale, *Eschrichtius robustus*. *Mar. Fish. Rev.* 36(4):38-45.

Fitch, J.E. and P.H. Young. 1948. Use and effect of explosives in California coastal waters. *Calif. Fish & Game* 34(2):53-70.

Flaherty, C. 1981. Apparent effects of boat traffic on harbor porpoise (*Phocoena phocoena*). p. 35 *In*: Abstr. 4th Bienn. Conf. Biol. Mar. Mamm., San Francisco, CA, Dec. 1981. 127 p.

Fleischer, G. 1976. Hearing in extinct cetaceans as determined by cochlear structure. *J. Paleontol.* 50(1):133-152.

Fleischer, G. 1978. Evolutionary principles of the mammalian middle ear. *Adv. Anat. Embryol. Cell Biol.* 55(5):1-70.

Fleischer, G. 1980. Low-frequency receiver of the middle ear in mysticetes and odontocetes. p. 891-893 *In*: R.-G. Busnel and J.F. Fish (eds.), Animal sonar systems. Plenum, New York. 1135 p.

Fletcher, H. 1940. Auditory patterns. *Rev. Mod. Phys.* 12(1):47-65.

Fletcher, J.L. and R.G. Busnel. (eds.). 1978. Effects of noise on wildlife. Academic Press, New York. 305 p.

Fobes, J.L. and C.C. Smock. 1981. Sensory capacities of marine mammals. *Psychol. Bull.* 89(2):288-307.

Fogden, S.C.L. 1971. Mother-young behaviour at grey seal breeding beaches. *J. Zool.* 164(1):61-92

Ford, J. 1977. White whale-offshore exploration acoustic study. Rep. from F.F. Slaney & Co. Ltd., Vancouver, B.C., for Imperial Oil Ltd., Calgary, Alb. 26 p. + fig., tables.

Ford, J.K.B. 1989. Acoustic behaviour of resident killer whales (*Orcinus orca*) off Vancouver Island, British Columbia. *Can. J. Zool.* 67(3):727-745.

Ford, J.K.B. 1991. Vocal traditions among resident killer whales (*Orcinus orca*) in coastal waters of British Columbia. *Can. J. Zool.* 69(6):1454-1483.

Ford, J.K.B. and H.D. Fisher. 1978. Underwater acoustic signals of the narwhal (*Monodon monoceros*). *Can. J. Zool.* 56(4, Pt. 1):552-560.

Ford, J.K.B. and H.D. Fisher. 1982. Killer whale (*Orcinus orca*) dialects as an indicator of stocks in British Columbia. *Rep. Int. Whal. Comm.* 32:671-679.

Ford, J.K.B. and H.D. Fisher. 1983. Group-specific dialects of killer whales (*Orcinus orca*) in British Columbia. p. 129-161 *In*: R. Payne (ed.), Communication and behavior of whales. AAAS Sel. Symp. 76. Westview Press, Boulder, CO. 643 p.

Ford, J.K.B., J.C. Cubbage and P. Norton. 1987. Distribution, abundance, and age segregation of bowhead whales in the southeast Beaufort Sea, August-September 1986. Rep. 089. Environ. Stud. Res. Funds, Can. Oil & Gas Lands Admin., Ottawa, Ont. 93 p.

Forestell, P.H., E.K. Brown, L.M. Herman and J.R. Mobley, Jr. 1991. Near-shore distribution of humpback whales near Maui, Hawaii: 1976-1991. p. 23 *In*: Abstr. 9th Bienn. Conf. Biol. Mar. Mamm., Chicago, IL, Dec. 1991. 76 p.

Foster, B.R. and E.Y. Rahs. 1983. Mountain goat response to hydroelectric exploration in northwestern British Columbia. *Environ. Manage.* 7(2):189-197.

Fraker, M.A. 1977a. The 1976 white whale monitoring program, Mackenzie Estuary, N.W.T. Rep. from F.F. Slaney & Co. Ltd., Vancouver, B.C., for Imperial Oil Ltd., Calgary, Alb. 76 p. + maps, tables, append.

Fraker, M.A. 1977b. The 1977 whale monitoring program/Mackenzie Estuary, N.W.T. Rep. from F.F. Slaney & Co. Ltd., Vancouver, B.C., for Imperial Oil Ltd., Calgary, Alb. 53 p. + maps.

Fraker, M.A. 1978. The 1978 whale monitoring program/Mackenzie Estuary, N.W.T. Rep. from F.F. Slaney & Co. Ltd., Vancouver, B.C., for Esso Resources Canada Ltd., Calgary, Alb. 28 p. + maps, photos.

Fraker, M.A. 1980. Status and harvest of the Mackenzie stock of white whales (*Delphinapterus leucas*). *Rep. Int. Whal. Comm.* 30:451-458.

Fraker, M.A. and P.N. Fraker. 1979. The 1979 whale monitoring program/Mackenzie Estuary. Rep. from LGL Ltd., Sidney, B.C., for Esso Resources Canada Ltd., Edmonton, Alb. 51 p.

Fraker, P.N. and M.A. Fraker. 1981. The 1980 whale monitoring program, Mackenzie Estuary. Rep. from LGL Ltd., Sidney, B.C., for Esso Resources Canada Ltd., Calgary, Alb. 98 p.

Frankel, A.S., J.R. Mobley, Jr., and L.M. Herman. 1995. Estimation of auditory response thresholds in humpback whales using biologically meaningful sounds. *In*: R.A. Kastelein, J.A. Thomas and P.E. Nachtigall (eds.), Sensory systems of aquatic mammals. De Spil Publ., Woerden, Netherlands. (in press).

Freddy, D.J., W.M. Bronaugh and M.C. Fowler. 1986. Responses of mule deer to disturbance by persons afoot and snowmobiles. *Wildl. Soc. Bull.* 14(1):63-68.

Fricke, J.R., J.M. Davis and D.H. Reed. 1985. A standard quantitative calibration procedure for marine seismic sources. *Geophysics* 50(10):1525-1532.

Freitag, L.E. and P.L. Tyack. 1993. Passive acoustic localization of the Atlantic bottlenose dolphin using whistles and echolocation clicks. *J. Acoust. Soc. Am.* 93(4, Pt. 1):2197-2205.

Friedl, W.A. and P.O. Thompson. 1981. Measuring acoustic noise around Kahoolawe Island. NOSC TR 732. U.S. Naval Ocean Systems Cent., San Diego, CA. 15 p. NTIS AD-A109485.

Frisk, G.V. 1993. Ocean and seabed acoustics: A theory of wave propagation. P T R Prentice Hall, Englewood Cliffs, NJ. 313 p.

Frost, K.J. and L.F. Lowry. 1988. Effects of industrial activities on ringed seals in Alaska, as indicated by aerial surveys. p. 15-25 *In*: W.M. Sackinger et al. (eds.), Port and ocean engineering under arctic conditions, vol. II. Geophys. Inst., Univ. Alaska, Fairbanks. 111 p.

Frost, K.J. and L.F. Lowry. 1990. Use of Kasegaluk Lagoon by marine mammals. p. 93-100 *In*: Alaska OCS Reg. 3rd Info. Transfer Meet. Conf. Proc. OCS Study MMS 90-0041. Rep. from MBC Appl. Environ. Sci., Costa Mesa, CA, for U.S. Minerals Manage. Serv., Anchorage, AK. 233 p.

Frost, K.J. and L.F. Lowry. 1993. Assessment of damages to harbor seals caused by the *Exxon Valdez* oil spill. p. 300-302 *In*: *Exxon Valdez* oil spill symposium/Abstract book, Anchorage, AK, Feb. 1993. *Exxon Valdez* Oil Spill Trustee Counc., Univ. Alaska Sea Grant Coll. Program, and Am. Fish Soc. Alaska Chap., Anchorage, AK.

Frost, K.J., L.F. Lowry and J.J. Burns. 1982 [publ. 1983]. Distribution of marine mammals in the coastal zone of the Bering Sea during summer and autumn.

Environ. Assess. Alaskan Cont. Shelf, Final Rep. Princ. Invest., NOAA, Juneau, AK 20:365-561. 650 p. NTIS PB85-201226.

Frost, K.J., L.F. Lowry and R.R. Nelson. 1984. Belukha whale studies in Bristol Bay, Alaska. p. 187-200 *In*: B.R. Melteff and D.H. Rosenberg (eds.), Proc. workshop on biological interactions among marine mammals and commercial fisheries in the southeastern Bering Sea, Oct. 1983, Anchorage, AK. Univ. Alaska Sea Grant Rep. 84-1. Univ. Alaska, Fairbanks.

Frost, K.J., L.F. Lowry, J.R. Gilbert and J.J. Burns. 1988 [publ. 1989]. Ringed seal monitoring: Relationships of distribution and abundance to habitat attributes and industrial activities. Outer Cont. Shelf Environ. Assess. Program, Final Rep. Princ. Invest., NOAA, Anchorage, AK 61:345-445. 536 p. OCS Study MMS 89-0026; NTIS PB89-234645.

Frost, K.J., L.F. Lowry and G. Carroll. 1993. Beluga whale and spotted seal use of a coastal lagoon system in the northeastern Chukchi Sea. *Arctic* 46(1):8-16.

Fuller, R.G. and J.B. Kirkwood. 1977. Ecological consequences of nuclear testing. p. 627-649 *In*: M.L. Merritt and R.G. Fuller (eds.), The environment of Amchitka Island, Alaska. TID-26712. Energy Res. & Dev. Admin. NTIS, Springfield, VA. 682 p.

Gagnon, G.J. and C.W. Clark. 1993. The use of U.S. Navy IUSS passive sonar to monitor the movement of blue whales. p. 50 *In*: Abstr. 10th Bienn. Conf. Biol. Mar. Mamm., Galveston, TX, Nov. 1993. 130 p.

Gales, R.S. 1982. Effects of noise of offshore oil and gas operations on marine mammals—An introductory assessment. NOSC TR 844, 2 vol. U.S. Naval Ocean Systems Cent., San Diego, CA. 79 + 300 p. NTIS AD-A123699 + AD-A123700.

Gallagher, M.L., J.D. Hall and K.D. Brewer. 1992a. Amoco Production Company Galahad exploration prospect/Site specific monitoring plan/90 day report. Rep. from Coastal & Offshore Pacific Corp., Walnut Creek, CA [for Amoco Prod. Co., Anchorage, AK]. 26 p.

Gallagher, M.L., K.D. Brewer and J.D. Hall. 1992b. ARCO Alaska, Inc. Cabot prospect/Site specific monitoring plan/Final report. Rep. from Coastal & Offshore Pacific Corp., Walnut Creek, CA, for ARCO Alaska Inc. [Anchorage, AK]. 78 p. + append.

Gallardo, V.A., D. Arcos, M. Salamanca and L. Pastene. 1983. On the occurrence of Bryde's whales (*Balaenoptera edeni* Anderson, 1878) in an upwelling area off central Chile. *Rep. Int. Whal. Comm.* 33:481-488.

Gambell, R. 1968. Aerial observations of sperm whale behaviour. *Norsk Hvalfangst-Tid.* 57(6):126-138.

Garciarena, D. 1988. The effects of whalewatching on right whales in Argentina. *Whalewatcher, J. Am. Cetac. Soc.* 22(3):3-5.

Gard, R. 1974. Aerial census of gray whales in Baja California lagoons, 1970 and 1973, with notes on behavior, mortality and conservation. *Calif. Fish & Game* 60(3):132-143.

Gardner, D.L. (convener). 1994. Abstracts of invited and contributed papers/ Acoustical oceanography and underwater acoustics: Use of naval facilities for ocean acoustics research. *J. Acoust. Soc. Am.* 95(5, Pt. 2):2851-2854.

Garrott, R.A., L.L. Eberhardt and D.M. Burn. 1993. Mortality of sea otters in Prince William Sound following the *Exxon Valdez* oil spill. *Mar. Mamm. Sci.* 9(4):343-359.

Garshelis, D.L. and J.A. Garshelis. 1984. Movements and management of sea otters in Alaska. *J. Wildl. Manage.* 48(3):665-678.

Gaskin, D.E. 1964. Recent observations in New Zealand waters on some aspects of behaviour of the sperm whale (*Physeter macrocephalus*). *Tuatara* 12(2): 106-114.

Gaskin, D.E. 1991. An update on the status of the right whale, *Eubalaena glacialis*, in Canada. *Can. Field-Nat.* 105(2):198-205.

Gaspin, J.B. 1983. Safe swimmer ranges from bottom explosions. NSWC/WOL TR-83-84. Naval Surf. Weap. Cent., White Oak Lab., Silver Spring, MD. 51 p. Def. Tech. Info. Cent. AD-B086375.

Gaunt, A.S. 1983. On sonograms, harmonics, and assumptions. *Condor* 85(2): 259-261.

Gentry, R.L. 1967. Underwater auditory localization in the California sea lion (*Zalophus californianus*). *J. Aud. Res.* 7:187-193.

Gentry, R.L., E.C. Gentry and J.F. Gilman. 1990. Responses of northern fur seals to quarrying operations. *Mar. Mamm. Sci.* 6(2):151-155.

George, J.C., L.M. Philo, K. Hazard, D. Withrow, G.M. Carroll and R. Suydam. 1994. Frequency of killer whale (*Orcinus orca*) attacks and ship collisions based on scarring on bowhead whales (*Balaena mysticetus*) of the Bering-Chukchi-Beaufort seas stock. *Arctic* 47(3):247-255.

Gerrodette, T. and W.G. Gilmartin. 1990. Demographic consequences of changed pupping and hauling sites of the Hawaiian monk seal. *Conserv. Biol.* 4(4): 423-430.

Gerstein, E.R., L.A. Gerstein, S.E. Forsythe and J.E. Blue. 1993. Underwater audiogram of a West Indian manatee (*Trichechus manatus*). p. 53 *In*: Abstr. 10th Bienn. Conf. Biol. Mar. Mamm., Galveston, TX, Nov. 1993. 130 p.

Gilmore, R.M. 1978. Seismic blasting in or near the path of southward migrating gray whales, San Diego, California/January 1955. *Newsl. Am. Cetac. Soc. San Diego Chap.* 3(2):6-7.

Glass, K. 1989. Are dolphins being deafened in the Pacific? *Oceanus* 32(4):83-85.

Glockner-Ferrari, D.A. and M.J. Ferrari. 1985. Individual identification, behavior, reproduction, and distribution of humpback whales, *Megaptera novaeangliae*, in Hawaii. MMC-83/06. U.S. Mar. Mamm. Comm., Washington, DC. 35 p. NTIS PB85-200772.

Glockner-Ferrari, D.A. and M.J. Ferrari. 1990. Reproduction in the humpback whale (*Megaptera novaeangliae*) in Hawaiian waters, 1975-1988: The life history, reproductive rates and behavior of known individuals identified through surface and underwater photography. *Rep. Int. Whal. Comm. (Spec. Issue)* 12:161-169.

Goertner, J.F. 1982. Prediction of underwater explosion safe ranges for sea mammals. NSWC/WOL TR-82-188. Naval Surf. Weap. Cent., White Oak Lab., Silver Spring, MD. 25 p. NTIS AD-A139823.

Goodson, A.D., R.H. Mayo, M. Klinowska and P.R.S. Bloom. 1994. Field testing passive acoustic devices designed to reduce the entanglement of small cetaceans in fishing gear. *Rep. Int. Whal. Comm. (Spec. Issue)* 15:597-605.

Goodyear, J. 1989. Feeding ecology, night behavior, and vessel collision risk of Bay of Fundy right whales. p. 24 *In*: Abstr. 8th Bienn. Conf. Biol. Mar. Mamm., Pacific Grove, CA, Dec. 1989. 81 p.

Goodyear, J.D. 1993. A sonic/radio tag for monitoring dive depths and underwater movements of whales. *J. Wildl. Manage.* 57(3):503-513.

Goodyear, J., B. Würsig and D.R. Schmidt. 1987. Movements of bowhead whales in the Beaufort Sea as determined by radio telemetry. p. 527-547 *In*: W.J. Richardson (ed.), Importance of the eastern Alaskan Beaufort Sea to feeding bowhead whales, 1985-86. OCS Study MMS 87-0037. Rep. from LGL Ecol. Res. Assoc. Inc., Bryan, TX, for U.S. Minerals Manage. Serv., Reston, VA. 547 p. NTIS PB88-150271.

Gordon, J., R. Leaper, F.G. Hartley and O. Chappell. 1992. Effects of whale-watching vessels on the surface and underwater acoustic behaviour of sperm whales off Kaikoura, New Zealand. Sci. & Res. Ser. 52. New Zealand Dep. Conserv., Wellington. 64 p.

Gourevitch, G. 1980. Directional hearing in terrestrial mammals. p. 357-373 *In*: A.N. Popper and R.R. Fay (eds.), Comparative studies of hearing in vertebrates. Springer-Verlag, New York. 457 p.

Grachev, G.A. 1983. Specific characteristics of signal attenuation in a shallow sea. *Sov. Phys. Acoust. (Engl. Transl.)* 29(2):160-161.

Graham, W.C. 1989. Southbound migrations of the gray whale near San Clemente Island in the southern California Bight—1986 to 1989. p. 24 *In*: Abstr. 8th Bienn. Conf. Biol. Mar. Mamm., Pacific Grove, CA, Dec. 1989. 81 p.

Green, G.A., J.J. Brueggeman, R.A. Grotefendt, C.E. Bowlby, M.L. Bonnell and K.C. Balcomb, III. 1992. Cetacean distribution and abundance off Oregon and Washington, 1989-1990. Chap. I *In*: J.J. Brueggeman (ed.), Oregon and Washington marine mammal and seabird surveys. OCS Study MMS 91-0093. Rep. from EBASCO Environmental, Bellevue, WA, and Ecological Consulting Inc., Portland, OR, for U.S. Minerals Manage. Serv., Pacific OCS Reg., Los Angeles, CA. 100 p.

Green, J.E. and S.R. Johnson. 1983. The distribution and abundance of ringed seals in relation to gravel island construction in the Alaskan Beaufort Sea. p. 1-28 *In*: B.J. Gallaway (ed.), Biological studies and monitoring at Seal Island, Beaufort Sea, Alaska 1982. Rep. from LGL Ecol. Res. Assoc. Inc., Bryan, TX, for Shell Oil Co., Houston, TX. 150 p.

Green, K. and H.R. Burton. 1988a. Annual and diurnal variations in the underwater vocalizations of Weddell seals. *Polar Biol.* 8(3):161-164.

Green, K. and H.R. Burton. 1988b. Do Weddell seals sing? *Polar Biol.* 8(3):165-166.

Green, M.L. 1990. The impact of parasail boats on the Hawaiian humpback whale (*Megaptera novaeangliae*). Unpubl. manuscr., presented at Mar. Mamm. Comm. Hearings, Honolulu, HI, March 1980. 11 p.

Green, M.L. and R.G. Green. 1990. Short-term impact of vessel traffic on the Hawaiian humpback whale (*Megaptera novaeangliae*). Unpubl. manuscr., presented at Annu. Meet. Anim. Behav. Soc., Buffalo, NY, June 1990. 9 p.

Green, R.H. 1979. Sampling design and statistical methods for environmental biologists. Wiley, New York. 257 p.

Greene, C.R. 1981. Underwater acoustic transmission loss and ambient noise in arctic regions. p. 234-258 *In*: N.M. Peterson (ed.), The question of sound from icebreaker operations: The proceedings of a workshop. Arctic Pilot Proj., Petro-Canada, Calgary, Alb. 350 p.

Greene, C.R. 1982. Characteristics of waterborne industrial noise. p. 249-346 *In*: W.J. Richardson (ed.), Behavior, disturbance responses and feeding of bowhead whales *Balaena mysticetus* in the Beaufort Sea, 1980-81. Chapter by Polar Res. Lab. Inc., in Rep. from LGL Ecol. Res. Assoc. Inc., Bryan, TX, for U.S. Bur. Land Manage., Washington, DC. 456 p. NTIS PB86-152170.

Greene, C.R. 1983. Characteristics of underwater noise during construction of Seal Island, Alaska 1982. p. 118-150 *In*: B.J. Gallaway (ed.), Biological studies and monitoring at Seal Island, Beaufort Sea, Alaska 1982. Rep. from LGL Ecol. Res. Assoc. Inc., Bryan, TX, for Shell Oil Co., Houston, TX. 150 p.

Greene, C.R. 1985a. Characteristics of waterborne industrial noise, 1980-84. p. 197-253 *In*: W.J. Richardson (ed.), Behavior, disturbance responses and distribution of bowhead whales *Balaena mysticetus* in the eastern Beaufort Sea, 1980-84. OCS Study MMS 85-0034. Rep. from LGL Ecol. Res. Assoc. Inc., Bryan, TX, for U.S. Minerals Manage. Serv., Reston, VA. 306 p. NTIS PB87-124376.

Greene, C.R., Jr. 1985b. A pilot study of possible effects of marine seismic airgun array operation on rockfish plumes. Rep. from Greeneridge Sciences Inc., Santa Barbara, CA, for Seismic Steering Committee. 50 p.

Greene, C.R. 1986. Underwater sounds from the semisubmersible drill rig SEDCO 708 drilling in the Aleutian Islands. Sect. 1 *In*: API Publ. 4438. Am. Petrol. Inst., Washington, DC. 69 p.

Greene, C.R. 1987a. Acoustic studies of underwater noise and localization of whale calls. Sect. 2 *In*: Responses of bowhead whales to an offshore drilling operation in the Alaskan Beaufort Sea, autumn 1986. Rep. from LGL Ltd., King City, Ont., and Greeneridge Sciences Inc., Santa Barbara, CA, for Shell Western E & P Inc., Anchorage, AK. 128 p.

Greene, C.R., Jr. 1987b. Characteristics of oil industry dredge and drilling sounds in the Beaufort Sea. *J. Acoust. Soc. Am.* 82(4):1315-1324.

Greene, C.R. (convener). 1995. Abstracts of invited and contributed papers/Underwater acoustics: Transient sounds: Their measurement and description. *J. Acoust. Soc. Am.* 97(5, Pt. 2):3366-3368.

Greene, C.R. and B.M. Buck. 1964. Arctic Ocean ambient noise. *J. Acoust. Soc. Am.* 36(6):1218-1220.

Greene, C.R., Jr., and W.J. Richardson. 1988. Characteristics of marine seismic survey sounds in the Beaufort Sea. *J. Acoust. Soc. Am.* 83(6):2246-2254.

Greene, G.D., F.R. Engelhardt and R.J. Paterson (eds.). 1985. Proceedings of the workshop on effects of explosives use in the marine environment, Halifax, N.S., Jan. 1985. Tech. Rep. 5. Can. Oil & Gas Lands Admin. Environ. Prot. Branch, Ottawa, Ont. 398 p.

Griffin, D.R., J.J.G. McCue and A.D. Grinnell. 1963. The resistance of bats to jamming. *J. Exp. Zool.* 152(3):229-250.

Guinee, L.N., K. Chu and E.M. Dorsey. 1983. Changes over time in the songs of known individual humpback whales (*Megaptera novaeangliae*). p. 59-80 *In*: R. Payne (ed.), Communication and behavior of whales. AAAS Sel. Symp. 76. Westview Press, Boulder, CO. 643 p.

Gunther, E.R. 1949. The habits of fin whales. *Discovery Rep.* 25:115-141.

Hall, J.D. and J. Francine. 1990. Underwater sound production of a bottom founded drilling platform (Concrete Island Drilling Structure) located in the Alaskan Beaufort Sea (Camden Bay). p. 181-183 *In*: Ext. Abstr., 5th Conf. Biol. Bowhead Whale, *Balaena mysticetus*, April 1990, Anchorage, AK. North Slope Borough, Barrow, AK. 244 p.

Hall, J.D. and J. Francine. 1991. Measurements of underwater sounds from a concrete island drilling structure located in the Alaskan sector of the Beaufort Sea. *J. Acoust. Soc. Am.* 90(3):1665-1667.

Hall, J.D. and C.S. Johnson. 1972. Auditory thresholds of a killer whale *Orcinus orca* Linnaeus. *J. Acoust. Soc. Am.* 51(2):515-517.

Hall, J.D., M.L. Gallagher, K.D. Brewer and D.K. Ljungblad. 1991. Passive acoustic monitoring program at the ARCO Alaska, Inc. "Fireweed" prospect September-October 1990. Rep. from Coastal & Offshore Pacific Corp., Walnut Creek, CA [for ARCO Alaska Inc., Anchorage, AK]. 41 p.

Hall, J.D., M.L. Gallagher, K.D. Brewer, P.R. Regos and P.E. Isert. 1994. ARCO Alaska, Inc. 1993 Kuvlum exploration area site specific monitoring program/ Final report. Rep. from Coastal & Offshore Pacific Corp., Walnut Creek, CA, for ARCO Alaska Inc. [Anchorage, AK]. 219 p. + Data Appendix vol. 1, 2.

Hammond, P.S., S.A. Mizroch and G.P. Donovan (eds.). 1990. Individual recognition of cetaceans: Use of photo-identification and other techniques to estimate population parameters. *Rep. Int. Whal. Comm. (Spec. Issue)* 12. Int. Whal. Comm., Cambridge, U.K. 440 p.

Hamson, R.M. 1985. The theoretical responses of vertical and horizontal line arrays to wind-induced noise in shallow water. *J. Acoust. Soc. Am.* 78(5): 1702-1712.

Hanggi, E.B. and R.J. Schusterman. 1992. Underwater acoustic displays by male harbor seals (*Phoca vitulina*): Initial results. p. 449-457 *In*: J.A. Thomas, R.A. Kastelein and A.Ya. Supin (eds.), Marine mammal sensory systems. Plenum, New York. 773 p.

Hanggi, E.B. and R.J. Schusterman. 1994. Underwater acoustic displays and individual variation in male harbour seals, *Phoca vitulina*. *Anim. Behav.* 48 (6):1275-1283.

Hargreaves, A.L. and G.D. Hutson. 1990. Changes in heart rate, plasma cortisol and haematocrit of sheep during a shearing procedure. *Appl. Anim. Behav. Sci.* 26(1-2):91-101.

Harlow, H.J., E.T. Thorne, E.S. Williams, E.L. Belden and W.A. Gern. 1987a. Adrenal responsiveness in domestic sheep (*Ovis aries*) to acute and chronic stressors as predicted by remote monitoring of cardiac frequency. *Can. J. Zool.* 65(8):2021-2027.

Harlow, H.J., E.T. Thorne, E.S. Williams, E.L. Belden and W.A. Gern. 1987b. Cardiac frequency: A potential predictor of blood cortisol levels during acute and chronic stress exposure in Rocky Mountain bighorn sheep (*Ovis canadensis canadensis*). *Can. J. Zool.* 65(8):2028-2034.

Harlow, H.J., F.G. Lindzey, W.D. Van Sickle and W.A. Gern. 1992. Stress response of cougars to nonlethal pursuit by hunters. *Can. J. Zool.* 70(1):136-139.

Harrington, F.H. and A.M. Veitch. 1991. Short-term impacts of low-level jet fighter training on caribou in Labrador. *Arctic* 44(4):318-327.

Harrington, F.H. and A.M. Veitch. 1992. Calving success of woodland caribou exposed to low-level jet fighter overflights. *Arctic* 45(3):213-218.

Hartman, D.S. 1979. Ecology and behavior of the manatee (*Trichechus manatus*) in Florida. *Am. Soc. Mammal., Spec. Publ.* 5. 153 p.

Harwood, J. and J.J.D. Greenwood. 1985. Competition between British grey seals and fisheries. p. 153-169 *In*: J.R. Beddington, R.J.H. Beverton and D.M. Lavigne (eds.), Marine mammals and fisheries. George Allen & Unwin, London. 354 p.

Hatakeyama, Y. and H. Soeda. 1990. Studies on echolocation of porpoises taken in salmon gillnet fisheries. p. 269-281 *In*: J.A. Thomas and R.A. Kastelein (eds.), Sensory abilities of cetaceans/Laboratory and field evidence. Plenum, New York. 710 p.

Hatakeyama, Y., K. Ishii, T. Akamatsu, H. Soeda, T. Shimamura and T. Kojima. 1994. A review of studies on attempts to reduce the entanglement of the Dall's porpoise, *Phocoenoides dalli*, in the Japanese salmon gillnet fishery. *Rep. Int. Whal. Comm. (Spec. Issue)* 15:549-563.

Hatler, D.F. and J.D. Darling. 1974. Recent observations of the gray whale in British Columbia. *Can. Field-Nat.* 88(4):449-459.

Hawkins, J.E., Jr., and S.S. Stevens. 1950. The masking of pure tones and of speech by white noise. *J. Acoust. Soc. Am.* 22(1):6-13.

Hediger, H. 1934. Zur Biologie und Psychologie der Flucht bei Tieren. *Biol. Zentralbl.* 54(1/2):21-40.

Heinsohn, G.E. 1979. Report on sirenians. p. 135-151 *In*: Mammals in the seas, vol. II. FAO Fish. Ser. (5) II. Food & Agric. Organiz., United Nations, Rome. 151 p.

Helweg, D.A., L.M. Herman, S. Yamamoto and B.G. Bays. 1991. Humpback whale sightings in the Kerama Retto, Ryukyuan Islands, Japan in the winter of 1990. p. 32 *In*: Abstr. 9th Bienn. Conf. Biol. Mar. Mamm., Chicago, IL, Dec. 1991. 76 p.

Helweg, D.A., A.S. Frankel, J.R. Mobley, Jr., and L.M. Herman. 1992. Humpback whale song: Our current understanding. p. 459-483 *In*: J.A. Thomas, R.A. Kastelein and A.Ya. Supin (eds.), Marine mammal sensory systems. Plenum, New York. 773 p.

Henderson, J.R. and T.C. Johanos. 1988. Effects of tagging on weaned Hawaiian monk seal pups. *Wildl. Soc. Bull.* 16(3):312-317.

Herald, E.S., R.L. Brownell, Jr., F.L. Frye, E.J. Morris, W.E. Evans and A.B. Scott. 1969. Blind river dolphin: First side-swimming cetacean. *Science* 166(3911): 1408-1410.

Herman, L.M. 1979. Humpback whales in Hawaiian waters: A study in historical ecology. *Pacific Sci.* 33(1):1-15.

Herman, L.M. 1994. Hawaiian humpback whales and ATOC: A conflict of interests. *J. Environ. Devel.* 3(2):63-76.

Herman, L.M. and W.R. Arbeit. 1972. Frequency difference limens in the bottlenose dolphin: 1-70 kc/s. *J. Aud. Res.* 12(2):109-120.

Herman, L.M. and W.N. Tavolga. 1980. The communication systems of cetaceans. p. 149-209 *In*: L.M. Herman (ed.), Cetacean behavior: Mechanisms and functions. Wiley-Interscience, New York. 463 p.

Herman, L.M., P.H. Forestell and R.C. Antinoja. 1980. The 1976/1977 migration of humpback whales into Hawaiian waters: Composite description. MMC-77/ 19. U.S. Mar. Mamm. Comm., Washington, DC. 55 p. NTIS PB80-162332.

Herrero, S. and S. Fleck. 1990. Injury to people inflicted by black, grizzly or polar bears: Recent trends and new insights. *Int. Conf. Bear Res. Manage.* 8:25-32.

Herter, D.R. and W.R. Koski. 1988. The effects of airport development and operation on waterbird and northern fur seal populations: A review from the perspective of the St. George airport project. Rep. from LGL Alaska Res. Assoc. Inc., Anchorage, AK, for Alaska Dep. Transp. & Public Facil., Anchorage, AK. 201 p.

Hewitt, R.P. 1985. Reaction of dolphins to a survey vessel: Effects on census data. *Fish. Bull.* 83(2):187-193.

Hill, S.H. 1978. A guide to the effects of underwater shock waves on arctic marine mammals and fish. Pacific Mar. Sci. Rep. 78-26. Inst. Ocean Sciences, Patricia Bay, Sidney, B.C. 50 p.

Hirsch, A.E. and A.K. Ommaya. 1972. Head injury caused by underwater explosion of a firecracker. *J. Neurosurg.* 37(1):95-99.

Hobbs, L.J. and M.E. Goebel. 1982. Bowhead whale radio tagging feasibility study and review of large cetacean tagging. NOAA Tech. Memo. NMFS F/NWC-21. U.S. Natl. Mar. Mamm. Lab., Seattle, WA. 68 p. NTIS PB82-193145.

Hoelzel A.R. and R.W. Osborne. 1986. Killer whale call characteristics: Implications for cooperative foraging strategies. p. 373-403 *In*: B.C. Kirkevold and J.S. Lockard (eds.), Behavioral biology of killer whales. Alan R. Liss, New York. 457 p.

Hoff, B.J. and F.B. Chemlik. 1982. Better shallow water seismic data. *Ocean Ind.* 17(6):19-23.

Holing, D. 1994. The sound and the fury/Debate gets louder over ocean noise pollution and marine mammals. *Amicus J.* 16(3):18-23.

Holliday, D.V., W.C. Cummings and W.T. Ellison. 1980. Underwater sound measurements from Barrow and Prudhoe regions, Alaska, May-June, 1980. T-80-SD-022-U. Rep. from Tracor Appl. Sci., San Diego, CA, for Alaska Eskimo Whal. Comm. [Barrow, AK]. 316 p.

Holliday, D.V., W.C. Cummings and B.J. Lee. 1984. Acoustic and vibration measurements related to possible disturbance of ringed seals, *Phoca hispida*. T-84-06-001-U. Rep. from Tracor Appl. Sci., San Diego, CA, for Outer Cont. Shelf Environ. Assess. Program, NOAA, Juneau, AK. 148 p.

Hollien, H. 1993. Hearing conservation underwater. p. 567-581 *In*: R.T. Sataloff and J. Sataloff (eds.), Occupational hearing loss, 2nd ed. Dekker, New York. 856 p.

Hoover, A.A. 1988. Harbor seal *Phoca vitulina*. p. 125-157 *In*: J.W. Lentfer (ed.), Selected marine mammals of Alaska/Species accounts with research and management recommendations. U.S. Mar. Mamm. Comm., Washington, DC. 275 p. NTIS PB88-178462.

Horejsi, B.L. 1981. Behavioral response of barren ground caribou to a moving vehicle. *Arctic* 34(2):180-185.

Horsley, L.E. 1989. Modification and deployment techniques for hand-deployed arctic long-life sonobuoys. *IEEE J. Oceanic Eng.* 14(2):211-220.

Horwood, J.W. 1981. Results from the IWC/IDCR minke marking and sightings cruise, 1979/80. *Rep. Int. Whal. Comm.* 31:287-313.

Hubbard, H.H. (ed.). 1995. Aeroacoustics of flight vehicles, theory and practice, vol. 1, Noise sources; vol. 2, Noise control. Acoust. Soc. Am., New York. 608 + 447 p.

Hubbs, C.L. 1965. Data on speed and underwater exhalation of a humpback whale accompanying ships. *Hvalrådets Skr.* 48:42-44.

Hubbs, C.L. and L.C. Hubbs. 1967. Gray whale censuses by airplane in Mexico. *Calif. Fish & Game* 53(1):23-27.

Hudimac, A.A. 1957. Ray theory solution for the sound intensity in water due to a point source above it. *J. Acoust. Soc. Am.* 29(8):916-917.

Hudnall, J. 1978. A report on the general behavior of humpback whales near Hawaii, and the need for the creation of a whale park. *Oceans* 11(2):8-15.

Hult, R.W. 1982. Another function of echolocation for bottlenosed dolphins (*Tursiops truncatus*). *Cetology* 47:1-7.

Huntley, A.C., D.P. Costa, G.A.J. Worthy and M.A. Castellini (eds.). 1987. Approaches to marine mammal energetics. Spec. Publ. 1. Soc. Mar. Mammal., Lawrence, KS. 253 p.

Hutchinson, D.R. and R.S. Detrick. 1984. Water gun vs air gun: A comparison. *Mar. Geophys. Res.* 6(3):295-310.

HWRT. 1991. Final recovery plan for the humpback whale (*Megaptera novaeangliae*). Rep. from Humpback Whale Recov. Team for U.S. Natl. Mar. Fish. Serv., Silver Spring, MD. 105 p.

Ingold, P., B. Huber, P. Neuhaus, B. Mainini, H. Marbacher, R. Schnidrig-Petrig and R. Zeller. 1993. Tourismus und Freizeitsport im Alpenraum—Ein gravierendes Problem für Wildtiere? *Rev. Suisse Zool.* 100(3):529-545.

Insley, S.J. 1989. Female-pup vocal recognition in northern elephant seals and northern fur seals. p. 30 *In*: Abstr. 8th Bienn. Conf. Biol. Mar. Mamm., Pacific Grove, CA, Dec. 1989. 81 p.

Irvine, A.B., M.D. Scott, R.S. Wells and J.H. Kaufmann. 1981. Movements and activities of the Atlantic bottlenose dolphin, *Tursiops truncatus*, near Sarasota, Florida. *Fish. Bull.* 79(4):671-688.

Ising, H., E. Rebentisch, W. Babisch, I. Curio, D. Sharp and H. Baumgärtner. 1990. Medically relevant effects of noise from military low-altitude flights—Results of an interdisciplinary pilot study. *Environ. Int.* 16(4-6):411-423.

I.W.C. 1982. Report of the special meeting on Southern Hemisphere minke whales, Cambridge, 22-26 June 1981. *Rep. Int. Whal. Comm.* 32:697-745.

I.W.C. 1990. Report of the sub-committee on stock estimation. *Rep. Int. Whal. Comm.* 40:131-143.

Jacobs, D.W. 1972. Auditory frequency discrimination in the Atlantic bottlenose dolphin, *Tursiops truncatus* Montague: A preliminary report. *J. Acoust. Soc. Am.* 52(2, Pt. 2):696-698.

Jacobs, D.W. and J.D. Hall. 1972. Auditory thresholds of a fresh water dolphin, *Inia geoffrensis* Blainville. *J. Acoust. Soc. Am.* 51(2, Pt. 2):530-533.

Jacobs, M., D.P. Nowacek, D.J. Gerhart, G. Cannon, S. Nowicki and R.B. Forward, Jr. 1993. Seasonal changes in vocalizations during behavior of the Atlantic bottlenose dolphin. *Estuaries* 16(2):241-246.

Jacobsen, N.K. 1979. Alarm bradycardia in white-tailed deer fawns (*Odocoileus virginianus*). *J. Mammal.* 60(2):343-349.

Jakosky, J.J. and J. Jakosky, Jr. 1956. Characteristics of explosives for marine seismic exploration. *Geophysics* 21(4):969-991.

Janik, V.M., G. Dehnhardt and D. Todt. 1994. Signature whistle variations in a bottlenosed dolphin, *Tursiops truncatus*. *Behav. Ecol. Sociobiol.* 35(4):243-248.

Jefferson, T.A. and B.E. Curry. 1994. Review and evaluation of potential acoustic methods of reducing or eliminating marine mammal-fishery interactions. Rep. from Mar. Mamm. Res. Program, Texas A & M Univ., College Station, TX, for U.S. Mar. Mamm. Comm., Washington, DC. 59 p. NTIS PB95-100384.

Jefferson, T.A., S. Leatherwood and M.A. Webber. 1993. Marine mammals of the world. FAO Species Ident. Guide. Food & Agric. Organiz., United Nations, Rome, Italy. 320 p.

Jenkins, P.F., D.A. Helweg and D.H. Cato. 1995. Humpback whale song in Tonga: Preliminary results. *In*: R.A. Kastelein, J.A. Thomas and P.E. Nachtigall (eds.), Sensory systems of aquatic mammals. De Spil Publ., Woerden, Netherlands. (in press).

Jensen, F.B. and W.A. Kuperman. 1980. Sound propagation in a wedge-shaped ocean with a penetratable bottom. *J. Acoust. Soc. Am.* 67(5):1564-1566.

Jensen, F.B., W.A. Kuperman, M.B. Porter and H. Schmidt. 1994. Computational ocean acoustics. Am. Inst. Phys. Press, New York. 612 p.

Jing Xianying, Xiao Youfu and Jing Rongcai. 1981. Acoustic signals and acoustic behaviour of Chinese river dolphin (*Lipotes vexillifer*). *Sci. Sinica (Engl. ed.)* 24(3):407-415.

Johnson, B.W. 1977. The effects of human disturbance on a population of harbor seals. Environ. Assess. Alaskan Cont. Shelf, Annu. Rep. Princ. Invest., NOAA, Boulder, CO, 1977(1):422-432. 708 p. NTIS PB-280934/1.

Johnson, C.S. 1967. Sound detection thresholds in marine mammals. p. 247-260 *In*: W.N. Tavolga (ed.), Marine bio-acoustics, vol. 2. Pergamon, Oxford, U.K. 353 p.

Johnson, C.S. 1968a. Relation between absolute threshold and duration-of-tone pulses in the bottlenosed porpoise. *J. Acoust. Soc. Am.* 43(4):757-763.

Johnson, C.S. 1968b. Masked tonal thresholds in the bottlenosed porpoise. *J. Acoust. Soc. Am.* 44(4):965-967.

Johnson, C.S. 1971. Auditory masking of one pure tone by another in the bottlenosed porpoise. *J. Acoust. Soc. Am.* 49(4, Pt. 2):1317-1318.

Johnson, C.S. 1979. Thermal-noise limit in delphinid hearing. NOSC TD 270. U.S. Naval Ocean Systems Cent., San Diego, CA. 4 p. NTIS AD-A076206.

Johnson, C.S. 1986. Dolphin audition and echolocation capacities. p. 115-136 *In*: R.J. Schusterman, J.A. Thomas and F.G. Wood (eds.), Dolphin cognition and behavior: A comparative approach. Erlbaum, Hillsdale, NJ. 393 p.

Johnson, C.S. 1991. Hearing thresholds for periodic 60-kHz tone pulses in the beluga whale. *J. Acoust. Soc. Am.* 89(6):2996-3001.

Johnson, C.S. 1992. Detection of tone glides by the beluga whale. p. 241-247 *In*: J.A. Thomas, R.A. Kastelein and A.Ya. Supin (eds.), Marine mammal sensory systems. Plenum, New York. 773 p.

Johnson, C.S., M.W. McManus and D. Skaar. 1989. Masked tonal hearing thresholds in the beluga whale. *J. Acoust. Soc. Am.* 85(6):2651-2654.

Johnson, S.R., C.R. Greene, R.A. Davis and W.J. Richardson. 1986. Bowhead whales and underwater noise near the Sandpiper Island drillsite, Alaskan Beaufort Sea, autumn 1985. Rep. from LGL Ltd., King City, Ont., and Greeneridge Sciences Inc., Santa Barbara, CA, for Shell Western E&P Inc., Anchorage, AK. 130 p.

Johnson, S.R., J.J. Burns, C.I. Malme and R.A. Davis. 1989. Synthesis of information on the effects of noise and disturbance on major haulout concentrations of Bering Sea pinnipeds. OCS Study MMS 88-0092. Rep. from LGL Alaska Res. Assoc. Inc., Anchorage, AK, for U.S. Minerals Manage. Serv., Anchorage, AK. 267 p. NTIS PB89-191373.

Johnston, R.C. and B. Cain. 1981. Marine seismic energy sources: Acoustic performance comparison. Manuscript presented at 102nd Meet. Acoust. Soc. Am., Miami Beach, FL, Dec. 1981. 35 p.

Johnston, R.C., D.H. Reed and J.F. Desler. 1988. Special report of the SEG technical standards committee, SEG standards for specifying marine seismic energy sources. *Geophysics* 53(4):566-575.

Jones, M.L. and S.L. Swartz. 1984. Demography and phenology of gray whales and evaluation of whale-watching activities in Laguna San Ignacio, Baja California Sur, Mexico. p. 309-374 *In*: M.L. Jones, S.L. Swartz and S. Leatherwood (eds.), The gray whale *Eschrichtius robustus*. Academic Press, Orlando, FL. 600 p.

Jones, M.L. and S.L. Swartz. 1986. Demography and phenology of gray whales and evaluation of human activities in Laguna San Ignacio, Baja California Sur, Mexico: 1978-1982. Rep. from Cetacean Res. Assoc., San Diego, CA, for U.S. Mar. Mamm. Comm., Washington, DC. 69 p. NTIS PB86-219078.

Jones, M.L., S.L. Swartz and M.E. Dahlheim. 1994. Census of gray whale abundance in San Ignacio Lagoon: A follow-up study in response to low whale counts recorded during an acoustic playback study of noise-effects on gray whales. Rep. for U.S. Mar. Mamm. Comm., Washington, DC. 32 p. NTIS PB94-195062.

Jordan, R.H. and G.M. Burghardt. 1986. Employing an ethogram to detect reactivity of black bears (*Ursus americanus*) to the presence of humans. *Ethology* 73(2):89-115.

Joyce, G.G., N. Øien, J. Calambokidis and J.C. Cubbage. 1989. Surfacing rates of minke whales in Norwegian waters. *Rep. Int. Whal. Comm.* 39:431-434.

Jurasz, C.M. and V.P Jurasz. 1979a. Ecology of humpback whale. Draft report for U.S. Natl. Park Serv. (Contr. No. CX-9000-7-0045). 118 p. + fig., tables.

Jurasz, C.M. and V.P. Jurasz. 1979b. Feeding modes of the humpback whale, *Megaptera novaeangliae*, in southeast Alaska. *Sci. Rep. Whales Res. Inst.* 31:69-83.

Kamminga, C. 1988. Echolocation signal types of odontocetes. p. 9-22 *In*: P.E. Nachtigall and P.W.B. Moore (eds.), Animal sonar/Processes and performance. Plenum, New York. 862 p.

Kamminga, C. and J.G. van Velden. 1987. Investigations on cetacean sonar VIII/ Sonar signals of *Pseudorca crassidens* in comparison with *Tursiops truncatus*. *Aquat. Mamm.* 13(2):43-49.

Kamminga, C. and H. Wiersma. 1981. Investigations on cetacean sonar II. Acoustical similarities and differences in odontocete sonar signals. *Aquat. Mamm.* 8(2):41-62.

Kamminga, C., H. Wiersma, W.H. Dudok van Heel and G.S. Tas'an. 1983. Investigations on cetacean sonar VI. Sonar sounds in *Orcaella brevirostris* of the Makaham River, East Kalimantan, Indonesia; first descriptions of acoustic behaviour. *Aquat. Mamm.* 10(3):83-94.

Kamminga, C., T. Kataoka and F.J. Engelsma. 1986. Investigations on cetacean sonar VII/Underwater sounds of *Neophocaena phocaenoides* of the Japanese coastal population. *Aquat. Mamm.* 12(2):52-60.

Kamminga, C., M.T. van Hove, F.J. Engelsma and R.P. Terry. 1993. Investigations on cetacean sonar X: A comparative analysis of underwater echolocation clicks of *Inia* spp. and *Sotalia* spp. *Aquat. Mamm.* 19(1):31-43.

Kanik, B., M. Winsby and R. Tanasichuk. 1980. Observations of marine mammal and sea bird interaction with icebreaking activities in the High Arctic July 2-

12, 1980. Rep. from Hatfield Consultants Ltd., West Vancouver, B.C., for Petro-Canada, Calgary, Alb. 53 p.

Kapel, F.O. 1979. Exploitation of large whales in West Greenland in the twentieth century. *Rep. Int. Whal. Comm.* 29:197-214.

Kastak, D. and R.J. Schusterman. 1995. Aerial and underwater hearing thresholds for 100 Hz pure tones in two pinniped species. *In*: R.A. Kastelein, J.A. Thomas and P.E. Nachtigall (eds.), Sensory systems of aquatic mammals. De Spil Publ., Woerden, Netherlands. (in press).

Kastelein, R.A., C.L. van Ligtenberg, I. Gjertz and W.C. Verboom. 1993. Free field hearing tests on wild Atlantic walruses (*Odobenus rosmarus rosmarus*) in air. *Aquat. Mamm.* 19(3):143-148.

Kastelein, R.A., A.D. Goodson, J. Lien and D. de Haan. 1995a. The effects of acoustic alarms on harbour porpoise (*Phocoena phocoena*) behaviour. p. 157-168 *In*: P.E. Nachtigall, J. Lien, W.W.L. Au and A.J. Read (eds.), Harbour porpoises—Laboratory studies to reduce bycatch. De Spil Publ., Woerden, Netherlands. (in press).

Kastelein, R.A., J. Postma and W.C. Verboom. 1995b. Airborne vocalizations of Pacific walrus pups (*Odobenus rosmarus divergens*). *In*: R.A. Kastelein, J.A. Thomas and P.E. Nachtigall (eds.), Sensory systems of aquatic mammals. De Spil Publ., Woerden, Netherlands. (in press).

Kasuya, T. 1985. Fishery-dolphin conflict in the Iki Island area of Japan. p. 253-272 *In*: J.R. Beddington, R.J.H. Beverton and D.M. Lavigne (eds.), Marine mammals and fisheries. George Allen & Unwin, London. 354 p.

Kaufman, G. and K. Wood. 1981. Effects of boat traffic, air traffic and military activity on Hawaiian humpback whales. p. 67 *In*: Abstr. 4th Bienn. Conf. Biol. Mar. Mamm., San Francisco, CA, Dec. 1981. 127 p.

Kelly, B.P., L.T. Quakenbush and J.R. Rose. 1986 [publ. 1989]. Ringed seal winter ecology and effects of noise disturbance. Outer Cont. Shelf Environ. Assess. Program, Final Rep. Princ. Invest., NOAA, Anchorage, AK 61:447-536. 536 p. OCS Study MMS 89-0026; NTIS PB89-234645.

Kelly, B.P., J.J. Burns and L.T. Quakenbush. 1988. Responses of ringed seals (*Phoca hispida*) to noise disturbance. p. 27-38 *In*: W.M. Sackinger et al. (eds.), Port and ocean engineering under arctic conditions, vol. II. Geophys. Inst., Univ. Alaska, Fairbanks. 111 p.

Kenney, R.D. and S.D. Kraus. 1993. Right whale mortality—A correction and an update. *Mar. Mamm. Sci.* 9(4):445-446.

Kennish, M.J. (ed.). 1989. Practical handbook of marine science. CRC Press, Boca Raton, FL. 710 p.

Kenyon, K.W. 1972. Man versus the monk seal. *J. Mammal.* 53(4):687-696.

Kenyon, K.W. 1981. Sea otter *Enhydra lutris* (Linnaeus, 1758). p. 209-223 *In*: S.H. Ridgway and R.J. Harrison (eds.), Handbook of marine mammals, vol. 1. Academic Press, London. 235 p.

Kenyon, K.W. and D.W. Rice. 1959. Life history of the Hawaiian monk seal. *Pacific. Sci.* 13(3):215-252.

Ketten, D.R. 1991. The marine mammal ear: Specializations for aquatic audition and echolocation. p. 717-750 *In*: D. Webster, R. Fay and A. Popper (eds.), The biology of hearing. Springer-Verlag, Berlin.

Ketten, D.R. 1992. The cetacean ear: Form, frequency, and evolution. p. 53-75 *In*: J.A. Thomas, R.A. Kastelein and A.Ya. Supin (eds.), Marine mammal sensory systems. Plenum, New York. 773 p.

Ketten, D.R. 1994. Functional analyses of whale ears: Adaptations for underwater hearing. *IEEE Proc. Underwat. Acoustics* 1:264-270.

Ketten, D.R. 1995. Estimates of blast injury and acoustic trauma zones for marine mammals from underwater explosions. *In*: R.A. Kastelein, J.A. Thomas and P.E. Nachtigall (eds.), Sensory systems of aquatic mammals. De Spil Publ., Woerden, Netherlands. (in press).

Ketten, D.R. and D. Wartzok. 1990. Three-dimensional reconstructions of the dolphin ear. p. 81-105 *In*: J.A. Thomas and R.A. Kastelein (eds.), Sensory abilities of cetaceans/Laboratory and field evidence. Plenum, New York. 710 p.

Ketten, D.R., D.K. Odell and D.P. Domning. 1992. Structure, function, and adaptation of the manatee ear. p. 77-95 *In*: J.A. Thomas, R.A. Kastelein and A.Ya. Supin (eds.), Marine mammal sensory systems. Plenum, New York. 773 p.

Ketten, D.R., J. Lien and S. Todd. 1993. Blast injury in humpback whale ears: Evidence and implications. *J. Acoust. Soc. Am.* 94(3, Pt. 2):1849-1850.

Ketten, D.R. 1995. Estimates of blast injury and acoustic trauma zones for marine mammals from underwater explosions. *In*: R.A. Kastelein, J.A. Thomas and P.E. Nachtigall (eds.), Sensory systems of aquatic mammals. De Spil Publ., Woerden, Netherlands. (in press).

Kibal'chich, A.A., G.A. Dzhamanov and M.V. Ivashin. 1986. Records of bowhead and gray whales in early winter in the Bering Sea. *Rep. Int. Whal. Comm.* 36:291-292.

Kibblewhite, A.C. and L.D. Hampton. 1980. A review of deep ocean sound attenuation data at very low frequencies. *J. Acoust. Soc. Am.* 67(1):147-157.

Kingsley, M.C.S. 1986. Distribution and abundance of seals in the Beaufort Sea, Amundsen Gulf, and Prince Albert Sound, 1984. Rep. 025. Environ. Stud. Revolv. Funds, Dep. Fish. & Oceans, Winnipeg. 16 p.

Kingsley, M.C.S., H.J. Cleator and M.A. Ramsay. 1994. Summer distribution and movements of narwhals (*Monodon monoceros*) in Eclipse Sound and adjacent waters, north Baffin Island, N.W.T. *Medd. Grønl., Biosci.* 39:163-174.

Kinsler, L.E., A.R. Frey, J.V. Sanders and A.B. Coppen. 1982. Fundamentals of acoustics, 3rd ed. Wiley, New York. 480 p.

Kishiro, T. and T. Kasuya. 1993. Review of Japanese dolphin drive fisheries and their status. *Rep. Int. Whal. Comm.* 43:439-452.

Klein, D.R. 1991. Caribou in the changing north. *Appl. Anim. Behav. Sci.* 29(1-4): 279-291.

Kleinenberg, S.E., A.V. Yablokov, B.M. Bel'kovich and M.N. Tarasevich. 1964. Beluga (*Delphinapterus leucas*) investigation of the species. Transl. from Russian by Israel Program Sci. Transl., Jerusalem, 1969. 376 p.

Klima, E.F., G.R. Gitschlag and M.L. Renaud. 1988. Impacts of the explosive removal of offshore petroleum platforms on sea turtles and dolphins. *Mar. Fish. Rev.* 50(3):33-42.

Klinowska, M. 1986. Diurnal rhythms in Cetacea—A review. *Rep. Int. Whal. Comm. (Spec. Issue)* 8:75-88.

Klinowska, M. 1991. Dolphins, porpoises and whales of the world/The IUCN red data book. Int. Union Conserv. Nat., Gland, Switz., and Cambridge, U.K. 429 p.

Klishin, V.O., R. Pezo Diaz, V.V. Popov and A.Ya. Supin. 1990. Some characteristics of hearing of the Brazilian manatee, *Trichechus inunguis*. *Aquat. Mamm.* 16(3):139-144.

Knowlton, A.R., C.W. Clark and S.D. Kraus. 1991. Sounds recorded in the presence of sei whales, *Balaenoptera borealis*. p. 40 *In*: Abstr. 9th Bienn. Conf. Biol. Mar. Mamm., Chicago, IL, Dec. 1991. 76 p.

Knudsen, V.O., R.S. Alford and J.W. Emling. 1948. Underwater ambient noise. *J. Mar. Res.* 7(3):410-429.

Kochman, H.I., G.B. Rathun and J.A. Powell. 1985. Temporal and spatial distribution of manatees in Kings Bay, Crystal River, Florida. *J. Wildl. Manage.* 49(4):921-924.

Koski, W.R. and S.R. Johnson. 1987. Behavioral studies and aerial photogrammetry. Sect. 4 *In*: Responses of bowhead whales to an offshore drilling operation in the Alaskan Beaufort Sea, autumn 1986. Rep. from LGL Ltd., King City, Ont., and Greeneridge Sciences Inc., Santa Barbara, CA, for Shell Western Expl. & Prod. Inc., Anchorage, AK. 371 p.

Koski, W.R., G.W. Miller and R.A. Davis. 1988. The potential effects of tanker traffic on the bowhead whale in the Beaufort Sea. Rep. from LGL Ltd., King City, Ont., for Dep. Indian Affairs & Northern Dev., Hull, Que. 150 p.

Kovacs, K.M. and S. Innes. 1990. The impact of tourism on harp seals (*Phoca groenlandica*) in the Gulf of St. Lawrence, Canada. *Appl. Anim. Behav. Sci.* 26(1-2):15-26.

Kramer, F.S., R.A. Peterson and W.C. Walter (eds.). 1968. Seismic energy sources/1968 handbook. Bendix-United Geophysical Corp. 57 p.

Kraus, S.D. 1990. Rates and potential causes of mortality in North Atlantic right whales (*Eubalaena glacialis*). *Mar. Mamm. Sci.* 6(4):278-291.

Krieger, K.J. and B.L. Wing. 1984. Hydroacoustic surveys and identification of humpback whale forage in Glacier Bay, Stephens Passage, and Frederick Sound, southeastern Alaska, summer 1983. NOAA Tech. Memo. NMFS F/NWC-66. U.S. Natl. Mar. Fish. Serv., Auke Bay, AK. 60 p. NTIS PB85-183887.

Krieger, K.J. and B.L. Wing. 1986. Hydroacoustic monitoring of prey to determine humpback whale movements. NOAA Tech. Memo. NMFS F/NWC-98. U.S. Natl. Mar. Fish. Serv., Auke Bay, AK. 62 p. NTIS PB86-204054.

Kruse, S. 1991. The interactions between killer whales and boats in Johnstone Strait, B.C. p. 148-159 *In*: K. Pryor and K.S. Norris (eds.), Dolphin societies/Discoveries and puzzles. Univ. Calif. Press, Berkeley. 397 p.

Kryter, K.D. 1985. The effects of noise on man, 2nd ed. Academic Press, Orlando, FL. 688 p.

Kryter, K.D., W.D. Ward, J.D. Miller and D.H. Eldredge. 1966. Hazardous exposure to intermittent and steady-state noise. *J. Acoust. Soc. Am.* 39(3):451-464.

Kuperman, W.A. and F.B. Jensen (eds.). 1980. Bottom-interacting ocean acoustics. Plenum, New York. 717 p.

Leaper, R., O. Chappell and J. Gordon. 1992. The development of practical techniques for surveying sperm whale populations acoustically. *Rep. Int. Whal. Comm.* 42:549-560.

Leatherwood, S. and R.R. Reeves (eds.). 1989. Marine mammal research and conservation in Sri Lanka 1985-1986. Mar. Mamm. Tech. Rep. 1. United Nations Environ. Programme, Oceans & Coastal Areas Programme Activ. Cent., Nairobi, Kenya. 138 p.

Leatherwood, S. and W.A. Walker. 1979. The northern right whale dolphin *Lissodelphis borealis* Peale in the eastern North Pacific. p. 85-141 *In*: H.E. Winn and B.L. Olla (eds.), Behavior of marine animals, vol. 3: Cetaceans. Plenum, New York. 438 p.

Leatherwood, S., F.T. Awbrey and J.A. Thomas. 1982. Minke whale response to a transiting survey vessel. *Rep. Int. Whal. Comm.* 32:795-802.

Leatherwood, S., R.R. Reeves, C.L. Hill and B. Würsig. 1991. Observations of river dolphins in the Amazon and Maranon rivers and tributaries, Peru, March, June and July 1991. p. 42 *In*: Abstr. 9th Bienn. Conf. Biol. Mar. Mamm., Chicago, IL, Dec. 1991. 76 p.

Leatherwood, S., T.A. Jefferson, J.C. Norris, W.E. Stevens, L.J. Hansen and K.D. Mullin. 1993. Occurrence and sounds of Fraser's dolphins (*Lagenodelphis hosei*) in the Gulf of Mexico. *Texas J. Sci.* 45(4):349-354.

Le Boeuf, B.J. and R.S. Peterson. 1969. Dialects in elephant seals. *Science* 166 (3913):1654-1656.

Le Boeuf, B.J. and L.F. Petrinovich. 1974. Dialects of northern elephant seals, *Mirounga angustirostris*: Origin and reliability. *Anim. Behav.* 22(3):656-663.

Lee, D. and G. Botseas. 1982. IFD: An implicit finite-difference computer model for solving the parabolic equation. NUSC Tech. Rep. 6659. U.S. Naval Underwater Systems Cent., Newport, RI. Var. pag. NTIS AD-A117701.

Leggat, L.J., H.M. Merklinger and J.L. Kennedy. 1981. LNG carrier underwater noise study for Baffin Bay. p. 115-155 *In*: N.M. Peterson (ed.), The question of sound from icebreaker operations: The proceedings of a workshop. Arctic Pilot Proj., Petro-Canada, Calgary, Alb. 350 p.

Lesage, V., C. Barrette and M.C.S. Kingsley. 1993. The effect of noise from an outboard motor and a ferry on the vocal activity of beluga (*Delphinapterus leucas*) in the St. Lawrence Estuary, Canada. p. 70 *In*: Abstr. 10th Bienn. Conf. Biol. Mar. Mamm., Galveston, TX, Nov. 1993. 130 p.

Levenson, C. 1974. Source level and bistatic target strength of the sperm whale (*Physeter catodon*) measured from an oceanographic aircraft. *J. Acoust. Soc. Am.* 55(5):1100-1103.

Lewis, J.P. 1987. An evaluation of a census-related disturbance of Steller sea lions. M.S. Thesis, Univ. Alaska, Fairbanks. 93 p.

LGL and Greeneridge. 1986. Reactions of beluga whales and narwhals to ship traffic and ice-breaking along ice edges in the eastern Canadian High Arctic: 1982-1984. Environ. Stud. 37. Indian & Northern Affairs Canada, Ottawa, Ont. 301 p.

LGL and Greeneridge. 1987. Responses of bowhead whales to an offshore drilling operation in the Alaskan Beaufort Sea, autumn 1986. Rep. from LGL Ltd., King City, Ont., and Greeneridge Sciences Inc., Santa Barbara, CA, for Shell Western E & P Inc., Anchorage, AK. 371 p.

Liebermann, L. 1949. Sound propagation in chemically active media. *Phys. Rev.* 76(10):1520-1524.

Lien, J., S. Todd and J. Guigne. 1990. Inferences about perception in large cetaceans, especially humpback whales, from incidental catches in fixed fishing gear, enhancement of nets by "alarm" devices, and the acoustics of fishing gear. p. 347-362 *In*: J.A. Thomas and R.A. Kastelein (eds.), Sensory abilities of cetaceans/Laboratory and field evidence. Plenum, New York. 710 p.

Lien, J., W. Barney, S. Todd, R. Seton and J. Guzzwell. 1992. Effects of adding sounds to cod traps on the probability of collisions by humpback whales. p. 701-708 *In*: J.A. Thomas, R.A. Kastelein and A.Ya. Supin (eds.), Marine mammal sensory systems. Plenum, New York. 773 p.

Lien, J., R. Barnaby and P. Morse. 1993a. Effectiveness of adding acoustic cues to groundfish gillnets to minimize harbour porpoise by-catch. p. 70 *In*: Abstr. 10th Bienn. Conf. Biol. Mar. Mamm., Galveston, TX, Nov. 1993. 130 p.

Lien, J., S. Todd, P. Stevick, F. Marques and D. Ketten. 1993b. The reaction of humpback whales to underwater explosions: Orientation, movements, and behavior. *J. Acoust. Soc. Am.* 94(3, Pt. 2):1849.

Lien, J., C. Hood, D. Pittman, P. Ruel, D. Borggaard, C. Chisholm, L. Wiesner, T. Mahon and D. Mitchell. 1995. Field tests of acoustic devices on groundfish gillnets: Assessment of effectiveness in reducing harbour porpoise by-catch. *In*: R.A. Kastelein, J.A. Thomas and P.E. Nachtigall (eds.), Sensory systems of aquatic mammals. De Spil Publ., Woerden, Netherlands. (in press).

Lilly, J.C. and A.M. Miller. 1961. Sounds emitted by the bottlenose dolphin. *Science* 133(3465):1689-1693.

Ling, J.K. and D.J. Needham. [1990]. Final report on aerial survey of southern right whales in the proposed marine reserve. Rep. from South Austral. Mus., Adelaide, S.A., for Austral. Natl. Parks & Wildl. Serv., Canberra, A.C.T. 18 p.

Ljungblad, D.K. 1986. Endangered whale aerial surveys in the Navarin Basin and St. Matthew Hall planning areas, Alaska. Appendix E *In*: D.K. Ljungblad et al., Aerial surveys of endangered whales in the northern Bering, eastern Chukchi, and Alaskan Beaufort seas, 1985: With a seven year review, 1979-85. NOSC TR 1111. U.S. Naval Ocean Systems Cent., San Diego, CA. 409 p. NTIS AD-A172753/6.

Ljungblad, D.K. and S.E. Moore. 1983. Killer whales (*Orcinus orca*) chasing gray whales (*Eschrichtius robustus*) in the northern Bering Sea. *Arctic* 36(4):361-364.

Ljungblad, D.K., S.E. Moore, D.R. Van Schoik and C.S. Winchell. 1982a. Aerial surveys of endangered whales in the Beaufort, Chukchi, and northern Bering seas. NOSC TD 486. U.S. Naval Ocean Systems Cent., San Diego, CA. 406 p. NTIS AD-A126542/0.

Ljungblad, D.K., P.D. Scoggins and W.G. Gilmartin. 1982b. Auditory thresholds of a captive eastern Pacific bottle-nosed dolphin, *Tursiops* spp. *J. Acoust. Soc. Am.* 72(6):1726-1729.

Ljungblad, D.K., P.O. Thompson and S.E. Moore. 1982c. Underwater sounds recorded from migrating bowhead whales, *Balaena mysticetus*, in 1979. *J. Acoust. Soc. Am.* 71(2):477-482.

Ljungblad, D.K., S.E. Moore and D.R. Van Schoik. 1983. Aerial surveys of endangered whales in the Beaufort, eastern Chukchi, and northern Bering seas, 1982. NOSC TD 605. U.S. Naval Ocean Systems Cent., San Diego, CA. 382 p. NTIS AD-A134772/3.

Ljungblad, D.K., S.E. Moore, J.T. Clarke and J.C. Bennett. 1987. Distribution, abundance, behavior and bioacoustics of endangered whales in the Alaskan Beaufort and eastern Chukchi seas, 1979-86. OCS Study MMS 87-0039. NOSC TR 1177. U.S. Naval Ocean Systems Cent., San Diego, CA, and SEACO Inc., San Diego, CA. 391 p. NTIS PB88-116470 or AD-A183934/9.

Ljungblad, D.K., B. Würsig, S.L. Swartz and J.M. Keene. 1988. Observations on the behavioral responses of bowhead whales (*Balaena mysticetus*) to active geophysical vessels in the Alaskan Beaufort Sea. *Arctic* 41(3):183-194.

Lockyer, C. 1977. Observations on diving behaviour of the sperm whale *Physeter catodon*. p. 591-609 *In*: M. Angel (ed.), A voyage of discovery. Pergamon, Oxford, U.K. 696 p.

Lockyer, C. 1981. Growth and energy budgets of large baleen whales from the Southern Hemisphere. p. 379-487 *In*: Mammals in the seas, vol. III. FAO Fish. Ser. (5) III. Food & Agric. Organiz., United Nations, Rome. 504 p.

Lockyer, C. 1986. Body fat condition in northeast Atlantic fin whales, *Balaenoptera physalus*, and its relationship with reproduction and food resource. *Can. J. Fish. Aquat. Sci.* 43(1):142-147.

Lockyer, C. 1990. Review of incidents involving wild, sociable dolphins, worldwide. p. 337-353 *In*: S. Leatherwood and R.R. Reeves (eds.), The bottlenose dolphin. Academic Press, San Diego, CA. 653 p.

Lockyer, C. 1992. Marine explosions. *Nature (London)* 358(6384):271.

Lockyer, C. and R.J. Morris. 1986. The history and behaviour of a wild, sociable bottlenose dolphin (*Tursiops truncatus*) off the north coast of Cornwall. *Aquat. Mamm.* 12(1):3-16.

Loughrey, A.G. 1959. Preliminary investigation of the Atlantic walrus *Odobenus rosmarus rosmarus* (Linnaeus). *Can. Wildl. Serv. Wildl. Manage. Bull.* (Ser. 1) 14. 123 p.

Lubard, S.C. and P.M. Hurdle. 1976. Experimental investigation of acoustic transmission from air into a rough ocean. *J. Acoust. Soc. Am.* 60(5):1048-1052.

Lubbock, B. 1937. The arctic whalers. Brown, Son & Ferguson, Glasgow, U.K. 483 p. Reprinted 1978.

Lugg, R. 1979. Marine seismic sources. p. 143-203 *In*: A.A. Fitch (ed.), Developments in geophysical exploration methods. Appl. Sci. Publ., London. 311 p.

Luz, G.A. and J.B. Smith. 1976. Reactions of pronghorn antelope to helicopter overflight. *J. Acoust. Soc. Am.* 59(6):1514-1515.

Lynn, S.K. and D.L. Reiss. 1992. Pulse sequence and whistle production by two captive beaked whales, *Mesoplodon* species. *Mar. Mamm. Sci.* 8(3):299-305.

MacArthur, R.A., R.H. Johnston and V. Geist. 1979. Factors influencing heart rate in free-ranging bighorn sheep: A physiological approach to the study of wildlife harassment. *Can. J. Zool.* 57(10):2010-2021.

MacArthur, R.A., V. Geist and R.H. Johnston. 1982. Cardiac and behavioral responses of mountain sheep to human disturbance. *J. Wildl. Manage.* 46(2): 351-358.

Macfarlane, J.A.F. [1981]. Reactions of whales to boat traffic in the area of the confluence of the Saguenay and St. Lawrence rivers, Quebec. Manuscript. 50 p.

Mainini, B., P. Neuhaus and P. Ingold. 1993. Behaviour of marmots *Marmota marmota* under the influence of different hiking activities. *Biol. Conserv.* 64 (2):161-164.

Majors, A.P. and A.C. Myrick, Jr. 1990. Effects of noise on animals: Implications for dolphins exposed to seal bombs in the Eastern Tropical Pacific purse-seine fishery/An annotated bibliography. Admin. Rep. LJ-90-06. U.S. Natl. Mar. Fish. Serv., La Jolla, CA. 55 p.

Makris, N.C. and D.H. Cato. 1994. Using singing whales to track nonsingers. *J. Acoust. Soc. Am.* 96(5, Pt. 2):3270.

Malme, C.I. and P.A. Krumhansl. 1993. A study of sound levels produced by MWRA outfall tunnel boring machine operations in Massachusetts Bay. BBN Tech. Memo. 1113. Rep. from BBN Systems & Technol. Corp., Cambridge, MA. 33 p.

Malme, C.I. and P.R. Miles. 1985. Behavioral responses of marine mammals (gray whales) to seismic discharges. p. 253-280 *In*: Proc. Workshop on Effects of Explosives Use in the Marine Environment, Jan. 1985, Halifax, N.S. Tech. Rep. 5. Can. Oil & Gas Lands Admin. Environ. Prot. Branch, Ottawa, Ont. 398 p.

Malme, C.I. and R. Mlawski. 1979. Measurements of underwater acoustic noise in the Prudhoe Bay area. BBN Tech. Memo. 513. Rep. from Bolt Beranek & Newman Inc., Cambridge, MA, for Exxon Prod. Res. Co., Houston, TX. 74 p.

Malme, C.I. and P.W. Smith, Jr. 1988. Analysis of the acoustic environment of selected pinniped haulout sites in the Alaskan Bering Sea. BBN Tech. Memo. 1012. Rep. from BBN Systems & Technol. Corp., Cambridge, MA, for LGL Alaska Res. Assoc., Anchorage, AK. Var. pag. (Also appears in slightly revised form as Appendix 1 *in* S.R. Johnson et al. 1989).

Malme, C.I., P.R. Miles and P.T. McElroy. 1981. The acoustic environment of humpback whales in Glacier Bay and Fredrick [sic] Sound, Alaska. *J. Acoust. Soc. Am.* 70(Suppl. 1):S85.

Malme, C.I., P.R. Miles, C.W. Clark, P. Tyack and J.E. Bird. 1983. Investigations of the potential effects of underwater noise from petroleum industry activities on migrating gray whale behavior. BBN Rep. 5366. Rep. from Bolt Beranek & Newman Inc., Cambridge, MA, for U.S. Minerals Manage. Serv., Anchorage, AK. Var. pag. NTIS PB86-174174.

Malme, C.I., P.R. Miles, C.W. Clark, P. Tyack and J.E. Bird. 1984. Investigations of the potential effects of underwater noise from petroleum industry activities on migrating gray whale behavior/Phase II: January 1984 migration. BBN Rep. 5586. Rep. from Bolt Beranek & Newman Inc., Cambridge, MA, for U.S. Minerals Manage. Serv., Anchorage, AK. Var. pag. NTIS PB86-218377.

Malme, C.I., P.R. Miles, P. Tyack, C.W. Clark and J.E. Bird. 1985. Investigation of the potential effects of underwater noise from petroleum industry activities on feeding humpback whale behavior. BBN Rep. 5851; OCS Study MMS 85-0019. Rep. from BBN Labs Inc., Cambridge, MA, for U.S. Minerals Manage. Serv., Anchorage, AK. Var. pag. NTIS PB86-218385.

Malme, C.I., P.W. Smith, Jr., and P.R. Miles. 1986a. Study of the effects of offshore geophysical acoustic survey operations on important commercial fisheries in California. BBN Rep. 6125; OCS Study MMS 86-0032. Rep. from BBN Labs Inc., Cambridge, MA, for Battelle Labs, Ventura, CA, and U.S. Minerals Manage. Serv., Los Angeles, CA. 106 p.

Malme, C.I., B. Würsig, J.E. Bird and P. Tyack. 1986b [publ. 1988]. Behavioral responses of gray whales to industrial noise: Feeding observations and predictive modeling. BBN Rep. 6265. Outer Cont. Shelf Environ. Assess. Progr., Final Rep. Princ. Invest., NOAA, Anchorage, AK 56:393-600. 600 p. OCS Study MMS 88-0048; NTIS PB88-249008.

Malme, C.I., B. Würsig, J.E. Bird and P. Tyack. 1988. Observations of feeding gray whale responses to controlled industrial noise exposure. p. 55-73 *In*: W.M. Sackinger et al. (eds.), Port and ocean engineering under arctic conditions, vol. II. Geophys. Inst., Univ. Alaska, Fairbanks. 111 p.

Malme, C.I., P.R. Miles, G.W. Miller, W.J. Richardson, D.G. Roseneau, D.H. Thomson and C.R. Greene, Jr. 1989. Analysis and ranking of the acoustic disturbance potential of petroleum industry activities and other sources of noise in the environment of marine mammals in Alaska. BBN Rep. 6945; OCS Study MMS 89-0006. Rep. from BBN Systems & Technol. Corp., Cambridge, MA, for U.S. Minerals Manage. Serv., Anchorage, AK. Var. pag. NTIS PB90-188673.

Mansfield, A.W. 1983. The effects of vessel traffic in the Arctic on marine mammals and recommendations for future research. *Can. Tech. Rep. Fish. Aquat. Sci.* 1186. 97 p.

Mansfield, A.W. and D.J. St. Aubin. 1991. Distribution and abundance of the Atlantic walrus, *Odobenus rosmarus rosmarus*, in the Southampton Island-Coats Island region of northern Hudson Bay. *Can. Field-Nat.* 105(1):95-100.

Marine Mammal Commission. 1979/80. Humpback whales in Glacier Bay National Monument, Alaska. MMC-79/01. U.S. Mar. Mamm. Comm., Washington, DC. 44 p. NTIS PB80-141559.

Marquette, W.M., H.W. Braham, M.K. Nerini and R.V. Miller. 1982. Bowhead whale studies, autumn 1980-spring 1981: Harvest, biology and distribution. *Rep. Int. Whal. Comm.* 32:357-370.

Marsh, H., A.V. Spain and G.E. Heinsohn. 1978. Physiology of the dugong. *Comp. Biochem. Physiol. A* 61(2):159-168.

Marsh, H.W. and M. Schulkin. 1962. Shallow-water transmission. *J. Acoust. Soc. Am.* 34(6):863-864.

Marten, K.L., K.S. Norris, M. Poole, C.R. Schilt and K. Newman. 1989. Big bang theory update: Debilitating fish with sound. p. 41 *In*: Abstr. 8th Bienn. Conf. Biol. Mar. Mamm., Pacific Grove, CA, Dec. 1989. 81 p.

Martin, M.L., M. Weinrich and J. Bower. 1993. The acoustic behavior of humpback whales, *Megaptera novaeangliae*, in a high latitude feeding ground. p. 74 *In*: Abstr. 10th Bienn. Conf. Biol. Mar. Mamm., Galveston, TX, Nov. 1993. 130 p.

Mason, W.P. (ed.). 1965. Physical acoustics, vol. II, Pt. A, p. 293-295. Academic Press, New York. 476 p.

Mate, B. 1993. Experiments with an acoustic harassment system to limit seal movements. *J. Acoust. Soc. Am.* 94(3, Pt. 2):1828.

Mate, B.R. and J.T. Harvey (eds.). 1987. Acoustical deterrents in marine mammal conflicts with fisheries. ORESU-W-86-001. Oregon State Univ. Sea Grant Coll. Program, Corvallis, OR. 116 p.

Mate, B.R., K.M. Stafford and D.K. Ljungblad. 1994. A change in sperm whale (*Physeter macrocephalus*) distribution correlated to seismic surveys in the Gulf of Mexico. *J. Acoust. Soc. Am.* 96(5, Pt. 2):3268-3269.

Mattila, D.K., L.N. Guinee and C.A. Mayo. 1987. Humpback whale songs on a North Atlantic feeding ground. *J. Mammal.* 68(4):880-883.

Maybaum, H.L. 1990. Effects of a 3.3 kHz sonar system on humpback whales, *Megaptera novaeangliae*, in Hawaiian waters. *Eos* 71(2):92.

Maybaum, H.L. 1993. Responses of humpback whales to sonar sounds. *J. Acoust. Soc. Am.* 94(3, Pt. 2):1848-1849.

Mayo, C.A. and M.K. Marx. 1990. Surface foraging behaviour of the North Atlantic right whale, *Eubalaena glacialis*, and associated zooplankton characteristics. *Can. J. Zool.* 68(10):2214-2220.

McCarty, S.L. 1982. Survey of the effects of outer continental shelf platforms on cetacean behavior. p. C-1 to C-31 *In*: R.S. Gales (ed.), Effects of noise of offshore oil and gas operations on marine mammals—An introductory assessment, vol. 2. NOSC TR 844. U.S. Naval Ocean Systems Cent., San Diego, CA. 300 p. NTIS AD-A123700.

McCauley, R.D. 1994. Seismic surveys. p. 19-121 *In*: J.M. Swan, J.M. Neff and P.C. Young (eds.), Environmental implications of offshore oil and gas development in Australia/The findings of an independent scientific review. Austral. Petrol. Explor. Assoc., Sydney, N.S.W. 696 p.

McDonald, M.A., J.A. Hildebrand, S. Webb, L. Dorman and C.G. Fox. 1993. Vocalizations of blue and fin whales during a midocean ridge airgun experiment. *J. Acoust. Soc. Am.* 94(3, Pt. 2):1849.

McLaren, M.A. and J.E. Green. 1985. The reactions of muskoxen to snowmobile harassment. *Arctic* 38(3):188-193.

McLeod, P.J. 1986. Observations during the stranding of one individual from a pod of pilot whales, *Globicephala melaena*, in Newfoundland. *Can. Field-Nat.* 100(1):137-139.

McLeod, S.A., F.C. Whitmore, Jr., and L.G. Barnes. 1993. Evolutionary relationships and classification. p. 45-70 *In*: J.J. Burns, J.J. Montague and C.J. Cowles (eds.), The bowhead whale. Spec. Publ. 2. Soc. Mar. Mammal., Lawrence, KS. 787 p.

McSweeney, D.J., K.C. Chu, W.F. Dolphin and L.N. Guinee. 1989. North Pacific humpback whale songs: A comparison of southeast Alaskan feeding ground songs with Hawaiian wintering ground songs. *Mar. Mamm. Sci.* 5(2):139-148.

Medwin, H. and J.D. Hagy, Jr. 1972. Helmholtz-Kirchhoff theory for sound transmission through a statistically rough plane interface between dissimilar fluids. *J. Acoust. Soc. Am.* 51(3, Pt. 2):1083-1090.

Mees, J. and P.J.H. Reijnders. 1994. The harbour seal, *Phoca vitulina*, in the Oosterschelde: Decline and possibilities for recovery. *Hydrobiologia* 283:547-555.

Mellen, R.H. 1952. The thermal-noise limit in the detection of underwater acoustic signals. *J. Acoust. Soc. Am.* 24(5):478-480.

Mellen, R.H., D.G. Browning and L. Goodman. 1976. Diffusion loss in a stratified sound channel. *J. Acoust. Soc. Am.* 60(5):1053-1055.

Michalak, R., H. Ising and E. Rebentisch. 1990. Acute circulatory effects of military low-altitude flight noise. *Int. Arch. Occup. Environ. Health* 62(5):365-372.

Mhenni, S. 1993. Interactions mammifères marins et engins de pêche: La dispersion des dauphins par des ondes ultra sonores. p. 89-93 *In*: La pêche en Tunisie: Pêche côtière et environnement. CERES Sér. Géogr. 9. Cent. Études Rech. Économ. Soc., Tunis.

Mikhalevsky, P.N., A.B. Baggeroer, A. Gavrilov and M. Slavinsky. 1994. Continuous wave and M-sequence transmissions across the Arctic. *J. Acoust. Soc. Am.* 96(5, Pt. 2):3235-3236.

Miles, P.R. 1984. Offshore seismic survey history in California and the migration of gray whales. Appendix A *In*: C.I. Malme, P.R. Miles, C.W. Clark, P. Tyack and J.E. Bird, Investigations of the potential effects of underwater noise from petroleum industry activities on migrating gray whale behavior/Phase II: January 1984 migration. BBN Rep. 5586. Rep. from Bolt Beranek & Newman Inc., Cambridge, MA, for U.S. Minerals Manage. Serv., Anchorage, AK. Var. pag. NTIS PB86-218377.

Miles, P.R. and C.I. Malme. 1983. The acoustic environment and noise exposure of humpback whales in Glacier Bay, Alaska. BBN Tech. Memo. 734. Rep. from Bolt Beranek & Newman Inc., Cambridge, MA, for U.S. Natl. Mar. Fish. Serv., Seattle, WA. 81 p.

Miles, P.R., C.I. Malme, G.W. Shepard, W.J. Richardson and J.E. Bird. 1986. Prediction of drilling site-specific interaction of industrial acoustic stimuli and endangered whales: Beaufort Sea (1985). BBN Rep. 6185; OCS Study

MMS 86-0046. Rep. from BBN Labs Inc., Cambridge, MA, for U.S. Minerals Manage. Serv., Anchorage, AK. 312 p. NTIS PB87-124343.

Miles, P.R., C.I. Malme and W.J. Richardson. 1987. Prediction of drilling site-specific interaction of industrial acoustic stimuli and endangered whales in the Alaskan Beaufort Sea. BBN Rep. 6509; OCS Study MMS 87-0084. Rep. from BBN Labs Inc., Cambridge, MA, and LGL Ltd., King City, Ont., for U.S. Minerals Manage. Serv., Anchorage, AK. 341 p. NTIS PB88-158498.

Miller, E.H. 1985. Airborne acoustic communication in the walrus *Odobenus rosmarus*. *Natl. Geogr. Res.* 1:124-145.

Miller, E.H. 1991. Communication in pinnipeds, with special reference to non-acoustic signalling. p. 128-235 *In*: D. Renouf (ed.), The behaviour of pinnipeds. Chapman & Hall, London. 410 p.

Miller, E.H. 1992. Acoustic signals of shorebirds/A survey and review of published information. Tech. Rep., R. Brit. Col. Mus., Victoria, B.C. 62 p.

Miller, E.H. and D.A. Job. 1992. Airborne acoustic communication in the Hawaiian monk seal, *Monachus schauinslandi*. p. 485-531 *In*: J.A. Thomas, R.A. Kastelein and A.Ya. Supin (eds.), Marine mammal sensory systems. Plenum, New York. 773 p.

Miller, E.H. and A.V. Murray. 1995. Structure, complexity and organization of vocalizations in pup harp seals, *Phoca groenlandica*. *In*: R.A. Kastelein, J.A. Thomas and P.E. Nachtigall (eds.), Sensory systems of aquatic mammals. De Spil Publ., Woerden, Netherlands. (in press).

Miller, F.L. and A. Gunn. 1980. Behavioral responses of muskox herds to simulation of cargo slinging by helicopter, Northwest Territories. *Can. Field-Nat.* 94 (1):52-60.

Miller, G.A., G.A. Heise and W. Lichten. 1951. The intelligibility of speech as a function of the context of the test materials. *J. Exp. Psychol.* 41(5):329-335.

Miller, G.W., R.A. Davis and W.J. Richardson. 1991. Behavior of bowhead whales of the Davis Strait and Bering/Beaufort stocks vs. regional differences in human activities. OCS Study MMS 91-0029. Rep. from LGL Ltd., King City, Ont., for U.S. Minerals Manage. Serv., Anchorage, AK. 111 p. NTIS PB91-235267.

Miller, M.W., N.T. Hobbs and M.C. Sousa. 1991. Detecting stress responses in Rocky Mountain bighorn sheep (*Ovis canadensis canadensis*): Reliability of cortisol concentrations in urine and feces. *Can. J. Zool.* 69(1):15-24.

Mills, A.W. 1958. On the minimum audible angle. *J. Acoust. Soc. Am.* 30(4):237-246.

Milne, A.R. and J.H. Ganton. 1964. Ambient noise under Arctic-sea ice. *J. Acoust. Soc. Am.* 36(5):855-863.

Mitchell, E.D. and L. Ghanimé. 1982. Evidence of whale-vessel interaction—North shore of the St. Lawrence Estuary. p. 3-1 to 3-32 *In*: Analysis of whale observations from the St-Lawrence Estuary. Rep. from André Marsan & Assoc. for Can. Dep. Fish. Oceans, Petro-Canada Arctic Pilot Proj., and Can. Dep. Supply Serv. Var. pag.

Mitson, R.B. 1990. Very-high-frequency acoustic emissions from the white-beaked dolphin (*Lagenorhynchus albirostris*). p. 283-294 *In*: J.A. Thomas and R.A.

Kastelein (eds.), Sensory abilities of cetaceans/Laboratory and field evidence. Plenum, New York. 710 p.

Moen, A.N., S. Whittemore and B. Buxton. 1982. Effects of disturbance by snowmobiles on heart rate of captive white-tailed deer. *N.Y. Fish & Game J.* 29 (2):176-183.

Møhl, B. 1964. Preliminary studies on hearing in seals. *Vidensk. Medd. Dansk Naturh. Foren.* 127:283-294.

Møhl, B. 1967. Frequency discrimination in the common seal and a discussion of the concept of upper hearing limit. p. 43-54 *In*: V.M. Albers (ed.), Underwater acoustics, vol. 2. Plenum, New York. 416 p.

Møhl, B. 1968a. Auditory sensitivity of the common seal in air and water. *J. Aud. Res.* 8(1):27-38.

Møhl, B. 1968b. Hearing in seals. p. 172-195 *In*: R.J. Harrison, R.C. Hubbard, R.S. Peterson, C.E. Rice and R.J. Schusterman (eds.), The behavior and physiology of pinnipeds. Appleton-Century-Crofts, New York. 411 p.

Møhl, B. 1981. Masking effects of noise; their distribution in time and space. p. 259-266 *In*: N.M. Peterson (ed.), The question of sound from icebreaker operations: The proceedings of a workshop. Arctic Pilot Proj., Petro-Canada, Calgary, Alb. 350 p.

Møhl, B. and S. Andersen. 1973. Echolocation: High-frequency component in the click of the harbour porpoise (*Phocoena ph.* L.). *J. Acoust. Soc. Am.* 54(5): 1368-1372.

Møhl, B. and K. Ronald. 1975. The peripheral auditory system of the harp seal, *Pagophilus groenlandicus*, (Erxleben, 1777). *Rapp. P.-V. Réun. Cons. Int. Explor. Mer* 169:516-523.

Møhl, B., J.M. Terhune and K. Ronald. 1975. Underwater calls of the harp seal, *Pagophilus groenlandicus*. *Rapp. P.-V. Réun. Cons. Int. Explor. Mer* 169:533-543.

Møhl, B., A. Surlykke and L.A. Miller. 1990. High intensity narwhal clicks. p. 295-303 *In*: J.A. Thomas and R.A. Kastelein (eds.), Sensory abilities of cetaceans/Laboratory and field evidence. Plenum, New York. 710 p.

Moore, K.E., W.A. Watkins and P.L. Tyack. 1993. Pattern similarity in shared codas from sperm whales (*Physeter catodon*). *Mar. Mamm. Sci.* 9(1):1-9.

Moore, P.W.B. 1975. Underwater localization of click and pulsed pure-tone signals by the California sea lion (*Zalophus californianus*). *J. Acoust. Soc. Am.* 57(2):406-410.

Moore, P.W.B. 1980. Cetacean obstacle avoidance. p. 97-108 *In*: R.-G. Busnel and J.F. Fish (eds.), Animal sonar systems. Plenum, New York. 1135 p.

Moore, P.W.B. and W.W.L. Au. 1975. Underwater localization of pulsed pure tones by the California sea lion (*Zalophus californianus*). *J. Acoust. Soc. Am.* 58(3):721-727.

Moore, P.W.B. and D.A. Pawloski. 1990. Investigations on the control of echolocation pulses in the dolphin (*Tursiops truncatus*). p. 305-316 *In*: J.A. Thomas and R.A. Kastelein (eds.), Sensory abilities of cetaceans/Laboratory and field evidence. Plenum, New York. 710 p.

Moore, P.W.B. and R.J. Schusterman. 1976. Discrimination of pure-tone intensities by the California sea lion. *J. Acoust. Soc. Am.* 60(6):1405-1407.

Moore, P.W.B. and R.J. Schusterman. 1987. Audiometric assessment of northern fur seals, *Callorhinus ursinus*. *Mar. Mamm. Sci.* 3(1):31-53.

Moore, S.E. and J.T. Clarke. 1992. Patterns of bowhead whale distribution and abundance near Barrow, Alaska, in fall 1982-1989. *Mar. Mamm. Sci.* 8(1):27-36.

Moore, S.E. and J.T. Clarke. in press. Potential impact of offshore human activities on gray whales. *Rep. Int. Whal. Comm. (Spec. Issue).*

Moore, S.E. and D.K. Ljungblad. 1984. Gray whales in the Beaufort, Chukchi, and Bering seas: Distribution and sound production. p. 543-559 *In*: M.L. Jones, S.L. Swartz and S. Leatherwood (eds.), The gray whale *Eschrichtius robustus*. Academic Press, Orlando, FL. 600 p.

Moore, S.E. and S.H. Ridgway. 1995. Whistles produced by common dolphins from the southern California Bight. *Aquat. Mamm.* 21(1):55-63.

Moore, S.E., D.K. Ljungblad and D.R. Schmidt. 1984. Ambient, industrial and biological sounds recorded in the northern Bering, eastern Chukchi and Alaskan Beaufort seas during the seasonal migrations of the bowhead whale (*Balaena mysticetus*), 1979-1982. Rep. from SEACO Inc., San Diego, CA, for U.S. Minerals Manage. Serv., Anchorage, AK. 111 p. NTIS PB86-168887.

Moore, S.E., J.K. Francine, A.E. Bowles and J.K.B. Ford. 1988. Analysis of calls of killer whales, *Orcinus orca*, from Iceland and Norway. *Rit Fisk.* 11:225-250.

Moore, S.E., J.C. Bennett and D.K. Ljungblad. 1989. Use of passive acoustics in conjunction with aerial surveys to monitor the fall bowhead whale (*Balaena mysticetus*) migration. *Rep. Int. Whal. Comm.* 39:291-295.

Morrice, M.G., H.R. Burton and K. Green. 1994. Microgeographic variation and songs in the underwater vocalisation repertoire of the Weddell seal (*Leptonychotes weddellii*) from the Vestfold Hills, Antarctica. *Polar Biol.* 14(7):441-446.

Morton, A.B., J.C. Gale and R.C. Prince. 1986. Sound and behavioral correlations in captive *Orcinus orca*. p. 303-333 *In*: B.C. Kirkevold and J.S. Lockard (eds.), Behavioral biology of killer whales. Alan R. Liss, New York. 457 p.

Moscrop, A. 1993. An assessment of threats to marine cetaceans resulting from the degradation of their habitats. M.Sc. Thesis, Univ. of Greenwich, London. 227 p.

Moulton, J.M. 1960. Swimming sounds and the schooling of fishes. *Biol. Bull. (Woods Hole, Mass.)* 119(2):210-223.

Mullin, K., R. Lohoefener, W. Hoggard, C. Roden and C. Rogers. 1989. Is the spatial distribution of bottlenose dolphin herds affected by petroleum platforms? p. 45 *In*: Abstr. 8th Bienn. Conf. Biol. Mar. Mamm., Pacific Grove, CA, Dec. 1989. 81 p.

Mullin, K., W. Hoggard, C. Roden, R. Lohoefener, C. Rogers and B. Taggart. 1991. Cetaceans on the upper continental slope in the north-central Gulf of Mexico. OCS Study MMS 91-0027. Rep. from U.S. Natl. Mar. Fish. Serv., Pascagoula, MS, for U.S. Minerals Manage. Serv., New Orleans, LA. 108 p.

Mullin, K.D., L.V. Higgins, T.A. Jefferson and L.J. Hansen. 1994a. Sightings of the Clymene dolphin (*Stenella clymene*) in the Gulf of Mexico. *Mar. Mamm. Sci.* 10(4):464-470.

Mullin, K.D., T.A. Jefferson, L.J. Hansen and W. Hoggard. 1994b. First sightings of melon-headed whales (*Peponocephala electra*) in the Gulf of Mexico. *Mar. Mamm. Sci.* 10(3):342-348.

Mullins, J., H. Whitehead and L.S. Weilgart. 1988. Behaviour and vocalizations of two single sperm whales, *Physeter macrocephalus*, off Nova Scotia. *Can. J. Fish. Aquat. Sci.* 45(10):1736-1743.

Munk, W.H. 1990. The Heard Island experiment. Int. Sci. Lect. Ser., U.S. Natl. Acad. Sci. and U.S. Navy Off. Naval Res. Natl. Acad Press, Washington, DC. 33 p.

Munk, W.H., R.C. Spindel, A. Baggeroer and T.G. Birdsall. 1994. The Heard Island Feasibility Test. *J. Acoust. Soc. Am.* 96(4):2330-2342.

Myrberg, A.A., Jr. 1978. Ocean noise and the behavior of marine animals: Relationships and implications. p. 169-208 *In*: J.L. Fletcher and R.G. Busnel (eds.), Effects of noise on wildlife. Academic Press, New York. 305 p.

Myrick, A.C., Jr., E.R. Cassano and C.W. Oliver. 1990a. Potential for physical injury, other than hearing damage, to dolphins from seal bombs used in the yellowfin tuna purse-seine fishery: Results from open-water tests. Admin. Rep. LJ-90-07. U.S. Natl. Mar. Fish. Serv., La Jolla, CA. 28 p.

Myrick, A.C., Jr., M. Fink and C.B. Glick. 1990b. Identification, chemistry, and behavior of seal bombs used to control dolphins in the yellowfin tuna purse-seine fishery in the Eastern Tropical Pacific: Potential hazards. Admin. Rep. LJ-90-08. U.S. Natl. Mar. Fish. Serv., La Jolla, CA. 25 p.

Nachtigall, P.E. 1986. Vision, audition, and chemoreception in dolphins and other marine mammals. p. 79-113 *In*: R.J. Schusterman, J.A. Thomas and F.G. Wood (eds.), Dolphin cognition and behavior: A comparative approach. Erlbaum, Hillsdale, NJ. 393 p.

Nachtigall, P.E. and P.W.B. Moore (eds.). 1988. Animal sonar processes and performance. Plenum, New York. 862 p.

Nachtigall, P.E., W.W.L. Au, J.L. Pawloski and P.W.B. Moore. 1995. Risso's dolphin (*Grampus griseus*) hearing thresholds in Kaneohe Bay, Hawaii. *In*: R.A. Kastelein, J.A. Thomas and P.E. Nachtigall (eds.), Sensory systems of aquatic mammals. De Spil Publ., Woerden, Netherlands. (in press).

Nair, R.V. and R.S. Lal Mohan. 1975. Studies on the vocalisation of the sea cow *Dugong dugon* in captivity. *Indian J. Fish.* 22:277-278.

Nielsen, R.O. 1991. Sonar signal processing. Artech House, Norwood, MA. 368 p.

Nilson, M.R., C.G. D'Vincent and F.A. Sharpe. 1989. Form and function of the feeding vocalization of the southeast Alaskan humpback whale (*Megaptera novaeangliae*). p. 46 *In*: Abstr. 8th Bienn. Conf. Biol. Mar. Mamm., Pacific Grove, CA, Dec. 1989. 81 p.

Nishiwaki, M. and H. Marsh. 1985. Dugong *Dugong dugon* (Müller, 1776). p. 1-31 *In*: S.H. Ridgway and R. Harrison (eds.), Handbook of marine mammals, vol. 3. Academic Press, London. 362 p.

Nishiwaki, M. and A. Sasao. 1977. Human activities disturbing natural migration routes of whales. *Sci. Rep. Whales Res. Inst.* 29:113-120.

NMFS (U.S. Natl. Mar. Fish. Serv.). 1987. Endangered fish and wildlife; approaching humpback whales in Hawaiian waters. *Fed. Regist.* 52(225, 23 Nov.):44912-44915 [50 CFR Part 222].

NMFS (U.S. Natl. Mar. Fish. Serv.). 1993. Protected species special exception permits/Proposed rule and request for comments. *Fed. Regist.* 58(197, 14 Oct.): 53320-53364.

Norris, J.C. and S. Leatherwood. 1981. Hearing in bowhead whale, *Balaena mysticetus*, as estimated by cochlear morphology. p. 745-787 *In*: T.F. Albert (ed.), Tissue structural studies and other investigations on the biology of endangered whales in the Beaufort Sea, vol. II. Rep. from Dep. Vet. Sci., Univ. Maryland, College Park, MD, for U.S. Bur. Land Manage., Anchorage, AK. 953 p. in 2 vol. NTIS PB86-153566.

Norris, K.S. 1969. The echolocation of marine mammals. p. 391-423 *In*: H.T. Andersen (ed.), The biology of marine mammals. Academic Press, New York. 511 p.

Norris, K.S. 1981. Marine mammals of the Arctic, their sounds and their relation to alterations in the acoustic environment by man-made noise. p. 304-309 *In*: N.M. Peterson (ed.), The question of sound from icebreaker operations: The proceedings of a workshop. Arctic Pilot Proj., Petro-Canada, Calgary, Alb. 350 p.

Norris, K.S. and T.P. Dohl. 1980. Behavior of the Hawaiian spinner dolphin, *Stenella longirostris*. *Fish. Bull.* 77(4):821-849.

Norris, K.S. and W.E. Evans. 1967. Directionality of echolocation clicks in the rough-tooth porpoise, *Steno bredanensis* (Lesson). p. 305-316 *In*: W.N. Tavolga (ed.), Marine bio-acoustics, vol. 2. Pergamon, Oxford, U.K. 353 p.

Norris, K.S. and G.W. Harvey. 1974. Sound transmission in the porpoise head. *J. Acoust. Soc. Am.* 56(2):659-664.

Norris, K.S. and B. Møhl. 1983. Can odontocetes debilitate prey with sound? *Am. Nat.* 122(1):85-104.

Norris, K.S. and R.R. Reeves (eds.). 1978. Report on a workshop on problems related to humpback whales (*Megaptera novaeangliae*) in Hawaii. MMC-77/03. Rep. from Sea Life Inc., Makapuu Pt., HI, for U.S. Mar. Mamm. Comm., Washington, DC. 90 p. NTIS PB-280794.

Norris, K.S. and W.A. Watkins. 1971. Underwater sounds of *Arctocephalus philippii*, the Juan Fernández fur seal. p. 169-171 *In*: W.H. Burt (ed.), Antarctic Pinnipedia. Antarct. Res. Ser. 18. Am. Geophys. Union, Washington, DC. 226 p.

Norris, K.S., G.W. Harvey, L.A. Burzell and T.D. Krishna Kartha. 1972. Sound production in the freshwater porpoises *Sotalia* cf. *fluviatilis* Gervais and Deville and *Inia geoffrensis* Blainville, in the Rio Negro, Brazil. *Invest. Cetacea* 4:251-259 + plates.

Norris, K.S., R.M. Goodman, B. Villa-Ramirez and L. Hobbs. 1977. Behavior of California gray whale, *Eschrichtius robustus*, in southern Baja California, Mexico. *Fish. Bull.* 75(1):159-172.

Norris, K.S., W.E. Stuntz and W. Rogers. 1978. The behavior of porpoises and tuna in the eastern tropical Pacific yellowfin tuna fishery—Preliminary studies. MMC-76/12. U.S. Mar. Mamm. Comm., Washington, DC. 86 p. NTIS PB-283970.

Norris, K.S., B. Villa-Ramirez, G. Nichols, B. Würsig and K. Miller. 1983. Lagoon entrance and other aggregations of gray whales (*Eschrichtius robustus*). p. 259-293 *In*: R. Payne (ed.), Communication and behavior of whales. AAAS Sel. Symp. 76. Westview Press, Boulder, CO. 643 p.

Norris, K.S., B. Würsig, R.S. Wells and M. Würsig, with S.M. Brownlee, C.M. Johnson and J. Solow. 1994. The Hawaiian spinner dolphin. Univ. Calif. Press, Berkeley. 408 p.

Norris, T.F. 1994. Effects of boat noise on the acoustic behavior of humpback whales. *J. Acoust. Soc. Am.* 96(5, Pt. 2):3251.

Northrop, J., W.C. Cummings and P.O. Thompson. 1968. 20-Hz signals observed in the central Pacific. *J. Acoust. Soc. Am.* 43(2):383-384.

Northrop, J., W.C. Cummings and M.F. Morrison. 1971. Underwater 20-Hz signals recorded near Midway Island. *J. Acoust. Soc. Am.* 49(6, Pt. 2):1909-1910.

Norton Fraker, P. and M.A. Fraker. 1982. The 1981 white whale monitoring program, Mackenzie Estuary. Rep. from LGL Ltd., Sidney, B.C. for Esso Resources Canada Ltd. (manager), Calgary, Alb. 74 p.

Noseworthy, E., D. Renouf and W.K. Jacobs. 1989. Acoustic breeding displays of harbour seals. p. 46 *In*: Abstr. 8th Bienn. Conf. Biol. Mar. Mamm., Pacific Grove, CA, Dec. 1989. 81 p.

NRC/OSB. 1994. Low-frequency sound and marine mammals/Current knowledge and research needs. U.S. Natl. Res. Counc., Ocean Stud. Board, Committee on low-frequency sound and marine mammals (D.M. Green, H.A. DeFerrari, D. McFadden, J.S. Pearse, A.N. Popper, W.J. Richardson, S.H. Ridgway and P.L. Tyack). Natl. Acad. Press, Washington, DC. 75 p.

Oelschläger, H.A. 1986a. Comparative morphology and evolution of the otic region in toothed whales (Cetacea, Mammalia). *Am. J. Anat.* 177(3):353-368.

Oelschläger, H.A. 1986b. Tympanohyal bone in toothed whales and the formation of the tympano-periotic complex (Mammalia: Cetacea). *J. Morphol.* 188(2):157-165.

Officer, C.B. 1958. Introduction to the theory of sound transmission with application to the ocean. McGraw-Hill, New York. 284 p.

Öhrström, E., M. Björkman and R. Rylander. 1990. Effects of noise during sleep with reference to noise sensitivity and habituation. *Environ. Int.* 16(4-6):477-482.

O'Keeffe, D.J. and G.A. Young. 1984. Handbook on the environmental effects of underwater explosions. NSWC/WOL TR-83-240. Naval Surf. Weap. Cent., White Oak Lab., Silver Spring, MD. 207 p. Def. Tech. Info. Cent. AD-B 093885.

Oliver, G.W. 1978. Navigation in mazes by a grey seal, *Halichoerus grypus* (Fabricius). *Behaviour* 67(1-2):97-114.

Osborn, L.S. 1985. Population dynamics, behavior, and the effect of disturbance on haulout patterns of the harbor seal *Phoca vitulina richardsi*/Elkhorn Slough, Monterey Bay, California. B.A. Thesis, Dep. Environ. Stud. & Dep. Biol., Univ. Calif., Santa Cruz. 75 p.

O'Shea, T.J., C.A. Beck, R.K. Bonde, H.I. Kochman and D.K. Odell. 1985. An analysis of manatee mortality patterns in Florida, 1976-81. *J. Wildl. Manage.* 49(1):1-11.

Ouellet, P. 1979. Northern whales. [LP phono. record]. Music Gallery Editions 19. Toronto, Ont.

Overstrom, N.A. 1983. Association between burst-pulse sounds and aggressive behavior in captive Atlantic bottlenosed dolphins (*Tursiops truncatus*). *Zoo Biol.* 2:93-103.

Ovsyanikov, N.G., L.L. Bove and A.A. Kochnev. 1994. [The factors causing mass death of walruses on coastal rookeries.] *Zool. Zh.* 73(5):80-87 (in Russian, Engl. summ.).

Palka, D.L. 1993. The presence of ship avoidance during a line transect survey of harbor porpoises in the Gulf of Maine. p. 84 *In*: Abstr. 10th Bienn. Conf. Biol. Mar. Mamm., Galveston, TX, Nov. 1993. 130 p.

Papastavrou, V., S.C. Smith and H. Whitehead. 1989. Diving behaviour of the sperm whale, *Physeter macrocephalus*, off the Galapagos Islands. *Can. J. Zool.* 67(4):839-846.

Parrott, R. 1991. Seismic and acoustic systems for marine survey used by the Geological Survey of Canada: Background information for environmental screening. Manuscript, Atlantic Geosci. Cent., Geol. Surv. Can., Dartmouth, N.S. 36 p.

Patten, D.R., W.F. Samaras and D.R. McIntyre. 1980. Whales, move over! *Whale-watcher, J. Am. Cetac. Soc.* 14(4):13-15.

Patterson, B. and G.R. Hamilton. 1964. Repetitive 20 cycle per second biological hydroacoustic signals at Bermuda. p. 125-146 *In*: W.N. Tavolga (ed.), Marine bio-acoustics. Pergamon, Oxford, U.K. 413 p.

Payne, K. and R. Payne. 1985. Large scale changes over 19 years in songs of humpback whales in Bermuda. *Z. Tierpsychol.* 68(2):89-114.

Payne, R.S. 1970. Songs of the humpback whale. Cat. No. ST-620. Capital Records, Hollywood, CA.

Payne, R. 1972. Swimming with Patagonia's right whales. *Natl. Geogr.* 142(4): 576-587.

Payne, R. 1978a. Behavior and vocalizations of humpback whales (*Megaptera* sp.). p. 56-78 *In*: K.S. Norris and R.R. Reeves (eds.), Report on a workshop on problems related to humpback whales (*Megaptera novaeangliae*) in Hawaii. MMC-77/03. Rep. from Sea Life Inc., Makapuu Pt., HI, for U.S. Mar. Mamm. Comm., Washington, DC. 90 p. NTIS PB-280794.

Payne, R. 1978b. A note on harassment. p. 89-90 *In*: K.S. Norris and R.R. Reeves (eds.), Report on a workshop on problems related to humpback whales (*Megaptera novaeangliae*) in Hawaii. MMC-77/03. Rep. from Sea Life Inc., Makapuu Pt., HI, for U.S. Mar. Mamm. Comm., Washington, DC. 90 p. NTIS PB-280794.

Payne, R. and L.N. Guinee. 1983. Humpback whale (*Megaptera novaeangliae*) songs as an indicator of "stocks". p. 333-358 *In*: R. Payne (ed.), Communication and behavior of whales. AAAS Sel. Symp. 76. Westview Press, Boulder, CO. 643 p.

Payne, R.S. and S. McVay. 1971. Songs of humpback whales. *Science* 173(3997): 585-597.

Payne, R. and D. Webb. 1971. Orientation by means of long range acoustic signaling in baleen whales. *Ann. N.Y. Acad. Sci.* 188:110-141.

Payne, R., O. Brazier, E.M. Dorsey, J.S. Perkins, V.J. Rowntree and A. Titus. 1983. External features in southern right whales (*Eubalaena australis*) and their use in identifying individuals. p. 371-445 *In*: R. Payne (ed.), Communication and behavior of whales. AAAS Sel. Symp. 76. Westview Press, Boulder, CO. 643 p.

Pearsons, K.S. 1966. The effects of duration and background noise level on perceived noisiness. FAA-ADS-78. Rep. from Bolt, Beranek & Newman Inc., Cambridge, MA, for U.S. Fed. Aviat. Agency, Washington, DC. Var. pag. NTIS AD-646025.

Pekeris, C.L. 1948. Theory of propagation of explosive sound in shallow water. *In*: Propagation of sound in the ocean. *Geol. Soc. Am. Memoir* 27. 200 p.

Penner, R.H., C.W. Turl and W.W. Au. 1986. Target detection by the beluga using a surface-reflected path. *J. Acoust. Soc. Am.* 80(6):1842-1843.

Perrin, W.F., G.P. Donovan and J. Barlow (eds.). 1994. Gillnets and cetaceans. Rep. Int. Whal. Comm. (Spec. Issue) 15. 629 p.

Perry, E. and D. Renouf. 1985. The vocalization of the harbour seal pup: A useful tool for identification and contact, especially in water. *In*: Abstr. 6th Bienn. Conf. Biol. Mar. Mamm., Vancouver, B.C., Nov. 1985. [86 p.]

Perry, E.A. and D. Renouf. 1988. Further studies of the role of harbour seal (*Phoca vitulina*) pup vocalizations in preventing separation of mother-pup pairs. *Can. J. Zool.* 66(4):934-938.

Peterson, N.M. (ed.). 1981. The question of sound from icebreaker operations: The proceedings of a workshop. Arctic Pilot Proj., Petro-Canada, Calgary, Alb. 350 p.

Peterson, R.S. 1968. Social behavior in pinnipeds with particular reference to the northern fur seal. p. 3-53 *In*: R.J. Harrison, R.C. Hubbard, R.S. Peterson, C.E. Rice and R.J. Schusterman (eds.), The behavior and physiology of pinnipeds. Appleton-Century-Crofts, New York. 411 p.

Peterson, R.S. and G.A. Bartholomew. 1967. The natural history and behavior of the California sea lion. *Am. Soc. Mammal., Spec. Publ.* 1. 79 p.

Peterson, R.S. and G.A. Bartholomew. 1969. Airborne vocal communication in the California sea lion, *Zalophus californianus. Anim. Behav.* 17(1):17-24.

Peterson, R.S., C.L. Hubbs, R.L. Gentry and R.L. DeLong. 1968. The Guadalupe fur seal: Habitat, behavior, population size, and field identification. *J. Mammal.* 49(4):665-675.

Petrinovich, L. 1974. Individual recognition of pup vocalization by northern elephant seal mothers. *Z. Tierpsychol.* 34(3):308-312.

Piercy, J.E. and T.F.W. Embleton. 1974. Effect of ground on near-horizontal sound propagation. *Trans. Soc. Automot. Eng., Sect. I* 83:928-936.

Pilleri, G., C. Kraus and M. Gihr. 1971. Physical analysis of the sounds emitted by *Platanista indi*. *Invest. Cetacea* 3:22-30 + plates.

Pilleri, G., K. Zbinden and C. Kraus. 1980. Characteristics of the sonar system of cetaceans with pterygoschisis/Directional properties of the sonar clicks of *Neophocaena phocaenoides* and *Phocoena phocoena* (Phocoenidae). *Invest. Cetacea* 11:157-188.

Pippard, L. 1985. Status of the St. Lawrence River population of beluga, *Delphinapterus leucas*. *Can. Field-Nat.* 99(3):438-450.

Polacheck, T. and L. Thorpe. 1990. The swimming direction of harbor porpoise in relationship to a survey vessel. *Rep. Int. Whal. Comm.* 40:463-470.

Popov, V. and A. Supin. 1990. Electrophysiological studies of hearing in some cetaceans and a manatee. p. 405-415 *In*: J.A. Thomas and R.A. Kastelein (eds.), Sensory abilities of cetaceans/Laboratory and field evidence. Plenum, New York. 710 p.

Popov, V.V., T.F. Ladygina and A.Ya. Supin. 1986. Evoked potentials of the auditory cortex of the porpoise, *Phocoena phocoena*. *J. Comp. Physiol. A* 158(5): 705-711.

Popov, V.V., A.Ya. Supin and V.O. Klishin. 1992. Electrophysiological study of sound conduction in dolphins. p. 269-276 *In*: J.A. Thomas, R.A. Kastelein and A.Ya. Supin (eds.), Marine mammal sensory systems. Plenum, New York. 773 p.

Popper, A.N. 1980a. Sound emission and detection by delphinids. p. 1-52 *In*: L.M. Herman (ed.), Cetacean behavior: Mechanisms and functions. Wiley-Interscience, New York. 463 p.

Popper, A.N. 1980b. Behavioral measures of odontocete hearing. p. 469-481 *In*: R.-G. Busnel and J.F. Fish (eds.), Animal sonar systems. Plenum, New York. 1135 p.

Potter, J.R. 1994. ATOC: Sound policy or enviro-vandalism? Aspects of a modern media-fueled policy issue. *J. Environ. Devel.* 3(2):47-62.

Poulter, T.C. 1963. Sonar signals of the sea lion. *Science* 139(3556):753-755.

Poulter, T.C. 1966. The use of active sonar by the California sea lion *Zalophus californianus* (Lesson). *J. Aud. Res.* 6:165-173.

Poulter, T.C. 1968. Underwater vocalization and behavior of pinnipeds. p. 69-84 *In*: R.J. Harrison, R.C. Hubbard, R.S. Peterson, C.E. Rice and R.J. Schusterman (eds.), The behavior and physiology of pinnipeds. Appleton-Century-Crofts, New York. 411 p.

Preen, A.R. 1992. Interactions between dugongs and seagrasses in a subtropical environment. Ph.D. Thesis, James Cook Univ., Townsville, Queensl. 392 p.

Price, G.R. 1986. Hazard from intense low-frequency acoustic impulses. *J. Acoust. Soc. Am.* 80(4):1076-1086.

Provancha, J.A. and M.J. Provancha. 1988. Long-term trends in abundance and distribution of manatees (*Trichechus manatus*) in the northern Banana River, Brevard County, Florida. *Mar. Mamm. Sci.* 4(4):323-338.

Pryor, K. and K.S. Norris. 1978. The tuna/porpoise problem: Behavioral aspects. *Oceanus* 21(2):31-37.

Pryor, K., J. Lindbergh, S. Lindbergh and R. Milano. 1990. A dolphin-human fishing cooperative in Brazil. *Mar. Mamm. Sci.* 6(1):77-82.

Pryor, T., K. Pryor and K.S. Norris. 1965. Observations on a pygmy killer whale (*Feresa attenuata* Gray) from Hawaii. *J. Mammal.* 46(3):450-461.

Ralls, K., P. Fiorelli and S. Gish. 1985. Vocalizations and vocal mimicry in captive harbor seals, *Phoca vitulina*. *Can. J. Zool.* 63(5):1050-1056.

Ramprashad, F. 1975. Aquatic adaptations in the ear of the harp seal *Pagophilus groenlandicus* (Erxleben, 1777). *Rapp. P.-V. Réun. Cons. Int. Explor. Mer* 169:102-111.

Rathbun, G.B. 1988. Fixed-wing airplane versus helicopter surveys of manatees (*Trichechus manatus*). *Mar. Mamm. Sci.* 4(1):71-75.

Rauch, D. 1980. Experimental and theoretical studies of seismic interface waves in coastal waters. p. 307-327 *In*: W.A. Kuperman and F.B. Jensen (eds.), Bottom-interacting ocean acoustics. Plenum, New York. 717 p.

Ray, [G.]C. 1970. Population ecology of Antarctic seals. p. 398-414 *In*: M.W. Holdgate (ed.), Antarctic ecology. Academic Press, London. 604 p.

Ray, G.C. and W.A. Watkins. 1975. Social function of underwater sounds in the walrus *Odobenus rosmarus*. *Rapp. P.-V. Réun. Cons. Int. Explor. Mer* 169:524-526.

Ray, [G.]C., W.A. Watkins and J.J. Burns. 1969. The underwater song of *Erignathus* (bearded seal). *Zoologica (N.Y.)* 54(2):79-83 + plates, phono. record.

Ray, G.C., E.D. Mitchell, D. Wartzok, V.M. Kozicki and R. Maiefski. 1978. Radio tracking of a fin whale (*Balaenoptera physalus*). *Science* 202(4367):521-524.

Reeves, R.R. 1977. The problem of gray whale (*Eschrichtius robustus*) harassment: At the breeding lagoons and during migration. MMC-76/06. U.S. Mar. Mamm. Comm. 60 p. NTIS PB-272506.

Reeves, R.R. 1992. Whale responses to anthropogenic sounds: A literature review. Sci. & Res. Ser. 47. New Zealand Dep. Conserv., Wellington. 47 p.

Reeves, R.R. and E. Mitchell. 1981. White whale hunting in Cumberland Sound. *Beaver* 312(3):42-49.

Reeves, R.R., D.K. Ljungblad and J.T. Clarke. 1984. Bowhead whales and acoustic seismic surveys in the Beaufort Sea. *Polar Rec.* 22(138):271-280.

Reeves, R.R., B.S. Stewart and S. Leatherwood. 1992. The Sierra Club handbook of seals and sirenians. Sierra Club, San Francisco, CA. 359 p.

Reeves, R.R., E. Mitchell and H. Whitehead. 1993. Status of the northern bottlenose whale, *Hyperoodon ampullatus*. *Can. Field-Nat.* 107(4):490-508.

Reijnders, P.J.H. 1981. Management and conservation of the harbour seal, *Phoca vitulina*, population in the international Wadden Sea area. *Biol. Conserv.* 19(3):213-221.

Reiter, G.A. 1981. Cold weather response F/V *Ryuyo Maru No. 2*[,] St. Paul, Pribiloff Islands, Alaska. p. 227-231 *In*: Proc. 1981 Oil Spill Conference. API Publ. 4334. Am. Petrol. Inst., Washington, DC. 742 p.

Renaud, D.L. and A.N. Popper. 1975. Sound localization by the bottlenose porpoise *Tursiops truncatus*. *J. Exp. Biol.* 63(3):569-585.

Renouf, D. 1980. Masked hearing thresholds of harbour seals (*Phoca vitulina*) in air. *J. Aud. Res.* 20(4):263-269.

Renouf, D. 1984. The vocalization of the harbour seal pup (*Phoca vitulina*) and its role in the maintenance of contact with the mother. *J. Zool.* 202(4):583-590.

Renouf, D. and M.B. Davis. 1982. Evidence that seals may use echolocation. *Nature (London)* 300(5893):635-637.

Renouf, D. and E. Perry. 1983. The harbour seal pup's vocalization and its role in the maintenance of contact with the mother. p. 86-87 *In*: Abstr. 5th Bienn. Conf. Biol. Mar. Mamm., Boston, MA, Nov. 1983. 112 p.

Renouf, D., G. Galway and L. Gaborko. 1980. Evidence for echolocation in harbour seals. *J. Mar. Biol. Assoc. U.K.* 60(4):1039-1042.

Renouf, D., L. Gaborko, G. Galway and R. Finlayson. 1981. The effect of disturbance on the daily movements of harbour seals and grey seals between the sea and their hauling grounds at Miquelon. *Appl. Anim. Ethol.* 7(4):373-379.

Repenning, C.A. 1972. Underwater hearing in seals: Functional morphology. p. 307-331 *In*: R.J. Harrison (ed.), Functional anatomy of marine mammals, vol. 1. Academic Press, London. 451 p.

Reynolds, J.E., III. 1985. Evaluation of the nature and magnitude of interactions between bottlenose dolphins, *Tursiops truncatus*, and fisheries and other human activities in coastal areas of the southeastern United States. MMC-84/07. Rep. from Eckerd Coll., St. Petersburg, FL, for U.S. Mar. Mamm. Comm., Washington, DC. 38 p. NTIS PB86-162203.

Reynolds, J.E., III, and D.K. Odell. 1991. Manatees and dugongs. Facts on File, New York. 192 p.

Reynolds, P.C. 1974. The effects of simulated compressor station sounds on Dall sheep using mineral licks on the Brooks Range, Alaska. Chap. II (82 p.) *In*: R.D. Jakimchuk (ed.), The reaction of some mammals to aircraft and compressor station noise disturbance. Arctic Gas Biol. Rep. Ser., vol. 23.

Rice, D.W. 1965. Offshore southward migration of gray whales off southern California. *J. Mammal.* 46(3):504-505.

Rice, D.W. and A.A. Wolman. 1971. The life history and ecology of the gray whale (*Eschrichtius robustus*). *Am. Soc. Mammal., Spec. Publ.* 3. 142 p.

Richardson, W.J. and K.J. Finley. 1989. Comparison of behavior of bowhead whales of the Davis Strait and Bering/Beaufort stocks. OCS Study MMS 88-0056. Rep. from LGL Ltd., King City, Ont., for U.S. Minerals Manage. Serv., Herndon, VA. 131 p. NTIS PB89-195556.

Richardson, W.J. and C.R. Greene, Jr. 1993. Variability in behavioral reaction thresholds of bowhead whales to man-made underwater sounds. *J. Acoust. Soc. Am.* 94(3, Pt. 2):1848.

Richardson, W.J. and C.I. Malme. 1993. Man-made noise and behavioral responses. p. 631-700 *In*: J.J. Burns, J.J. Montague and C.J. Cowles (eds.), The bowhead whale. Spec. Publ. 2. Soc. Mar. Mammal., Lawrence, KS. 787 p.

Richardson, W.J. and B. Würsig. in press. Influences of man-made noise and other human actions on cetacean behaviour. *Mar. Freshwat. Behav. Physiol.*

Richardson, W.J., R.A. Davis, C.R. Evans and P. Norton. 1985a. Distribution of bowheads and industrial activity, 1980-84. p. 255-306 *In*: W.J. Richardson (ed.), Behavior, disturbance responses and distribution of bowhead whales *Balaena mysticetus* in the eastern Beaufort Sea, 1980-84. OCS Study MMS 85-0034. Rep. from LGL Ecol. Res. Assoc. Inc., Bryan, TX, for U.S. Minerals Manage. Serv., Reston, VA. 306 p. NTIS PB87-124376.

Richardson, W.J., M.A. Fraker, B. Würsig and R.S. Wells. 1985b. Behaviour of bowhead whales *Balaena mysticetus* summering in the Beaufort Sea: Reactions to industrial activities. *Biol. Conserv.* 32(3):195-230.

Richardson, W.J., R.S. Wells and B. Würsig. 1985c. Disturbance responses of bowheads, 1980-84. p. 89-196 *In*: W.J. Richardson (ed.), Behavior, disturbance responses and distribution of bowhead whales *Balaena mysticetus* in the eastern Beaufort Sea, 1980-84. OCS Study MMS 85-0034. Rep. from LGL Ecol. Res. Assoc. Inc., Bryan, TX, for U.S. Minerals Manage. Serv., Reston, VA. 306 p. NTIS PB87-124376.

Richardson, W.J., B. Würsig and C.R. Greene, Jr. 1986. Reactions of bowhead whales, *Balaena mysticetus*, to seismic exploration in the Canadian Beaufort Sea. *J. Acoust. Soc. Am.* 79(4):1117-1128.

Richardson, W.J., R.A. Davis, C.R. Evans, D.K. Ljungblad and P. Norton. 1987a. Summer distribution of bowhead whales, *Balaena mysticetus*, relative to oil industry activities in the Canadian Beaufort Sea, 1980-84. *Arctic* 40(2):93-104.

Richardson, W.J., B. Würsig and G.W. Miller. 1987b. Bowhead distribution, numbers and activities. p. 257-368 *In*: W.J. Richardson (ed.), Importance of the eastern Alaskan Beaufort Sea to feeding bowhead whales, 1985-86. OCS Study MMS 87-0037. Rep. from LGL Ecol. Res. Assoc. Inc., Bryan, TX, for U.S. Minerals Manage. Serv., Reston, VA. 547 p. NTIS PB88-150271.

Richardson, W.J., C.R. Greene, J.P. Hickie, R.A. Davis and D.H. Thomson. 1989. Effects of offshore petroleum operations on cold water marine mammals: A literature review, 2nd ed. API Publ. 4485. Am. Petrol. Inst., Washington, DC. 385 p.

Richardson, W.J., C.R. Greene, Jr., W.R. Koski, C.I. Malme, G.W. Miller, M.A. Smultea and B. Würsig. 1990a. Acoustic effects of oil production activities on bowhead and white whales visible during spring migration near Pt. Barrow, Alaska—1989 phase. OCS Study MMS 90-0017. Rep. from LGL Ltd., King City, Ont., for U.S. Minerals Manage. Serv., Herndon, VA. 284 p. NTIS PB91-105486.

Richardson, W.J., B. Würsig and C.R. Greene, Jr. 1990b. Reactions of bowhead whales, *Balaena mysticetus*, to drilling and dredging noise in the Canadian Beaufort Sea. *Mar. Environ. Res.* 29(2):135-160.

Richardson, W.J., C.R. Greene, Jr., W.R. Koski and M.A. Smultea, with G. Cameron, C. Holdsworth, G. Miller, T. Woodley and B. Würsig. 1991a. Acoustic effects of oil production activities on bowhead and white whales visible during spring migration near Pt. Barrow, Alaska—1990 phase. OCS Study MMS 91-0037. Rep. from LGL Ltd., King City, Ont., for U.S. Minerals Manage. Serv., Herndon, VA. 311 p. NTIS PB92-170430.

Richardson, W.J., C.R. Greene, Jr., C.I. Malme and D.H. Thomson, with S.E. Moore and B. Würsig. 1991b. Effects of noise on marine mammals. OCS

Study MMS 90-0093. Rep. from LGL Ecol. Res. Assoc. Inc., Bryan, TX, for U.S. Minerals Manage. Serv., Atlantic OCS Reg., Herndon, VA. 462 p. NTIS PB91-168914.

Richardson, W.J., K.J. Finley, G.W. Miller, R.A. Davis and W.R. Koski. 1995. Feeding, social and migration behavior of bowhead whales, *Balaena mysticetus*, in Baffin Bay vs. the Beaufort Sea—Regions with different amounts of human activity. *Mar. Mamm. Sci.* 11(1):1-45.

Richens, V.B. and G.R. Lavigne. 1978. Response of white-tailed deer to snowmobiles and snowmobile trails in Maine. *Can. Field-Nat.* 92(4):334-344.

Ridgway, S.H. 1980. Electrophysiological experiments on hearing in odontocetes. p. 483-493 *In*: R.-G. Busnel and J.F. Fish (eds.), Animal sonar systems. Plenum, New York. 1135 p.

Ridgway, S.H. 1983. Dolphin hearing and sound production in health and illness. p. 247-296 *In*: R.R. Fay and G. Gourevitch (eds.), Hearing and other senses: Presentations in honor of E.G. Wever. Amphora Press, Groton, CT. 405 p.

Ridgway, S.H. and D.A. Carder. 1983. Audiograms for large cetaceans: A proposed method for field studies. *J. Acoust. Soc. Am.* 74(Suppl. 1):S53.

Ridgway, S.H. and D.A. Carder. 1993. High-frequency hearing loss in old (25+ years old) male dolphins. *J. Acoust. Soc. Am.* 94(3, Pt. 2):1830.

Ridgway, S.H. and R.J. Harrison (eds.). 1981a. Handbook of marine mammals, vol. 1: The walrus, sea lions, fur seals and sea otter. Academic Press, London. 235 p.

Ridgway, S.H. and R.J. Harrison (eds.). 1981b. Handbook of marine mammals, vol. 2: Seals. Academic Press, London. 359 p.

Ridgway, S.H. and R. Harrison (eds.). 1985. Handbook of marine mammals, vol. 3: The sirenians and baleen whales. Academic Press, London. 362 p.

Ridgway, S.H. and P.L. Joyce. 1975. Studies on seal brain by radiotelemetry. *Rapp. P.-V. Réun. Cons. Int. Explor. Mer* 169:81-91.

Ridgway, S.H., T.H. Bullock, D.A. Carder, R.L. Seeley, D. Woods and R. Galambos. 1981. Auditory brainstem response in dolphins. *Proc. Natl. Acad. Sci. USA* 78(3):1943-1947.

Riedman, M.L. 1983. Studies of the effects of experimentally produced noise associated with oil and gas exploration and development on sea otters in California. Rep. from Cent. Coastal Mar. Stud., Univ. Calif. Santa Cruz, CA, for U.S. Minerals Manage. Serv., Anchorage, AK. 92 p. NTIS PB86-218575.

Riedman, M.L. 1984. Effects of sounds associated with petroleum industry activities on the behavior of sea otters in California. p. D-1 to D-12 *In*: C.I. Malme, P.R. Miles, C.W. Clark, P. Tyack and J.E. Bird, Investigations of the potential effects of underwater noise from petroleum industry activities on migrating gray whale behavior/Phase II: January 1984 migration. BBN Rep. 5586. Rep. from Bolt Beranek & Newman Inc., Cambridge, MA, for U.S. Minerals Manage. Serv., Anchorage, AK. Var. pag. NTIS PB86-218377.

Riedman, M. 1990. The pinnipeds/Seals, sea lions, and walruses. Univ. Calif. Press, Berkeley. 439 p.

Robinson, D.W., J.M. Bowsher and W.C. Copeland. 1963. On judging the noise from aircraft in flight. *Acustica* 13(5):324-336.

Robinson, N.H. 1979. Recent records of southern right whales in New South Wales. *Victorian Nat.* 96:168-169.

Rogers, P.H. 1977. Weak-shock solution for underwater explosive shock waves. *J. Acoust. Soc. Am.* 62(6):1412-1419.

Rogers, T., D.H. Cato and M.M. Bryden. 1995. Underwater vocal repertoire of the leopard seal (*Hydrurga leptonyx*) in Prydz Bay, Antarctica. *In*: R.A. Kastelein, J.A. Thomas and P.E. Nachtigall (eds.), Sensory systems of aquatic mammals. De Spil Publ., Woerden, Netherlands. (in press).

Romanenko, E.V. and V.Ya. Kitain. 1992. The functioning of the echolocation system of *Tursiops truncatus* during noise masking. p. 415-419 *In*: J.A. Thomas, R.A. Kastelein and A.Ya. Supin (eds.), Marine mammal sensory systems. Plenum, New York. 773 p.

Ross, D. 1976. Mechanics of underwater noise. Pergamon, New York. 375 p. (Reprinted 1987, Peninsula Publ., Los Altos, CA).

Rowlett, R.A., M.A. Smultea, J. Brueggeman, G.A. Green, C.C. Swanson, R.A. Grotefendt, D.P. Volsen and J.J. Burns. 1993. Polar bear reactions to icebreaker operations associated with offshore drilling explorations. p. 94 *In*: Abstr. 10th Bienn. Conf. Biol. Mar. Mamm., Galveston, TX, Nov. 1993. 130 p.

Rueggeberg, H. and J. Booth. 1989. Interactions between wildlife and salmon farms in British Columbia: Results of a survey. Tech. Rep. 67. Can. Wildl. Serv. Pacific & Yukon Reg., Delta, B.C. 84 p.

Rugh, D.J., K.E.W. Shelden, D.E. Withrow, H.W. Braham and R.P. Angliss. 1993. Spotted seal summer distribution and abundance in Alaska. p. 94 *In*: Abstr. 10th Bienn. Conf. Biol. Mar. Mamm., Galveston, TX, Nov. 1993. 130 p.

RWRT. 1991. Recovery plan for the northern right whale (*Eubalaena glacialis*). Rep. from Right Whale Recov. Team for U.S. Natl. Mar. Fish. Serv., Silver Spring, MD. 86 p.

Saayman, G.S. and C.K. Tayler. 1973. Some behaviour patterns of the southern right whale *Eubalaena australis*. *Z. Säugetierk.* 38:172-183.

Salden, D.R. 1988. Humpback whale encounter rates offshore of Maui, Hawaii. *J. Wildl. Manage.* 52(2):301-304.

Salden, D.R. 1993. Effects of research boat approaches on humpback whale behavior off Maui, Hawaii, 1989-1993. p. 94 *In*: Abstr. 10th Bienn. Conf. Biol. Mar. Mamm., Galveston, TX, Nov. 1993. 130 p.

Salter, R.E. 1978. Normal behavior and disturbance responses of walruses (*Odobenus rosmarus* L.) during terrestrial haul-out, eastern Bathurst Island, N.W.T., July-August 1977. Rep. from LGL Ltd., Toronto, Ont., for Polar Gas Proj., Toronto, Ont. 68 p.

Salter, R.E. 1979. Site utilization, activity budgets, and disturbance responses of Atlantic walruses during terrestrial haul-out. *Can. J. Zool.* 57(6):1169-1180.

Sandegren, F.E. 1976. Agonistic behavior in the male northern elephant seal. *Behaviour* 57(1-2):136-158.

Sandegren, F.E., E.W. Chu and J.E. Vandevere. 1973. Maternal behavior in the California sea otter. *J. Mammal.* 54(3):668-679.

Santoro, A.K., K.L. Marten and T.W. Cranford. 1989. Pygmy sperm whale sounds (*Kogia breviceps*). p. 59 *In*: Abstr. 8th Bienn. Conf. Biol. Mar. Mamm., Pacific Grove, CA, Dec. 1989. 81 p.

Sauer, E.G.F. 1963. Courtship and copulation of the gray whale in the Bering Sea at St. Lawrence Island, Alaska. *Psychol. Forsch.* 27:157-174.

Sayigh, L.S., P.L. Tyack, R.S. Wells and M.D. Scott. 1990. Signature whistles of free-ranging bottlenose dolphins *Tursiops truncatus*: Stability and mother-offspring comparisons. *Behav. Ecol. Sociobiol.* 26(4):247-260.

Sayigh, L.S., P.L. Tyack and R.S. Wells. 1993a. Recording underwater sounds of free-ranging dolphins while underway in a small boat. *Mar. Mamm. Sci.* 9 (2):209-213.

Sayigh, L.S., P.L. Tyack, R.S. Wells, M.D. Scott and A.B. Irvine. 1993b. Individual recognition in free-ranging bottlenose dolphins: A field test using playback experiments. p. 95 *In*: Abstr. 10th Bienn. Conf. Biol. Mar. Mamm., Galveston, TX, Nov. 1993. 130 p.

Scharf, B. 1970. Critical bands. p. 157-202 *In*: J.V. Tobias (ed.), Foundations of modern auditory theory, vol. 1. Academic Press, New York. 466 p.

Schevill, W.E. 1968a. Sea lion echo ranging? *J. Acoust. Soc. Am.* 43(6):1458-1459.

Schevill, W.E. 1968b. Quiet power whaleboat. *J. Acoust. Soc. Am.* 44(4):1157-1158.

Schevill, W.E. and B. Lawrence. 1949. Underwater listening to the white porpoise (*Delphinapterus leucas*). *Science* 109(2824):143-144.

Schevill, W.E. and W.A. Watkins. 1965. Underwater calls of *Trichechus* (manatee). *Nature (London)* 205(4969):373-374.

Schevill, W.E. and W.A. Watkins. 1966. Sound structure and directionality in *Orcinus* (killer whale). *Zoologica (N.Y.)* 51(6):71-76 + plates.

Schevill, W.E. and W.A. Watkins. 1971a. Pulsed sounds of the porpoise *Lagenorhynchus australis*. *Breviora* 366:1-10.

Schevill, W.E. and W.A. Watkins. 1971b. Directionality of the sound beam in *Leptonychotes weddelli* (Mammalia: Pinnipedia). p. 163-168 *In*: W.H. Burt (ed.), Antarctic pinnipedia. Am. Geophys. Union, Washington, DC. 226 p.

Schevill, W.E and W.A. Watkins. 1972. Intense low-frequency sounds from an Antarctic minke whale, *Balaenoptera acutorostrata*. *Breviora* 388:1-8.

Schevill, W.E., W.A. Watkins and C. Ray. 1963. Underwater sounds of pinnipeds. *Science* 141(3575):50-53.

Schevill, W.E., W.A. Watkins and C. Ray. 1966. Analysis of underwater *Odobenus* calls with remarks on the development and function of the pharyngeal pouches. *Zoologica (N.Y.)* 51(10):103-106 + plates, phono. record.

Schevill, W.E., W.A. Watkins and C. Ray. 1969. Click structure in the porpoise, *Phocoena phocoena*. *J. Mammal.* 50(4):721-728.

Schilling, M.R., M.T. Weinrich and T.L. Ledder. 1989. Reaction of humpback whales to vessel approaches in New England waters. p. 60 *In*: Abstr. 8th Bienn. Conf. Biol. Mar. Mamm., Pacific Grove, CA, Dec. 1989. 81 p.

Schulberg, S., I. Show and D.[R.] Van Schoik. 1989. Results of the 1987-1988 gray whale migration and Landing Craft Air Cushion interaction study program.

U.S. Navy Contr. N62474-87-C-8669. Rep. from SRA Southwest Res. Assoc., Cardiff, CA, for Naval Facil. Eng. Comm., San Bruno, CA. 45 p.

Schulberg, S., I. Show and R. Van Schoik. 1991. Results of the 1988-89 gray whale migration and Landing Craft Air Cushion interaction study program. U.S. Navy Contr. N62474-87-C-8669. Rep. from SRA Southwest Res. Assoc. Inc., Carlsbad, CA, for Naval Facil. Eng. Comm., San Bruno, CA. 65 p.

Schultz, K.W. and P.J. Corkeron. 1994. Interspecific differences in whistles produced by inshore dolphins in Moreton Bay, Queensland, Australia. *Can. J. Zool.* 72(6):1061-1068.

Schultz, K.W., D.H. Cato, P.J. Corkeron and M.M. Bryden. in press. Low frequency narrow-band sounds produced by bottlenose dolphins. *Mar. Mamm. Sci.*

Schultz, R.D. and J.A. Bailey. 1978. Responses of national park elk to human activity. *J. Wildl. Manage.* 42(1):91-100.

Schusterman, R.J. 1974. Auditory sensitivity of a California sea lion to airborne sound. *J. Acoust. Soc. Am.* 56(4):1248-1251.

Schusterman, R.J. 1981a. Behavioral capabilities of seals and sea lions: A review of their hearing, visual, learning and diving skills. *Psychol. Rec.* 31(2):125-143.

Schusterman, R.J. 1981b. Steller sea lion *Eumetopias jubatus* (Schreber, 1776). p. 119-141 *In*: S.H. Ridgway and R.J. Harrison (eds.), Handbook of marine mammals, vol. 1. Academic Press, London. 235 p.

Schusterman, R.J. and R.F. Balliet. 1969. Underwater barking by male sea lions (*Zalophus californianus*). *Nature (London)* 222(5199):1179-1181.

Schusterman, R.J. and P.W. Moore. 1978. The upper limit of underwater auditory frequency discrimination in the California sea lion. *J. Acoust. Soc. Am.* 63(5):1591-1595.

Schusterman, R.J., R. Gentry and J. Schmook. 1966. Underwater vocalization by sea lions: Social and mirror stimuli. *Science* 154(3748):540-542.

Schusterman, R.J., R. Gentry and J. Schmook. 1967. Underwater sound production by captive California sea lions, *Zalophus californianus*. *Zoologica (N.Y.)* 52(3):21-24 + plates.

Schusterman, R.J., R.F. Balliet and J. Nixon. 1972. Underwater audiogram of the California sea lion by the conditioned vocalization technique. *J. Exp. Anal. Behav.* 17(3):339-350.

Scrimger, P. and R.M. Heitmeyer. 1991. Acoustic source-level measurements for a variety of merchant ships. *J. Acoust. Soc. Am.* 89(2):691-699.

Scronce, B.L. and S.H. Ridgway. 1980. Grey seal, *Halichoerus*: Echolocation not demonstrated. p. 991-993 *In*: R.-G. Busnel and J.F. Fish (eds.), Animal sonar systems. Plenum, New York. 1135 p.

Seaman, G.A. and J.J. Burns. 1981. Preliminary results of recent studies of belukhas in Alaskan waters. *Rep. Int. Whal. Comm.* 31:567-574.

Seeley, R.L., W.F. Flanigan, Jr., and S.H. Ridgway. 1976. A technique for rapidly assessing the hearing of the bottlenosed porpoise, *Tursiops truncatus*. NUC-TP-522. U.S. Naval Undersea Cent., San Diego, CA. 15 p. NTIS AD-A 029178.

Selye, H. 1973. The evolution of the stress concept. *Am. Sci.* 61(6):692-699.

Sergeant, D.E. 1981. On permissible exploitation rates of Monodontidae. *Rep. Int. Whal. Comm.* 31:583-588.

Sergeant, D. 1986. Present status of white whales *Delphinapterus leucas* in the St. Lawrence Estuary. *Naturaliste Can.* 113(1):61-81.

Sergeant, D.E. and W. Hoek. 1988. An update of the status of white whales *Delphinapterus leucas* in the Saint Lawrence Estuary, Canada. *Biol. Conserv.* 45 (4):287-302.

Shallenberger, E.E. 1978. Activities possibly affecting the welfare of humpback whales. p. 81-85 *In*: K.S. Norris and R.R. Reeves (eds.), Report on a workshop on problems related to humpback whales (*Megaptera novaeangliae*) in Hawaii. MMC-77/03. Rep. from Sea Life Inc., Makapuu Pt., HI, for U.S. Mar. Mamm. Comm., Washington, DC. 90 p. NTIS PB-280794.

Shane, S.H. 1980. Occurrence, movements, and distribution of bottlenose dolphin, *Tursiops truncatus*, in southern Texas. *Fish. Bull.* 78(3):593-601.

Shane, S.H. 1983. Abundance, distribution, and movements of manatees (*Trichechus manatus*) in Brevard County, Florida. *Bull. Mar. Sci.* 33(1):1-9.

Shane, S.H. 1984. Manatee use of power plant effluents in Brevard County, Florida. *Florida Sci.* 47(3):180-187.

Shane, S.H. 1990. Behavior and ecology of the bottlenose dolphin at Sanibel Island, Florida. p. 245-265 *In*: S. Leatherwood and R.R. Reeves (eds.), The bottlenose dolphin. Academic Press, San Diego, CA. 653 p.

Shane, S.H., R.S. Wells and B. Würsig. 1986. Ecology, behavior and social organization of the bottlenose dolphin: A review. *Mar. Mamm. Sci.* 2(1):34-63.

Shank, C.C. 1979. Human-related behavioral disturbance to northern large mammals: A bibliography and review. Rep. for Foothills Pipe Lines (South Yukon) Ltd., Calgary, Alb. 254 p.

Shaughnessy, P.D. 1985. Interactions between fisheries and Cape fur seals in southern Africa. p. 119-134 *In*: J.R. Beddington, R.J.H. Beverton and D.M. Lavigne (eds.), Marine mammals and fisheries. George Allen & Unwin, London. 354 p.

Shaughnessy, P.D., A. Semmelink, J. Cooper and P.G.H. Frost. 1981. Attempts to develop acoustic methods of keeping Cape fur seals *Arctocephalus pusillus* from fishing nets. *Biol. Conserv.* 21(2):141-158.

Shaver, H.N. and T.C. Poulter. 1967. Sea lion echo ranging. *J. Acoust. Soc. Am.* 42(2):428-437.

Shideler, D. 1993. Deterrent methods. p. 35-50 *In*: J.C. Truett (ed.), Guidelines for oil and gas operations in polar bear habitats. OCS Study MMS 93-0008. Rep. from LGL Ecol. Res. Assoc. Inc., Bryan, TX, for U.S. Minerals Manage. Serv., Anchorage, AK. 104 p.

Shipley, C., M. Hines and J.S. Buchwald. 1981. Individual differences in threat calls of northern elephant seal bulls. *Anim. Behav.* 29(1):12-19.

Shipley, C., M. Hines and J.S. Buchwald. 1986. Vocalizations of northern elephant seal bulls: Development of adult call characteristics during puberty. *J. Mammal.* 67(3):526-536.

Shipley, C., B.S. Stewart and J. Bass. 1992. Seismic communication in northern elephant seals. p. 553-562 *In*: J.A. Thomas, R.A. Kastelein and A.Ya. Supin (eds.), Marine mammal sensory systems. Plenum, New York. 773 p.

Shochi, Y., K. Zbinden, C. Kraus, M. Gihr and G. Pilleri. 1982. Characteristics and directional properties of the sonar signals emitted by the captive Commerson's dolphin, *Cephalorhynchus commersoni* (Gray, 1846). *Invest. Cetacea* 13:177-201.

Shockley, R.C., J. Northrop, P.G. Hansen and C. Hartdegen. 1982. SOFAR propagation paths from Australia to Bermuda: Comparison of signal speed algorithms and experiments. *J. Acoust. Soc. Am.* 71(1):51-60.

Silber, G.K. 1986. The relationship of social vocalizations to surface behavior and aggression in the Hawaiian humpback whale (*Megaptera novaeangliae*). *Can. J. Zool.* 64(10):2075-2080.

Silber, G.K. 1991. Acoustic signals of the vaquita (*Phocoena sinus*). *Aquat. Mamm.* 17(3):130-133.

Silber, G.K., M.W. Newcomer and G.J. Barros. 1988. Observations on the behavior and ventilation cycles of the vaquita, *Phocoena sinus*. *Mar. Mamm. Sci.* 4(1):62-67.

Silber, G.K., K.A. Waples and P.A. Nelson. 1994. Response of free-ranging harbour porpoises to potential gillnet modifications. *Rep. Int. Whal. Comm.* (*Spec. Issue*) 15:579-584.

Simmonds, M.P. and L.F. Lopez-Jurado. 1991. Whales and the military. *Nature* (*London*) 351(6326):448.

Sinnott, J.M. and R.N. Aslin. 1985. Frequency and intensity discrimination in human infants and adults. *J. Acoust. Soc. Am.* 78(6):1986-1992.

Sivian, L.J. and S.D. White. 1933. On minimum audible sound fields. *J. Acoust. Soc. Am.* 4(4):288-321.

Sjare, B.L. and T.G. Smith. 1986a. The vocal repertoire of white whales, *Delphinapterus leucas*, summering in Cunningham Inlet, Northwest Territories. *Can. J. Zool.* 64(2):407-415.

Sjare, B.L. and T.G. Smith. 1986b. The relationship between behavioral activity and underwater vocalizations of the white whale, *Delphinapterus leucas*. *Can. J. Zool.* 64(12):2824-2831.

Slaney, F.F. 1975. Bell Voyageur 002 ACV environmental assessment. Prepared for Transport Canada, Transportation Dev. Agency.

Slay, C.K., A.R. Knowlton and S.D. Kraus. 1993. Right whales and dredging in the southeast US: One approach to conservation management. p. 100 *In*: Abstr. 10th Bienn. Conf. Biol. Mar. Mamm., Galveston, TX, Nov. 1993. 130 p.

Slijper, E.J. 1962. Whales. Hutchinson & Co., London. 511 p.

Smith, B.D. 1993. 1990 status and conservation of the Ganges river dolphin *Platanista gangetica* in the Karnali River, Nepal. *Biol. Conserv.* 66(3):159-169.

Smith, M.J.T. 1989. Aircraft noise. Cambridge Univ. Press, Cambridge, U.K. 359 p.

Smith, P.F. 1985. Toward a standard for hearing conservation for underwater and hyperbaric environments. *J. Aud. Res.* 25(4):221-238.

Smith, P.W., Jr. 1974. Averaged sound transmission in range-dependent channels. *J. Acoust. Soc. Am.* 55(6):1197-1204.

Smolker, R.A., J. Mann and B.B. Smuts. 1993. Use of signature whistles during separations and reunions by wild bottlenose dolphin mothers and infants. *Behav. Ecol. Sociobiol.* 33(6):393-402.

Sonn, M. 1969. Psychoacoustical terminology. Raytheon Co., Submarine Signal Div., Portsmouth, RI. 67 p. Written for inclusion in "Handbook of Psychoacoustical Data".

Sopuck, L.G., C.E. Tull, J.E. Green and R.E. Salter. 1979. Impacts of development on wildlife: A review from the perspective of the Cold Lake project. Rep. from LGL Ltd., Edmonton, Alb., for Esso Resources Canada Ltd., Calgary, Alb. 400 p.

Sorensen, P.W., R.J. Medved, M.A.M. Hyman and H.E. Winn. 1984. Distribution and abundance of cetaceans in the vicinity of human activities along the continental shelf of the northwestern Atlantic. *Mar. Environ. Res.* 12(1):69-81.

Spaling, H. and B. Smit. 1993. Cumulative environmental change: Conceptual frameworks, evaluation approaches, and institutional perspectives. *Environ. Manage.* 17(5):587-600.

Sparks, T.D., J.C. Norris and W.E. Evans. 1993. Acoustically determined distributions of sperm whales in the northwestern Gulf of Mexico. p. 102 *In*: Abstr. 10th Bienn. Conf. Biol. Mar. Mamm., Galveston, TX, Nov. 1993. 130 p.

Sparrow, V.W. 1995. The effect of supersonic aircraft speed on the penetration of sonic boom noise into the ocean. *J. Acoust. Soc. Am.* 97(1):159-162.

Spero, D. 1981. Vocalizations and associated behavior of northern right whales *Eubalaena glacialis*. p. 108 *In*: Abstr. 4th Bienn. Conf. Biol. Mar. Mamm., San Francisco, CA, Dec. 1981. 127 p.

Spieth, W. 1956. Annoyance threshold judgments of bands of noise. *J. Acoust. Soc. Am.* 28(5):872-877.

Spindel, R.C. and P.F. Worcester. 1990. Ocean acoustic tomography. *Sci. Am.* 263 (4):94-99.

Spofford, C.W., R.R. Green and J.B. Hersey. 1983. The estimation of geo-acoustic ocean sediment parameters from measured bottom-loss data. Rep. SAI-83-879-WA. Rep. from Science Applic. Inc., McLean, VA, for U.S. Nav. Ocean Res. Dev. Activ., NSTL Station, MS. Var. pag.

SRA. 1988. Results of the 1986-1987 gray whale migration and landing craft, air cushion interaction study program. U.S. Navy Contr. N62474-86-M-0942. Rep. from SRA Southwest Res. Assoc., Cardiff by the Sea, CA, for Naval Facil. Eng. Comm., San Bruno, CA. 31 p.

Staal, P.R. 1985. Acoustic effects of underwater explosive discharges. p. 89-111 *In*: Proc. Workshop on Effects of Explosives Use in the Marine Environment, Jan. 1985, Halifax, N.S. Tech. Rep. 5. Can. Oil & Gas Lands Admin. Environ. Prot. Branch, Ottawa, Ont. 398 p.

Staal, P.R. and D.M.F. Chapman. 1986. Observations of interface waves and low-frequency acoustic propagation over a rough granite seabed. p. 643-652 *In*: T. Akal and J.M. Berkson (eds.), Ocean seismo-acoustics. Plenum, New York. 915 p.

Stacey, P.J. and R.W. Baird. 1991. Status of the false killer whale, *Pseudorca crassidens*, in Canada. *Can. Field-Nat.* 105(2):189-197.

Stafford, K.M., C.G. Fox and B.R. Mate. 1994. Acoustic detection and location of blue whales (*Balaenoptera musculus*) from SOSUS data by matched filtering. *J. Acoust. Soc. Am.* 96(5, Pt. 2):3250-3251.

Stark, C. 1988. Two DAT portables/A special test report. *Stereo Rev.* 1988(10, Oct.):68-71.

St. Aubin, D.J. and J.R. Geraci. 1988. Capture and handling stress suppresses circulating levels of thyroxine (T4) and triiodothyronine (T3) in beluga whales *Delphinapterus leucas*. *Physiol. Zool.* 61(2):170-175.

Steel, C. and J.G. Morris. 1982. The West Indian manatee: An acoustic analysis. *Am. Zool.* 22(4):925.

Steiner, W.W. 1981. Species-specific differences in pure tonal whistle vocalizations of five western North Atlantic dolphin species. *Behav. Ecol. Sociobiol.* 9(4):241-246.

Steiner, W.W., J.H. Hain, H.E. Winn and P.J. Perkins. 1979. Vocalizations and feeding behavior of the killer whale (*Orcinus orca*). *J. Mammal.* 60(4):823-827.

Stewart, B.S. 1981. Behavioral response of northern elephant seals and California sea lions on San Nicolas Island, California, to loud impulse noise. *J. Acoust. Soc. Am.* 70(Suppl. 1):S84.

Stewart, B.S. 1982. Behavioral response of northern elephant seals (*Mirounga angustirostris*) and California sea lions (*Zalophus californianus*) on San Nicolas Island to loud impulse noise. p. 4-35 *In*: Studies on the pinnipeds of the southern California Channel Islands, 1980-1981. HSWRI Tech. Rep. 82-137. Rep. from Hubbs/Sea World Res. Inst., San Diego, CA, for U.S. Air Force Space & Missile Syst. Org. and U.S. Natl. Mar. Fish. Serv., Washington, DC. Var. pag.

Stewart, B.S. 1993. Behavioral and hearing responses of pinnipeds to rocket launch noise and sonic boom. *J. Acoust. Soc. Am.* 94(3, Pt. 2):1828.

Stewart, B.S., W.E. Evans and F.T. Awbrey. 1982. Effects of man-made water-borne noise on behavior of belukha whales (*Delphinapterus leucas*) in Bristol Bay, Alaska. HSWRI Tech. Rep. 82-145. Rep. from Hubbs/Sea World Res. Inst., San Diego, CA, for U.S. Natl. Oceanic & Atmos. Admin., Juneau, AK. 29 p. + fig., tables.

Stewart, B.S., F.T. Awbrey and W.E. Evans. 1983 [publ. 1986]. Belukha whale (*Delphinapterus leucas*) responses to industrial noise in Nushagak Bay, Alaska: 1983. Outer Cont. Shelf Environ. Assess. Program, Final Rep. Princ. Invest., NOAA, Anchorage, AK 43:587-616. 702 p. OCS Study MMS 86-0057; NTIS PB87-192118.

Stewart, B.S., J.K. Francine and P.H. Thorson. 1993. Biological effects of launch-specific related noise and sonic boom from the Titan IV rocket at San Miguel Island and South Vandenberg Air Force Base on 2 August 1993. HSWRI Tech. Rep. 93-246. Rep. from Hubbs/Sea World Res. Inst., San Diego, CA, for U.S. Air Force Space & Missile Syst. Cent., Los Angeles, CA. 22 p.

Stewart, R.E.A. and D.M. Lavigne. 1984. Energy transfer and female condition in nursing harp seals *Phoca groenlandica*. *Holarctic Ecol.* 7(2):182-194.

Stirling, I. 1971. Studies on the behaviour of the South Australian fur seal, *Arctocephalus forsteri* (Lesson)/I. Annual cycle, postures and calls, and adult males during the breeding season. *Austral. J. Zool.* 19(3):243-266.

Stirling, I. 1972. Observations on the Australian sea lion, *Neophoca cinerea* (Peron). *Austral. J. Zool.* 20(3):271-279.

Stirling, I. 1973. Vocalization in the ringed seal (*Phoca hispida*). *J. Fish. Res. Board Can.* 30(10):1592-1594.

Stirling, I. 1988a. Polar bears. Univ. Michigan Press, Ann Arbor. 220 p.

Stirling, I. 1988b. Attraction of polar bears *Ursus maritimus* to offshore drilling sites in the eastern Beaufort Sea. *Polar Rec.* 24(148):1-8.

Stirling, I. and D.B. Siniff. 1979. Underwater vocalizations of leopard seals (*Hydrurga leptonyx*) and crabeater seals (*Lobodon carcinophagus*) near the South Shetland Islands, Antarctica. *Can. J. Zool.* 57(6):1244-1248.

Stirling, I. and R.M. Warneke. 1971. Implications of a comparison of the airborne vocalizations and some aspects of the behaviour of the two Australian fur seals, *Arctocephalus* spp., on the evolution and present taxonomy of the genus. *Austral. J. Zool.* 19(3):227-241.

Stirling, I., W. Calvert and H. Cleator. 1983. Underwater vocalizations as a tool for studying the distribution and relative abundance of wintering pinnipeds in the high Arctic. *Arctic* 36(3):262-274.

Stirling, I., W. Calvert and C. Spencer. 1987. Evidence of stereotyped underwater vocalizations of male Atlantic walruses (*Odobenus rosmarus rosmarus*). *Can. J. Zool.* 65(9):2311-2321.

Stockwell, C.A., G.C. Bateman and J. Berger. 1991. Conflicts in national parks: A case study of helicopters and bighorn sheep time budgets at the Grand Canyon. *Biol. Conserv.* 56(3):317-328.

Stone, G.S., S.K. Katona, A. Mainwaring, J.M. Allen and H.D. Corbett. 1992. Respiration and surfacing rates of fin whales (*Balaenoptera physalus*) observed from a lighthouse tower. *Rep. Int. Whal. Comm.* 42:739-745.

Sullivan, R.M. 1982. Agonistic behavior and dominance relationships in the harbor seal, *Phoca vitulina*. *J. Mammal.* 63(4):554-569.

Sumich, J.L. 1983. Swimming velocities, breathing patterns, and estimated costs of locomotion in migrating gray whales, *Eschrichtius robustus*. *Can. J. Zool.* 61(3):647-652.

Supin, A. and V. Popov. 1990. Frequency-selectivity of the auditory system in the bottlenose dolphin, *Tursiops truncatus*. p. 385-393 *In*: J.A. Thomas and R.A. Kastelein (eds.), Sensory abilities of cetaceans/Laboratory and field evidence. Plenum, New York. 710 p.

Supin, A.Ya. and V.V. Popov. 1993. Direction-dependent spectral sensitivity and interaural spectral difference in a dolphin: Evoked potential study. *J. Acoust. Soc. Am.* 93(6):3490-3495.

Supin, A.Y., V.V. Popov and V.O. Klishin. 1993. ABR frequency tuning curves in dolphins. *J. Comp. Physiol. A* 173(5):649-656.

Suryan, R.M. 1993. Pupping phenology and disturbance of harbor seals (*Phoca vitulina richardsi*) in the northern San Juan Islands, Washington. p. 104 *In*: Abstr. 10th Bienn. Conf. Biol. Mar. Mamm., Galveston, TX, Nov. 1993. 130 p.

Swartz, S.L. and W.C. Cummings. 1978. Gray whales, *Eschrichtius robustus*, in Laguna San Ignacio, Baja California, Mexico. MMC-77/04. Rep. from San Diego Nat. Hist. Museum for U.S. Mar. Mamm. Comm., Washington, DC. 38 p. NTIS PB-276319.

Swartz, S.L. and R.J. Hofman. 1991. Marine mammal and habitat monitoring: Requirements; principles; needs; and approaches. U.S. Mar. Mamm. Comm., Washington, DC. 16 p. NTIS PB91-215046.

Swartz, S.L. and M.L. Jones. 1978. The evaluation of human activities on gray whales, *Eschrichtius robustus*, in Laguna San Ignacio, Baja California, Mexico. MMC-78/03. U.S. Mar. Mamm. Comm., Washington, DC. 34 p. NTIS PB-289737.

Swartz, S.L. and M.L. Jones. 1981. Demographic studies and habitat assessment of gray whales, *Eschrichtius robustus*, in Laguna San Ignacio, Baja California Sur, Mexico. MMC-81/05. U.S. Mar. Mamm. Comm., Washington, DC. 56 p. NTIS PB82-123373.

Swift, R. and L. Morgan. 1993. The effect of disturbance on harbor seal haul out in Bolinas Lagoon, California. p. 105 *In*: Abstr. 10th Bienn. Conf. Biol. Mar. Mamm., Galveston, TX, Nov. 1993. 130 p.

Swingle, W.M., S.G. Barco, T.D. Pitchford, W.A. McLellan and D.A. Pabst. 1993. Appearance of juvenile humpback whales feeding in the nearshore waters of Virginia. *Mar. Mamm. Sci.* 9(3):309-315.

Szymanski, M.D., D.E. Bain and K.R. Henry. 1995. Auditory evoked potentials of a killer whale (*Orcinus orca*): Preliminary results. *In*: R.A. Kastelein, J.A. Thomas and P.E. Nachtigall (eds.), Sensory systems of aquatic mammals. De Spil Publ., Woerden, Netherlands. (in press).

Tappert, F.D. 1977. The parabolic approximation method. p. 224-287 *In*: J.B. Keller and J.S. Papadakis (eds.), Wave propagation and underwater acoustics. Springer-Verlag, New York. 287 p.

Taruski, A.G. 1979. The whistle repertoire of the North Atlantic pilot whale (*Globicephala melaena*) and its relationship to behavior and environment. p. 345-368 *In*: H.E. Winn and B.L. Olla (eds.), Behavior of marine animals, vol. 3: Cetaceans. Plenum, New York. 438 p.

Taylor, B.L. and P.K. Dawson. 1984. Seasonal changes in density and behavior of harbor porpoise (*Phocoena phocoena*) affecting census methodology in Glacier Bay National Park, Alaska. *Rep. Int. Whal. Comm.* 34:479-483.

Terhune, J.M. 1974. Directional hearing of a harbor seal in air and water. *J. Acoust. Soc. Am.* 56(6):1862-1865.

Terhune, J.M. 1976. Audibility aspects of sonic tracking of marine mammals. *J. Mammal.* 57(1):179-180.

Terhune, J.M. 1981. Influence of loud vessel noises on marine mammal hearing and vocal communication. p. 270-286 *In*: N.M Peterson (ed.), The question of sound from icebreaker operations: The proceedings of a workshop. Arctic Pilot Proj., Petro-Canada, Calgary, Alb. 350 p.

Terhune, J.M. 1985. Scanning behavior of harbor seals on haul-out sites. *J. Mammal.* 66(2):392-395.

Terhune, J.M. 1988. Detection thresholds of a harbour seal to repeated underwater high-frequency, short-duration sinusoidal pulses. *Can. J. Zool.* 66(7): 1578-1582.

Terhune, J.M. 1989a. Can seals alter the acoustical impedance of the outer and middle ears? p. 131-133 *In*: A.J. Cohen (ed.), Proc. Annu. Meet. Can. Acoust. Assoc., Oct. 1989, Halifax, N.S. 169 p.

Terhune, J.M. 1989b. Underwater click hearing thresholds of a harbour seal, *Phoca vitulina. Aquat. Mamm.* 15(1):22-26.

Terhune, J.M. 1991. Masked and unmasked pure tone detection thresholds of a harbour seal listening in air. *Can. J. Zool.* 69(8):2059-2066.

Terhune, J.M. 1994. Geographical variation of harp seal underwater vocalizations. *Can. J. Zool.* 72(5):892-897.

Terhune, J.M. and K. Ronald. 1970. The audiogram and calls of the harp seal (*Pagophilus groenlandicus*) in air. p. 133-140 *In*: Proc. 7th Annu. Conf. Biol. Sonar & Diving Mammals, Stanford Res. Inst., Menlo Park, CA, Oct. 1970.

Terhune, J.M. and K. Ronald. 1971. The harp seal, *Pagophilus groenlandicus* (Erxleben, 1777). X. The air audiogram. *Can. J. Zool.* 49(3):385-390.

Terhune, J.M. and K. Ronald. 1972. The harp seal, *Pagophilus groenlandicus* (Erxleben, 1777). III. The underwater audiogram. *Can. J. Zool.* 50(5):565-569.

Terhune, J.M. and K. Ronald. 1973. Some hooded seal (*Cystophora cristata*) sounds in March. *Can. J. Zool.* 51(3):319-321 + plates.

Terhune, J.M. and K. Ronald. 1974. Underwater hearing of phocid seals. C.M. 1974/N:5. Int. Counc. Explor. Sea. 11 p.

Terhune, J.M. and K. Ronald. 1975a. Underwater hearing sensitivity of two ringed seals (*Pusa hispida*). *Can. J. Zool.* 53(3):227-231.

Terhune, J.M. and K. Ronald. 1975b. Masked hearing thresholds of ringed seals. *J. Acoust. Soc. Am.* 58(2):515-516.

Terhune, J.M. and K. Ronald. 1976a. Examining harp seal behavioural patterns via their underwater vocalizations. *Appl. Anim. Ethol.* 2:261-264.

Terhune, J.M. and K. Ronald. 1976b. The upper frequency limit of ringed seal hearing. *Can. J. Zool.* 54(7):1226-1229.

Terhune, J.M. and K. Ronald. 1986. Distant and near-range functions of harp seal underwater calls. *Can. J. Zool.* 64(5):1065-1070.

Terhune, J. and S. Turnbull. 1995. Variation in the psychometric functions and hearing thresholds of a harbour seal. *In*: R.A. Kastelein, J.A. Thomas and P.E. Nachtigall (eds.), Sensory systems of aquatic mammals. De Spil Publ., Woerden, Netherlands. (in press).

Terhune, J.M., R.E.A. Stewart and K. Ronald. 1979. Influence of vessel noises on underwater vocal activity of harp seals. *Can. J. Zool.* 57(6):1337-1338.

Terhune, J.M., H. Burton and K. Green. 1993. Classification of diverse call types using cluster analysis techniques. *Bioacoustics* 4(4):245-258.

Terhune, J.M., H. Burton and K. Green. 1994a. Weddell seal in-air call sequences made with closed mouths. *Polar Biol.* 14(2):117-122.

Terhune, J.M., N.C. Grandmaitre, H.R. Burton and K. Green. 1994b. Weddell seals lengthen many underwater calls in response to conspecific vocalizations. *Bioacoustics* 5:223-226.

Thiele, L. 1981. Underwater noise from the icebreaker M/S "Voima". Rep. 81.42. Rep. from Ødegaard & Danneskiold-Samsøe K/S, Copenhagen, for Greenl. Fish. Invest., Copenhagen, Denmark. 35 p.

Thiele, L. 1984. Preliminary results of underwater noise measurements on the icebreaker "John A. MacDonald". Note 84.108. Rep. from Ødegaard & Danneskiold-Samsøe K/S, Copenhagen, for Greenl. Fish. Invest., Copenhagen, Denmark. 21 p.

Thiele, L. 1988. Underwater noise study from the icebreaker "John A. MacDonald". Rep. 85.133. Rep. from Ødegaard & Danneskiold-Samsøe ApS, Copenhagen, Denmark. 133 p.

Thiele, L. and J. Ødegaard. 1983. Underwater noise from the propellers of a triple screw container ship. Rep. 82.54. Rep. from Ødegaard & Danneskiold-Samsøe K/S, Copenhagen, for Greenl. Fish. Invest., Copenhagen, Denmark. 51 p.

Thomas, J.A. and D.P. DeMaster. 1982. An acoustic technique for determining diurnal activities in leopard (*Hydruga leptonyx*) and crabeater (*Lobodon carcinophagus*) seals. *Can. J. Zool.* 60(8):2028-2031.

Thomas, J.A. and C.L. Golladay. 1995. Geographic variation in leopard seal (*Hydrurga leptonyx*) underwater vocalizations. *In*: R.A. Kastelein, J.A. Thomas and P.E. Nachtigall (eds.), Sensory systems of aquatic mammals. De Spil Publ., Woerden, Netherlands. (in press).

Thomas, J.A. and V.B. Kuechle. 1982. Quantitative analysis of Weddell seal (*Leptonychotes weddelli*) underwater vocalizations at McMurdo Sound, Antarctica. *J. Acoust. Soc. Am.* 72(6):1730-1738.

Thomas, J.A. and I. Stirling. 1983. Geographic variation in the underwater vocalizations of Weddell seals (*Leptonychotes weddelli*) from Palmer Peninsula and McMurdo Sound, Antarctica. *Can. J. Zool.* 61(10):2203-2212.

Thomas, J.A. and C.W. Turl. 1990. Echolocation characteristics and range detection threshold of a false killer whale (*Pseudorca crassidens*). p. 321-334 *In*: J.A. Thomas and R.A. Kastelein (eds.), Sensory abilities of cetaceans/Laboratory and field evidence. Plenum, New York. 710 p.

Thomas, J.A., S. Leatherwood, W.E. Evans, J.R. Jehl, Jr., and F.T. Awbrey. 1981. Ross Sea killer whale distribution, behavior, color pattern, and vocalizations. *Antarct. J. U.S.* 16:157-158.

Thomas, J.A., S.R. Fisher, W.E. Evans and F.T. Awbrey. 1983a. Ultrasonic vocalizations of leopard seals (*Hydrurga leptonyx*). *Antarct. J. U.S.* 17(5):186.

Thomas, J.A., K.C. Zinnel and L.M. Ferm. 1983b. Analysis of Weddell seal (*Leptonychotes weddelli*) vocalizations using underwater playbacks. *Can. J. Zool.* 61(7):1448-1456.

Thomas, J.A., S.R. Fisher and F.A. Awbrey. 1986a. Use of acoustic techniques in studying whale behavior. *Rep. Int. Whal. Comm. (Spec. Issue)* 8:121-138.

Thomas, J.A., S.R. Fisher, L.M. Ferm and R.S. Holt. 1986b. Acoustic detection of cetaceans using a towed array of hydrophones. *Rep. Int. Whal. Comm. (Spec. Issue)* 8:139-148.

Thomas, J., N. Chun, W. Au and K. Pugh. 1988a. Underwater audiogram of a false killer whale (*Pseudorca crassidens*). *J. Acoust. Soc. Am.* 84(3):936-940.

Thomas, J.A., R.A. Puddicombe, M. George and D. Lewis. 1988b. Variations in underwater vocalizations of Weddell seals (*Leptonychotes weddelli*) at the Vestfold Hills as a measure of breeding population discreteness. *Hydrobiologia* 165:279-284.

Thomas, J., M. Stoermer, C. Bowers, L. Anderson and A. Garver. 1988c. Detection abilities and signal characteristics of echolocating false killer whales (*Pseudorca crassidens*). p. 323-328 *In*: P.E. Nachtigall and P.W.B. Moore (eds.), Animal sonar/Processes and performance. Plenum, New York. 862 p.

Thomas, J.A., R.A. Kastelein and F.T. Awbrey. 1990a. Behavior and blood catecholamines of captive belugas during playbacks of noise from an oil drilling platform. *Zoo Biol.* 9(5):393-402.

Thomas, J., P. Moore, R. Withrow and M. Stoermer. 1990b. Underwater audiogram of a Hawaiian monk seal (*Monachus schauinslandi*). *J. Acoust. Soc. Am.* 87(1):417-420.

Thomas, J.A., J.L. Pawloski and W.W.L. Au. 1990c. Masked hearing abilities in a false killer whale (*Pseudorca crassidens*). p. 395-404 *In*: J.A. Thomas and R.A. Kastelein (eds.), Sensory abilities of cetaceans/Laboratory and field evidence. Plenum, New York. 710 p.

Thomas, J.A., K.T. Ramirez, D.P. Tremel, G.S. Dye and D.L. Dale. 1993. Low-frequency hearing in a Pacific white-sided dolphin. p. 106 *In*: Abstr. 10th Bienn. Conf. Biol. Mar. Mamm., Galveston, TX, Nov. 1993. 130 p.

Thompson, D. and M.A. Fedak. 1993. Cardiac responses of grey seals during diving at sea. *J. Exp. Biol.* 174:139-154.

Thompson, P.M. 1992. The conservation of marine mammals in Scottish waters. *Proc. R. Soc. Edinburgh, Sect. B* 100:123-140.

Thompson, P.O., W.C. Cummings and S.J. Ha. 1986. Sounds, source levels, and associated behavior of humpback whales, southeast Alaska. *J. Acoust. Soc. Am.* 80(3):735-740.

Thompson, P.O., L.T. Findley and O. Vidal. 1987. Doublet stereotyped and other blue whale phonations recorded in the Gulf of California, Mexico. p. 70 *In*: Abstr. 7th Bienn. Conf. Biol. Mar. Mamm., Miami, FL, Dec. 1987. 88 p.

Thompson, P.O., L.T. Findley and O. Vidal. 1992. 20-Hz pulses and other vocalizations of fin whales, *Balaenoptera physalus*, in the Gulf of California, Mexico. *J. Acoust. Soc. Am.* 92(6):3051-3057.

Thompson, R.K.R. and L.M. Herman. 1975. Underwater frequency discrimination in the bottlenosed dolphin (1-140 kHz) and the human (1-8 kHz). *J. Acoust. Soc. Am.* 57(4):943-948.

Thompson, T.J., H.E. Winn and P.J. Perkins. 1979. Mysticete sounds. p. 403-431 *In*: H.E. Winn and B.L. Olla (eds.), Behavior of marine animals, vol. 3: Cetaceans. Plenum, New York. 438 p.

Thomson, C.A. and J.R. Geraci. 1986. Cortisol, aldosterone, and leucocytes in the stress response of bottlenose dolphins, *Tursiops truncatus*. *Can. J. Fish. Aquat. Sci.* 43(5):1010-1016.

Thomson, D.H., D.B. Fissel, J.R. Marko, R.A. Davis and G.A. Borstad. 1986. Distribution of bowhead whales in relation to hydrometeorological events in the Beaufort Sea. Rep. 028. Environ. Stud. Revolv. Funds, Can. Oil & Gas Lands Admin., Ottawa, Ont. 119 p.

Thomson, J.A. 1958. Biological effects of the Ripple Rock explosion. Prog. Rep. Pacific Coast Station 111. Fish. Res. Board Can., Nanaimo, B.C. 8 p.

Thorp, W.H. 1967. Analytic description of the low-frequency attenuation coefficient. *J. Acoust. Soc. Am.* 42(1):270.

Thorpe, W.H. 1963. Learning and instinct in animals, 2nd ed. Methuen, London. 558 p.

Tillman, M.F. and G.P. Donovan (eds.). 1986. Behaviour of whales in relation to management: Report of the workshop. *Rep. Int. Whal. Comm. (Spec. Issue)* 8:1-56.

Tilt, W.C. 1985. Whales and whalewatching in North America with special emphasis on the issue of harassment. Yale School of Forestry & Environ. Stud., New Haven, CT. 122 p.

Tinney, R.T., Jr. 1988. Review of information bearing upon the conservation and protection of humpback whales in Hawaii. Rep. for U.S. Mar. Mamm. Comm., Washington, DC. 56 p. NTIS PB88-195359.

Todd, S., J. Lien and A. Verhulst. 1992. Orientation of humpback whales (*Megaptera novaeangliae*) and minke whales (*Balaenoptera acutorostrata*) to acoustic alarm devices designed to reduce entrapment in fishing gear. p. 727-739 *In*: J.A. Thomas, R.A. Kastelein and A.Ya. Supin (eds.), Marine mammal sensory systems. Plenum, New York. 773 p.

Tolstoy, I. 1955. Dispersion and simple harmonic point sources in wave ducts. *J. Acoust. Soc. Am.* 27(5):897-907.

Tolstoy, I. 1960. Guided waves in a fluid with continuously variable velocity overlying an elastic solid: Theory and experiment. *J. Acoust. Soc. Am.* 32(1):81-87.

Tønnessen, J.N. and A.O. Johnsen. 1982. The history of modern whaling. (Transl. by R.I. Christophersen.) Univ. Calif. Press, Berkeley. 798 p.

Trasky, L.L. 1976. Environmental impact of seismic exploration and blasting in the aquatic environment. Rep. from Alaska Dep. Fish & Game, Anchorage, AK. 23 p.

Trillmich, F. 1981. Mutual mother-pup recognition in Galápagos fur seals and sea lions: Cues used and functional significance. *Behaviour* 78(1):21-42.

Trillmich, F. and P. Majluf. 1981. First observations on colony structure, behavior, and vocal repertoire of the South American fur seal (*Arctocephalus australis* Zimmermann, 1783) in Peru. *Z. Säugetierk.* 46(5):310-322.

Tucker, M.J. and R.A. Puddicombe. 1988. Protection status of marine mammals in Commonwealth waters. p. 79-85 *In*: M.L. Augee (ed.), Marine mammals of Australasia/Field biology and captive management. R. Zool. Soc. New South Wales, Mosman, N.S.W. 140 p.

Turl, C.W.   1993.   Low-frequency sound detection by a bottlenose dolphin.   *J. Acoust. Soc. Am.* 94(5):3006-3008.

Turl, C.W. and R.H. Penner.   1989.   Differences in echolocation click patterns of the beluga (*Delphinapterus leucas*) and the bottlenose dolphin (*Tursiops truncatus*).   *J. Acoust. Soc. Am.* 86(2):497-502.

Turl, C.W., R.H. Penner and W.W.L. Au.   1987.   Comparison of target detection capabilities of the beluga and bottlenose dolphin.   *J. Acoust. Soc. Am.* 82(5): 1487-1491.

Turnbull, S.D. and J.M. Terhune.   1990.   White noise and pure tone masking of pure tone thresholds of a harbour seal listening in air and underwater.   *Can. J. Zool.* 68(10):2090-2097.

Turnbull, S.D. and J.M. Terhune.   1993.   Repetition enhances hearing detection thresholds in a harbour seal (*Phoca vitulina*).   *Can. J. Zool.* 71(5):926-932.

Turnbull, S.D. and J.M. Terhune.   1994.   Descending frequency swept tones have lower thresholds than ascending frequency swept tones for a harbor seal (*Phoca vitulina*) and human listeners.   *J. Acoust. Soc. Am.* 96(5, Pt. 1):2631-2636.

Tyack, P.   1981.   Interactions between singing Hawaiian humpback whales and conspecifics nearby.   *Behav. Ecol. Sociobiol.* 8(2):105-116.

Tyack, P.   1983.   Differential response of humpback whales, *Megaptera novaeangliae*, to playback of song or social sounds.   *Behav. Ecol. Sociobiol.* 13(1):49-55.

Tyack, P.   1985.   An optical telemetry device to identify which dolphin produces a sound.   *J. Acoust. Soc. Am.* 78(5):1892-1895.

Tyack, P.   1986a.   Population biology, social behavior and communication in whales and dolphins.   *Trends Ecol. Evol.* 1(6):144-150.

Tyack, P.   1986b.   Whistle repertoires of two bottlenosed dolphins, *Tursiops truncatus*: Mimicry of signature whistles?   *Behav. Ecol. Sociobiol.* 18(4):251-257.

Tyack, P.L.   1987.   Do untrained dolphins imitate signature whistles to call each other?   p. 71 *In*: Abstr. 7th Bienn. Conf. Biol. Mar. Mamm., Miami, FL, Dec. 1987.   88 p.

Tyack, P.L.   1989.   Let's have less public relations and more ecology.   *Oceanus* 32 (1):103-108.

Tyack, P. and H. Whitehead.   1983.   Male competition in large groups of wintering humpback whales.   *Behaviour* 83(1/2):132-154.

Tyack, P.L., R. Wells, A. Read, T. Howald and T. Spradlin.   1993.   Experimental playback of low frequency noise to bottlenose dolphins, *Tursiops truncatus*. p. 3 *In*: Abstr. 10th Bienn. Conf. Biol. Mar. Mamm., Galveston, TX, Nov. 1993.   130 p.

Tyrrell, W.A.   1964.   Design of acoustic systems of obtaining bio-acoustic data. p. 65-86 *In*: W.N. Tavolga (ed.), Marine bio-acoustics.   Pergamon, Oxford, U.K.   413 p.

Udevitz, M.S., J.L. Bodkin and D.P. Costa.   1995.   Detection of sea otters in boat-based surveys of Prince William Sound, Alaska.   *Mar. Mamm. Sci.* 11(1):59-71.

Urick, R.J.   1971.   The noise of melting icebergs.   *J. Acoust. Soc. Am.* 50(1, Pt. 2): 337-341.

Urick, R.J. 1972. Noise signature of an aircraft in level flight over a hydrophone in the sea. *J. Acoust. Soc. Am.* 52(3, Pt. 2):993-999.

Urick, R.J. 1982. Sound propagation in the sea. Peninsula Publ., Los Altos, CA. Var. pag.

Urick, R.J. 1983. Principles of underwater sound, 3rd ed. McGraw-Hill, New York. 423 p.

Urick, R.J. 1986. Ambient noise in the sea. Peninsula Publ., Los Altos, CA. Var. pag.

U.S. Navy. 1979. Military specification, sonobuoy AN/SSQ-41B. MIL-S-22793 E(AS). Naval Air Syst. Comm., Washington, DC. 24 p.

U.S. Navy. 1985. Military specification, sonobuoy AN/SSQ-57A. MIL-S-81478 C(AS). Naval Air Syst. Comm., Washington, DC.

U.S. Navy. 1993. Request for a Letter of Authorization for the incidental take of marine mammals associated with Navy projects involving underwater detonations in the Outer Sea Test Range of the Naval Air Warfare Cent., Weapons Division Pt. Mugu, California, June 1993 ed. Request from Chief of Naval Operations [to U.S. Natl. Mar. Fish. Serv., Off. Prot. Resour., Silver Spring, MD]. 153 p.

Verboom, W.C. 1992. Bio-acoustics: Standardization, reference levels and data notation for underwater sound measurements. p. 741-751 *In*: J.A. Thomas, R.A. Kastelein and A.Ya. Supin (eds.), Marine mammal sensory systems. Plenum, New York. 773 p.

Verboom, W.C. and R.A. Kastelein. 1995. Rutting whistles of a male Pacific walrus (*Odobenus rosmarus divergens*). *In*: R.A. Kastelein, J.A. Thomas and P.E. Nachtigall (eds.), Sensory systems of aquatic mammals. De Spil Publ., Woerden, Netherlands. (in press).

Voronov, V.A. and I.M. Stosman. 1983. On sound perception in the dolphin *Phocoena phocoena*. *J. Evol. Biochem. Physiol.* 18(5):352-357 (Transl. from *Zh. Evol. Biokhim. Fiziol.* 18(5):499-506, 1982).

Wagstaff, R.A. 1973. Ambient noise: Comments on its causes, variability, and measurement. NUC TN 1039. U.S. Naval Undersea Cent., San Diego, CA. 52 p.

Wainwright, W.N. 1958. Comparison of hearing thresholds in air and in water. *J. Acoust. Soc. Am.* 30(11):1025-1029.

Walker, L.W. 1949. Nursery of the gray whales. *Nat. Hist.* 58(6):248-256.

Wang Ding et al. 1992. [published as Ding Wang et al. 1992 (*q.v.*)]

Wang Ding, B. Würsig and W. Evans. 1995. Comparisons of whistles among seven odontocete species. *In*: R.A. Kastelein, J.A. Thomas and P.E. Nachtigall (eds.), Sensory systems of aquatic mammals. De Spil Publ., Woerden, Netherlands. (in press).

Ward, J.G. and E. Pessah. 1986. Marine mammal observations in the Beaufort Sea, 1985 season, with a discussion of bowhead whales sightings, 1976-1985. Dome/Canmar Tech. Rep. Dome Petrol. Ltd., Calgary, Alb. 54 p.

Ward, J.G. and E. Pessah. 1988. Industry observations of bowhead whales in the Canadian Beaufort Sea, 1976-1985. p. 75-88 *In*: W.M. Sackinger et al. (eds.),

Port and ocean engineering under arctic conditions, vol. II. Geophys. Inst., Univ. Alaska, Fairbanks. 111 p.

Ward, W.D. (ed.). 1968. Proposed damage-risk criterion for impulse noise (gunfire). Committee on Hearing, Bioacoustics, and Biomechanics, Natl. Res. Counc., Natl. Acad. Sci., Washington, DC. 8 p.

Wartzok, D., R.J. Schusterman and J. Gailey-Phipps. 1984. Seal echolocation? *Nature (London)* 308(5961):753.

Wartzok, D., W.A. Watkins, B. Würsig and C.I. Malme. 1989. Movements and behaviors of bowhead whales in response to repeated exposures to noises associated with industrial activities in the Beaufort Sea. Rep. from Purdue Univ., Fort Wayne, IN, for Amoco Production Co., Anchorage, AK. 228 p.

Wartzok, D., R. Elsner, H. Stone, B.P. Kelly and R.W. Davis. 1992a. Under-ice movements and the sensory basis of hole finding by ringed and Weddell seals. *Can. J. Zool.* 70(9):1712-1722.

Wartzok, D., S. Sayegh, H. Stone, J. Barchak and W. Barnes. 1992b. Acoustic tracking system for monitoring under-ice movements of polar seals. *J. Acoust. Soc. Am.* 92(2, Pt. 1):682-687.

Waters, J.F. 1972. Computer programs for underwater sound fields due to airborne sources. Tech. Note 144. Contr. No. N00014-70-C-0301 for U.S. Navy Off. Naval Res., Arlington, VA. 74 p.

Waters, S.L. 1992. Non-consumptive utilisation of marine mammals in Canada: International and national regulation. p. 141-172 *In*: D. VanderZwaag (ed.), Canadian ocean law and policy. Butterworths, Toronto, Ont. 546 p.

Watkins, W.A. 1967a. Air-borne sounds of the humpback whale, *Megaptera novaeangliae*. *J. Mammal.* 48(4):573-578.

Watkins, W.A. 1967b. The harmonic interval: Fact or artifact in spectral analysis of pulse trains. p. 15-43 *In*: W.N. Tavolga (ed.), Marine bio-acoustics, vol. 2. Pergamon, Oxford, U.K. 353 p.

Watkins, W.A. 1977. Acoustic behavior of sperm whales. *Oceanus* 20(2):50-58.

Watkins, W.A. 1980a. Acoustics and the behavior of sperm whales. p. 283-290 *In*: R.-G. Busnel and J.F. Fish (eds.), Animal sonar systems. Plenum, New York. 1135 p.

Watkins, W.A. 1980b. Click sounds from animals at sea. p. 291-297 *In*: R.-G. Busnel and J.F. Fish (eds.), Animal sonar systems. Plenum, New York. 1135 p.

Watkins, W.A. 1981a. Reaction of three species of whales *Balaenoptera physalus*, *Megaptera novaeangliae*, and *Balaenoptera edeni* to implanted radio tags. *Deep-Sea Res.* 28A(6):589-599.

Watkins, W.A. 1981b. Activities and underwater sounds of fin whales. *Sci. Rep. Whales Res. Inst.* 33:83-117.

Watkins, W.A. 1986. Whale reactions to human activities in Cape Cod waters. *Mar. Mamm. Sci.* 2(4):251-262.

Watkins, W.A. and C.A. Goebel. 1984. Sonar observations explain behaviors noted during boat maneuvers for radio tagging of humpback whales (*Megaptera novaeangliae*) in the Glacier Bay area. *Cetology* 48:1-8.

Watkins, W.A. and K.E. Moore. 1982. An underwater acoustic survey for sperm whales (*Physeter catodon*) and other cetaceans in the southeast Caribbean. *Cetology* 46:1-7.

Watkins, W.A. and K.E. Moore. 1983. Three right whales (*Eubalaena glacialis*) alternating at the surface. *J. Mammal.* 64(3):506-508.

Watkins, W.A. and G.C. Ray. 1977. Underwater sounds from ribbon seal, *Phoca* (*Histriophoca*) *fasciata*. *Fish. Bull.* 75(2):450-453.

Watkins, W.A. and G.C. Ray. 1985. In-air and underwater sounds of the Ross seal, *Ommatophoca rossi*. *J. Acoust. Soc. Am.* 77(4):1598-1600.

Watkins, W.A. and W.E. Schevill. 1972. Sound source location by arrival-times on a non-rigid three-dimensional hydrophone array. *Deep-Sea Res.* 19(10):691-706.

Watkins, W.A. and W.E. Schevill. 1974. Listening to Hawaiian spinner porpoises, *Stenella* cf. *longirostris*, with a three-dimensional hydrophone array. *J. Mammal.* 55(2):319-328.

Watkins, W.A. and W.E. Schevill. 1975. Sperm whales (*Physeter catodon*) react to pingers. *Deep-Sea Res.* 22(3):123-129.

Watkins, W.A. and W.E. Schevill. 1976. Right whale feeding and baleen rattle. *J. Mammal.* 57(1):58-66.

Watkins, W.A. and W.E. Schevill. 1977a. Spatial distribution of *Physeter catodon* (sperm whales) underwater. *Deep-Sea Res.* 24(7):693-699.

Watkins, W.A. and W.E. Schevill. 1977b. Sperm whale codas. *J. Acoust. Soc. Am.* 62(6):1485-1490 + phono. record.

Watkins, W.A. and W.E. Schevill. 1979a. Aerial observation of feeding behavior in four baleen whales: *Eubalaena glacialis*, *Balaenoptera borealis*, *Megaptera novaeangliae*, and *Balaenoptera physalus*. *J. Mammal.* 60(1):155-163.

Watkins, W.A. and W.E. Schevill. 1979b. Distinctive characteristics of underwater calls of the harp seal, *Phoca groenlandica*, during the breeding season. *J. Acoust. Soc. Am.* 66(4):983-988.

Watkins, W.A. and D. Wartzok. 1985. Sensory biophysics of marine mammals. *Mar. Mamm. Sci.* 1(3):219-260.

Watkins, W.A., W.E. Schevill and P.B. Best. 1977. Underwater sounds of *Cephalorhynchus heavisidii* (Mammalia: Cetacea). *J. Mammal.* 58(3):316-320.

Watkins, W.A., K.E. Moore, D. Wartzok and J.H. Johnson. 1981. Radio tracking of finback (*Balaenoptera physalus*) and humpback (*Megaptera novaeangliae*) whales in Prince William Sound, Alaska. *Deep-Sea Res.* 28A(6):577-588.

Watkins, W.A., K.E. Moore and P. Tyack. 1985a. Sperm whale acoustic behaviors in the southeast Caribbean. *Cetology* 49:1-15.

Watkins, W.A., K. Moore and P. Tyack. 1985b. Codas shared by Caribbean sperm whales. *In*: Abstr. 6th Bienn. Conf. Biol. Mar. Mamm., Vancouver, B.C., Nov. 1985. [86 p.]

Watkins, W.A., P. Tyack, K.E. Moore and J.E. Bird. 1987. The 20-Hz signals of finback whales (*Balaenoptera physalus*). *J. Acoust. Soc. Am.* 82(6):1901-1912.

Watkins, W.A., M.A. Daher, K.M. Fristrup, T.J. Howald and G. Notarbartolo di Sciara. 1993. Sperm whales tagged with transponders and tracked underwater by sonar. *Mar. Mamm. Sci.* 9(1):55-67.

Watson, C.S. 1963. Masking of tones by noise for the cat. *J. Acoust. Soc. Am.* 35 (2):167-172.

Watts, A.J. (ed.). 1994. Jane's underwater warfare systems 1994-95, 6th ed. Jane's Information Group Inc., Surrey, U.K. 383 p.

Weigle, B.L., I.E. Beeler-Wright and J.A. Huff. 1993. Responses of manatees to an approaching boat: A pilot study. p. 111 *In*: Abstr. 10th Bienn. Conf. Biol. Mar. Mamm., Galveston, TX, Nov. 1993. 130 p.

Weilgart, L.S. and H. Whitehead. 1988. Distinctive vocalizations from mature male sperm whales (*Physeter macrocephalus*). *Can. J. Zool.* 66(9):1931-1937.

Weilgart, L.S. and H. Whitehead. 1990. Vocalizations of the North Atlantic pilot whale (*Globicephala melas*) as related to behavioral contexts. *Behav. Ecol. Sociobiol.* 26(6):399-402.

Weilgart, L. and H. Whitehead. 1993. Coda communication by sperm whales (*Physeter macrocephalus*) off the Galápagos Islands. *Can. J. Zool.* 71(4):744-752.

Weinstein, M.S. and A.G. Henney. 1965. Wave solution for air-to-water sound transmission. *J. Acoust. Soc. Am.* 37(5):899-901.

Wenz, G.M. 1962. Acoustic ambient noise in the ocean: Spectra and sources. *J. Acoust. Soc. Am.* 34(12):1936-1956.

Weston, D.E. 1960. Underwater explosions as acoustic sources. *Proc. Phys. Soc., London* 76(2):233-249.

Weston, D.E. 1976. Propagation in water with uniform sound velocity but variable-depth lossy bottom. *J. Sound Vib.* 47(4):473-483.

Westworth, D.A. 1977. Impact of seismic activity on muskrat populations on the Mackenzie Delta. Environ. Stud. 1, North of 60. QS-8139-OOO-EE-A1. Dep. Indian & Northern Affairs, Ottawa, Ont. 70 p.

Wever, E.G., J.G. McCormick, J. Palin and S.H. Ridgway. 1971a. The cochlea of the dolphin, *Tursiops truncatus*: General morphology. *Proc. Natl. Acad. Sci. USA* 68(10):2381-2385.

Wever, E.G., J.G. McCormick, J. Palin and S.H. Ridgway. 1971b. Cochlea of the dolphin, *Tursiops truncatus*: The basilar membrane. *Proc. Natl. Acad. Sci. USA* 68(11):2708-2711.

Wever, E.G., J.G. McCormick, J. Palin and S.H. Ridgway. 1971c. The cochlea of the dolphin, *Tursiops truncatus*: Hair cells and ganglion cells. *Proc. Natl. Acad. Sci. USA* 68(12):2908-2912.

Wever, E.G., J.G. McCormick, J. Palin and S.H. Ridgway. 1972. Cochlear structure in the dolphin, *Lagenorhynchus obliquidens*. *Proc. Natl. Acad. Sci. USA* 69(3):657-661.

White, M.J., Jr., J. Norris, D. Ljungblad, K. Baron and G. di Sciara. 1978. Auditory thresholds of two beluga whales (*Delphinapterus leucas*). HSWRI Tech. Rep. 78-109. Rep. from Hubbs/Sea World Res. Inst., San Diego, CA, for U.S. Naval Ocean Systems Cent., San Diego, CA. 35 p.

Whitehead, H. and L. Weilgart. 1990. Click rates from sperm whales. *J. Acoust. Soc. Am.* 87(4):1798-1806.

Whitehead, H. and L. Weilgart. 1991. Patterns of visually observable behaviour and vocalizations in groups of female sperm whales. *Behaviour* 118(3/4):275-296.

Whitehead, H., J. Gordon, E.A. Mathews and K.R. Richard. 1990. Obtaining skin samples from living sperm whales. *Mar. Mamm. Sci.* 6(4):316-326.

Wickens, P.[A.] 1994. Operational interactions between seals and fisheries in South Africa. Rep. from Mar. Biol. Res. Inst., Univ. Cape Town, Rondebosch, S. Afr., for S. Afr. Dep. Environ. Aff. and S. Afr. Nature Found. 162 p.

Wickens, P.A., P.A. Shelton, J.H.M. David, J.G. Field, W.H. Oosthuizen, J.-P. Roux and A.M. Starfield. 1992a. A fur seal simulation model to explore alternative management strategies. *Can. J. Fish. Aquat. Sci.* 49(7):1396-1405.

Wickens, P.A., D.W. Japp, P.A. Shelton, F. Kriel, P.C. Goosen, B. Rose, C.J. Augustyn, C.A.R. Bross, A.J. Penney and R.G. Krohn. 1992b. Seals and fisheries in South Africa—Competition and conflict. *S. Afr. J. Mar. Sci.* 12:773-789.

Wiener, F.M. and Staff of BBN Inc. 1954. Capabilities and limitations of long range public address equipment, Final Report, Phase I. BBN Rep. 312. Rep. from Bolt Beranek & Newman Inc., Cambridge, MA, for U.S. Army Signal Corps, Ft. Monmouth, NJ. Var. pag.

Wier, C.C., W. Jesteadt and D.M. Green. 1977. Frequency discrimination as a function of frequency and sensation level. *J. Acoust. Soc. Am.* 61(1):178-184.

Wiley, D.N., R.A. Asmutis, T.D. Pitchford and D.P. Gannon. 1995. Stranding and mortality of humpback whales, *Megaptera novaeangliae*, in the mid-Atlantic and southeast United States, 1985-1992. *Fish. Bull.* 93(1):196-205.

Wille, P.C. and D. Geyer. 1984. Measurements on the origin of the wind-dependent ambient noise variability in shallow water. *J. Acoust. Soc. Am.* 75(1):73-185.

Williams, T.M., W.A. Friedl, M.L. Fong, R.M. Yamada, P. Sedivy and J.E. Haun. 1992. Travel at low energetic cost by swimming and wave-riding bottlenose dolphins. *Nature (London)* 355(6363):821-823.

Wilson, O.B., Jr., S.N. Wolf and F. Ingenito. 1985. Measurements of acoustic ambient noise in shallow water due to breaking surf. *J. Acoust. Soc. Am.* 78 (1):190-195.

Winn, H.E. and P.J. Perkins. 1976. Distribution and sounds of the minke whale, with a review of mysticete sounds. *Cetology* 19:1-12.

Winn, H.E., P.J. Perkins and T.C. Poulter. 1970a. Sounds of the humpback whale. p. 39-52 *In*: Proc. 7th Annu. Conf. Biol. Sonar & Diving Mammals, Stanford Res. Inst., Menlo Park, CA.

Winn, H.E., P.J. Perkins and L. Winn. 1970b. Sounds and behavior of the northern bottle-nosed whale. p. 53-59 *In*: Proc. 7th Annu. Conf. Biol. Sonar & Diving Mammals, Stanford Res. Inst., Menlo Park, CA.

Winn, H.E., R.K. Edel and A.G. Taruski. 1975. Population estimate of the humpback whale (*Megaptera novaeangliae*) in the West Indies by visual and acoustic techniques. *J. Fish. Res. Board Can.* 32(4):499-506.

Winn, H.E., T.J. Thompson, W.C. Cummings, J. Hain, J. Hudnall, H. Hays and W.W. Steiner. 1981. Song of the humpback whale—Population comparisons. *Behav. Ecol. Sociobiol.* 8(1):41-46.

Winn, L.K. and H.E. Winn. 1985. Wings in the sea/The humpback whale. Univ. Press of New England, Hanover, NH. 151 p.

Withrow, D.E. 1983. Gray whale research in Scammon's Lagoon (Laguna Ojo de Liebre). *Cetus* 5(1):8-13.

Withrow, D.E., G.C. Bouchet and L.L. Jones. 1985. Response of Dall's porpoise (*Phocoenoides dalli*) to survey vessels in both offshore and nearshore waters: Results of 1984 research. Int. N. Pacific Fish. Comm. Doc. U.S. Natl. Mar. Mamm. Lab., Seattle, WA. 16 p.

Wolfson, F.H. 1977. Gray whale behavior [letter to editor]. *Science* 195(4278): 534-535.

Wood, F.G., Jr. 1953. Underwater sound production and concurrent behavior of captive porpoises, *Tursiops truncatus* and *Stenella plagiodon*. *Bull. Mar. Sci. Gulf Caribb.* 3(2):120-133.

Wood, F.G. and W.E. Evans. 1980. Adaptiveness and ecology of echolocation in toothed whales. p. 381-425 *In*: R.-G. Busnel and J.F. Fish (eds.), Animal sonar systems. Plenum, New York. 1135 p.

Wooldridge, D.R. and P. Belton. 1980. Natural and synthesized aggressive sounds as polar bear repellents. *Int. Conf. Bear Res. Manage.* 4:85-91.

Woolley, B.L. and W.T. Ellison. 1993. Low frequency mechanoreceptors in man: A preliminary investigation into the acoustical/physical basis for human physiological response to low frequency water borne noise. Rep. from Marine Acoustics Inc., Newport, RI, for U.S. Navy, NCCOSC, RDT & E Div., San Diego, CA. Not paginated.

Worley, R.D. and R.A. Walker. 1982. Low-frequency ambient ocean noise and sound transmission over a thinly sedimented rock bottom. *J. Acoust. Soc. Am.* 71(4):863-870.

Wright, D.G. 1982. A discussion paper on the effects of explosives on fish and marine mammals in the waters of the Northwest Territories. *Can. Tech. Rep. Fish. Aquat. Sci.* 1052. 16 p.

Wright, D.G. 1985. A history and scientific rationale of the development of guidelines to cover the use of explosives in the marine environment in Canada and other nations. p. 2-15 *In*: Proc. Workshop on Effects of Explosives Use in the Marine Environment, Jan. 1985, Halifax, N.S. Tech. Rep. 5. Can. Oil & Gas Lands Admin. Environ. Prot. Branch, Ottawa, Ont. 398 p.

Wright, R.A. and W.H. Allton. 1971. Sea otter studies in the vicinity of Amchitka Island. *BioScience* 21(12):673-677.

Wright, S.D., B.B. Ackerman, R.K. Bonde, C.A. Beck and D.J. Banowetz. 1991. A retrospective analysis of watercraft-related mortality of the West Indian manatee in Florida (1979-1989). p. 75 *In*: Abstr. 9th Bienn. Conf. Biol. Mar. Mamm., Chicago, IL, Dec. 1991. 76 p.

Würsig, B. and C. Clark. 1993. Behavior. p. 157-199 *In*: J.J. Burns, J.J. Montague and C.J. Cowles (eds.), The bowhead whale. Spec. Publ. 2. Soc. Mar. Mammal., Lawrence, KS. 787 p.

Würsig, B. and S. Lynn. in press. Behavior of cetaceans relative to census vessels. *In*: Proc. 14th Annu. Gulf of Mexico Info. Transfer Meet., Nov. 1994. U.S. Minerals Manage. Serv., New Orleans, LA.

Würsig, B. and M. Würsig. 1980. Behavior and ecology of the dusky dolphin, *Lagenorhynchus obscurus*, in the south Atlantic. *Fish. Bull.* 77(4):871-890.

Würsig, B., C.W. Clark, E.M. Dorsey, M.A. Fraker and R.S. Payne. 1982. Normal behavior of bowheads. p. 33-143 *In*: W.J. Richardson (ed.), Behavior, disturbance responses and feeding of bowhead whales *Balaena mysticetus* in the Beaufort Sea, 1980-81. Chapter by New York Zool. Soc. in Rep. from LGL Ecol. Res. Assoc. Inc., Bryan, TX, for U.S. Bur. Land Manage., Washington, DC. 456 p. NTIS PB86-152170.

Würsig, B., E.M. Dorsey, M.A. Fraker, R.S. Payne and W.J. Richardson. 1985a. Behavior of bowhead whales, *Balaena mysticetus*, summering in the Beaufort Sea: A description. *Fish. Bull.* 83(3):357-377.

Würsig, B., E.M. Dorsey, W.J. Richardson, C.W. Clark and R. Payne. 1985b. Normal behavior of bowheads, 1980-84. p. 13-88 *In*: W.J. Richardson (ed.), Behavior, disturbance responses and distribution of bowhead whales *Balaena mysticetus* in the eastern Beaufort Sea, 1980-84. Rep. from LGL Ecol. Res. Assoc. Inc., Bryan, TX, for U.S. Minerals Manage. Serv., Reston, VA. 306 p. NTIS PB87-124376.

Würsig, B., E.M. Dorsey, W.J. Richardson and R.S. Wells. 1989. Feeding, aerial and play behaviour of the bowhead whale, *Balaena mysticetus*, summering in the Beaufort Sea. *Aquat. Mamm.* 15(1):27-37.

Wyrick, R.F. 1954. Observations on the movements of the Pacific gray whale *Eschrichtius glaucus* (Cope). *J. Mammal.* 35(4):596-598.

Xiao Youfu and Jing Rongcai. 1989. Underwater acoustic signals of the baiji, *Lipotes vexillifer*. p. 129-136 *In*: W.F. Perrin, R.L. Brownell, Jr., Zhou Kaiya and Liu Jiankang (eds.), Biology and conservation of the river dolphins. Occas. Pap. IUCN Species Surv. Comm. 3. Int. Union Conserv. Nat., Gland, Switzerland. 173 p.

Yeager, E., F.H. Fisher, J. Miceli and R. Bressel. 1973. Origin of the low-frequency sound absorption in sea water. *J. Acoust. Soc. Am.* -53(6):1705-1707.

Yelverton, J.T. 1981. Underwater explosion damage risk criteria for fish, birds, and mammals. Manuscript, presented at 102nd Meet. Acoust. Soc. Am., Miami Beach, FL, Dec. 1981. 32 p.

Yelverton, J.T., D.R. Richmond, E.R. Fletcher and R.K. Jones. 1973. Safe distances from underwater explosions for mammals and birds. DNA 3114T. Rep. from Lovelace Foundation for Medical Educ. and Res., Albuquerque, NM, for Defense Nuclear Agency, Washington, DC. 67 p. NTIS AD-766952.

Young, G.A. 1991. Concise methods for predicting the effects of underwater explosions on marine life. NSWC/WOL MP-91-220. Naval Surf. Weap. Cent., White Oak Lab., Silver Spring, MD. 13 p. DTIC/NTIS AD-A241310.

Young, N.M. 1989. Dive and ventilation patterns correlated to behavior of fin whales, *Balaenoptera physalus*, in Cape Cod and Massachusetts bays. p. 74 *In*: Abstr. 8th Bienn. Conf. Biol. Mar. Mamm., Pacific Grove, CA, Dec. 1989. 81 p.

Young, R.W. 1973. Sound pressure in water from a source in air and vice versa. *J. Acoust. Soc. Am.* 53(6):1708-1716.

Young, R.W. and C.N. Miller. 1960. Noise data for two outboard motors in air and in water. *Noise Control* 6(1):22-25.

Zagaeski, M. 1987. Some observations on the prey stunning hypothesis. *Mar. Mamm. Sci.* 3(3):275-279.

Zaitseva, K.A., A.I. Akopian and V.P. Morozov. 1975. Noise resistance of the dolphin auditory analyzer as a function of noise direction. *Biofizika* 20(3):519-521 (Transl. JPRS-65762, NTIS 297212, 4 p.).

Zaitseva, K.A., V.P. Morozov and A.I. Akopian. 1980. Comparative characteristics of spatial hearing in the dolphin *Tursiops truncatus* and man. *Neurosci. Behav. Physiol.* 10(2):180-182 (Transl. from *Zh. Evol. Biokhim. Fiziol.* 14(1): 80-83, 1978).

Zakarauskas, P. 1986. Ambient noise in shallow water: A literature review. *Can. Acoust.* 14(3):3-17.

Zakarauskas, P., D.M.F. Chapman and P.R. Staal. 1990. Underwater acoustic ambient noise levels on the eastern Canadian continental shelf. *J. Acoust. Soc. Am.* 87(5):2064-2071.

Zhou Kaiya and Zhang Xingduan. 1991. Baiji/The Yangtze river dolphin and other endangered animals of China. Stone Wall Press and Yilin Press, Washington, DC, and Nanjing, China. 129 p.

Zimushko, V.V. and M.V. Ivashin. 1980. Some results of Soviet investigations and whaling of gray whales (*Eschrichtius robustus*, Lilljeborg, 1961). *Rep. Int. Whal. Comm.* 30:237-246.

Zwicker, E., G. Flottorp and S.S. Stevens. 1957. Critical band width in loudness summation. *J. Acoust. Soc. Am.* 29(5):548-557.

APPENDIX 1

COMMON AND SCIENTIFIC NAMES
OF MARINE MAMMALS

WHALES and DOLPHINS	**Order CETACEA**
TOOTHED WHALES (ODONTOCETES)	**Suborder ODONTOCETI**
Dolphins & small toothed whales	**Superfamily Delphinoidea**
Narwhal and Beluga	**Family Monodontidae**
Narwhal	- *Monodon monoceros*
Beluga (White) Whale	- *Delphinapterus leucas*
Dolphins (Delphinids)	**Family Delphinidae**
	Subfamily Orcaellinae
Irrawaddy Dolphin	- *Orcaella brevirostris*
	Subfamily Globicephalinae
Melon-headed Whale	- *Peponocephala electra*
Pygmy Killer Whale	- *Feresa attenuata*
False Killer Whale	- *Pseudorca crassidens*
Killer Whale	- *Orcinus orca*
Long-finned Pilot Whale	- *Globicephala melas* (= *melaena*)
Short-finned Pilot Whale	- *Globicephala macrorhynchus*
	Subfamily Steninae
Rough-toothed Dolphin	- *Steno bredanensis*
Tucuxi	- *Sotalia fluviatilis*
Indo-Pacific Hump-backed Dolphin	- *Sousa chinensis*
Atlantic Hump-backed Dolphin	- *Sousa teuszii*
	Subfamily Delphininae
White-beaked Dolphin	- *Lagenorhynchus albirostris*
Atlantic White-sided Dolphin	- *Lagenorhynchus acutus*
Dusky Dolphin	- *Lagenorhynchus obscurus*
Pacific White-sided Dolphin	- *Lagenorhynchus obliquidens*
Hourglass Dolphin	- *Lagenorhynchus cruciger*
Peale's Dolphin	- *Lagenorhynchus australis*
Fraser's Dolphin	- *Lagenodelphis hosei*
Common Dolphin (Short-beaked)	- *Delphinus delphis*
Long-beaked Common Dolphin	- *Delphinus capensis*
Risso's Dolphin (Grampus)	- *Grampus griseus*
Bottlenose Dolphin	- *Tursiops truncatus*

Atlantic Spotted Dolphin	- *Stenella frontalis*
Pantropical Spotted Dolphin	- *Stenella attenuata*
Spinner Dolphin (Long-snouted)	- *Stenella longirostris*
Clymene (Short-snouted Spinner) Dolphin	- *Stenella clymene*
Striped Dolphin	- *Stenella coeruleoalba*

Subfamily Lissodelphinae

Northern Right Whale Dolphin	- *Lissodelphis borealis*
Southern Right Whale Dolphin	- *Lissodelphis peronii*

Subfam. Cephalorhynchinae

Commerson's Dolphin	- *Cephalorhynchus commersonii*
Black Dolphin	- *Cephalorhynchus eutropia*
Heaviside's Dolphin	- *Cephalorhynchus heavisidii*
Hector's Dolphin	- *Cephalorhynchus hectori*

Porpoises **Family Phocoenidae**

Dall's Porpoise	- *Phocoenoides dalli*
Spectacled Porpoise	- *Australophocaena dioptrica*
Harbor Porpoise	- *Phocoena phocoena*
Vaquita (Gulf of Calif. Harbor Porp.)	- *Phocoena sinus*
Burmeister's Porpoise	- *Phocoena spinipinnis*
Finless Porpoise	- *Neophocaena phocaenoides*

River Dolphins and Franciscana **Superfamily Platanistoidea**

Boutu (Boto, Amazon River Dolphin)	- *Inia geoffrensis*
Baiji (Chinese River Dolphin)	- *Lipotes vexillifer*
Franciscana (La Plata Dolphin)	- *Pontoporia blainvillei*
Indus Susu (Indus River Dolphin)	- *Platanista minor*
Ganges Susu (Ganges River Dolphin)	- *Platanista gangetica*

Sperm Whales **Superfamily Physeteroidea**

Sperm Whale	- *Physeter catodon*
	(= *P. macrocephalus*)
Pygmy Sperm Whale	- *Kogia breviceps*
Dwarf Sperm Whale	- *Kogia simus*

Beaked Whales **Superfamily Ziphioidea**

Baird's Beaked Whale	- *Berardius bairdii*
Arnoux's Beaked Whale	- *Berardius arnuxii*
Northern Bottlenose Whale	- *Hyperoodon ampullatus*
Southern Bottlenose Whale	- *Hyperoodon planifrons*
Cuvier's Beaked (Goosebeaked) Whale	- *Ziphius cavirostris*
Tasman (Shepherd's) Beaked Whale	- *Tasmacetus shepherdi*
Blainville's Beaked Whale	- *Mesoplodon densirostris*
Sowerby's Beaked Whale	- *Mesoplodon bidens*
Gervais' Beaked Whale	- *Mesoplodon europaeus*
True's Beaked Whale	- *Mesoplodon mirus*
Strap-toothed [Beaked] Whale	- *Mesoplodon layardii*

Gray's Beaked Whale	- *Mesoplodon grayi*
Andrews' Beaked Whale	- *Mesoplodon bowdoini*
Longman's Beaked Whale	- *Mesoplodon pacificus*
Hector's Beaked Whale	- *Mesoplodon hectori*
Ginkgo-toothed Beaked Whale	- *Mesoplodon ginkgodens*
Stejneger's Beaked Whale	- *Mesoplodon stejnegeri*
Hubbs' Beaked Whale	- *Mesoplodon carlhubbsi*
Pygmy Beaked Whale	- *Mesoplodon peruvianus*

BALEEN WHALES (MYSTICETES) — Suborder MYSTICETI

Right Whales — **Family Balaenidae**
- Bowhead Whale — - *Balaena mysticetus*
- Northern Right Whale — - *Eubalaena glacialis*
- Southern Right Whale — - *Eubalaena australis*

Pygmy Right Whale — **Family Neobalaenidae**
- Pygmy Right Whale — - *Caperea marginata*

Rorquals — **Family Balaenopteridae**
- Blue Whale — - *Balaenoptera musculus*
- Fin Whale — - *Balaenoptera physalus*
- Sei Whale — - *Balaenoptera borealis*
- Bryde's Whale — - *Balaenoptera edeni*
- Minke Whale — - *Balaenoptera acutorostrata,*
    B. bonaerensis
- Humpback Whale — - *Megaptera novaeangliae*

Gray Whale — **Family Eschrichtiidae**
- Gray Whale — - *Eschrichtius robustus*

CARNIVORES (in part) — Order CARNIVORA

True = Earless = Hair Seals (Phocids) — **Family Phocidae**

Phocinids — **Subfamily Phocinae**
- Ringed Seal — - *Phoca hispida*
- Caspian Seal — - *Phoca caspica*
- Baikal Seal — - *Phoca sibirica*
- Harbor (Common) Seal — - *Phoca vitulina*
- Spotted (Largha) Seal — - *Phoca largha*
- Ribbon Seal — - *Phoca fasciata*
- Harp Seal — - *Phoca (Pagophilus) groenlandica*
- Bearded Seal — - *Erignathus barbatus*
- Hooded Seal — - *Cystophora cristata*
- Gray Seal — - *Halichoerus grypus*

Monachids — **Subfamily Monachinae**
- Crabeater Seal — - *Lobodon carcinophagus*
- Ross Seal — - *Ommatophoca rossii*

Leopard Seal	-	*Hydrurga leptonyx*
Weddell Seal	-	*Leptonychotes weddellii*
Northern Elephant Seal	-	*Mirounga angustirostris*
Southern Elephant Seal	-	*Mirounga leonina*
Mediterranean Monk Seal	-	*Monachus monachus*
Caribbean (W. Indian) Monk Seal	-	*Monachus tropicalis* Extinct?
Hawaiian Monk Seal	-	*Monachus schauinslandi*

Eared Seals (Otariids)   **Family Otariidae**

Fur Seals   **Subfamily Arctocephalinae**

Northern Fur Seal	-	*Callorhinus ursinus*
Guadalupe Fur Seal	-	*Arctocephalus townsendi*
Juan Fernández Fur Seal	-	*Arctocephalus philippii*
Galápagos Fur Seal	-	*Arctocephalus galapagoensis*
South American Fur Seal	-	*Arctocephalus australis*
South African & Australian Fur Seal	-	*Arctocephalus pusillus*
New Zealand (W. Australian) Fur Seal	-	*Arctocephalus forsteri*
Antarctic (Kerguelen) Fur Seal	-	*Arctocephalus gazella*
Subantarctic (Amsterdam I.) Fur Seal	-	*Arctocephalus tropicalis*

Sea Lions   **Subfamily Otariinae**

Northern (Steller) Sea Lion	-	*Eumetopias jubatus*
California, Galápagos, and Japanese (extinct) Sea Lion	-	*Zalophus californianus*
South American (Southern) Sea Lion	-	*Otaria byronia* (=*O. flavescens*)
Australian Sea Lion	-	*Neophoca cinerea*
New Zealand (Hooker's) Sea Lion	-	*Phocarctos hookeri*

Odobenids   **Family Odobenidae**

| Walrus | - | *Odobenus rosmarus* |

Otters (Mustelids, in part)   **Family Mustelidae**

| Sea Otter | - | *Enhydra lutris* |
| Marine Otter | - | *Lutra felina* |

Bears (in part)   **Family Ursidae**

| Polar Bear | - | *Ursus maritimus* |

MANATEES & DUGONGS (SEA COWS)   Order SIRENIA

Manatees   **Family Trichechidae**

West Indian (Florida, Carib.) Manatee	-	*Trichechus manatus*
Amazonian Manatee	-	*Trichechus inunguis*
West African Manatee	-	*Trichechus senegalensis*

Dugongs   **Family Dugongidae**

| Dugong | - | *Dugong dugon* |
| Steller's Sea Cow | - | *Hydrodamalis gigas* Extinct |

APPENDIX 2

A GLOSSARY OF ACOUSTICAL TERMS

The following definitions should serve most readers. More comprehensive definitions and notes are contained in several American National Standard Institute (ANSI) standards on acoustics, for example ANSI (1971), ANSI (1986), and especially ANSI (1994): *American National Standard Acoustical Terminology*, ANSI S1.1-1994 (ASA Catalog No. 111-1994). These are all published by the Standards Secretariat, Acoustical Society of America, 120 Wall Street, 32nd Floor, New York, New York 10005-3993.

absorption. Process by which sound energy is converted into heat in the water or air.

acoustic energy. Energy in an acoustic wave, measured in joules or watt-seconds; proportional to the product of pressure squared and time.

acoustic impulse. Integral over time of the initial positive acoustic pressure pulse, measured in pascal-seconds (Pa·s); used in describing sound pulses (Section 6.7.2).

acoustic intensity. Acoustic power crossing a unit area; pressure squared divided by acoustic impedance (ρc, where ρ represents the density of the medium and c the sound speed).

acoustic power. Energy per unit time, in watts, proportional to acoustic pressure squared.

acoustic pressure. Very small pressure variations (compared to shock or blast wave pressures) around an ambient static pressure at acoustic frequencies.

aliasing. Process by which artifactual out-of-band components appear in a signal spectrum if sampling is not fast enough (2x the highest frequency in the waveform) (Section 3.4.3).

ambient noise. Environmental background noise not of direct interest during a measurement or observation; may be from sources near and far, distributed and discrete, but excludes sounds produced by measurement equipment, such as cable flutter.

audiogram. Graph showing an animal's absolute auditory threshold (threshold in the absence of much background noise) versus frequency. **Behavioral audiograms** are determined by tests with trained animals. *Cf.* evoked potential.

auditory threshold. Minimum sound level that can be perceived by an animal in the absence of significant background noise. Varies with frequency and is inversely related to auditory sensitivity.

A-weighted level. A measure of airborne noise level relevant to human sound perception. Determined by integrating the weighted mean square pressure across all frequencies, where the weighting factors approximate the in-air auditory sensitivity curve for humans (see Fig. 5.5 in Section 5.6).

band-pass filter. Filter with high- and low-pass cutoff frequencies to pass only a specified range of frequencies.

bar-meter. Unit used in seismic survey industry for peak-to-peak (*q.v.*) source level of strong acoustic sources. For a sinusoid, 1 bar-m_{p-p} = 220 dB re 1 µPa-m_{p-p} = 214 dB re 1 µPa-m_{peak} = 211 dB re 1 µPa-m_{rms} [see equation (6.3) in Section 6.5].

best frequency. Frequency where an animal's auditory sensitivity is highest (threshold lowest).

blade-rate. Number of turns of propeller or turbine per second multiplied by number of blades; often the fundamental frequency of a harmonic family of tones in a sound spectrum.

cavitation. Cavities form in a liquid when local static pressure is reduced sufficiently to rupture the liquid; bubbles appear (e.g., during explosions; frequent adjacent to ship propellers).

continuous wave. Sound whose waveform continues with time. *Cf.* transient wave.

convergence zones. Annular regions of elevated sound pressure that sometimes occur at evenly spaced distances (~60 km in temperate-zone oceans) from a shallow source in deep water.

critical band. Frequency band within which background noise has strong effects on detection of a sound signal at a particular frequency.

critical ratio. Difference between sound level for a barely audible tone and the spectrum level of background noise at nearby frequencies.

cylindrical spreading. Sound spreading for cylindrical waves. Transmission loss $10 \log_{10} (R/R_0)$, where R is range and R_0 is a reference range. Received level diminishes by 3 dB when range doubles, and by 10 dB for a 10-fold range increase.

cylindrical wave. Sound with cylindrically shaped wavefronts. Does not occur close to point sources of sound. *Cf.* plane wave, spherical wave.

Damage Risk Criterion (DRC). Received level or other acoustic measure above which a specified type of injury is likely (Section 10.6.2).

decibel (dB). Unit of level (*q.v.*); one-tenth of a **bel**. A logarithmic measure of sound strength, calculated as $20 \log_{10} (P/P_{ref})$, where P is sound pressure and P_{ref} is a reference pressure (e.g., 1 µPa). Note that $20 \log(P)$ is identical to $10 \log(P^2)$, where P^2 is the mean square sound pressure and is proportional to power, intensity, or energy.

delay. Time by which one waveform lags behind another. For example, reflected sound is delayed in reaching a receiver compared to directly traveling sound. *Cf.* time delay.

difference limen (DL). Minimum frequency difference, in Hz, required to perceive two tones as being at separate frequencies, or a single tone as being frequency modulated. *Cf.* Weber ratio.

directivity index (DI). Measure of the concentration of emitted sound in specific directions, or of the enhanced sensitivity of a receiver for sounds arriving from some directions.

doppler shift. Change in received signal frequency caused by radial motion of the source, the receiver, or both.

DRC. See Damage Risk Criterion.

duty cycle. Percent of time a given periodic event or activity occurs.

effective sound pressure. See sound pressure, effective.

electrical noise. Noise generated by electronic circuits, as distinct from acoustic noise.

evoked potential (EP). Electrical signal emitted by an animal's nervous or sensory systems in response to applied stimulus such as a sound. Strength of EP versus sound frequency gives information about *relative* sensitivity versus frequency. *Cf.* audiogram/behavioral.

faired cable. A cable with many ribbon- or hair-like attachments to eliminate strumming in currents.

far field. Receiver is in the "far field" of a spatially extended source when the source appears to have point source properties. *Cf.* near field, point source.

filter. Instrument or mechanism for altering the frequency range or shape of a waveform.

free field. Propagation medium without effective boundaries; no surface or bottom interactions.

frequency. Rate at which a repetitive event occurs, measured in hertz (cycles per second).

fundamental frequency. Lowest frequency of a harmonic series; generally equals the rotation or blade rate (*q.v.*), in Hz, of the source.

habituation (behavioral). Gradual waning of behavioral responsiveness over time as animals learn that a repeated or ongoing stimulus lacks significant consequences for the animal (*cf.* sensitization).

harmonics. Tones at integer multiples of fundamental frequency; fundamental = first harmonic.

hertz (Hz). Measure of frequency corresponding to one cycle per second.

high-pass filter. Filter passing only sounds above a specified frequency, eliminating lower-frequency sounds. *Cf.* low-pass filter.

hydrophone. Transducer for detecting underwater sound pressures; an underwater microphone.

image source. In sound transmission analysis, a perfect reflector may be replaced by an imaginary "image" source as far behind the reflector as the real source is in front. Algebraic sign of sound from image source is negative for a soft boundary (water-air) and positive for a hard boundary (water-rock).

impulse. See Acoustic impulse.

infrasonic. Sound at frequencies too low to be audible to humans—generally, below 20 Hz.

intensity level. Acoustic intensity expressed in decibels.

level. Logarithm-based measure of sound amplitude, power, energy, or intensity. The base-10 logarithm of the ratio of one such quantity to a reference quantity of the same kind, for example,

$\log_{10} (P/P_{ref})$. Usually expressed in decibels (*q.v.*) by multiplying by 10 (for power or energy) or 20 (for amplitude).

Lloyd mirror effect. Diminished or augmented pressure of a sound from an underwater source either located near the water/air boundary or when received near that boundary. Caused by interference between direct and surface-reflected waves (Section 4.5.2).

low-pass filter. Filter passing only sounds below a specified frequency, eliminating higher-frequency sounds. *Cf.* high-pass filter.

masking. Obscuring of sounds of interest by interfering sounds, generally at similar frequencies (Section 8.5).

mean square pressure. Average of pressure squared. Acoustic power, intensity, and energy are proportional to mean square acoustic pressure.

microbar (µbar). Unit of pressure previously used as a reference pressure in decibel level measurements; 1 µbar equals 1 dyne/cm^2, 0.1 pascal, or 10^5 µPa.

micropascal (µPa). Usual reference pressure for underwater sound levels; 1 µPa = 10^{-5} µbar.

minimum audible angle (MAA). Smallest detectable angular displacement of a sound source (Section 8.4).

mode theory. Short for **normal mode theory**. Generally, useful in predicting sound propagation in shallow water of constant depth where the sound velocity structure and bottom materials do not change with distance from the source. *Cf.* PE model.

near field. Receiver is in the "near field" of a spatially extended source when sound from different parts of the source can be resolved spatially. *Cf.* far field, point source.

octave band. Frequency band whose upper limit in hertz is twice the lower limit.

one-third octave band. Frequency band whose upper limit in hertz is $2^{1/3}$ (1.26) times the lower limit; bandwidth is proportional to center frequency. Three adjacent ⅓-octave bands span one octave.

particle velocity. Physical manifestation of sound; a measure of the particle motion associated with sound energy. Measured in distance per unit time (e.g., cm/s). A sound wave can be detected by sensing either pressure (*q.v.*) or particle motion.

pascal. Unit of pressure equal to 1 newton per square meter; equals 10 dynes/cm^2 or 10 µbars.

PE model. Parabolic Equation model for sound propagation; it can allow for variations in water depth, sound velocity structure, and bottom materials with distance from source (e.g., Fig. 4.7). Facilitates rapid solution on computers. *Cf.* mode theory.

peak level. Sound level (in dB) associated with the maximum amplitude of a sound.

peak to peak. Algebraic difference between positive and negative extremes, as for a waveform.

period. Time (in s) after which a cyclic activity repeats. In acoustics, period (in s/cycle) is the reciprocal of frequency (cycles/s).

phase. Angular measure of the displacement in time of some periodic function with respect to a reference time. *Cf.* relative phase.

plane wave. For a plane wave, the wavefronts (points of constant phase) are planes. *Cf.* cylindrical wave, spherical wave.

point source. Hypothetical single point from which sound radiates. *Cf.* source level.

power density spectrum. Distribution of power in a signal versus frequency, where continuously distributed sound (not tones) is the important component. Correct units are watts/Hz but the usual units in acoustics are $\mu Pa^2/Hz$; power is proportional to the mean square pressure and pressure is the measured quantity.

power spectrum. Distribution of power in a signal versus frequency, where tones are the important components. Correct units are watts but the usual units in acoustics are μPa^2; power is proportional to pressure squared and pressure is the measured quantity.

pressure, acoustic. Physical manifestation of sound, measured as force per unit area (e.g., in micropascals; $1 \mu Pa = 10^{-5}$ dynes/cm^2). *Cf.* particle velocity.

pressure release effect. See Lloyd mirror effect.

projector. An underwater transducer used to project sounds; an underwater loudspeaker.

propagation loss. Loss of sound power with increasing distance from source; equals transmission loss. In decibels re level at reference distance such as 1 m. Includes spreading+absorption+scattering losses (*q.v.*).

proportional bandwidth filter. Filter whose bandwidth is proportional to the filter center frequency, for example, octave and ⅓-octave filters (*q.v.*).

pure tone. See tone.

ray. Path of a point on a sound wavefront propagating through a medium. **Ray theory** is a form of solution to the wave equation. *Cf.* mode theory.

reflection. Process by which a traveling wave is deflected by a boundary between two media. Angle of reflection equals angle of incidence.

refraction. Bending of a sound wave passing through a boundary between two media; may also occur when physical properties of a single medium change along the propagation path. If the second medium has higher sound speed, sound rays are bent away from the perpendicular to the boundary, and vice versa. Snell's law governs refraction: $c_2 \sin \theta_1 = c_1 \sin \theta_2$, where c is sound speed, subscripts 1 and 2 refer to the first and second media, and angles are measured from the perpendicular to the boundary.

relative phase. Phase (*q.v.*) of a periodic waveform with respect to a reference waveform.

scattering. Process by which sound energy is diverted from a regular path by inhomogeneities in the medium (volume scattering) or roughness at a boundary (boundary scattering).

sea state (SS). Index of wave action, related to wind speed: for example, 0=calm, 3=small whitecaps/moderate breeze, 6=very rough/gale, 9=hurricane (see Table 5.1 in Section 5.2).

seismic noise. Noise attributable to earth movements (tectonics) or volcanic activity; also applied to man-made noise from high-energy sources used in geophysical exploration.

sensitization (behavioral). Increased behavioral responsiveness over time when animals learn that a repeated or ongoing stimulus has significant consequences for the animal (*cf.* habituation).

shadow zone. Region in a sound transmission medium not reached by sound rays transmitted directly from a source. May result from refraction (*q.v.*) or presence of a high-loss sound barrier. Weak sound energy usually penetrates the zone via reflections and scattering ("leakage").

Snell's Law. See refraction.

SOFAR channel. SOund Fixing And Ranging channel or deep sound channel, where sound rays propagating close to horizontally are trapped by refraction, reducing spreading loss and avoiding surface and bottom losses.

sonagram or **sonogram**.   Graph showing presence/absence (and sometimes level) of sound energy for each combination of frequency (Y axis) versus time (X axis); commonly used to illustrate transient sounds.   Sound level may be shown by gray-scale or color (*cf.* waterfall display; Section 3.4.4).

SOSUS.   SOund SUrveillance System, a navy system based on bottom-mounted hydrophones.   Capable of monitoring many low-frequency sounds, including baleen whale calls (Section 3.2.4).

sound.   Form of energy manifested by small pressure and/or particle velocity variations in a continuous medium.

sound pressure.   Pressure associated with a sound wave.   Equals total instantaneous pressure with a sound wave minus static pressure.

sound pressure, effective.   Square root of mean square (rms) pressure.   Quantifies the effective power in a sound wave of arbitrary waveshape (random or sinusoidal).   Averaging must be over an integer or large number of periods for a sinusoid, and over a long period compared to the rate of variation of a random sound wave.

sound pressure density spectrum.   Distribution of sound pressure versus frequency, appropriate for signals with a continuous distribution of energy within the frequency range under consideration; pressure at any frequency is infinitesimal, but integration over a frequency band results in a nonzero quantity.   Dimensions are pressure squared per unit frequency (e.g., $\mu Pa^2/Hz$).   *Cf.* power density spectrum.

sound pressure density spectrum level, SPDSL (= spectrum level).   Decibel measure of sound pressure density spectrum, generally in dB re $(1 \ \mu Pa)^2/Hz$.   *Cf.* sound pressure spectrum level, SPSL.

sound pressure level, SPL.   Decibel measure of sound pressure (*q.v.*).

sound pressure spectrum.   Distribution of sound pressure versus frequency for a waveform dominated by tones.   Dimension is rms (root mean square) pressure (e.g., in μPa).

sound pressure spectrum level, SPSL. Decibel measure of sound pressure spectrum, generally in dB re 1 µPa. *Cf.* sound pressure density spectrum level, SPDSL.

source level. Acoustic pressure that would be measured at a standard reference distance (usually 1 m) away from an ideal point source (*q.v.*) radiating the same amount of sound as the actual source. Units may be dB re 1 µPa at 1 m, often abbreviated as dB re 1 µPa-m. Source level may vary with frequency (see source spectrum level); may be given for some band of frequencies.

source spectrum level. Acoustic source strength versus frequency; meaningful for sources of tones. Described in dB re a unit pressure at a unit distance (e.g., dB re 1 µPa-m).

spectrum level. Abbreviation for sound pressure density spectrum level (*q.v.*) or, less often, for sound pressure spectrum level (*q.v.*); often used ambiguously.

spherical spreading. Sound spreading for spherical waves. Transmission loss $20 \log_{10} (R/R_0)$, where R is range and R_0 is a reference range. Received level diminishes by 6 dB when range doubles, and by 20 dB for a 10-fold range increase.

spherical wave. Sound wave with spherically shaped wavefronts; forms in free space without reflecting boundaries or refraction. Typically emitted by a point source; retains sphericity until modified by reflection or refraction. *Cf.* cylindrical wave, plane wave.

spreading loss. Loss of acoustic pressure with increasing distance from the source owing to the spreading wavefronts. There is no spreading loss with plane waves. Spreading loss is distinct from absorption and scattering losses.

stress. "an environmental effect on an individual which overtaxes its [physiological] control systems and reduces its fitness or appears likely to do so" (Broom and Johnson 1993:72).

thermal noise. Ambient noise component caused by molecular agitation; mainly above 30 kHz.

thermocline. Part of water column where water temperature decreases rapidly with increasing depth. Sound rays are strongly refracted downward when passing through a thermocline.

threshold of audibility. Level at which a sound is just detectable; depends on listener and frequency.

time delay. Time difference between related events, such as the arrivals of a sound wave at two receivers, or sound transmission and return of an echo. *Cf.* delay.

tone. Sinusoidal waveform without harmonic components; all power is at a specific frequency.

transducer. Device that changes energy from one form to another. Acoustic transducers change pressure waveform to electrical waveform, or vice versa. Examples include microphones, hydrophones, loudspeakers, and projectors.

transient wave. Wave that starts and ends in a relatively short time. *Cf.* continuous wave.

transmission loss. Same as propagation loss (*q.v.*).

ultrasonic. Sound at frequencies too high to be audible to humans— generally, above 20 kHz.

waterfall display. Graph showing frequency, time, and relative sound level in 3-dimensional format; commonly used to illustrate transient sounds (*cf.* sonagram; Section 3.4.4).

waveform. Functional form, or shape, of a signal or noise versus time (e.g., a graph of pressure or voltage versus time).

wavelength. Length of a single cycle of a periodic waveform. The wavelength λ, frequency f, and speed of sound c are related by the expression $c = f\lambda$.

Weber ratio. Relative difference limen (*q.v.*), calculated as DL/frequency (Section 8.3.1).

white noise. Noise whose spectrum level is largely independent of frequency over a specified frequency range. Need not be random.

INDEX

marine mammal (*continued*)
  radii of noise influence, **325-386**, 445-449
  significance of responses & impacts, 387-424, 449-452
Marine Mammal Protection Act, U.S. (MMPA), 4, 8-10, 12
Marmot, *Marmota marmota*, 409, 413
Marsh-Schulkin model, 71, 85
masking, **226-236**, **359**-366, 390-392, 437-439, 448
  adaptations that reduce, 233-236, 239, 256, 288, 364-366, 391-392, 411, 415-416, 417
  ambient noise effects on, **360**-362
  band, 31-32, **229-233**, 238-239, 538
  critical band, 31-32, 231-232, 239, 538
  critical ratio, 31, 206, **226-229**, 327-328, 331, 538
  cumulative effects, 406
  definition, 32, 226, 541
  equal power assumption, **230-233**, 239
  importance of, 1, 6-7, 205-206, 325-328, 359, 390-392
  in terrestrial mammals, 227, **229**, **231**-233, 411
  low-frequency, 227-**228**, 232, 238-239, 328, 374-375, 391
  of calls, 256, 264, 271, 285, 288, 319, **359**-366
  of tone by a tone, 232-233
  radius of, 325, **359-366**, 385, 446-447
  signal-to-noise ratio, 362
  & hearing threshold, 326-328
  & radius of audibility, 326-329, **359**-366
Massachusetts, *see* Cape Cod
mean square pressure, 17, 541
measurement procedures, **33-58**
  ambient noise, 48-**49**
  calls, 54-55
  citations of reviews, 34
  echolocation, 54
  hearing, 34, 55-56
  hydrophone, 36-37
  man-made noise, 49-52, 101
  meters, sound level, 35, 44

measurement procedures (*continued*)
  microphone, 35-36
  propagation loss, 51, 52-54
  proportional bandwidth spectra, 46
  sound pressure density spectrum level, SPDSL, 46
  sound spectrum, 46-47
  source level, 49-52, 101-102, 357-358
  transient sound, 19, 26, 44-**45**, 47, 50, 54-55
mechanical & flow noise, 37, 111
Mediterranean Sea, 302
Megaptera novaeangliae, *see* Whale, Humpback
Mesoplodon carlhubbsi, *see* Beaked Whale, Hubb's
  densirostris, *see* Beaked Whale, Blainville's
Mexico, 169, 250, 260, 261, 263-264, 280, 288, 400
microbar, definition, 17-19, 541
micropascal, definition, 16-19, *18*, 541
microphone, 35-36
Minerals Management Service, U.S., xiii-xv, 9
Minimum Audible Angle, **223-226**, 541
Mirounga angustirostris, *see* Seal, Northern Elephant
mitigation
  call modification, 233-236, 239, 256, 288, 364-366, 391-392, 411, 415-416
  design of equipment, 418-419
  directional hearing, 416
  displacement, 416-417
  habituation, 417
  monitoring to determine effectiveness, 418-423
  operational procedures, 421-422
  routing & positioning, 420-421, 450
  seasonal & hourly timing, 420
  source level reduction, 422
mitigation of
  aircraft disturbance, 420-421
  collisions with boats, 418, 422
  drilling disturbance, 418-420
  explosion injury/mortality, 420-422
  ocean science disturbance, 419, 421-422

Oregon, 300
oscilloscope, 44
Otaria byronia (=O. flavescens), see Sea
   Lion, South American (Southern)
Otter, Sea, *see* Sea Otter
outboard engine noise, **112**-*113*
Ovibos moschatus, *see* Muskox

P

Pacific Ocean
   calls, 166, 168
   disturbance, 260, 265, 303, 309, 311,
      321, 399
   man-made noise, 155, 399
   propagation loss, 66, 345
parabolic equation model, *see* PE model
particle velocity, 541
pascal, definition, 16-17, *18*, 541
PE model, 61, 68-**70**, 542
peak level, definition, 26, 542
peak to peak, 136, 185, 542
Peponocephala electra, *see* Whale,
   Melon-headed
periodic waveform, 20
period, definition, 15, 542
Permanent Threshold Shift, *see* PTS
permits, incidental take, *see* incidental
   take authorization
permits, scientific research (Australia,
   Canada, U.S.), 11-12, 34, 424
phase, definition, 29-30, 542
Phoca fasciata, *see* Seal, Ribbon
   hispida, *see* Seal, Ringed
   largha, *see* Seal, Spotted (Largha)
   vitulina, *see* Seal, Harbor (Common)
   groenlandica, *see* Seal, Harp
Phocarctos hookeri, *see* Sea Lion, New
   Zealand (Hooker's)
Phocoena phocoena, *see* Porpoise, Harbor
   sinus, *see* Vaquita (Gulf of California
   Harbor Porpoise)
Phocoenoides dalli, *see* Porpoise, Dall's
Physeter catodon, *see* Whale, Sperm
physiological effects of noise on terrestrial mammals, 411-413
pile-driving, *see* noise, hammering
pinger disturbance, 301-303

pinnipeds (*see also* under species names)
   aircraft disturb., 242-247, 318-322,
      339-340, 350-351, 397-398, 400
   calls, 159, *189-201* (*see also* phocids,
      otariids, Walrus)
   collisions with ships & boats, 254
   construction disturb., 277, 280-281
   drilling disturb., 281-282, **352**-353
   echolocation? 198-199
   explosion disturbance, 281, 304, 319
   explosion injury/mortality, 306-307,
      323
   habituation, 244, 246, 255, 291, 304,
      312-313, 315, 319-320
   hearing, otariids, 208, **213-216**, **220**-
      221, **223**, **225-230**, 240, **330**, **348**-
      351, 438
   hearing, phocids, *18*, 208, **211-216**,
      218, **220**-223, **225-232**, 235, 240,
      328-**330**, 438
   hearing impairment, 368-369, 399
   hovercraft disturbance, 278
   human disturbance to mammals,
      315-318, 321
   hunting disturbance, 253-255, 276,
      276, 315, 317, 321
   icebreaker disturbance, **253**, 274-275,
      282, 322, 441
   ocean science disturb., 309, 323-324
   production disturbance, 290, 354-**355**
   purposeful scaring, 291, 304, 311-
      314, 320, 414
   seismic exploration disturb., 291-292,
      313, 323, **356**-357, 420, 441, 445
   sensitization, 243, 254, 321
   ship & boat disturbance, **252**-255,
      319-322, 339-340, 394
   sonar disturbance, 303, 323
   sonic boom disturbance, 243, 245
   tolerance of noise & disturbance, 253-
      255, 282, 291, 304, 311, 318-320,
      323
pitch, 15
plane wave, 542
Platanista gangetica, *see* Susu, Ganges
   (Ganges River Dolphin)
   minor, *see* Susu, Indus (Indus River
   Dolphin)